RUSSIA
St. Petersburg
Moscow
FINLAND
ESTONIA
LATVIA
LITHUANIA
BELARUS
UKRAINE
POLAND
ROMANIA
BULGARIA
GEORGIA
AZER.
ARM.
TURKEY
Istanbul
GREECE
CYPRUS
SYRIA
LEB.
ISRAEL
IRAQ
JORDAN
Cairo
Baghdad
KUWAIT
Tehran
IRAN
TURKMENISTAN
UZBEKISTAN
KYRGYZSTAN
TAJIKISTAN
KAZAKHSTAN
MONGOLIA
CHINA
Beijing (Peking)
Shenyang
Tianjin
NORTH KOREA
Seoul
SOUTH KOREA
JAPAN
Tokyo
Osaka
Wuhan
Chongqing
Shanghai
Hong Kong
TAIWAN
PACIFIC
OCEAN
Tropic of Cancer
Lahore
Delhi
NEPAL
BHUTAN
PAKISTAN
Karachi
Ahmadabad
BANGLA DESH
Kolkata (Calcutta)
Dacca
BURMA (Myanmar)
LAOS
THAILAND
CAMBODIA
VIETNAM
Ho Chi Minh City
Manila
PHILIPPINES
Guam (U.S.A.)
NORTHERN MARIANAS
FEDERATED STATES OF MICRONESIA
PALAU
Mumbai (Bombay)
INDIA
Hyderabad
Bangalore
Chennai (Madras)
Bangkok
SRI LANKA
MALDIVES
MALAYSIA
SINGAPORE
BRUNEI
Borneo
Equator
INDONESIA
Jakarta
EAST TIMOR
New Guinea
PAPUA NEW GUINEA
Christmas Island (Australia)
Cocos Islands (Australia)
INDIAN
OCEAN
Oceania
AUSTRALIA
Sydney
New Caledonia (Fr.)
Tropic of Capricorn
NEW ZEALAND
Africa
LIBYA
EGYPT
SAUDI ARABIA
OMAN
YEMEN
DJIBOUTI
ERITREA
ETHIOPIA
SOMALI REP
KENYA
SUDAN
CHAD
NIGER
NIGERIA
CENTRAL AFRICAN REP
CAMEROON
GABON
CONGO
CONGO (Dem. Rep. of the)
RWANDA
BURUNDI
TANZANIA
SEYCHELLES
COMOROS
ANGOLA
MALAWI
ZAMBIA
MOZAMBIQUE
MADAGASCAR
MAURITIUS
Réunion (Fr.)
ZIMBABWE
NAMIBIA
BOTSWANA
SWAZILAND
SOUTH AFRICA
LESOTHO
Prince Edward Islands (South Africa)
Crozet Is. (Fr.)
Kerguelen Is. (Fr.)
SOUTHERN OCEAN
Antarctica
Antarctic Circle
Tropic of Cancer
Equator
Tropic of Capricorn
COPYRIGHT PHILIP'S

D1021454

Copyright © 2008 Philip's

Philip's, a division of Octopus Publishing Group Limited
2–4 Heron Quays, London E14 4JP
www.octopusbooks.co.uk
An Hachette Livre UK Company
www.hachettelivre.co.uk

Cartography by Philip's

CITY PLANS
Page 29, Dublin: The town plan of Dublin is based on Ordnance Survey Ireland by permission of the Government Permit Number 8408. © Ordnance Survey Ireland and Government of Ireland.

Ordnance Survey®

Page 31, London: This product includes mapping data licensed from Ordnance Survey® with the permission of the Controller of Her Majesty's Stationery Office. © Crown copyright 2008. All rights reserved. Licence number 100011710.

Vector data: Courtesy of Gräfe and Unser Verlag GmbH, München, Germany (city-center maps of Bangkok, Cape Town, Mexico City, Singapore, Sydney, and Tokyo).

Published in North America by Oxford University Press, Inc., 198 Madison Avenue, New York, NY 10016

www.oup.com/us/atlas

OXFORD UNIVERSITY PRESS

Oxford is a registered trademark of Oxford University Press

All rights reserved. No part of this publication may be reproduced, stored in a retrieval system, or transmitted in any form or by any means, electronic, electrical, chemical, mechanical, optical, photocopying, recording, or otherwise, without the prior permission of the Publisher.

Library of Congress Cataloging-in-Publication Data available

ISBN 978-0-19-537453-7

Printing (last digit): 9 8 7 6 5 4 3 2 1

Printed in Hong Kong

CONTENTS

WORLD STATISTICS

4–7 Countries
8–9 Cities
10–11 Time zones
12–13 Flight paths
14–15 Distance table
16–19 World climate

CITY PLANS

20 City plans – legend
21 Amsterdam
22 Athens
23 Bangkok
24 Barcelona
25 Berlin
26 Brussels
27 Cape Town
28 Chicago
29 Dublin
30 Hong Kong
31 London
32 Madrid
33 Mexico City
34 Moscow
35 Mumbai
36 New York
37 Paris
38 Prague
39 Rio de Janeiro
40 Rome
41 San Francisco
42 Singapore
43 Sydney
44 Tokyo
45 Toronto
46 Vienna

GAZETTEER OF NATIONS

47 Gazetteer of Nations – contents
48–72 Country-by-country profiles

NOTE:
For reasons of safety or politics, there may be times when it is not advisable, or desirable, to visit one or more of the countries described in the Gazetteer of Nations section. If in doubt, please check with the US Department of State (www.state.gov/travel).

WORLD MAPS

1 World Maps – general reference
2–3 The Land Hemisphere 1:133.3M
4–5 The Water Hemisphere 1:133.3M

EUROPE

6–7 Europe 1:26.7M
8–9 Scandinavia and the Baltic Lands 1:13.3M
10–11 British Isles 1:6.7M
12–13 France 1:6.7M
14–15 Germany and Benelux 1:6.7M
16–17 Central Europe 1:6.7M
18–19 Spain and Portugal 1:6.7M
20–21 Italy and the Adriatic 1:6.7M
22–23 Greece and the Balkans 1:6.7M
24–25 Eastern Europe 1:13.3M

ASIA

26–27 Asia 1:67M
28–29 Western Russia and Central Asia 1:26.7M
30–31 Eastern Siberia 1:26.7M
32–33 Japan 1:8.5M
34–35 China 1:26.7M
36–37 Philippines and Eastern Indonesia 1:16.7M
38–39 Southeast Asia 1:16.7M
40–41 Eastern India, Bangladesh and Burma 1:13.3M
42–43 Western India, Pakistan and Sri Lanka 1:13.3M
44–45 Persian Gulf, Iran and Afghanistan 1:13.3M
46–47 The Middle East and Turkey 1:13.3M
48–49 Arabia and the Horn of Africa 1:20M

AFRICA

50–51 Africa 1:56M
52–53 Northwest Africa 1:20M
54–55 Northeast Africa 1:20M
56–57 Central Africa 1:20M
58–59 Southern Africa 1:20M

AUSTRALASIA

60–61 Australia 1:26.7M
62–63 Southeast Australia 1:10.7M
64–65 New Zealand 1:8M
Central and Southwest Pacific

NORTH AMERICA

66–67 North America 1:46.7M
68–69 Western Canada and Alaska 1:20M
70–71 Eastern Canada 1:20M
72–73 Northwest USA 1:8M
74–75 North-central USA 1:8M
76–77 Northeast USA 1:8M
78–79 Southwest USA 1:8M
80–81 Southern USA 1:8M
82–83 Southeast USA 1:8M
84–85 Mexico 1:20M
86–87 Caribbean and Central America 1:20M

SOUTH AMERICA

88–89 South America 1:46.7M
90–91 South America – Northwest 1:21.3M
92–93 South America – Northeast 1:21.3M
94–95 South America – South 1:21.3M

POLAR REGIONS

96 Antarctica 1:46.7M

INDEX

97–160 Index to World Maps

Country/Territory	Area (1,000 sq km)	Area (1,000 sq mi)	Population (1,000s)	Density (persons per sq km)	Capital City	Annual Income US$
Afghanistan	652	252	31,890	49	Kabul	800
Albania	28.7	11.1	3,601	125	Tirana	5,500
Algeria	2,382	920	33,333	14	Algiers	8,100
American Samoa (US)	0.20	0.08	58	290	Pago Pago	5,800
Andorra	0.47	0.18	72	153	Andorra La Vella	38,800
Angola	1,247	481	12,264	10	Luanda	6,500
Anguilla (UK)	0.10	0.04	14	134	The Valley	8,800
Antigua & Barbuda	0.44	0.17	69	157	St John's	10,900
Argentina	2,780	1,074	40,302	15	Buenos Aires	13,000
Armenia	29.8	11.5	2,972	100	Yerevan	5,700
Aruba (Netherlands)	0.19	0.07	100	518	Oranjestad	21,800
Australia	7,741	2,989	20,434	3	Canberra	37,500
Austria	83.9	32.4	8,200	98	Vienna	39,000
Azerbaijan	86.6	33.4	8,120	94	Baku	9,000
Azores (Portugal)	2.2	0.86	236	107	Ponta Delgada	15,000
Bahamas	13.9	5.4	306	22	Nassau	22,700
Bahrain	0.69	0.27	709	1,066	Manama	34,700
Bangladesh	144	55.6	150,448	1,045	Dhaka	1,400
Barbados	0.43	0.17	281	652	Bridgetown	19,700
Belarus	208	80.2	9,725	47	Minsk	10,200
Belgium	30.5	11.8	10,392	340	Brussels	36,500
Belize	23.0	8.9	294	13	Belmopan	7,800
Benin	113	43.5	8,078	72	Porto-Novo	1,500
Bermuda (UK)	0.05	0.02	66	1,196	Hamilton	69,900
Bhutan	47.0	18.1	2,328	50	Thimphu	1,400
Bolivia	1,099	424	9,119	8	La Paz/Sucre	4,400
Bosnia-Herzegovina	51.2	19.8	4,552	89	Sarajevo	6,600
Botswana	582	225	1,816	3	Gaborone	14,700
Brazil	8,514	3,287	190,011	22	Brasília	9,700
Brunei	5.8	2.2	372	65	Bandar Seri Begawan	25,600
Bulgaria	111	42.8	7,323	66	Sofia	11,800
Burkina Faso	274	106	14,326	52	Ouagadougou	1,200
Burma (= Myanmar)	677	261	47,374	70	Rangoon/Naypyidaw	1,900
Burundi	27.8	10.7	8,391	301	Bujumbura	800
Cambodia	181	69.9	13,996	77	Phnom Penh	1,800
Cameroon	475	184	18,060	38	Yaoundé	2,300
Canada	9,971	3,850	33,390	3	Ottawa	38,200
Canary Is. (Spain)	7.2	2.8	1,682	234	Las Palmas/Santa Cruz	19,900
Cape Verde Is.	4.0	1.6	424	105	Praia	7,000
Cayman Is. (UK)	0.26	0.10	47	178	George Town	43,800
Central African Republic	623	241	4,369	7	Bangui	700
Chad	1,284	496	9,886	8	Ndjamena	1,600
Chile	757	292	16,285	22	Santiago	14,400
China	9,597	3,705	1,321,852	138	Beijing	5,300
Colombia	1,139	440	44,380	39	Bogotá	7,200
Comoros	2.2	0.86	711	328	Moroni	600
Congo	342	132	3,801	11	Brazzaville	3,700
Congo (Dem. Rep. of the)	2,345	905	65,752	28	Kinshasa	300
Cook Is. (NZ)	0.24	0.09	22	91	Avarua	9,100
Costa Rica	51.1	19.7	4,134	79	San José	13,500
Croatia	56.5	21.8	4,493	80	Zagreb	15,500
Cuba	111	42.8	11,394	103	Havana	4,500
Cyprus	9.3	3.6	788	85	Nicosia	24,600
Czech Republic	78.9	30.5	10,229	130	Prague	24,400
Denmark	43.1	16.6	5,468	127	Copenhagen	37,400

Listed above are the principal countries and territories of the world. If a territory is not completely independent, then the country it is associated with is named. The area figures give the total area of land, inland water, and ice. The population figures are 2007 estimates. The annual income is the Gross Domestic Product per capita in US dollars. [Gross Domestic Product per capita has been measured

Country/Territory	Area (1,000 sq km)	Area (1,000 sq mi)	Population (1,000s)	Density (persons per sq km)	Capital City	Annual Income US$
Djibouti	23.2	9.0	496	22	Djibouti	1,000
Dominica	0.75	0.29	72	96	Roseau	3,800
Dominican Republic	48.5	18.7	9,366	192	Santo Domingo	9,200
East Timor	14.9	5.7	1,085	72	Dili	800
Ecuador	284	109	13,756	49	Quito	7,100
Egypt	1,001	387	80,335	80	Cairo	5,400
El Salvador	21.0	8.1	6,948	330	San Salvador	5,200
Equatorial Guinea	28.1	10.8	551	20	Malabo	4,100
Eritrea	118	45.4	4,907	40	Asmara	1,000
Estonia	45.1	17.4	1,316	29	Tallinn	21,800
Ethiopia	1,104	426	76,512	68	Addis Ababa	700
Faroe Is. (Denmark)	1.4	0.54	48	34	Tórshavn	31,000
Fiji	18.3	7.1	919	50	Suva	4,100
Finland	338	131	5,238	16	Helsinki	35,500
France	552	213	60,876	111	Paris	33,800
French Guiana (France)	90.0	34.7	196	1	Cayenne	8,300
French Polynesia (France)	4.0	1.5	279	67	Papeete	17,500
Gabon	268	103	1,455	5	Libreville	13,800
Gambia, The	11.3	4.4	1,688	149	Banjul	800
Gaza Strip	0.36	0.14	1,482	4,118	–	1,100
Georgia	69.7	26.9	4,646	67	Tbilisi	4,200
Germany	357	138	82,401	231	Berlin	34,400
Ghana	239	92.1	22,931	96	Accra	1,400
Gibraltar (UK)	0.006	0.002	28	4,303	Gibraltar Town	38,200
Greece	132	50.9	10,706	81	Athens	30,500
Greenland (Denmark)	2,176	840	56	0.03	Nuuk (Godthåb)	20,000
Grenada	0.34	0.13	90	262	St George's	3,900
Guadeloupe (France)	1.7	0.66	449	264	Basse-Terre	7,900
Guam (US)	0.55	0.21	173	316	Agana	15,000
Guatemala	109	42.0	12,728	117	Guatemala City	5,400
Guinea	246	94.9	9,948	40	Conakry	1,000
Guinea-Bissau	36.1	13.9	1,473	41	Bissau	600
Guyana	215	83.0	769	4	Georgetown	5,300
Haiti	27.8	10.7	8,706	314	Port-au-Prince	1,900
Honduras	112	43.3	7,484	67	Tegucigalpa	3,300
Hong Kong (China)	1.1	0.42	6,980	6,392	–	42,000
Hungary	93.0	35.9	9,956	107	Budapest	19,500
Iceland	103	39.8	302	3	Reykjavik	39,400
India	3,287	1,269	1,129,866	344	New Delhi	2,700
Indonesia	1,905	735	234,694	122	Jakarta	3,400
Iran	1,648	636	65,398	40	Tehran	12,300
Iraq	438	169	27,500	63	Baghdad	3,600
Ireland	70.3	27.1	4,109	58	Dublin	45,600
Israel	20.6	8.0	6,427	309	Jerusalem	28,800
Italy	301	116	58,148	193	Rome	31,000
Ivory Coast (= Côte d'Ivoire)	322	125	18,013	56	Yamoussoukro	1,800
Jamaica	11.0	4.2	2,780	253	Kingston	4,800
Japan	378	146	127,433	337	Tokyo	33,800
Jordan	89.3	34.5	6,053	66	Amman	4,700
Kazakhstan	2,725	1,052	15,285	6	Astana	11,100
Kenya	580	224	36,914	63	Nairobi	1,600
Kiribati	0.73	0.28	108	133	Tarawa	1,800
Korea, North	121	46.5	23,302	193	Pyŏngyang	1,900
Korea, South	99.3	38.3	49,045	498	Seoul	24,600
Kosovo	10.9	4.2	2,127	195	Priština	1,800

using the purchasing power parity method. This enables comparisons to be made between countries through their purchasing power (in US dollars), showing real price levels of goods and services rather than using currency exchange rates.] The figures are the latest available, usually 2007 estimates. *OPT = Occupied Palestinian Territory; N/A = Not available.

Country/Territory	Area (1,000 sq km)	Area (1,000 sq mi)	Population (1,000s)	Density (persons per sq km)	Capital City	Annual Income US$
Kuwait	17.8	6.9	2,506	141	Kuwait City	55,300
Kyrgyzstan	200	77.2	5,284	27	Bishkek	2,000
Laos	237	91.4	6,522	28	Vientiane	1,900
Latvia	64.6	24.9	2,260	35	Riga	17,700
Lebanon	10.4	4.0	3,926	377	Beirut	10,400
Lesotho	30.4	11.7	2,125	70	Maseru	1,500
Liberia	111	43.0	3,196	29	Monrovia	500
Libya	1,760	679	6,037	3	Tripoli	13,100
Liechtenstein	0.16	0.06	34	214	Vaduz	25,000
Lithuania	65.2	25.2	3,575	55	Vilnius	16,700
Luxembourg	2.6	1.0	480	186	Luxembourg	80,800
Macau (China)	0.02	0.007	457	18,280	–	24,300
Macedonia (FYROM)	25.7	9.9	2,056	81	Skopje	8,400
Madagascar	587	227	19,449	33	Antananarivo	1,000
Madeira (Portugal)	0.78	0.30	241	309	Funchal	22,700
Malawi	118	45.7	13,603	115	Lilongwe	800
Malaysia	330	127	24,821	75	Kuala Lumpur/Putrajaya	14,400
Maldives	0.30	0.12	369	1,230	Malé	3,900
Mali	1,240	479	11,995	10	Bamako	1,200
Malta	0.32	0.12	402	1,272	Valletta	23,200
Marshall Is.	0.18	0.07	62	342	Majuro	2,900
Martinique (France)	1.1	0.43	433	394	Fort-de-France	14,400
Mauritania	1,026	396	3,270	3	Nouakchott	1,800
Mauritius	2.0	0.79	1,251	613	Port Louis	11,900
Mexico	1,958	756	108,701	55	Mexico City	12,500
Micronesia, Fed. States of	0.70	0.27	108	154	Palikir	2,300
Moldova	33.9	13.1	4,320	128	Chişinău	2,200
Monaco	0.001	0.0004	33	33,000	Monaco	30,000
Mongolia	1,567	605	2,952	2	Ulan Bator	2,900
Montenegro	14.0	5.4	685	49	Podgorica	3,800
Montserrat (UK)	0.10	0.04	10	94	Plymouth	3,400
Morocco	447	172	33,757	76	Rabat	3,800
Mozambique	802	309	20,906	26	Maputo	900
Namibia	824	318	2,055	2	Windhoek	5,200
Nauru	0.02	0.008	14	644	Yaren District	5,000
Nepal	147	56.8	28,902	205	Katmandu	1,100
Netherlands	41.5	16.0	16,571	399	Amsterdam/The Hague	38,600
Netherlands Antilles (Neths)	0.80	0.31	224	233	Willemstad	16,000
New Caledonia (France)	18.6	7.2	222	12	Nouméa	15,000
New Zealand	271	104	4,116	15	Wellington	27,300
Nicaragua	130	50.2	5,675	44	Managua	3,200
Niger	1,267	489	12,895	10	Niamey	700
Nigeria	924	357	135,031	146	Abuja	2,200
Northern Mariana Is. (US)	0.46	0.18	85	177	Saipan	12,500
Norway	324	125	4,628	14	Oslo	55,600
Oman	310	119	3,205	15	Muscat	19,100
Pakistan	796	307	164,742	205	Islamabad	2,600
Palau	0.46	0.18	21	46	Melekeok	7,600
Panama	75.5	29.2	3,242	41	Panamá	9,000
Papua New Guinea	463	179	5,796	13	Port Moresby	2,900
Paraguay	407	157	6,669	16	Asunción	4,000
Peru	1,285	496	28,675	22	Lima	7,600
Philippines	300	116	91,077	304	Manila	3,300
Poland	323	125	38,518	123	Warsaw	16,200
Portugal	88.8	34.3	10,643	115	Lisbon	21,800
Puerto Rico (US)	8.9	3.4	3,944	433	San Juan	19,600
Qatar	11.0	4.2	907	79	Doha	29,400
Réunion (France)	2.5	0.97	777	311	St-Denis	6,200

Country/Territory	Area (1,000 sq km)	Area (1,000 sq mi)	Population (1,000s)	Density (persons per sq km)	Capital City	Annual Income US$
Romania	238	92.0	22,276	94	Bucharest	11,100
Russia	17,075	6,593	141,378	8	Moscow	14,600
Rwanda	26.3	10.2	9,908	376	Kigali	1,000
St Kitts & Nevis	0.26	0.10	39	151	Basseterre	8,200
St Lucia	0.54	0.21	171	277	Castries	4,800
St Vincent & Grenadines	0.39	0.15	118	304	Kingstown	3,600
Samoa	2.8	1.1	214	73	Apia	2,100
San Marino	0.06	0.02	30	485	San Marino	34,100
São Tomé & Principe	0.96	0.37	200	199	São Tomé	1,200
Saudi Arabia	2,150	830	27,601	14	Riyadh	20,700
Senegal	197	76.0	12,522	64	Dakar	1,700
Serbia	77.5	29.9	8,024	104	Belgrade	7,700
Seychelles	0.46	0.18	82	180	Victoria	18,400
Sierra Leone	71.7	27.7	6,155	86	Freetown	800
Singapore	0.68	0.26	4,553	6,570	Singapore City	48,900
Slovak Republic	49.0	18.9	5,448	112	Bratislava	19,800
Slovenia	20.3	7.8	2,009	99	Ljubljana	27,300
Solomon Is.	28.9	11.2	567	20	Honiara	600
Somalia	638	246	9,119	14	Mogadishu	600
South Africa	1,221	471	43,998	36	Cape Town/Pretoria	10,600
Spain	498	192	40,448	80	Madrid	33,700
Sri Lanka	65.6	25.3	20,926	319	Colombo	4,100
Sudan	2,506	967	39,379	16	Khartoum	2,500
Suriname	163	63.0	471	3	Paramaribo	7,800
Swaziland	17.4	6.7	1,133	65	Mbabane	4,800
Sweden	450	174	9,031	20	Stockholm	36,900
Switzerland	41.3	15.9	7,555	183	Bern	39,800
Syria	185	71.5	19,315	104	Damascus	4,500
Taiwan	36.0	13.9	22,859	635	Taipei	29,800
Tajikistan	143	55.3	7,077	49	Dushanbe	1,600
Tanzania	945	365	39,384	42	Dodoma	1,100
Thailand	513	198	65,068	127	Bangkok	8,000
Togo	56.8	21.9	5,702	100	Lomé	900
Tonga	0.65	0.25	117	156	Nuku'alofa	2,200
Trinidad & Tobago	5.1	2.0	1,057	206	Port of Spain	21,700
Tunisia	164	63.2	10,276	63	Tunis	7,500
Turkey	775	299	71,159	91	Ankara	7,500
Turkmenistan	488	188	5,097	10	Ashkhabad	9,200
Turks & Caicos Is. (UK)	0.43	0.17	22	51	Cockburn Town	11,500
Tuvalu	0.03	0.01	12	461	Fongafale	1,600
Uganda	241	93.1	30,263	128	Kampala	1,100
Ukraine	604	233	46,300	77	Kiev	6,900
United Arab Emirates	83.6	32.3	4,444	53	Abu Dhabi	55,200
United Kingdom	242	93.4	60,776	248	London	35,300
United States of America	9,629	3,718	301,140	31	Washington, DC	46,000
Uruguay	175	67.6	3,461	20	Montevideo	10,700
Uzbekistan	447	173	27,780	62	Tashkent	2,200
Vanuatu	12.2	4.7	212	17	Port-Vila	2,900
Venezuela	912	352	26,024	29	Caracas	12,800
Vietnam	332	128	85,262	259	Hanoi	2,600
Virgin Is. (UK)	0.15	0.06	24	154	Road Town	38,500
Virgin Is. (US)	0.35	0.13	108	308	Charlotte Amalie	14,500
Wallis & Futuna Is. (France)	0.20	0.08	16	60	Mata-Utu	3,800
West Bank (OPT)*	5.9	2.3	2,536	433	–	1,100
Western Sahara	266	103	383	1	El Aaiún	N/A
Yemen	528	204	22,231	42	Sana'	2,400
Zambia	753	291	11,477	15	Lusaka	1,400
Zimbabwe	391	151	12,311	32	Harare	500

	Population (1,000s)
Afghanistan	
Kabul	3,288
Algeria	
Algiers	3,260
Angola	
Luanda	2,839
Argentina	
Buenos Aires	13,349
Córdoba	1,592
Rosario	1,312
Mendoza	1,072
Armenia	
Yerevan	1,103
Australia	
Sydney	4,388
Melbourne	3,663
Brisbane	1,769
Perth	1,484
Adelaide	1,137
Austria	
Vienna	2,260
Azerbaijan	
Baku	1,856
Bangladesh	
Dhaka	12,560
Chittagong	4,171
Khulna	1,497
Rajshahi	1,035
Belarus	
Minsk	1,778
Belgium	
Brussels	1,012
Bolivia	
La Paz	1,533
Santa Cruz	1,352
Brazil	
São Paulo	18,333
Rio de Janeiro	11,469
Belo Horizonte	5,304
Pôrto Alegre	3,795
Recife	3,527
Brasília	3,341
Salvador	3,331
Fortaleza	3,261
Curitiba	2,871
Campinas	2,640
Belém	2,097
Goiânia	1,878
Manaus	1,673
Santos	1,634
Vitória	1,602
Maceió	1,137
Natal	1,049
Bulgaria	
Sofia	1,093
Burma (= Myanmar)	
Rangoon	4,107
Cambodia	
Phnom Penh	1,364
Cameroon	
Douala	1,980
Yaoundé	1,727
Canada	
Toronto	5,312
Montréal	3,640
Vancouver	2,188
Ottawa	1,156
Calgary	1,058
Edmonton	1,015
Chile	
Santiago	5,683

	Population (1,000s)
China	
Shanghai	14,503
Beijing	10,717
Guangzhou	8,425
Shenzhen	7,233
Wuhan	7,093
Hong Kong	7,041
Tianjin	7,040
Chongqing	6,363
Shenyang	4,720
Dongguan	4,320
Chengdu	4,065
Xi'an	3,926
Harbin	3,695
Nanjing	3,621
Guiyang	3,447
Dalian	3,073
Changchun	3,046
Zibo	2,982
Kunming	2,837
Hangzhou	2,831
Qingdao	2,817
Taiyuan	2,794
Jinan	2,743
Zhengzhou	2,590
Fuzhou	2,453
Changsha	2,451
Lanzhou	2,411
Xiamen	2,371
Shijiazhuang	2,275
Jinxi	2,268
Jilin	2,255
Wenzhou	2,212
Nanchang	2,188
Zaozhuang	2,096
Nanchong	2,046
Nanning	2,040
Linyi	2,035
Ürümqi	2,025
Yantai	1,991
Wanxian	1,963
Xuzhou	1,960
Baotou	1,920
Hefei	1,916
Suzhou	1,849
Nanyang	1,830
Tangshan	1,825
Ningbo	1,810
Datong	1,763
Yancheng	1,678
Tianmen	1,676
Shangqui	1,650
Lu'an	1,647
Wuxi	1,646
Luoyang	1,644
Hohhot	1,644
Anshan	1,611
Qiqihar	1,607
Tai'an	1,598
Daqing	1,594
Xinghua	1,587
Pingxiang	1,562
Handan	1,535
Xiantao	1,528
Zhanjiang	1,514
Weifang	1,498
Shantou	1,495
Fushun	1,456
Xianyang	1,450
Luzhou	1,447
Neijiang	1,441

	Population (1,000s)
Changde	1,429
Huainan	1,420
Liuzhou	1,409
Suining, Sichuan	1,401
Quanzhou	1,377
Xintai	1,334
Mianyang	1,322
Heze	1,318
Yiyang	1,318
Yueyang	1,286
Suqian	1,258
Changzhou	1,249
Huaian	1,243
Chifeng	1,238
Jingmen	1,228
Yuzhou	1,226
Zaoyang	1,210
Huzhou	1,203
Tianshui	1,199
Yongzhou	1,182
Mudanjiang	1,171
Liupanshui	1,149
Leshan	1,143
Jining, Shandong	1,143
Xiaoshan	1,130
Yixing	1,129
Zigong	1,087
Xianyang	1,072
Fuyu	1,068
Yulin	1,060
Baoding	1,042
Xinyi, Jiangsu	1,022
Zhuzhou	1,016
Jixi	1,012
Linqing	1,009
Jiamusi	1,006
Xiangfan	1,006
Zhangjiakou	1,001
Colombia	
Bogotá	7,594
Medellín	3,236
Cali	2,583
Barranquilla	1,918
Bucaramanga	1,069
Cartagena	1,002
Congo	
Brazzaville	1,173
Congo (Dem. Rep.)	
Kinshasa	6,049
Kolwezi	1,207
Lubumbashi	1,179
Costa Rica	
San José	1,217
Croatia	
Zagreb	1,067
Cuba	
Havana	2,192
Czech Republic	
Prague	1,171
Denmark	
Copenhagen	1,091
Dominican Republic	
Santo Domingo	2,563
Ecuador	
Guayaquil	2,387
Quito	1,514
Egypt	
Cairo	11,146
Alexandria	3,760

	Population (1,000s)
El Salvador	
San Salvador	1,517
Ethiopia	
Addis Ababa	2,899
Finland	
Helsinki	1,091
France	
Paris	9,820
Lyons	1,403
Marseilles	1,382
Lille	1,029
Georgia	
Tbilisi	1,406
Germany	
Berlin	3,387
Hamburg	1,705
Munich	1,195
Ghana	
Accra	1,981
Kumasi	1,517
Greece	
Athens	3,238
Guatemala	
Guatemala City	3,242
Guinea	
Conakry	1,465
Haiti	
Port-au-Prince	2,129
Honduras	
Tegucigalpa	1,061
Hungary	
Budapest	1,693
India	
Mumbai	18,336
Delhi	15,334
Kolkata	14,299
Chennai	6,915
Bangalore	6,532
Hyderabad	6,145
Ahmedabad	5,171
Pune	4,485
Surat	3,671
Kanpur	3,040
Jaipur	2,796
Lucknow	2,589
Nagpur	2,359
Patna	2,066
Indore	1,941
Vadodara	1,686
Bhopal	1,656
Coimbatore	1,628
Ludhiana	1,583
Agra	1,526
Visakhapatnam	1,468
Cochin	1,461
Nashik	1,408
Meerut	1,340
Faridabad	1,330
Varanasi	1,300
Ghaziabad	1,277
Asansol	1,272
Jamshedpur	1,246
Madurai	1,245
Jabalpur	1,234
Rajkot	1,205
Dhanbad	1,195
Amritsar	1,162
Allahabad	1,153
Vijayawada	1,093
Srinagar	1,093
Aurangabad	1,065

	Population (1,000s)
Bhilainagar-Durg	1,051
Solapur	1,012
Indonesia	
Jakarta	13,215
Bandung	4,126
Surabaya	2,992
Medan	2,287
Palembang	1,733
Ujung Pandang	1,284
Iran	
Tehran	7,352
Mashhad	2,147
Esfahan	1,547
Tabriz	1,396
Karaj	1,235
Shiraz	1,230
Qom	1,045
Iraq	
Baghdad	5,910
Mosul	1,236
Basra	1,187
Ireland	
Dublin	1,037
Israel	
Tel Aviv-Yafo	3,025
Italy	
Rome	3,348
Milan	2,953
Naples	2,245
Turin	1,660
Ivory Coast (= Côte d'Ivoire)	
Abidjan	3,516
Japan	
Tokyo	12,064
Yokohama	6,427
Osaka	2,599
Nagoya	2,172
Sapporo	1,922
Kobe	1,493
Kyoto	1,468
Fukuoka	1,341
Kawasaki	1,250
Hiroshima	1,126
Kitakyushu	1,011
Sendai	1,008
Jordan	
Amman	1,292
Kazakhstan	
Almaty	1,156
Kenya	
Nairobi	2,818
Korea, North	
Pyŏngyang	3,351
N'ampo	1,102
Korea, South	
Seoul	9,888
Busan	3,830
Incheon	2,884
Daegu	2,675
Daejeon	1,522
Gwangju	1,379
Seongnam	1,353
Ulsan	1,340
Lebanon	
Beirut	2,070
Libya	
Tripoli	2,098

	Population (1,000s)
Benghazi	1,114
Madagascar	
Antananarivo	1,808
Malaysia	
Kuala Lumpur	1,405
Mali	
Bamako	1,379
Mexico	
Mexico City	19,013
Guadalajara	3,905
Monterrey	3,517
Toluca	1,987
Puebla	1,880
Tijuana	1,570
Ciudad Juárez	1,469
León	1,438
Torreón	1,057
Morocco	
Casablanca	3,743
Rabat	1,859
Fès	1,032
Mozambique	
Maputo	1,316
Nepal	
Katmandu	1,176
Netherlands	
Amsterdam	1,157
Rotterdam	1,112
New Zealand	
Auckland	1,152
Nicaragua	
Managua	1,165
Nigeria	
Lagos	11,135
Kano	2,884
Ibadan	2,375
Kaduna	1,329
Benin City	1,022
Pakistan	
Karachi	11,819
Lahore	6,373
Faisalabad	2,533
Rawalpindi	1,794
Gujranwala	1,466
Multan	1,459
Hyderabad	1,392
Peshawar	1,255
Panama	
Panamá	1,216
Paraguay	
Asunción	1,858
Peru	
Lima	8,180
Philippines	
Manila	10,677
Davao	1,326
Poland	
Warsaw	1,680
Portugal	
Lisbon	2,761
Porto	1,309
Puerto Rico	
San Juan	2,604
Romania	
Bucharest	1,934
Russia	
Moscow	10,672
Saint Petersburg	5,315

	Population (1,000s)
Novosibirsk	1,425
Nizhniy Novgorod	1,288
Yekaterinburg	1,281
Samara	1,140
Omsk	1,132
Kazan	1,108
Rostov	1,081
Chelyabinsk	1,067
Ufa	1,035
Volgograd	1,016
Perm	1,014
Saudi Arabia	
Riyadh	5,514
Jedda	3,807
Mecca	1,529
Medina	1,044
Senegal	
Dakar	2,313
Serbia	
Belgrade	1,116
Sierra Leone	
Freetown	1,007
Singapore	
Singapore City	4,372
Somalia	
Mogadishu	1,320
South Africa	
Johannesburg	3,254
Cape Town	3,083
Durban	2,631
Pretoria	1,271
Vereeniging	1,027
Port Elizabeth	1,006
Spain	
Madrid	5,608
Barcelona	4,795
Sudan	
Khartoum	4,518
Sweden	
Stockholm	1,729
Syria	
Aleppo	2,505
Damascus	2,317
Taiwan	
Taipei	2,606
Kaohsiung	1,515
T'aichung	1,033
Tanzania	
Dar es Salaam	2,683
Thailand	
Bangkok	6,604
Togo	
Lomé	1,337
Tunisia	
Tunis	2,063
Turkey	
Istanbul	9,712
Ankara	3,573
Izmir	2,487
Bursa	1,414
Adana	1,245
Uganda	
Kampala	1,345
Ukraine	
Kiev	2,621
Kharkov	1,521
Dnepropetrovsk	1,122
Donetsk	1,065

	Population (1,000s)
Odessa	1,027
United Arab Emirates	
Dubai	1,330
United Kingdom	
London	8,505
Birmingham	2,280
Manchester	2,228
Liverpool	1,519
Glasgow	1,159
United States of America	
New York	18,718
Los Angeles	12,298
Chicago	8,814
Miami	5,434
Philadelphia	5,392
Dallas–Fort Worth	4,655
Boston	4,361
Houston	4,320
Atlanta	4,304
Washington	4,238
Detroit	4,034
Phoenix–Mesa	3,416
San Francisco	3,385
Seattle	2,989
San Diego	2,852
Minneapolis–St Paul	2,556
Tampa–St Petersburg	2,252
Denver	2,239
Baltimore	2,205
St Louis	2,159
Cleveland	1,855
Portland	1,810
Pittsburgh	1,806
Las Vegas	1,720
San Bernardino	1,690
San Jose	1,631
Cincinnati	1,599
Sacramento	1,555
Norfolk–Virginia Beach	1,460
Kansas City	1,437
San Antonio	1,436
Indianapolis	1,387
Milwaukee	1,316
Orlando	1,306
Providence	1,248
Columbus	1,236
Austin	1,107
Memphis	1,053
New Orleans	1,010
Uruguay	
Montevideo	1,353
Uzbekistan	
Tashkent	2,181
Venezuela	
Caracas	3,276
Valencia	2,330
Maracaibo	2,182
Maracay	1,138
Vietnam	
Ho Chi Minh City	5,065
Hanoi	4,164
Haiphong	1,873
Yemen	
Sana'	1,801
Zambia	
Lusaka	1,450
Zimbabwe	
Harare	1,527

Listed above are the principal cities with more than 1,00,000 inhabitants. The figures are taken from the most recent census or estimate available (usually 2007), and as far as possible are for the metropolitan area or urban agglomeration.

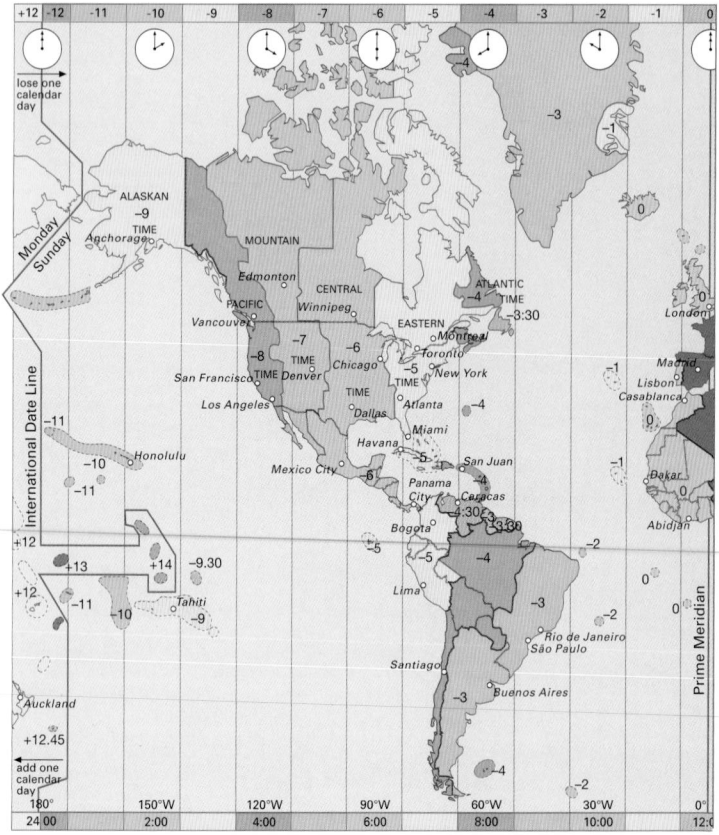

The world is divided into 24 time zones, each centered on meridians at 15° intervals, which is the longitudinal distance the Sun travels every hour. The Prime Meridian running through Greenwich in London, England, passes through the middle of the first time zone. Zones to the east of Greenwich are ahead of Universal Time (UT) by one hour for every 15° of longitude, while zones to the west are behind UT by one hour.

When it is 12 noon at the Greenwich meridian, 180° east it is midnight of the same day, while at 180° west the day is only just beginning. To overcome this, the International Date Line was established in 1883 – an imaginary line which approximately follows the 180th meridian. Therefore, if one traveled eastward from Japan (140° East) toward Samoa (170° West), one would pass from Sunday night straight into Sunday morning.

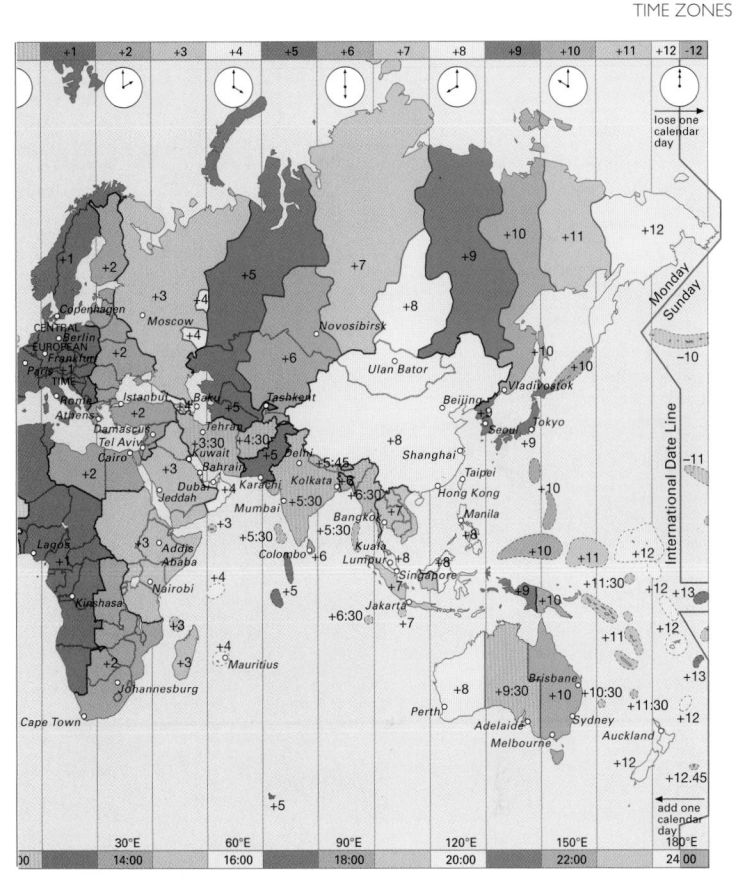

TIME DIFFERENCES FROM EASTERN STANDARD TIME

BEIJING	+13	LONDON	+5
CAIRO	+7	LOS ANGELES	–3
CHICAGO	–1	MOSCOW	+8
DALLAS	–1	MEXICO CITY	–1
DELHI	+10.5	SANTIAGO	+1
DENVER	–2	SYDNEY	+15
HONOLULU	–5	TOKYO	+14
KUWAIT	+8	VANCOUVER	–3

KEY TO TIME ZONES MAP

10	Hours behind or ahead of UT or Coordinated Universal Time		Zones ahead of UT (GMT)
	Zones using UT (GMT)		Half-hour zones
	Zones behind UT (GMT)		Time zone boundaries
	International boundaries		International Date Line
	Actual solar time, when time at Greenwich is 12:00 (noon)		**Note:** Certain time zones are affected by the incidence of daylight saving time in countries where it is adopted.

WORLD'S BUSIEST AIRPORTS

TOTAL NUMBER OF PASSENGERS IN MILLIONS (2006)

ATLANTA HARTSFIELD INTL. (ATL)	84.8
CHICAGO O'HARE INTL. (ORD)	77.0
LONDON HEATHROW (LHR)	67.5
TOKYO HANEDA (HND)	65.8
LOS ANGELES INTL. (LAX)	61.0
DALLAS/FORT WORTH INTL. (DFW)	60.2
PARIS CHARLES DE GAULLE (CDG)	56.8
FRANKFURT INTL. (FRA)	52.8
BEIJING CAPITAL INTL (PEK)	48.7

The flight paths shown on the maps above usually follow the shortest, most direct route from A to B, known as the ***great-circle route***. A great circle is any circle that divides the globe into equal halves. Aircraft do not always fly along great-circle routes, however. Lack of search and rescue and emergency landing provisions, together with limits on fuel consumption and minimum flying altitudes, mean that commercial aircraft do not usually fly across Antarctica.

FLIGHT TIMES FROM NEW YORK

FRANKFURT	8hrs 35mins
JOHANNESBURG	17hrs 45mins
MEXICO CITY	5hrs 45mins
PARIS	8hrs 15mins
ROME	9hrs 35mins
SANTIAGO	12hrs 55mins
SINGAPORE	23hrs 10mins
TOKYO	14hrs 35mins
VANCOUVER	7hrs 25mins

FLIGHT TIMES FROM LONDON

ATHENS	4hrs 05mins
AUCKLAND	24hrs 20mins
BANGKOK	14hrs 30mins
BUENOS AIRES	14hrs 20mins
HONG KONG	14hrs 10mins
LOS ANGELES	12hrs 00mins
MOSCOW	3hrs 50mins
MUMBAI (BOMBAY)	11hrs 15mins
NEW YORK	6hrs 50mins

Kms	Beijing	Buenos Aires	Cairo	Caracas	Chicago	Hong Kong	Honolulu	Johannesburg	Kolkata	Lagos	London	Los Angeles
Beijing		11972	4688	8947	6588	1220	5070	7276	2031	7119	5057	6251
Buenos Aires	19268		7341	3167	5599	11481	7558	5025	10268	4919	6917	6122
Cairo	7544	11814		6340	6127	5064	8838	3894	3541	2432	2180	7580
Caracas	14399	5096	10203		2502	10166	6009	6847	9609	4810	4664	3612
Chicago	10603	9011	3206	4027		7783	4247	8689	7978	5973	3949	1742
Hong Kong	1963	18478	8150	16360	12526		5543	6669	1653	7360	5980	7232
Honolulu	8160	12164	14223	9670	6836	8921		11934	7048	10133	7228	2558
Johannesburg	11710	8088	6267	11019	13984	10732	19206		5256	2799	5637	10362
Kolkata	3269	16524	5699	15464	12839	2659	11343	8459		5727	4946	8152
Lagos	11457	7916	3915	7741	9612	11845	16308	4505	9216		3118	7713
London	8138	11131	3508	7507	6356	9623	11632	9071	7961	5017		5442
Los Angeles	10060	9852	12200	5812	2804	11639	4117	16676	13120	12414	8758	
Mexico City	12460	7389	12372	3586	2726	14122	6085	14585	15280	11071	8936	2493
Moscow	5794	13477	2902	9938	8000	7144	11323	9161	5534	6254	2498	9769
Mumbai	4757	14925	4355	14522	12953	4317	12914	6974	1664	7612	7190	14000
Nairobi	9216	10402	3536	11544	12883	8776	17282	2927	6179	3807	6819	15544
New York	10988	8526	9020	3430	1145	12950	7980	12841	12747	8477	5572	3936
Paris	8217	11051	3210	7625	6650	9630	11968	8732	7858	4714	342	9085
Rio de Janeiro	17338	1953	9896	4546	8547	17704	13342	7113	15073	6035	9299	10155
Rome	8126	11151	2133	8363	7739	9284	12916	7743	7219	4039	1431	10188
Singapore	4478	15879	8267	18359	15078	2599	10816	8660	2897	11145	10852	14123
Sydney	8949	11800	14418	15343	14875	7374	8168	11040	9138	15519	16992	12073
Tokyo	2099	18362	9571	14164	10137	2874	6202	13547	5141	13480	9562	8811
Wellington	10782	9981	16524	13122	13451	9427	7513	11761	11354	16050	18814	10814

The table above shows air distances in miles and kilometers between 30 major cities.

	Mexico City	Moscow	Mumbai	Nairobi	New York	Paris	Rio de Janeiro	Rome	Singapore	Sydney	Tokyo	Wellington	Miles
Beijing	7742	3600	2956	5727	6828	5106	10773	5049	2783	5561	1304	6700	
Buenos Aires	4591	8374	9275	6463	5298	6867	1214	6929	9867	7332	11410	6202	
Cairo	7687	1803	2706	2197	5605	1994	6149	1325	5137	8959	5947	10268	
Caracas	2228	6175	9024	7173	2131	4738	2825	5196	11407	9534	8801	8154	
Chicago	1694	4971	8048	8005	711	4132	5311	4809	9369	9243	6299	8358	
Hong Kong	8775	4439	2683	5453	8047	5984	11001	5769	1615	4582	1786	5857	
Honolulu	3781	7036	8024	10739	4958	7437	8290	8026	6721	5075	3854	4669	
Johannesburg	9063	5692	4334	1818	7979	5426	4420	4811	5381	6860	8418	7308	
Kolkata	9494	3438	1034	3839	7921	4883	9366	4486	1800	5678	3195	7055	
Lagos	6879	3886	4730	2366	5268	2929	3750	2510	6925	9643	8376	9973	
London	5552	1552	4467	4237	3463	212	5778	889	6743	10558	5942	11691	
Los Angeles	1549	6070	8700	9659	2446	5645	6310	6331	8776	7502	5475	6719	
Mexico City		6664	9728	9207	2090	5717	4780	6365	10321	8058	7024	6897	
Moscow			3126	3942	4666	1545	7184	1477	5237	9008	4651	10283	
Mumbai				2816	7793	4356	8332	3837	2432	6313	4189	7686	
Nairobi					7358	4029	5548	3350	4635	7552	6996	8490	
New York	10724					3626	4832	4280	9531	9935	6741	8951	
Paris	15656	5031					5708	687	6671	10539	6038	11798	
Rio de Janeiro	14818	6344	4532					5725	9763	8389	11551	7367	
Rome	3264	7510	12541	11842					6229	10143	6127	11523	
Singapore	9200	2486	7010	6485	5836					3915	3306	5298	
Sydney	7693	11562	13409	8928	7777	9187					4861	1383	
Tokyo	10243	2376	6175	5391	6888	1105	9214					5762	
Wellington	16610	8428	3914	7460	15339	10737	15712	10025					
Miles	12969	14497	10160	12153	15989	16962	13501	16324	6300				
	11304	7485	6742	11260	10849	9718	18589	9861	5321	7823			
	11100	16549	12370	13664	14405	18987	11855	18545	8526	2226	9273		

Known as "great-circle" distances, these measure the shortest routes between the cities.

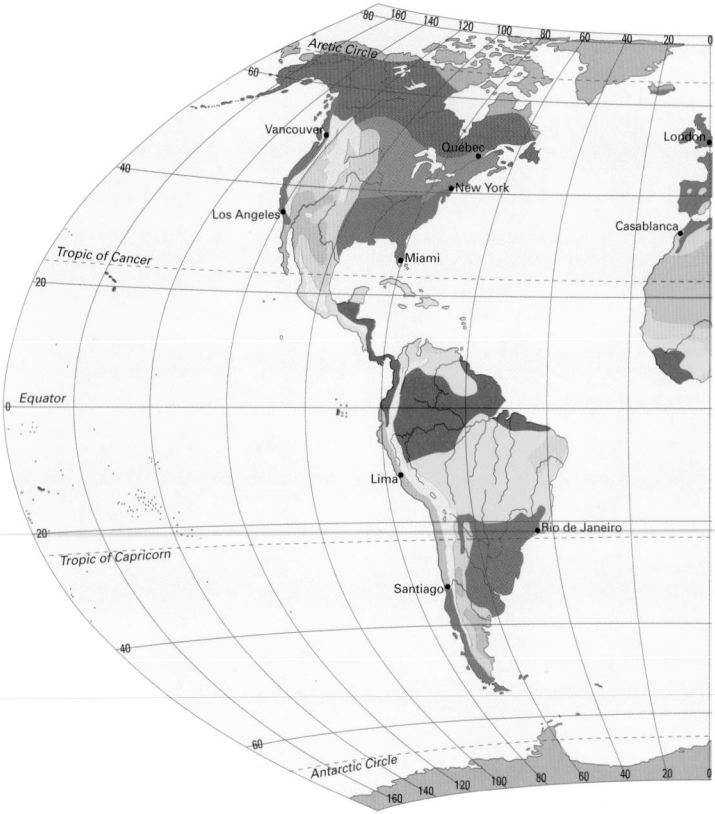

Climate is weather in the long term: the seasonal pattern of temperature and precipitation averaged over a period of time. Temperature roughly follows latitude, and is warmest near the equator and coldest near the poles. The interplay of various factors, however, namely the differential heating of land and sea, the influence of landmasses and mountain ranges on winds and ocean currents, and the effect of vegetation, all combine to add complexity. Thus New York and Naples share almost the same latitude, but their resulting climates are quite different. Most scientists are now in agreement that the world's climate is changing, due partly to atmospheric pollution. By the year 2050, average world temperatures are predicted to rise by approximately 3°F to make the climate hotter than it has been at any time during the last 120,000 years. Climate graphs for 24 cities are given on pages 18 and 19.

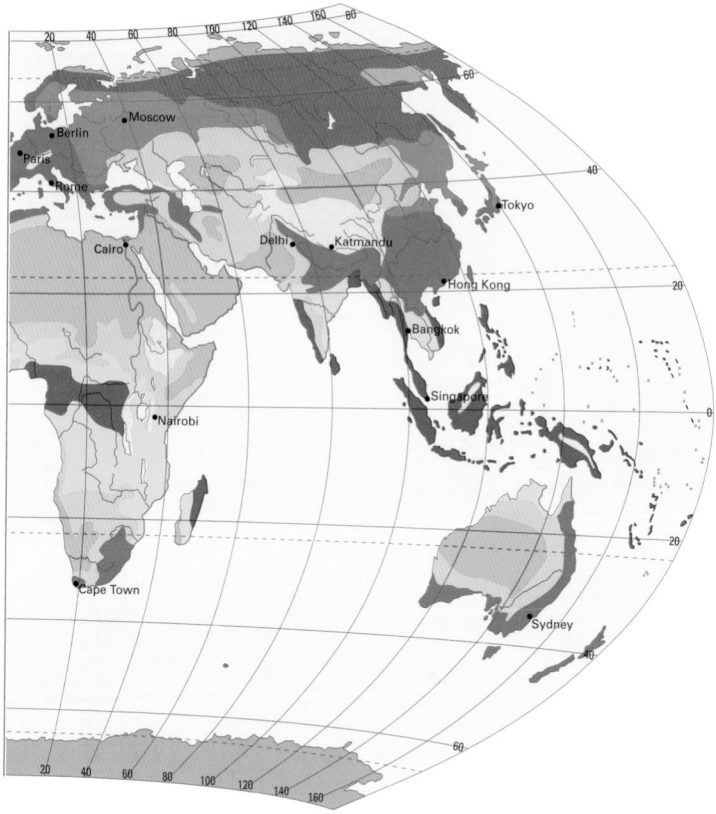

SEASONAL WEATHER EXTREMES

- **Caribbean**
  Hurricanes – August to October
- **Northern Latitudes**
  Blizzards – November to March
- **Southern Asia**
  Cyclones and typhoons – June to November
- **Southern Asia**
  Monsoon rains – July to October

CLIMATIC REGIONS

- Tropical climate (hot and wet)
- Desert climate (hot and very dry)
- Savanna climate (hot with dry season)
- Steppe climate (Warm and dry)
- Mild climate (Warm and wet)
- Continental climate (cold with wet winter)
- Subarctic climate (very cold winter)
- Polar climate (very cold and dry)
- Mountainous climate (altitude affects climate)
- Lima • Climate graphs on pages 18 and 19

Note: Climate comprises a description of the condition of the atmosphere over a considerable area for a long time (at least 30 years).

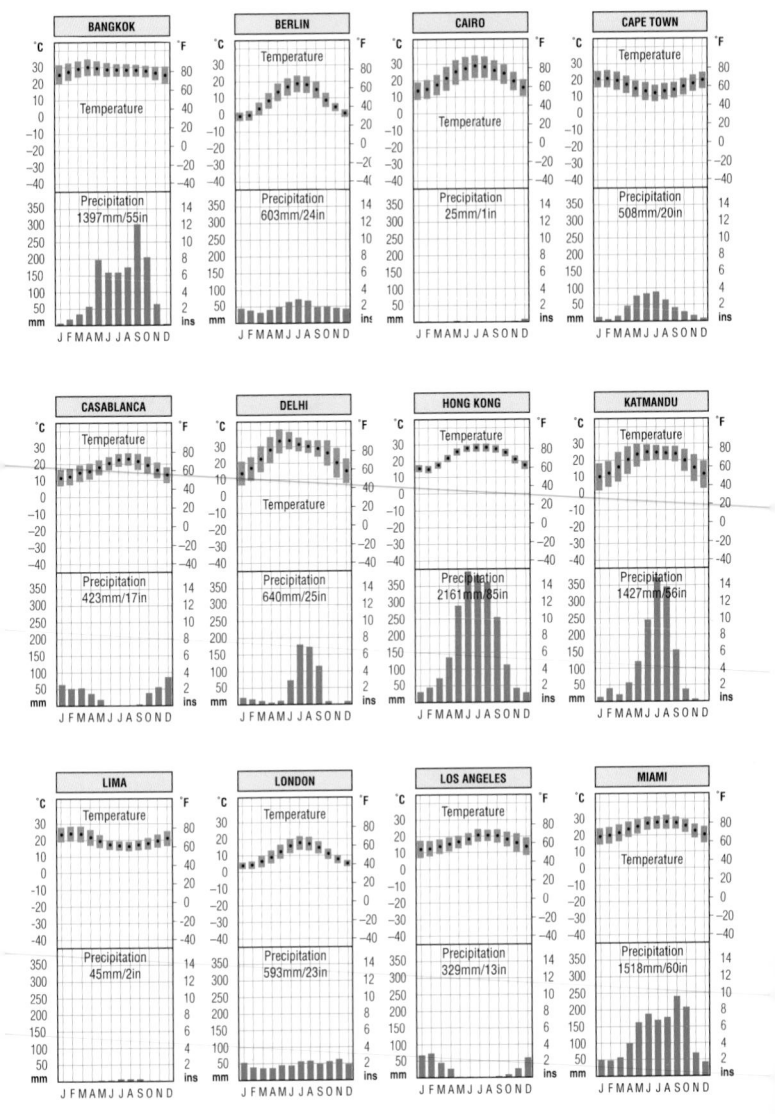
BANGKOK
Temperature
Precipitation
1397mm/55in
BERLIN
Temperature
Precipitation
603mm/24in
CAIRO
Temperature
Precipitation
25mm/1in
CAPE TOWN
Temperature
Precipitation
508mm/20in
CASABLANCA
Temperature
Precipitation
423mm/17in
DELHI
Temperature
Precipitation
640mm/25in
HONG KONG
Temperature
Precipitation
2161mm/85in
KATMANDU
Temperature
Precipitation
1427mm/56in
LIMA
Temperature
Precipitation
45mm/2in
LONDON
Temperature
Precipitation
593mm/23in
LOS ANGELES
Temperature
Precipitation
329mm/13in
MIAMI
Temperature
Precipitation
1518mm/60in
°C
°F
mm
ins
J F M A M J J A S O N D

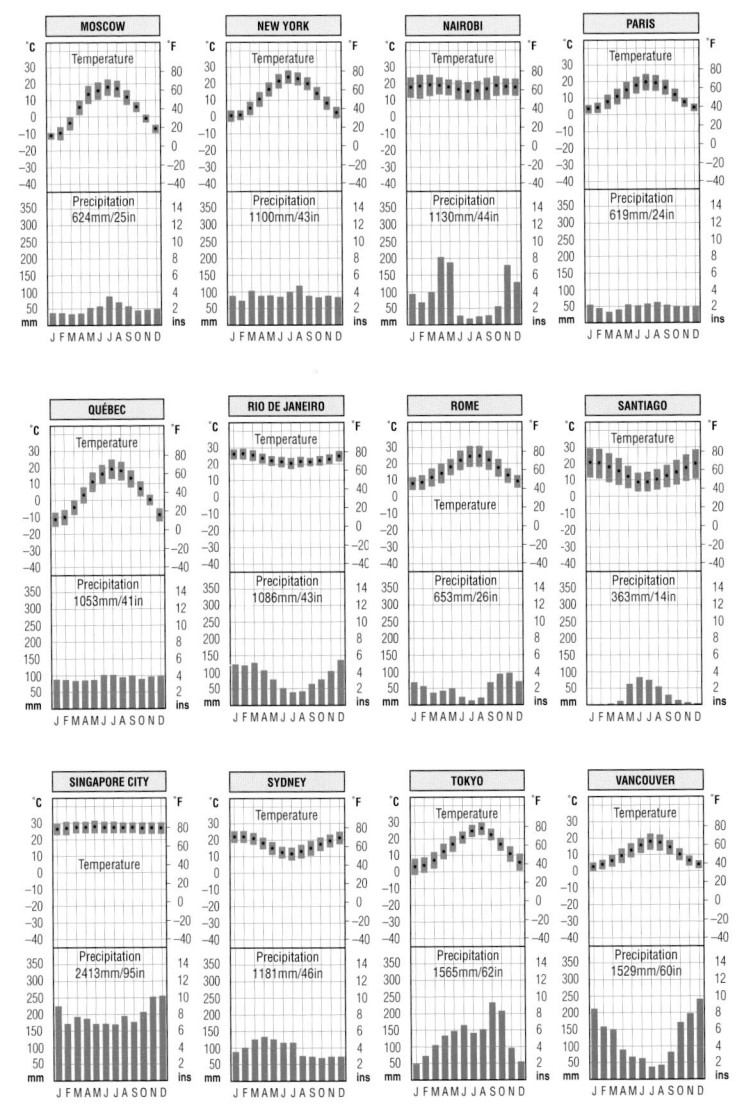
MOSCOW
Temperature
Precipitation
624mm/25in
NEW YORK
Temperature
Precipitation
1100mm/43in
NAIROBI
Temperature
Precipitation
1130mm/44in
PARIS
Temperature
Precipitation
619mm/24in
QUÉBEC
Temperature
Precipitation
1053mm/41in
RIO DE JANEIRO
Temperature
Precipitation
1086mm/43in
ROME
Temperature
Precipitation
653mm/26in
SANTIAGO
Temperature
Precipitation
363mm/14in
SINGAPORE CITY
Temperature
Precipitation
2413mm/95in
SYDNEY
Temperature
Precipitation
1181mm/46in
TOKYO
Temperature
Precipitation
1565mm/62in
VANCOUVER
Temperature
Precipitation
1529mm/60in
°C
°F
mm
ins
J F M A M J J A S O N D

CITY PLANS

21 Amsterdam
22 Athens
23 Bangkok
24 Barcelona
25 Berlin
26 Brussels
27 Cape Town
28 Chicago
29 Dublin
30 Hong Kong
31 London
32 Madrid
33 Mexico City
34 Moscow
35 Mumbai
36 New York
37 Paris
38 Prague
39 Rio de Janeiro
40 Rome
41 San Francisco
42 Singapore
43 Sydney
44 Tokyo
45 Toronto
46 Vienna

LEGEND TO CITY PLANS

	Motorway		Abbey/cathedral
	Through route		Church of interest
	Secondary road		Hospital
	Other road		Mosque
	Limited access / pedestrian road		Shrine
			Synagogue
	Railroad		Temple
	Tramway/monorail		Tourist information center
	Elevated rail lines		
	Rail/bus station		Public building
U M S	Underground/Metro station	Museum	Place of interest

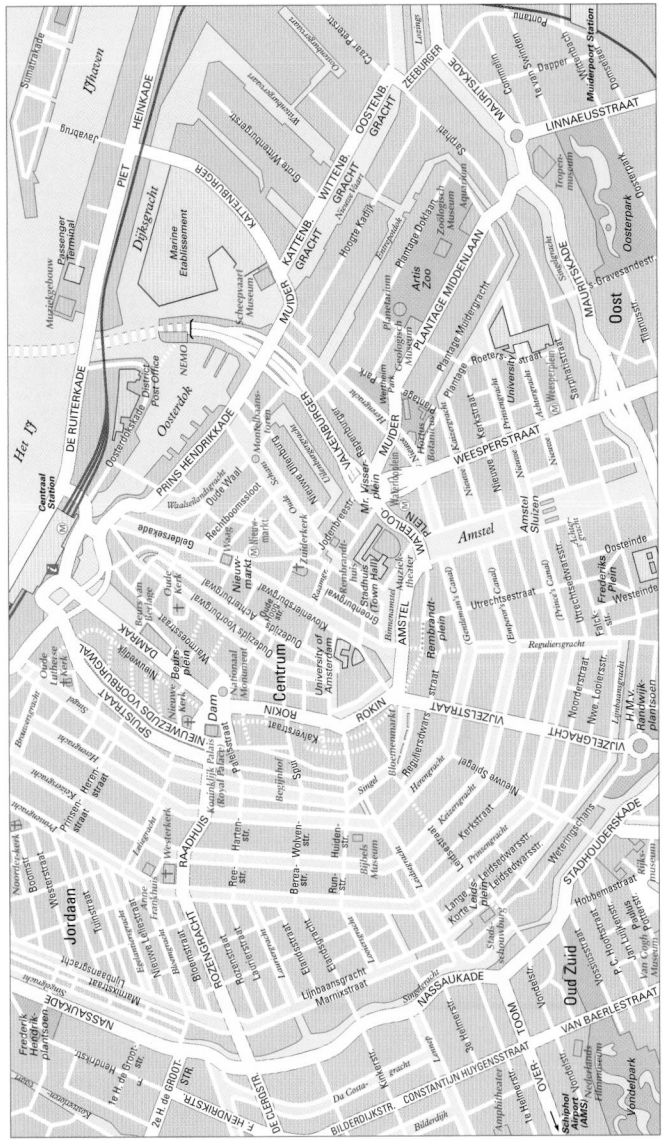
0 km 1
Het IJ
Centraal Station
Passenger Terminal
Musiekgebouw
Oosterdok
Post Office
NEMO
Marina Etablissement
Schepenvaart Museum
Dijksgracht
Javaplein
Sumatrakade
Theaters
PIET HEINKADE
DE RUITERKADE
PRINS HENDRIKKADE
Oosterdokskade
Gelderlandkade
Rechtboomsloot
Oude Waal
Nieuwe Uilenburg
Waterlooplein
Nieuwe Kerk
Nieuwe Kerkstraat
Oude Lutherse Kerk
Dam
Nationale Monumenten
Koninklijk Paleis (Royal Palace)
Beurs van Berlage
Damrak
Nieuwendijk
Warmoesstraat
Oude Zijds Voorburgwal
Oude Zijds Achterburgwal
Nieuwezijds Voorburgwal
Nieuwezijds Achterburgwal
Oude Kerk
Centrum
Nieuwmarkt
Zeedijk
Kloveniersburgwal
Amstel
Rembrandtplein
Muziektheater
Stadhuis (Town Hall)
Amstel Station
Waterlooplein
Mr. Visserplein
Weesperstraat
Nieuwe Herengracht
Nieuwe Keizersgracht
Nieuwe Prinsengracht
Nieuwe Spiegel
Nieuwe Uilenburgerstr.
Nieuwe Leliestraat

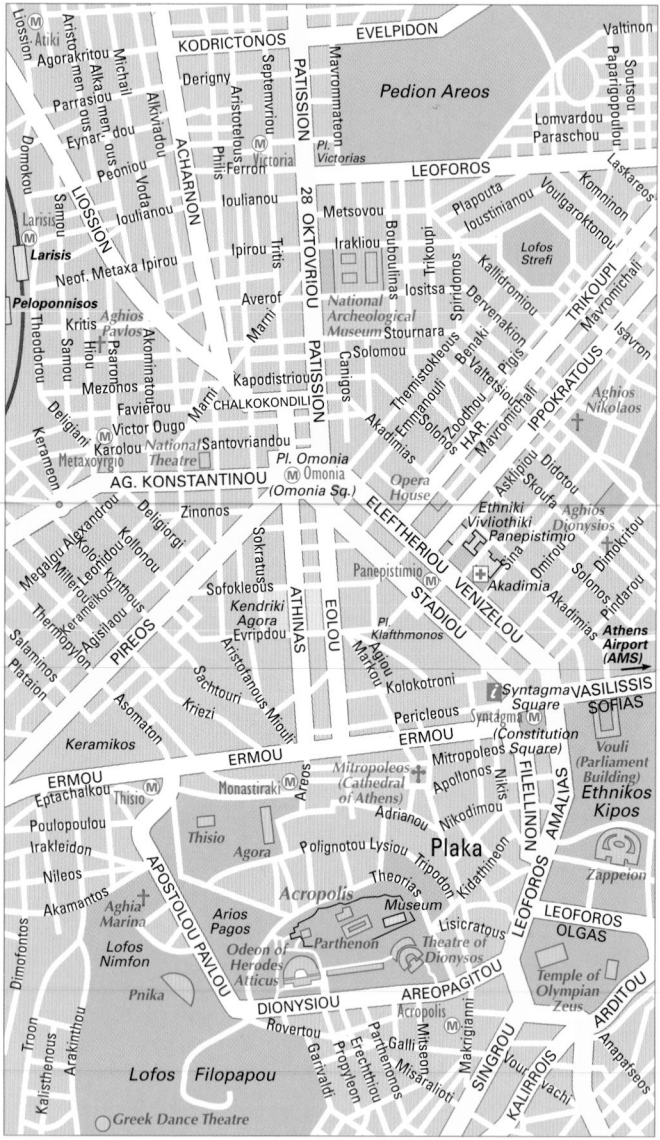
0 km 1
Liossion
Ⓜ Atiki
Aristomenous
Agorakritou
Alkamenous
Michail
Parrasiou
Eynardou
Alkiviadou
Peoniou
Voda
Domokou
Samou
Ioulianou
LIOSSION
Larisiou
Ⓜ Larisis
Peloponnisos
Neof. Metaxa
Ipirou
Theodorou
Kritis
Aghios Pavlos
Samou
Hiou
Psaronou
Akominatou
Mezonos
Favierou
Deligiani
Victor Ougo
Karolou
Ⓜ National Theatre
Santovriandou
Metaxourgio
Keramеon
AG. KONSTANTINOU
Zinonos
Deligiorgi
Megalou Alexandrou
Kolonou
Millerou
Leonidou
Keramikou
Kynthous
Thermopylon
Agisilaou
Salaminos
Plataion
PIREOS
Asomaton
Keramikos
ERMOU
Eptachalkou
Ⓜ Thisio
Poulopoulou
Irakleidon
Nileos
Akamantos
Aghia Marina
Lofos Nimfon
Dimofontos
Troon
Arakinthou
Kalisthenous
Lofos Filopapou
Greek Dance Theatre
KODRICTONOS
Derigny
Aristotelous
Phillis
Ferron
Ⓜ Victoria
Septemvriou
Mavromateon
Pl. Victorias
Pedion Areos
EVELPIDON
Valtinon
Papariggopoulou
Soutsou
Lomvardou
Paraschou
Lasfareos
LEOFOROS
Komninon
Voulgaroktonou
Plapouta
Ioustinianou
Lofos Strefi
Kallidromiou
Dervenakion
TRIKOUPI
Mavromichali
Isavron
Benaki
Pigis
Valaitsou
IPPOKRATOUS
Aghios Nikolaos
Didotou
Skoufa
Ethniki Vivliothiki
Panepistimio
Aghios Dionysios
Dimokritou
Omirou
Solonos
Pindarou
Akadimia
Akadimias
Athens Airport (AMS)
VASILISSIS SOFIAS
Syntagma Square
Ⓜ Syntagma (Constitution Square)
Vouli (Parliament Building)
Ethnikos Kipos
Zappeion
FILELLINON
AMALIAS
LEOFOROS OLGAS
Temple of Olympian Zeus
ARDITOU
Anapafseos
SINGROU
Vou
Vachi
KALIRROIS
Makrigianni
Mitseon
Misaraliotou
Galliou
Parthenonos
Erechthiou
Propileon
Garivaldi
Rovertou
DIONYSIOU
AREOPAGITOU
Acropolis
Theatre of Dionysos
Odeon of Herodes Atticus
Parthenon
Acropolis Museum
Plaka
Polignotou
Lysiou
Tripodon
Kidathineon
Theorias
Lisicratous
Mitropoleos
Apollonos
Nikis
Nikodimou
Adrianou
Mitropoleos (Cathedral of Athens)
Monastiraki
Thisio
Agora
APOSTOLOU PAVLOU
Arios Pagos
Pnika
ATHINAS
Sokratous
Sofokleous
Kendriki Agora
Evripidou
Aristofanous
Mnouli
Sachtouri
Kriezi
EOLOU
Pl. Klafthmonos
Agiou Markou
Kolokotroni
Panepistimio
Ⓜ Omonia
Pl. Omonia
(Omonia Sq.)
Opera House
ELEFTHERIOU VENIZELOU
STADIOU
Pericleous
Ioulianou
Ipirou
Tritis
Marni
Kapodistriou
CHALKOKONDILI
Averof
Metsovou
Irakliou
Bouboulinas
Iroon Polytechniou
Iositsa
Spiridonos
National Archeological Museum
Stournara
Solomou
Carnigos
Themistokleous
Emmanouil
Zoodhou
Solonos
Akademias
HAR. Mavromichali

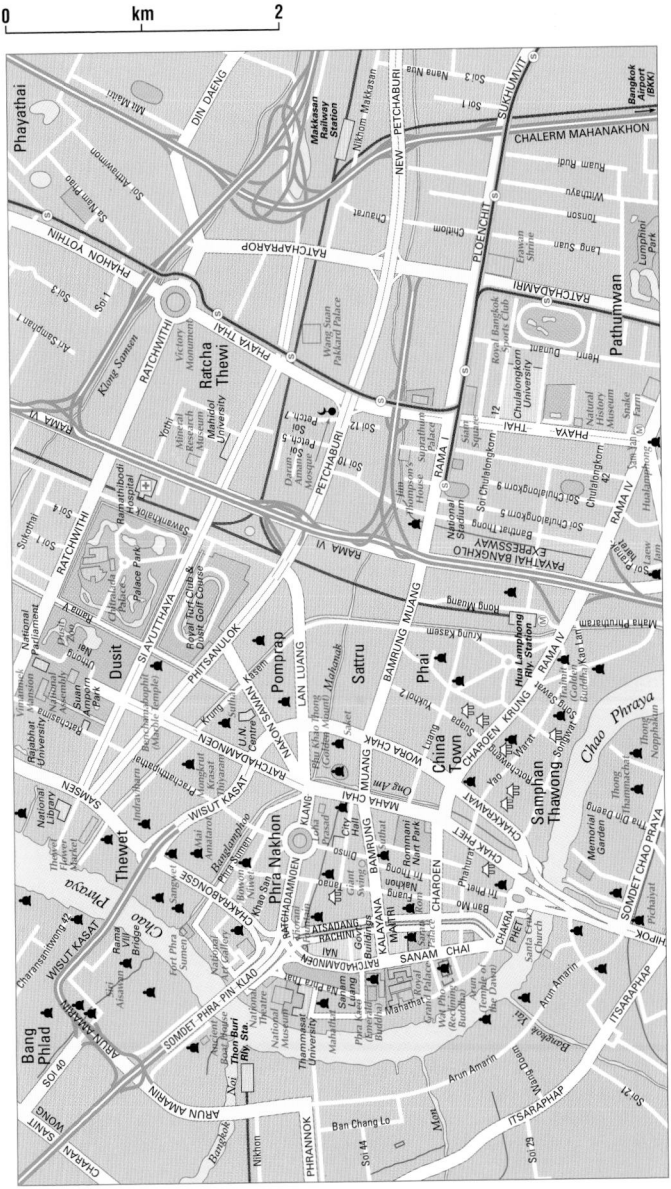

COPYRIGHT PHILIPS

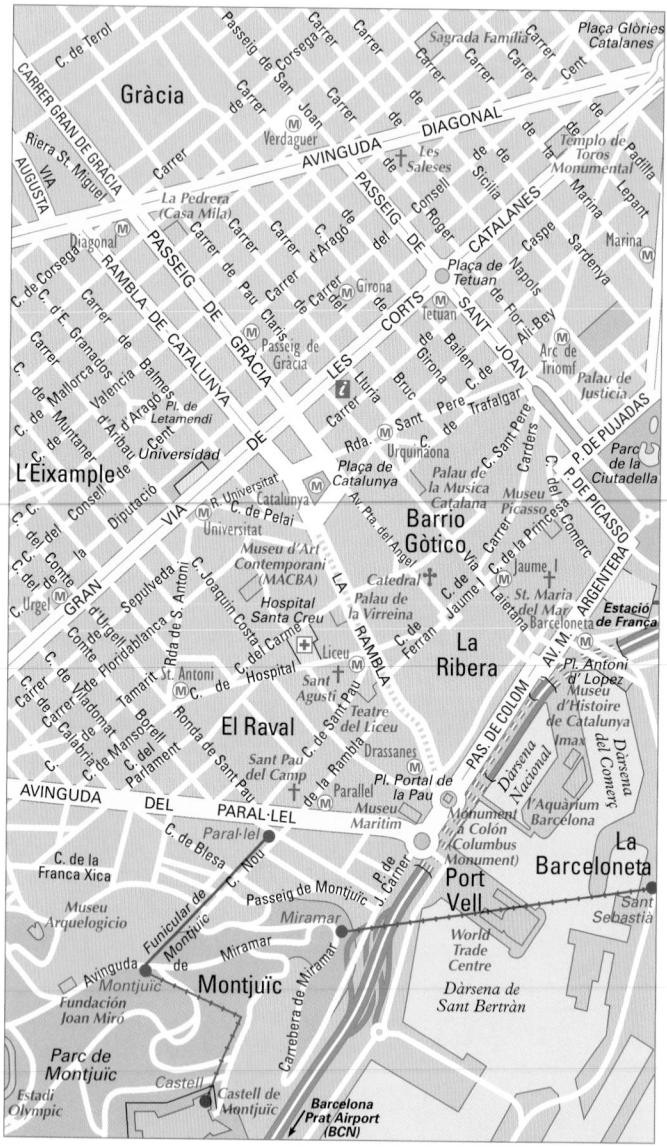

COPYRIGHT PHILIP'S

0 km 1

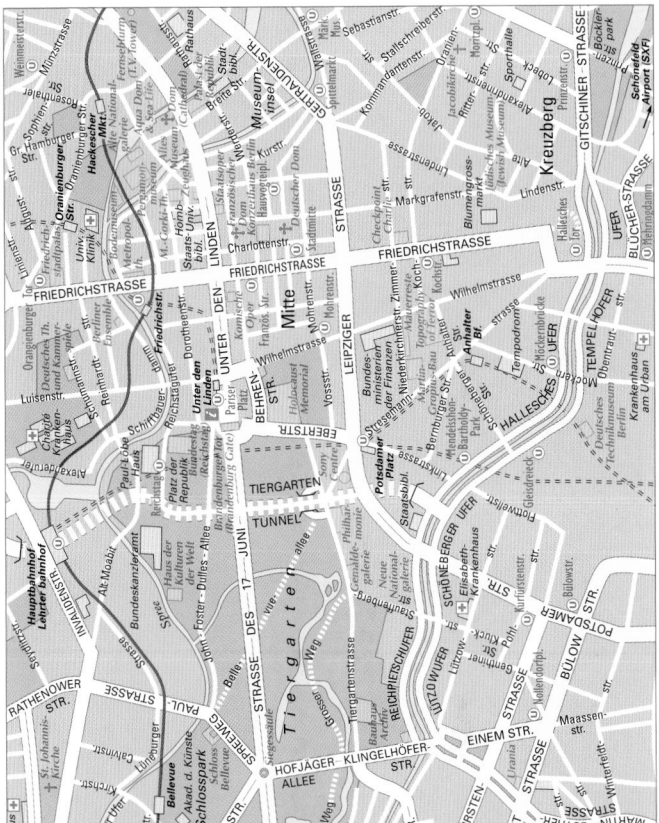

COPYRIGHT PHILIP'S

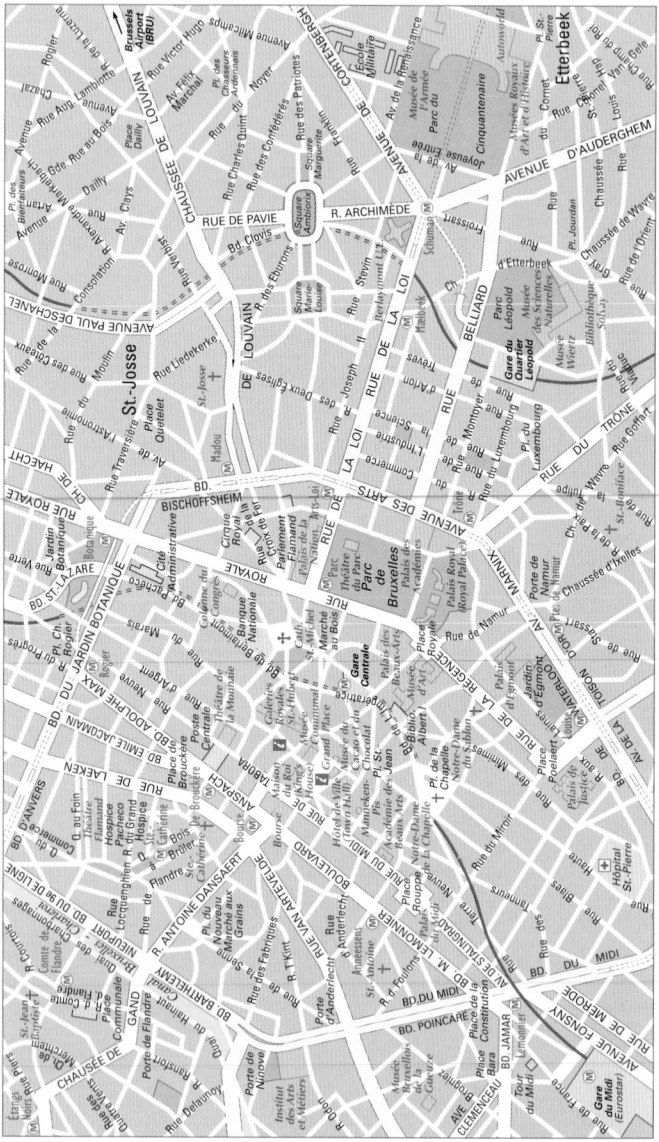
0
km
1
Brussels Airport (BRU)
Etterbeek
St-Josse
Parc de Bruxelles
Gare Centrale
Gare du Midi (Eurostar)
Gare du Quartier Léopold
Parc Léopold
Musée Wiertz
Bibliothèque Solvay
Musée des Sciences Naturelles
Musées Royaux d'Art et d'Histoire
Musée de l'Armée
Parc du Cinquantenaire
Autoworld
Palais Royal / Koninklijk Paleis
Palais des Académies
Palais de Justice
Palais des Beaux-Arts
Musée d'Art Moderne
Musée Bruxellois de la Gaufrette
Musée Bruxellois de la Gueuze
Musée Bruxellois de la Bière
Musée du Chocolat
Musée du Cacao et du Chocolat
Maison du Roi (Kings House)
Grand Place
Hôtel de Ville (Town Hall)
Manneken-Pis
Cathédrale St-Michel
Marché aux Poissons
Marché aux Fleurs
Marché aux Grains
Marché aux Oiseaux
Galeries Royales St-Hubert
Théâtre de la Monnaie
Théâtre Royal Flamand
Théâtre National
Cirque Royal
Centre Administratif
Centre Culturel du Congrès
Parlement Flamand
Parlement Wallon
Banque Nationale
Poste Centrale
Place de Brouckère
Place Rogier
Place Dailly
Place Quetelet
Place Poelaert
Place Ste-Catherine
Place Jourdan
Place Communale
Place de la Constitution
Place de la Chapelle
Place Royale
Place Bara

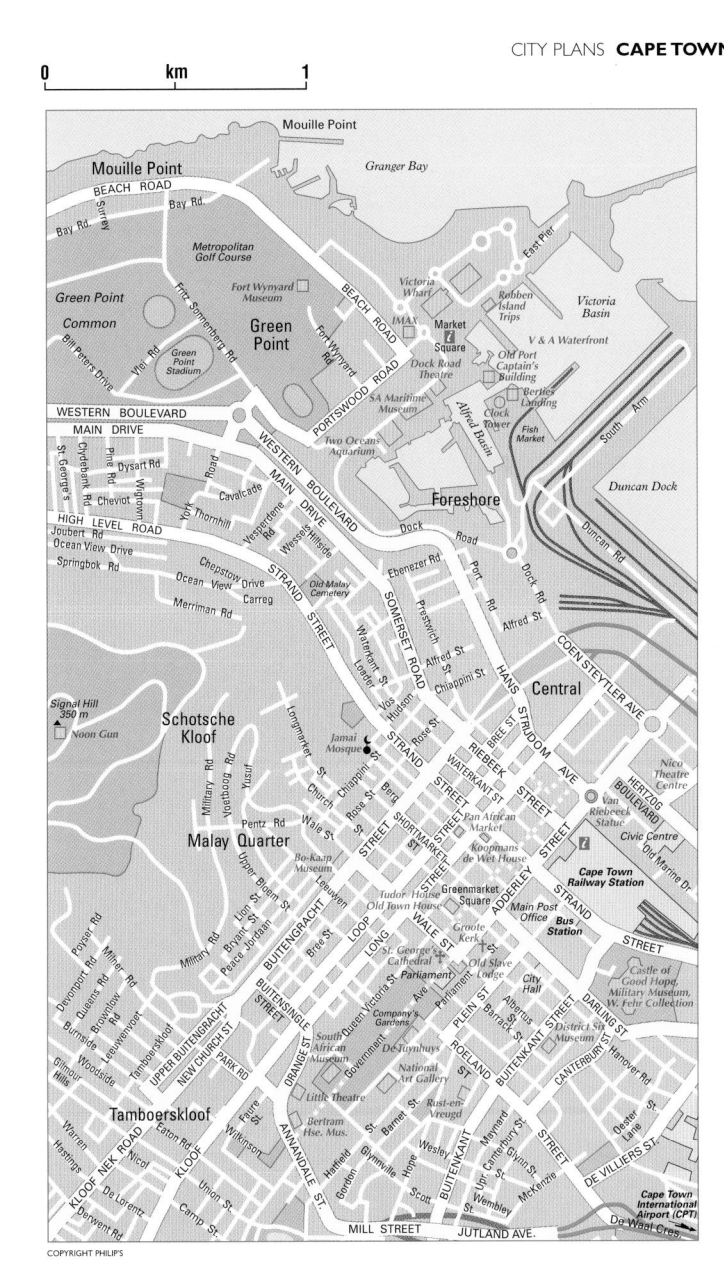

COPYRIGHT PHILIP'S

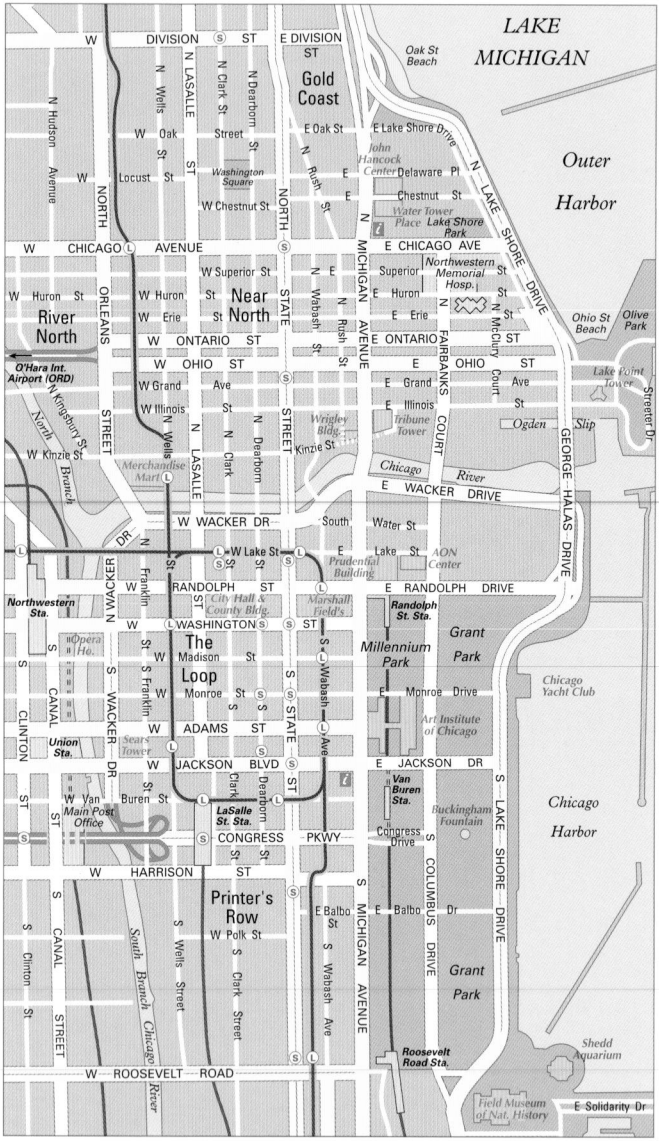
0 km 0.5
LAKE MICHIGAN
Outer Harbor
Chicago Harbor
Oak St Beach
Gold Coast
E DIVISION ST
W DIVISION ST
N LASALLE
N Clark St
N Dearborn
N Wells
N Hudson Avenue
W Oak Street
E Oak St
E Lake Shore Drive
John Hancock Center
Washington Square
W Locust St
W Chestnut St
E Chestnut St
Delaware Pl
Water Tower Place
Lake Shore Park
N LAKE SHORE DRIVE
W CHICAGO AVENUE
E CHICAGO AVE
Northwestern Memorial Hosp.
W Superior St
Superior St
W Huron St
E Huron St
Near North
River North
W Erie St
E Erie St
Ohio St Beach
Olive Park
W ONTARIO ST
E ONTARIO ST
W OHIO ST
E OHIO ST
O'Hara Int. Airport (ORD)
W Grand Ave
E Grand Ave
W Illinois St
E Illinois St
Lake Point Tower
Streeter Dr
Wrigley Bldg.
Tribune Tower
Ogden Slip
W Kinzie St
Kinzie St
Merchandise Mart
Chicago River
E WACKER DRIVE
W WACKER DR
South Water St
W Lake St
E Lake St
AON Center
Prudential Building
GEORGE HALAS DRIVE
N WACKER DR
W RANDOLPH ST
E RANDOLPH DRIVE
Northwestern Sta.
City Hall & County Bldg.
Marshall Field's
Randolph St. Sta.
W WASHINGTON ST
Opera Hs.
The Loop
Millennium Park
Grant Park
Chicago Yacht Club
W Madison St
W Monroe St
E Monroe Drive
Art Institute of Chicago
Union Sta.
Sears Tower
W ADAMS ST
W JACKSON BLVD
E JACKSON DR
Van Buren Sta.
W Van Buren St
Main Post Office
LaSalle St. Sta.
Buckingham Fountain
CONGRESS PKWY
Congress Drive
W HARRISON ST
Printer's Row
W Polk St
E Balbo St
E Balbo Dr
S MICHIGAN AVENUE
S COLUMBUS DRIVE
S LAKE SHORE DRIVE
S CANAL STREET
S Clinton St
South Branch Chicago River
Roosevelt Road Sta.
Shedd Aquarium
W ROOSEVELT ROAD
Field Museum of Nat. History
E Solidarity Dr
Elevated rail lines
COPYRIGHT PHILIP'S

0 km 0.5

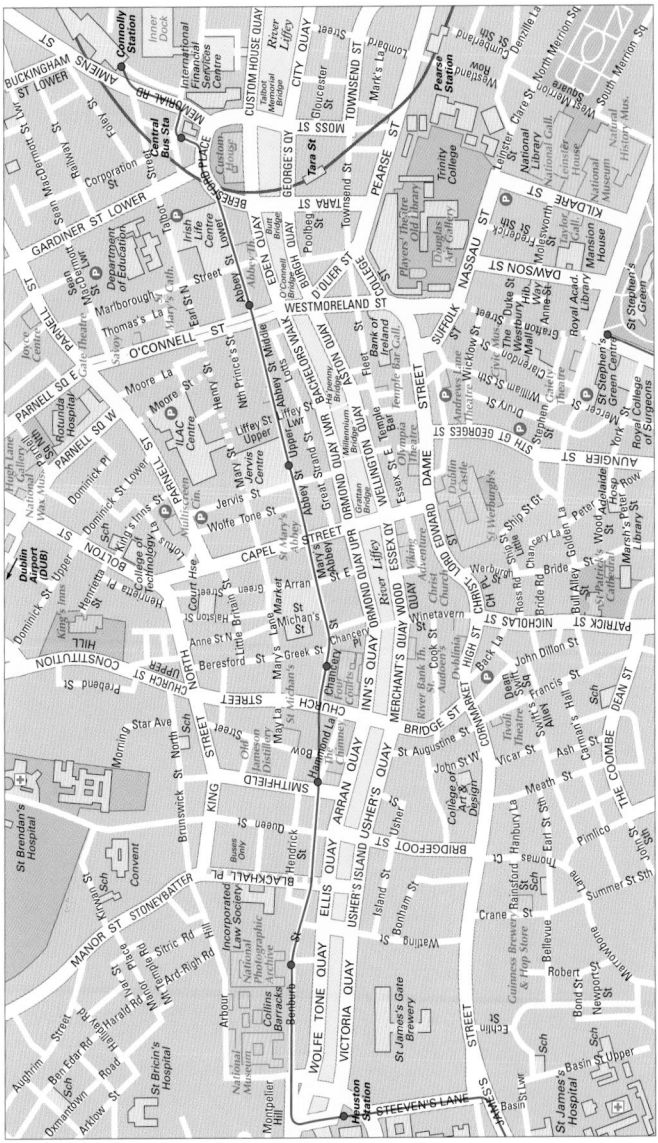
Connolly Station
Inner Dock
International Financial Services Centre
Liffey
River
CUSTOM HOUSE QUAY
Millennium Bridge
CITY QUAY
Gloucester St
TOWNSEND ST
Mark's La
Lombard
Westland Row
Pearse Station
Denzille La
Clare St
North Merrion Sq
South Merrion Sq
BUCKINGHAM ST LOWER
AMIENS ST
MEDICAL PL
Central Bus Station
Custom House
GEORGE'S QY
MOSS ST
Tara St
PEARSE ST
Trinity College
Leinster House
National Library
National Museum
Natural History Mus.
Merrion Sq
West Merrion Sq
Foley St
Railway
Corporation
Seán McDermott St Lwr
BERESFORD PL
TARA ST
Pooley St
Townsend St
Players Theatre
Old Museum
Douglas Hyde Gallery
KILDARE ST
Taylor Gall.
Mansion House
GARDINER ST LOWER
Department of Education
Irish Life Centre
Abbey St Lower
Abbey St
Abbey Tl
Blurt Bridge
O'Connell Bridge
EDEN QUAY
COLLEGE ST
DULOR ST
WESTMORELAND ST
NASSAU ST
DAWSON ST
Frederick St
Molesworth St
Duke St
The Westbury Hotel
Grafton St
Royal Acad. Library
St Stephen's Green
Marlborough
Thomas's La
Earl St N
Mary's Cath.
O'CONNELL ST
Sackville Pl
Bank of Ireland
Fleet
Temple Bar Gall.
SUFFOLK ST
Wicklow St
Clarendon St
Grafton St
Stephen's Green Shop Centre
Royal College of Surgeons
PARNELL SQ E
Moore La
Moore St
Nth Prince's St
Liffey St Upper
Upper Abbey St
Middle Abbey St
Lwr Abbey St
SACKVILLE (O'CONNELL) BRIDGE
ORMOND QUAY UPR
Millennium Bridge
Grattan Bridge
WELLINGTON QUAY
Temple Bar
Essex St E
Temple Bar Theatre
Dublin Theatre
Mansion House
William St S
Drury St
Stephen's Gallery
AUGHRIM ST
PARNELL SQ W
Rotunda Hospital
Gate Theatre
Parnell Sq. Cinema
Dominick Pl
Dominick St Lower
Dominick St Upper
Jervis St
Mary's Abbey Centre
Abbey St
Great Strand St
ORMOND QUAY LWR
Ha'penny Bridge
Merrion Row
Merrion Sq
Dublin Castle
Wolfe Tone St
CAPEL ST
Mary's Abbey
St Mary's Abbey
Liffey
ESSEX QY
Temple Bar
Adventure
Christ Church Cathedral
Marsh's Library
Peter Row
Wood
Adelaide
Golden La
Peter St
Chatsery La
Ship St Gt
Ship St Little
Bull Alley
Ross Rd
Bride Rd
Bride St
Werburgh St
Dublin Castle
St Werburgh's
Dublin Airport (DUB)
Dominick St Upper
Henrietta St
Henrietta Pl
Bolton St
College of Technology
Green St
Court House
Arran
Market
Mary's Lane
Little Britain St
Haslam St
Anne St N
Beresford St
Greek St
St Michan's
Chancery Pl
Four Courts
Inns Quay
Chancery
Christ Church
Dublin Castle
Wine Tavern
Werburgh St
Cook St
River Bank Th.
Aungier St
Dublin Castle
Back La
Dean St
Francis St
John Dillon St
Wood St
Adelaide Rd
PATRICK ST
NICHOLAS ST
CHRIST CH PL
CONSTITUTION HILL
Prebend St
CHURCH ST UPPER
NORTH CHURCH STREET
Morning Star Ave
Star Ave
Mary's La
Hammond La
Smithfield
Chimney
Jameson Distillery
Old Jameson Distillery
MERCHANT'S QUAY WOOD QUAY
INN'S QUAY
ORMOND QUAY UPR
River Liffey
HIGH ST
CHRIST CH PL
CORNMARKET
Dean St
Swift's Alley
Francis St
Ivoli Theatre
Vicar St
Ash St
Carman's Hall
DEAN ST
THE COOMBE
Meath St
Pimlico
Thomas St
Earl St Sth
Summer St Sth
Hanbury La
Rainsford St
Crane St
Bellevue
Robert St
Bond St
Newport St
Basin St Upper
Basin St Low
Basin St
Metrowave
Guinness Brewery & Hop Store
Coleman St
Sch
St James's Hospital
Sarsfield Quay
Kilmainham Ct
Bridge
BRIDGE ST
St Augustine St
John's Lw
Vicar St
College of Art & Design
BRIDGEFOOT
Usher's Island
Usher St
Usher's Quay
Ellis Quay
Bonham St
Island St
Watling St
Wolfe Tone Quay
Victoria Quay
Houston Station
STEVEN'S LANE
Montpelier Hill
Collins Barracks
Benburb St
Arbour Hill
Stirc Rd
Ard Righ Rd
Manor Pl
Manor St
Aughrim Street
Ben Edar Rd
Oxmantown Road
Arkow St
St Brendan's Hospital
Brunswick St North
KING STREET
Queen St
Hendrick St
Blackhall Pl
Stoneybatter
Manor St
Incorporated Law Society
National Photographic Archive
National Museum
St Bricin's Hospital
Convent
Sch
Buses Only
Sch
Sch
Sch

0 km 1

The width of Victoria Harbour has been compressed so that the land area is better represented.

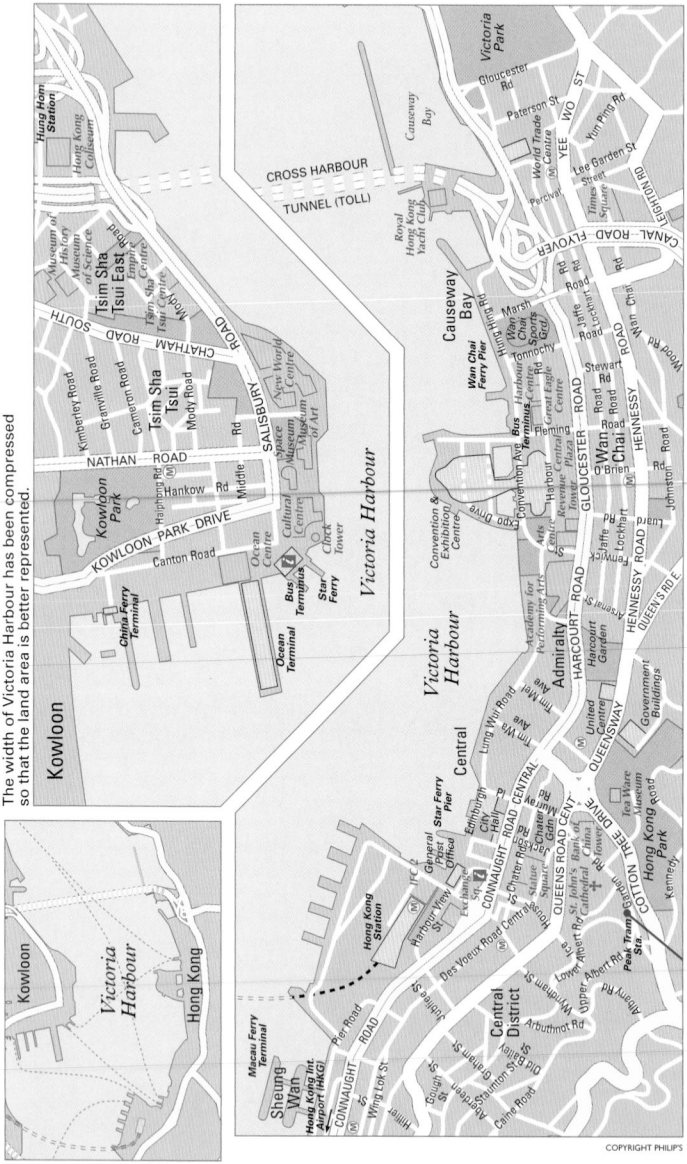
Kowloon
Victoria Harbour
Hong Kong
Hong Ham Station
Hong Kong Coliseum
Museum of History
Museum of Science
Tsim Sha Tsui East
Tsim Sha Tsui Centre
Tsim Sha Tsui
Kimberley Road
Granville Road
Cameron Road
Mody Road
CHATHAM ROAD SOUTH
NATHAN ROAD
Hankow Rd
Middle Rd
SALISBURY
Kowloon Park
KOWLOON PARK DRIVE
Canton Road
Ocean Centre
Cultural Centre
Clock Tower
Museum of Art
Star Ferry
Bus Terminus
Ocean Terminal
China Ferry Terminal
CROSS HARBOUR TUNNEL (TOLL)
Causeway Bay
Royal Hong Kong Yacht Club
Victoria Park
Gloucester Rd
Paterson St
World Trade Centre
Yin Ping Rd
Lee Garden St
Times Square
ELDERTON RD
CANAL ROAD FLYOVER
Causeway Bay
Wan Chai Ferry Pier
Hung Hing Rd
Wan Chai Sports Centre
Tonnochy Rd
Marsh Rd
Lockhart Road
Stewart Rd
Great Eagle Centre
Fleming Rd
Bus Terminus
Convention Ave
Convention & Exhibition Centre
EXPO Drive
Harbour Centre
Revenue Plaza
Arts Centre
Academy for Performing Arts
Wan Chai
GLOUCESTER ROAD
O'Brien Rd
Fenwick St
Lockhart Rd
HENNESSY ROAD
HENNESSY Road
Johnston Rd
Luard Rd
Wood Rd
Admiralty
HARCOURT ROAD
Tim Wa Ave
Lung Wui Road
Central
Harcourt Garden
United Centre
QUEENSWAY
Government Buildings
QUEEN'S RD E
Tai Wan Rd
Tai Hang Rd
Star Ferry Pier
General Post Office
Exchange Sq
City Hall
Edinburgh Pl
CONNAUGHT ROAD CENTRAL
Charter Rd
Queen's Gdn
Chater Rd
QUEENS ROAD CENTRAL
Des Voeux Road Central
Hong Kong Station
Harbour View St
Macau Ferry Terminal
Sheung Wan
Hong Kong Int. Airport (HKG)
CONNAUGHT ROAD
Pier Road
Wing Lok St
Hillier St
Jervois St
Sai Ying Pun
Central District
Arbuthnot Rd
Queen's Rd Central
Lower Albert Rd
Upper Albert Rd
Wyndham St
Albany Rd
Cotton Tree Drive
Hong Kong Park
Tea Ware Museum
Kennedy Rd
Pedestrian Tram Stn
Old Bailey St
Caine Road
Cochrane St
Aberdeen St
Bonham Str
Ladder St
Cat Street
Hollywood Rd
Bonham Rd
Pottinger St
Queen's Road East
Wan Chai Road
Tai Yuen St

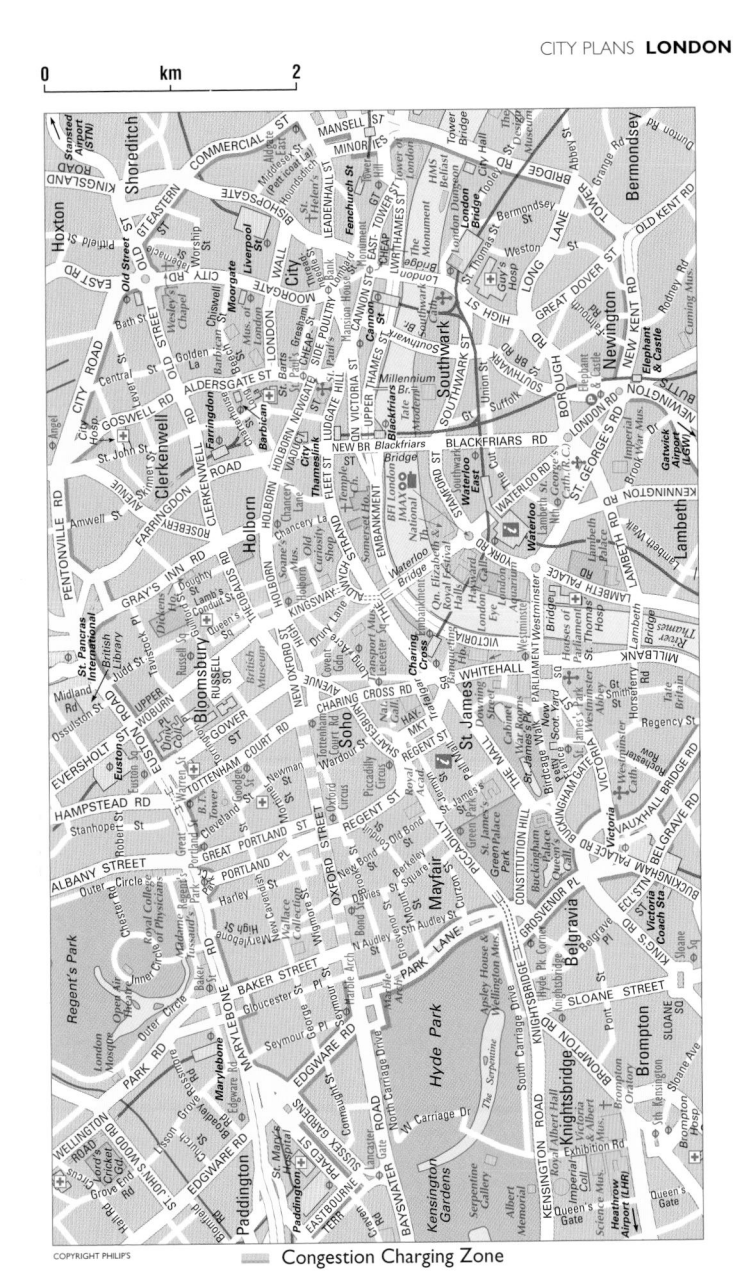
0
km
2
Hoxton
Shoreditch
Bermondsey
Clerkenwell
Holborn
Bloomsbury
Soho
St James
Mayfair
Belgravia
Regent's Park
Hyde Park
Paddington
Knightsbridge
Brompton
Lambeth
Newington
Southwark
City
Kensington Gardens
Stansted Airport (STN)
Heathrow Airport (LHR)
Gatwick Airport (LGW)
COPYRIGHT PHILIP'S
Congestion Charging Zone

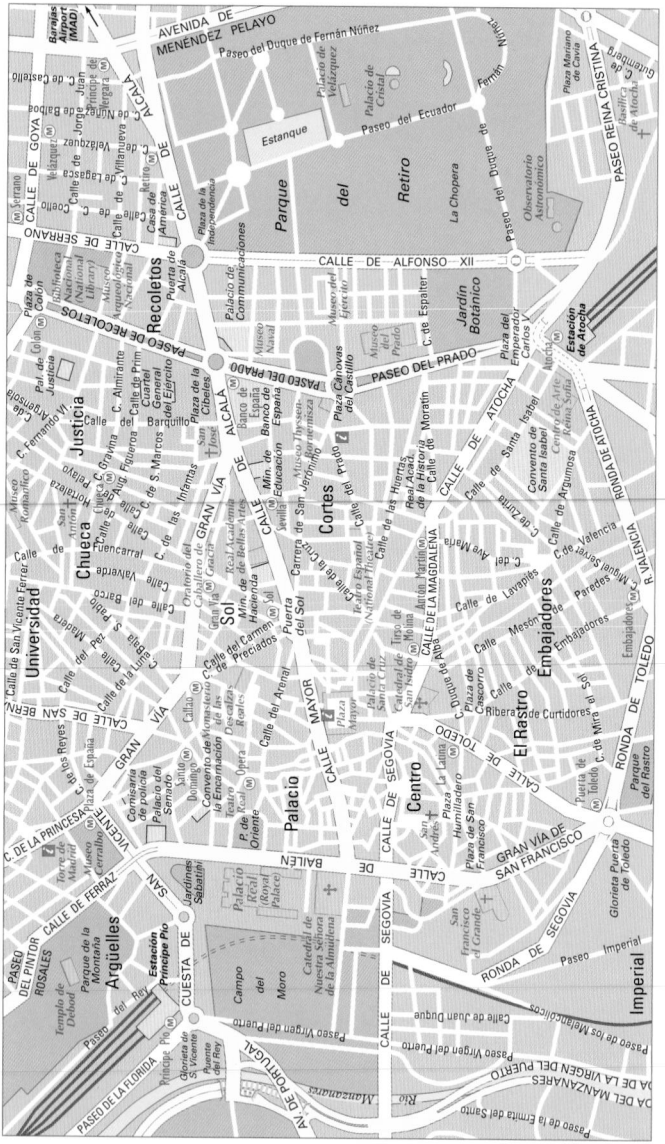
0
km
1
Barajas Airport (MAD)
AVENIDA DE MENÉNDEZ PELAYO
Paseo del Duque de Fernán Núñez
Estanque
Palacio de Velázquez
Palacio de Cristal
Parque del Retiro
Paseo del Ecuador
La Chopera
Observatorio Astronómico
Plaza Mariano de Cavia
PASEO REINA CRISTINA
Basílica de Atocha
Glorieta de Ambrosio Gutiérrez
CALLE DE ALFONSO XII
Jardín Botánico
Plaza del Emperador Carlos V
Estación de Atocha
PASEO DEL PRADO
Museo del Prado
Museo del Ejército
Museo Naval
Palacio de Comunicaciones
Plaza de la Independencia
Puerta de Alcalá
Plaza de Cánovas del Castillo
Plaza de la Cibeles
Banco de España
Min. de Educación
Museo Thyssen-Bornemisza
Recoletos
Justicia
Chueca
Universidad
Cortes
Sol
Palacio
Centro
Embajadores
El Rastro
Argüelles
Imperial
PASEO DE RECOLETOS
CALLE DE SERRANO
CALLE DE GOYA
CALLE DE ALCALA
GRAN VIA
CALLE DE ATOCHA
RONDA DE ATOCHA
CALLE DE SEGOVIA
RONDA DE SEGOVIA
CALLE DE TOLEDO
RONDA DE TOLEDO
CALLE DE FERRAZ
CALLE DE SAN BERNARDO
GRAN VIA DE SAN FRANCISCO
Palacio Real (Royal palace)
Catedral de Nuestra Señora de la Almudena
Campo del Moro
Parque del Rey
Estación Príncipe Pío
Templo de Debod
Parque de la Montaña
Museo Reina Sofía
Museo Nacional (National Library)
Museo Arqueológico Nacional
Museo Romántico
Museo Cerralbo
Museo Thyssen-Bornemisza
Centro de Arte Reina Sofía
Real Academia de Bellas Artes
Real Academia de la Historia
Teatro Real (Royal Opera)
Teatro Español (National Theatre)

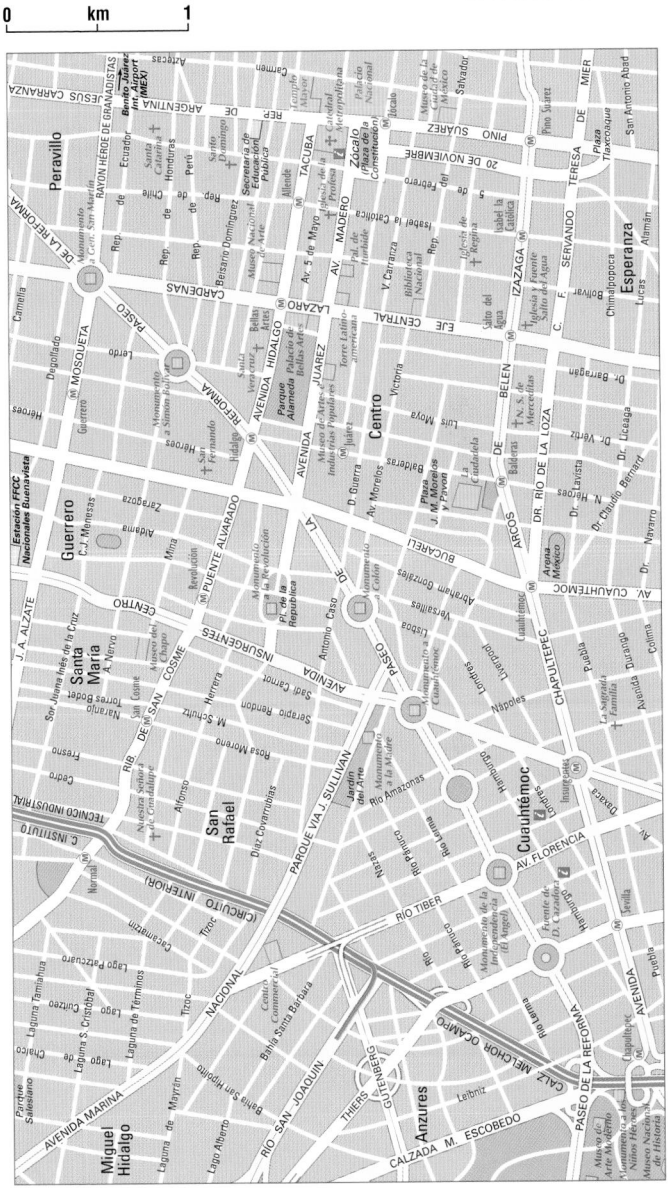
0 km 1
Peravillo
Guerrero
Santa Maria
San Rafael
Cuauhtémoc
Centro
Esperanza
Miguel Hidalgo
Anzures
Benito Juárez Int. Airport (MEX)
Estación FFCC Nacionales Buenavista
Arena México
Zócalo (Plaza de la Constitución)
Palacio Nacional
Catedral Metropolitana
Templo Mayor
Museo Nacional de Arte
Secretaría de Educación Pública
Museo de la Ciudad de México
Monumento a Cuauhtémoc
Monumento a Colón
Monumento a la Revolución
Monumento a Simón Bolívar
Monumento a la Madre
Monumento a la Independencia (El Angel)
Fuente de D. Quixote
Museo de Arte Moderno
Museo Nacional de Historia
Parque Alameda
Palacio de Bellas Artes
Torre Latinoamericana
Jardín del Arte
Plaza J. M. Morelos y Pavón
Plaza de la República
Bolsa Mexicana de Valores
Centro Comercial
Iglesia y Fuente Salto del Agua
Iglesia de Regina
Iglesia de San Fernando
Iglesia de Santa Veracruz
Iglesia de Santa Cecilia
Iglesia de Nuestra Señora de Guadalupe
Iglesia de Santo Domingo
Iglesia de San Cosme
Iglesia de San Antonio Abad

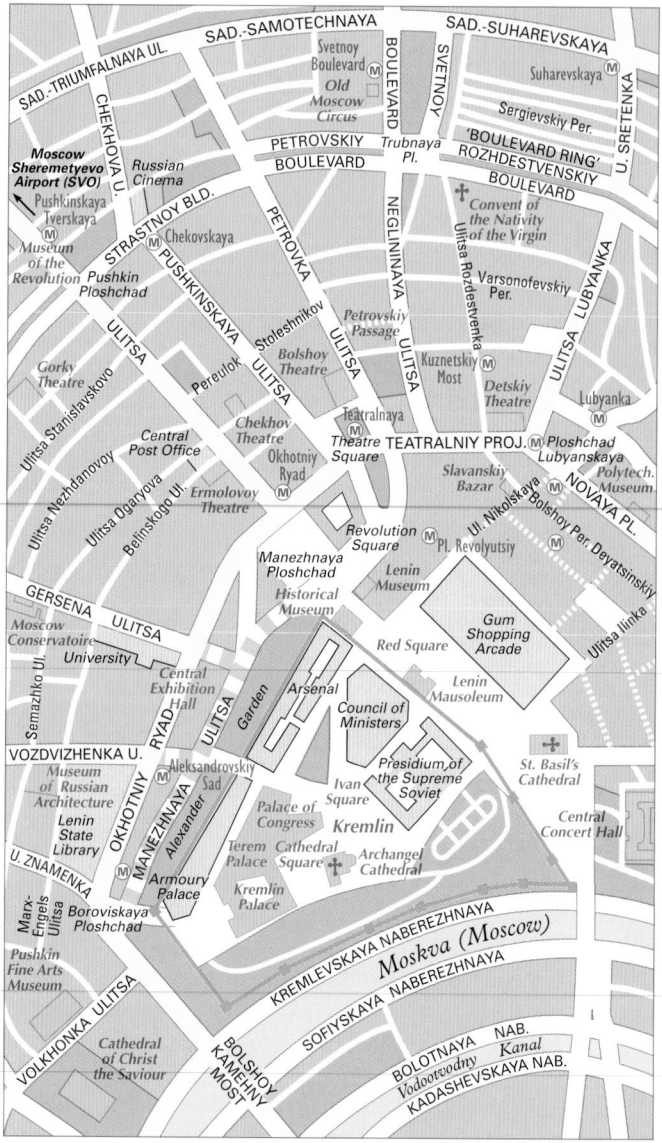

COPYRIGHT PHILIP'S

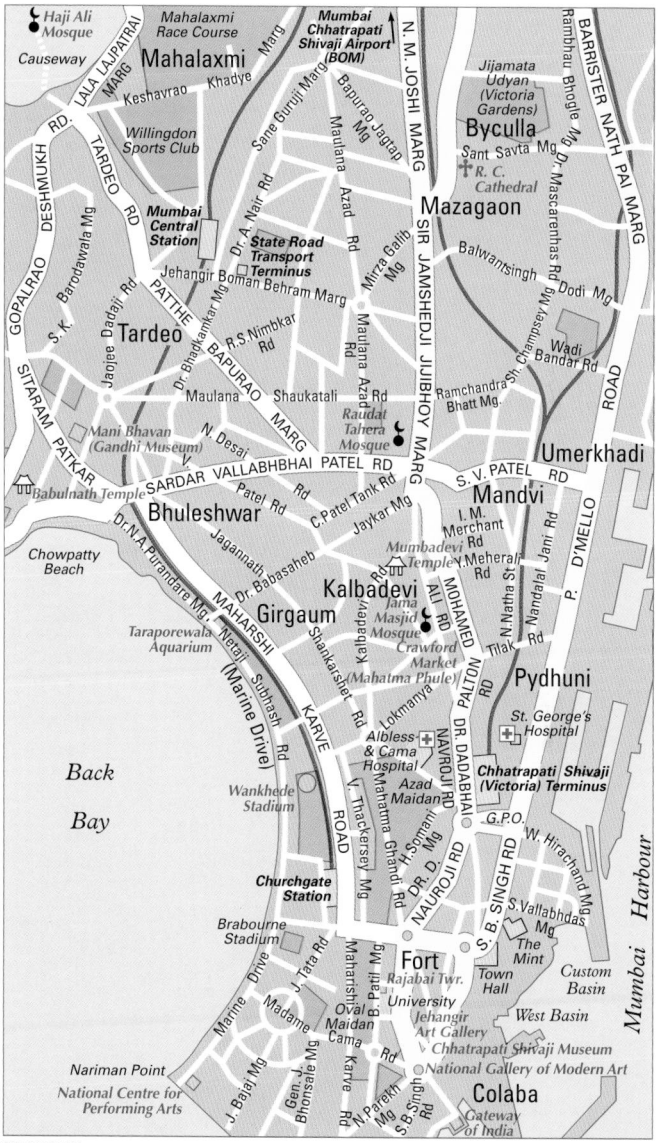

COPYRIGHT PHILIP'S

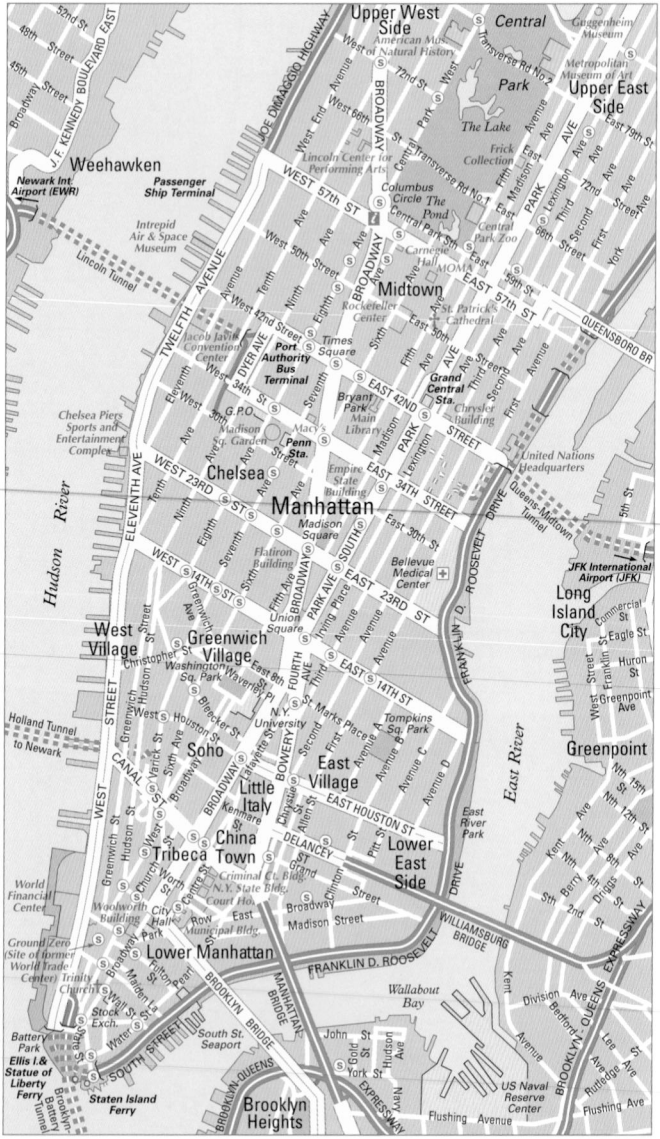
0 km 2
Upper West Side
Central Park
Upper East Side
Guggenheim Museum
Metropolitan Museum of Art
American Museum of Natural History
The Lake
Frick Collection
Lincoln Center for Performing Arts
Columbus Circle
The Pond
Central Park Zoo
Carnegie Hall
MOMA
Weehawken
Newark Int Airport (EWR)
Passenger Ship Terminal
Intrepid Air & Space Museum
Lincoln Tunnel
Midtown
Rockefeller Center
St. Patrick's Cathedral
Jacob Javits Convention Center
Port Authority Bus Terminal
Times Square
Grand Central Sta.
Bryant Park
Main Library
Chrysler Building
G.P.O.
Madison Sq. Garden
Penn Sta.
Macy's
Empire State Building
United Nations Headquarters
Chelsea Piers Sports and Entertainment Complex
Chelsea
Manhattan
Madison Square
Flatiron Building
Bellevue Medical Center
Union Square
Hudson River
West Village
Greenwich Village
Washington Sq. Park
N.Y. University
Tompkins Sq. Park
Soho
East Village
Little Italy
Kenmare St
China Town
Tribeca Town
Lower East Side
Holland Tunnel to Newark
World Financial Center
Ground Zero (Site of former World Trade Center)
Trinity Church
Criminal Cts. Bldg.
N.Y. State Bldg.
Court Ho.
Woolworth Building
City Hall Park
Row
East Municipal Bldg.
Lower Manhattan
Stock Ex.
South Seaport
Battery Park
Ellis I.& Statue of Liberty Ferry
Staten Island Ferry
Brooklyn Heights
Wallabout Bay
US Naval Reserve Center
JFK International Airport (JFK)
Long Island City
Greenpoint
East River
East River Park
Queens-Midtown Tunnel
QUEENSBORO BR
FDR DRIVE
WILLIAMSBURG BRIDGE
BROOKLYN BRIDGE
MANHATTAN BRIDGE
BROOKLYN-QUEENS EXPRESSWAY
Flushing Avenue
Bedford Avenue
Lexington Avenue
Third Avenue
Second Avenue
First Avenue
York Street
Madison Street
Broadway
Canal Street
Houston St
Delancey St
Grand St
Chambers St
Fulton St
Wall St
Liberty St
Cortlandt St
Rector St
Battery Tunnel
Brooklyn Tunnel
Holland Tunnel
Williamsburg Br
Manhattan Br
Brooklyn Br
Central Park
Flushing
Long Island City
Greenpoint
Williamsburg
Brooklyn Heights
Staten Island
East River
Hudson River

0 km 1

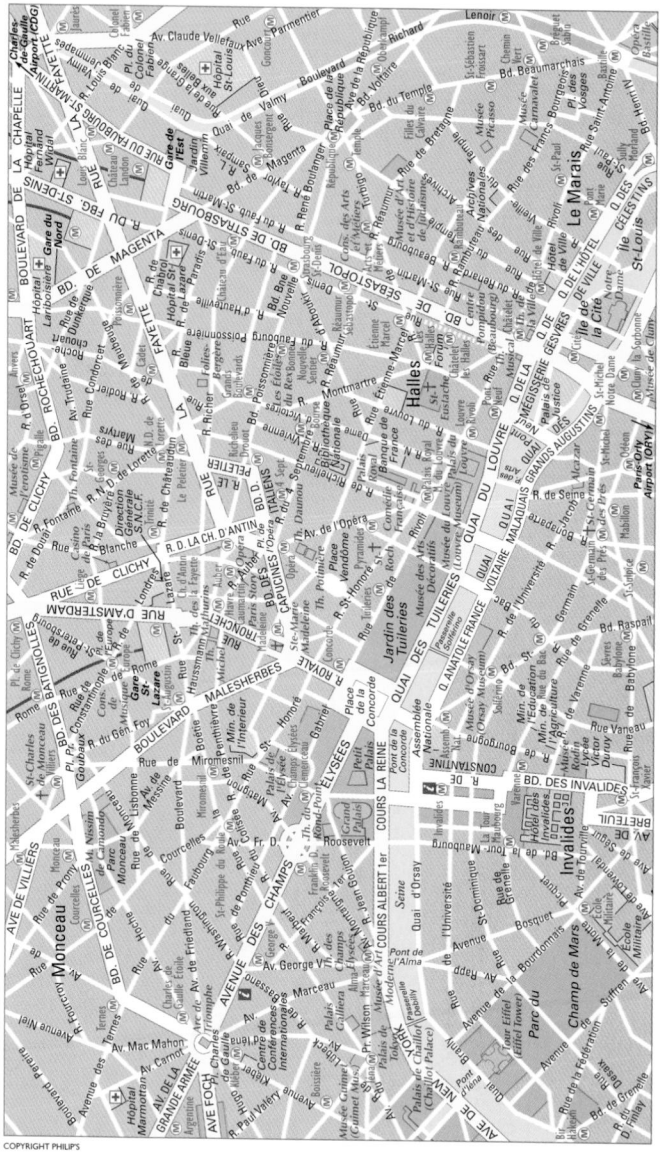
Monceau
Le Marais
Halles
Jardin des Tuileries
Invalides
Champ de Mars
Parc du
Ile de la Cité
Ile St-Louis
Gare de l'Est
Gare du Nord
Gare St-Lazare
Charles-de-Gaulle Airport (CDG)
Paris-Orly Airport (ORY)
Hôpital St-Louis
Hôpital Fernand Widal
Hôpital Lariboisière
Hôpital Marmottan
Hôpital Cochin
Hôpital Bichat
Hôpital Tenon
Hôpital Saint-Antoine
Musée d'Art Moderne
Musée Rodin
Musée Picasso
Musée Carnavalet
Musée de Cluny
Musée d'Orsay
Musée du Louvre (Louvre Museum)
Musée des Arts Décoratifs
Musée National d'Art Moderne
Musée National Rodin
Musée Nissim de Camondo

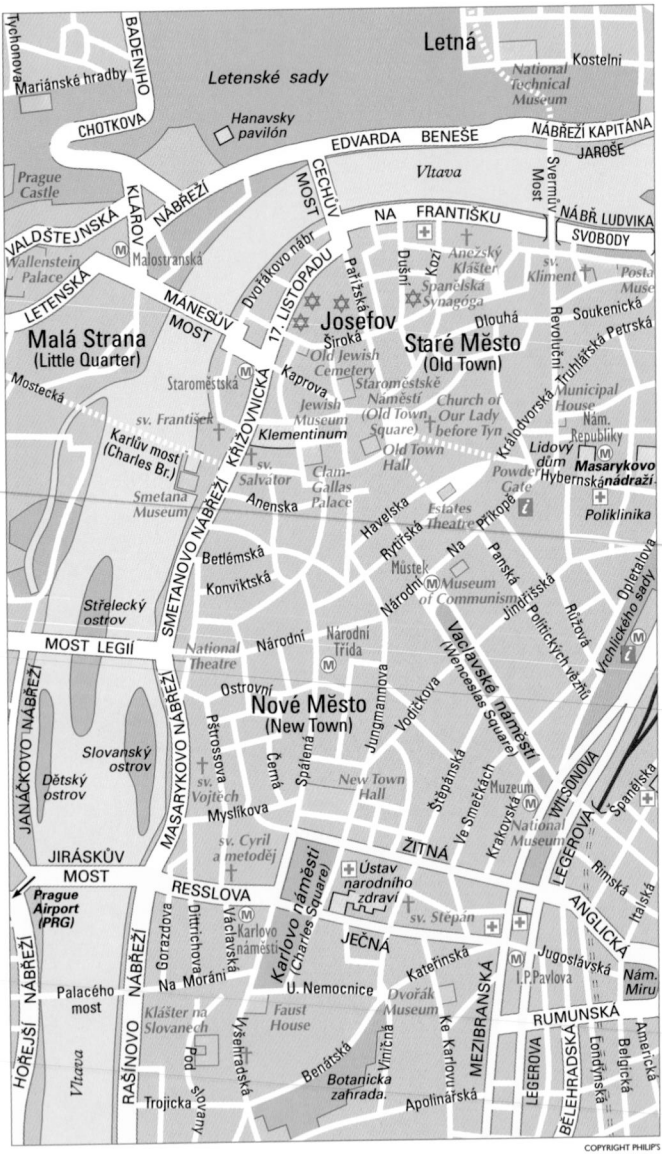
0
km
0.5
Letná
Letenské sady
Mariánské hradby
Hanavsky pavilón
National Technical Museum
Kostelní
BADENIHO
CHOTKOVA
EDVARDA BENEŠE
NÁBŘEŽÍ KAPITÁNA JAROŠE
Vltava
Prague Castle
VALDŠTEJNSKÁ
KLÁROV
NÁBŘEŽÍ
CECHŮV MOST
Švermův Most
NA FRANTIŠKU
NÁBŘ. LUDVÍKA SVOBODY
Wallenstein Palace
Malostranská
LETENSKÁ
MANESŮV MOST
Dvořákovo nábř.
17. LISTOPADU
Pařížská
Dušní
Kozí
Anežský Klášter
Španělská Synagóga
sv. Kliment
Poštovní Muse
Josefov
Dlouhá
Soukenická
Revoluční
Truhlářská
Petrská
Malá Strana
(Little Quarter)
Široká
Old Jewish Cemetery
Staré Město
(Old Town)
Mostecká
Staroměstská
KŘIŽOVNICKÁ
Kaprova
Staroměstské Náměstí (Old Town Square)
Church of Our Lady before Týn
Municipal House
Nám. Republiky
sv. František
Klementinum
Jewish Museum
Karlův most (Charles Br.)
sv. Salvator
Old Town Hall
Královská
Lidový dům
Masarykovo nádraží
Hybernská
Smetana Museum
Clam-Gallas Palace
Anenská
Powder Gate
Příkopy
Estates Theatre
Havelská
Rytířská
Poliklinika
Betlémská
Konviktská
Na Poříčí
Panská
Jindřišská
Opletalova
SMETANOVO NÁBŘEŽÍ
Střelecký ostrov
Národní
Museum of Communism
Politických vězňů
Růžová
Vrchlického sady
MOST LEGIÍ
National Theatre
Národní Třída
Ostrovní
Nové Město
(New Town)
Václavské náměstí
(Wenceslas Square)
JANÁČKOVO NÁBŘEŽÍ
MASARYKOVO NÁBŘEŽÍ
Slovanský ostrov
Dětský ostrov
Petrossova
Černá
Spálená
Jungmannova
Vodičkova
Štěpánská
Ve Smečkách
Krakovská
WILSONOVA
Španělská
sv. Vojtěch
New Town Hall
Myslíkova
Muzeum
National Museum
LEGEROVA
JIRÁSKŮV MOST
sv. Cyril a metoděj
ŽITNÁ
Prague Airport (PRG)
RESSLOVA
Ústav národního zdraví
sv. Štěpán
Římská
Italská
ANGLICKÁ
Gorazdova
Dittrichova
Václavská
Karlovo náměstí
Karlovo náměstí (Charles Square)
JEČNÁ
Jugoslávská
Nám. Míru
Palacého most
Na Moráni
U. Nemocnice
Kateřinská
I.P.Pavlova
NÁBŘEŽÍ
Klášter na Slovanech
Faust House
Dvořák Museum
RUMUNSKÁ
HOŘEJŠÍ NÁBŘEŽÍ
RAŠÍNOVO NÁBŘEŽÍ
Vltava
Vyšehradská
Pod slovany
Benátská
Vinařická
Ke Karlovu
MEZIBRANSKÁ
LEGEROVA
BĚLEHRADSKÁ
Belgická
Americká
Botanická zahrada
Trojická
Apolinářská
COPYRIGHT PHILIP'S

0 km 0.5

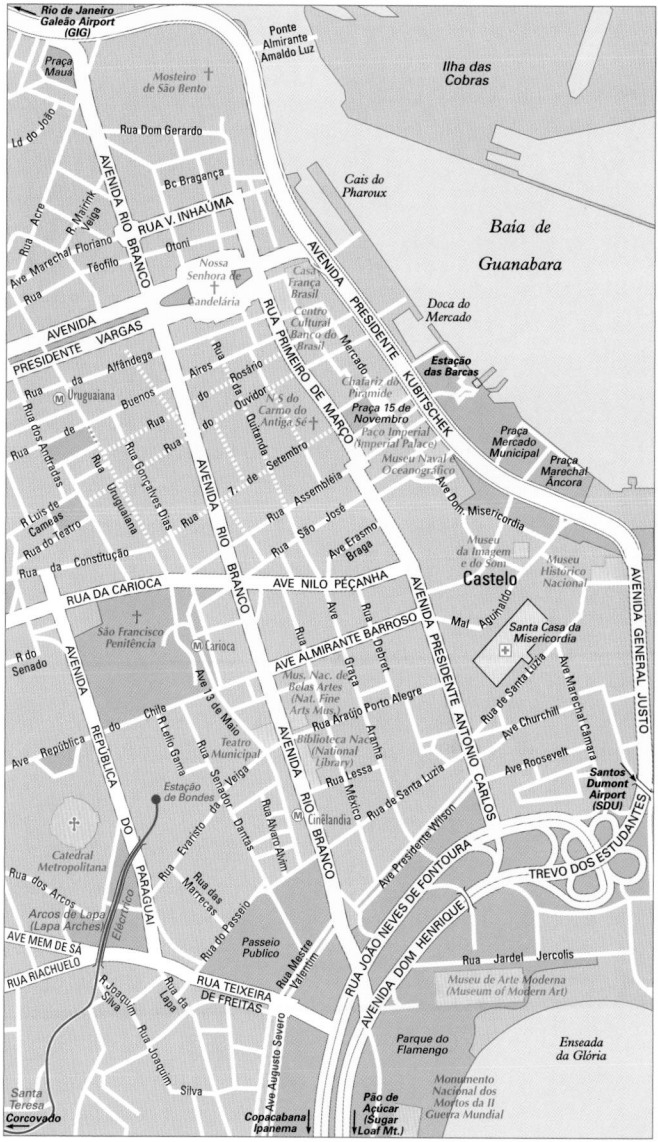

COPYRIGHT PHILIP'S

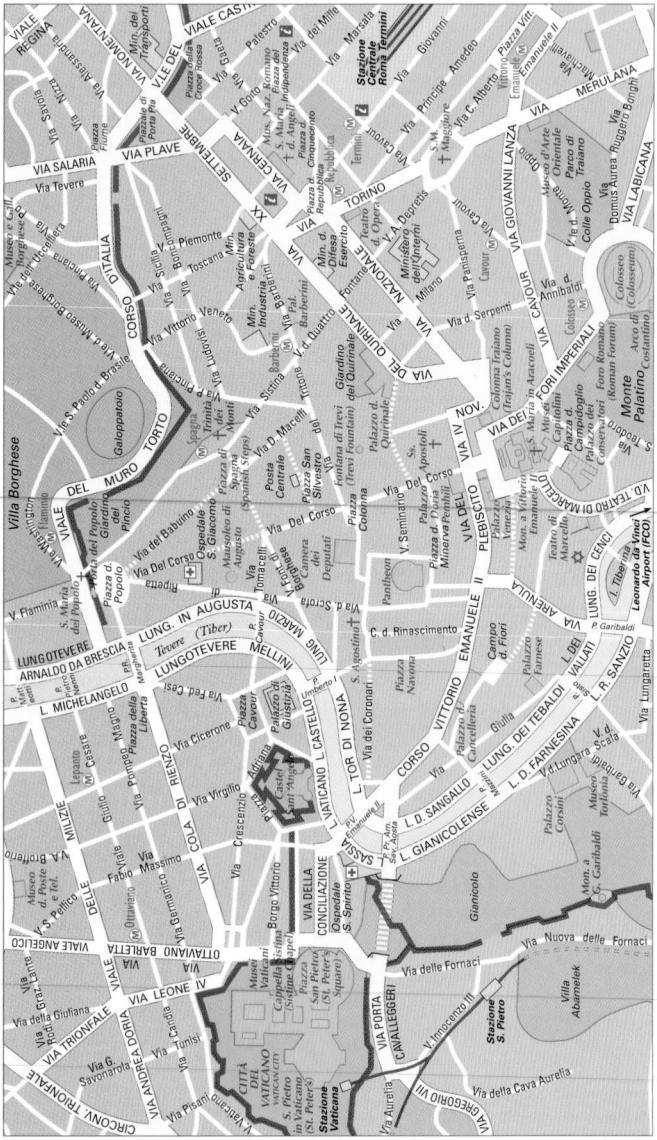
0
km
1
Villa Borghese
Galoppatoio
Giardino del Pincio
Piazza del Popolo
Piazza di Spagna (Spanish Steps)
Piazza Barberini
Piazza San Silvestro
Piazza Colonna
Piazza di Trevi (Fontana di Trevi)
Piazza Venezia
Piazza Navona
Piazza Farnese
Piazza Cavour
Piazza della Libertà
Piazza Fiume
Piazza Esquilino
Piazza Vittorio Emanuele II

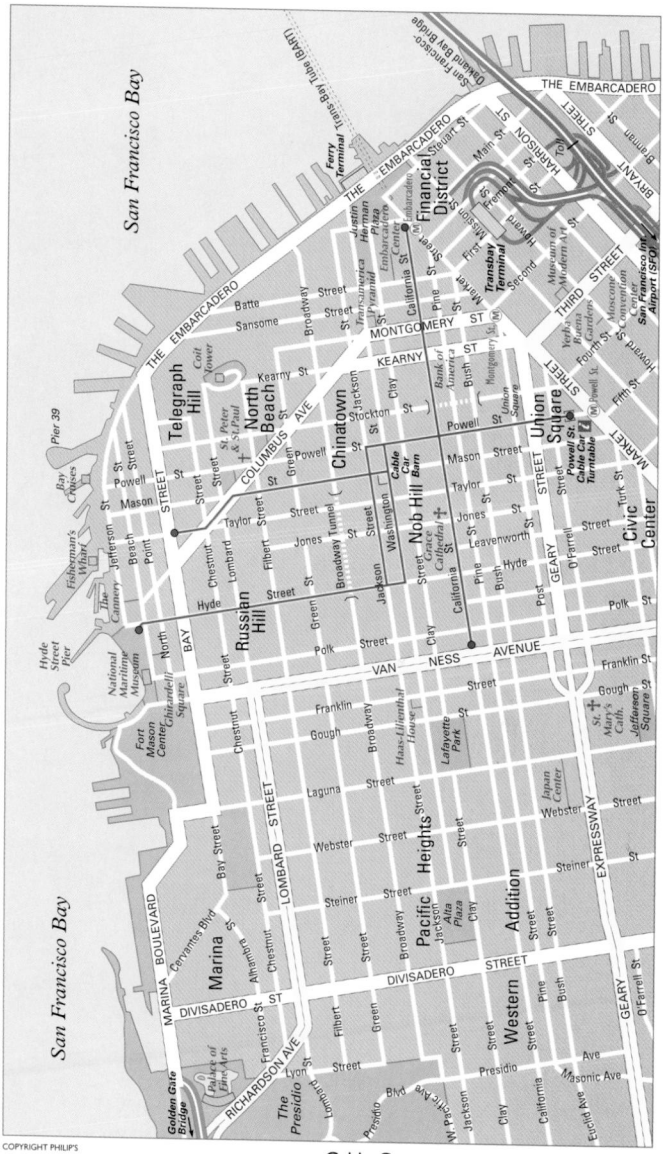
0
km
0.5
San Francisco Bay
San Francisco Bay
Golden Gate Bridge
Palace of Fine Arts
The Presidio
Presidio Blvd
Presidio Ave
Lyon St
Francisco St
Marina Blvd
Cervantes Blvd
Marina
Marina Boulevard
Divisadero St
Richardson Ave
Lombard Street
Bay Street
Chestnut
Fillmore St
Webster
Steiner
Laguna
Pacific Heights
Jackson St
Alta Plaza
Clay
Broadway
Western Addition
Presidio
California
Masonic Ave
Euclid Ave
Geary
O'Farrell St
Japan Center
Webster
Steiner
Expressway
Van Ness Avenue
Franklin
Gough
Haas-Lilienthal House
Lafayette Park
St. Mary's Cathedral
Jefferson Square
Polk
Russian Hill
Hyde
Lombard
Chestnut
Fort Mason Center
Chirardelli Square
North Beach
Fisherman's Wharf
Jefferson
Beach
Pier 39
Bay Cruises
Powell
Mason
Taylor
Jones
Leavenworth
Hyde
Bush
Pine
Post
Geary
O'Farrell
Turk
Eddy
Ellis
Olive
Market
Hayes
Fulton
Grove
Hyde Street Pier
The Cannery
National Maritime Museum
Telegraph Hill
Coit Tower
St. Peter & St. Paul
Kearny St
Columbus Ave
Green
Chinatown
Stockton
Grant
Jackson
Washington
Broadway Tunnel
Cable Car Barn
Nob Hill
Grace Cathedral
California St
Powell
Clay
Sacramento
Bank of Canton Tower
Union Square
Union Square
Powell St.
Cable Car Turntable
Civic Center
Hyde
Larkin
Polk
Van Ness Avenue
Franklin
Gough
Market St
Fourth St
Moscone Convention Center
Yerba Buena Gardens
Third Street
Howard St
Fifth St
Mission St
Second
Museum of Modern Art
Transbay Terminal
Harrison St
Bryant St
Brannan St
Embarcadero
Pyramid
Transamerica
Embarcadero Center
Justin Herman Plaza
Ferry Terminal
Financial District
Sansome
Battery
Montgomery St
Kearny
Stockton
Grant

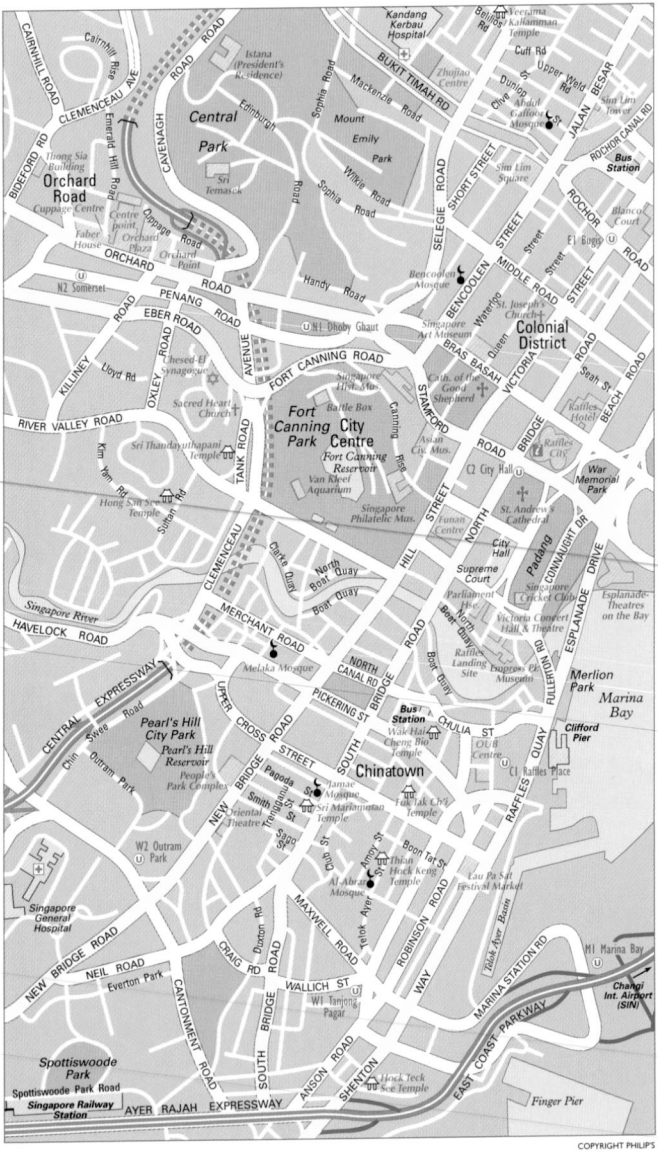

COPYRIGHT PHILIPS

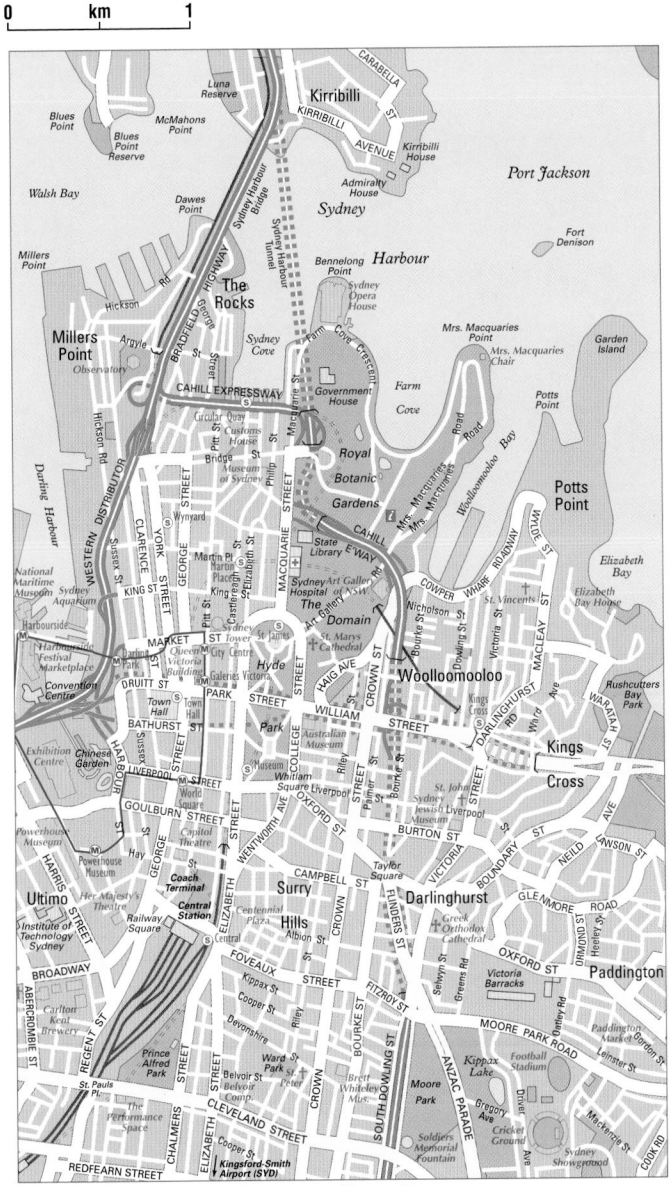

COPYRIGHT PHILIP'S

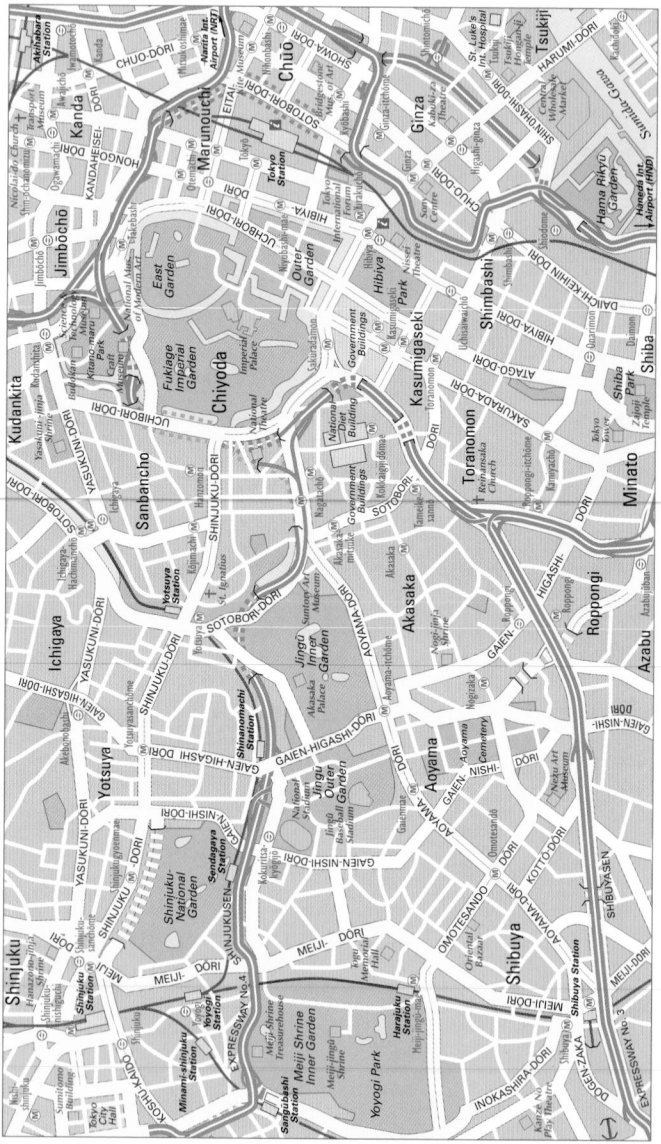
0
km
2
Shinjuku
Shinjuku-Gyoen
Shinjuku-National Garden
Meiji Shrine Inner Garden
Meiji-jingū Shrine
Yoyogi Park
Yotsuya
Ichigaya
Kudankita
Sanbancho
Chiyoda
Fukiage Imperial Garden
East Garden
Jimbōchō
Kanda
Marunouchi
Chūō
Outer Garden
Hibiya
Kasumigaseki
Shimbashi
Ginza
Tsukiji
Toranomon
Minato
Shiba
Shiba Park
Kasumigaseki
Akasaka
Aoyama
Aoyama Cemetery
Shibuya
Roppongi
Azabu
Tokyo Station
Shinjuku Station
Shinanomachi Station
Sendagaya Station
Yoyogi Station
Harajuku Station
Shibuya Station
Sangubashi Station
Minami-shinjuku Station
Meiji-jingū-mae Station
Nishi-Shinjuku Station
Tokyo City Hall
Tokyo Metro
Toei Subway
COPYRIGHT PHILIP'S

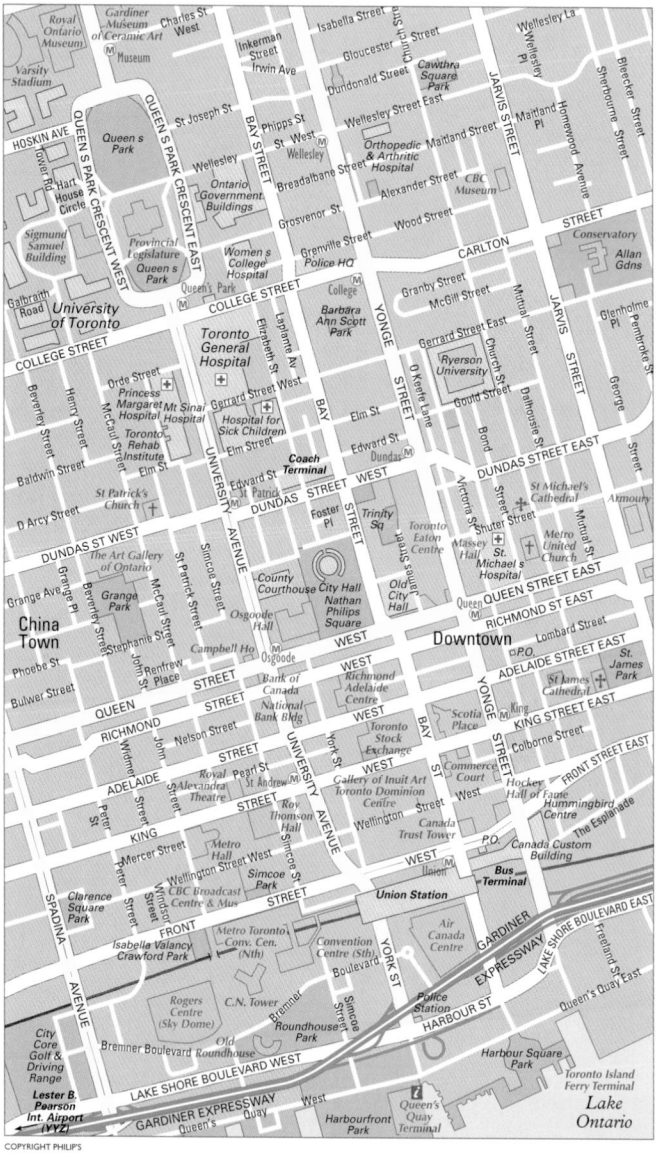

COPYRIGHT PHILIP'S

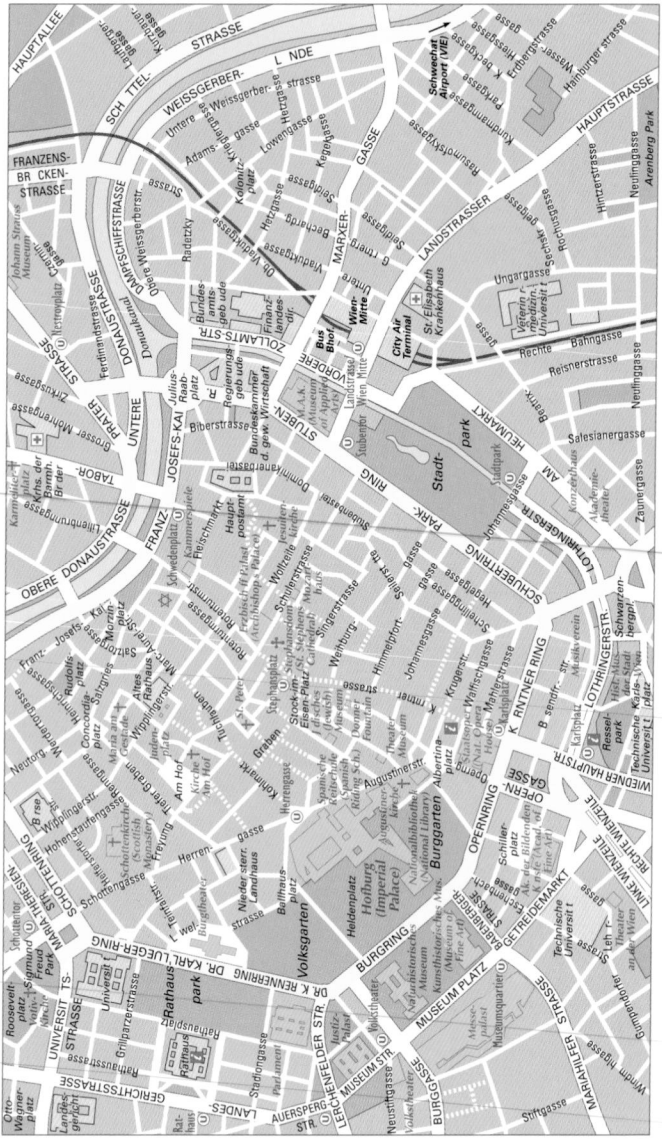
0
km
1
HAUPTALLEE
SCHÖTTELDORFER STRASSE
WEISSGERBER-LÄNDE
FRANZENS-BRÜCKEN-STRASSE
DONAUFERSCHIFFSTRASSE
DONAUSTRASSE
Donauwasserstr.
Ferdinandstrasse
Johann Strauss Museum
Czerninplatz
Ottakringer Bräu
Kaiser-Ebersdorfer Str.
Kaiserwasserstr.
Lichtenwerder Str.
Donaukanal
Radetzky-Brücke
Radetzky-platz
Bundesamtsgebäude
Finanzlandesdir.
Regierungsgebäude
Bundeskammer d. gew. Wirtschaft
ZOLLAMTS-STR.
Vorgartenstr.

GAZETTEER OF NATIONS

48 Afghanistan
Albania
Algeria
American Samoa
Andorra
Angola

49 Anguilla
Antigua & Barbuda
Argentina
Armenia
Aruba
Australia

50 Austria
Azerbaijan
Azores
Bahamas
Bahrain
Bangladesh

51 Barbados
Belarus
Belgium
Belize
Benin
Bermuda

52 Bolivia
Bosnia-Herzegovina
Botswana
Brazil
Bulgaria
Burma

53 Cambodia
Canada
Canary Is.
Cape Verde
Cayman Is.
Chad

54 Chile
China
Colombia
Comoros
Costa Rica
Croatia

55 Cuba
Cyprus
Czech Rep.
Denmark
Dominica
Dominican Rep.

56 Ecuador
Egypt
El Salvador
Estonia
Ethiopia
Fiji Is.

57 Finland
France
French Polynesia
Gambia, The
Georgia
Germany

58 Gibraltar
Greece
Grenada
Guadeloupe
Hong Kong
Hungary

59 Iceland
India
Indonesia
Iran
Ireland
Israel

60 Italy
Jamaica
Japan
Jordan
Kenya
Korea, South

61 Kuwait
Latvia
Lebanon
Libya
Liechtenstein
Lithuania

62 Luxembourg
Madagascar
Malawi
Malaysia
Maldives
Malta

63 Martinique
Mauritius
Mexico
Mongolia
Montenegro
Morocco

64 Namibia
Nepal
Netherlands
Neth. Antilles
New Zealand
Nigeria

65 Norway
Oman
Pakistan
Paraguay
Peru
Philippines

66 Poland
Portugal
Puerto Rico
Qatar
Réunion
Romania

67 Russia
St Kitts & Nevis
St Lucia
St Vincent
Samoa
Saudi Arabia

68 Serbia
Seychelles
Singapore
Slovak Rep.
Slovenia
South Africa

69 Spain
Sri Lanka
Sweden
Switzerland
Syria
Taiwan

70 Tanzania
Thailand
Trinidad & T.
Tunisia
Turkey
Uganda

71 Ukraine
UAE
UK
USA
Uruguay
Venezuela

72 Vietnam
Virgin Is., British
Virgin Is., US
Yemen
Zambia
Zimbabwe

AFGHANISTAN

GOVERNMENT Transitional
LANGUAGES Pashtu, Dari/Persian, Uzbek
CURRENCY Afghani = 100 puls
MEDICAL Visitors should protect against yellow fever, polio, typhoid and malaria
TRAVEL Most governments currently advise against all travel to Afghanistan. The security situation remains serious, with danger away from main roads from mines and unexploded ordnance
WEATHER Jun to Aug very hot; Dec to Mar very cold; Jun to Sep scanty rainfall; mild at other times
BANKING 0800–1200 and 1300–1630 Sat to Wed; 0830–1330 Thu. However, at the time of writing, many banks are closed
EMERGENCY Unavailable
TIME ZONE GMT +4.30
INTERNATIONAL DIALING CODE Unavailable

ALBANIA

GOVERNMENT Multiparty republic
LANGUAGES Albanian (official)
CURRENCY Lek = 100 qindars
MEDICAL Water is untreated and not safe to drink. Medical facilities in the country are poor
TRAVEL Crime is high throughout parts of the country and visitors should remain vigilant at all times. It is advisable to dress down and avoid carrying expensive items. Street demonstrations against the government are common
WEATHER Jun to Sep warm and dry; Oct to May cool and wet
BANKING 0700–1500 Mon to Fri
EMERGENCY Police 24445; Fire 23333; Ambulance 22235
TIME ZONE GMT +1
INTERNATIONAL DIALING CODE 355

ALGERIA

GOVERNMENT Socialist republic
LANGUAGES Arabic and Berber (both official), French
CURRENCY Algerian dinar = 100 centimes
MEDICAL There is a risk of yellow fever, malaria, hepatitis A, typhoid, and polio
TRAVEL Most governments currently advise against all tourist and non-essential travel to Algeria. Travel by public transport should be avoided and only secure accommodation used
WEATHER Jun to Sep in the north is usually hot with high humidity along the coast; Oct to Feb wet and mild
BANKING 0900–1630 Sun to Thu
EMERGENCY Unavailable
TIME ZONE GMT +1
INTERNATIONAL DIALING CODE 213

AMERICAN SAMOA

GOVERNMENT US overseas territory
LANGUAGES Samoan, English
CURRENCY US dollar = 100 cents
MEDICAL Water is untreated and is unsafe to drink. Vaccination against polio and typhoid is recommended
TRAVEL Most visits to American Samoa are trouble-free and crime is low. Tourists should respect local culture and take usual precautions, especially in the towns
WEATHER Hot, tropical climate with heavy rainfall from Dec to Apr. The most comfortable time to visit is May to Sep
BANKING 0900–1500 Mon to Fri
EMERGENCY All services 911
TIME ZONE GMT –11
INTERNATIONAL DIALING CODE 1 684

ANDORRA

GOVERNMENT Parliamentary co-princedom
LANGUAGES Catalan, Spanish, French
CURRENCY Euro = 100 cents
MEDICAL There are no specific health risks
TRAVEL In Andorra, visitors will find some of the most stunning scenery and the best skiing in the Pyrenees. Shopping around, prices may often be up to 30% below those in France and Spain
WEATHER Jun to Sep warm and pleasant; Dec to Apr sunny but cold with abundant snow; rain falls throughout the year; snow often remains on the peaks of mountains until July
BANKING 0900–1300 and 1500–1700 Mon to Fri; 0900–1200 Sat
EMERGENCY Police 110; Fire/Ambulance 118
TIME ZONE GMT +1
INTERNATIONAL DIALING CODE 376

ANGOLA

GOVERNMENT Multiparty republic
LANGUAGES Portuguese (official), many others
CURRENCY Kwanza = 100 lwei
MEDICAL There is a risk of yellow fever, hepatitis A, polio, typhoid, and malaria
TRAVEL Most governments currently advise against tourist and non-essential travel to Angola due to the aftermath of civil war. Visitors should remain vigilant, particularly after dark. Crime levels are high and land mines are widely distributed and unmarked
WEATHER Warm to hot all year; Nov to Apr wet; cooler and wetter climate in the south
BANKING 0845–1600 Mon to Fri
EMERGENCY Unavailable
TIME ZONE GMT +1
INTERNATIONAL DIALING CODE 244

ANGUILLA

GOVERNMENT UK overseas territory
LANGUAGES English (official)
CURRENCY East Caribbean dollar = 100 cents
MEDICAL There are no specific health risks, but medical facilities are limited on the island
TRAVEL Most visits are trouble-free, but beachwear should be confined to resort areas. Travelers should take normal precautions, such as locking doors and securing valuables
WEATHER Tropical climate. Hurricane risk from Jun to Nov; Oct to Dec is the rainy season. Optimum diving conditions in summer months
BANKING 0800–1500 Mon to Thu; 0800–1700 Fri
EMERGENCY All services 911
TIME ZONE GMT –4
INTERNATIONAL DIALING CODE 1 264

ANTIGUA & BARBUDA

GOVERNMENT Constitutional monarchy
LANGUAGES English (official), English patois
CURRENCY East Caribbean dollar = 100 cents
MEDICAL Visitors should take normal precautions against mosquito bites. Vaccinations recommended against polio and typhoid
TRAVEL Generally trouble-free, but visitors should avoid isolated areas, including beaches, after dark
WEATHER Tropical with little variation between the seasons; rainfall is minimal. The islands are at risk from hurricanes from Jun to Nov
BANKING 0800–1400 Mon to Thu; 0800–1700 Fri
EMERGENCY All services 999/911
TIME ZONE GMT –4
INTERNATIONAL DIALING CODE 1 268

ARGENTINA

GOVERNMENT Federal republic
LANGUAGES Spanish (official)
CURRENCY Argentine peso = 10,000 australs
MEDICAL Cholera is a risk in the subtropical northern region
TRAVEL Occasional outbreaks of social unrest. It is inadvisable to walk in isolated, poorly-lit areas. Visitors should avoid carrying too much cash or wearing jewelry. Avoid military areas, which usually allow no stopping
WEATHER Jun to Aug cool in Buenos Aires area; Dec to Feb hot and humid; rain falls all year round
BANKING 1000–1500 Mon to Fri
EMERGENCY Police 101/107
TIME ZONE GMT –3
INTERNATIONAL DIALING CODE 54

ARMENIA

GOVERNMENT Multiparty republic
LANGUAGES Armenian (official)
CURRENCY Dram = 100 couma
MEDICAL Visitors should protect against hepatitis and bacterial infection
TRAVEL The border areas with Azerbaijan should be avoided at all times. Crime remains relatively low in Armenia, but occasional thefts from cars and pickpocketing may occur. The local standard of driving is poor, but most visits are generally trouble-free
WEATHER Apr to Oct hot and sunny; Jul to Sep little rainfall; Dec to Feb cold with heavy snow
BANKING 0930–1730 Mon to Fri
EMERGENCY Unavailable
TIME ZONE GMT +4
INTERNATIONAL DIALING CODE 374

ARUBA

GOVERNMENT Parliamentary democracy
LANGUAGES Dutch, English, Spanish, Papiamento
CURRENCY Aruba florin = 100 cents
MEDICAL Water is purified and should be safe; normal precautions should be taken with food
TRAVEL Beachwear should be confined to the beach. Travelers should take normal precautions, such as avoiding isolated areas after dark
WEATHER Tropical marine climate, warm and dry with average temperatures of 82°F [28°C]. Nov and Dec experience short showers
BANKING 0800–1200 and 1300–1600 Mon to Fri
EMERGENCY Police 11 000; Ambulance 74 300; Fire 115
TIME ZONE GMT –4
INTERNATIONAL DIALING CODE 297

AUSTRALIA

GOVERNMENT Federal constitutional monarchy
LANGUAGES English (official)
CURRENCY Australian dollar = 100 cents
MEDICAL No vaccinations required. There are few health hazards, but visitors should protect against sunburn, spider, and snake bites
TRAVEL Visitors should exercise caution in major urban areas, particularly after dark
WEATHER Tropical to temperate; Nov to Mar warm or hot in all areas; Jun to Aug mild in south-eastern region; Sep to May warm to hot; rain falls all year round and is heaviest Mar to Jul
BANKING 0930–1600 Mon to Thu; 0930–1700 Fri, but hours vary throughout the country
EMERGENCY Emergency Services 000
TIME ZONE East GMT +10; Cen. +9.30; West +8
INTERNATIONAL DIALING CODE 61

AUSTRIA

GOVERNMENT Federal republic
LANGUAGES German (official)
CURRENCY Euro = 100 cents
MEDICAL There are no specific health risks in Austria
TRAVEL Visitors to the Alps should contact the Austrian Tourist Agency for advice on safety. Austria benefits all year round by providing summer sightseeing and winter sports
WEATHER Jun to Aug warm and pleasant; Oct to Apr cold; Mar to Aug higher rainfall
BANKING 0800–1230 and 1330–1500 Mon, Tue, Wed and Fri; Thu 0800–1230 and 1330–1730
EMERGENCY Emergency Services 112; Police 133; Ambulance 144
TIME ZONE GMT +1
INTERNATIONAL DIALING CODE 43

AZERBAIJAN

GOVERNMENT Federal multiparty republic
LANGUAGES Azerbaijani (official), Russian
CURRENCY Azerbaijani manat = 100 gopik
MEDICAL Visitors should protect against malaria, yellow fever, diptheria, tick-borne encephalitis, hepatitis, rabies, and typhoid fever
TRAVEL Travel to the western region of Nagorno-Karabakh and surrounding occupied area should be avoided. Passport photocopies should be carried at all times. Do not enter or leave the country via the land borders with Russia
WEATHER May to Sep sunny, warm, and dry; Oct to Apr mild with some rain
BANKING 0930–1730 Mon to Fri
EMERGENCY Unavailable
TIME ZONE GMT +4
INTERNATIONAL DIALING CODE 994

AZORES

GOVERNMENT Portuguese autonomous region
LANGUAGES Portuguese
CURRENCY Euro = 100 cents
MEDICAL There are no specific health risks in the Azores
TRAVEL Most visits to the Azores are trouble-free. The nine large islands and numerous small ones are situated in the middle of the Atlantic Ocean and offer the traveler a wealth of stunning scenery
WEATHER Mild throughout the year; Jun to Sep sunny and warm; Jan to Apr changeable; Oct to Mar wet
BANKING Visitors should check at their hotel
EMERGENCY Unavailable
TIME ZONE GMT –1
INTERNATIONAL DIALING CODE Unavailable

BAHAMAS

GOVERNMENT Constitutional parliamentary democracy
LANGUAGES English (official), Creole
CURRENCY Bahamian dollar = 100 cents
MEDICAL Visitors should protect against dehydration, sunburn, tetanus, and jellyfish
TRAVEL Most visits are trouble-free, but crime exists in the cities of Nassau and Freeport. Keep valuables hidden and avoid walking alone
WEATHER Mild throughout the year; May to Oct warm and wet; Dec to Mar cooler and drier; Jun to Nov hurricanes occur
BANKING 0930–1500 Mon to Thu; 0930–1700 Fri, but hours on each island vary
EMERGENCY All Services 911
TIME ZONE GMT –5
INTERNATIONAL DIALING CODE 1 242

BAHRAIN

GOVERNMENT Monarchy (emirate) with a cabinet appointed by the Emir
LANGUAGES Arabic (official), English, Farsi, Urdu
CURRENCY Bahrain dinar = 1,000 fils
MEDICAL There are no specific health risks
TRAVEL Generally calm, but any increase in regional tension may affect travel advice. Visitors should avoid village areas, particularly after dark. Keep cash and valuables out of sight at all times
WEATHER Jun to Sep very hot; Nov to Mar milder and pleasant
BANKING 0800–1200 and 1600–1800 Sat to Wed; 0800–1100 Thu
EMERGENCY All Services 999
TIME ZONE GMT +3
INTERNATIONAL DIALING CODE 973

BANGLADESH

GOVERNMENT Multiparty republic
LANGUAGES Bengali (official), English
CURRENCY Taka = 100 paisas
MEDICAL Visitors should protect against cholera, dysentery, hepatitis, malaria, and meningitis
TRAVEL Avoid political gatherings. Driving conditions are very poor. Visitors should keep valuables hidden and avoid travel after dark
WEATHER Jun to Sep monsoon with heavy rain and very high humidity; Nov to Feb sunny and cool; Mar to Jun hot with thunderstorms
BANKING 0830–1430 Sun to Wed; 0830–1300 Thu. Closed Fri and Sat
EMERGENCY Police Dhaka 866 551–3; Fire and Ambulance Service Dhaka 9 555 555
TIME ZONE GMT +6
INTERNATIONAL DIALING CODE 880

BARBADOS

GOVERNMENT Parliamentary democracy
LANGUAGES English (local Bajan dialect also spoken)
CURRENCY Barbados dollar = 100 cents
MEDICAL The sun is intense and visitors should wear strong sunscreen at all times. Other health risks include dengue fever
TRAVEL Travel is generally risk-free, but visitors should avoid deserted beaches at night
WEATHER Warm all year round; Jun to Dec wet season; Feb to May cooler and drier
BANKING 0800–1500 Mon to Thu; 0800–1300 and 1500–1700 Fri
EMERGENCY Police 112; Ambulance 115; All Services 119
TIME ZONE GMT –4
INTERNATIONAL DIALING CODE 1 246

BELARUS

GOVERNMENT Multiparty republic
LANGUAGES Belarusian and Russian (both official)
CURRENCY Belarusian rouble = 100 kopecks
MEDICAL Visitors should avoid eating dairy produce, mushrooms, and fruits of the forests which can carry high levels of radiation. Other health risks include hepatitis A and B, and typhoid
TRAVEL Pickpocketing and theft from vehicles or hotel rooms is common. Visitors should avoid demonstrations and rallies, and remain vigilant at all times
WEATHER May to Aug mild; Oct to Apr cold; Jan to Mar snow cover; rain falls all year round
BANKING 0900–1730 Mon to Fri
EMERGENCY Police 02; Ambulance 03
TIME ZONE GMT +2
INTERNATIONAL DIALING CODE 375

BELGIUM

GOVERNMENT Federal constitutional monarchy
LANGUAGES Dutch, French, German (all official)
CURRENCY Euro = 100 cents
MEDICAL There are no specific health risks, but medical care is expensive
TRAVEL Most visits are trouble-free, but visitors should take sensible precautions to avoid the increasing threat of mugging, bag-snatching, and pickpocketing, particularly in Brussels
WEATHER May to Sep mild; Nov to Mar cold; rain falls all year round, often as snow in winter
BANKING 0900–1200 and 1400–1600 Mon to Fri. Some banks open 0900–1200 Sat
EMERGENCY Police 101; Emergency Services 112 Fire/Ambulance 100 (112 from a mobile phone)
TIME ZONE GMT +1
INTERNATIONAL DIALING CODE 32

BELIZE

GOVERNMENT Constitutional monarchy
LANGUAGES English (official), Spanish, Creole
CURRENCY Belizean dollar = 100 cents
MEDICAL Precautions should be taken against polio, typhoid, and cholera. Malaria is present throughout the year, excluding urban areas
TRAVEL Nov to May is the best time to visit, but this is the busy tourist season when prices rise and hotels fill up. Belize has one of the longest barrier reefs in the world
WEATHER Hot and humid climate. Monsoon and hurricane season runs from Jun to Sep
BANKING 0800–1300 Mon to Thu; 0800–1200 and 1500–1800 Fri
EMERGENCY All services 911
TIME ZONE GMT –6
INTERNATIONAL DIALING CODE 501

BENIN

GOVERNMENT Multiparty republic
LANGUAGES French (official), Fon, Adja, Yoruba
CURRENCY CFA franc = 100 centimes
MEDICAL Visitors should protect against cholera and malaria. Yellow fever vaccination certificates are required for entry. Water is unsafe to drink
TRAVEL Travel is generally safe, but driving out of towns at night should be avoided due to poor street lighting. Occasional incidents of mugging and armed robberies occur in Cotonou
WEATHER Warm to hot all year round; Mar to Jul and Sep to Oct are rainy seasons in the south
BANKING 0800–1100 and 1500–1600 Mon to Fri
EMERGENCY Consult foreign embassy
TIME ZONE GMT +1
INTERNATIONAL DIALING CODE 229

BERMUDA

GOVERNMENT Self-governing British dependency
LANGUAGES English (some Portuguese is also spoken)
CURRENCY Bermuda dollar = 100 cents
MEDICAL There are no specific health risks
TRAVEL Most visits to Bermuda are trouble-free. Accommodation can be up to 40% cheaper between Nov and Mar, but events and entertainment are less plentiful at this time
WEATHER Jun to Sep very warm; Nov to Apr mild; rainfall is abundant and evenly distributed all year round
BANKING 0930–1500 Mon to Thu; 0930–1500 and 1630–1730 Fri
EMERGENCY All Services 911
TIME ZONE GMT –4
INTERNATIONAL DIALING CODE 1 441

BOLIVIA

GOVERNMENT Multiparty republic
LANGUAGES Spanish, Aymara, Quechua (official)
CURRENCY Boliviano = 100 centavos
MEDICAL Altitude sickness is common. Visitors should drink plenty of water and protect against cholera, hepatitis, malaria, polio, and tetanus
TRAVEL Pickpocketing is common and visitors are advised to remain vigilant at all times. The country is going through a period of unrest
WEATHER Average max. daily temperature of 62–66°F [17–19°C] all year round; low annual rainfall, most falling Dec to Mar
BANKING 0930–1500 Mon to Thu; 0930–1500 and 1630–1730 Fri
EMERGENCY All Services 911
TIME ZONE GMT –4
INTERNATIONAL DIALING CODE 591

BOSNIA-HERZEGOVINA

GOVERNMENT Federal republic
LANGUAGES Bosnian, Serbian, Croatian
CURRENCY Convertible marka = 100 convertible pfenniga
MEDICAL Medical facilities are limited. There is a risk of hepatitis and typhoid fever
TRAVEL Crime level is generally low, but isolated incidents of violence can flare up. Unexploded land mines and other ordnance still remain in certain areas
WEATHER Jun to Sep warm; Dec to Feb cold; spring and fall mild; rain falls all year round
BANKING 0730–1530 Mon to Fri
EMERGENCY Consult foreign office in country of residence before departure
TIME ZONE GMT +1
INTERNATIONAL DIALING CODE 387

BOTSWANA

GOVERNMENT Multiparty republic
LANGUAGES English (official), Setswana
CURRENCY Pula = 100 thebe
MEDICAL There are no specific health risks, but visitors should protect against malaria
TRAVEL Most visits are trouble-free, but there is an increasing incidence of crime. Prolonged rainfall may cause flooding and block roads from Dec to Apr
WEATHER In the east, May to Sep mild with little rainfall; Nov to Mar warm, rainy season but nights can be cold
BANKING 0900–1430 Mon, Tue, Thu and Fri; 0815–1200 Wed; 0815–1045 Sat
EMERGENCY Police 351161
TIME ZONE GMT +2
INTERNATIONAL DIALING CODE 267

BRAZIL

GOVERNMENT Federal republic
LANGUAGES Portuguese (official)
CURRENCY Real = 100 centavos
MEDICAL Visitors should take precautions against AIDS, malaria, meningitis, and yellow fever
TRAVEL High crime rate in major cities of Rio de Janeiro and São Paulo. Dress down and avoid wearing jewelry
WEATHER Jun to Sep pleasant in southeast; Dec to Mar hot and humid with high rainfall
BANKING 1000–1630 Mon to Fri
EMERGENCY All Services 0
TIME ZONE Eastern GMT –3; North East and East Pará –3; Western –4; Amapa and West Para –4; Acre State –5; Fernando de Noronha Archipelago –2
INTERNATIONAL DIALING CODE 55

BULGARIA

GOVERNMENT Multiparty republic
LANGUAGES Bulgarian (official), Turkish
CURRENCY Lev = 100 stotinki
MEDICAL There are no specific health risks
TRAVEL Most visits to Bulgaria are trouble-free, but there is a risk of robbery. Pickpockets operate in downtown Sofia and in the Black Sea resorts. Car theft is commonplace
WEATHER May to Sep warm with some rainfall; Nov to Mar cold with snow; rain falls frequently during spring and fall
BANKING 0800–1130 and 1400–1800 Mon to Fri; 0830–1130 Sat
EMERGENCY Police 166; Fire 160; Ambulance 150
TIME ZONE GMT +2
INTERNATIONAL DIALING CODE 359

BURMA (= MYANMAR)

GOVERNMENT Military regime
LANGUAGES Burmese (official); minority ethnic groups have their own languages
CURRENCY Kyat = 100 pyas
MEDICAL Visitors should protect against cholera, dysentery, hepatitis, malaria, rabies, and typhoid
TRAVEL Politically unsettled. Visitors should avoid large crowds and should not visit Aung San Suu Kyi without prior arrangement. Terrorist attacks have been reported in some areas
WEATHER Monsoon climate; Feb to May hot with very little rain; May to Oct wet; Nov to Feb cooler and drier
BANKING 1000–1400 Mon to Fri
EMERGENCY Unavailable
TIME ZONE GMT +6.30
INTERNATIONAL DIALING CODE 95

CAMBODIA

GOVERNMENT Constitutional monarchy
LANGUAGES Khmer (official), French, English
CURRENCY Riel = 100 sen
MEDICAL Visitors should protect against cholera, hepatitis, malaria, typhoid, and rabies
TRAVEL Visitors should seek advice before traveling. The greatest risks are from traffic accidents and armed robbery after dark. Land mines exist in certain rural areas
WEATHER Tropical monsoon climate; May to Oct monsoon; Dec to Jan lower humidity and little rainfall; Feb to Apr hot; temperatures are constant throughout the country
BANKING 0800–1500 Mon to Fri
EMERGENCY Unavailable
TIME ZONE GMT +7
INTERNATIONAL DIALING CODE 855

CANADA

GOVERNMENT Federal multiparty constitutional monarchy
LANGUAGES English and French (both official)
CURRENCY Canadian dollar = 100 cents
MEDICAL Medical treatment is expensive and it is essential that visitors have travel insurance. Blackfly and mosquitoes can cause problems in areas near water
TRAVEL Most visits to Canada are trouble-free
WEATHER Varies considerably; Jul to Aug tend to be warm all round the country; Nov to Mar very cold everywhere except west coast
BANKING 1000–1500 Mon to Fri
EMERGENCY Emergency Services 911 or 0
TIME ZONE Six zones exist from GMT –3.30 in Newfoundland to –8 on the Pacific coast
INTERNATIONAL DIALING CODE 1

CANARY ISLANDS

GOVERNMENT Spanish autonomous region
LANGUAGES Spanish
CURRENCY Euro = 100 cents
MEDICAL The Canary Islands are part of Spain and there are no specific health risks
TRAVEL The islands are volcanic and the landscape is varied. Many resorts suffer the effects of mass tourism, but beyond these areas there are stunning, peaceful regions to be enjoyed
WEATHER Subtropical climate; generally hot and sunny all year round, but Dec to Feb slightly cooler than rest of year
BANKING Visitors should enquire at hotel
EMERGENCY Unavailable
TIME ZONE GMT
INTERNATIONAL DIALING CODE 34

CAPE VERDE

GOVERNMENT Multiparty republic
LANGUAGES Portuguese, Creole
CURRENCY Cape Verde escudo = 100 centavos
MEDICAL Water is untreated and unsafe to drink. Avoid dairy products as they are unpasteurized. Polio and typhoid vaccinations are recommended; there is a risk of cholera and malaria
TRAVEL Most visits to Cape Verde are trouble-free. Visitors should avoid carrying valuables in public and remain vigilant at all times
WEATHER Warm and temperate climate with a dry summer. The islands suffer periodically from drought
BANKING 0800–1400 Mon to Fri
EMERGENCY All services 87
TIME ZONE GMT –1
INTERNATIONAL DIALING CODE 238

CAYMAN ISLANDS

GOVERNMENT British crown colony
LANGUAGES English (local dialects also spoken)
CURRENCY Cayman Islands dollar = 100 cents
MEDICAL There is a risk of sunburn and poisonous plants are present
TRAVEL Most visits to the Cayman Islands are trouble-free. Car hire is a good way to move around the islands
WEATHER Warm tropical climate all year round; May to Oct wet season with usually brief showers
BANKING 0900–1600 Mon to Thu; 0900–1630 Fri
EMERGENCY Police 911; Ambulance 555; All Services 911
TIME ZONE GMT –5
INTERNATIONAL DIALING CODE 1 345

CHAD

GOVERNMENT Multiparty republic
LANGUAGES French and Arabic (both official)
CURRENCY CFA franc = 100 centimes
MEDICAL Visitors should be vaccinated against yellow fever, tetanus, cholera, and hepatitis A
TRAVEL Visitors to Chad should remain vigilant at all times especially in the southwest region along the border with Cameroon. Areas to avoid include the Aozou Strip and the Tibesti area on the border with Libya, where minefields exist
WEATHER Hot tropical climate; Mar to May very hot; May to Oct wet in south; Jun to Sep wet in central areas; little rain in northern regions
BANKING 0900–1400 Mon to Fri
EMERGENCY Unavailable
TIME ZONE GMT +1
INTERNATIONAL DIALING CODE 235

CHILE

GOVERNMENT Multiparty republic
LANGUAGES Spanish (official)
CURRENCY Chilean peso = 100 centavos
MEDICAL Visitors should protect themselves against cholera
TRAVEL Most visits are trouble-free, but visitors are advised to keep in groups and avoid walking alone, particularly after dark. Pickpockets and muggers are active in cities. Passport photocopies should be carried at all times
WEATHER Variable climate; Sep to Nov and Feb to Apr pleasant temperatures; Dec to Mar hotter; skiing is popular from Jun to Aug
BANKING 0900–1400 Mon to Fri
EMERGENCY Police 133; Fire 132
TIME ZONE GMT –4; Easter Island –6
INTERNATIONAL DIALING CODE 56

CHINA

GOVERNMENT Single-party Communist republic
LANGUAGES Mandarin Chinese (official)
CURRENCY Renminbi yuan = 10 jiao = 100 fen
MEDICAL Rabies is widespread. A virulent strain of viral pneumonia has emerged in the southeast and malaria is common in southern areas
TRAVEL Violent crimes are rare. Crime occurs in cities, and extra care should be taken around street markets and popular bar areas at night
WEATHER Climate varies; Apr to Sep humid and hot; Jan to Mar very cold; rainfall high in central areas; Jul to Sep typhoon season in the south
BANKING 0930–1200 and 1400–1700 Mon to Fri; 0900–1700 Sat
EMERGENCY Police 110; Fire 119
TIME ZONE GMT +8
INTERNATIONAL DIALING CODE 86

COLOMBIA

GOVERNMENT Multiparty republic
LANGUAGES Spanish (official)
CURRENCY Colombian peso = 100 centavos
MEDICAL Visitors should protect against altitude sickness, cholera, hepatitis A, B and D, and malaria
TRAVEL Guerrilla and criminal attacks close to Bogota are increasing. Violence and kidnapping are serious problems in Colombia. The border area with Panama and the Uraba region of Antioquia are particularly dangerous
WEATHER Hot and humid; May to Nov rainy season; cooler in upland areas
BANKING 0900–1500 Mon to Fri
EMERGENCY All Services 112 (01 in smaller towns and rural areas)
TIME ZONE GMT –5
INTERNATIONAL DIALING CODE 57

COMOROS

GOVERNMENT Multiparty republic
LANGUAGES Arabic and French (both official)
CURRENCY CFA franc = 100 centimes
MEDICAL Strict food hygiene precautions are essential. Cholera and malaria are prevalant and medical facilities are basic and limited
TRAVEL Generally crime-free, but be aware of pickpockets. Visitors should not walk around town centres unaccompanied at night
WEATHER Tropical climate with average temperatures of 77°F [25°C]. Cyclone risk between Jan and Apr
BANKING 0730–1300 Mon to Thu; 0730–1100 Fri
EMERGENCY Unavailable
TIME ZONE GMT +3
INTERNATIONAL DIALING CODE 269

COSTA RICA

GOVERNMENT Multiparty republic
LANGUAGES Spanish (official), English
CURRENCY Costa Rican colón = 100 céntimos
MEDICAL Cases of dengue fever have been confirmed. Visitors should protect themselves against malaria, cholera, and hepatitis
TRAVEL Daylight muggings can occur. Do not wear jewelry or carry large amounts of cash. Riptides are very common on all beaches
WEATHER Coastal areas warmer than inland low-lying regions; Dec to Apr warm and dry; May to Nov rainy season; landslides can occur
BANKING 0900–1500 Mon to Fri
EMERGENCY Police 104; Fire 103; Ambulance 225/1436 and 228/2187
TIME ZONE GMT –7
INTERNATIONAL DIALING CODE 506

CROATIA

GOVERNMENT Multiparty republic
LANGUAGES Croatian
CURRENCY Kuna = 100 lipas
MEDICAL No specific health risks, although the health system is severely stretched at present
TRAVEL Exercise caution in the areas bordering Bosnia-Herzegovina, Serbia, and Montenegro. There continue to be incidents of violence and many unexploded land mines remain undetected. It is inadvisable to use the Debelli Brijeg crossing-points into Montenegro
WEATHER Continental climate in the north and Mediterranean on the Adriatic Coast
BANKING 0700–1500 Mon to Fri
EMERGENCY Police 92; Fire 93; Ambulance 94
TIME ZONE GMT +1
INTERNATIONAL DIALING CODE 385

CUBA

GOVERNMENT Socialist republic
LANGUAGES Spanish (official)
CURRENCY Cuban peso = 100 centavos
MEDICAL Tap water is unsafe to drink, with a risk of contracting hepatitis A
TRAVEL Street theft occurs, especially in Old Havana and major tourist sites. Do not carry large amounts of cash or jewelry. Do not travel with anyone other than your recognized tour operator. Avoid military zones
WEATHER May to Oct hot rainy season; Aug to Nov hurricane season; Dec to Apr cooler
BANKING 0830–1200 and 1330–1500 Mon to Fri; 0830–1030 Sat
EMERGENCY All Services 26811
TIME ZONE GMT –4
INTERNATIONAL DIALING CODE 53

CYPRUS

GOVERNMENT Multiparty republic
LANGUAGES Greek and Turkish (both official)
CURRENCY Euro = 100 cents
MEDICAL There are no specific health risks, but visitors should be protected against hepatitis
TRAVEL Travel is generally trouble-free, but attempts to pass overland from the northern Turkish sector into the southern Greek region are not recommended
WEATHER Apr to May and Sep to Oct cool and pleasant; Jun to Aug hot and dry; Nov to Mar rainfall is heavier, but temperatures remain warm
BANKING 0815–1230 in tourist areas; 1530–1730 in winter; 1630–1830 in summer
EMERGENCY All Services 199
TIME ZONE GMT +2
INTERNATIONAL DIALING CODE 357

CZECH REPUBLIC

GOVERNMENT Multiparty republic
LANGUAGES Czech (official)
CURRENCY Czech koruna = 100 haler
MEDICAL Visitors to forested areas should seek advice about immunization against tick-borne encephalitis and lyme disease
TRAVEL Most visits are trouble-free, but petty theft is a growing problem, particularly in Prague. Pickpocketing is very common at tourist attractions
WEATHER May to Sep mild; Apr and Oct much cooler
BANKING 0800–1800 Mon to Fri
EMERGENCY Police 158; Fire 150; Ambulance 155
TIME ZONE GMT +1
INTERNATIONAL DIALING CODE 42

DENMARK

GOVERNMENT Parliamentary monarchy
LANGUAGES Danish (official), English
CURRENCY Danish krone = 100 øre
MEDICAL There are no specific health risks in Denmark
TRAVEL Visits to Denmark are generally trouble-free. Visitors will enjoy relatively low prices compared to other European countries
WEATHER Jun to Aug warm summer season; Oct to Mar cold and wet with chance of frost; spring and fall are usually mild and pleasant
BANKING 0930–1700 Mon, Tue, Wed and Fri; 0930–1800 Thu. Some foreign exchange bureaux remain open until midnight
EMERGENCY Emergency Services 112
TIME ZONE GMT +1
INTERNATIONAL DIALING CODE 45

DOMINICA

GOVERNMENT Parliamentary democracy
LANGUAGES English (official), Creole, French
CURRENCY East Caribbean dollar = 100 cents
MEDICAL Dengue fever is prevalent and visitors should guard against mosquito bites
TRAVEL Most visits are trouble-free. Visitors are advised to take sensible precautions and be vigilant at all times
WEATHER Tropical climate with heavy rainfall, particularly in Jun to Oct, which is also the hottest period. Tropical storms and hurricanes can occur between Jun and Nov
BANKING 0800–1500 Mon to Thu; 0800–1700 Fri
EMERGENCY All services 999
TIME ZONE GMT –4
INTERNATIONAL DIALING CODE 1 767

DOMINICAN REPUBLIC

GOVERNMENT Multiparty republic
LANGUAGES Spanish (official)
CURRENCY Dominican peso = 100 centavos
MEDICAL Tourists should protect against polio and typhoid. There are occasional outbreaks of malaria and dengue fever; anti-mosquito skin repellants are recommended
TRAVEL Border areas should be avoided while the political unrest in neighbouring Haiti continues. Avoid any excursions that are not recommended by tour operators
WEATHER Hot tropical climate; Jun to Nov rainy season with the risk of hurricanes
BANKING 0800–1600 Mon to Fri
EMERGENCY Emergency Services 711
TIME ZONE GMT –4
INTERNATIONAL DIALING CODE 1 809

ECUADOR

GOVERNMENT Multiparty republic
LANGUAGES Spanish (official), Quechua
CURRENCY US dollar = 100 cents
MEDICAL There is a risk of dengue fever, hepatitis, malaria, typhoid, diptheria, and rabies
TRAVEL Street crimes such as muggings and pickpocketing are common in the cities. Visitors should avoid travel to the provinces bordering Colombia due to incidents of kidnapping
WEATHER Jan to Apr warm and rainy on mainland and Galapagos; Jun to Aug cold; Jun to Aug dry in Highlands; Aug to Feb dry in Oriente
BANKING 0900–1330 and 1430–1830 Mon to Fri
EMERGENCY Police 101; Ambulance 131
TIME ZONE GMT –5; Galapagos Islands –6
INTERNATIONAL DIALING CODE 593

EL SALVADOR

GOVERNMENT Republic
LANGUAGES Spanish (official)
CURRENCY US dollar = 100 cents
MEDICAL Tourists should protect against cholera, hepatitis, malaria, rabies, and typhoid
TRAVEL El Salvador is more politically stable than ever, but has high levels of violent crime. Visitors traveling alone should be vigilant at all times
WEATHER Hot subtropical climate; Nov to Apr dry season; May to Oct rainy season with cooler evenings
BANKING 0900–1300 and 1345–1600 Mon to Fri
EMERGENCY All Services 123/121
TIME ZONE GMT –6
INTERNATIONAL DIALING CODE 503

ETHIOPIA

GOVERNMENT Federation of nine provinces
LANGUAGES Amharic (official), many others
CURRENCY Birr = 100 cents
MEDICAL Water-borne diseases and malaria are prevalent. Medical facilities outside the capital are extremely poor
TRAVEL Most governments advise against travel to the Gambella region and the Eritrean border. There is currently a high risk of terrorism throughout the country
WEATHER Lowlands are hot and humid, it is warm in the hills and cool in the upland areas
BANKING 0800–1200 and 1300–1700 Mon to Thu; 0830–1100 and 1300–1700 Fri
EMERGENCY Not available
TIME ZONE GMT +3
INTERNATIONAL DIALING CODE 251

EGYPT

GOVERNMENT Republic
LANGUAGES Arabic (official), French, English
CURRENCY Egyptian pound = 100 piastres
MEDICAL There are no specific health risks in Egypt
TRAVEL Due to continuing tensions, visitors should keep in touch with developments in the Middle East and remain vigilant at all times. Particular care should be taken when traveling in Luxor and beyond in the Nile Valley
WEATHER Jun to Aug very hot and dry; Sep to May dry and cooler; spring and fall months are pleasant; dusty Saharan winds during Apr
BANKING 0830–1400 Sun to Thu
EMERGENCY Unavailable
TIME ZONE GMT +2
INTERNATIONAL DIALING CODE 20

ESTONIA

GOVERNMENT Multiparty republic
LANGUAGES Estonian (official), Russian
CURRENCY Estonian kroon = 100 senti
MEDICAL There are no specific health risks
TRAVEL Most visits are trouble-free. Despite independence in 1991, much tradition exists in Estonia. Skiing, skating, and ice fishing are popular during the winter months
WEATHER Large temperature variations; Apr to May warm and pleasant; Jun to Sep hot.; Dec to Mar very cold with heavy snowfall; rain falls all year round
BANKING 0930–1630 Mon to Fri
EMERGENCY Police 02; Fire 01; Ambulance 03 (dial an extra 0 first if in Tallinn)
TIME ZONE GMT +2
INTERNATIONAL DIALING CODE 372

FIJI ISLANDS

GOVERNMENT Transitional
LANGUAGES English (official), various Fijian dialects
CURRENCY Fijian dollar = 100 cents
MEDICAL Visitors should protect against dengue fever and should avoid mosquito bites
TRAVEL There has been an increase in petty crime due to the unsettled economic and political situations
WEATHER Tropical climate; Dec to Apr humid, rainy season with a risk of tropical cyclones; May to Oct cooler, dry season
BANKING 0930–1500 Mon to Thu; 0930–1600 Fri
EMERGENCY All Services 000
TIME ZONE GMT +12
INTERNATIONAL DIALING CODE 679

FINLAND

GOVERNMENT Multiparty republic
LANGUAGES Finnish and Swedish (both official)
CURRENCY Euro = 100 cents
MEDICAL There are no specific health risks, but if mushroom-picking/eating, seek advice on safety
TRAVEL Visits to Finland are generally trouble-free
WEATHER Temperate climate; May to Sep warm with midnight sun; Oct to Mar very cold; Nov to May snow cover in the north; skiing starts in Feb, the coldest month, and continues until Jun in Lapland
BANKING 0915–1615 Mon to Fri
EMERGENCY Police 002; Fire/Ambulance 000; Emergency Services 112; Doctor 008
TIME ZONE GMT +2
INTERNATIONAL DIALING CODE 358

FRENCH POLYNESIA

GOVERNMENT French overseas territory
LANGUAGES French and Polynesian (both official)
CURRENCY French Pacific franc = 100 cents
MEDICAL Water is untreated and dairy foods are unpasteurized. Vaccinations against polio and typhoid are recommended
TRAVEL Most visits are trouble-free, but visitors should remain vigilant at al times. French Polynesia is made up of 130 islands, Tahiti being the most popular
WEATHER Tropical but moderate climate with occasional cyclonic storms in Jan. Cool and dry Mar to Nov
BANKING 0745–1530 Mon to Fri
EMERGENCY Dial operator
TIME ZONE GMT –9 to GMT –10
INTERNATIONAL DIALING CODE 689

GEORGIA

GOVERNMENT Multiparty republic
LANGUAGES Georgian (official), Russian
CURRENCY Lari = 100 tetri
MEDICAL Diptheria and rabies cases have been reported. Tap water is unsafe to drink. Anthrax has been reported in the east. Medical care is poor and visitors should carry their own syringes
TRAVEL The regions of Abkhazia and South Ossetia should be avoided. Do not attempt access across the land borders with Russia
WEATHER Jul to Sep hot; Dec to Mar mild, especially in the southwest; low temperatures in alpine areas; rainfall heavy in southwest
BANKING 0930–1730 Mon to Fri
EMERGENCY Police 02; Fire 01; Ambulance 03
TIME ZONE GMT +4
INTERNATIONAL DIALING CODE 995

FRANCE

GOVERNMENT Multiparty republic
LANGUAGES French (official)
CURRENCY Euro = 100 cents
MEDICAL There are no specific health risks
TRAVEL Most visits to France are trouble-free. There have been sporadic bomb attacks on the island of Corsica and care should be exercised
WEATHER Temperate climate in the north; rain falls all year round; Mediterranean climate in the south; mild in the west; May to Sep hot and sunny; Oct to Nov pleasant temperatures
BANKING 0900–1200 and 1400–1600 Mon to Fri. Some banks close on Mondays
EMERGENCY Police 17; Fire 18; Ambulance 15; Emergency Services 112
TIME ZONE GMT +1
INTERNATIONAL DIALING CODE 33

GAMBIA, THE

GOVERNMENT Military regime
LANGUAGES English (official), Mandinka, Wolof
CURRENCY Dalasi = 100 butut
MEDICAL Water-borne diseases and malaria are common. Other health risks include yellow fever, hepatitis, rabies, and typhoid
TRAVEL Exercise caution when walking at night. Do not travel with valuables and dress modestly
WEATHER Nov to Mar dry and cool with winds from the Sahara; Jun to Oct rainy season; inland the cool season is shorter and temperatures are hot from Mar to Jun
BANKING 0800–1330 Mon to Thu; 0800–1100 Fri
EMERGENCY Consult foreign embassy
TIME ZONE GMT
INTERNATIONAL DIALING CODE 220

GERMANY

GOVERNMENT Federal multiparty republic
LANGUAGES German (official)
CURRENCY Euro = 100 cents
MEDICAL There are no specific health risks, but medical care is expensive
TRAVEL Visits to Germany are generally trouble-free. Travelers are able to enjoy a wealth of arts and culture, plus stunning natural scenery
WEATHER Very variable, temperate climate throughout the country; May to Oct warm; Nov to Apr cold; rain falls all year round
BANKING 0830–1300 and 1400/30–1600 Mon to Fri
EMERGENCY Police 110; Fire 112; Emergency Services 112
TIME ZONE GMT +1
INTERNATIONAL DIALING CODE 49

GIBRALTAR

GOVERNMENT UK overseas territory
LANGUAGES English and Spanish
CURRENCY Gibraltar pound = 100 pence
MEDICAL There are no specific health risks in Gibraltar
TRAVEL Most visits to Gibraltar are trouble-free. The country was recognized as a British possession in 1713, and despite Spanish claims, its population has consistently voted to retain its contacts with Britain
WEATHER Warm all year round; Jun to Sep hot and can be humid; Nov to Mar mild
BANKING 0900–1530 and 1630–1800 Mon to Fri
EMERGENCY All Services 999
TIME ZONE GMT +1
INTERNATIONAL DIALING CODE 350

GREECE

GOVERNMENT Multiparty republic
LANGUAGES Greek (official)
CURRENCY Euro = 100 cents
MEDICAL There is a risk of sunburn
TRAVEL Visitors should exercise normal precautions regarding safety and security. Tourists are strongly advised not to hire motorcycles, scooters, or mopeds
WEATHER Mediterranean climate; Aug to Nov pleasant temperatures; Nov to Mar heavy rainfall; Apr to Jun hot
BANKING 0800–1400 Mon to Fri
EMERGENCY Police 100; Fire 199; Ambulance 166; Emergency Services 112
TIME ZONE GMT +2
INTERNATIONAL DIALING CODE 30 + 1 for Athens; 31 Thessaloniki; 81 Heraklion; 661 Corfu

GRENADA

GOVERNMENT Constitutional monarchy
LANGUAGES English (official)
CURRENCY East Caribbean dollar = 100 cents
MEDICAL Tourists should protect against polio and typhoid. Anti-mosquito repellants are recommended
TRAVEL Trips are mostly trouble-free; however, tourists should remain vigilant at all times
WEATHER Tropical climate, rainy season is Jun to Sep when tropical storms and hurricanes occur. Jan to May is drier and less humid
BANKING 0800–1400 Mon to Thu; 0800–1300 and 1400–1700 Fri
EMERGENCY Police 112; Ambulance 434; Emergency services 911
TIME ZONE GMT –4
INTERNATIONAL DIALING CODE 1 473

GUADELOUPE

GOVERNMENT French overseas territory
LANGUAGES French (official), Creole
CURRENCY Euro = 100 cents
MEDICAL Polio and typhoid vaccinations are recommended. Water is untreated and unsafe to drink
TRAVEL Visits to Guadeloupe are generally trouble-free, and the French culture and influence is clearly evident. Soufriere de Guadeloupe is an active volcano
WEATHER Warm, humid weather all year round. Rainy season from Jun to Oct, when there is a risk of hurricanes
BANKING 0800–1600 Mon to Fri
EMERGENCY Police 17; Fire and Ambulance 18
TIME ZONE GMT –4
INTERNATIONAL DIALING CODE 590

HONG KONG

GOVERNMENT Special administrative region of China
LANGUAGES Chinese and English; Cantonese is most widely spoken
CURRENCY Hong Kong dollar = 100 cents
MEDICAL Visitors should protect against polio and typhoid. Slight risk of malaria in rural areas
TRAVEL Most visits are trouble-free
WEATHER Nov to Dec warm with pleasant breeze; Jan to Feb much cooler; Mar to Apr warmer; May to Sep very humid and uncomfortable, with a risk of cyclones in Sep
BANKING 0900–1630 Mon to Fri; 0900–1330 Sat
EMERGENCY All Services 999
TIME ZONE GMT +8
INTERNATIONAL DIALING CODE 852

HUNGARY

GOVERNMENT Multiparty republic
LANGUAGES Hungarian (official)
CURRENCY Forint = 100 fillér
MEDICAL There are no specific health risks in Hungary
TRAVEL Street theft is common in tourist areas, particularly in Budapest. It is illegal to drive having consumed alcohol. Passports to be carried at all times. Do not take photographs of anything connected with the military
WEATHER Jun to Aug very warm and sunny; spring and fall mild and pleasant; Jan to Mar very cold
BANKING 0900–1400 Mon to Fri
EMERGENCY Police 107; Fire/Ambulance 104
TIME ZONE GMT +1
INTERNATIONAL DIALING CODE 36

ICELAND

GOVERNMENT Multiparty republic
LANGUAGES Icelandic (official)
CURRENCY Icelandic króna = 100 aurar
MEDICAL There is a risk of hypothermia if trekking during the winter months
TRAVEL Visitors planning to travel off-road do so at their own risk and must contact the local authorities (Vegagerdin) prior to departure. Interior roads are closed in winter
WEATHER Weather is highly changeable all year round; May to Aug is mild with nearly 24 hours of daylight in Reykjavik; Sep to Apr is cold
BANKING 0915–1600 Mon to Fri
EMERGENCY Unavailable
TIME ZONE GMT
INTERNATIONAL DIALING CODE 354

INDIA

GOVERNMENT Multiparty federal republic
LANGUAGES Hindi, English, Telugu, Bengali, Marathi, Tamil, Urdu, Gujarati, Malayalam, Kannada, Oriya, Punjabi, Assamese, Kashmiri, Sindhi and Sanskrit (all official)
CURRENCY Indian rupee = 100 paisa
MEDICAL There is a risk of malaria, AIDS, and intestinal problems. Precautions should be taken
TRAVEL Visitors are advised to avoid the Pakistan border areas, as well as Jammu and Kashmir
WEATHER Hot tropical climate that varies from region to region; Apr to Sep very hot with monsoon rains
BANKING 1000–1400 Mon to Fri
EMERGENCY Unavailable
TIME ZONE GMT +5.30
INTERNATIONAL DIALING CODE 91

INDONESIA

GOVERNMENT Multiparty republic
LANGUAGES Bahasa Indonesian (official)
CURRENCY Indonesian rupiah = 100 sen
MEDICAL There is a risk of polio, typhoid, hepatitis B, yellow fever, and TB. Unpasteurized dairy produce should be avoided
TRAVEL Non-essential travel to Indonesia is not recommended due to the risk of terrorism against Western interests
WEATHER Tropical, varying climate; May to Oct dry weather from eastern monsoon; Nov to Apr rains from western monsoon. In northern Sumatra this pattern is reversed
BANKING 0800–1500 Mon to Fri
EMERGENCY Police 110; Ambulance 118
TIME ZONE West GMT +7; Central +8; East +9
INTERNATIONAL DIALING CODE 62

IRAN

GOVERNMENT Islamic republic
LANGUAGES Persian, Turkic, Kurdish
CURRENCY Iranian rial = 100 dinars
MEDICAL There is a risk of polio, typhoid, malaria and cholera
TRAVEL Visitors should monitor media reports before traveling. Any increase in regional tension will affect travel advice. Visitors should exercise caution and avoid carrying large sums of money since robbery and bag-snatching are common
WEATHER Dec to Mar very cold; Apr to Jun and Sep to Nov warm; Jun to Sep extremely hot
BANKING 0900–1600 Sat to Wed; 0900–1200 Thu. Closed on Fri
EMERGENCY Unavailable
TIME ZONE GMT +3.30
INTERNATIONAL DIALING CODE 98

IRELAND

GOVERNMENT Multiparty republic
LANGUAGES Irish (Gaelic) and English (both official)
CURRENCY Euro = 100 cents
MEDICAL There are no specific health risks
TRAVEL The Irish usually have close community bonds. Visitors should find people very friendly. Strong economic growth continues
WEATHER Rain falls all year round; Jul to Sep warm; Nov to Mar wet and cold; spring and fall mild
BANKING 1000–1600 Mon to Fri. Banks may open later in Dublin
EMERGENCY Emergency Services 112; All Services 999
TIME ZONE GMT
INTERNATIONAL DIALING CODE 353

ISRAEL

GOVERNMENT Multiparty republic
LANGUAGES Hebrew and Arabic (both official)
CURRENCY New Israeli shekel = 100 agorat
MEDICAL There are no specific health risks
TRAVEL Most governments currently strongly advise against travel to the West Bank, Gaza, and Jerusalem, or near their border areas with Israel. Visitors should keep car doors locked when traveling and avoid carrying large sums of cash
WEATHER Jul to Sep hot and windy; Dec to Mar cool in the north; spring and fall are warm and pleasant
BANKING 0830–1230 and 1600–1730 Mon, Tue and Thu; 0830–1230 Wed; 0830–1200 Fri
EMERGENCY Police/Fire 100; Ambulance 101
TIME ZONE GMT +2
INTERNATIONAL DIALING CODE 972

ITALY

GOVERNMENT Multiparty republic
LANGUAGES Italian (official), German, French, Slovene
CURRENCY Euro = 100 cents
MEDICAL There are no specific health risks
TRAVEL Crime is rare, but visitors in tourist areas and city centres should remain vigilant after dark
WEATHER Apr to May and Oct to Nov warm and pleasant; Jun to Sep hot; Dec to Mar colder temperatures with heavy snow in mountain areas; warmer in the south
BANKING Generally 0830–1330 and 1530–1930 Mon to Fri
EMERGENCY Police 112; Fire 115; Ambulance 113; Emergency Services 112
TIME ZONE GMT +1
INTERNATIONAL DIALING CODE 39

JAMAICA

GOVERNMENT Constitutional monarchy
LANGUAGES English (official), patois English
CURRENCY Jamaican dollar = 100 cents
MEDICAL There are no specific health risks
TRAVEL Most visits are trouble-free, but violent crime does exist, mainly in Kingston. Visitors should avoid walking alone in isolated areas, and be particularly alert after dark and using public transport
WEATHER Tropical climate; temperatures remain high all year round; May to Oct rainy season, but showers can occur at any time
BANKING 0900–1400 Mon to Thu; 0900–1500 Fri
EMERGENCY Police 119; Fire/Ambulance 110
TIME ZONE GMT –5
INTERNATIONAL DIALING CODE 1 876

JAPAN

GOVERNMENT Constitutional monarchy
LANGUAGES Japanese (official)
CURRENCY Yen = 100 sen
MEDICAL Health and hygiene standards are high and visitors are not required to have vaccinations
TRAVEL Most visits remain trouble-free. There is a high risk of earthquakes and typhoons which often hit the country
WEATHER Sep to Nov typhoons and rain; Jun to Sep warm/very hot with rain in Jun; Mar to May pleasant; Dec to Feb cold winds and snow in western areas, but dry and clear on Pacific coast
BANKING 0900–1500 Mon to Fri
EMERGENCY Tokyo English Life Line 3403 7106; Japan Helpline 0120 461 997
TIME ZONE GMT +9
INTERNATIONAL DIALING CODE 81

JORDAN

GOVERNMENT Constitutional monarchy
LANGUAGES Arabic (official)
CURRENCY Jordan dinar = 1,000 fils
MEDICAL There are no specific health risks, but visitors should consider vaccination against hepatitis, polio, tetanus, typhoid, and diptheria
TRAVEL Before traveling, visitors should monitor media reports for any increase in regional tension. Crime is low, but visitors should dress modestly and respect local customs
WEATHER Jun to Sep hot and dry with cool evenings; Nov to Mar cooler with rainfall
BANKING 0830–1230 and 1530–1730 Sat to Thu; 0830–1000 during Ramadan
EMERGENCY Police 192; Fire/Ambulance 193
TIME ZONE GMT +2
INTERNATIONAL DIALING CODE 962

KENYA

GOVERNMENT Multiparty republic
LANGUAGES Kiswahili and English (both official)
CURRENCY Kenyan shilling = 100 cents
MEDICAL Malaria is endemic and AIDS is widespread. Water is unsafe to drink
TRAVEL Be alert at all times, particularly in Nairobi and Mombasa. Avoid traveling after dark and in isolated areas
WEATHER Complex and changeable; Jan to Feb hot and dry; Mar to May hot and wet; Jun to Oct warm and dry; Nov to Dec warm and wet; Cooler with rain at any time at higher altitudes
BANKING 0900–1500 Mon to Fri; 0900–1100 on first and last Sat of each month
EMERGENCY All Services 336886/501280
TIME ZONE GMT +3
INTERNATIONAL DIALING CODE 254

KOREA, SOUTH

GOVERNMENT Multiparty republic
LANGUAGES Korean (official)
CURRENCY South Korean won = 100 chon
MEDICAL There are no specific health risks, but medical and dental treatment can be expensive
TRAVEL Travel to South Korea is generally trouble-free, but some form of identification should be carried at all times
WEATHER Jul to Aug hot with heavy rainfall and a chance of typhoons; Sep to Nov and Apr to May mild and dry; Dec to Mar cold but dry, with good skiing
BANKING 0930–1630 Mon to Fri; 0930–1330 Sat
EMERGENCY Unavailable
TIME ZONE GMT +9
INTERNATIONAL DIALING CODE 82

KUWAIT

GOVERNMENT Constitutional monarchy
LANGUAGES Arabic (official), English
CURRENCY Kuwaiti dinar = 1,000 fils
MEDICAL Vaccinations against polio, typhoid, and cholera are recommended
TRAVEL Visitors should monitor media reports before traveling. Any increase in regional tension will affect travel advice. There is a danger from unexploded bombs and land mines on beaches and in rural areas. All Islamic laws should be respected. Photography permits are required
WEATHER Apr to Oct hot, humid with little rain; Nov to Mar cool and dry
BANKING 0800–1200 Sun to Thu
EMERGENCY Unavailable
TIME ZONE GMT +3
INTERNATIONAL DIALING CODE 965

LEBANON

GOVERNMENT Multiparty republic
LANGUAGES Arabic (official), French, English
CURRENCY Lebanese pound = 100 piastres
MEDICAL Protection against polio and typhoid is recommended
TRAVEL Visitors should remain alert to international developments in the Middle East. Most governments currently advise against travel to areas within the Israeli Occupied Zone
WEATHER Jun to Sep hot and dry, but humid along the coast; Dec to May high rainfall with snow in mountains; spring and fall pleasant
BANKING 0830–1200 Mon to Sat
EMERGENCY Police 386 440 425; Fire 310 105; Ambulance 386 675
TIME ZONE GMT +2
INTERNATIONAL DIALING CODE 961

LIECHTENSTEIN

GOVERNMENT Hereditary constitutional monarchy
LANGUAGES German (official)
CURRENCY Swiss franc = 100 centimes
MEDICAL There is a risk of altitude sickness, sunburn, and hypothermia in the Alps
TRAVEL Most visits to Liechtenstein are trouble-free. The country is culturally and economically extremely similar to Switzerland. Winter sports are very popular in the Alps from Nov to Apr
WEATHER Temperate climate; Nov to Apr cool or cold; Jun to Sep warm with high rainfall
BANKING 0800–1630 Mon to Fri
EMERGENCY Police 117; Ambulance 144
TIME ZONE GMT +1
INTERNATIONAL DIALING CODE 41 75

LATVIA

GOVERNMENT Multiparty republic
LANGUAGES Latvian (official), Lithuanian, Russian
CURRENCY Latvian lat = 10 santimi
MEDICAL Visitors should protect themselves against tick-borne encephalitis, particularly if visiting forested areas
TRAVEL Most visits are trouble-free, but tourists should exercise caution since muggings and pickpocketing have increased recently. Use guarded car parks and keep valuables hidden
WEATHER Temperate climate; Apr to Sep warm and clear; Nov to Mar extremely cold; spring and fall mild
BANKING 1000–1800 Mon to Fri
EMERGENCY Police 02; Fire 01; Ambulance 03
TIME ZONE GMT +2
INTERNATIONAL DIALING CODE 371

LIBYA

GOVERNMENT Single-party socialist state
LANGUAGES Arabic (official), Berber
CURRENCY Libyan dinar = 1,000 dirhams
MEDICAL There is a slight risk of malaria, cholera, and hepatitis
TRAVEL Most visits to Libya are trouble-free, but any increase in regional tension will affect travel advice
WEATHER Warm all year round; Nov to Mar occasional rainfall; Apr to Sep can be very hot; May to Jun severe sandstorms from the south
BANKING 0800–1200 Sat to Wed (during winter); 0800–1200 Sat to Thu; 1600–1700 Sat and Wed (during summer)
EMERGENCY Unavailable
TIME ZONE GMT +1
INTERNATIONAL DIALING CODE 218

LITHUANIA

GOVERNMENT Multiparty republic
LANGUAGES Lithuanian (official), Russian, Polish
CURRENCY Litas = 100 centai
MEDICAL Travelers to forested areas should seek advice about protection against rabies and tick-borne encephalitis
TRAVEL There is a risk of pickpocketing, mugging, and bag-snatching, particularly on public transport. Be alert at all times and avoid quiet areas after dark
WEATHER Temperate climate; May to Sep warm; Oct to Nov mild; Nov to Mar can be very cold with snowfall common
BANKING 0900–1700 Mon to Fri
EMERGENCY Police 02; Fire 01; Ambulance 03
TIME ZONE GMT +2
INTERNATIONAL DIALING CODE 370

LUXEMBOURG

GOVERNMENT Constitutional monarchy (Grand Duchy)
LANGUAGES Luxembourgish (official), French, German
CURRENCY Euro = 100 cents
MEDICAL There are no specific health risks
TRAVEL Most travel to Luxembourg is trouble-free. The country is prosperous with a very high quality of life. Visitors may find it expensive compared to other European countries
WEATHER May to Sep warm with rainfall; Oct to Apr cold with snow
BANKING Varies greatly but generally 0900–1200 and 1330–1630 Mon to Fri
EMERGENCY Police 113; Fire/Ambulance 112
TIME ZONE GMT +1
INTERNATIONAL DIALING CODE 352

MADAGASCAR

GOVERNMENT Republic
LANGUAGES Malagasy and French (both official)
CURRENCY Malagasy franc = 100 centimes
MEDICAL There is a risk of polio, typhoid, bilharzia, cholera, rabies, and hepatitis. Precautions should be taken. Water is unsafe to drink and unpasteurized dairy products should be avoided
TRAVEL Locals are very welcoming and have a relaxed attitude toward time. Local culture should be respected
WEATHER Generally hot and subtropical with varying temperatures. Inland is more temperate, and the south is dry and arid
BANKING 0800–1300 Mon to Fri
EMERGENCY Unavailable
TIME ZONE GMT +3
INTERNATIONAL DIALING CODE 261

MALAWI

GOVERNMENT Multiparty republic
LANGUAGES Chichewa and English (both official)
CURRENCY Malawian kwacha = 100 tambala
MEDICAL AIDS and malaria are very common. Outbreaks of cholera do occur, particularly during the rainy season
TRAVEL Be alert at all times, particularly after dark. Avoid travel out of town at night since the condition of roads is poor. Cases of muggings and bag-snatching are increasing. Do not resist demands since attacks can be very violent
WEATHER Apr to Oct hot and dry; May to Jul cool and cold at night; Nov to Apr rainy season
BANKING 0800–1300 Mon to Fri
EMERGENCY Unavailable
TIME ZONE GMT +2
INTERNATIONAL DIALING CODE 265

MALAYSIA

GOVERNMENT Federal constitutional monarchy
LANGUAGES Malay (official), Chinese, English
CURRENCY Ringgit (Malaysian dollar) = 100 cents
MEDICAL No vaccinations required, but visitors should be up-to-date with typhoid, tetanus, and hepatitis B. Also check malarial status of region
TRAVEL The penalty for all drug offences is harsh. There has been a recent increase in street crime in Kuala Lumpur
WEATHER Nov to Feb heavy rains in eastern areas; Apr to May and Oct thunderstorms in western areas; showers can occur all year round
BANKING 1000–1500 Mon to Fri
EMERGENCY All Services 999
TIME ZONE GMT +8
INTERNATIONAL DIALING CODE 60

MALDIVES

GOVERNMENT Republic
LANGUAGES Maldivian Dhivehi, English
CURRENCY Rufiyaa = 100 laari
MEDICAL There is a high risk of sunburn all year round
TRAVEL Travel to the Maldives is generally trouble-free, but visitors should be aware that there are very harsh penalties for drug offences. Visitors should respect the Islamic religion and act accordingly
WEATHER Hot, tropical climate; May to Oct warm, but humid and wet from the southwest monsoon; Nov to Apr hot and dry
EMERGENCY Police 119; Fire 118; Ambulance 102
TIME ZONE GMT +5
INTERNATIONAL DIALING CODE 960

MALTA

GOVERNMENT Multiparty republic
LANGUAGES Maltese and English (both official)
CURRENCY Euro = 100 cents
MEDICAL There are no specific health risks
TRAVEL Most visits are trouble-free and crime is rare. However, bag-snatching and pickpocketing can occur. Caution should be exercised when traveling by car since many roads are poorly maintained. Visitors should dress modestly when visiting churches
WEATHER Jul to Sep hot with cool breezes; Feb to Jun mild; occasional sudden bursts of rain
BANKING 0800–1200 Mon to Thu; 0800–1200 and 1430–1600 Fri; 0800–1130 Sat
EMERGENCY Police 191; Ambulance 196
TIME ZONE GMT +1
INTERNATIONAL DIALING CODE 356

MARTINIQUE

GOVERNMENT Overseas department of France
LANGUAGES French, French Creole patois, English
CURRENCY Euro = 100 cents
MEDICAL There is a risk of sunburn and intestinal parasites. Bilharzia (schistosomiasis) may be present in fresh water
TRAVEL Travel to Martinique is generally trouble-free
WEATHER Warm all year round; Sep can be very humid; Feb to May cooler and dry; Oct to Dec higher rainfall; upland areas are cooler than lowlands
BANKING 0800–1600 Mon to Fri
EMERGENCY Police 17; Fire/Ambulance 18
TIME ZONE GMT –4
INTERNATIONAL DIALING CODE 596

MEXICO

GOVERNMENT Federal republic
LANGUAGES Spanish (official)
CURRENCY Mexican peso = 100 centavos
MEDICAL Visitors should protect themselves against polio, tetanus, typhoid, and hepatitis A
TRAVEL Most visits are trouble-free, but visitors should remain aware of incidents of armed robbery in urban areas, particularly Mexico City, and should dress down accordingly
WEATHER May to Oct humid, rainy season; Oct to May warm and dry; lowland areas are warmer and upland areas are cooler all year round
BANKING 0900–1330 Mon to Fri
EMERGENCY All Services 08
TIME ZONE Spans three time zones from GMT –6 to –8
INTERNATIONAL DIALING CODE 52

MONTENEGRO

GOVERNMENT Republic
LANGUAGES Serbian
CURRENCY Euro = 100 cents
MEDICAL There are no specific health risks, but the health system suffers from widespread shortages of medicines and other essentials
TRAVEL Most visits to Montenegro are trouble free but sensible precautions should be taken. Visitors should be vigilant for pickpocketing in public places and on public transport.
WEATHER Montenegro has a continental climate; Nov to Mar very cold; Jun to Sep warm with colder conditions in the mountain regions
BANKING 0700–1500 Mon to Fri; 0800-1400 Sat
EMERGENCY Police 92; Fire 93; Ambulance 94
TIME ZONE GMT +1
INTERNATIONAL DIALING CODE 382

MAURITIUS

GOVERNMENT Multiparty democracy
LANGUAGES French (official), Creole, English
CURRENCY Mauritian rupee = 100 cents
MEDICAL Malaria exists in the northern rural areas and there is a risk of bilharzia
TRAVEL Visitors should always respect local customs and traditions. Most visits are trouble-free, crime levels are low, but sensible precautions should be taken
WEATHER The weather is warm with a year-round sea breeze. Jan to May are the best months to visit. Tropical storms are likely to occur from Dec to Mar
BANKING 0930–1430 Mon to Fri; 0930–1130 Sat
EMERGENCY Unavailable
TIME ZONE GMT +4
INTERNATIONAL DIALING CODE 230

MONGOLIA

GOVERNMENT Multiparty republic
LANGUAGES Khalkha Mongolian (official), Turkic, Russian
CURRENCY Tugrik = 100 möngös
MEDICAL Visitors should protect against brucellosis, cholera, and meningitis
TRAVEL Petty street crime is increasing. Visitors should avoid traveling alone after dark. In rural areas always carry a GPS and satellite phone
WEATHER May to Oct dry and mild; Nov to Apr bitterly cold. Note that between Oct and May sudden snowstorms can block roads and bring transport systems to a standstill
BANKING 1000–1500 Mon to Fri
EMERGENCY Unavailable
TIME ZONE GMT +9
INTERNATIONAL DIALING CODE 976

MOROCCO

GOVERNMENT Constitutional monarchy
LANGUAGES Arabic (official), Berber, French
CURRENCY Moroccan dirham = 100 centimes
MEDICAL There are no specific health risks, but malaria is present in northern coastal areas
TRAVEL Visits are usually trouble-free, but visitors should only use authorized guides. Theft is increasing in major cities and valuables should be hidden at all times
WEATHER Winter cool and wet in north; Oct to Apr warm to hot in lowlands; Dec to Mar very cold in upland areas
BANKING 0830–1130 and 1430–1700 Mon to Fri (winter); 0800–1530 Mon to Fri (summer)
EMERGENCY Police 19; Fire/Ambulance 15
TIME ZONE GMT
INTERNATIONAL DIALING CODE 212

NAMIBIA

GOVERNMENT Multiparty republic
LANGUAGES English (official), Afrikaans, German
CURRENCY Namibian dollar = 100 cents
MEDICAL Malaria and bilharzia are endemic in the north and east respectively
TRAVEL Most visits are trouble-free. The Angola border should be avoided because of land mines left undetected after the civil war. Visitors should seek advice before traveling to townships
WEATHER Oct to Apr rain inland; May to Oct hot and dry; the coast is cool and relatively free of rain all year round
BANKING 0900–1530 Mon to Fri
EMERGENCY Police 1011; Fire 2032270; Ambulance 2032276
TIME ZONE GMT +2
INTERNATIONAL DIALING CODE 264

NEPAL

GOVERNMENT Multiparty republic
LANGUAGES Nepali (official), local languages
CURRENCY Nepalese rupee = 100 paisa
MEDICAL There is a risk of altitude sickness, hepatitis A, malaria (in lowland areas), and typhoid
TRAVEL Trekkers are advised to use professional guides and should obtain up-to-date advice regarding the safety of their chosen route
WEATHER Oct to Nov clear and dry, and not too cold at higher altitudes; Dec to Jan cool; Feb to Apr warm; Jun to Sep monsoon season
BANKING 1000–1450 Sun to Thu; 1000–1230 Fri
EMERGENCY Unavailable
TIME ZONE GMT +5.45
INTERNATIONAL DIALING CODE 977

NETHERLANDS

GOVERNMENT Constitutional monarchy
LANGUAGES Dutch (official), Frisian
CURRENCY Euro = 100 cents
MEDICAL There are no specific health risks in the Netherlands
TRAVEL Most visits to the Netherlands are trouble-free. Attitudes here are very liberal. Locals are extremely welcoming and speak very good English
WEATHER Jun to Sep usually warm but changeable; Nov to Mar can be bitterly cold with some snow; rain falls all year round; Apr is best for daffodils and May is best for tulips
BANKING 0900–1600 Mon to Fri
EMERGENCY Emergency Services 112
TIME ZONE GMT +1
INTERNATIONAL DIALING CODE 31

NETHERLANDS ANTILLES

GOVERNMENT Parliamentary democracy
LANGUAGES Dutch (official), French, English, Spanish, many others
CURRENCY Netherlands Antillean gilder = 100 cents
MEDICAL Polio and typhoid vaccinations are recommended. Water is considered drinkable and normal precautions should be taken with food
TRAVEL Most visits to the Netherlands Antilles are trouble-free
WEATHER Hot and tropical climate with cool sea breezes
BANKING 0830–1530 Mon to Fri
EMERGENCY Police 599/5/22222; Ambulance 599/5/22111
TIME ZONE GMT –4
INTERNATIONAL DIALING CODE 599

NEW ZEALAND

GOVERNMENT Constitutional monarchy
LANGUAGES English and Maori (both official)
CURRENCY New Zealand dollar = 100 cents
MEDICAL There are no specific health risks
TRAVEL Most visits are trouble-free, but visitors should take precautions against street crime in urban areas after dark. Travel within the country is relatively cheap and efficient, and accommodation is varied and affordable
WEATHER Subtropical climate in North Island; no extremes of heat or cold, but Nov to Apr warmer; temperate in South Island with cool temperatures; rainfall occurs all year round
BANKING 0900–1630 Mon to Fri
EMERGENCY All Services 111
TIME ZONE GMT +12
INTERNATIONAL DIALING CODE 64

NIGERIA

GOVERNMENT Federal multiparty republic
LANGUAGES English (official), Hausa, Yoruba, Ibo
CURRENCY Naira = 100 kobo
MEDICAL Visitors must have a yellow fever vaccination and protect against cerebral malaria
TRAVEL Incidences of kidnapping are increasing. Violent street crime, armed robberies, and car theft are common throughout the country. Visitors should avoid using public transport and traveling after dark outside tourist areas
WEATHER Mar to Nov hot, humid and wet; Apr to Sep wet; Dec to Mar dusty winds, but cooler
BANKING 0800–1500 Mon; 0800–1330 Tue to Fri
EMERGENCY Unavailable
TIME ZONE GMT +1
INTERNATIONAL DIALING CODE 234

NORWAY

GOVERNMENT Constitutional monarchy
LANGUAGES Norwegian (official)
CURRENCY Norwegian krone = 100 ore
MEDICAL There are no specific health risks in Norway
TRAVEL Most visits to Norway remain trouble-free. The country offers beautiful mountain scenery and year-round skiing
WEATHER May to Sep sunny and warm with long daylight hours; Dec to Mar very cold and dark; midnight sun occurs from 13 May to 29 Jul, and from 28 May to 14 Jul in the Lofoten Islands
BANKING 0900–1700 Mon to Thu; 0900–1530 Fri
EMERGENCY Police (Oslo) 002; Ambulance 003
TIME ZONE GMT +1
INTERNATIONAL DIALING CODE 47

OMAN

GOVERNMENT Monarchy with consultative council
LANGUAGES Arabic (official), Baluchi, English
CURRENCY Omani rial = 100 baizas
MEDICAL Visitors should protect against malaria
TRAVEL Most visits to Oman are trouble-free, but visitors should remain informed of developments in the Middle East. There are harsh penalties, including the death penalty, for drug offences. Driving conditions are hazardous
WEATHER Jun to Sep very hot; Oct to Mar pleasant; the rest of the year is cooler
BANKING 0800–1200 Sat to Wed; 0800–1130 Thu
EMERGENCY All Services 999
TIME ZONE GMT +4
INTERNATIONAL DIALING CODE 698

PAKISTAN

GOVERNMENT Military regime
LANGUAGES Urdu (official), many others
CURRENCY Pakistan rupee = 100 paisa
MEDICAL Visitors should protect against dengue fever, hepatitis A, and malaria. There is also a risk of encephalitis in rural regions
TRAVEL Due to the threat from terrorism, most Western governments advise against all travel to Pakistan, except for their nationals of Pakistan origin
WEATHER Nov to Apr warm; Apr to Jul hot; Jul to Sep monsoon with high rainfall in upland areas
BANKING 0900–1300 and 1500–2000 Sun to Thu; closed on Fri. Some banks open on Sat
EMERGENCY Unavailable
TIME ZONE GMT +5
INTERNATIONAL DIALING CODE 92

PARAGUAY

GOVERNMENT Multiparty republic
LANGUAGES Spanish and Guaraní (both official)
CURRENCY Guaraní = 100 céntimos
MEDICAL There is a risk of cholera, hepatitis, hookworm, typhoid, malaria, and tuberculosis
TRAVEL Most visits to Paraguay are trouble-free, but there is economic recession and some political instability. Attractions include several national parks, including the Chaco – South America's great wilderness
WEATHER Subtropical climate; Dec to Mar is the hottest and wettest season, but rain falls all year round
BANKING 0845–1215 Mon to Fri
EMERGENCY All Services 00
TIME ZONE GMT +5
INTERNATIONAL DIALING CODE 595

PERU

GOVERNMENT Transitional republic
LANGUAGES Spanish and Quechua (both official), Aymara
CURRENCY New sol = 100 centavos
MEDICAL Visitors should protect against altitude sickness, cholera, typhoid, hepatitis, and malaria
TRAVEL Tourist areas are generally safe, but visitors should exercise caution, particularly in Lima and Cuzco, where crime has become a serious problem for foreign visitors
WEATHER Oct to Apr hot and dry in coastal areas, but much rainfall in highlands; May to Sep is dry and the best time to visit the highlands
BANKING 0930–1600 Mon to Fri
EMERGENCY All Services 011/5114
TIME ZONE GMT –5
INTERNATIONAL DIALING CODE 51

PHILIPPINES

GOVERNMENT Multiparty republic
LANGUAGES Filipino (Tagalog) and English (both official), Spanish, many others
CURRENCY Philippine peso = 100 centavos
MEDICAL Visitors should protect against cholera, malaria, rabies and hepatitis
TRAVEL Visitors should check developments before traveling. Bomb explosions and kidnapping by organized gangs or terrorists have occurred in Manila and Mindanao
WEATHER Tropical climate with sea breeze; Jun to Sep wet; Oct to Feb cool and dry; Mar to May hot and dry; Jun to Sep typhoons occur
BANKING 0900–1600 Mon to Fri
EMERGENCY Unavailable
TIME ZONE GMT +8
INTERNATIONAL DIALING CODE 63

POLAND

GOVERNMENT Multiparty republic
LANGUAGES Polish (official)
CURRENCY Zloty = 100 groszy
MEDICAL Medical care is generally poor, particularly in rural regions
TRAVEL Most visits to Poland are trouble-free, but there is a serious risk of robbery when using public transport. Locals are very hospitable and welcoming
WEATHER Temperate climate; May to Sep warm; Nov to Mar cold and dark; spring and fall are warm and pleasant; rain falls all year round
BANKING 0800–1800 Mon to Fri
EMERGENCY Police 997; Ambulance 999
TIME ZONE GMT +1
INTERNATIONAL DIALING CODE 48

PORTUGAL

GOVERNMENT Multiparty republic
LANGUAGES Portuguese (official)
CURRENCY Euro = 100 cents
MEDICAL Sunburn is a risk during summer
TRAVEL Most visits are trouble-free. Children under 18 years traveling to Portugal should be accompanied by parents/guardians, or someone in the country should be authorized to have responsibility for them
WEATHER Apr to Oct hot and sunny; Nov to Mar wetter, particularly in the north; summers are hotter and winters are longer in the north
BANKING 0830–1500 Mon to Fri
EMERGENCY Emergency Services 112; All Services 115
TIME ZONE GMT
INTERNATIONAL DIALING CODE 351

PUERTO RICO

GOVERNMENT Commonwealth of the United States
LANGUAGES Spanish and English (both official)
CURRENCY US dollar = 100 cents
MEDICAL There is a risk of sunburn and a slight risk of hepatitis and bilharzia
TRAVEL Most visits to Puerto Rico are trouble-free
WEATHER Tropical climate with little variation in temperature all year round; May to Nov hurricane season; cooler in upland regions
BANKING 0900–1430 Mon to Thu; 0900–1430 and 1530–1700 Fri
EMERGENCY Police 787 343 2020; Fire 787 343 2330; All Services 911
TIME ZONE GMT –4
INTERNATIONAL DIALING CODE 1 787

QATAR

GOVERNMENT Constitutional absolute monarchy
LANGUAGES Arabic (official), English,
CURRENCY Qatari riyal = 100 dirhams
MEDICAL There are no specific health risks
TRAVEL Visitors should keep informed of international developments before traveling. It is prohibited to bring drugs, alcohol, religious material, or pork products into the country; videos may be censored. Visitors should dress modestly and respect local customs
WEATHER Jun to Sep very hot and dry; Apr to May and Dec to Feb frequent sandstorms; Nov and Feb to Mar warm with little wind
BANKING 0730–1130 Sat to Thu
EMERGENCY All Services 999
TIME ZONE GMT +3
INTERNATIONAL DIALING CODE 974

RÉUNION

GOVERNMENT Overseas department of France
LANGUAGES French (official), Creole
CURRENCY Euro = 100 cents
MEDICAL Precautions should be taken against typhoid and rabies. Water is unsafe to drink and dairy products should be avoided as they are unpasteurized
TRAVEL Most trips to Réunion are trouble-free. Its society and culture are similar to Western Europe. Usual precautions should be taken
WEATHER Hot and tropical with cooler temperatures in the hills. Cool and dry from May to Nov; hot and wet from Dec to Apr
BANKING 0800–1600 Mon to Fri
EMERGENCY Police 17; Fire 18; Ambulance 15
TIME ZONE GMT +4
INTERNATIONAL DIALING CODE 262

ROMANIA

GOVERNMENT Multiparty republic
LANGUAGES Romanian (official), Hungarian
CURRENCY Leu = 100 bani
MEDICAL Visitors should protect against rabies, typhoid, and encephalitis
TRAVEL Petty theft is common in urban areas. It is illegal to exchange money on the street. Corruption is widespread. Roads are poorly maintained
WEATHER May to Oct warm, but coastal areas are cooled by sea breezes; Nov to Apr harsh winter with snow, but milder along the coast
BANKING 0900–1200 Mon to Fri; 1300–1500 Mon to Fri (currency exchange only)
EMERGENCY Police 955; Fire 981; Ambulance 961
TIME ZONE GMT +2
INTERNATIONAL DIALING CODE 40

RUSSIA

GOVERNMENT Federal multiparty republic
LANGUAGES Russian (official), many others
CURRENCY Russian ruble = 100 kopeks
MEDICAL Visitors should protect against diptheria, hepatitis A, typhoid, and encephalitis
TRAVEL Travel to the Chechen Republic and northern Caucasus is inadvisable. Visitors should keep all valuables out of sight
WEATHER Variable climate in north and central regions; Jul to Aug warm and wet; May to Jun and Sep to Oct dry; Nov to Apr very cold with snow
BANKING 0930–1730 Mon to Fri
EMERGENCY Police 02; Fire 01; Ambulance 03
TIME ZONE GMT +3 in Moscow and St Petersburg. Other areas vary
INTERNATIONAL DIALING CODE 7

ST KITTS & NEVIS

GOVERNMENT Constitutional monarchy
LANGUAGES English
CURRENCY East Caribbean dollar = 100 cents
MEDICAL Visitors should protect against mosquito bites as dengue fever is present. Water is untreated and is unsafe to drink
TRAVEL Most visits are trouble-free. The islands are now commercialized and tourists are welcomed. Usual precautions should be taken
WEATHER Hot and tropical with cooling sea breezes. There is little seasonal temperature variation. Hurricane season is Aug to Oct
BANKING 0800–1500 Mon to Thu; 0800-1500/1700 Fri; 0830–1100 Sat
EMERGENCY All Services 911
TIME ZONE GMT –4
INTERNATIONAL DIALING CODE 1 869

ST LUCIA

GOVERNMENT Parliamentary democracy
LANGUAGES English (official), French patois
CURRENCY East Caribbean dollar = 100 cents
MEDICAL Dengue fever is present; precautions should be taken against mosquito bites. Polio and typhoid vaccinations are recommended
TRAVEL Most trips to St Lucia are trouble-free, but sensible precautions should be taken. Beachwear should not be worn in towns
WEATHER Tropical climate moderated by trade winds. Temperatures are uniform at about 79°F [26°C]. St Lucia lies in the hurricane belt
BANKING 0800–1500 Mon to Thu; 0800–1700 Fri; 0800–1200 Sat
EMERGENCY All Services 999
TIME ZONE GMT –4
INTERNATIONAL DIALING CODE 1 758

ST VINCENT & THE GRENADINES

GOVERNMENT Parliamentary democracy
LANGUAGES English
CURRENCY East Caribbean dollar = 100 cents
MEDICAL Protection from polio, typhoid, and mosquito bites are recommended
TRAVEL Sensible precautions should be taken. There is a relaxed society and most visits are trouble-free. Excellent West Indian cuisine can be found on St Vincent
WEATHER Tropical climate with cooling trade winds. Hottest months are Jun and Jul. Tropical storms may occur from Jun to Nov
BANKING 0800–1500 Mon to Thu; 0800–1700 Fri
EMERGENCY All Services 999
TIME ZONE GMT –4
INTERNATIONAL DIALING CODE 1 809

SAMOA

GOVERNMENT Mix of parliamentary democracy and constitutional monarchy
LANGUAGES Samoan (Polynesian), English
CURRENCY Samoan dollar = 100 sene
MEDICAL Vaccination against polio and typhoid are recommended. Water is untreated and is unsafe to drink
TRAVEL Most visits are trouble-free, but traditional moral and religious codes are very important. Beachwear should not be worn outside resorts
WEATHER Tropical climate with cooler temperatures in the evenings. The rainy season is from Dec to Apr
BANKING 0900–1500 Mon to Fri; 0830–1130 Sat
EMERGENCY All services 999
TIME ZONE GMT –11
INTERNATIONAL DIALING CODE 685

SAUDI ARABIA

GOVERNMENT Absolute monarchy with consultative assembly
LANGUAGES Arabic (official)
CURRENCY Saudi riyal = 100 halalas
MEDICAL Cases of cerebral malaria have been reported in Jizan, southwest Saudi Arabia
TRAVEL Visitors should seek advice on recent developments. Islamic customs must be followed. Bombings have occurred in Riyadh and visitors should remain extremely vigilant
WEATHER Desert climate; extremely dry; May to Oct very hot; Nov to Feb mild
BANKING 0830–1200 and 1700–1900 Sat to Wed; 0830–1200 Thu
EMERGENCY Unavailable
TIME ZONE GMT +3
INTERNATIONAL DIALING CODE 966

SERBIA

GOVERNMENT Republic
LANGUAGES Serbian (official), Albanian
CURRENCY New dinar = 100 paras
MEDICAL The medical system is suffering from widespread shortages. Visitors should protect themselves against hepatitis and rabies.
TRAVEL The situation in Serbia is calm at present, though visitors should seek advice on developments before traveling. Travel to Kosovo is still inadvisable
WEATHER Serbia has a continental climate with a gradual transition between the four seasons. Nov to Mar very cold; Jun to Sep warm
BANKING 0700–1500 Mon to Fri; 0800-1400 Sat
EMERGENCY Police 92; Fire 93; Ambulance 94
TIME ZONE GMT +1
INTERNATIONAL DIALING CODE 381

SEYCHELLES

GOVERNMENT Democratic republic
LANGUAGES English, French, French Creole
CURRENCY Seychelles rupee = 100 cents
MEDICAL There are no specific health risks
TRAVEL Crime is relatively rare, but incidents of theft do occur in tourist areas. Visitors, particularly women, should remain vigilant and avoid walking in quiet areas after dark. Roads often have sheer drops and no barriers
WEATHER Nov to Feb hot, humid monsoon; very warm temperatures all year round; May and Oct breezy at the start and finish of the trade winds
BANKING 0830–1430 Mon to Fri
EMERGENCY Unavailable
TIME ZONE GMT +4
INTERNATIONAL DIALING CODE 248

SINGAPORE

GOVERNMENT Multiparty republic
LANGUAGES Chinese, Malay, Tamil and English (all official)
CURRENCY Singapore dollar = 100 cents
MEDICAL There are no specific health risks
TRAVEL The crime rate is very low in Singapore and most visits remain trouble-free. There are harsh penalties, including the death penalty, for all drug offences. Smoking is illegal in public places
WEATHER Hot and humid all year round; Nov to Jan cool with most rainfall
BANKING 1000–1500 Mon to Fri; 1100–1600 Sat
EMERGENCY All Services 999
TIME ZONE GMT +8
INTERNATIONAL DIALING CODE 65

SLOVAK REPUBLIC

GOVERNMENT Multiparty republic
LANGUAGES Slovak (official), Hungarian
CURRENCY Slovak koruna = 100 halierov
MEDICAL There is risk from rabies and tick-borne encephalitis in forested areas during summer months
TRAVEL Pickpockets operate around the main tourist areas, and foreigners are easily identified and targeted. Sensible precautions should be taken
WEATHER A temperate climate with cold winters and mild summers
BANKING 0800–1700 Mon to Fri
EMERGENCY Fire 150; Ambulance 155; Police 158
TIME ZONE GMT +1 in winter; GMT +2 in summer
INTERNATIONAL DIALING CODE 42

SLOVENIA

GOVERNMENT Multiparty republic
LANGUAGES Slovene (official), Serbo-Croatian
CURRENCY Euro = 100 cents
MEDICAL Summer visitors to forested areas should seek advice about protection against tick-borne encephalitis
TRAVEL Harsh fines are given for traffic offences and jaywalking. Passports and international driving licences should be carried at all times
WEATHER Continental climate inland; Jun to Sep warm; Nov to Mar cold; Mediterranean climate in coastal areas; Sep is the best time for hiking and climbing
BANKING 0800–1800 Mon to Fri
EMERGENCY Police 92; Fire 93; Ambulance 94
TIME ZONE GMT +1
INTERNATIONAL DIALING CODE 386

SOUTH AFRICA

GOVERNMENT Multiparty republic
LANGUAGES Afrikaans, English, Ndebele, Pedi, Sotho, Swazi, Tsonga, Tswana, Venda, Xhosa and Zulu (all official)
CURRENCY Rand = 100 cents
MEDICAL There is a high incidence of HIV/AIDS. Malaria is a risk in certain areas. Hygiene and water standards are high in tourist areas
TRAVEL Violent crime is high in the townships. There is a risk of car-jacking and armed robbery. Visitors should hide valuables and seek advice about which areas to avoid
WEATHER Generally warm and sunny all year
BANKING 0830–1530 Mon to Fri
EMERGENCY Police 1011; Ambulance 10222
TIME ZONE GMT +2
INTERNATIONAL DIALING CODE 27

SPAIN

GOVERNMENT Constitutional monarchy
LANGUAGES Castilian Spanish (official), Catalan, Galician, Basque
CURRENCY Euro = 100 cents
MEDICAL There are no specific health risks in Spain
TRAVEL Most visits to Spain are trouble-free. The country is rich in arts and culture
WEATHER Temperate in north; Apr to Oct hot and dry, particularly in the south; central plateau can by very cold during winter
BANKING 0900–1400 Mon to Fri; 0900–1300 Sat (but not during summer)
EMERGENCY Police 091; Fire/Ambulance 085; Emergency Services 112
TIME ZONE GMT +1
INTERNATIONAL DIALING CODE 34

SWEDEN

GOVERNMENT Constitutional monarchy
LANGUAGES Swedish (official), Finnish, Sami
CURRENCY Swedish krona = 100 öre
MEDICAL There are no specific health risks
TRAVEL Most visits to Sweden are generally trouble-free. Since devaluation of the Swedish currency, the country has become considerably more affordable
WEATHER May to Jul hot and dry, but Aug can be wet; the midnight sun can be seen from May to Jun above the Arctic Circle; Nov to Apr extremely cold, particularly in the north
BANKING 0930–1500 Mon to Fri
EMERGENCY Emergency Services 112; All Services 90 000/112
TIME ZONE GMT +1
INTERNATIONAL DIALING CODE 46

SYRIA

GOVERNMENT Multiparty republic
LANGUAGES Arabic (official), Kurdish, Armenian
CURRENCY Syrian pound = 100 piastres
MEDICAL Visitors should vaccinate against polio, hepatitis A and B, and tetanus
TRAVEL Visitors should keep informed of developments in the Middle East. They should dress modestly and avoid driving out of main cities at night. Harsh penalties exist for drug offences
WEATHER Apr to Jun mild and dry; Jun to Sep hot; Dec to Mar very cold, particularly in coastal and upland regions
BANKING 0800–1400 Sat and Thu
EMERGENCY Contact hotel operator
TIME ZONE GMT +2
INTERNATIONAL DIALING CODE 963

SRI LANKA

GOVERNMENT Multiparty republic
LANGUAGES Sinhala and Tamil (both official)
CURRENCY Sri Lankan rupee = 100 cents
MEDICAL There is a risk of cholera and malaria. Rabies is widespread
TRAVEL The northern region and the eastern coast remain heavily mined. A cease-fire between the Tamil Tigers and the government was signed in February 2002
WEATHER Tropical climate; May to Jul and Dec to Jan monsoon seasons; coastal regions are cool due to sea breezes
BANKING 0900–1300 Mon to Sat; 0900–1500 Tue to Fri
EMERGENCY All Services 1 691095/699935
TIME ZONE GMT +5.30
INTERNATIONAL DIALING CODE 94

SWITZERLAND

GOVERNMENT Federal republic
LANGUAGES French, German, Italian and Romansch (all official)
CURRENCY Swiss franc = 100 centimes
MEDICAL There is a risk of altitude sickness, sunburn and hypothermia in the Alps
TRAVEL Most visits to Switzerland remain trouble-free
WEATHER Climate varies from region to region; Alpine regions have lower temperatures; Jun to Sep warm and sunny; Nov to Apr cold with snow which starts to melt in Apr
BANKING 0830–1630 Mon to Fri
EMERGENCY Police 117; Fire 118; Ambulance 144
TIME ZONE GMT +1
INTERNATIONAL DIALING CODE 41

TAIWAN

GOVERNMENT Unitary multiparty republic
LANGUAGES Mandarin Chinese (official)
CURRENCY New Taiwan dollar = 100 cents
MEDICAL There are no specific health risks, but visitors should be vaccinated against hepatitis
TRAVEL Most visits to Taiwan are trouble-free. Petty crime exists, but is not common. Some roads in central and southern areas may still be blocked by landslides following the 1999 earthquake
WEATHER Subtropical climate with moderate temperatures in the north; Jun to Sep very hot and humid; Jun to Oct typhoon season
BANKING 0900–1530 Mon to Fri; 0900–1230 Sat
EMERGENCY Police 110
TIME ZONE GMT +8
INTERNATIONAL DIALING CODE 886

TANZANIA

GOVERNMENT Multiparty republic
LANGUAGES Swahili and English (both official)
CURRENCY Tanzanian shilling = 100 cents
MEDICAL There is a risk of yellow fever, malaria, cholera, and hepatitis. AIDS is widespread
TRAVEL Most visits are trouble-free, but crime does occur, particularly on public transport and in tourist areas. There are increased risks in Zanzibar where bomb explosions have occurred
WEATHER Tropical climate; Mar to May rainy season in coastal areas; Jan to Feb hot and dry; Nov to Dec and Feb to May rainy season in highland areas
BANKING 0830–1600 Mon to Fri
EMERGENCY Unavailable
TIME ZONE GMT +3
INTERNATIONAL DIALING CODE 255

TRINIDAD & TOBAGO

GOVERNMENT Parliamentary democracy
LANGUAGES English (official), Spanish
CURRENCY Trinidad & Tobago dollar = 100 cents
MEDICAL Dengue fever has become a problem in recent years. Medical facilities are basic and limited
TRAVEL While most visits are trouble-free, attacks on travelers are on the increase. Visitors should remain vigilant and alert at all times, and take sensible precautions
WEATHER Tropical climate with cooling trade winds. Hottest and wettest time is Jun to Nov
BANKING 0900–1400 Mon to Thu; 0900–1200 and 1500–1700 Fri
EMERGENCY Police 999; Ambulance/Fire 990
TIME ZONE GMT –4
INTERNATIONAL DIALING CODE 1 868

TURKEY

GOVERNMENT Multiparty republic
LANGUAGES Turkish (official), Kurdish, Arabic
CURRENCY New Turkish lira = 100 kurus
MEDICAL Contagious diseases are increasing and visitors should keep inoculations up-to-date
TRAVEL Most visits are trouble-free, but visitors should exercise caution, particularly in the tourist areas of Istanbul where street robbery is common, and seek recent advice before traveling
WEATHER Mediterranean climate; summers are hot and winters are mild
BANKING 0830–1200 and 1300–1700 Mon to Fri
EMERGENCY Police 155; Fire 111; Ambulance 112
TIME ZONE GMT +2
INTERNATIONAL DIALING CODE 90

THAILAND

GOVERNMENT Constitutional monarchy
LANGUAGES Thai (official), English, local dialects
CURRENCY Baht = 100 satang
MEDICAL Visitors should protect against malaria, dengue fever, AIDS, and cholera
TRAVEL Harsh penalties exist for drug offences. Tourists should use licensed taxis with yellow number plates. Visitors should seek advice before traveling to border areas with Burma or Cambodia. Riptides occur off the coast of Phuket
WEATHER Jun to Oct hot and rainy monsoon; Nov to Feb dry and pleasant; Mar to May hot; temperatures are more consistent in the south
BANKING 0830–1530 Mon to Fri
EMERGENCY Unavailable
TIME ZONE GMT +7
INTERNATIONAL DIALING CODE 66

TUNISIA

GOVERNMENT Multiparty republic
LANGUAGES Arabic (official), French
CURRENCY Tunisian dinar = 1,000 millimes
MEDICAL There is a risk of yellow fever and malaria
TRAVEL Travel to Tunisia is generally trouble-free, but visitors to southern desert areas and to areas close to the Algerian border should exercise caution. Tunisian laws and customs should be respected. Drug offences carry harsh penalties
WEATHER Jun to Aug hot and humid; Jan to Feb. cooler; hotter inland; higher rainfall in winter
BANKING 0830–1200 and 1300–1700 Mon to Fri
EMERGENCY Unavailable
TIME ZONE GMT +1
INTERNATIONAL DIALING CODE 216

UGANDA

GOVERNMENT Republic in transition
LANGUAGES English and Swahili (both official)
CURRENCY Ugandan shilling = 100 cents
MEDICAL There is a risk of AIDS, yellow fever, and malaria
TRAVEL Most visits to Uganda are trouble-free, but visitors should seek recent advice before traveling. It is inadvisable to travel to areas bordering the Democratic Republic of the Congo or Sudan, and visitors should remain cautious if traveling to areas bordering Rwanda
WEATHER Dec to Feb and Jun to Aug hot and dry; Mar to May and Oct to Nov heavy rain
BANKING 0830–1400 Mon to Fri
EMERGENCY Unavailable
TIME ZONE GMT +3
INTERNATIONAL DIALING CODE 256

UKRAINE

GOVERNMENT Multiparty republic
LANGUAGES Ukrainian (official), Russian
CURRENCY Hryvnia = 100 kopiykas
MEDICAL There is a risk of diptheria in western Ukraine. Tick-borne encephalitis is common in forested areas. Do not drink tap water without first boiling it
TRAVEL Crime in the Ukraine remains low, but visitors should remain vigilant and keep valuables out of sight, particularly in crowded areas where pickpocketing and bag-snatching can occur
WEATHER Jun to Aug warm; Oct to Nov sunny but cold; Dec to Mar cold with snowfall
BANKING 0900–1600 Mon to Fri
EMERGENCY Unavailable
TIME ZONE GMT +2
INTERNATIONAL DIALING CODE 380

UNITED ARAB EMIRATES

GOVERNMENT Federation of seven emirates, each with its own government
LANGUAGES Arabic (official), English
CURRENCY Dirham = 100 fils
MEDICAL There is a risk of hepatitis A and B
TRAVEL Visitors should remain informed of recent international developments before traveling. They should dress modestly and respect local customs. Penalties for all drug offences are harsh and can include the death penalty
WEATHER Jun to Sep very hot and dry; Oct to May cooler and is the best time to visit
BANKING 0800–1200 Sat to Wed and 0800–1100 Thu
EMERGENCY All Services 344 663
TIME ZONE GMT +4
INTERNATIONAL DIALING CODE 971

UNITED KINGDOM

GOVERNMENT Constitutional monarchy
LANGUAGES English (official), Welsh, Gaelic
CURRENCY Pound sterling = 100 pence
MEDICAL No vaccinations are required in the UK and citizens of all EU countries are entitled to free medical treatment at National Health Service hospitals
TRAVEL Most visits are trouble-free, but visitors should exercise caution in urban areas after dark
WEATHER May to Aug warm and wet; Sep to Apr mild and wet
BANKING 0900–1730 Mon to Fri. Some bank branches open on Saturday mornings
EMERGENCY Police/Fire/Ambulance 999; Emergency Services 112
TIME ZONE GMT
INTERNATIONAL DIALING CODE 44

UNITED STATES OF AMERICA

GOVERNMENT Federal republic
LANGUAGES English (official), Spanish, more than 30 others
CURRENCY US dollar = 100 cents
MEDICAL There are no specific health risks, but medical treatment is expensive
TRAVEL Most visits to the USA are trouble-free, but visitors should remain vigilant and avoid wearing valuable jewelry or walking through isolated urban areas after dark
WEATHER Varies considerably; check climate before traveling
BANKING 0900–1500 Mon to Fri
EMERGENCY Emergency Services 911
TIME ZONE USA has six time zones from GMT –5 on East coast to –10 in Hawai'i
INTERNATIONAL DIALING CODE 1

URUGUAY

GOVERNMENT Multiparty republic
LANGUAGES Spanish (official)
CURRENCY Uruguayan peso = 100 centésimos
MEDICAL There are no specific health risks, but medical treatment can be expensive
TRAVEL Most visits to Uruguay are trouble-free, but street crime exists in urban areas, including Montevideo. It is, however, less common than in other Latin American countries
WEATHER Dec to Mar hot, but nights can be cool; Apr to Nov mild
BANKING 1330–1730 Mon to Fri (summer); 1300–1700 Mon to Fri (winter)
EMERGENCY Police 109; Fire 104; Ambulance 105; All Services 999
TIME ZONE GMT –3
INTERNATIONAL DIALING CODE 598

VENEZUELA

GOVERNMENT Federal republic
LANGUAGES Spanish (official), local dialects
CURRENCY Bolívar = 100 céntimos
MEDICAL There is a risk of yellow fever, cholera, dengue fever, and hepatitis
TRAVEL The incidence of violent crime is high and the political situation is volatile. Visitors should take precautions. Terrorist and narcotic gangs are active in areas bordering Colombia, where there is the risk of kidnapping
WEATHER May to Dec rainy season; Jan to Apr pleasant temperatures
BANKING 0830–1130 and 1400–1630 Mon to Fri
EMERGENCY Doctor 02 483 7021; Ambulance 02 545 4545
TIME ZONE GMT –4
INTERNATIONAL DIALING CODE 58

VIETNAM

GOVERNMENT Socialist republic
LANGUAGES Vietnamese (official), English, Chinese
CURRENCY Dong = 10 hao = 100 xu
MEDICAL Malaria, dengue fever, and encephalitis are common throughout the country. Visitors should avoid mosquito bites. Typhoid is common in the Mekong Delta
TRAVEL Take care if traveling in border areas. Unexploded mines and bombs still exist in certain areas. Drug smuggling carries the death penalty. Serious flooding can occur in central areas
WEATHER May to Oct tropical monsoons; Nov to Apr hot and dry
BANKING 0800–1630 Mon to Fri
EMERGENCY Police 13; Fire 14; Ambulance 15
TIME ZONE GMT +7
INTERNATIONAL DIALING CODE 84

VIRGIN ISLANDS, BRITISH

GOVERNMENT UK overseas territory
LANGUAGES English (official)
CURRENCY US dollar = 100 cents
MEDICAL Medical facilities are limited. Precautions should be taken against polio, typhoid and dengue fever
TRAVEL There is a low crime rate, but sensible precautions should be taken. Backpacking is discouraged throughout the 60 islands
WEATHER Subtropical and humid climate moderated by trade winds. Hurricanes are a risk from Jul to Oct
BANKING 0900–1500 Mon to Thu; 0900–1700 Fri
EMERGENCY Police 114; Ambulance 112
TIME ZONE GMT –4
INTERNATIONAL DIALING CODE 1 284

VIRGIN ISLANDS, US

GOVERNMENT US overseas territory
LANGUAGES English, Spanish, French, Creole
CURRENCY US dollar = 100 cents
MEDICAL Visitors should protect against typhoid and polio. Water is generally considered drinkable
TRAVEL Most visit are trouble-free and normal precautions should be taken. There is a large selection of hotel accommodation available
WEATHER Hot climate with cool winds. Low humidity with little seasonal temperature variation. The rainy season is Sep to Nov
BANKING 0900–1430 Mon to Thu; 0900–1400 and 1530–1700 Fri
EMERGENCY All services 911
TIME ZONE GMT –4
INTERNATIONAL DIALING CODE 1 340

YEMEN

GOVERNMENT Multiparty republic
LANGUAGES Arabic (official)
CURRENCY Yemeni rial = 100 fils
MEDICAL Visitors should protect against hepatitis A and B
TRAVEL Most governments currently strongly advise against travel to Yemen. Random armed kidnapping is common, and foreigners remain targets for crime and terrorism
WEATHER Varies with altitude; Oct to Mar nights can be very cold in upland regions; Apr to Sep very hot; Oct to Apr cool, dry and dusty
BANKING 0800–1200 Sat to Wed; 0800–1100 Thu. Closed on Fridays
EMERGENCY Unavailable
TIME ZONE GMT +3
INTERNATIONAL DIALING CODE 967

ZAMBIA

GOVERNMENT Multiparty republic
LANGUAGES English (official), Bemba, Nyanja
CURRENCY Zambian kwacha = 100 ngwee
MEDICAL Outbreaks of cholera and dysentery are common. Malaria is endemic, and cases of AIDS and tuberculosis are very high
TRAVEL Visitors should avoid traveling to areas bordering Angola and the Democratic Republic of the Congo. Armed robbery, bag-snatching and mugging are increasing, particularly in downtown areas. Keep valuables out of sight
WEATHER May to Sep very cool and dry; Oct to Nov hot and dry; Dec to Apr hot and wet
BANKING 0815–1430 Mon to Fri
EMERGENCY All Services 1 2 25067/254798
TIME ZONE GMT +2
INTERNATIONAL DIALING CODE 260

ZIMBABWE

GOVERNMENT Multiparty republic
LANGUAGES English (official), Shona, Ndebele
CURRENCY Zimbabwean dollar = 100 cents
MEDICAL There is a risk of bilharzia, cholera, malaria, yellow fever, and rabies. Incidences of HIV/AIDS are very high
TRAVEL There is currently political and social unrest throughout the country, in both rural and urban areas. Visitors should exercise caution and avoid large crowds and demonstrations
WEATHER May to Oct warm and dry, but cold at night; Nov to Apr wet and hot
BANKING 0800–1500 Mon, Tue, Thu and Fri. 0800–1300 Wed and 0800–1130 Sat
EMERGENCY Police 995; Ambulance 994
TIME ZONE GMT +2
INTERNATIONAL DIALING CODE 263

World Maps – general reference

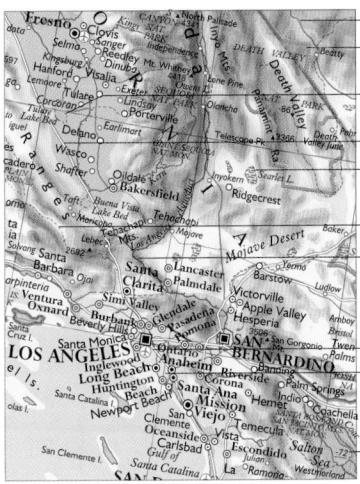

Settlements

Capital cities have red infills

Settlement symbols and type styles vary according to the scale of each map and indicate the importance of towns rather than specific population figures.

PACIFIC OCEAN
ARCTIC OCEAN
ATLANTIC OCEAN
North America
Asia
Europe
RUSSIA
CHINA
INDIA
UNITED STATES
CANADA
MEXICO
JAPAN
Tokyo
Osaka
Seoul
Pyongyang
Shenyang
Beijing
Tianjin
Shanghai
Wuhan
Hong Kong
Xi'an
Chongqing
Hanoi
Bangkok
Rangoon
Dhaka
Kolkata (Calcutta)
Chennai (Madras)
Hyderabad
Bangalore
Mumbai (Bombay)
Colombo
New Delhi
Islamabad
Lahore
Karachi
Kabul
Tehran
Baghdad
Muscat
Riyadh
Mecca
Cairo
Tripoli
Algiers
Tunis
Rabat
Casablanca
Madrid
Lisbon
Paris
London
Rome
Athens
Ankara
Moscow
St. Petersburg
Warsaw
Budapest
Istanbul
Tashkent
Astana
Ulan Bator
Anchorage
Alaska (USA)
Vancouver
Seattle
San Francisco
Los Angeles
San Diego
Phoenix
Dallas
Houston
Chicago
Detroit
Toronto
Ottawa
Montreal
Boston
New York
Philadelphia
Washington
Atlanta
Miami
Havana
Kingston
Santo Domingo
Port of Spain
Caracas
Bogota
Quito
Lima
Medellin
Mexico City
Monterrey
Guadalajara
Reykjavik
Nuuk
Newfoundland
Bermuda (U.K.)
Azores (Port)
Madeira
Canary Is.
Gibraltar
Svalbard (Norway)
Franz Josef Land
Novaya Zemlya
Kuril Is.
Sakhalin
Aleutian Is.
Hawaii Is.
Lakshadweep Is.
Andaman Is.
Maldives
Sri Lanka
North Pole
Arctic Circle
Tropic of Cancer
International Dateline
PROJECTION CENTERED ON LONDON

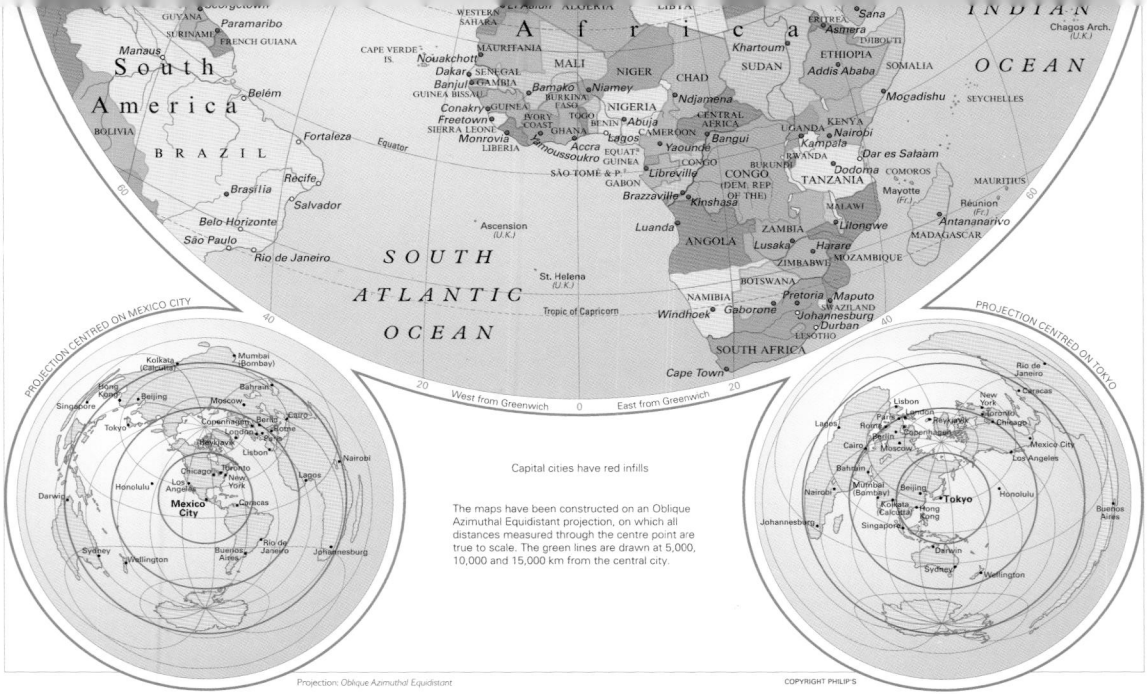

Capital cities have red infills

The maps have been constructed on an Oblique Azimuthal Equidistant projection, on which all distances measured through the centre point are true to scale. The green lines are drawn at 5,000, 10,000 and 15,000 km from the central city.

Projection: *Oblique Azimuthal Equidistant*

COPYRIGHT PHILIP'S

PROJECTION CENTRED ON THE ANTIPODES OF LONDON
East from Greenwich
West from Greenwich
PACIFIC OCEAN
INDIAN OCEAN
SOUTHERN OCEAN
Oceania
AUSTRALIA
International Dateline
Tropic of Cancer
Tropic of Capricorn
Equator
Antarctic Circle
Midway I. (U.S.A.)
Honolulu
Hawaiian Is. (U.S.A.)
Wake I. (U.S.A.)
MARSHALL IS.
KIRIBATI
SAMOA
TUVALU
FIJI
TONGA
Cook Is. (N.Z.)
Tahiti (Fr.)
FRENCH POLYNESIA
Marquesas Is. (Fr.)
Tuamotu Arch. (Fr.)
Pitcairn I. (U.K.)
Easter I. (Chile)
Galapagos Is. (Ecuador)
Kermadec Is. (N.Z.)
Auckland
Wellington
NEW ZEALAND
Chatham Is. (N.Z.)
Antipodes Is. (N.Z.)
Auckland Is. (N.Z.)
Macquarie Is. (Austral.)
Victoria Land
Adelie
Magnetic Pole
Northern Marianas (U.S.A.)
Guam (U.S.A.)
Bonin Is. (Japan)
FED. STATES OF MICRONESIA
SOLOMON IS.
VANUATU
New Caledonia (Fr.)
PAPUA NEW GUINEA
Port Moresby
PALAU
PHILIPPINES
Manila
Brisbane
Sydney
Canberra
Melbourne
Adelaide
Perth
Tasmania
Uluru
Pandang
Borneo
Jakarta
Kuala Lumpur
Ho Chi Minh City
VIETNAM
BRUNEI
MALAYSIA
SINGAPORE
INDONESIA
TIMOR
Cocos Is. (Austral.)

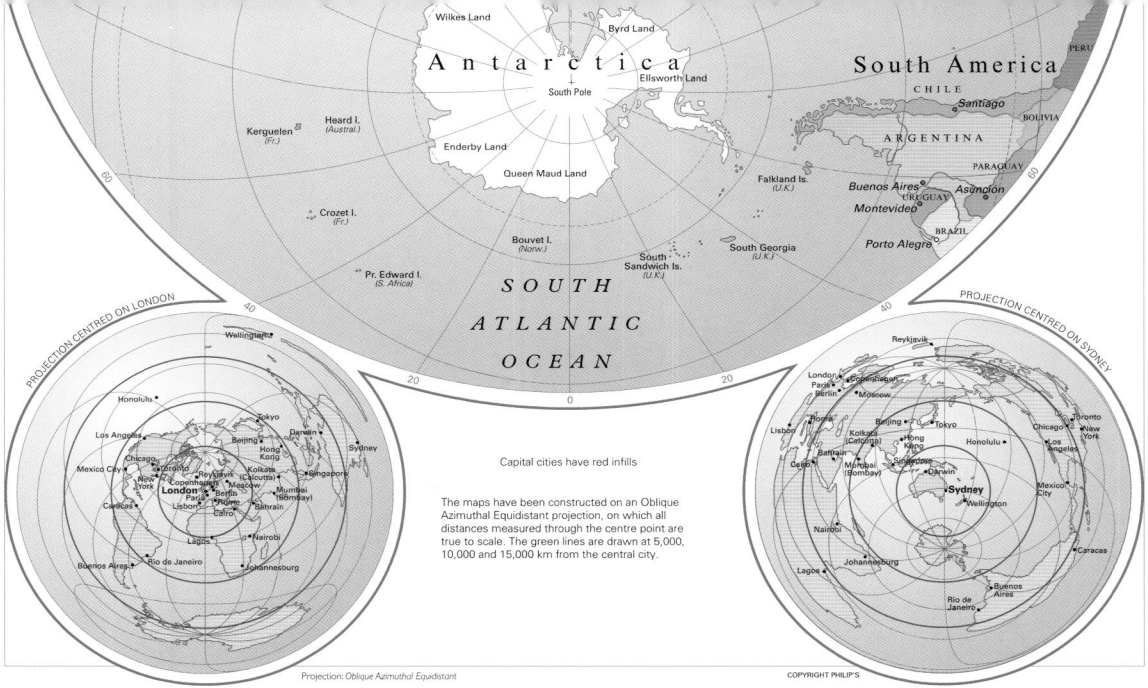

Capital cities have red infills

The maps have been constructed on an Oblique Azimuthal Equidistant projection, on which all distances measured through the centre point are true to scale. The green lines are drawn at 5,000, 10,000 and 15,000 km from the central city.

Projection: *Oblique Azimuthal Equidistant*

COPYRIGHT PHILIP'S

6 EUROPE

ICELAND
Reykjavik
Arctic Circle
Norwegian Sea
Faroe Is. (Den.)
Shetland Is.
Orkney Is.
Hebrides
UNITED KINGDOM
SCOTLAND
Aberdeen
Glasgow
Dundee
Edinburgh
N. IRELAND
Belfast
IRELAND
Dublin
Cork
Manchester
Liverpool
Leeds
Sheffield
Newcastle upon Tyne
WALES
Cardiff
Bristol
ENGLAND
Birmingham
Plymouth
Southampton
LONDON
ATLANTIC OCEAN
English Channel
Channel Is.
Le Havre
Brest
Rouen
PARIS
Seine
Loire
Nantes
Bay of Biscay
FRANCE
Amsterdam
The Hague
Rotterdam
NETHERLANDS
Antwerp
BELGIUM
Brussels
Lille
Meuse
Luxembourg
LUX.
Bonn
Rhine
Cologne
Essen
Dortmund
Hamburg
Bremen
Hannover
Kiel
Berlin
Magdeburg
Leipzig
Halle
Chemnitz
Dresden
GERMANY
Frankfurt am Main
Nuremberg
Stuttgart
Munich
Strasbourg
Dijon
Zürich
BASEL
SWITZERLAND
Geneva
Lyon
St-Étienne
Limoges
Bordeaux
Garonne
Toulouse
Rhône
Grenoble
Milan
Turin
Genoa
Bologna
Venice
Trieste
Nice
MONACO
Marseilles
Toulon
Corsica
Ajaccio
Sardinia
Cagliari
Rome
ITALY
Florence
SAN MARINO
Naples
Taranto
Palermo
Messina
Sicily
Catania
Pantelleria (Italy)
MALTA
Valletta
Tyrrhenian Sea
Adriatic Sea
Ionian Sea
Mediterranean Sea
Bilbao
Vitoria
Pamplona
Zaragoza
Barcelona
Valencia
Palma
Minorca
Majorca
Ibiza
Alicante
Murcia
Granada
Málaga
Gibraltar
Str. of Gibraltar
Ceuta
Tangier
Melilla
Cádiz
Seville
Córdoba
Guadalquivir
Guadiana
Badajoz
Vigo
La Coruña
Porto
Douro
Valladolid
Madrid
Tagus
Lisbon
PORTUGAL
SPAIN
ANDORRA
Andorra-la-Vella
Algiers
Annaba
Constantine
ALGERIA
TUNISIA
Tunis
MOROCCO
Africa
Sweden
Tromsø
Narvik
Trondheim
NORWAY
Bergen
Stavanger
Oslo
Gävle
Uppsala
Örebro
Stockholm
Vänern
Vättern
Jönköping
Skagerrak
Kattegat
Aalborg
Aarhus
Gothenburg
DENMARK
Copenhagen
Malmö
Baltic Sea
Gdańsk
Szczecin
Bydgoszcz
Poznań
Łódź
Wrocław
Katowice
Prague
CZECH REP.
Ostrava
Vienna
Linz
Salzburg
Innsbruck
Graz
AUSTRIA
Bratislava
Budapest
HUNG.
SLOVENIA
Ljubljana
Zagreb
CROATIA
BOSNIA-HERZ.
Split
Sarajevo
MONTENEGRO
Podgorica
Bari
Tirana
ALB.
Corfu
Elbe
Oder
North Sea
Gotland
Malaga
Balearic Is.

100 0 100 200 300 400 500 600 700 800 km
100 0 100 200 300 400 500 miles
10 11 12 13 14 15 16 17 18 19
C D E F G H J
Hammerfest
Murmansk
White Sea
Arkhangelsk
KOMI
Ob
Luleå
KARELIA
N. Dvina
FINLAND
Vaasa
Kotlas
L. Onega
Perm
Nizhniy Tagil
Yekaterinburg
Chelyabinsk
Vyborg
L. Ladoga
Kirov
UDMURTIA
Turku
Helsinki
ST. PETERSBURG
Vologda
Rybinsk Res.
Kostroma
Yaroslavl
Ivanovo
Nizhny Novgorod
MARI EL
Kazan
CHUVASHIA
TATARSTAN
UFA
BASHKORTOSTAN
Magnitogorsk
Tallinn
ESTONIA
L. Chudskoye
RUSSIA
MOSCOW
LATVIA
Riga
Simbirsk
Samara
Orenburg
MORDVINIA
Penza
Volga
Uralsk
LITHUANIA
Kaunas
W. Dvina
Vitebsk
Smolensk
Tula
Tambov
Saratov
Kaliningrad
Vilnius
Mahilyow
Minsk
Orel
Voronezh
KAZAKHSTAN
Ural
Atyrau
Białystok
BELARUS
Gomel
Kursk
Brest
Pripet
Warsaw
Chernihiv
Volgograd
Lublin
Dnepr
Kharkov
Kiev
Zhytomyr
UKRAINE
Lvov
Donetsk
Taganrog
Don
Rostov
Astrakhan
Caspian Sea
Dniester
Dnepropetrovsk
Zaporozhye
Krivoy Rog
Kherson
Prut
KALMYKIA
Miskolc
Debrecen
MOLDOVA
Nikolayev
Kishinev
Odessa
Stavropol
NORTH OSSETIA
CHECHNIA
Makhachkala
Cluj-Napoca
ROMANIA
Timişoara
Galaţi
Brasov
Ploieşti
CRIMEA
Krasnodar
ADYGEA
KARACHAI CHERKESSIA
KABARDINO BALKARIA
INGUSHETIA
DAGESTAN
GEORGIA
Tbilisi
Baku
Sevastopol
Constanta
Bucharest
Black Sea
Danube
Varna
ARMENIA
AZERBAIJAN
Yerevan
Pristina
Sofia
Samsun
Bosporus
Erzerum
Tabriz
BULGARIA
Plovdiv
Skopje
MACEDONIA
ISTANBUL
Thessaloniki
Bursa
Ankara
TURKEY
IRAN
Kayseri
Diyarbakir
GREECE
Izmir
Konya
Adana
Tigris
IRAQ
Patra
Athens
Antalya
Aleppo
Euphrates
SYRIA
Baghdad
Rhodes
CYPRUS
Nicosia
Crete
COPYRIGHT PHILIP'S

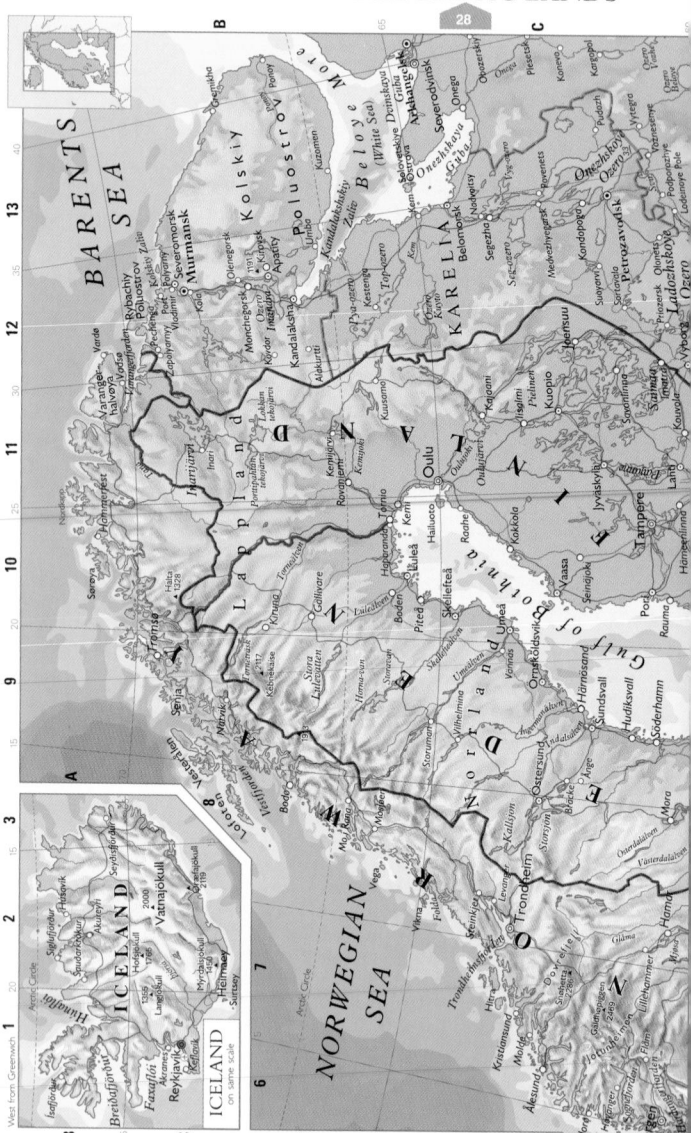
28
BARENTS SEA
Murmansk
Kolskiy Poluostrov
Kandalaksha
Apatity
Kirovsk
Monchegorsk
Severomorsk
Rybachiy Poluostrov
Vardø
Varangerhalvøya
Kirkenes
Nordkapp
Honningsvåg
Hammerfest
Alta
Karasjok
Kautokeino
Lakselv
Finnmark
Lappland
Kiruna
Gällivare
Jokkmokk
Arjeplog
Arvidsjaur
Luleå
Piteå
Skellefteå
Umeå
Vilhelmina
Storuman
Lycksele
Hemavan
Mo i Rana
Mosjøen
Bodø
Narvik
Tromsø
Hammerfest
Vesterålen
Lofoten
Svolvær
Sørfjorden
Tromsø
Hetta
Sørøya
Inari
Ivalo
Kittilä
Pello
Muonio
Kolari
Pajala
Haparanda
Tornio
Kemi
Oulu
Kajaani
Kuopio
Joensuu
Jyväskylä
Tampere
Vaasa
Pori
Turku
Helsinki
Lahti
Kouvola
Lappeenranta
Imatra
Savonlinna
Mikkeli
Rovaniemi
Kemijärvi
Kuusamo

Oslo
Hønefoss
Hougesund
Drammen
Stavanger
Skien
Fredrikstad
Kristiansand
Arendal
Mandal
Lindesnes
Skagerrak
Falun
Gävle
Svealand
Karlstad
Uppsala
Avesta
Sala
Vasterås
Hälsingborg
Halmstad
Orebro
Eskilstuna
STOCKHOLM
Göteborg
(Gothenburg)
Skagen
Frederikshavn
Aalborg
Varberg
Borås
Jönköping
Göta Kanal
Norrköping
Linköping
Gotland
Visby
Vastervik
Oskarshamn
Kattegat
Halmstad
Kalmar
Oland
Helsingborg
Karlskrona
Arhus
Randers
Holstebro
Esbjerg
Odense
Sjælland
Fyn
KOBENHAVN
(Copenhagen)
Lund
Malmö
Bornholm
DENMARK
Flensburg
Kiel
Gedser
Rügen
Sassnitz
Helgoland
Stralsund
Lübeck
Rostock
Emden
HAMBURG
Bremen
Osnabrück
Hannover
Braunschweig
Potsdam
BERLIN
Münster
Magdeburg
Dortmund
Kassel
Halle
Erfurt
Leipzig
Chemnitz
Plauen
Fulda
Frankfurt
Darmstadt
Würzburg
Heidelberg
Nürnberg
Dresden
Görlitz
Legnica
Wrocław
Walbrzych
Opole
Częstochowa
Katowice
Kraków
Chorzów
Tychy
Ostrava
Hradec Králové
PRAHA
(Prague)
Plzeň
CZECH REP.
Zilina
Cremon
Tarnów
Przemyśl
Rzeszów
Lviv
Ostrava
Poznań
Frankfurt
Szczecin
Koszalin
Świnoujście
Gdańsk
Gdynia
Elbląg
Olsztyn
Suwałki
Bydgoszcz
Toruń
Łomża
Płock
WARSZAWA
(Warsaw)
Kalisz
Łódź
Radom
Kielce
Lublin
Chełm
Białystok
POLAND
GERMANY
Turku
Vantaa
Helsinki
Espoo
Kotka
Aland
(Ahvenanmaa)
Hanko
Gulf of Finland
Tallinn
Hiiumaa
(Dagö)
Saaremaa
(Oesel)
Kohtla-Jarve
ESTONIA
Parnu
Tartu
Gulf of Riga
Ventspils
Riga
LATVIA
Jelgava
Liepāja
Rēzekne
Daugavpils
Šiauliai
Panevėžys
Klaipėda
LITHUANIA
Kaunas
Vilnius
Kaliningrad
(Russia)
Sovetsk
Nemunas
Kronshtadt
SANKT-PETERBURG
Narva (St. Petersburg)
Kolpino
Novaya Ladoga
Tikhvin
Belozersk
Kirillov
Cherepovets
Gdov
Luga
Novgorod
Pskov
Dno
Staraya Russa
Valdaysk
Vozvyshennost
Kholm
Tver
Kimry
Staritsa
Rzhev
Zelenograd
MOSKVA
(Moscow)
Odintsovo
Torbpets
Velikiye Luki
Nevel
Vyazma
Kaluga
Smolensk
Polatsk
Vitsyebsk
Lyepyel
Orsha
Dnepr
Roslavl
Belev
Mahilyow
MINSK
Barysaw
Babruysk
Zhlobin
Homyel
Bryansk
Orel
Seltso
Baranavichy
Slutsk
Pinsk
Pripyat
Mazyr
Brest
Kovel
Korosten
Rivne
Lutsk
Zhytomyr
Chernihiv
Novhorod-Siverskyy
Konotop
Nizhyn
Sumy
Pryluky
Okhtyrka
Chornobyl
Kyivskye Vdsch
KYIV
(Kiev)
Pereyaslav-Khmelnytskyy
Bila Tserkva
Berdychiv
Cherkasy
Poltava
Chervonohrad
BELARUS
UKRAINE
RUSSIA
Vyshniy Volochek
Borovichi
Rybinsk Res.
Bologoye
Maloya Vishera
Cherepovets
Gulf of Finland
BALTIC SEA
Bug
Dnepr
Desna
Pripyat
Nemunas
Daugava
Volga
Oka

10
BRITISH ISLES
ATLANTIC OCEAN
NORTH SEA
SCOTLAND
NORWAY
Shetland Is. (U.K.)
Yell
Unst
Fetlar
Mainland
Lerwick
Foula
Fair Isle
Orkney Is.
Westray
Sanday
Stronsay
Mainland
Kirkwall
Hoy
South Ronaldsay
Pentland Firth
Thurso
Wick
C. Wrath
Helmsdale
Lewis
Stornoway
Harris
St. Kilda (U.K.)
North Uist
Benbecula
South Uist
Barra
Outer Hebrides
Sea of the Hebrides
Inner Hebrides
North Minch
North West Highlands
Ullapool
Lairg
Golspie
Tain
Invergordon
Dingwall
Portree
Skye
Glen More
Inverness
L. Ness
Loch Ness
Aviemore
Nairn
Elgin
Moray Firth
Buckie
Banff
Fraserburgh
Peterhead
Huntly
Inverurie
Aberdeen
Stonehaven
Ballater
Deeside
CAIRNGORMS
Grampian Mts.
Ben Nevis
Fort William
Mallaig
Rhum
Eigg
Coll
Tobermory
Tiree
Mull
Oban
L. Etive
Colonsay
Jura
Islay
Campbeltown
Arran
Kilmarnock
Ayr
Girvan
Ailsa Craig
Galloway Hills
Southern Uplands
Jedburgh
Hawick
Galashiels
Berwick-upon-Tweed
Alnwick
Cheviot Hills
Edinburgh
Glasgow
Motherwell
Hamilton
East Kilbride
Paisley
Greenock
Dumbarton
Dunfermline
Kirkcaldy
Dunbar
Stirling
L. Lomond
L. Katrine
L. Tay
Perth
Dundee
Arbroath
Montrose
Forfar
St. Andrews
Glenrothes
Aberdeenshire
Bergen
Askøyna
Osøyro
Stord
Bømlo
Leirvik
Haugesund
Kopervik
Åkrahamn
Bokna fjordet
Stavanger
Sandnes
Bryne
Nærbe
Giants Causeway
Malin Hd.
Ballycastle
1224
316
789
1182
1311
1442
1214
238
840
816
A
B
C
9
2
3
4
5
6
7
8
9

UNITED KINGDOM
IRELAND
NORTHERN IRELAND
Belfast
Dublin
Dun Laoghaire
Cork
Limerick
Galway
Sligo
Waterford
Wexford
Rosslare
Arklow
Dundalk
Drogheda
Athlone
Tullamore
Portlaroise
Kilkenny
Carlow
Tipperary
Clonmel
Mallow
Killarney
Tralee
Ennis
Athy
Bray
Navan
Kilrush
Ballina
Castlebar
Westport
Roscommon
Longford
Mullingar
Cavan
Leitrim
Letterkenny
Londonderry
Ballymena
Lisburn
Newry
Omagh
Enniskillen
Portadown
Armagh
Coleraine
Larne
Bangor
Antrim
Donegal
Bundoran
Ballyshannon
Tuam
Ballinasloe
Galway B.
Aran Is.
Shannon
Lough Neagh
Lough Erne
Lough Mask
Lough Corrib
Lough Ree
Lough Derg
Connemara
Burren
Dingle
Tralee
Killarney
Cork
Youghal
Kinsale
Bantry
Clonakilty
Macgillycuddy's Reeks
Valencia
C. Clear
Cobh
Dungarvan
Carrick-on-Suir
Clonmel
Nenagh
Thurles
Limerick
Ennis
Athlone
Tullamore
Mullingar
Navan
Dublin
Wicklow Mts
Irish Sea
Anglesey
Holyhead
Caernarfon
Bangor
Colwyn Bay
Chester
Wrexham
Shrewsbury
Welshpool
Aberystwyth
Cardigan Bay
Pwllheli
Snowdon
Cambrian Mts
WALES
Cardiff
Swansea
Newport
Rhondda
Llanelli
Carmarthen
Haverfordwest
Milford Haven
Pembroke
Fishguard
Brecon
Merthyr Tydfil
Neath
Barry
Port Talbot
Bristol Channel
St. George's Channel
Celtic Sea
Land's End
Isles of Scilly
Penzance
Truro
Falmouth
St. Austell
Newquay
Plymouth
Torbay
Exmouth
Exeter
Barnstaple
Bude
Taunton
Yeovil
Bournemouth
Poole
Weymouth
Southampton
Portsmouth
Isle of Wight
Salisbury
Winchester
Fareham
Havant
Chichester
Worthing
Brighton
Eastbourne
Hastings
Crawley
Guildford
Dorking
Reigate
Ashford
Folkestone
Dover
Canterbury
Margate
Ramsgate
Chatham
Maidstone
Rochester
Southend-on-Sea
Chelmsford
Colchester
Harwich
Ipswich
Felixstowe
Bury St. Edmunds
Thetford
Ely
Cambridge
Bedford
Milton Keynes
Stevenage
Luton
Harlow
Hertford
Watford
Basildon
Hemel Hempstead
Aylesbury
High Wycombe
Reading
Slough
Windsor
Basingstoke
Newbury
Swindon
Oxford
Cheltenham
Gloucester
Cwmbran
Stratford
Leamington Spa
Coventry
Rugby
Northampton
Royal Leamington Spa
Worcester
Hereford
Kidderminster
Wolverhampton
BIRMINGHAM
Reddrich
Nuneaton
Leicester
Corby
Peterborough
Stamford
Grantham
Lincoln
Boston
Skegness
Louth
Grimsby
Cleethorpes
Doncaster
Rotherham
Sheffield
Mansfield
Nottingham
Derby
Stoke-on-Trent
Stafford
Telford
Shrewsbury
Chesterfield
Crewe
Stockport
Warrington
Liverpool
MANCHESTER
Oldham
Huddersfield
Barnsley
Bradford
Leeds
Halifax
Burnley
Blackburn
Bolton
Preston
Blackpool
Keighley
Harrogate
York
Beverley
Kingston upon Hull
Scunthorpe
Humber
Wash
Cromer
King's Lynn
Norwich
Great Yarmouth
Lowestoft
THE BROADS
Haarlem
Alkmaar
Texel
Den Helder
NETHERLANDS
's-Gravenhage (Den Haag)
Hoek van Holland
ROTTERDAM
Dordrecht
Vlissingen
Zeebrugge
Oostende
Antwerpen
Brugge
Gent
Mechelen
BELGIUM
Brussel (Bruxelles)
Dunkerque
Calais
Tournai
Lille
Tourcoing
Roubaix
Valenciennes
Cambrai
St-Quentin
Laon
Amiens
Abbeville
Le Tréport
Dieppe
Pays de Caux
Fécamp
Rouen
Le Havre
Bolbec
Trouville-sur-Mer
Deauville
Caen
Lisieux
Bayeux
Elbeuf
Seine
Le Touquet-Paris-Plage
Boulogne-sur-Mer
St-Omer
Béthune
Bruay-la-Buissière
Lens
Villeneuve d'Ascq
Picardie
Flandre
FRANCE
Channel Is. (U.K.)
Guernsey
St. Peter Port
Sark
Jersey
St. Helier
Alderney
C. de la Hague
Pte. de Barfleur
Cherbourg
Valognes
Cotentin
Channel
English
Newcastle-upon-Tyne
South Shields
Sunderland
Durham
Hartlepool
Redcar
Middlesbrough
Stockton-on-Tees
Darlington
Gateshead
Hexham
Carlisle
Workington
Whitehaven
Cumbrian Mts
Barrow-in-Furness
Lancaster
Douglas
I. of Man
Dumfries
Annan
Kirkcudbright
Stranraer
Mull of Galloway
Ayr
Bridlington
Scarborough
Cleveland Hills
Yorkshire Dales
Lake District
Peak District
Malvern Hills
Cotswold Hills
Exmoor
Dartmoor
Pembrokeshire Coast
Brecon Beacons
Snowdonia
Norfolk Broads
Pennines
Solway Firth
Mersey
Thames
Humber
Tyne
Shannon
Severn
Trent
Ouse
Tees
Brussel
Projection: Conical with two standard parallels
National Parks
West from Greenwich
East from Greenwich
COPYRIGHT PHILIP'S
12
14
2
3
4
5
6
7
D
E
F
G
50
54
52
16
36
99
963
918
893
976
Miles
Kilometres
0
25
50
75
100
125
150
175 km

12 FRANCE

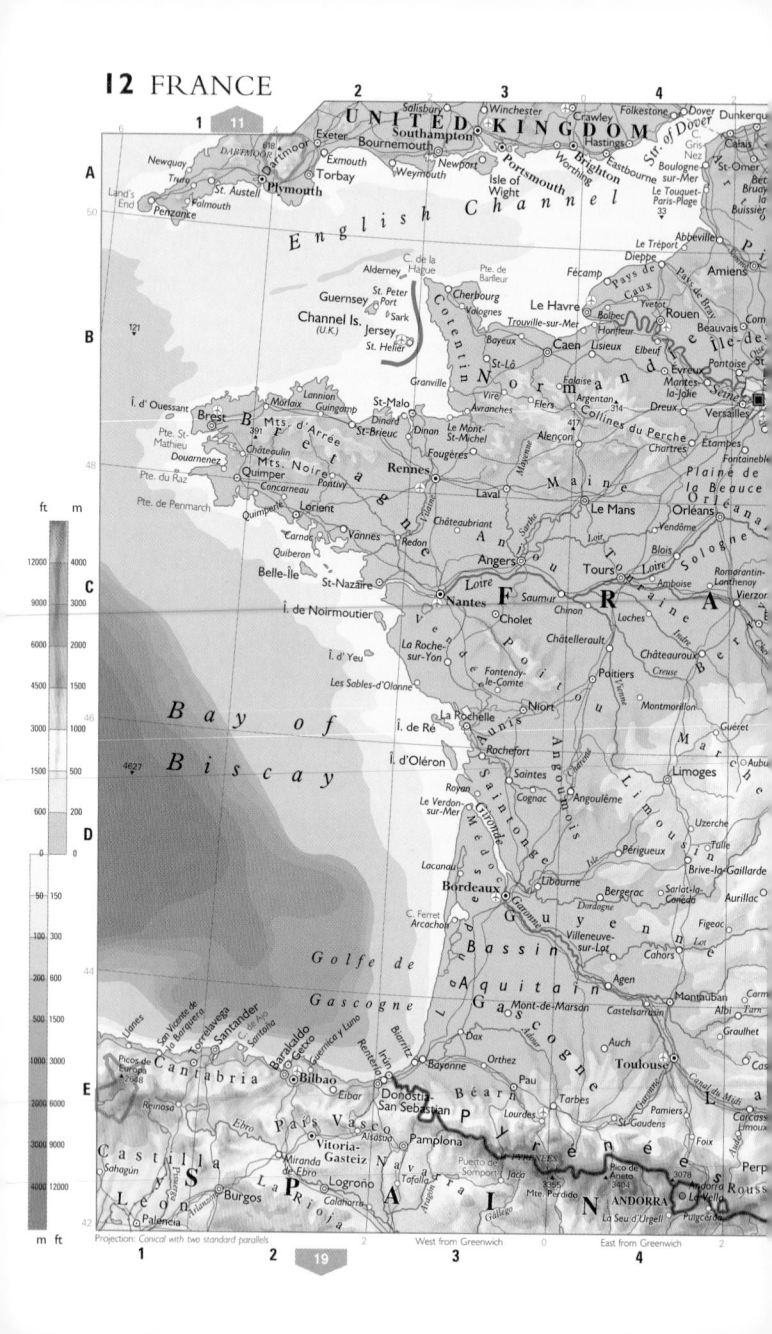
UNITED KINGDOM
English Channel
Bay of Biscay
Golfe de Gascogne
FRANCE
Salisbury
Winchester
Southampton
Bournemouth
Exeter
Torbay
Plymouth
Newquay
Truro
St. Austell
Falmouth
Penzance
Land's End
Dartmoor
Exmoor
Newport
Weymouth
Portsmouth
Isle of Wight
Brighton
Worthing
Hastings
Eastbourne
Folkestone
Dover
Dunkerque
Str. of Dover
Calais
Boulogne
Le Touquet-Paris-Plage
St. Omer
Abbeville
Le Tréport
Dieppe
Fécamp
Amiens
Pays de Caux
Pays de Bray
Le Havre
Bolbec
Yvetot
Rouen
Honfleur
Beauvais
Alderney
C. de la Hague
Pte. de Barfleur
Cherbourg
Valognes
Guernsey
St. Peter Port
Sark
Channel Is. (U.K.)
Jersey
St. Helier
Trouville-sur-Mer
Bayeux
Caen
Lisieux
Elbeuf
Evreux
Pontoise
St. Germain
Granville
St-Lô
Falaise
Argentan
Mantes-la-Jolie
Versailles
Cotentin
Normandie
île-de-France
Vire
Avranches
Flers
Dreux
Collines du Perche
Chartres
Étampes
Fontainebleau
Alençon
Mayenne
Ouessant
Morlaix
Lannion
Guingamp
St-Malo
Dinard
St-Brieuc
Dinan
Le Mont-St-Michel
Fougères
Brest
Bretagne
Mts. d'Arrée
Pte. St. Matheu
Douarnenez
Châteaulin
Mts. Noires
Quimper
Pontivy
Pte. du Raz
Concarneau
Pte. de Penmarch
Quimperlé
Lorient
Vannes
Redon
Carnac
Quiberon
Belle-Île
St-Nazaire
Rennes
Vilaine
Loire
Laval
Mayenne
Maine
Le Mans
Sarthe
Loir
Vendôme
Orléans
Plaine de la Beauce
Orléanais
Châteaubriant
Angers
Anjou
Tours
Touraine
Blois
Sologne
Loire
Amboise
Romorantin-Lanthenay
Vierzon
Nantes
Saumur
Chinon
Cholet
Loches
Châtellerault
Châteauroux
Indre
Berry
Cher
Vendée
Poitou
La Roche-sur-Yon
Fontenay-le-Comte
Poitiers
Vienne
Creuse
Montmorillon
Niort
Sèvre Niortaise
Les Sables-d'Olonne
Î. de Noirmoutier
Î. d'Yeu
Î. de Ré
La Rochelle
Aunis
Rochefort
Saintes
Saintonge
Charente
Angoumois
Angoulême
Limoges
Limousin
Marche
Guéret
Aubusson
Uzerche
Tulle
Périgueux
Brive-la-Gaillarde
Aurillac
Figeac
Lot
Cahors
Agen
Montauban
Tarn
Albi
Graulhet
Castelsarrasin
Mont-de-Marsan
Landes
Dax
Adour
Auch
Toulouse
Garonne
Canal du Midi
Carcassonne
Limoux
Aude
Pamiers
Foix
Perpignan
Roussillon
Andorra la Vella
Puigcerdà
ANDORRA
Pyrénées
Pic de Aneto 3404
3078
Mte. Perdido
3355
La Seu d'Urgell
Puerto de Somport
Jaca
Gave
Pau
Tarbes
Lourdes
St-Gaudens
Bayonne
Orthez
Béarn
Aquitaine
Gascogne
Bordeaux
Libourne
Bergerac
Sarlat-la-Canéda
Villeneuve-sur-Lot
Dordogne
Lot
Garonne
Gironde
Médoc
C. Ferret
Arcachon
Dax
Bayonne
Biarritz
Adour
Nive
Nivelle
Bidasoa
Donostia San Sebastián
Irún
Hondarribia
Pamplona
Navarra
Tafalla
Aragón
Pueto de Somport
Huesca
Zaragoza
Ebro
Alsasua
Vitoria-Gasteiz
País Vasco
Miranda de Ebro
Logroño
La Rioja
Calahorra
Bilbao
Eibar
Guernica y Luno
Gernika
Bermeo
Mundaca
Baracaldo
Getxo
Santander
Santoña
Torrelavega
San Vicente de la Barquera
Llanes
Cantabria
Picos de Europa
2648
Reinosa
Burgos
Palencia
Castilla y León
Sahagún
Duero
Pisuerga
Carrión
Golfe de Gascogne

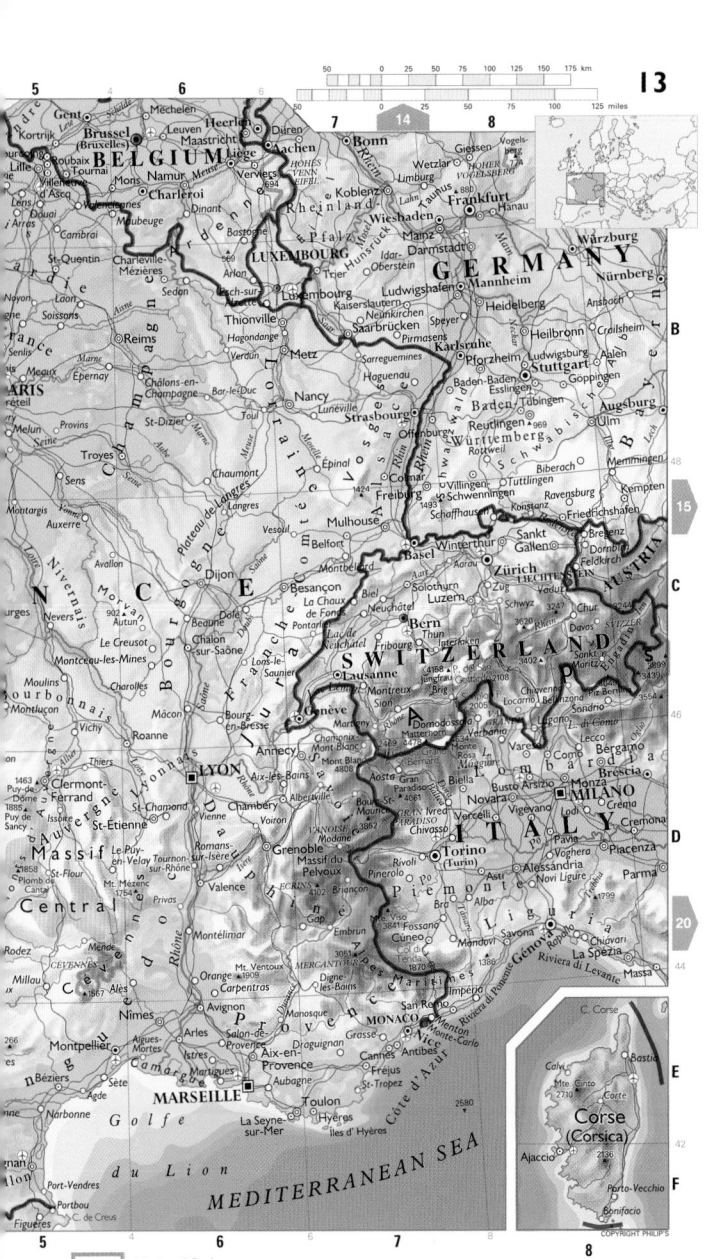
13
50 0 25 50 75 100 125 150 175 km
50 0 25 50 75 100 125 miles
14
15
20
5
6
7
8
B
C
D
E
F
BELGIUM
LUXEMBOURG
GERMANY
SWITZERLAND
AUSTRIA
LIECHTENSTEIN
FRANCE
ITALY
Brussel (Bruxelles)
Gent
Antwerpen
Mechelen
Leuven
Maastricht
Liège
Namur
Mons
Charleroi
Kortrijk
Roubaix
Tournai
Lille
Douai
Lens
Arras
Valenciennes
Maubeuge
Cambrai
St. Quentin
Charleville-Mézières
Sedan
Laon
Soissons
Reims
Épernay
Meaux
PARIS
Melun
Provins
Sens
Troyes
Chaumont
Langres
Vesoul
Montargis
Auxerre
Avallon
Dijon
Beaune
Autun
Nevers
Le Creusot
Montceau-les-Mines
Chalon-sur-Saône
Charolles
Moulins
Montluçon
Vichy
Roanne
Mâcon
Bourg-en-Bresse
Thiers
Clermont-Ferrand
Puy-de-Dôme
Puy de Sancy
St-Étienne
St-Chamond
Le Puy-en-Velay
St-Flour
Mt. Mézenc
Massif Central
Romans-sur-Isère
Tournon-sur-Rhône
Valence
Privas
Montélimar
Mende
Millau
Alès
Nîmes
Montpellier
Béziers
Sète
Agde
Narbonne
Carcassonne
Aigues-Mortes
Arles
Salon-de-Provence
Istres
Marseille
Aix-en-Provence
Marignane
Aubagne
Toulon
Hyères
Iles d' Hyères
La Seyne-sur-Mer
St-Tropez
Fréjus
Cannes
Antibes
Grasse
Draguignan
Nice
Monaco
Menton
Monte-Carlo
Ventimiglia
San Remo
Imperia
Savona
Genova
Riviera di Levante
Riviera di Ponente
La Spezia
Massa
Chiavari
Rapallo
Portofino
Alessandria
Novi Ligure
Asti
Alba
Bra
Cuneo
Mondovì
Fossano
Torino (Turin)
Pinerolo
Rivoli
Chivasso
Ivrea
Biella
Vercelli
Novara
Busto Arsizio
Varese
Como
Bergamo
Brescia
Lecco
Milano
Monza
Crema
Cremona
Lodi
Pavia
Piacenza
Parma
Voghera
Vigevano
Lugano
Locarno
Bellinzona
Sondrio
Chiavenna
Sankt Moritz
Davos
Chur
Vaduz
Zug
Luzern
Zürich
Sankt Gallen
Winterthur
Schaffhausen
Konstanz
Friedrichshafen
Bregenz
Dornbirn
Feldkirch
Basel
Solothurn
Biel
Neuchâtel
Fribourg
Bern
Thun
Interlaken
Brig
Montreux
Lausanne
Sion
Genève
Annecy
Chambéry
Albertville
Grenoble
Briançon
Gap
Embrun
Digne-les-Bains
Orange
Carpentras
Avignon
Manosque
Frejus

14 GERMANY AND BENELUX

UNITED KINGDOM
NORTH SEA
NETHERLANDS
AMSTERDAM
's-Gravenhage (Den Haag)
ROTTERDAM
Hoek van Holland
BELGIUM
Brussel (Bruxelles)
Antwerpen
Gent
Brugge
Oostende
Liège
Namur
Charleroi
Mons
Lille
Roubaix
Tourcoing
Calais
Boulogne-sur-Mer
Dunkerque
Amiens
Beauvais
Reims
Metz
Nancy
Strasbourg
Mulhouse
Colmar
Freiburg
Karlsruhe
Mannheim
Heidelberg
Stuttgart
Frankfurt
Wiesbaden
Mainz
Koblenz
Bonn
Köln (Cologne)
Aachen
Düsseldorf
Essen
Dortmund
Duisburg
Bielefeld
Münster
Osnabrück
Bremen
Hamburg
Hannover
Kassel
Frankfurt
Würzburg
Nürnberg
Ulm
Augsburg
Regensburg
Erfurt
Leipzig
Dresden
Berlin
Rostock
Wismar
Schwerin
Lübeck
Hamburg
Kiel
Flensburg
Sylt
Esbjerg
Aabenraa
Wilhelmshaven
Bremerhaven
Emden
Groningen
Leeuwarden
Amsterdam
Rotterdam
Den Haag
Utrecht
Arnhem
Nijmegen
Eindhoven
Tilburg
Breda
Antwerpen
Gent
Brugge
Oostende
Boulogne
Le Havre
Lyon
Saint-Etienne
Grenoble
Annecy
Chambéry
Dijon
Besançon
Paris
Rouen
Caen
Cherbourg
Luxembourg
Trier
Basel
Zürich
Bern
Luzern
Lausanne
Genève
Sion
Chur
Davos
Bolzano
Trento
Verona
Milano
Como

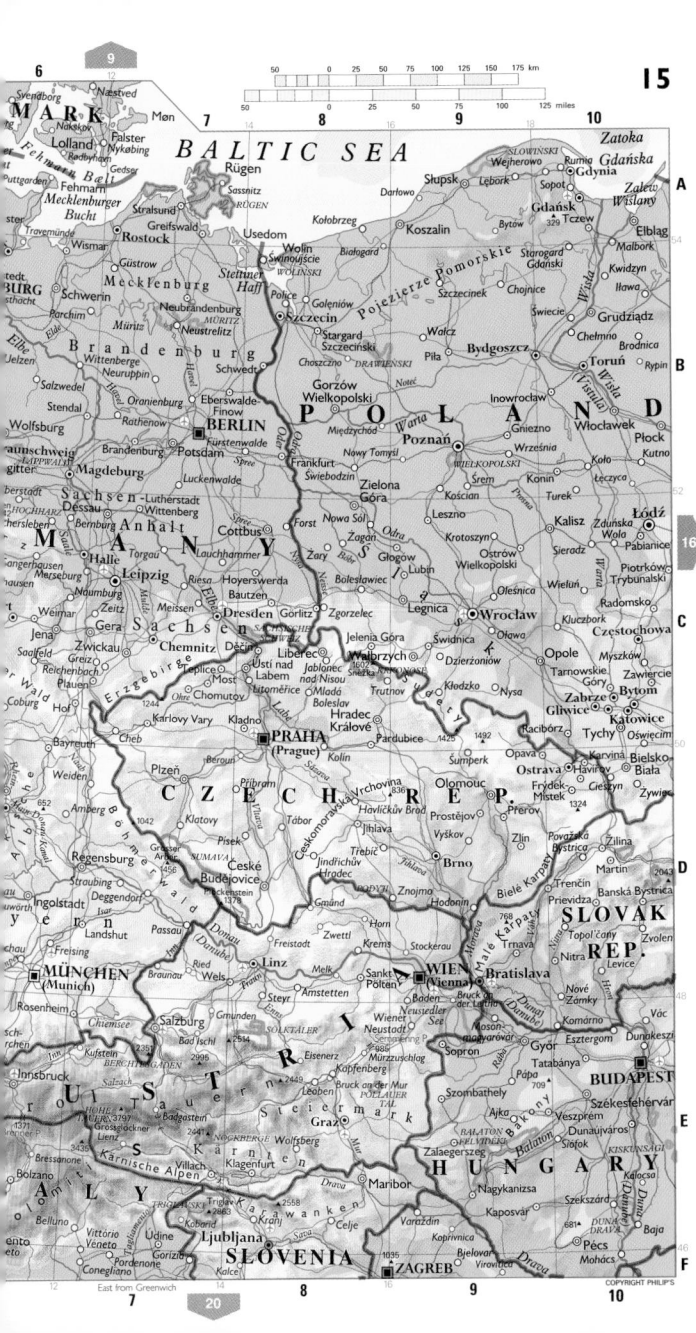
15
BALTIC SEA
Zatoka Gdańska
Zalew Wiślany
Rügen
Stralsund
Greifswald
Rostock
Wismar
Usedom
Wolin
Świnoujście
Szczecin
Koszalin
Kołobrzeg
Słupsk
Lębork
Darłowo
Gdańsk
Gdynia
Sopot
Tczew
Elbląg
Malbork
Starogard Gdański
Chojnice
Świecie
Grudziądz
Chełmno
Brodnica
Toruń
Rypin
Włocławek
Płock
Kutno
Łęczyca
Łódź
Pabianice
Piotrków Trybunalski
Radomsko
Częstochowa
Myszków
Zawiercie
Tarnowskie Góry
Bytom
Zabrze
Gliwice
Katowice
Tychy
Oświęcim
Bielsko-Biała
Żywiec
Karviná
Havířov
Frýdek-Místek
Ostrava
Opava
Racibórz
Olomouc
Přerov
Prostějov
Vyškov
Zlín
Povážská Bystrica
Žilina
Martin
Trenčín
Banská Bystrica
Prievidza
Topoľčany
Zvolen
Nitra
Levice
Nové Zámky
Komárno
Esztergom
Dunaújváros
Székesfehérvár
Veszprém
Tatabánya
Győr
Sopron
Mosonmagyaróvár
Vác
Dunakeszi
BUDAPEST
Szolnok
Szeged
Kecskemét
Debrecen
Miskolc
Eger
Nyíregyháza
Szekszárd
Pécs
Mohács
Baja
Kaposvár
Nagykanizsa
Zalaegerszeg
Szombathely
Pápa
Ajka
Sopron
Graz
Leoben
Bruck an der Mur
Kapfenberg
Mürzzuschlag
Eisenerz
Steyr
Amstetten
Wiener Neustadt
Baden
Bruck an der Leitha
Sankt Pölten
Krems
Stockerau
Mistelbach
Znojmo
Hodonín
Brno
Třebíč
Jihlava
Tábor
Jindřichův Hradec
Česká Budějovice
Písek
Klatovy
Cheb
Karlovy Vary
Kladno
Mladá Boleslav
Liberec
Jablonec nad Nisou
Ústí nad Labem
Teplice
Most
Chomutov
Děčín
Hradec Králové
Pardubice
Chrudim
Kolín
Mělník
Jelenia Góra
Świdnica
Wałbrzych
Dzierżoniów
Kłodzko
Nysa
Opole
Brzeg
Oława
Legnica
Wrocław
Głogów
Lubin
Bolesławiec
Zgorzelec
Zielona Góra
Żary
Nowa Sól
Zagań
Forst
Cottbus
Hoyerswerda
Bautzen
Görlitz
Meissen
Dresden
Pirna
Freiberg
Chemnitz
Zwickau
Plauen
Gera
Jena
Weimar
Erfurt
Halle
Leipzig
Merseburg
Naumburg
Zeitz
Dessau
Wittenberg
Bernburg
Lutherstadt Wittenberg
Magdeburg
Luckenwalde
Potsdam
Brandenburg
Fürstenwalde
Frankfurt
Świebodzin
Nowy Tomyśl
Poznań
Gniezno
Konin
Turek
Kalisz
Leszno
Krotoszyn
Ostrów Wielkopolski
Sieradz
Wieluń
Kluczbork
Oleśnica
Głubczyce
Trutnov
Praha (Prague)
Plzeň

16 CENTRAL EUROPE

Zatoka Gdańska
Kaliningrad (Russia)
Gdynia
Gdańsk
Elbląg
Słupsk
Koszalin
Szczecin
Stettiner Haff
Usedom
Wolin
Świnoujście
Pojezierze Pomorskie
Pojezierze Mazurskie
Olsztyn
Grudziądz
Bydgoszcz
Toruń
Włocławek
Płock
WARSZAWA (Warsaw)
Poznań
Gorzów Wielkopolski
Zielona Góra
BERLIN
GERMANY
POLAND
Łódź
Wrocław
Legnica
Dresden
Chemnitz
Liberec
Jelenia Góra
Katowice
Kraków
Częstochowa
Kielce
Opole
Gliwice
Zabrze
Bytom
Sosnowiec
Ostrava
Olomouc
PRAHA (Prague)
CZECH REP.
Brno
Bratislava
WIEN (Vienna)
SLOVAK REP.
Košice
Miskolc
Debrecen
BUDAPEST
HUNGARY
Graz
Klagenfurt
Maribor
Ljubljana
SLOVENIA
ZAGREB
CROATIA
Trieste
Rijeka
Osijek
SERBIA
Vojvodina
Novi Sad
Timisoara
Szeged
Arad
Debrecen
Eger
Salgótarján
Nyíregyháza
Szolnok
Kecskemét
Szombathely
Sopron
Győr
Veszprém
Pécs
Baja
Subotica
Karlovac
Varaždin
Celje
Koper
Bielovar
Virovitica
Sisak
Vukovar
Zrenjanin
Karlovy Vary
Plzeň
Prague
Vienna
Kaliningrad
Minsk
Vilnius

50 0 25 50 75 100 125 150 175 km
50 0 25 50 75 100 125 miles
B E L A R U S
MINSK
Marijampolė
Alytus
Druskininkai
Lida
Hrodna
Navahrudak
Dzyarzhynsk
Hrozyanka
Bykhaw
Slawharad
Augustów
Suwałki
Sokółka
Białystok
Masty
Dzyatlava
Stowbtsy
Nyasvizh
Slutsk
Babruysk
Asipovichy
Rahachow
Zhlobin
Vawkavysk
Slonim
Baranavichy
Klyetsk
Lyakhovichy
Hantsavichy
Salihorsk
Glusk
Aktsyabrski
Homyel
Svyetlahorsk
Rechytsa
Vasilevichi
Swisłach
Hajnówka
Bielsk Podlaski
Watsevichy
Tsyelyakhany
Byaroza
Pruzhany
Kobryn
Drogichyn
Luninyets
Pyetrykaw
Kalinkavichy
Mazyr
Khoyniki
Loyew
Zhabinka
Pinsk
Yelsk
Biała Podlaska
Siedlce
Brest
Malaryta
Międzyrzec Podlaski
Kamin-Kashyrskyy
Dubrovytsya
Ovruch
Chornobyl
Włodawa
Olevsk
Korosten
Oster
Kyyivske Vdskh.
Lublin
Chełm
Lyuboml
Kovel
Starvy Chartoryisk
Kostopil
Belokorovichi
Dymer
Irpin
KYIVIV (Kiev)
Świdnik
Krasnik
Novovolynsk
Volodymyr-Volynskyy
Rozhyshche
Kivertsi
Oleksandriya
Lutsk
Rivne
Zdolbuniv
Karets
Novohrad-Volynskyy
Malyn
Radomyshl
Korostyshev
Vasylkiv
Zamość
Stalowa Wola
Sokal
Chervonohrad
Horokhiv
Dubno
Ostroh
Zhytomyr
Pershotravensk
Fastiv
Rava-Ruska
Radekhiv
Berestechko
Krementsk
Shepetivka
Slavuta
Polonne
Berdychiv
Rzeszów
Nesterov
Kamyanka-Buzka
Brody
Izyaslav
Bila Tserkva
Skvyra
Tarashcha
Jarosław
Yavoriv
Mostyska
Lviv (Lvov)
Zolochiv
Starokonstyantyniv
Khmelnik
Kozyatyn
Tetiyev
Przemyśl
Horodok
Ternopil
Zbarazh
Khmelnytskyy
Lipovets
Zhashkiv
Sanok
Sambir
Khodoriv
Berezhany
Skalat
Hrymayliv
Vinnytsya
Borislav
Drohobych
Rogatyn
Terebovlya
Horodok
Bar
Zhmerynka
Haysyn
Stryy
Truskavets
Kalush
Dnestr
Buchach
Kopychyntsi
Chortkiv
Tulchyn
Uman
Skole
Bolekhiv
Skala-Podilska
Kamyanets-Podilskyy
Ivano-Frankivsk
Horodenka
Zalishchyky
Mohyliv-Podilskyy
Vapnyarka
Hayvoron
Bershad
Michalowce
Uzhhorod
Velyatyn
Nadvirna
Kolomyya
Pechenizhyn
Snyatyn
Yaremcha
Chernivtsi
Khotyn
Novoselytsya
Lipcani
Ocnita
Yampil
Drochia
Soroca
Edineț
Florești
Bălți
Râbnița
Bolta
Ananyiv
Kotovsk
Mukacheve
Berehove
Khust
Vynohradiv
Tyachiv
Rakhiv
Yasinya
Storozhynets
Hlyboka
Dorohoi
Sighetul Marmației
Rădăuți
Suceava
Botoșani
Falticeni
Pașcani
Falești
Orhei
Dubăsari
Nyíregyháza
Satu Mare
Baia Mare
Borșa
Vatra-Dornei
Bistrița
Iași
Roman
Târgu Frumos
Hârlău
Chișinău
Tiraspol
Carei
Oradea
Zalău
Dej
Piatra Neamț
Vaslui
Husi
Leova
Cimișlia
Tighina
Cahul
Comrat
Bilhorod Dnistrovskyy
Salonta
Cluj-Napoca
Reghin
Târgu Mureș
Bacău
Miercurea-Ciuc
Odorheiu Secuiesc
Onești
Bârlad
Cantemir
Cahul
Artsyz
Turda
Mintiu Bihor
Abrud
Aiud
Târnăveni
Sighișoara
Sfântu Gheorghe
Tecuci
Tatarbunary
Alba-Iulia
Mediaș
Focșani
Galați
Izmayil
Kiliya
Ozero Katyk Volkove
Deva
Simeria
Sibiu
Brașov
Săcele
Râmnicu Sărat
Reni
Sulina
Lugoj
Hunedoara
Petroșani
Câmpulung
Curtea de Argeș
Câmpina
Buzău
Brăila
Caransebeș
Vulcan
Pitești
Slatina
Vf. Moldoveanu
Vf. Omul
Vf. Peleaga
Parângul Mare
Carpații Meridionali
Munții Bihorului

18 SPAIN AND PORTUGAL

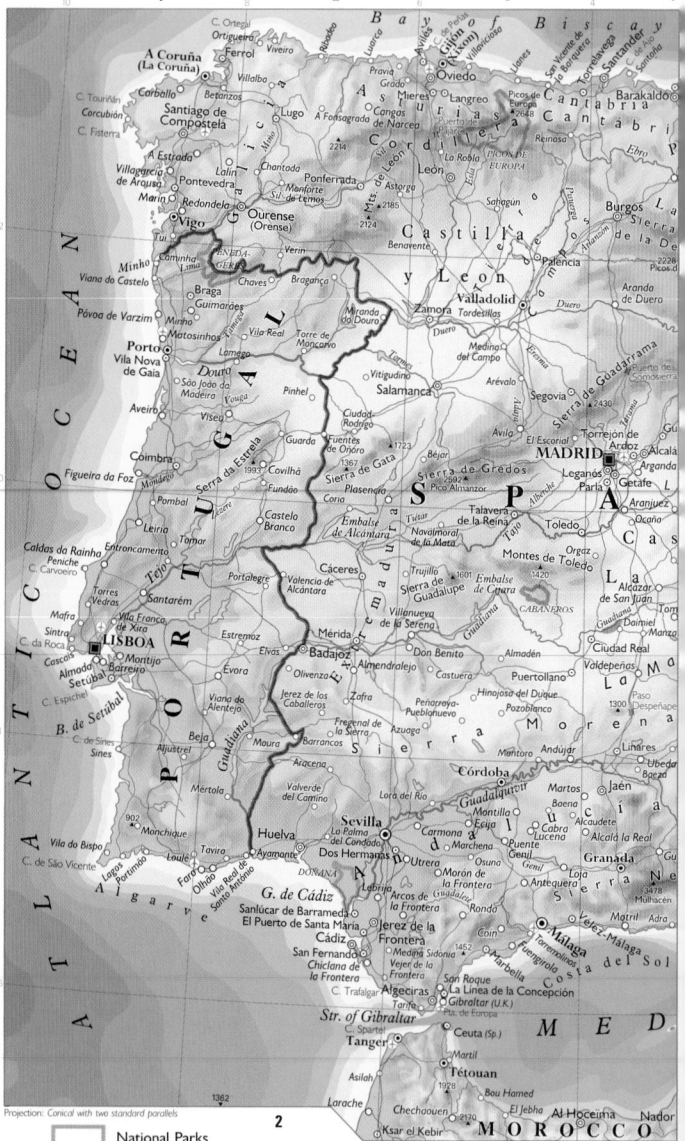
Bay of Biscay
A Coruña (La Coruña)
Ferrol
Ortigueira
Viveiro
Ribadeo
Luarca
Avilés
Gijón (Xixón)
Cabo de Peñas
Villaviciosa
Oviedo
Pravia
Grado
Mieres
Langreo
Cangas de Narcea
A Fonsagrada
Lugo
Santiago de Compostela
Carballo
Betanzos
C. Touriñán
Corcubión
C. Finisterra
Vigo
Pontevedra
Marín
Redondela
Villagarcía de Arousa
A Estrada
Lalín
Chantada
Ponferrada
Ourense (Orense)
Astorga
León
Sahagún
Benavente
Zamora
Tordesillas
Valladolid
Palencia
Burgos
Aranda de Duero
Viana do Castelo
Braga
Guimarães
Póvoa de Varzim
Matosinhos
Porto
Vila Nova de Gaia
Vila Real
Chaves
Bragança
Miranda do Douro
Torre de Moncorvo
Lamego
Medina del Campo
Salamanca
Vitigudino
Arévalo
Segovia
Sierra de Guadarrama
Avila
El Escorial
Torrejón de Ardoz
MADRID
Alcalá
Aveiro
Viseu
Pinhel
Ciudad Rodrigo
Guarda
Fuentes de Oñoro
Coimbra
Figueira da Foz
Serra da Estrela
Covilhã
Fundão
Sierra de Gata
Plasencia
Coria
Bejar
Sierra de Gredos
Pico Almanzor
Leganés
Parla
Getafe
Aranjuez
Ocaña
Leiria
Pombal
Tomar
Castelo Branco
Embalse de Alcántara
Talavera de la Reina
Navalmoral de la Mata
Toledo
Montes de Toledo
Orgaz
Caldas da Rainha
Peniche
C. Carvoeiro
Entroncamento
Torres Vedras
Santarem
Portalegre
Valencia de Alcantara
Cáceres
Trujillo
Sierra de Guadalupe
Embalse de Cíjara
Alcázar de San Juan
Daimiel
Mafra
Vila Franca de Xira
Sintra
C. da Roca
LISBOA
Cascais
Almada
Setúbal
Barreiro
Montijo
C. Espichel
B. de Setúbal
Estremoz
Elvas
Badajoz
Mérida
Villanueva de la Serena
Don Benito
Almendralejo
Almadén
Ciudad Real
Valdepeñas
Puertollano
Evora
Olivenza
Castuera
Hinojosa del Duque
Pozoblanco
Viana do Alentejo
Jerez de los Caballeros
Peñarroya-Pueblonuevo
Fregenal de la Sierra
Azuaga
Paso Despeñaperros
C. de Sines
Sines
Beja
Aljustrel
Mértola
Moura
Barrancos
Aracena
Valverde del Camino
Lora del Rio
Montoro
Andújar
Linares
Úbeda
Baeza
Córdoba
Jaén
Martos
Baena
Alcaudete
Montilla
Cabra
Lucena
Alcalá la Real
Granada
Loja
Antequera
Sierra Nevada
Matrit
Adra
Vila do Bispo
C. de São Vicente
Monchique
Lagos
Portimão
Tavira
Faro
Olhão
Vila Real de Santo António
Loulé
Ayamonte
Huelva
Sevilla
La Palma del Condado
Carmona
Marchena
Osuna
Utrera
Morón de la Frontera
Dos Hermanas
Puente Genil
Arcos de la Frontera
Ronda
Coín
Málaga
Fuengirola
Marbella
Costa del Sol
Algarve
G. de Cádiz
Sanlúcar de Barrameda
El Puerto de Santa María
Cádiz
Jerez de la Frontera
San Fernando
Chiclana de la Frontera
Medina Sidonia
Vejer de la Frontera
San Roque
La Línea de la Concepción
C. Trafalgar
Algeciras
Tarifa
Gibraltar (U.K.)
Str. of Gibraltar
Pta. de Europa
Ceuta (Sp.)
Tanger
Martil
Tétouan
Asilah
Larache
Chechaouen
Bou Hamed
El Jebha
Al Hoceima
Nador
Ksar el Kebir
MOROCCO
ATLANTIC OCEAN
PORTUGAL
SPAIN
Sierra Morena
Sierra de Cazorla
Sierra de Segura
Sierra de Alcaraz
Sierra de Gredos
Sierra de Guadarrama
Sierra de la Demanda
Sierra de Gata
Sierra da Estrela
Sierra de Cabañeros
Sierra de Aracena
Sierra de Monchique
Mts. de León
Cordillera Cantábrica
Picos de Europa
Picos de Europa
Pico del Almanzor
Tajo
Duero
Ebro
Guadiana
Guadalquivir
Miño
Douro
Tejo
Mondego
Vouga
Lima
Guadiana
Guadalquivir
Guadalete

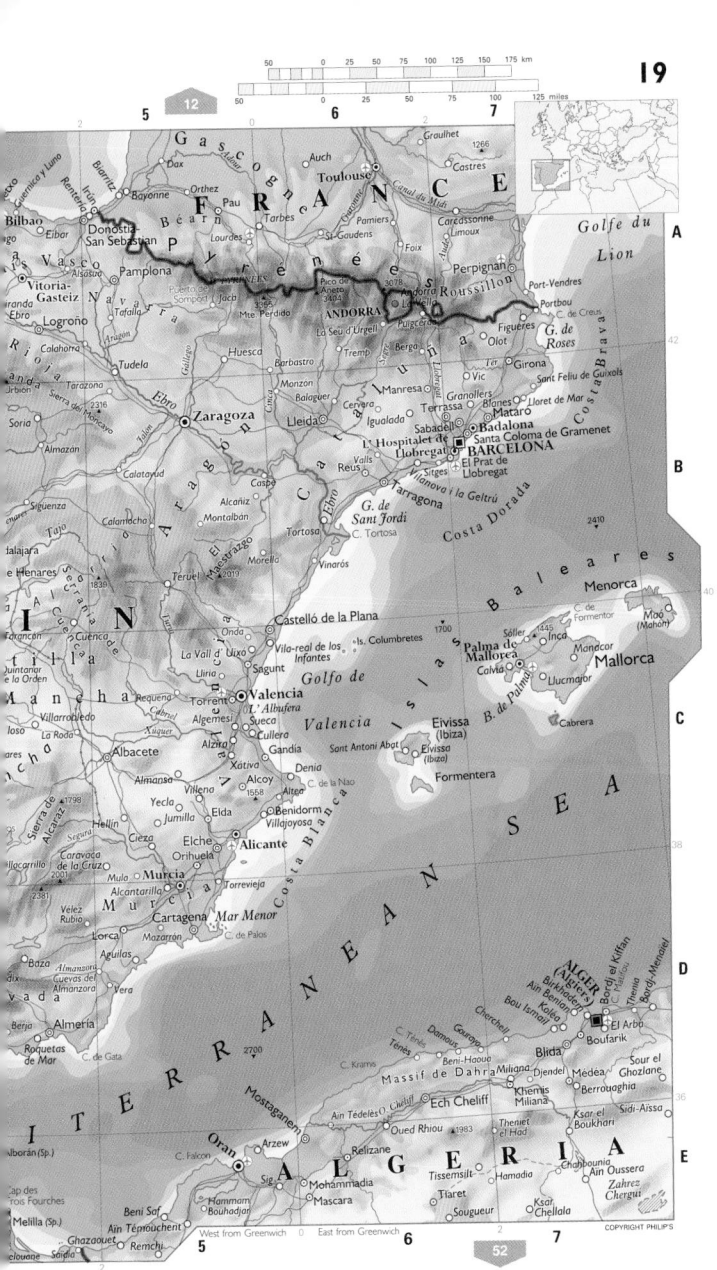
50 0 25 50 75 100 125 150 175 km
50 0 25 50 75 100 125 miles
12
5
6
7
A
B
C
D
E
42
40
38
36
52
Gascogne
FRANCE
Pyrénées
Navarra
Rioja
Aragón
Cataluña
Valencia
Murcia
Andalucía
Castilla-La Mancha
Castilla y León
Vasco
Baleares
Mediterranean Sea
Golfe du Lion
Costa Brava
Costa Dorada
Costa Blanca
Golfo de Valencia
Graulhet
Auch
Toulouse
Castres
Dax
Bayonne
Orthez
Pau
Tarbes
Pamiers
Carcassonne
Limoux
Bilbao
Eibar
Donostia San Sebastián
Béarn
Lourdes
St. Gaudens
Foix
Perpignan
Roussillon
Vitoria-Gasteiz
Pamplona
Alsasua
Tafalla
Puerto de Somport
Jaca
Pico de Aneto 3404
Mte. Perdido
ANDORRA
La Seu d'Urgell
Puigcerdá
Port-Vendres
Portbou
C. de Creus
G. de Roses
Figueres
Olot
Logroño
Calahorra
Huesca
Tremp
Berga
Girona
Sant Feliu de Guixols
Tudela
Barbastro
Vic
Tarazona
Sierra del Moncayo
Monzon
Balaguer
Manresa
Granollers
Blanes
Lloret de Mar
Soria
Zaragoza
Cervera
Terrassa
Mataró
Almazán
Lleida
Igualada
Sabadell
Badalona
Santa Coloma de Gramenet
L'Hospitalet de Llobregat
BARCELONA
Valls
Reus
El Prat de Llobregat
Calatayud
Caspe
Vilanova y la Geltrú
Siguenza
Alcañiz
Tarragona
Calamocha
Montalban
G. de Sant Jordi
Tortosa
C. Tortosa
Tajo
Morella
Vinarós
Teruel
Sagunto
Menorca
C. de Formentor
Mahón (Mahon)
Castelló de la Plana
Cuenca
Vila-real de los Infantes
Is. Columbretes
Sóller
Inca
Palma de Mallorca
Mondoñor
Mallorca
Llucmajor
Calvia
B. de Palma
Llíria
La Vall d'Uixó
Valencia
Cabrera
Manchuela
Requena
Torrent
Algemesí
Sueca
L'Albufera
Eivissa (Ibiza)
Villarrobledo
La Roda
Yuste
Cullera
Gandía
Sant Antoni Abat
Albacete
Alzira
Xátiva
Denia
Formentera
Almansa
Villena
Alcoy
C. de la Nao
Altea
Yecla
Jumilla
Elda
Benidorm
Villajoyosa
Hellín
Cieza
Elche
Alicante
Caravaca de la Cruz
Orihuela
Mula
Murcia
Alcantarilla
Torrevieja
Vélez Rubio
Cartagena
Mar Menor
Lorca
Mazarrón
C. de Palos
Aguilas
Almanzora
Cuevas de Almanzora
Vera
Almería
Roquetas de Mar
C. de Gata
ALGER (Algiers)
Bordj el Kiffan
Bordj-Menaiel
Ain Benian
Birkhadem
Kolea
Bou Ismaïl
El Arbo
Boufarik
Blida
Sour el Ghozlane
Medéa
Berroughia
Djendel
Chemis Miliana
Miliana
Ech Cheliff
Ksar el Boukhari
Sidi-Aïssa
Ain Tedeles
Oued Rhiou
Theniet el Had
Mostaganem
Oran
Arzew
Relizane
Sig
Mohammadia
Mascara
Tissemsilt
Hamadia
Tiaret
Ksar Chellala
Chebounia
Ain Oussera
Zahrez Chergui
Saugueur
Beni Saf
Hammam Bouhadjar
Ain Témouchent
Ghazaouet
Remchi
Melilla (Sp.)
Alborán (Sp.)
C. Falcon
C. Tenès
C. Krims
Cherchell
Damous
Gouraya
Tenès
Beni-Haoua
Massif de Dahra
West from Greenwich
East from Greenwich
COPYRIGHT PHILIP'S

20
14
16
22
SWITZERLAND
AUSTRIA
HUNGARY
SLOVENIA
CROATIA
BOSNIA-HERZEGOVINA
FRANCE
MONACO
VATICAN CITY
SAN MARINO
Steiermark
Kärnten
Salzburg
Tirol
Vorarlberg
Piemonte
Lombardia
Liguria
Veneto
Friuli-Venezia Giulia
Trentino-Alto Adige
Emilia-Romagna
Toscana
Umbria
Marche
Lazio
Abruzzi
Molise
Campania
Puglia
Basilicata
Calabria
Sicilia
Sardegna
Corsica
Corse (Corsica)
LIGURIAN SEA
ADRIATIC SEA
Golfo di Genova
Golfo di Venezia
Istria
Dalmacija
Bouches de Bonifacio
Golfo dell'Asinara
Côte d'Azur
Riviera di Levante
Riviera di Ponente
Dolomiti
Alpi Giulie
Karnische Alpen
Karawanken
Julische Alpen
Gran Sasso d'Italia
Monte Rosa
Monte Bianco
Massif du Pelvoux
Grenoble
Chambéry
Annecy
Torino (Turin)
MILANO
Brescia
Bergamo
Verona
Venezia (Venice)
Trieste
Ljubljana
ZAGREB
Genova
La Spezia
Bologna
Firenze (Florence)
Pisa
Livorno
Roma
Napoli
Bari
Palermo
Catania
Cagliari
Sarajevo
Split
Dubrovnik
Ancona
Pescara
Foggia
Bari
Messina
Ajaccio
Bastia
Olbia
Porto Torres
Asinara
Porto-Vecchio
Bonifacio
Maddalena
Elba
Capraia
Pianosa
Giglio
Montecristo
Pula
Rijeka
Zadar
Dubrovnik
Mostar
Banja Luka
Osijek
Vukovar
Graz
Klagenfurt
Bolzano
Trento
Udine
Pordenone
Treviso
Padova
Mantova
Cremona
Parma
Modena
Ferrara
Ravenna
Rimini
Pesaro
Ancona
Perugia
Terni
Rieti
L'Aquila
Pescara
Chieti
Campobasso
Benevento

Sardegna (Sardinia)
Alghero
Sassari
Nuoro
Oristano
G. di Oristano
Cagliari
G. di Cagliari
San Pietro
Sant' Antioco
Iglesias
Quartu Sant' Elena
Carbonia
Arbatax
TYRRHENIAN SEA
Napoli
Ischia
Capri
Salerno
Battipaglia
Potenza
Taranto
Golfo di Taranto
Brindisi
Lecce
Gallipoli
Otranto
Cosenza
Crotone
Catanzaro
Reggio di Calabria
Messina
Isole Eolie
Stromboli
Lipari
Vulcano
Milazzo
Palermo
Trapani
Marsala
Mazara del Vallo
Sciacca
Agrigento
Catania
Siracusa
Augusta
Ragusa
Pantelleria (Italy)
Lampedusa
Isole Pelagie (Italy)
Valletta
MALTA
Gozo
Tunis
TUNISIA
ALGERIA
Annaba
Bizerte
Golfe de Tunis
Golfe de Hammamet
Sousse
Kairouan
Sfax
Gabès
Djerba
Tripoli
Malta
MEDITERRANEAN SEA
IONIAN SEA
Projection: Conical with two standard parallels
East from Greenwich
COPYRIGHT PHILIP'S
m 4000 3000 2000 1000 500 200 100 0 200 500 1000 2000 3000 4000
ft 12000 9000 6000 3000 1500 600 300 150 0 600 1500 3000 6000 9000 12000
National Parks

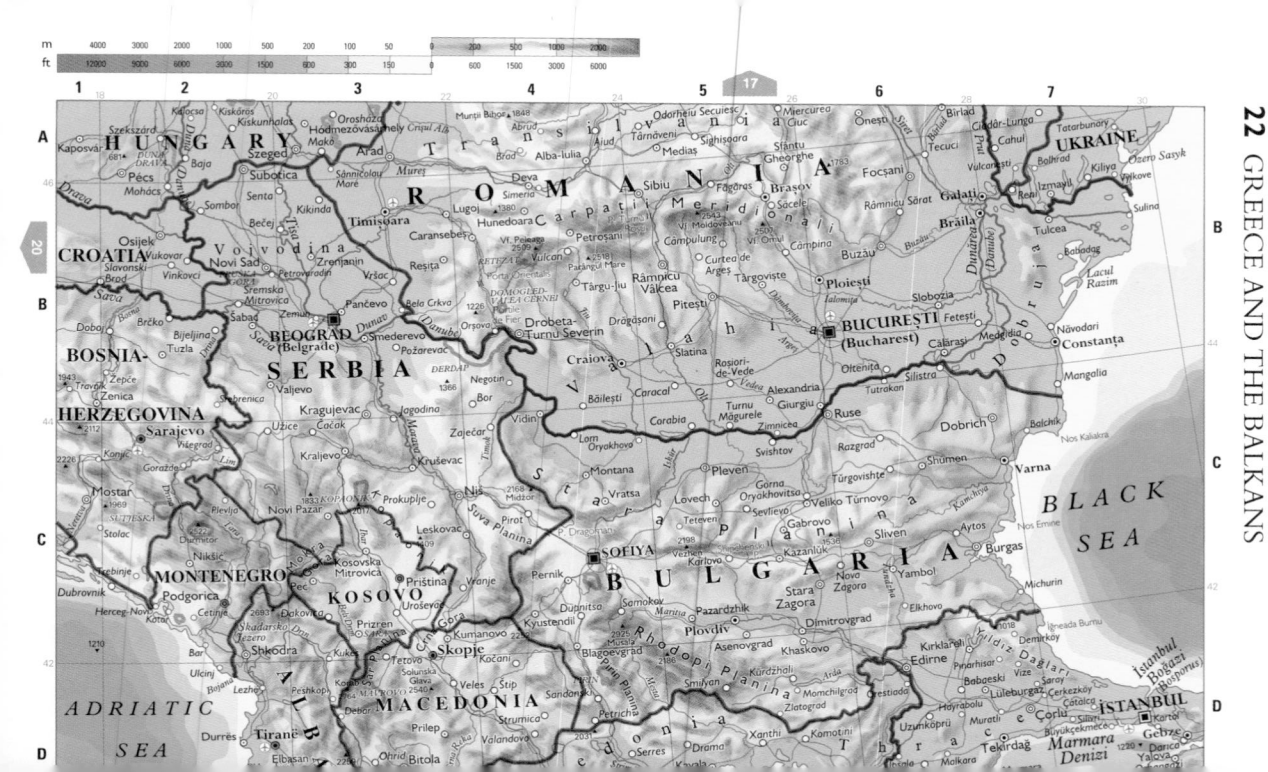
m
ft.
HUNGARY
ROMANIA
UKRAINE
CROATIA
Vojvodina
SERBIA
BOSNIA-HERZEGOVINA
MONTENEGRO
KOSOVO
MACEDONIA
BULGARIA
ALBANIA
BELGRADE (Belgrade)
BUCUREŞTI (Bucharest)
SOFIYA
ISTANBUL
BLACK SEA
ADRIATIC SEA
Marmara Denizi
Carpatii Meridionali
Munţii Bihor
Munţii Apuseni
Munţii Retezat

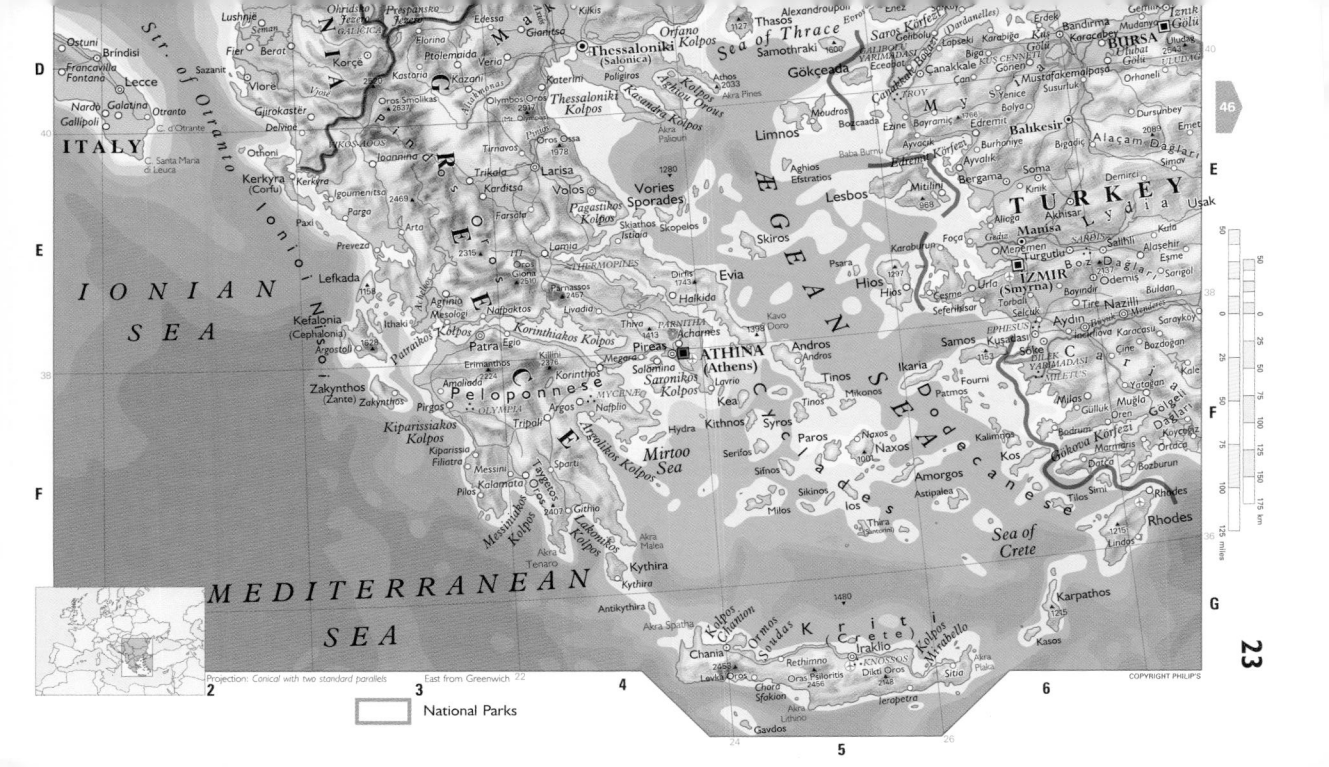
ITALY
Brindisi
Lecce
Otranto
Gallipoli
Galatina
Francavilla Fontana
Ostuni
Sazanit
Str. of Otranto
Santa Maria di Leuca
C. d'Otrante
Lushnje
Fier
Berat
Vlorë
Gjirokaster
Delvina
Korçë
Kastoria
Kozani
Verio
Ptolemaida
Florina
Edessa
Giannitsa
Thessaloniki (Salonica)
Katerini
Olympos
Larisa
Volos
Trikala
Karditsa
Farsala
Lamia
Thermopylae
Livadia
Thiva
Chalcis
Halkida
Evia
Skiros
Skopelos
Skiathos
Sporades
Vories Sporades
Thasos
Samothraki
Alexandroupoli
Sea of Thrace
Gökçeada
Limnos
Lesbos
Chios
Samos
Ikaria
Patmos
Fourni
Kos
Kalimnos
Leros
Amorgos
Astipalea
Naxos
Paros
Antiparos
Syros
Tinos
Andros
Mykonos
Kea
Kythnos
Serifos
Sifnos
Milos
Sikinos
Ios
Thira (Santorini)
Rhodes
Lindos
Karpathos
Kasos
Crete (Kriti)
Chania
Rethimno
Iraklio
Sitia
Ierapetra
Gavdos
Kythira
Antikythira
Kythira
Zakynthos (Zante)
Kefalonia (Cephalonia)
Argostoli
Lefkada
Ithaki
Paxi
Corfu (Kerkyra)
Igoumenitsa
Ioannina
Preveza
Arta
Patras
Pirgos
Kalamata
Tripoli
Sparti
Argos
Nafplio
Corinth
Megara
Piraeus
ATHINA (Athens)
Salamina
Aigina
Mesolongi
Nafpaktos
Agrinion
Amfissa
Delphi
Kozani
Florina
Ioannina
Tirnavos
Orei Ossa
Orei Parnassos
Orei Giona
Orei Taygetos
Orei Parnitha

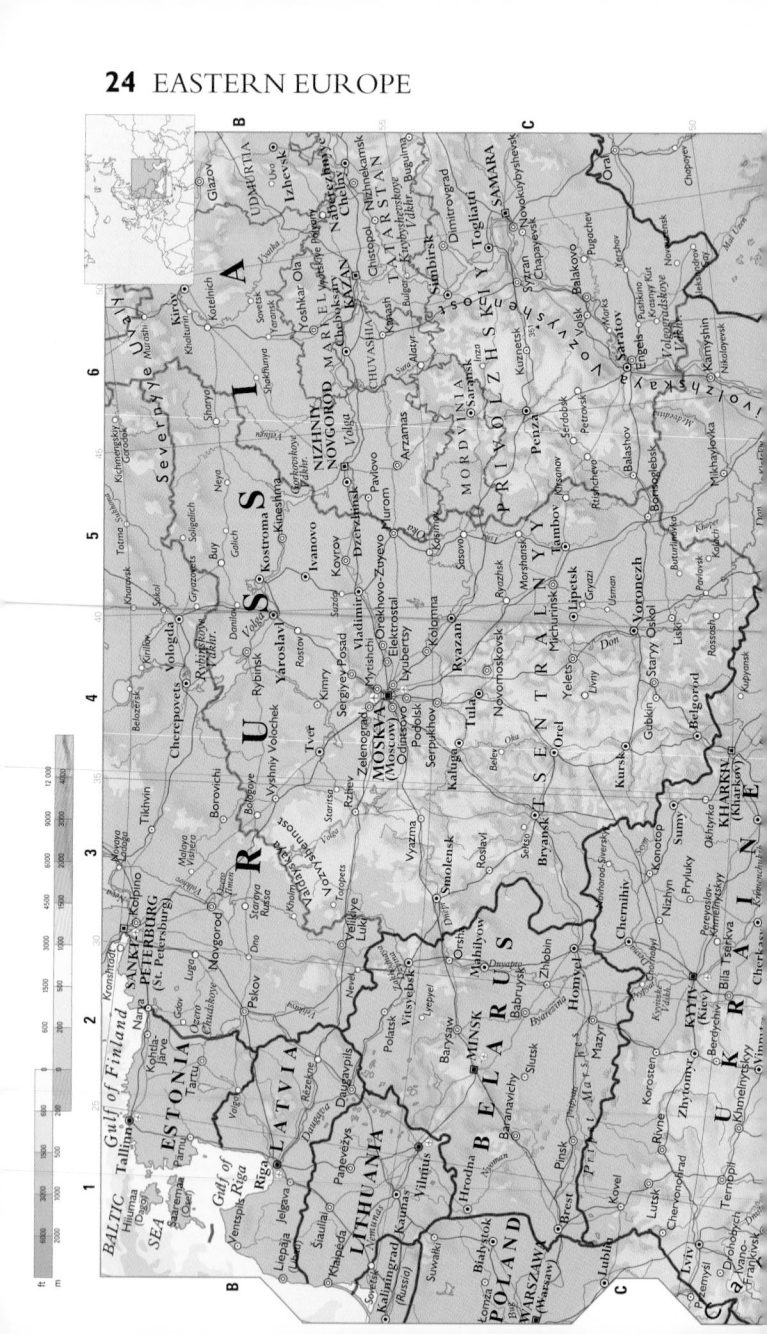
BALTIC SEA
Gulf of Finland
Gulf of Riga
ESTONIA
LATVIA
LITHUANIA
BELARUS
POLAND
UKRAINE
RUSSIA
Severnyye Uvaly
Vozvyshennost'
SANKT-PETERBURG (St. Petersburg)
MOSKVA (Moscow)
MINSK
KYIV (Kiev)
KHARKIV (Kharkov)
WARSZAWA (Warsaw)
Tallinn
Riga
Vilnius
Kaunas
Kaliningrad (Russia)
Suwałki
Białystok
Lublin
Brest
Lutsk
Chernovtsy
Lviv
Przemyśl
Ivanovo
Kostroma
Yaroslavl
Vologda
Cherepovets
Tver
Smolensk
Bryansk
Kursk
Voronezh
Belgorod
Sumy
Chernihiv
Homyel
Mahilyow
Vitsyebsk
Polatsk
Hrodna
Pinsk
Rivne
Ternopil
Khmelnytskyy
Zhytomyr
Cherkasy
Poltava
Kharkiv
Donetsk
Dnipropetrovsk
Zaporozhye
Kherson
Mykolayiv
Odesa
Simferopol
Sevastopol
Kerch
Yalta
Donetsk
Luhansk
Mariupol
Kyzyl Kut
Krasnyy Kut
Volgograd
Kamyshin
Ivolzhskaya

ROMANIA
MOLDOVA
BULGARIA
UKRAINE
RUSSIA
KAZAKHSTAN
GEORGIA
ARMENIA
AZERBAIJAN
TURKEY
IRAN
BLACK SEA
Sea of Azov
Caspian Sea
Caspian Depression
Caucasus Mountains
Kuzey Anadolu Dağları
Anadolu
Pontic Mountains
Carpathians
Transylvanian Alps
Dnieper Upland
Donetsk Ridge
Volga Upland
Tsimlyanskoye Vdkhr.
Kakhovske Vdkhr.
Dnipro
Don
Volga
Kuma
Terek
Kura
Aras
Danube
Dunărea
Bosporus
Istanbul Boğazı
Marmara Denizi
Dardanelles
Çanakkale Boğazı
Sea of Marmara
Lake Van
Lake Sevan
Lake Urmia
Lake Tuz
Lake Eğirdir
Lake Beyşehir

26 ASIA

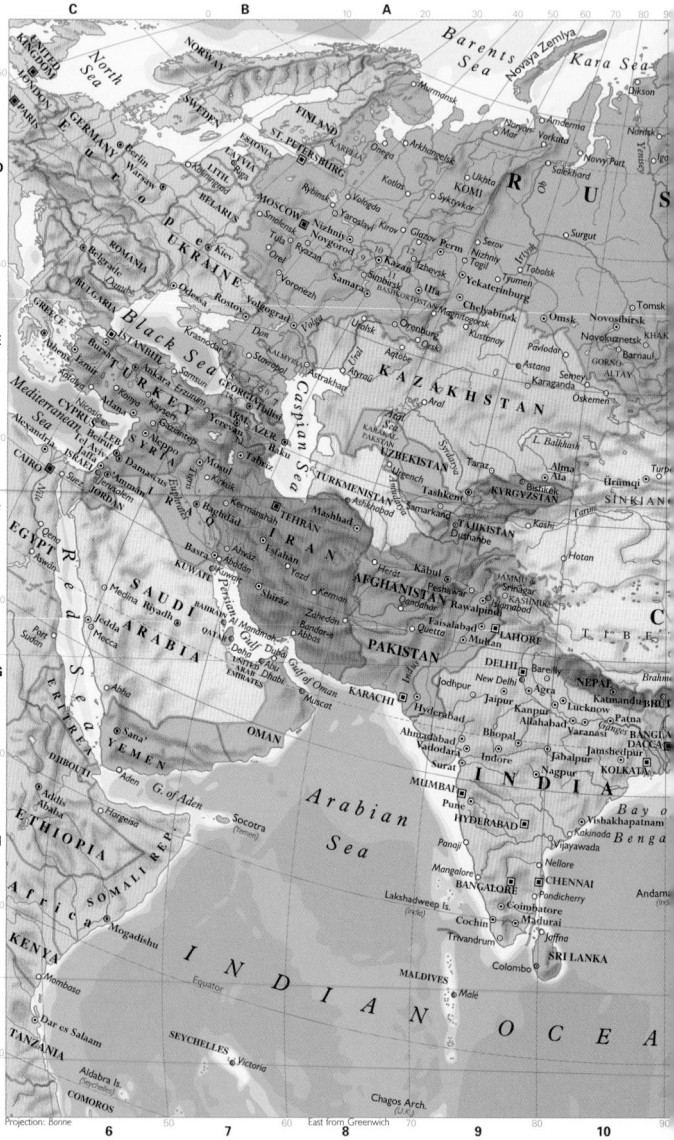
100 0 200 400 600 800 1000 1200 1400 km
100 0 200 400 600 800 1000 miles
C B A
D E F G H J
6 7 8 9 10
Barents Sea
Kara Sea
Novaya Zemlya
North Sea
Black Sea
Caspian Sea
Mediterranean Sea
Red Sea
Arabian Sea
INDIAN OCEAN
Bay of Bengal
Persian Gulf
Gulf of Oman
Gulf of Aden
Aral Sea
L. Balkhash
L. Urmia
Socotra (Yemen)
Lakshadweep Is. (India)
Andaman Is. (India)
Chagos Arch. (U.K.)
Aldabra Is. (Seychelles)
Equator
Projection: Bonne
East from Greenwich
m ft
0 200 600
1000 3000
2000 6000
4000 12000
6000 18000
8000 24000
UNITED KINGDOM
LONDON
PARIS
GERMANY
Berlin
Warsaw
NORWAY
SWEDEN
FINLAND
ESTONIA
LATVIA
Riga
LITHUANIA
BELARUS
ST. PETERSBURG
KARELIA
MOSCOW
Murmansk
Arkhangelsk
Onega
Kodas
Vologda
Yaroslavl
Kirov
Nizhniy Novgorod
Kazan
Izhevsk
Samara
Ufa
Perm
Yekaterinburg
Tyumen
Tobolsk
Surgut
Nizhniy Tagil
Serov
Ukhta
KOMI
Syktyvkar
Nenets Aut.
Vorkuta
Amderma
Dikson
Norilsk
Novy Port
Salekhard
Yenisey
Ob
RUSSIA
UKRAINE
Kiev
Odessa
Dnepr
Donetsk
Rostov
Volgograd
Volga
Voronezh
Orel
Smolensk
Tula
Ryazan
Saratov
Tambov
Penza
Ulyanovsk
Simbirsk
BASHKORTOSTAN
Ufa
Magnitogorsk
Chelyabinsk
Kustanay
Omsk
Novosibirsk
Tomsk
Novokuznetsk
KHAK
Barnaul
ALTAY
GORNO
Pavlodar
Astana
Karaganda
Semey
Oskemen
Omsk
Tobolsk
Tyumen
Ural
Aqtöbe
Aqtau
Atyrau
Astrakhand
KALMYKIA
Volgograd
Dnepr
Donetsk
Rostov
Krasnodar
Stavropol
Grozny
Makhachkala
Baku
Tbilisi
GEORGIA
ARMENIA
AZERBAIJAN
Yerevan
Gyumri
Nakhichevan
Tabriz
Mosul
Kirkuk
Erbil
Baghdad
Karbala
Kermanshah
TEHRAN
Mashhad
Esfahan
Yazd
Kerman
Shiraz
Zahedan
Bandar-e Abbas
Basra
Al Ahwaz
Abadan
Al Kuwayt
KUWAIT
BAHRAIN
QATAR
Doha
Dhahran
Al Dhahran
Abu Dhabi
UNITED ARAB EMIRATES
Muscat
OMAN
Al Mukalla
Mecca
Jeddah
Medina
Riyadh
SAUDI ARABIA
Al Ma'ani
Al Ma'an
Amman
JORDAN
Damascus
SYRIA
Aleppo
Latakia
Homs
Hama
Ankara
Eskişehir
Konya
Adana
Kayseri
Gaziantep
TURKEY
ISTANBUL
Bursa
Izmir
Denizli
Antalya
Samsun
Trabzon
Erzurum
Van
Diyarbakır
Batman
Mardin
Şanlıurfa
Kars
Erzincan
Sivas
Tokat
Zonguldak
Kastamonu
Sinop
Samsun

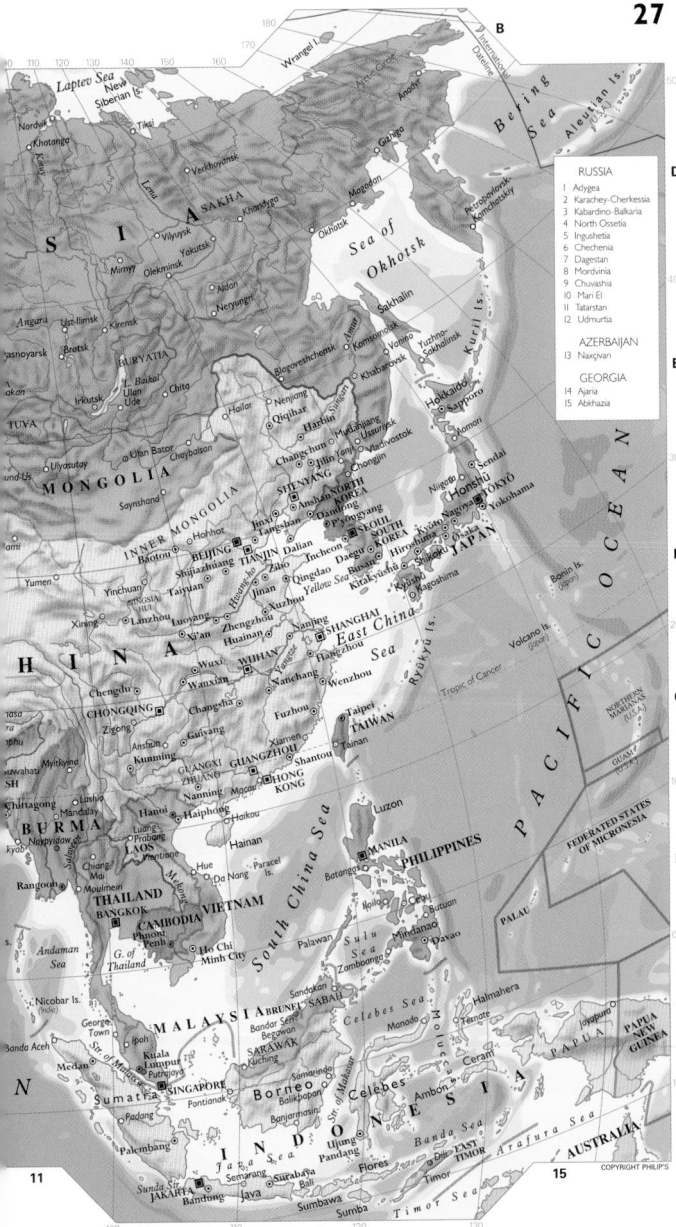
RUSSIA
1 Adygea
2 Karachey-Cherkessia
3 Kabardino-Balkaria
4 North Ossetia
5 Ingushetia
6 Chechenia
7 Dagestan
8 Mordvinia
9 Chuvashia
10 Mari El
11 Tatarstan
12 Udmurtia
AZERBAIJAN
13 Naxçivan
GEORGIA
14 Ajaria
15 Abkhazia
Laptev Sea
New Siberian Is.
Wrangel I.
Arctic Circle
International Dateline
Anadyr
Bering Sea
Aleutian Is.
Nordvik
Tiksi
Khatanga
Lena
Verkhoyansk
Gizhiga
Magadan
Petropavlovsk-Kamchatskiy
SIBERIA
SAKHA
Khandyga
Vilyuysk
Yakutsk
Okhotsk
Sea of Okhotsk
Sakhalin
Kuril Is.
Mirnyy
Olekminsk
Aldan
Neryungri
Angara
Ust-Ilimsk
Kirensk
Bratsk
Krasnoyarsk
BURYATIA
Ulan-Ude
Baikal
Chita
Irkutsk
Blagoveshchensk
Amur
Komsomolsk
Yuzhno-Sakhalinsk
Khabarovsk
Hokkaido
Sapporo
Kunashiri
Nenjiang
Qiqihar
Harbin
Mudanjiang
Ussuriysk
Vladivostok
Changchun
Jilin
Yanji
Chongjin
Niigata
Sendai
Honshu
TOKYO
Yokohama
Nagoya
Kyoto
Osaka
Kobe
JAPAN
Hiroshima
Kyushu
Kitakyushu
Fukuoka
Nagasaki
Kagoshima
Ryukyu Is.
Volcano Is. (Japan)
Bonin Is. (Japan)
Tropic of Cancer
NORTHERN MARIANAS (USA)
GUAM (USA)
FEDERATED STATES OF MICRONESIA
PALAU
PACIFIC OCEAN
TUVA
Ulyasutay
Ulan Bator
Choybalsan
MONGOLIA
Saynshand
INNER MONGOLIA
Hohhot
Baotou
BEIJING
Shijiazhuang
TIANJIN
Dalian
Zhao
Qingdao
Jinan
Yellow Sea
Taiyuan
Yinchuan
Xining
Lanzhou
Luoyang
Zhengzhou
Xuzhou
Xi'an
Huainan
Nanjing
SHANGHAI
East China Sea
Hangzhou
Wenzhou
Wuxi
WUHAN
Nanchang
Wanxian
Changsha
Chengdu
CHONGQING
Zigong
Kunming
Guiyang
Anshun
Fuzhou
Taipei
TAIWAN
Tainan
Xiamen
GUANGZHOU
Shantou
HONG KONG
Nanning
Macao
Haikou
Hainan
Hanoi
Haiphong
Luang Prabang
LAOS
Vientiane
Hue
Da Nang
Paracel Is.
Chittagong
Mandalay
Myitkyina
BURMA
Rangoon
Moulmein
Chiang Mai
THAILAND
BANGKOK
CAMBODIA
Phnom Penh
VIETNAM
Ho Chi Minh City
Andaman Sea
G. of Thailand
South China Sea
Luzon
MANILA
PHILIPPINES
Batangas
Iloilo
Cebu
Butuan
Mindanao
Davao
Palawan
Sulu Sea
Zamboanga
Sandakan
BRUNEI
SABAH
Bandar Seri Begawan
SARAWAK
Kuching
Celebes Sea
Halmahera
Ternate
Manado
Molucca Sea
Ceram
Ambon
Jayapura
PAPUA
PAPUA NEW GUINEA
Nicobar Is. (India)
George Town
Ipoh
Kuala Lumpur
Putrajaya
MALAYSIA
Banda Aceh
Medan
Sumatra
Padang
Palembang
SINGAPORE
Pontianak
Borneo
Samarinda
Balikpapan
Banjarmasin
Celebes
Sea of Makassar
INDONESIA
Banda Sea
Ujung Pandang
Flores
Dili
EAST TIMOR
Timor
Arafura Sea
AUSTRALIA
Java Sea
Sunda Str.
JAKARTA
Bandung
Semarang
Surabaya
Bali
Java
Sumbawa
Sumba
Timor Sea
COPYRIGHT PHILIP'S
11
15

28 WESTERN RUSSIA AND CENTRAL ASIA

RUSSIA
1 Adygea
2 Karachay-Cherkessia
3 Kabardino-Balkaria
4 North Ossetia
5 Ingushetia
6 Chechenia
7 Dagestan
8 Kalmykia
9 Chuvashia
10 Mari El
11 Tatarstan
12 Udmurtia
13 Khakassia
14 AZERBAIJAN Nakhichevan
15 GEORGIA Ajaria
16 Abkhazia
UKRAINE 17 Crimea
ARCTIC OCEAN
Barents Sea
Kara Sea
Novaya Zemlya
Zemlya Georga
Zemlya Frantsa Iosifa
Ostrov Rudolfa
Ostrov Green-Bell
Ostrov Bely
Ostrov Kolguyev
Ostrov Vaygach
Ostrov Vaskin
Ostrov Kamenny
Poluostrov Yamal
Poluostrov Gydanskiy
Poluostrov Kanin
Poluostrov Kola
Poluostrov Rybachiy
Poluostrov Kanin Nos
Mys Sporiy Navolok
Mys Kanin Nos
Pik Sidorova
Nordkapp
Hammerfest
Vardo
Murmansk
Petsamo
Gremikha
Kolvitsa
Kandalaksha
Apatity
Polyarnyy
Kuzomen
Arkhangelsk
Mezen
Onega
Belomorsk
Kem
Kostomuksha
Severodvinsk
Belomorskaya Gryada
Nordkapp
Nordstad
Narvik
Gallivare
Haparanda
Oulu
Ylivieska
Kajaani
Kuopio
Joensuu
Lappeenranta
Vyborg
Petrozavodsk
Medvezhyegorsk
Lodeynoye Pole
Ozerskiy
Cherepovets
Vologda
Kostroma
Gorkiy
Kirovo-Chepetsk
Kirov
Vyatka
Sosnovka
Kotelnich
Yaranskiy
Sovetskiy
Yoshkar-Ola
Cheboksary
Kazan
Yelabuga
Nizhnekamsk
Almetyevsk
Bugulma
Buzuluk
Sarapul
Izhevsk
Ufa
Sterlitamak
Beloretsk
Magnitogorsk
Kyshtym
Chelyabinsk
Zlatoust
Miass
Kurgan
Ishim
Tobolsk
Nizhnevartovsk
Surgut
Nizhnyaya Tunguska
Yenisey
Ob
Nadym
Novy Urengoy
Tazovskiy
Tarko Sale
Krasnoselkup
Igarka
Garmaso

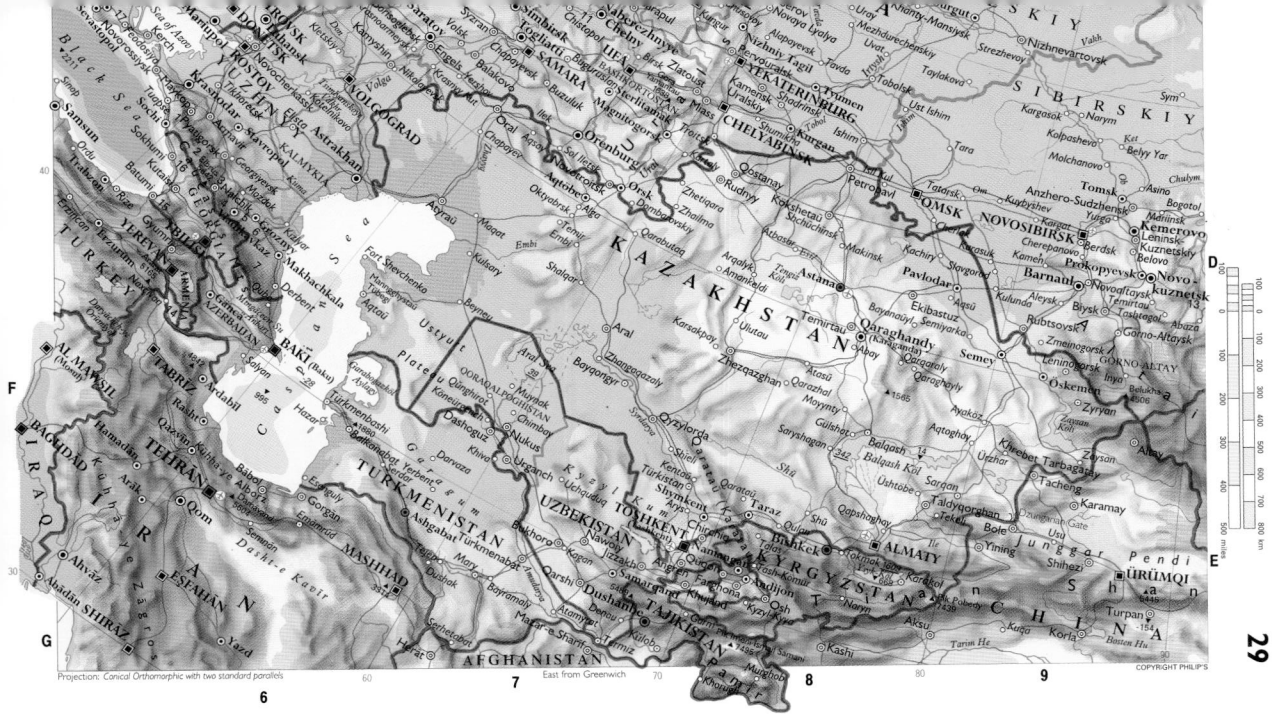
KAZAKHSTAN
TURKMENISTAN
UZBEKISTAN
KYRGYZSTAN
TAJIKISTAN
AFGHANISTAN
CHINA
IRAN
IRAQ
TURKEY
ARMENIA
AZERBAIJAN
GEORGIA
RUSSIA
MONGOLIA
Black Sea
Caspian Sea
Aral Sea
Sea of Azov
Persian Gulf
Ural Mts
Caucasus Mts
Kuh-e Zagros
Kuh-e Kavir
Dasht-e Kavir
Plateau Ustyurt
Plateau Ustyurt
Kyzyl Kum
Kyzyl Kum
Pendi Turpan
Jungar Pendi
Khyber Pass
Tarbagatay
Tacheng
Karamay
Bole
Yining
Shihezi
Turpan
Aksu
Kashi
Korla
Kuqa
Tarim He
Bishkek
Almaty
Taldyqorghan
Ashgabat
Mashhad
Esfahan
Shiraz
Yazd
Tehran
Tabriz
Baghdad
Al Mawsil
Baku
Yerevan
Tbilisi
Kutaisi
Sochi
Sukhumi
Trabzon
Samsun
Erzurum
Kars
Ankara
Kayseri
Adana
Mersin
Antakya
Gaziantep
Diyarbakir
Van
Batumi
Kerch
Simferopol
Sevastopol
Yalta
Mariupol
Donetsk
Rostov
Volgograd
Astrakhan
Stavropol
Krasnodar
Kalmykia
Saratov
Samara
Ufa
Orenburg
Aktobe
Orsk
Magnitogorsk
Chelyabinsk
Kurgan
Ekaterinburg
Tyumen
Tobolsk
Omsk
Novosibirsk
Barnaul
Biysk
Kemerovo
Novokuznetsk
Tomsk
Karaganda
Astana
Pavlodar
Semey
Oskemen
Almaty
Bishkek
Dushanbe
Tashkent
Samarkand
Bukhara
Khiva
Urgench
Nukus

30 EASTERN SIBERIA

31
100 0 100 200 300 400 500 600 700 800 km
100 0 100 200 300 400 500 miles
C
B
D
E
14
15
16
9
10
11
Mys Dezhneva (East C.)
St. Lawrence I. (USA)
Chukchi Sea
Ostrov Vrangelya
East Siberian Sea
Ostrov Novaya Sibir
Ostrov Bennetovskiy
Ostrov Geleniyakh
Ostrov Zhanetty
Ostrov Delongi
Ostrov Zemlya Bunge
Ostrov Fadeyevskiy
Ostrov Belkovskiy
Ostrov Malyy Lyakhovskiy
Ostrov Kotelnyy
Proliv Dmitriyya Laptieva
Mys Buorkhaya
Ostrov Ayan
Ostrov Matvevshi
Ambarchik
Chersky
Nizhne Kolymsk
Bolshoy Anyuy
Olenek
Tiksi
Bulun
Yakutsk
Pevek
Ust Chaun
Chokurdakh
Mazozhe
Ust Kunga
Druzhina
Deputatskiy
Verkhoyansk
Batagay
Verkhoyanskiy Khrebet
Khrebet Chekanovskogo
Khrebet Dzhugdzur
Khrebet Stanovoy
Khrebet Sikhote Alin
Da Hinggan Ling
Sredne Kolymsk
Zyryanka
Kolyma
Ust Nera
Susuman
Ust Omchug
Omsukchan
Magadan
Okhotsk
Ulya
Ust Maya
Aldan
Tommot
Nerungri
Tyndo
Skovorodino
Zeya
Ust Myukzha
Kolokan
Magdagachi
Shilka
Nerchinsk
Aginskoye
Olovyannaya
Borzya
Zabaykalsk
Manchouli
Hailar
Hailar Nar
Nenjiang
Beian
Hegang
Yichun
Jiamusi
QIQIHAR
DAQING
HARBIN
JIXI
Mudanjiang
Harbin
Bucheng
Yanji
Koskino
Nakhodka
Vladivostok
Ussuriysk
Artem
Dalnegorsk
Dalnerechensk
Lesozavodsk
Ternay
Olga
Dolinsk
Poronaysk
Sakhalinskiy Zaliv
Sakhalin
Okha
Nikolayevsk-na-Amure
Sovetskaya Gavan
Vanino
Komsomolsk
Khabarovsk
Birobidzhan
Smidovich
Obluchye
Roychikhinsk
Zavitinsk
Belogorsk
Shimanovsk
Svobodnyy
Tyndinskiy
Ust Ulma
Ust Nera
Ust Omchug
Ust Khoryuzovka
Ust Bolsheretsk
Petropavlovsk-Kamchatskiy
Kirovskiy
Ust Kamchatsk
Poluostrov Kamchatka
Khrebet Kamchatka
Sea of Okhotsk
Kurilskiye Ostrova
Ostrov Paramushir
Ostrov Onekotan
Ostrov Simushir
Ostrov Urup
Ostrov Iturup
Ostrov Kunashir
Ostrov Shikotan
Ostrov Zelenyy
Ostrov Tyuleniy
Ostrov Moneron
Ostrov Rebun
Ostrov Rishiri
Ostrov Sakhalin
Tatarskiy Proliv
Hokkaido
SAPPORO
Otaru
Obihiro
Kushiro
Abashiri
Rumoi
Wakkanai
Hakodate
Aomori
Hachinohe
JAPAN
Ostrov Sado
Ostrov Hokkaido

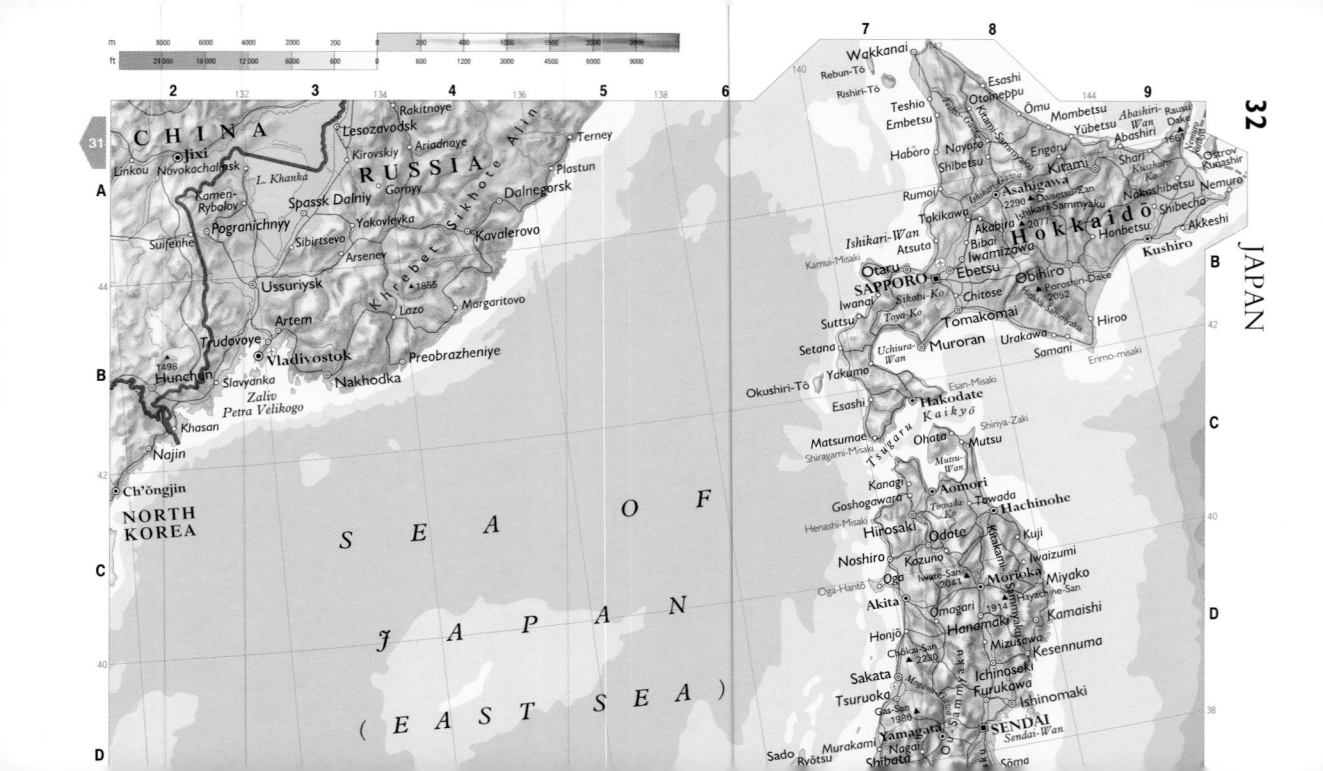
m 8000 6000 4000 2000 200 0 200 400 1000 1500 2000 3000
ft 24000 18000 12000 6000 600 0 600 1200 3000 4500 6000 9000
CHINA
Jixi
Linkou
Novokachalinsk
L. Khanka
Kamen-Rybalov
Pogranichnyy
Suifenhe
Spassk Dalniy
Rakitnoye
Lesozavodsk
Kirovskiy
Ariadnoye
Gornyy
Yakovlevka
Sibirtsevo
Arseniev
RUSSIA
Khrebet Sikhote Alin
Terney
Plastun
Dalnegorsk
Kavalerovo
Ussuriysk
1855
Lazo
Margaritovo
Artem
Trudovoye
Vladivostok
Preobrazheniye
Nakhodka
Hunchun
1498
Slavyanka
Zaliv Petra Velikogo
Khasan
Najin
Ch'ongjin
NORTH KOREA
SEA OF JAPAN (EAST SEA)
Wakkanai
Rebun-Tō
Rishiri-Tō
Esashi
Otaheppu
Teshio
Embetsu
Ōmu
Mombetsu
Yubetsu
Abashiri-Wan
Abashiri
Rausu Dake
1660
Haboro
Nayoro
Shibetsu
Engaru
Kitami
Shari
Kushiro-Ko
Ōgaro Kuasshir
Nemuro
Rumoi
Ishikari-Sammyaku
Asahigawa
2290
Daisetsu-San
Ishikari-Sammyaku
Nakashibetsu
Shibecha
Takikawa
Akabira
2077
Hokkaidō
Honbetsu
Akkeshi
Ishikari-Wan
Atsuta
Bibai
Iwamizawa
Kushiro
Kamui-Misaki
Otaru
SAPPORO
Ebetsu
Obihiro
Iwanai
Shikotsu-Ko
Chitose
Porosh-Dake
2052
Suttsu
Toya-Ko
Tomakomai
Hiroo
Setana
Uchiura-Wan
Muroran
Urakawa
Samani
Enimo-misaki
Okushiri-Tō
Yakumo
Esan-Misaki
Esashi
Hakodate
Kaikyō
Shirya-Zaki
Matsumae
Shiragami-Misaki
Ohata
Mutsu
Tsugaru
Mutsu-Wan
Kanagi
Aomori
Goshogawara
Tsugaru-Kō
Towada
Hachinohe
Henashi-Misaki
Hirosaki
Odate
Kuji
Kitakami
Noshiro
Kazuno
Iwaizumi
Ōga
Iwate-San
2041
Morioka
Miyako
Ōga-Hantō
Hayachine-San
Akita
Ōu-Sammyaku
Kamaishi
Omagari
1914
Honjō
Hanamaki
Mizusawa
Chōkai-San
2236
Kesennuma
Sakata
Ichinoseki
Furukawa
Tsuruoka
Ishinomaki
Gas-San
1386
Yamagata
SENDAI
Sendai-Wan
Murakami
Nagai
Shibata
Sado
Ryōtsu
Sōma
132
134
136
138
140
144
31
32
A
B
C
D
2
3
4
5
6
7
8
9
42
44
40
38

JAPAN
Honshū
Hokkaidō
Kyūshū
Shikoku
SOUTH KOREA
Korea Strait
PACIFIC OCEAN
Nampō Shotō
Ulleungdo (S. Korea)
Liancourt Rocks (Dokdo, Takeshima)
Oki-Shotō (Japan)
Tsushima (Japan)
Yeongdeok
Pohang
ULSAN
Aikawa
Niigata
Niitsu
Sanjo
Aizuwakamatsu
Fukushima
Koriyama
Iwaki
Nagaoka
Tokamachi
Sukagawa
Kitaibaraki
Hitachi
Wajima
Suzu
Nanao
Himi
Hakui
Takaoka
Kanazawa
Toyama
Takada
Iiyama
Nagano
Maebashi
Kusatsu
Kiryū
Hitsumoiya
Mito
Oyama
Tsuchiura
Komatsu
Tokuyama
Matsumoto
Kamagaya
Kawagoe
Kawaguchi
Funabashi
Chiba
Ichihara
TŌKYŌ
KAWASAKI
YOKOHAMA
Yokosuka
Fukui
Takefu
Gero
Tsuruga
Ōgaki
Ichinomiya
Gifu
Iida
Ina
Kofu
Odawara
Numazu
Tateyama
Itō
Ō-Shima
Izu-Shotō
Nii-Jima
Miyake-Jima
Hachijō-Jima
Aogashima
Matsue
Yonago
Tottori
Toyooka
Izumo
Ōda
Hamada
Masuda
Miyoshi
Fuchū
HIROSHIMA
Fukuyama
Kure
Hagi
Yamaguchi
Iwakuni
Ube
Hofu
Tokuyama
Shimonoseki
Katsumoto
Nōgata
KITAKYŪSHŪ
FUKUOKA
Karatsu
Buzen
Beppu
Saga
Imari
Kurume
Ōita
Omuta
Sasebo
Kumamoto
Saiki
Isahaya
Nagasaki
Yatsushiro
Nobeoka
Hyūga
Fukue-Shima
Hondo
Amakusa-Shotō
Ushibuka
Minamata
Kurino
Miyazaki
Miyakonojō
Sendai
Kagoshima
Makurazaki
Nichinan
Kanoya
Ibusuki
Koshiki-Rettō
Gotō-Rettō
Sukumo
Ashizuri-Zaki
Nakamura
Uwajima
Yawatahama
Shikoku
Matsuyama
Imabari
Ikeda
Tokushima
Naruto
Takamatsu
Kōchi
Muroto
Nankoku
Tosa-Wan
Muroto-Misaki
Shio-no-Misaki
Tanabe
Shingū
Kushimoto
Owase
Wakayama
Izumi-Sano
Matsusaka
OSAKA
Higashiōsaka
Amagasaki
KOBE
Himeji
Nishinomiya
Okayama
KYŌTO
Otsu
Yokkaichi
NAGOYA
Toyota
Okazaki
Toyohashi
Iwata
Hamamatsu
Shizuoka
Fuji
Tsuruga
Obama
Maizuru
Ayabe
Fukuchiyama
Tsuyama
Echizen-Misaki
Wakasa-Wan
Kyō-ga-Saki
Daiō-Misaki
Sata-Misaki
Ashizuri-Misaki
Tsurugi-San
Kuju-San
Aso-San
Daisen
Hakusan
Ontake-San
Fuji-San
Tsukuba-San
Nasu-Dake
Hodaka-Dake
Yatsugatake
Kiso-Sanchi
Kinki-Sanchi
Chūgoku-Sanchi
Kyūshū-Sanchi
Shikoku-Sanchi
Bungo-Suidō
Kii-Sanchi
Ise-Wan
Suruga-Wan
Kanto-Sanchi
Tanakura
Yaita
Shirane-San
Tsumagoi-Kō

34 CHINA

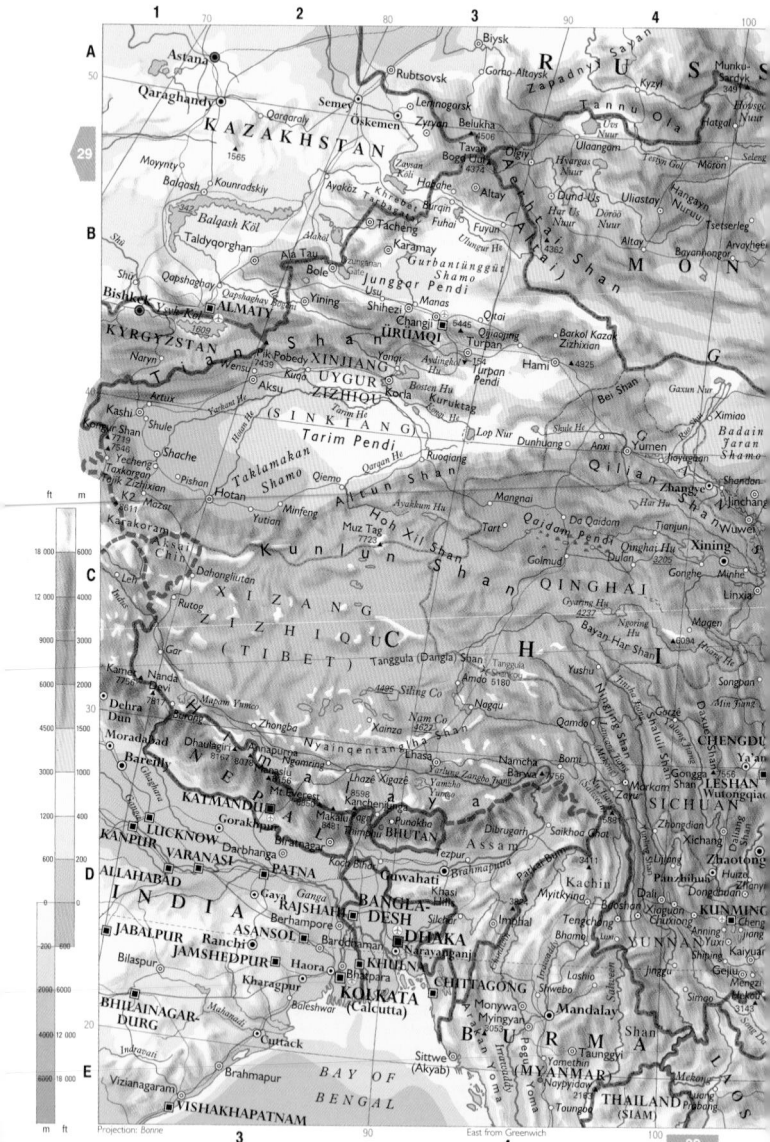
Astana
Qaraghandy
KAZAKHSTAN
Semey
Öskemen
Biysk
Rubtsovsk
Gorno-Altaysk
RUSSIA
Zapadnyy Sayan
Munku-Sardyk
Tannu Ola
Kyzyl
Hatgal
Ulaangom
Uvs Nuur
Hovsgol Nuur
Moron
Saleng
Mayynty
Balqash
Kounradskiy
Balqash Köl
Taldyqorghan
Ayakoz
Tacheng
Altay
Altai Shan
Dund-Us
Uliastay
Hangayn Nuruu
Tsetserleg
Arvayheer
Bayanhongor
MONGOLIA
Ala Tau
Bole
Yining
Shihezi
Junggar Pendi
Gurbantünggüt Shamo
Karamay
Fuhai
Fuyun
Qapshagbay
Bishkek
Issyk Kul
ALMATY
KYRGYZSTAN
Tian Shan
Naryn
Pobeda
Wensu
Kuqa
Aksu
Artux
Changji
ÜRÜMQI
Qitai
Qijiaping
Turpan
Barkol Kazak Zizhixian
Turpan Pendi
Hami
Bei Shan
Gaxun Nur
XINJIANG UYGUR ZIZHIQU (SINKIANG)
Kashi
Shule
Kashgar Shan
Shache
Yecheng
Taxkorgan
Tajik Zizhixian
K2
Mazar
Pishan
Hotan
Minfeng
Yutian
Karakoram
Aksai Chin
Dahongliutan
Tarim Pendi
Taklamakan Shamo
Kuqa He
Yarkand He
Hotan He
Keriya He
Niya He
Kuruktag
Bosten Hu
Lop Nur
Shule He
Dunhuang
Ruoqiang
Qarqan He
Qiemo
Altun Shan
Anxi
Yumen
Jiayuguan
Badain Jaran Shamo
Qilian Shan
Zhangye
Shandan
Jinchang
Wuwei
Mangnai
Tart
Da Qaidam
Qaidam Pendi
Muz Tag
Hoh Xil Shan
Kunlun Shan
Golmud
Dulan
Qinghai Hu
Xining
Minhe
Gonghe
Linxia
QINGHAI
Gyaring Hu
Ngoring Hu
Magen
Bayan Har Shan
Huang He
Yushu
Songpan
XIZANG ZIZHIQU (TIBET)
Tanggula (Dangla) Shan
Tanggula
Amdo 5180
Siling Co
Nagqu
Nam Co
Xainza
Nyainqentanglha Shan
Lhasa
Namcha Barwa
Bomi
Nujiang He
Jinsha Jiang
Dadu He
Min Jiang
Qamdo
Gonjo
Shaluli Shan
Gongga Shan
Kangding
Ya'an
CHENGDU
LESHAN
Wutongqiao
SICHUAN
Markam
Zerong
Zhongdian
Xichang
Zhaotong
Huize
Panzhihua
Dongchuan
Dali
Baoshan
Xiaoguan
Chuxiong
Chenggong
Jiang
KUNMING
Anning
Yuxi
Shiping
Kaiyuan
YUNNAN
Jingxi
Geiju
Mengzi
Simao
Lashio
Shwebo
Mandalay
Myingyan
Taungdwin
Yamethin
Naypyidaw
Taungoo
BURMA (MYANMAR)
Shan
Salween
Mekong
Mae Nam Chao Phraya
THAILAND (SIAM)
Tanlwin
Irrawaddy
Chindwin
Pegu Yoma
Arakan Yoma
Kaladan
Kabaw
Mahanadi
Indravati
Godavari
Bilaspur
Raipur
Nanded
Dehra Dun
Moradabad
Dhaulagiri
Bareilly
Pokhara
Annapurna
Manaslu
Ganesh Himal
Dhaulagiri
Lucknow
Gorakhpur
Lumbini
Makalu
Everest
Lhaze
Xigaze
Kanchenjunga
Pumo Ri
Thimphu
BHUTAN
Dibrugarh
Saikhoa Ghat
Assam
Kanpur
Varanasi
Darbhanga
Patna
Allahabad
Gaya
Ganga
Tezpur
Brahmaputra
Guwahati
Khasi Hills
Kachin
Myitkyina
Imphal
Chindwin
Tengchong
Bhamo
INDIA
Rajshahi
BANGLADESH
DHAKA
Sylhet
Berhampore
Barddhaman
Narayanganj
Asansol
Ranchi
Jabalpur
Jamshedpur
Haora
Bhatpara
KHULNA
CHITTAGONG
Kharagpur
KOLKATA (Calcutta)
Baleshwar
Bhilainagar-Durg
Cuttack
Sittwe (Akyab)
Brahmapur
Vizianagaram
VISHAKHAPATNAM
BAY OF BENGAL
Andaman Islands
Nicobar Islands
Projection: Bonne
East from Greenwich
ft
m
18 000
12 000
9000
6000
4500
3000
1200
600
0
200
2000
4000
6000
5500
4000
3000
2000
1500
400
200
0
600
6000
12 000
18 000

100 0 100 200 300 400 500 600 700 800 km
100 0 100 200 300 400 500 miles
31
5
6
7
8
A
B
C
D
Irkutsk
Ulan Ude
Chita
Oz. Baykal
Bukachacha
Sretensk
Nerchinsk
Olovyannaya
Borzoya
Pokrovsk
Zabaykalsky
Nauchnogorsky
Kyakhta
Ulanbulag
Darhan
Henteyn Nuurtu
Erdenet
Bulgan
Ulaanbaatar
Choybalsan
Ondorhaan
Dzamnmod
Tamsagbulag
Baruun-Urt
Kerulen
Hailar
Zalantun
Hanzhouli
Yakeshi
Bei'an
Fuyu
Nenjiang
Heihe (Aihui)
Yilehuli Shan
Oroqen Zizhiqi
Blagoveshchensk
Bureya
Obluchye
Birobidzhan
Khabarovsk
Komsomolsk
Cheedomyn
Svobodnyy
Shimanovsk
Xiao Hinggan Ling
Da Hinggan Ling
Mudanjiang
Ussuriysk
Vladivostok
Nakhodka
Ch'ŏngjin
Kimch'aek
Hŭngnam
Wŏnsan
Kaesŏng
Chŏrchŏn
Gangneung
Haeju
Namp'o
PYŏNGYANG
SEOUL
INCHEON
DAEJEON
DAEGU
BUSAN
Masan
Gunsan
Jeonju
GWANGJU
Mokpo
Tsushima
FUKUOKA
Nagasaki
Jeju-do (S. Korea)
Jeju
Korea Strait
JAPAN
Ryukyu-retto
Naha
Okinawa-Jima
Senkaku-Shotō
Sakishima-Gunto
Miyako-Jima
Ishigaki-Shima
Iriomote-Jima
Tropic of Cancer
TAIWAN
Yu Shan (FORMOSA)
T'aitung
P'ingtung
KAOHSIUNG
T'aichung
Changhua
T'aipei
Hsinchu
Chilung
Tainan
Chiayi
Hualien
Taitung
Putian
Quanzhou
Xiamen
Zhangzhou
Longyan
Yong'an
Sanming
Nanping
FUZHOU
Min Jiang
Wuyi Shan
Jiangxi
Jian
Ganzhou
Ruijin
Meizhou
Chaozhou
Shantou
Shaoguan
Guilin
Liuzhou
Wuzhou
Zhaoqing
Foshan
Jiangmen
Yangjiang
Macao
GUANGZHOU (Canton)
Huizhou
SHENZHEN
HONG KONG (Xianggang)
Batan Is.
Babuyan Is.
Luzon Str.
PHILIPPINES
Luzon
Laoag
2048
SOUTH CHINA SEA
Hainan Dao
HAINAN
Sanya
Haikou
Bandao
Leizhou
Zhanjiang
Maoming
Qinzhou
Beihai
Nam Dinh
HANOI
HAIPHONG
VIETNAM
Tonkin
G. of Tonkin
Pingxiang
Wenshan
KUNMING
Zhuzhou
Yichun
Jiujiang
Jingdezhen
Quzhou
Shangrao
Linhai
WENZHOU
Xinyang
Zhumadian
Nanyang
Shiyan
Yichang
Jingzhou
Jiaxing
Hangzhou Wan
HANGZHOU
NINGBO
EAST CHINA SEA
Ma'anshan
Wuhu
Anqing
Huangshan
Shaoxing
Tongling
Huainan
Bengbu
Huaibei
Suzhou
Changzhou
Nantong
Yangzhou
Lianyungang
Yancheng
Xinghua
Jiangyin
Wuxi
SHANGHAI
Kunshan
Qidong
Jinhua

35
38
PHILIPPINES
Luzon
MANILA
Quezon City
Olongapo
Cabanatuan
Tuguegarao
Baguio
Legaspi
Naga
Lucena
Batangas
Catanduanes
Mindoro
Palawan
Puerto Princesa
Cuyo Is.
Cagayan Is.
Calamian Group
Coron
Culion
Tawi-Tawi
Sulu Group
Jolo
Basilan
Zamboanga
Cotabato
DAVAO
General Santos
Mindanao
Bohol
Negros
Cebu
Leyte
Samar
Tacloban
Iloilo
Bacolod
Cagayan de Oro
Surigao
Butuan
Dumaguete
Tagbilaran
Kalibo
Roxas City
Tacloban
Sorsogon
Catarman
Calbayog
Ormoc
Maasbate
Tablas
Romblon

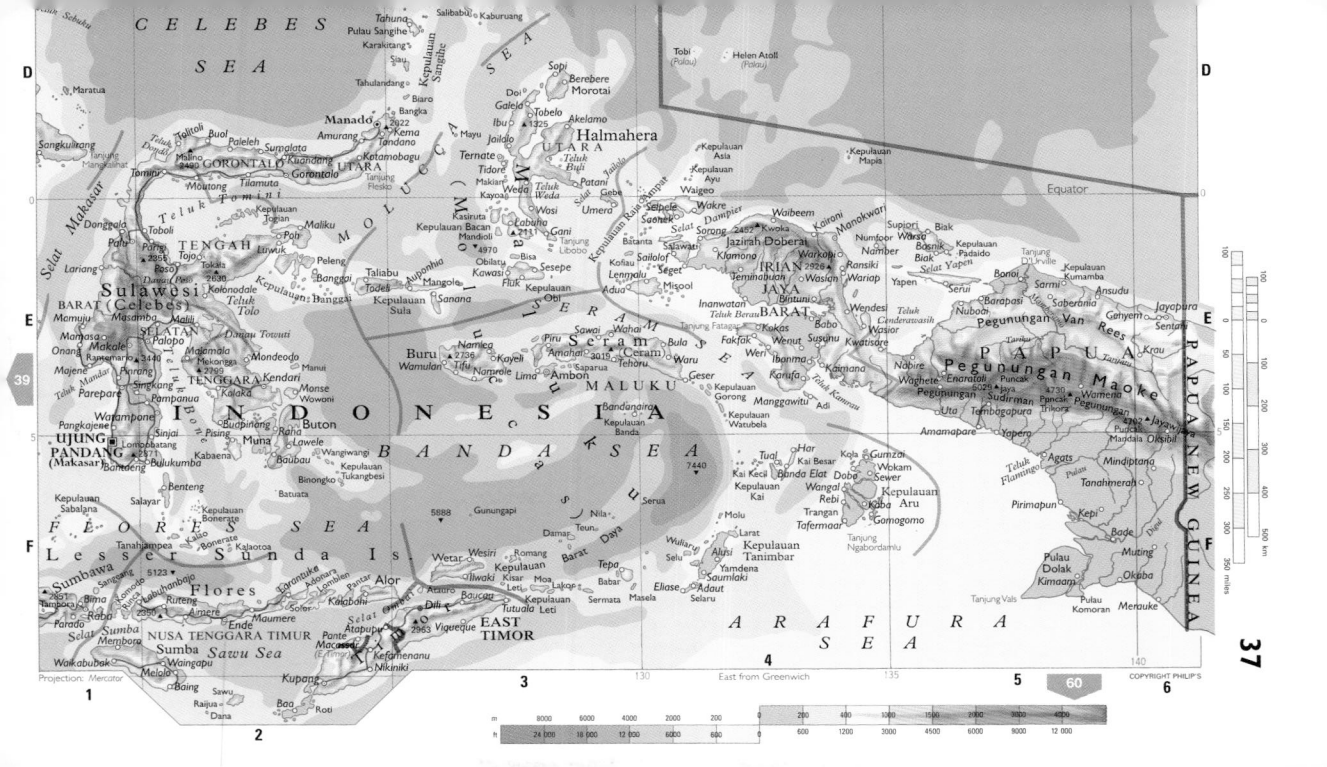
CELEBES SEA
Halmahera
Sulawesi
INDONESIA
BANDA SEA
FLORES SEA
Les Petites Sunda Is
ARAFURA SEA
PAPUA NEW GUINEA
Pegunungan Maoke
Pegunungan Van Rees
Equator
Selat Makassar
Selat Sumba
Sumba Sawu Sea
NUSA TENGGARA TIMUR
EAST TIMOR
Flores
Sumbawa
Alor
Seram
Buru
Sumba
Kupang
Manado
Ternate
Tidore
Jayapura
Sorong
Merauke
Projection: Mercator
East from Greenwich
COPYRIGHT PHILIP'S
37
39
60

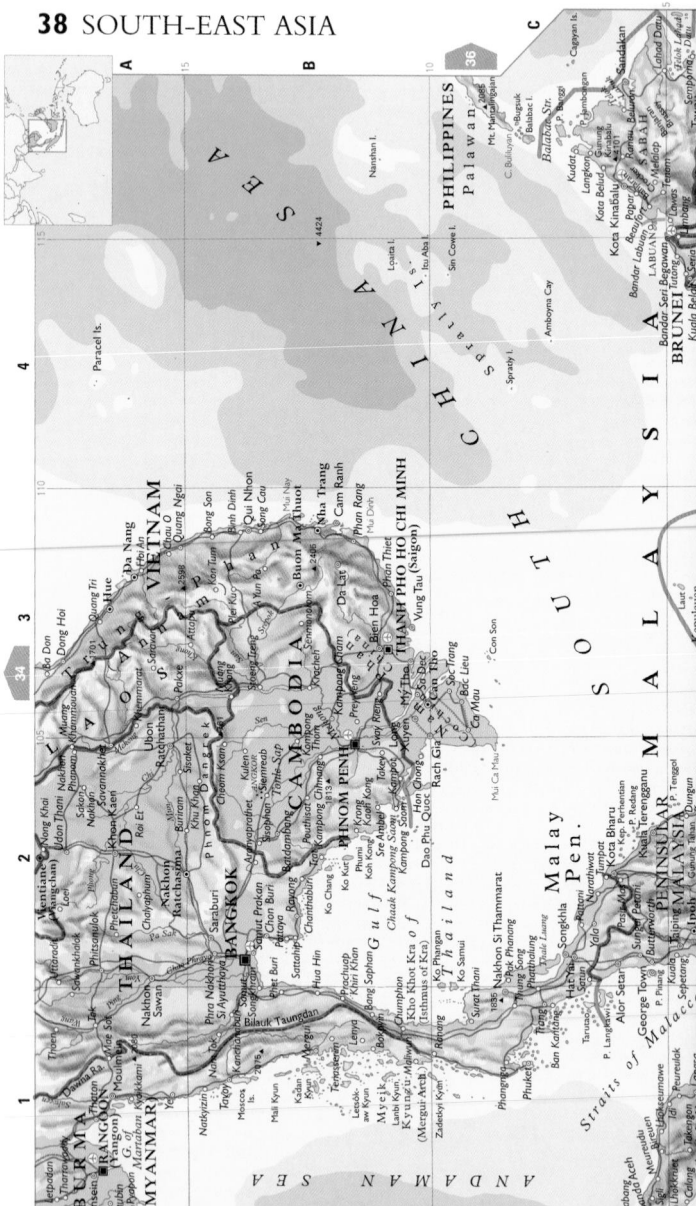
BURMA
(MYANMAR)
RANGOON
THAILAND
BANGKOK
LAOS
VIETNAM
CAMBODIA
PHNOM PENH
THANH PHO HO CHI MINH
(Saigon)
PHILIPPINES
Palawan
SOUTH CHINA SEA
Spratly Is.
Paracel Is.
Gulf of Thailand
Malay Pen.
Straits of Malacca
ANDAMAN SEA
MALAYSIA
PENINSULAR
SABAH
BRUNEI
Kuala Belait
Bandar Seri Begawan
Kota Kinabalu
Kota Bharu
Kuala Terengganu
Kuala Lumpur
Singapore
Medan
Banda Aceh
Sandakan
Tawau
Kuching
Miri
Bintulu
Kuantan
Mergui Arch.
Tenasserim
Mae Sot
Chiang Mai
Mandalay
Pegu
Moulmein
Tavoy
Mergui
Phuket
Hat Yai
Songkhla
Nakhon Si Thammarat
Surat Thani
Ban Karfakhee
Alor Setar
Ipoh
Seremban
Johor Bahru
Pekanbaru
Dumai
Sibolga
Pematangsiantar
Lhokseumawe
Sabang
Pulau Weh
Nanthan I.
Natuna Is.
Anambas Is.
Tioman I.
Pulau Pinang
Pulau Langkawi

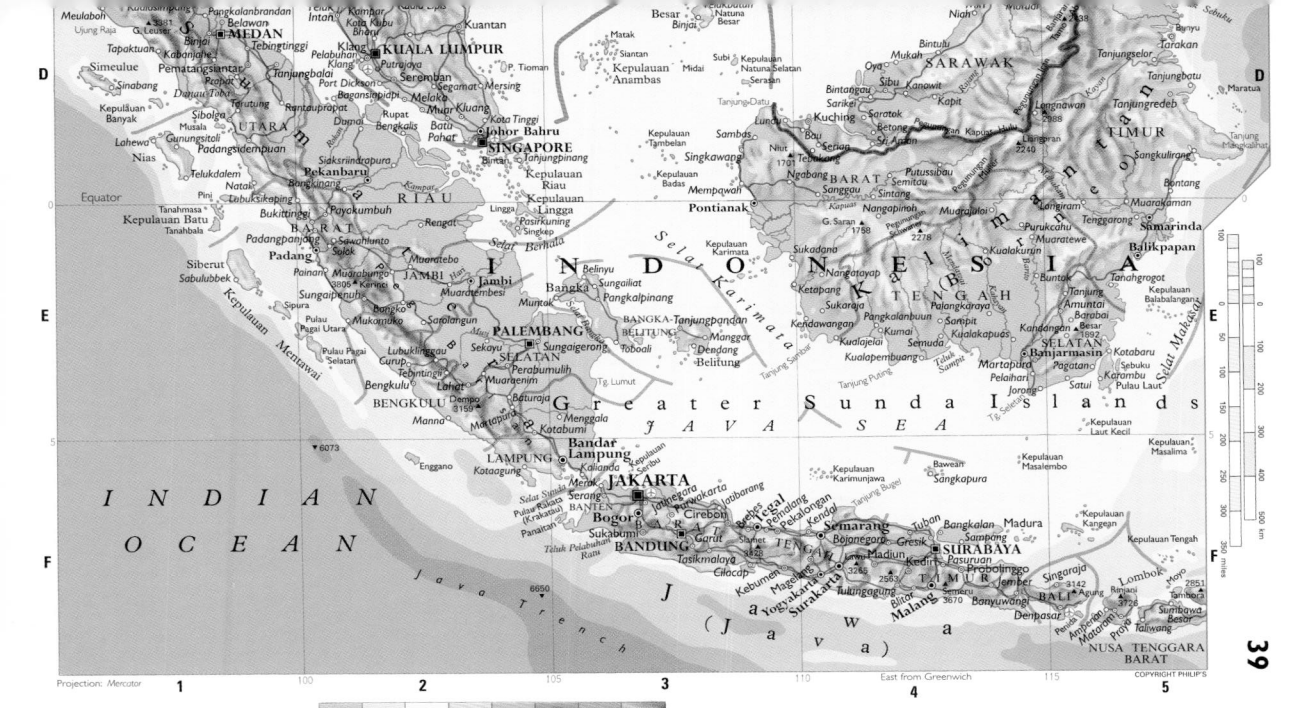
I N D O N E S I A
Greater Sunda Islands
INDIAN OCEAN
JAVA SEA
Java Trench
Selat Karimata
Selat Makassar
Selat Berhala
Selat Sunda
Kepulauan Mentawai
Kepulauan Riau
Kepulauan Natuna
Kepulauan Anambas
Kepulauan Tambelan
Kepulauan Badas
Kepulauan Karimata
Kepulauan Karimunjawa
Kepulauan Masalembo
Kepulauan Laut Kecil
Kepulauan Masalima
Kepulauan Balabalangan
Kepulauan Tengah
Kepulauan Kangean
Kepulauan Sangkapura
Kepulauan Natuna Besar
Kepulauan Natuna Selatan
Kepulauan Banyak
Kepulauan Batu
Kepulauan Nias
Kepulauan Mentawai
MEDAN
KUALA LUMPUR
SINGAPORE
Johor Bahru
Pekanbaru
RIAU
JAMBI
Jambi
PALEMBANG
BENGKULU
LAMPUNG
Bandar Lampung
JAKARTA
Bogor
BANDUNG
Cirebon
Semarang
SURABAYA
Madiun
Malang
Jember
Surakarta
Yogyakarta
Cilacap
Tasikmalaya
Pontianak
Singkawang
Sambas
Sintang
Putussibau
Nanga Pinoh
Sukadana
Ketapang
Sukaraya
Pangkalanbuun
Kuala Kapuas
Kuala Pembuang
Kumai
Sampit
Palangkaraya
Kendawangan
Tanjungpandan
Manggar
Toboali
Sungailiat
Pangkalpinang
Belinyu
Muntok
Muara Teweh
Purukcahu
Kuala Kurun
Tanjung Redeb
Tarakan
Nunukan
Sebatik
Tawau
Sandakan
Kota Kinabalu
Kuching
Sibu
Bintulu
Miri

40 EASTERN INDIA, BANGLADESH AND BURMA

X I Z A N G
Z I Z H I Q U
T I B E T
Xainza
Ngangla Ringco
Gangdise Shan
Nyainqentanglha Shan
Lhasa
Shigatse
Gyangze
Zhongba
Saga
Mustang
Thakhola
Pokhara
Annapurna
Gorkha
Nawakot
Kathmandu
Bhaktapur
Ramechhap
Dhankuta
Darjiling
Kanchenjunga
Everest
Gamba
Dingye
Thaze
Maqian L.
Ngamring
Tingri
Nepalganj
Lakhimpur
Sitapur
Bahraich
Gonda
Basti
Gorakhpur
Deoria
Muzaffarpur
Darbhanga
Bhagalpur
Purnea
Kishanganj
Siliguri
Jalpaiguri
Cooch Behar
Rangpur
Bogra
Dinajpur
Sylhet
Chittagong
Cox's Bazar
Kaptai
Rangamati
Bandarban
Mizoram
Aizawl
Lunglei
Chittagong Hills
Tripura
Agartala
Dhaka
Mymensingh
Jamalpur
Tangail
Gaibandha
Bangladesh

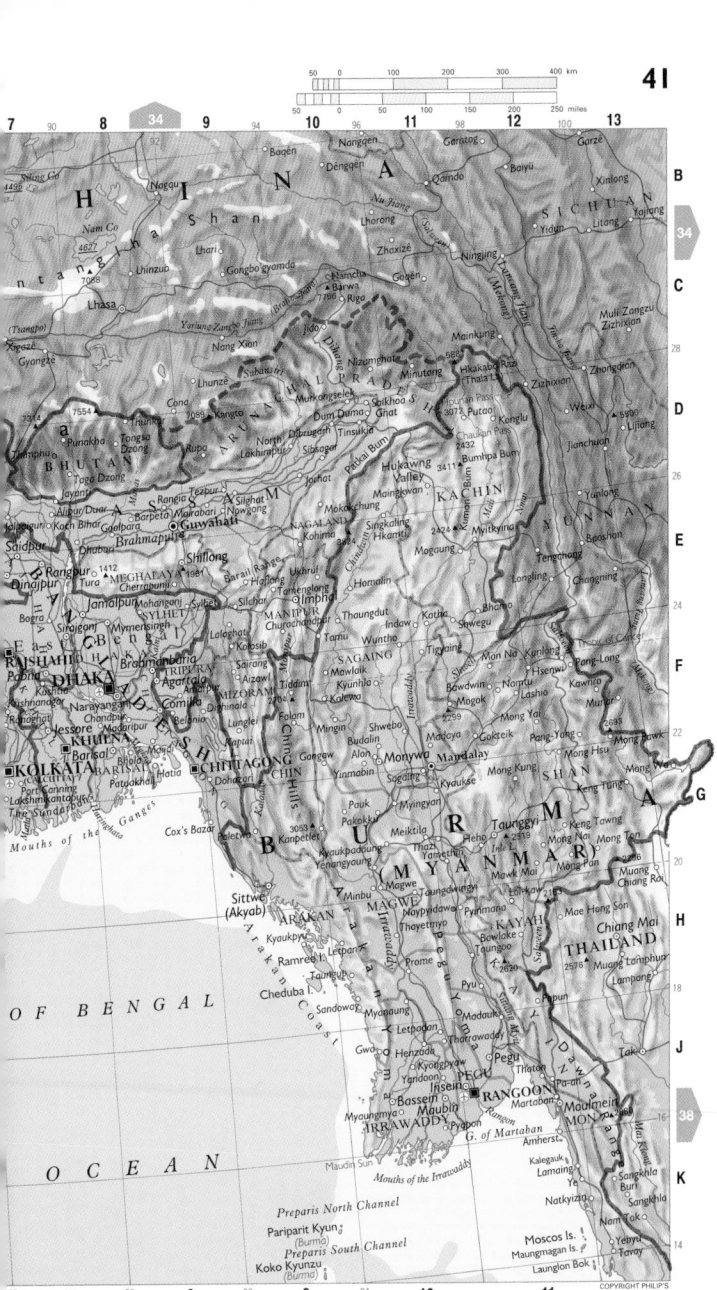
50 0 100 200 300 400 km
50 0 50 100 150 200 250 miles
CHINA
Shan
SICHUAN
Nagqu
Nam Co
Lhari
Lhinzub
Gongbo'gyamda
Lhasa
Yarlung Zangbo Jiang
Nang Xian
Gyangze
Xigaze
Tsangpo
Lhunze
Cona
Tsuntang
Kangto
Punakha
Tongsa Dzong
Thimphu
BHUTAN
Tago Dzong
Jayanti
Alipur Duar
Kalimpong
Kach Bihar
Gaibandha
Saidpur
Dinajpur
Rangpur
Jamalpur
Mymensingh
Sylhet
Sirajganj
Bogra
Rajshahi
Pabna
Khulna
Bangladesh
DHAKA
Narayanganj
Comilla
Chandpur
Jessore
KHULNA
Barisal
Bhola
Mongla
KOLKATA
Port Canning
Lakshmikantapur
The Sundarbans
Mouths of the Ganges
Hooghly
Hatia
Patuakhali
CHITTAGONG
Cox's Bazar
Teknaf
Sittwe (Akyab)
ARAKAN
Kyaukpyu
Ramree I.
Cheduba
Arakan Coast
OF BENGAL
OCEAN
Preparis North Channel
Paripari Kyun (Burma)
Preparis South Channel
Koko Kyunzu (Burma)
Mouths of the Irrawaddy
Maudin Sun
Moscos Is.
Maungmagan Is.
Launglon Bok
Nagqu
Baqen
Dengqen
Nangqen
Garntog
Qamdo
Baiyu
Gorze
Xinlong
Yajiang
Litang
Yidun
Lhorong
Zhoxizê
Ningjing
Gêgên
Nanchu
Barwa
Rigê
Jiulong
Mupi Zangzu Zizhixian
Zhongdian
Weixi
Lijiang
Jianchuan
Yunlong
Baoshan
Tengchong
Longling
Changning
Bhamo
Kachin
Myitkyina
Mogaung
Hukawng Valley
Mainkwan
Mohnyin
Bumhpa Bum
Hkakabo Razi
Putao
Kunlong
Lashio
Hsenwi
Kyaukme
Mogok
Mandalay
Monywa
Kyaukse
Myingyan
Pakokku
Meiktila
Taungdwingyi
Thayetmyo
Prome
Pyu
Pyinmana
Pyay
Pegu
Thaton
Moulmein
Mawlamyine
Tavoy
Mergui
Kawthoung
Ye
Natkyizin
Sittang
Salween
Irrawaddy
Chindwin
Mekong
Nu Jiang
Lancang Jiang
Jinsha Jiang
Yangtze
Brahmaputra
Tista
Teesta
Manas
Kosi
Ganges
Hooghly
Meghna
Karnaphuli
Kaladan
Mekong

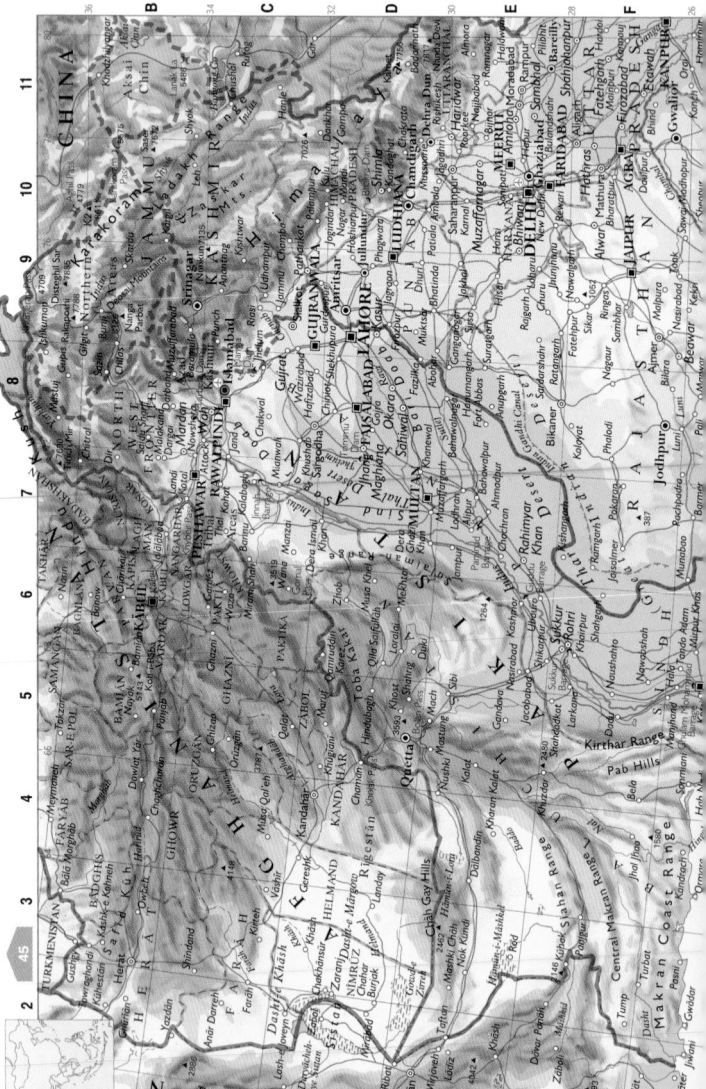
CHINA
Aksai Chin
Leh
Srinagar
KASHMIR
JAMMU
Jammu
Rawalpindi
Islamabad
PESHAWAR
KABUL
Jalalabad
Kandahar
HERAT
Quetta
Chaman
Zahedan
Khuzdar
Sukkur
Hyderabad
Karachi
Thatta
Jodhpur
Bikaner
Jaisalmer
Bahawalpur
Multan
Lahore
Amritsar
Ludhiana
Chandigarh
Shimla
Dehra Dun
DELHI
Meerut
Agra
Mathura
Gwalior
Kanpur
Lucknow
Allahabad
Varanasi
Patna
Ranchi
Jamshedpur
Kolkata
Durgapur
Bhopal
Indore
Ahmedabad
Surat
Mumbai
Pune
Nagpur
Hyderabad
Vijayawada
Chennai
Bangalore
Mysuru
Kochi
Thiruvananthapuram
Madurai
Tiruchirapalli
Salem
Coimbatore
Kolhapur
Aurangabad
Nashik
Vadodara
Rajkot
Bhuj
Kandla
Porbandar
Jaipur
Ajmer
Udaipur
Kota
Ujjain
Jabalpur
Raipur
Bhubaneswar
Cuttack
Vishakhapatnam
Guntur
Tirupati
Kozhikode
Thiruvananthapuram
Kandy
Colombo
Galle
Jaffna
Trincomalee
Hambantota
Indus
Ganges
Brahmaputra
Narmada
Tapti
Godavari
Krishna
Cauvery
Mahanadi

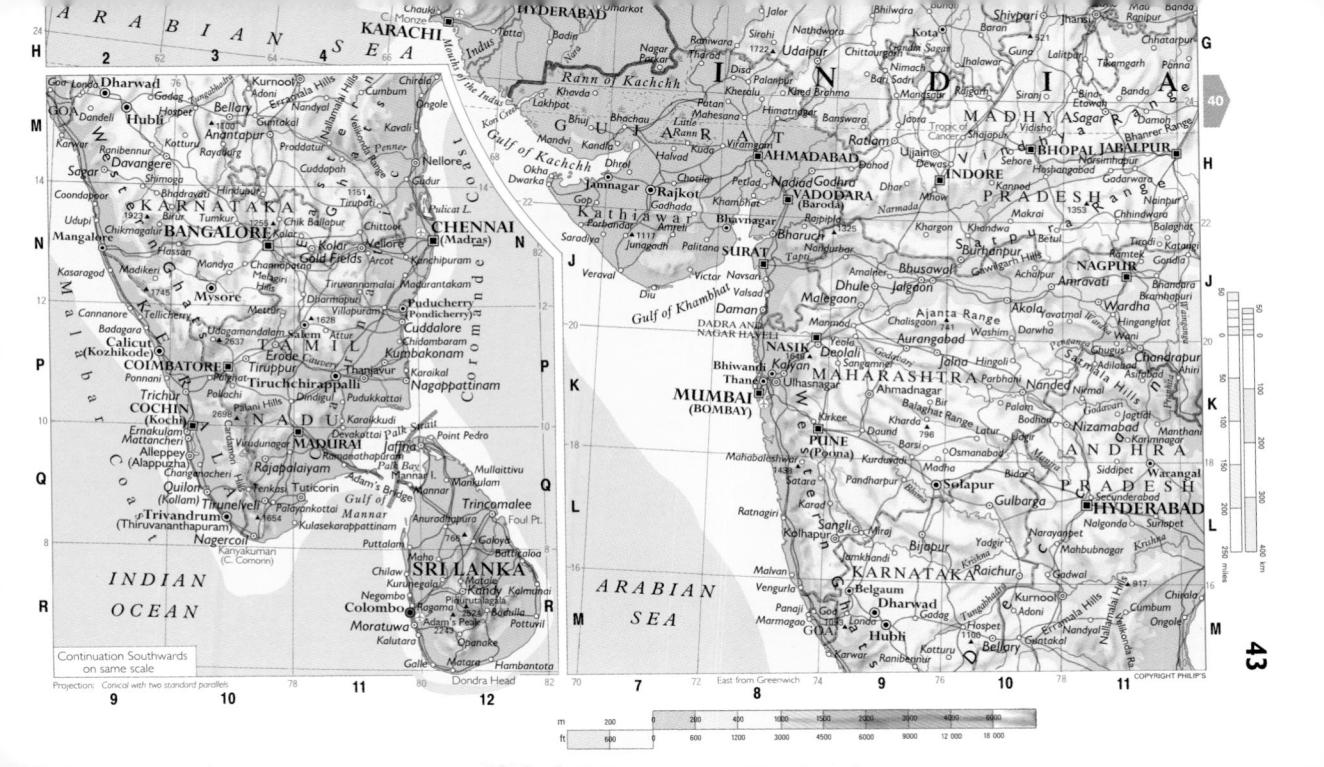
ARABIAN SEA
KARACHI
HYDERABAD
Indus
Mouth of the Indus
Rann of Kachchh
Gulf of Kachchh
INDIA
GUJARAT
AHMADABAD
Kathiawar
Rajkot
Jamnagar
Porbandar
Junagadh
Bhavnagar
Bhuj
Kandla
Dhrol
Okha
Dwarka
VADODARA
(Baroda)
Godhra
Nadiad
Anand
Bharuch
SURAT
Navsari
Valsad
Daman
DADRA AND NAGAR HAVELI
Gulf of Khambhat
MADHYA PRADESH
BHOPAL
JABALPUR
INDORE
Ujjain
Dewas
Ratlam
Indore
Khandwa
Burhanpur
Betul
Chhindwara
Nagpur
NAGPUR
Amravati
Wardha
Akola
Ajanta Range
Aurangabad
Jalna
Parbhani
Nanded
Latur
Osmanabad
Solapur
Gulbarga
Bidar
Raichur
Bijapur
Belgaum
Dharwad
Hubli
Goa
Panaji
Karwar
Ratnagiri
Kolhapur
Sangli
Miraj
Satara
Pune
(Poona)
Ahmednagar
Nasik
Deolali
Thane
Kalyan
Bhiwandi
Ulhasnagar
MUMBAI
(BOMBAY)
MAHARASHTRA
Malegaon
Dhule
Jalgaon
Amalner
Bhusawal
Chandrapur
Warangal
Secunderabad
HYDERABAD
Nizamabad
Karimnagar
Nalgonda
Suryapet
Mahbubnagar
Gadwal
Kurnool
Adoni
Bellary
Hospet
Gulbarga
ANDHRA PRADESH
KARNATAKA
Nandyal
Hingoli
Washim
Darwha
Yavatmal
Bhandara
Gondia
Ramtek
Dhar
Mhow
Sehore
Hoshangabad
Narsimhapur
Sagar
Damoh
Chhatarpur
Panna
Vidisha
Guna
Shivpuri
Datia
Jhansi
Lalitpur
Tikamgarh
Banda
Etawah
Bundi
Kota
Baran
Jhalawar
Chittaurgarh
Udaipur
Banswara
Jalore
Sirohi
Nathdwara
Bhilwara
Mandla
Seoni
Gwalior
Tikamgar

44 PERSIAN GULF, IRAN AND AFGHANISTAN

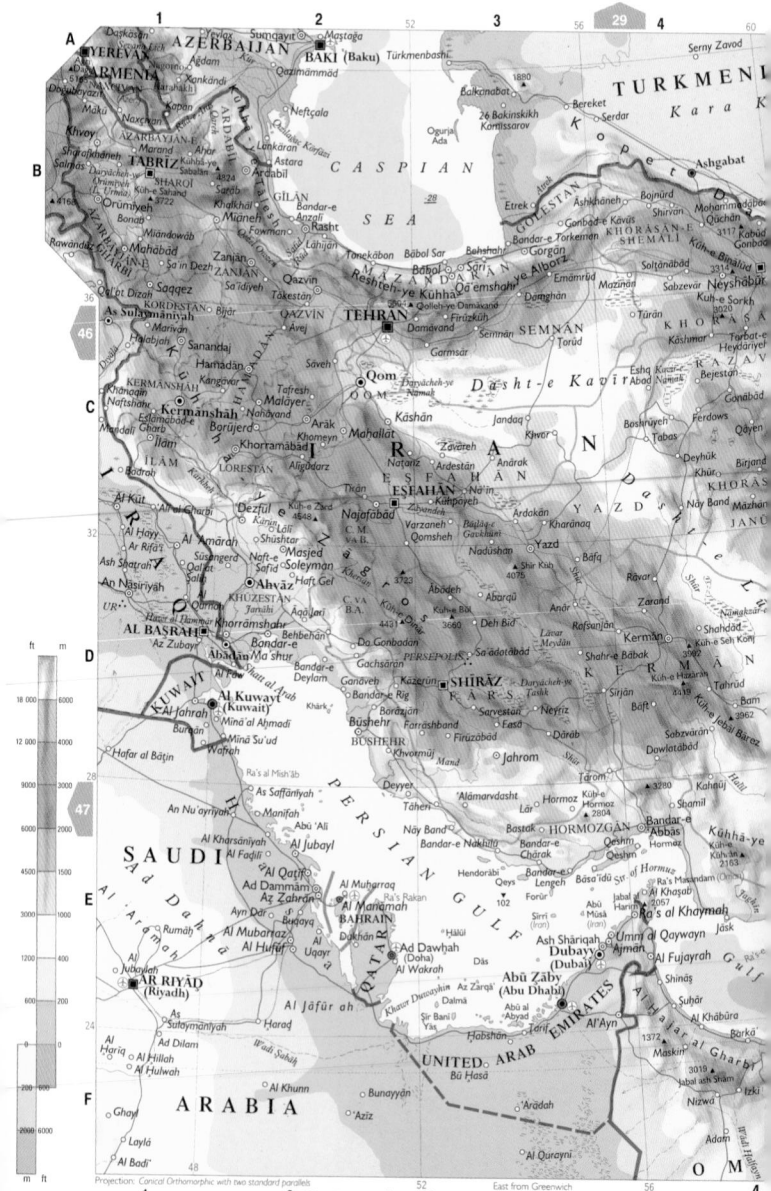
YEREVAN
ARMENIA
AZERBAIJAN
BAKI (Baku)
Türkmenbashi
TURKMENI
Kara K
Serny Zavod
Balkanabat
Bereket
Serdar
26 Bakinskikh Komissarov
Ashgabat
CASPIAN SEA
Astara
Ardabil
Lankaran
Neftçala
Sumqayit
Mastaga
Qazimämmäd
Aqdam
Jolfa
Naxçıvan
Nakhichevan
Culfa
Marand
Ahar
TABRIZ
Kuh-e Sahand
Sahand
Sarab
Mäku
Khvoy
Shaqlawa
Salmas
Dariyacheh-ye Urumiyeh
Urmia
Urumiyeh
Bonab
Miandowab
Mahabad
Sa'in Dezh
Saqqez
Lut Dizah
As Sulaymaniyah
Marivan
Halabjah
Sanandaj
Hamadan
Kangavar
Malayer
Tafresh
Nahavand
Arak
Khomeyn
Mahallat
Qazvin
Takestan
Zanjan
ZANJAN
Bandar-e Anzali
Rasht
Lahijan
Babol Sar
Tonekabon
Babol
Sari
Behshahr
Gorgan
Bandar-e Torkeman
Etrek
Ashkhaneh
Bojnurd
Shirvan
Gonbad-e Kavus
Mohammadabad
Quchan
Kabud Gonbad
Sabzevar
Neyshabur
Mazinan
Damghan
Semnan
Garmsar
Damavand
Firuzkuh
Qolleh-ye Damavand
Reshteh-ye Kuhha
Qa'emshahr
TEHRAN
Qom
Dariycheh-ye Namak
Kashan
Jandaq
Zaveh
Natanz
Ardestan
Anarak
Najafabad
Varzaneh
Qomsheh
Nadushan
Yazd
Ardakan
Kharanaq
Bafq
Rafsanjan
Kerman
Shahdad
Kuh-e Seh Koh
Sirjan
Bam
Tahrud
Kuh-e Jebal Barez
Sabzvaran
Dowlatabad
Jahrom
Lar
Bastak
HORMOZGAN
Bandar-e Abbas
Qeshm
Hormoz
Kuh-e Kuhban
Kuh-e Hazaran
Kuh-e Lalezar
Kuh-e Shah Kuh
Kuh-e Zard
Kuh-e Dena
Kuh-e Bul
Kuh-e Bidak
Kuh-e Sefid
Kuh-e Sabalan
Kuh-e Urmia
Kuh-e Binalud
Kuh-e Shah Jahan
Kuh-e Bashakerd
Kuh-e Bibak

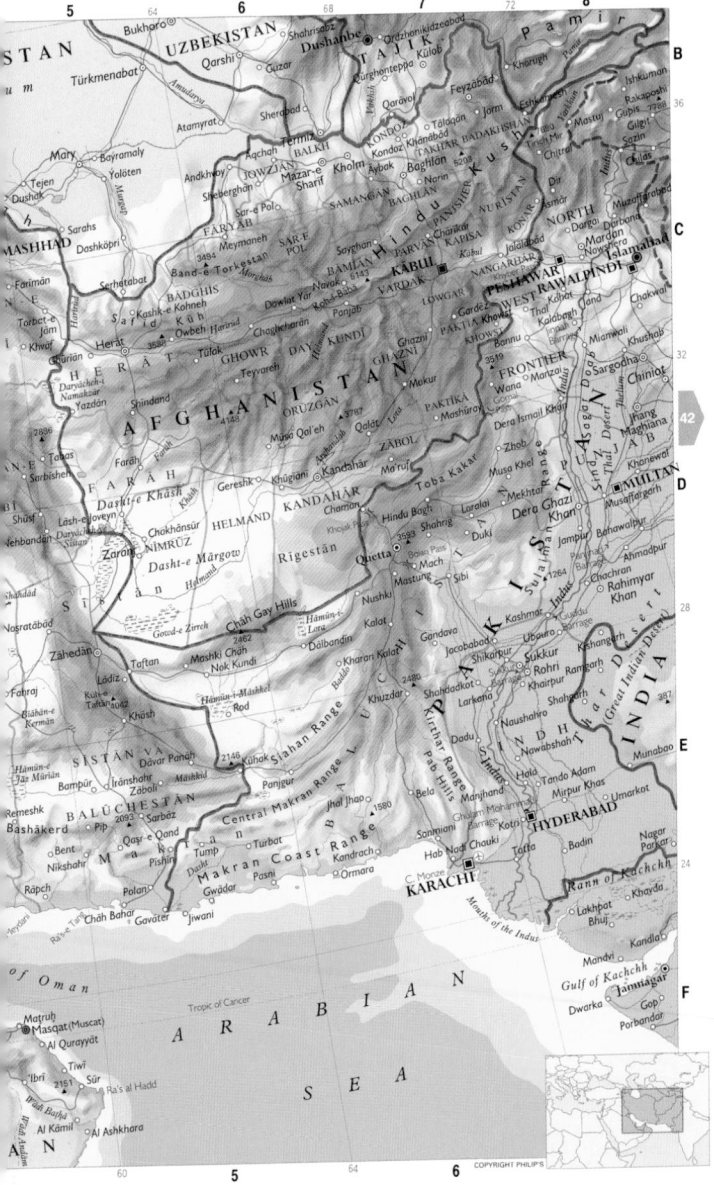
UZBEKISTAN
TAJIKISTAN
AFGHANISTAN
PAKISTAN
INDIA
IRAN
ARABIAN SEA
Dushanbe
Kābul
Herāt
Kandahār
Quetta
Zaranj
Peshāwar
Rawalpindi
Islamabad
Multān
Hyderābād
Karāchi
Mashhad
Mary
Tashkent
Bukhara
Samarqand
Qarshi
Mazār-e Sharīf
Kunduz
Jalālābād
Gardez
Ghazni
Farāh
Lashkar Gāh
Chaman
Khuzdār
Sukkur
Rohri
Jaisalmer
Bhuj
Jamnagar
Gulf of Kachchh
Rann of Kachchh
Tropic of Cancer
Tropic of Oman
Strait of Hormuz
Mouths of the Indus
Makran Coast Range
Central Makran Range
Siahan Range
Kirthar Range
Pab Hills
Sulaiman Range
Toba Kakar
Khyber Pass
Bolan Pass
Great Indian Desert
Thar Desert
Dasht-e Kavīr
Dasht-e Lūt
Dasht-e Margow
Registān
Chāh Gay Hills
Hindu Kush
Pamir
Tropic of Cancer
COPYRIGHT PHILIP'S

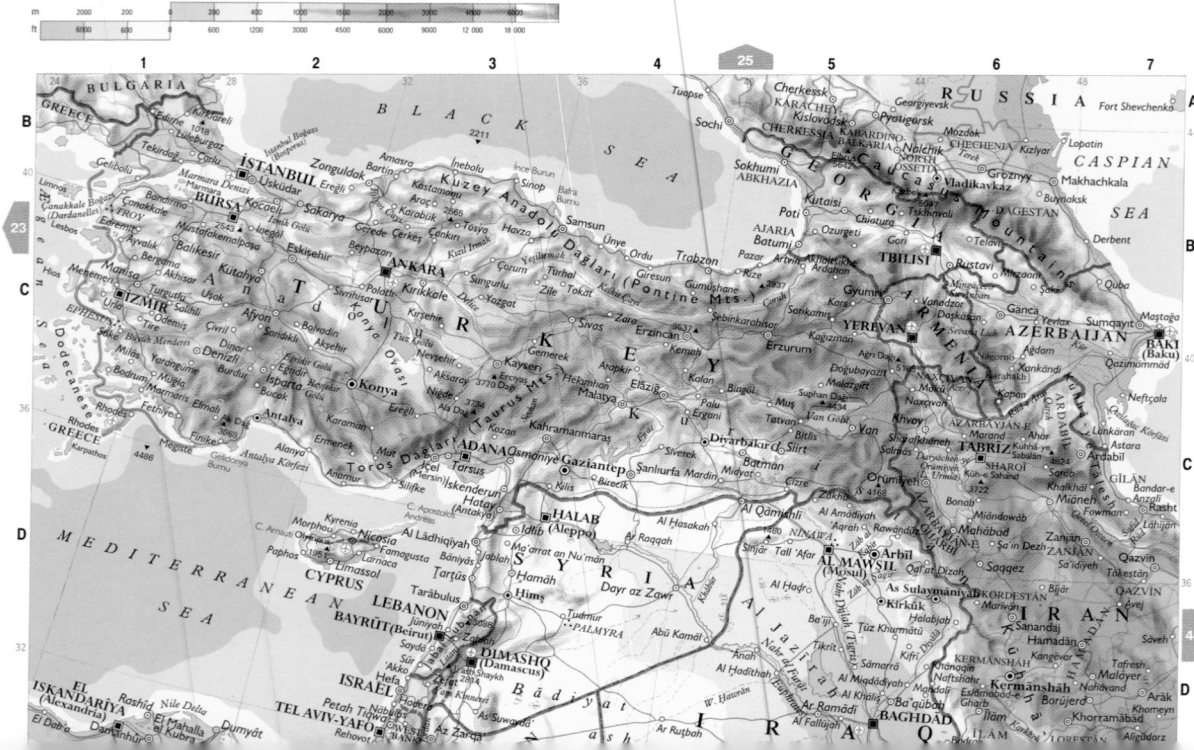
m 2000 200 0 200 400 1000 1500 2000 3000 4000
ft 6000 600 0 600 1200 3000 4500 6000 9000 12 000 18 000
1 2 3 4 5 6 7
A B C D
23 25 44
BULGARIA
GREECE
BLACK SEA
RUSSIA
Fort Shevchenko
Cherkessk
KARACHEY-CHERKESSIA
Georgiyevsk
Pyatigorsk
Mozdok
SHECHENIA
Kizlyar
Lopatin
CASPIAN SEA
Sochi
Tuapse
Sokhumi
ABKHAZIA
GEORGIA
Caucasus Mountains
Groznyy
Vladikavkaz
Makhachkala
DAGESTAN
Buynaksk
Derbent
Kutaisi
Poti
Ozurgeti
Batumi
AJARIA
Tbilisi
Rustavi
Mingechaur
Quba
Gyumri
YEREVAN
Vanadzor
Dashkasan
Gäncä
Yevlax
Sumqayıt
Maştağa
AZERBAIJAN
BAKI (Baku)
Qazımammäd
Neftçala
Lankaran
Astara
Ardabil
ARMENIA
NAKHICHEVAN
Julfa
Khoy
AZARBAYJAN-E
TABRIZ
Marand
Ahar
Sahabad
SHAROI
Sarab
GILAN
Bandar-e Anzali
Rasht
Lahijan
Khalkhal
Miāneh
Fowman
Zanjan
ZANJAN
Qazvin
QAZVIN
Tākestān
Āvej
Sāveh
Malāyer
Arāk
Khomeyn
Borujerd
Nahāvand
Tafresh
Khorramābād
Alīgūdarz
LORESTAN
Kermānshāh
KERMANSHAH
Eslāmābād-e Gharb
Gilān-e Gharb
Ilām
ILAM
Qasr-e Shirīn
Mandalī
Khānaqīn
Naft Khāneh
Sanandaj
Hamadān
Kangāvar
Bijār
Mārīvān
KURDISTAN
IRAN
Kirkuk
Halabjah
Tuz Khurmatū
Sāmarrā
Kifrī
Tikrit
Al Mīqdādiyah
Ba'qūbah
Al Khāliş
Ar Ramādī
Al Fallujah
BAGHDAD
Al Ḥillah
Ar Ruthbah
Al Ḥadīthah
Anah
Al Qā'im
Al Ḥaḍr
Al Ḥajjī
Al Ḥasakah
Al Qamishli
Al Ḥawl
Al Ḥawījah

EGYPT
SUDAN
Es Sahrā' en Nūbiya
Es Sinā'
Es Sahrā' Esh Sharqiyah
Aṭ Ṭubayq
Al Ḥamad
Ash Shām
Al Ḥajārah
Aṣ Ṣaḥrā' al Ḥijārah
An Nafūd
Jabal Shammar
Ḥarrat Khaybar
Ḥarrat al Kishb
Ḥarrat Nawāṣif
Ḥarrat 'Uwairidh
Al Qaṣīm
Ad Dahnā'
Al 'Arūmah
Al Ḥafar

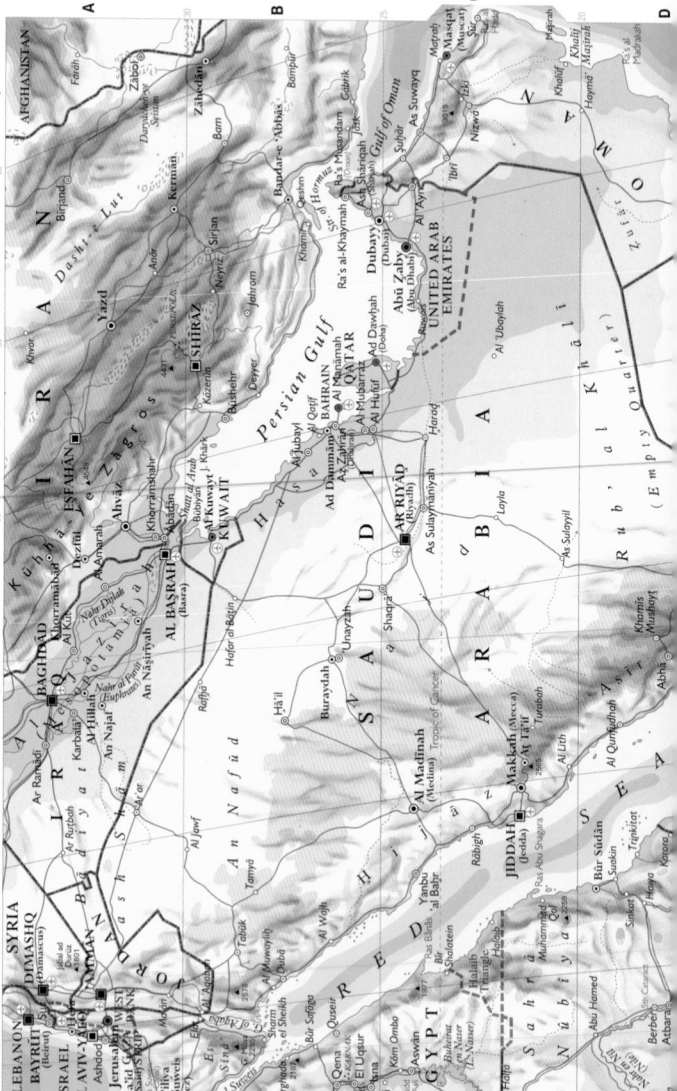
SYRIA
DIMASHQ
LEBANON
BAYRUT
ISRAEL
TEL AVIV-YAFO
Jerusalem
AMMAN
JORDAN
Al Ma'dinah (Medina)
Makkah (Mecca)
JIDDAH (Jeddah)
Al Ta'if
Tropic of Cancer
Bur Sudan

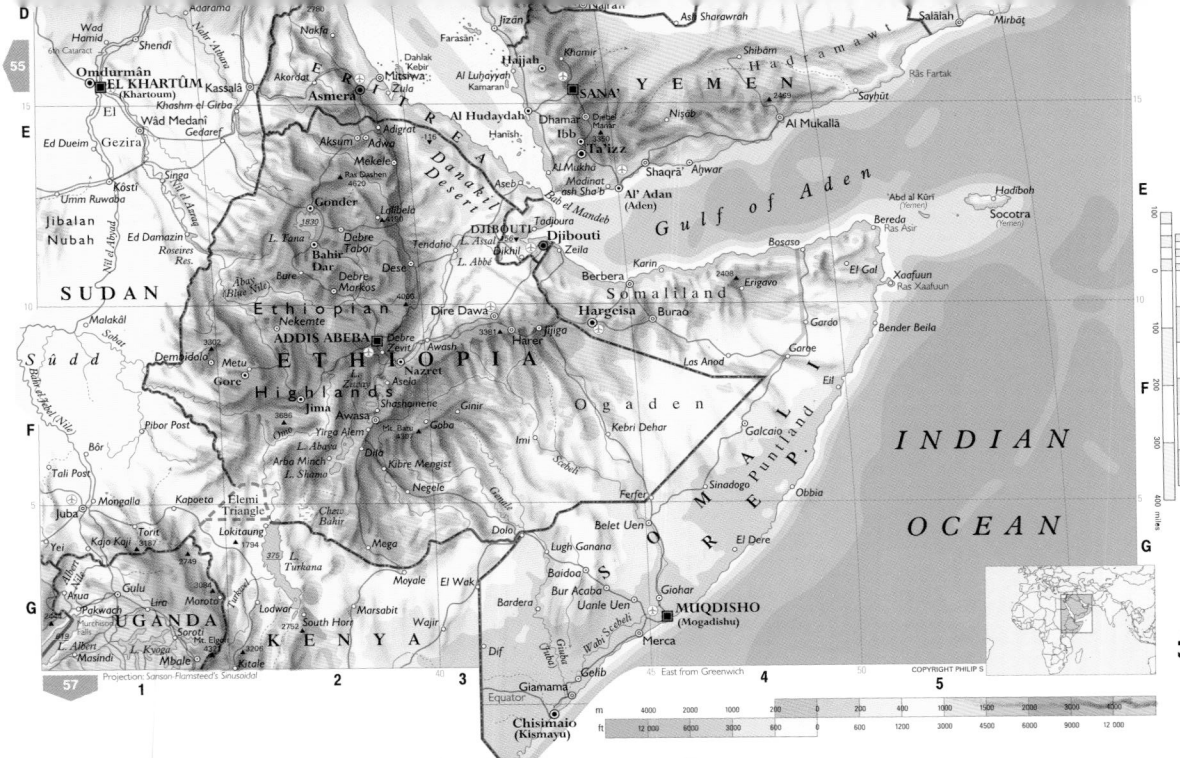
SUDAN
ETHIOPIA
KENYA
UGANDA
SOMALIA
Somaliland
Puntland
Ogaden
Gulf of Aden
INDIAN OCEAN
YEMEN
Hadramawt
Danakil Desert
Ethiopian Highlands
Omdurmān
EL KHARTŪM (Khartoum)
Asmera
SANA'
Al Hudaydah
Ta'izz
Al' Adan (Aden)
DJIBOUTI
Djibouti
Hargeisa
Burao
Berbera
ADDIS ABEBA
Dire Dawa
Harar
Jijiga
Gonder
Bahir Dar
Mekele
Aksum
Asosa
Gore
Jimma
Nekemte
Juba
Kampala
Mombasa
Nairobi
Kisumu
Eldoret
Lodwar
Kitale
Mbale
Gulu
Lira
Moroto
Pakwach
Masindi
Mogadishu
MUQDISHO (Mogadishu)
Merca
Kismayu
Chisimaio (Kismayu)
Giamama
Gelib
Dif
Belet Uen
Baidoa
Bur Acaba
Uanle Uen
Giohar
Kebri Dehar
Galcaio
Garowe
Bosaso
Bereda
Ras Asir
Socotra (Yemen)
Hadiboh
Xaafuun
Ras Xaafuun
Bender Beila
Gardo
Erigavo
Hargeisa
Berbera
Zeila
Djibouti
Tadjoura
Obbia
Sinadogo
Ferfer
Dolo
Mega
Moyale
El Wak
Marsabit
South Horn
Wajir
Lokitaung
Kapoeta
Torit
Juba
Mongalla
Bor
Malakāl
Dembidolo
Metu
Pibor Post
Tali Post
Kassalā
Khartoum
Shendi
Wad Hamid
Gezira
Ed Dueim
Kosti
Umm Ruwaba
Jibalan Nubah
Ed Damazin
Roseires Res.
Gedaref
Wād Medanī
Khashm el Girba
Adigrat
Adwa
Dahlak Kebir
Massawa
Zula
Akordat
Nakfa
Farasan
Jizān
Hajjah
Khamir
Al Luhayyah
Kamaran
Dhamar
Ibb
Al Mukallā
Nisab
Shibam
Sayhūt
Rās Fartak
Mirbāt
Salālah
Aṣ Ṣarawrah
Shaqrā
Al Wajh
Al Mukhā
Madīnat ash Sha'b
Bab el Mandeb
Aseb
Tendaho
Dese
Debre Markos
Debre Tabor
Debre Zeyit
Awash
Nazret
Asela
Shashamene
Ginir
Goba
Yirga Alem
Dilla
Kibre Mengist
Negele
Imi
Scebeli
Gomeli
Jubba
Wabi Scebeli
Karin
Los Anod
Gorge
Elt
El Gal
Sahel
Ṣûdd
Bahr el Abiyad
Nile
Bahr el Jebel
Sobat
Baro
Gambela
Lake Turkana
Lake Victoria
Lake Albert
Lake Kyoga
Lake Mobutu Sese Seko
Lake Tana
Lake Abaya
Lake Chamo
Lake Abbe
Lake Zwai
Lake Nyasa

NORTH ATLANTIC OCEAN
Mediterranean Sea
Black Sea
Caspian Sea
Red Sea
Persian Gulf
Adriatic Sea
Tyrrhenian Sea
Sahara
RUSSIA
KAZAKHSTAN
UKRAINE
GERMANY
POLAND
FRANCE
SPAIN
PORTUGAL
ITALY
TURKEY
IRAN
IRAQ
SAUDI ARABIA
YEMEN
EGYPT
SUDAN
LIBYA
ALGERIA
TUNISIA
MOROCCO
CHAD
NIGER
MALI
MAURITANIA
NIGERIA
SENEGAL
GAMBIA
GUINEA
SIERRA LEONE
IVORY COAST
GHANA
BURKINA FASO
BENIN
ETHIOPIA
DJIBOUTI
ERITREA
Nile
White Nile
Blue Nile
Niger
Congo
Tropic of Cancer
Azores
Madeira
Canary Is.
CAPE VERDE IS.
Socotra
Crete
Corsica
Sardinia
Sicily
Cyprus
Malta
LONDON
PARIS
ROME
MADRID
LISBON
ATHENS
CAIRO
TEHRAN
BAGHDAD
DAMASCUS
JERUSALEM
ANKARA
MOSCOW
KIEV
WARSAW
PRAGUE
BERLIN
BRUSSELS
AMSTERDAM
VIENNA
BUDAPEST
BELGRADE
SOFIA
ZAGREB
SARAJEVO
TIRANA
SKOPJE
ZURICH
BERN
MUNICH
ALGIERS
TUNIS
TRIPOLI
RABAT
KHARTOUM
ADDIS ABABA
NAIROBI
KAMPALA
DAKAR
BAMAKO
ABIDJAN
ACCRA
LAGOS
KANO
NIAMEY
N'DJAMENA
ABUJA
MOGADISHU
MECCA
MEDINA
RIYADH
JIDDA
ADEN
SANA'A
MUSCAT
DOHA
MANAMA
KUWAIT
BAKU
ST. PETERSBURG
KOLGEGRAD
ODESSA
ATHENS
DAMASCUS
JERUSALEM
TEL AVIV
ALEXANDRIA
PORT SAID
SUEZ
ASWAN
BENGHAZI
TRIPOLI
MISRATAH
GHADAMES
SABHA
MERZUQ
ALGIERS
ORAN
CONSTANTINE
TUNIS
SFAX
FEZ
RABAT
CASABLANCA
MARRAKESH
TOMBOUCTOU
MOPTI
BISSAU
CONAKRY
FREETOWN
ABUJA
LAGOS
ENUGU
KANO
MAIDUGURI
NIAMEY
ABECHE
ELFASHER
ELOBEID
KHARTOUM
OMDURMAN
ASMARA
ADDIS ABABA
MASSAWA
KUWAIT
BASRA

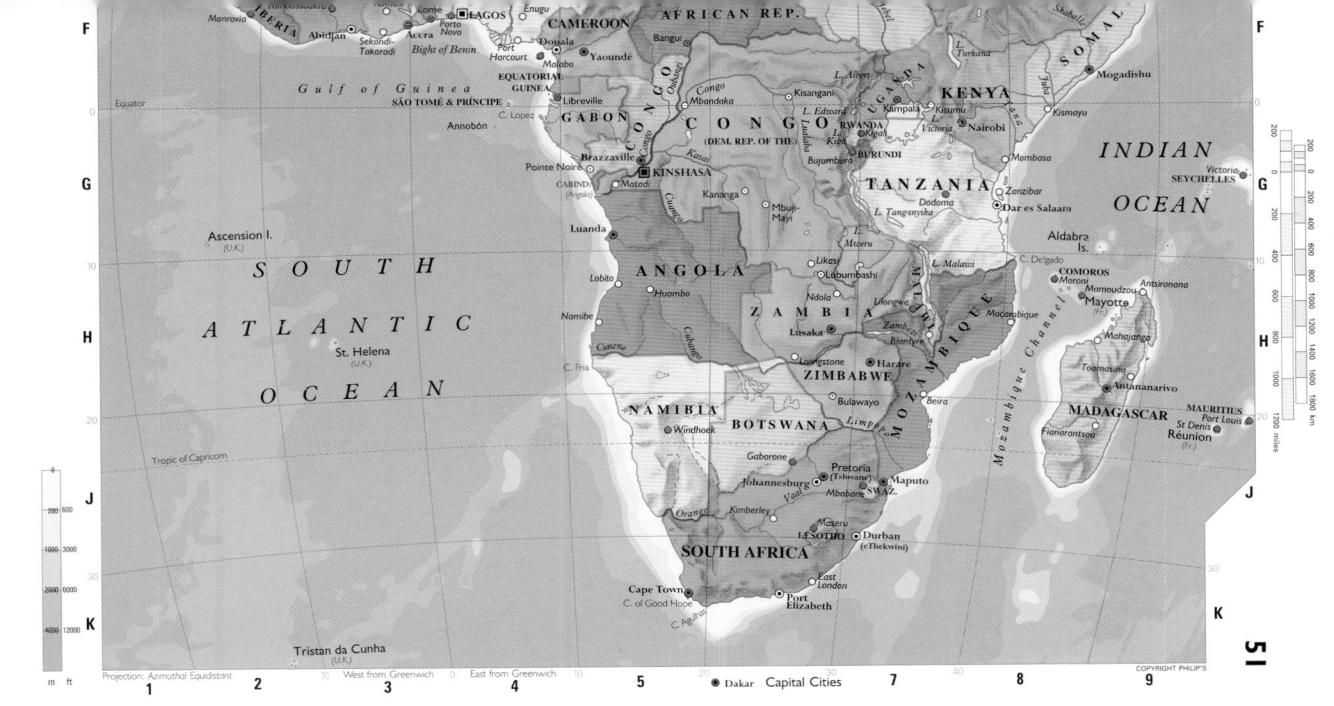
AFRICAN REP.
CAMEROON
LAGOS
Monrovia
LIBERIA
Abidjan
Sekondi-Takoradi
Accra
Porto Novo
Bight of Benin
Lome
Enugu
Port Harcourt
Douala
Malabo
Yaounde
Bangui
EQUATORIAL GUINEA
Gulf of Guinea
SÃO TOMÉ & PRÍNCIPE
Libreville
GABON
Annobón
C. Lopez
Equator
CONGO
Congo
Mbandaka
Kisangani
L. Albert
L. Edward
UGANDA
KENYA
Kampala
Kisumu
Nairobi
Kismayu
Mogadishu
SOMALIA
Turkana
Tana
Jubba
Shabelle
Kigali
RWANDA
Kivu
Goma
BURUNDI
Bujumbura
Victoria
Mombasa
INDIAN OCEAN
SEYCHELLES
Victoria
Brazzaville
Pointe Noire
KINSHASA
Matadi
CABINDA (Angola)
Kasai
Kananga
Mbuji-Mayi
TANZANIA
Zanzibar
Dodoma
Dar es Salaam
L. Tanganyika
L. Mweru
Luanda
Ascension I. (U.K.)
SOUTH ATLANTIC OCEAN
Lobito
ANGOLA
Huambo
Namibe
Cuanza
Cubango
Likasi
Lubumbashi
L. Malawi
Ndola
ZAMBIA
Lusaka
Zambezi
Lilongwe
MALAWI
Blantyre
Mozambique
Aldabra Is.
C. Delgado
COMOROS
Moroni
Mamoudzou
Antsiranana
Mayotte (Fr.)
Mozambique Channel
Mahajanga
Toamasina
Antananarivo
MADAGASCAR
Fianarantsoa
MAURITIUS
Port Louis
St. Denis
Réunion (Fr.)
St. Helena (U.K.)
C. Fria
Livingstone
Harare
ZIMBABWE
Bulawayo
Beira
Limpopo
NAMIBIA
BOTSWANA
Windhoek
Gaborone
Tropic of Capricorn
Pretoria (Tshwane)
Johannesburg
Maputo
Vaal
Mbabane
SWAZ.
Orange
Kimberley
Maseru
LESOTHO
Durban (eThekwini)
SOUTH AFRICA
East London
Cape Town
C. of Good Hope
Port Elizabeth
C. Agulhas
Tristan da Cunha (U.K.)
Projection: Azimuthal Equidistant
West from Greenwich
East from Greenwich
Dakar Capital Cities
COPYRIGHT PHILIP'S
m ft
miles
km
51

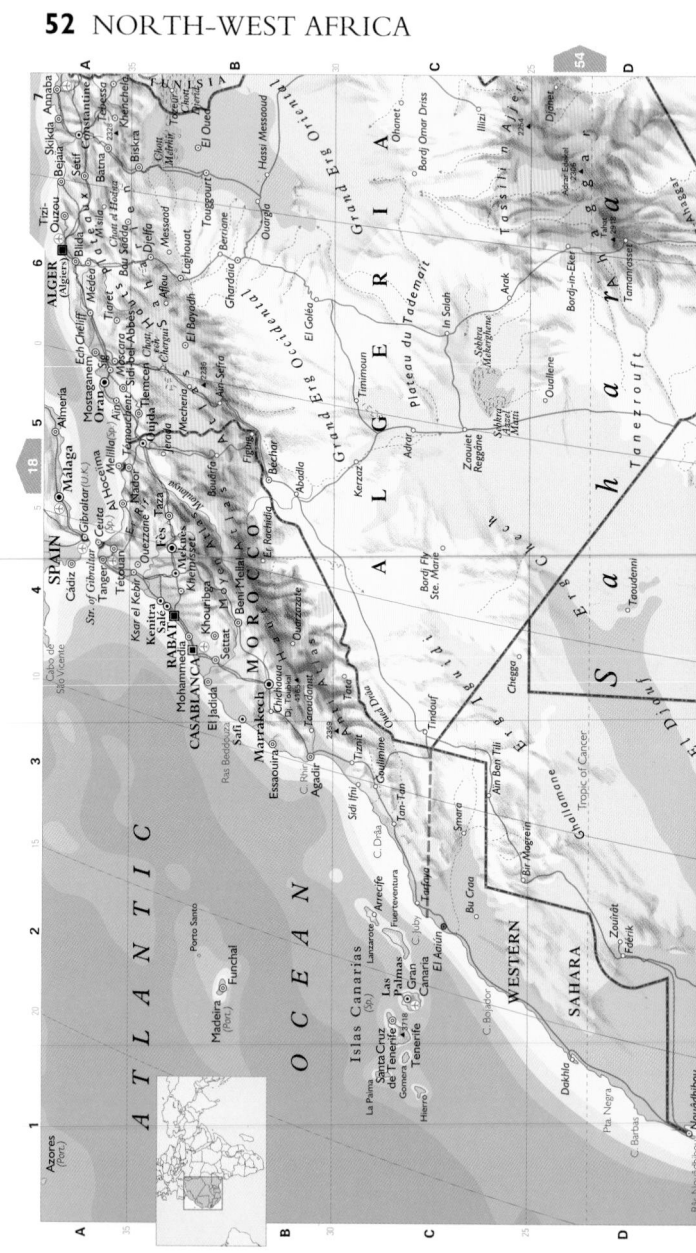
ATLANTIC OCEAN
SPAIN
MOROCCO
ALGERIA
WESTERN SAHARA
Sahara
Islas Canarias
Madeira (Port.)
Azores (Port.)
Cabo de São Vicente
Str. of Gibraltar
Cádiz
Gibraltar (U.K.)
Tangier
Ceuta
Tetuan
Málaga
Almeria
Mostaganem
Oran
Melilla
Algiers
Tipaza
Blida
Médéa
Tiaret
Sidi-bel-Abbès
Tlemcen
Ouezzane
Meknès
Fès
Taza
Kenitra
RABAT
Mohammedia
CASABLANCA
El Jadida
Safi
Khouribga
Settat
Beni Mellal
Marrakech
Essaouira
Agadir
Taroudannt
Ouarzazate
Tiznit
Tafraoute
Tindouf
Chegga
Tanezrouft
Tamanrasset
Djanet
Ghardaia
Laghouat
Touggourt
Biskra
Batna
Tébessa
Constantine
Annaba
Skikda
Bejaia
Setif
Ouzou
Trzi-
ALGER (Algiers)
Chlef
Mostaganem
Porto Santo
Funchal
Madeira (Port.)
Islas Canarias (Sp.)
Lanzarote
Arrecife
Fuerteventura
Las Palmas
Gran Canaria
Santa Cruz de Tenerife
Tenerife
La Palma
Gomera
Hierro
Dakhla
Pta. Negra
C. Barbas
Nouadhibou
Pta. Nouadhibou
C. Bojador
Bu Craa
Smara
Laayoune
Tan-Tan
Sidi Ifni
Tiznit
Goulimine
Tindouf
Ain Ben Tili
Bir Moghrein
Zouirat
Fderik
Atar
Chinguetti
Tropic of Cancer
Grand Erg Occidental
Grand Erg Oriental
Hamada de Tindouf
Hamada du Guir
Plateau du Tademaït
Tassili n Ajjer
Tassili n Ahaggar
Adrar
Tanezrouft
Tamanrasset
Tindouf
Tabelbala
Bechar
Beni Ounif
Figuig
Boudnib
Ouarzazate
Ouarzazate
Ouargla
Hassi Messaoud
El Oued
Touggourt
Berriane
Ghardaia
El Goléa
Timimoun
Adrar
Kerzaz
In Salah
Arak
Ilizi
Djanet
Bordj Omar Driss
Ohanet
Bordj-in-Eker
Ouallene
Zaouiet Reggene
Sebkra Mekerghene
Sebkra Azel Matti
Bordj Fly Ste. Marie
Mecheria
Aïn Sefra
Malaga
Cadiz

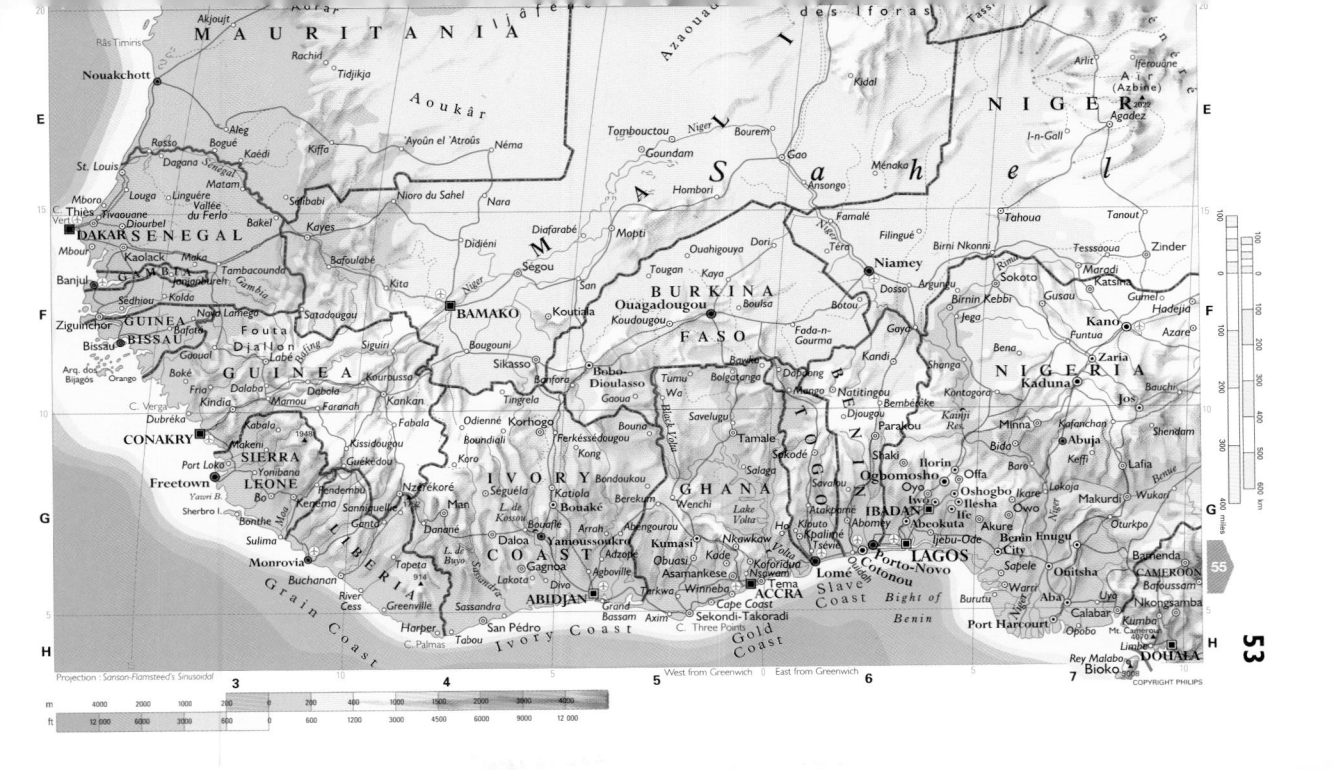
MAURITANIA
Nouakchott
Rās Timirīs
Akjoujt
Rachid
Tidjikja
Aoukâr
Azaouak
Air (Azbine)
Agadez
NIGER
Arlit
Iferouane
I-n-Gall
Tahoua
Tanout
Zinder
Maradi
Katsina
Gumel
Hadejia
Kano
Azare
Funtua
Zaria
Kaduna
NIGERIA
Jos
Bauchi
Abuja
Lafia
Makurdi
Wukari
Oturkpo
Benue
Niger
Kidal
Tombouctou
Goundam
Gao
Ménaka
Ansongo
Hombori
Bourem
Mopti
Diafarabé
Ouahigouya
Dori
Tera
Filingué
Birni Nkonni
Tessaoua
Niamey
Dosso
Argungu
Birnin Kebbi
Sokoto
Jega
Gaya
Kandi
Shanga
Bena
Kontagora
Bembèrèke
Natitingou
Djougou
Parakou
Kainji Res.
Minna
Bida
Kafanchan
Keffi
Shendam
Baro
Lokoja
Ilorin
Offa
Oyo
Ogbomosho
Iwo
Ilesha
Ife
Oshogbo
Ikare
Owo
IBADAN
Abeokuta
Abomey
Akure
Ijebu-Ode
Benin City
Enugu
Onitsha
Awka
Aba
Port Harcourt
Calabar
Oyobo
Mt. Cameroun
Limbe
DOUALA
Bamenda
CAMEROON
Bafoussam
Nkongsamba
Kumba
Bioko
Rey Malabo
Burutu
Warri
Sapele
Ura
Niger Delta
Bight of Benin
Slave Coast
Porto-Novo
Cotonou
LAGOS
Lomé
Tema
ACCRA
Cape Coast
Sekondi-Takoradi
Gold Coast
Kumasi
Obuasi
Asamankese
Koforidua
Nsawam
Kade
Nkawkaw
Tamale
Sekodé
Salaga
Savalou
Atakpamé
Kpalimé
Kpalimé
Tsévié
Kpalimé
Ho
Yeji
Lake Volta
Volta
Wenchi
Berekum
Sunyani
Techiman
GHANA
Bouaké
Katiola
Séguéla
Man
Danané
Bouaflé
Yamoussoukro
Daloa
Gagnoa
Divo
Lakota
Sassandra
Grand Bassam
Aixim
Tarkwa
Winneba
Cape Coast
C. Three Points
ABIDJAN
Aboisso
Adzopé
Abengourou
Arrah
Bondoukou
Odienné
Korhogo
Boundiali
Ferkéssédougou
Kong
Bouna
Tingréla
Tumu
Wa
Bolgatanga
Bawku
Dapaong
Mango
Savelugu
Gaoua
Bobo-Dioulasso
Banfora
Sikasso
Koutiala
Bougouni
Siguiri
Kouroussa
Kankan
Faranah
Mamou
Dabola
Dalaba
Kindia
Fria
Bokè
Gaoual
Labé
Pita
Koundara
Boké
Kamsar
Kissidougou
Guéckédou
Nzérékoré
Tapeta
Greenville
Harper
San Pédro
Tabou
C. Palmas
Sinoe
Buchanan
Monrovia
Sulima
Bonthe
Sherbro I.
Freetown
Port Loko
Yonibana
Kenema
Bo
Pendembu
Sangaredi
Gantá
Yaoun B.
Mano
Kabala
Makeni
CONAKRY
Dubréka
Coyah
Forécariah
Fabala
Odienné

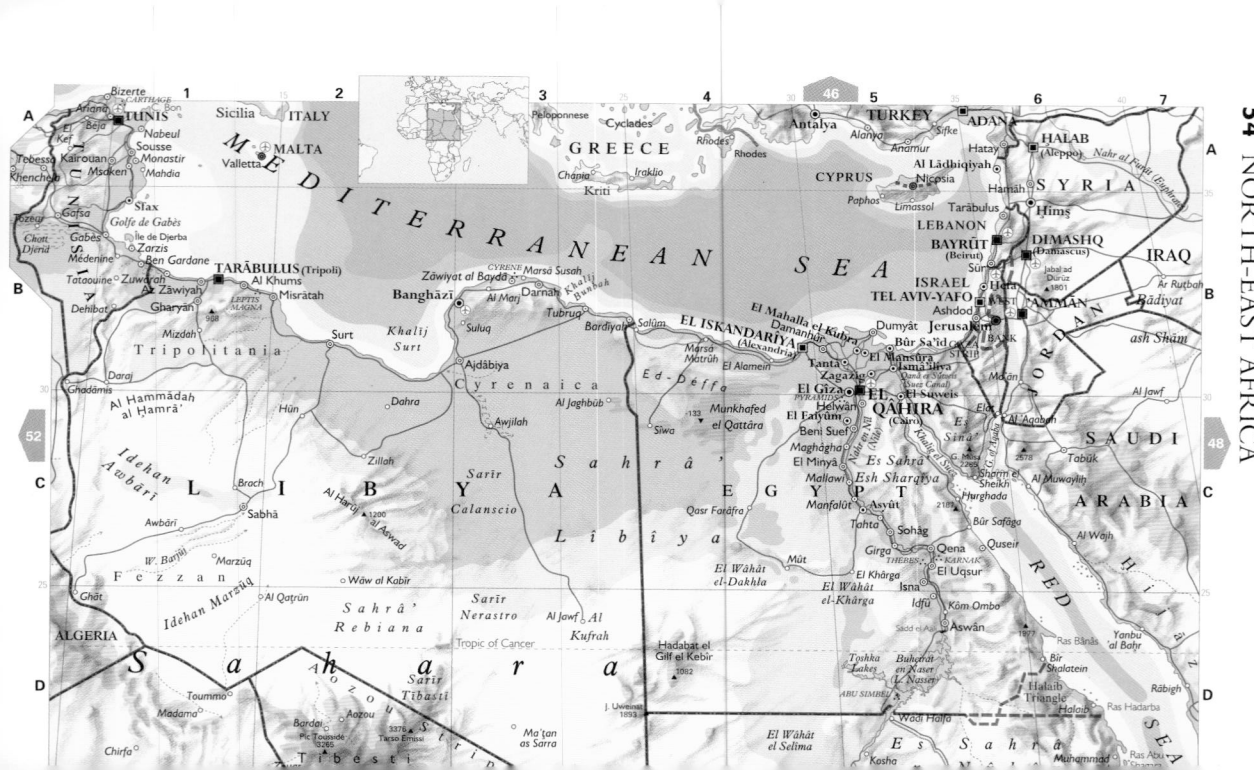
MEDITERRANEAN SEA
RED SEA
Sahara
Libya
Sahrâ' Libîya
Sahrâ' Rebiana
Sahrâ' Nerastro
Sarîr Calanscio
Sarîr Tibesti
Sarîr Tibasti
Tibesti
Fezzan
Tripolitania
Cyrenaica
Idehan Awbârî
Idehan Marzûq
Ed-Deffa
Es Sahra
Es Sahrâ
Tropic of Cancer
Golfe de Gabès
Chott Djerid
Chott Djerid
Khalij Surt
Khalij Burkah
Wâdi Halfa
Halaib Triangle
Halaib
Ras Hadarba
Ras Bânâs
Ras Abu Madi
Ras Abu Kaznah
Muhammad
Kosha
Abu Simbel
Lake Nasser
Toshka Lakes
Buhayrat en Nasser
Hadabat el Gilf el Kebir
Ma'ţan as Sarra
Al Kufrah
Al Jawf
Wâw al Kabîr
Al Qaţrûn
Ghât
Chirfa
Madama
Toummo
Aozou
Bardai
Pic Toussidé
Tarso Emissi
Marzûq
Sabhâ
Awbârî
Brach
Zillah
Al Hawj
Al Aswad
Hûn
Dahra
Awjilah
Ajdâbiya
Al Jaghbûb
Siwa
Marsa Matrûh
El Alamein
Al Mansûra
Tanta
Zagazig
Damanhûr
Dumyât
Bûr Sa'id
Ismâ'îlîya
Suez Canal
El Giza
Helwân
El Fayyûm
Beni Suef
Maghâgha
El Minya
Mallawî
Manfalût
Asyût
Tahta
Girga
Sohâg
Qena
Qûseir
Isna
Idfû
Kôm Ombo
Aswân
Hurghada
Sharm el Sheikh
Al Muwaylih
Tabûk
Al Jawf
Al Aqabah
Ma'ân
Al Ḥammâdah al Ḥamrâ'
Daraj
Ghadâmis
Mizdah
Gharyan
Zuwârah
Az Zâwiyah
Al Khums
Misrâtah
Tarābulus (Tripoli)
Zawîyat al Baydâ
Banghāzī
Darnah
Al Marj
Tubruq
Suluq
Bardiyah
Salûm
Surt
Ben Gardane
Zarzis
Médenine
Tataouine
Dehibat
Gabès
Gafsa
Tozeur
Sfax
Kairouan
Sousse
Monastir
Mahdia
Msaken
Nabeul
Tunis
Bizerte
Béja
Le Kef
Tebessa
Khenchela
Sicilia
ITALY
MALTA
Valletta
Peloponnese
Cyclades
GREECE
Kriti
Iraklio
Chania
Rhodes
Antalya
Alanya
Anamur
Sifke
TURKEY
ADANA
HALAB (Aleppo)
Hatay
Al Lādhiqiyah
Nicosia
CYPRUS
Paphos
Limassol
Hamāh
SYRIA
Ḥimṣ
Tarābulus
LEBANON
BAYRŪT (Beirut)
DIMASHQ (Damascus)
Ṣūr
Ḥaifa
ISRAEL
TEL AVIV-YAFO
Ashdod
Jerusalem
AMMAN
IRAQ
Ar Rutbah
Bādiyat ash Shām
JORDAN
Al Jawf
SAUDI ARABIA
Tabûk
Al Wajh
Yanbu' al Bahr
Rābigh
Al Ḥawiyah

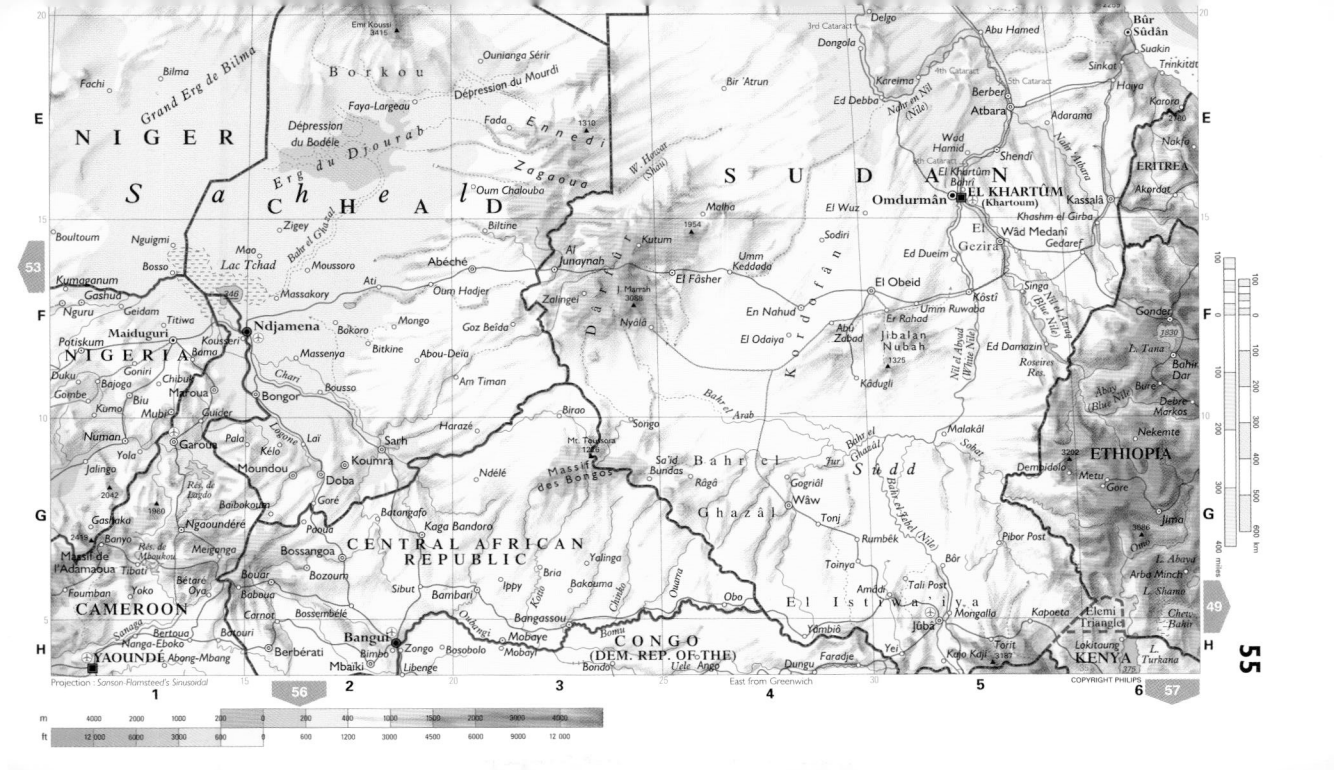
NIGER
Borkou
Grand Erg de Bilma
Bilma
Fachi
Dépression du Mourdi
Ounianga Sérir
Faya-Largeau
Dépression du Bodélé
Erg du Djourab
Fada
Ennedi
Zagaoua
Sachel
Oum Chalouba
Biltine
Zigey
Boultoum
Nguigmi
Mao
Lac Tchad
Bahr el Ghazal
Moussoro
Bosso
Abéché
Ati
Massakory
Oum Hadjer
Kumaganum
Gashua
Nguru
Geidam
Titiwa
Maiduguri
Ndjamena
Bakoro
Mongo
Goz Beida
Patiskum
Kousseri
Sama
NIGERIA
Massenya
Bitkine
Abou-Deia
Duku
Goniri
Chibuk
Bajoga
Gombe
Biu
Matroua
Bongor
Charri
Bousso
Am Timan
Kumo
Mubi
Guider
Numan
Garoua
Pala
Lagone
Lai
Kélo
Yola
Jalingo
Koumra
Sarh
Harazé
Moundou
Doba
Ndélé
Baibokoum
Goré
Batangafo
Gashaka
Ngaoundéré
Paoua
Kaga Bandoro
Banyo
Mts. de Mandara
Massif de l'Adamaoua
Meiganga
Bossangoa
CENTRAL AFRICAN REPUBLIC
Tibati
Foumban
Yoko
Bétaré Oya
Bouar
Bozoum
Bria
Yalinga
Sibut
Bambari
Ippy
Bakouma
Bossembélé
Carnot
Babouá
Bangassou
Mobaye
Mobayi
Bertoua
Batouri
Nanga-Eboko
Berberati
Bangui
Zongo
Bosobolo
Bimbo
Mbaiki
Libenge
YAOUNDÉ
Abong-Mbang
CAMEROON
CONGO
(DEM. REP. OF THE)
Bondo
Uele
Ango
Emi Koussi
3415
Massif des Bongos
Mt. Toubsora
1730
Birao
Bir 'Atrun
Kutum
Al Junaynah
Zalingei
Nyala
Mornah
3088
Malha
1954
El Fāsher
Umm Keddada
Sodiri
Kordofān
Dārfūr
El Odaiya
Abu Zabad
Kadugli
Bahr el Arab
Songa
Sa'id Bundas
Rāgā
Bahr el Ghazāl
Gogriāl
Wāw
Tonj
Tur
Bahr el Ghazāl
Bahr el Zeraf
Bahr el Jebel (Nile)
Sobat
Malakāl
Rumbēk
Toinya
Bōr
Pibor Post
Amadi
Tali Post
Mongalla
Yambiō
Yei
Torit
3187
Kapoeta
Lokitaung
Elemi Triangle
KENYA
L. Turkana
Faradje
Dungu
Juba
Kajo Kaji
Bahr el Jebel
Nile
Sudd
El Istiwā'iyā
Obo
Ouanda
Kotto
Chinko
Ouaka
Mbomu
Uele
Dongola
Delgo
3rd Cataract
Abu Hamed
Kareima
4th Cataract
5th Cataract
Ed Debba
Nahr an Nil (Nile)
Berber
Atbara
Wād Hamid
Shendi
Nile Atbara
El Khartūm Bahrī
EL KHARTŪM
(Khartoum)
Omdurmān
Kassalā
El Wuz
Khashm el Girba
Wād Madanī
Gedaref
El Gezira
Ed Dueim
El Obeid
Kōstī
Er Rahad
Umm Ruwaba
Singa
Blue Nile
Nile el Azrak
Jibalan Nubah
1325
Nile el Abyad (White Nile)
Ed Damazin
Roseires Res.
Gondar
1830
L. Tana
Bahir Dar
Abay (Blue Nile)
Bure
Debre Markos
Nekemte
ETHIOPIA
Dembidolo
3208
Metu
Gore
Jima
3580
Chew Bahir
L. Abaya
Arba Minch
L. Shamo
Bür Sūdān
Suakin
Trinkitat
Sinkat
Haya
Karora
Nakfa
ERITREA
Akordat
Boundary
Projection : Sanson-Flamsteed's Sinusoidal
East from Greenwich
COPYRIGHT PHILIPS
m
ft
55

56 CENTRAL AFRICA

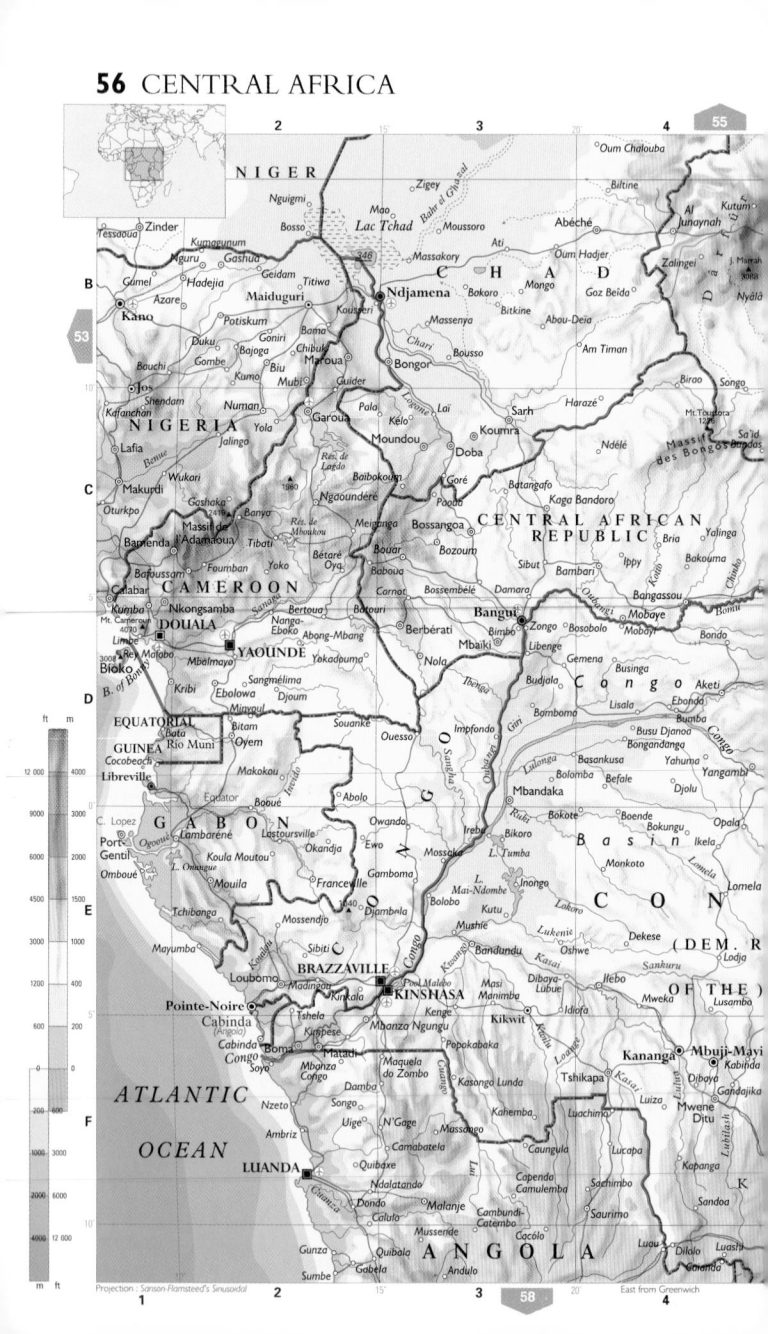

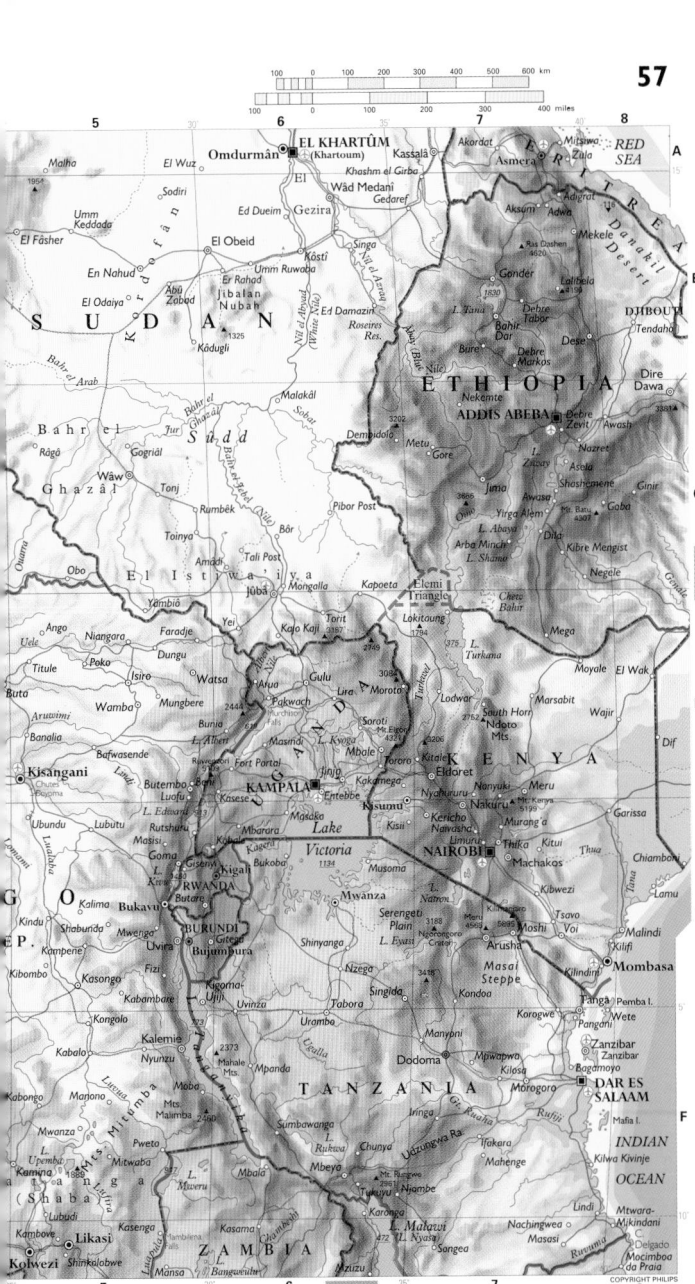
100 0 100 200 300 400 500 600 km
100 0 100 200 300 400 miles
5 6 7 8
A B C D E F
EL KHARTÛM (Khartoum)
Omdurmân
Kassalâ
Asmera
Massawa
Zula
RED SEA
ERITREA
Danakil Desert
Akordat
Aksum
Adwa
Adigrat
Mekele
Ras Dashen 4620
Gondar
Lalibela
Debre Tabor
L. Tana
Bahir Dar
Dese
Debre Markos
Buré
DJIBOUTI
Tendaho
ETHIOPIA
Dire Dawa
ADDIS ABEBA
Debre Zeyit
Awash
Nazret
L. Zwai
Asela
Shashemene
Ginir
Jimma
Awasa
Yirga Alem
Mts. Bale
Goba
L. Abaya
Dila
Arba Minch
L. Shala
Kibre Mengist
Negele
Gogrial
Wâw
Tonj
Rumbêk
Pibor Post
Bôr
Toinya
Amadi
Tali Post
Jûba
Mongalla
Kapoeta
Elemi Triangle
Chete Bahir
Lokitaung
Mega
Moyale
El Wak
Marsabit
Wajir
Dif
Mandera
Garissa
Malindi
Kilifi
Mombasa
Tanga
Pemba I.
Wete
Pangani
Zanzibar
Bagamoyo
Kilosa
Morogoro
DAR ES SALAAM
Mafia I.
INDIAN OCEAN
Kilwa Kivinje
Mtwara
Mikindani
Delgado
Mocimboa da Praia
Lindi
Nachingwea
Masasi
Ruvuma
Songea
Mtwara
Ndjamena
Kosti
Umm Ruwaba
Er Rahad
Jibalan Nubah
Abu Zabad
El Odaiya
En Nahud
El Fâsher
Umm Keddada
Sodiri
Malha
El Wuz
Ed Dueim
Gezira
Wâd Medanî
Gedaref
Khashm el Girba
El Obeid
Kadugli
Malakâl
Sobat
Bahr el Ghazal
Bahr el Arab
Bahr el Jebel
Nile
Blue Nile
White Nile
Atbara
Tekeze
Ed Damazin
Roseires Res.
Singa
Gondar
Dembidolo
Metu
Gore
Tepi
Bonga
Yambiô
Yei
Kajo Kaji
Tarit
Lokitaung
Kitale
Eldoret
Kakamega
Nyahururu
Nanyuki
Meru
Nakuru
Kericho
Nanyuki
Murang'a
Thika
Kitui
Machakos
Kibwezi
Tsavo
Voi
Moshi
Arusha
Kilimanjaro
Masai Steppe
Kilindini
Singida
Kondoa
Tabora
Korogwe
Manyoni
Dodoma
Mpwapwa
Iringa
Mahenge
Ifakara
Mbeya
Tukuyu
Mpanda
Mbala
Sumbawanga
Kasama
Kasenga
Kambove
Likasi
Kolwezi
Shinkolobwe
Mansa
Bangweulu
Mpika
Nzega
Shinyanga
Musoma
Mwanza
Bukoba
Kigali
Butare
Gitega
Bujumbura
Uvira
Kigoma
Ujiji
Kabambare
Kasongo
Kindu
Kabalo
Kongolo
Kalemie
Nyunzu
Mahale Mts.
Tunduma
Uramba
Mikumi
Ruaha
Rufiji
Kilombero
Ruvuma
Lake Victoria
Lake Tanganyika
Lake Malawi
Lake Rukwa
Lake Turkana
Lake Rudolf
Lake Edward
Lake Albert
Lake Kivu
Lake Natron
Lake Eyasi
Lake Manyara
Lake Mweru
Lake Nyasa
Ngorongoro Crater
Serengeti Plain
Mt. Kenya 5199
Mt. Elgon 4321
Mt. Rungwe 2961
Mt. Kilimanjaro 5895
Mt. Meru 4566
Mt. Bale 4307
Mt. Elgon
Mt. Kenya
Mt. Rungwe
Mt. Kilimanjaro
Mt. Meru
Mt. Bale

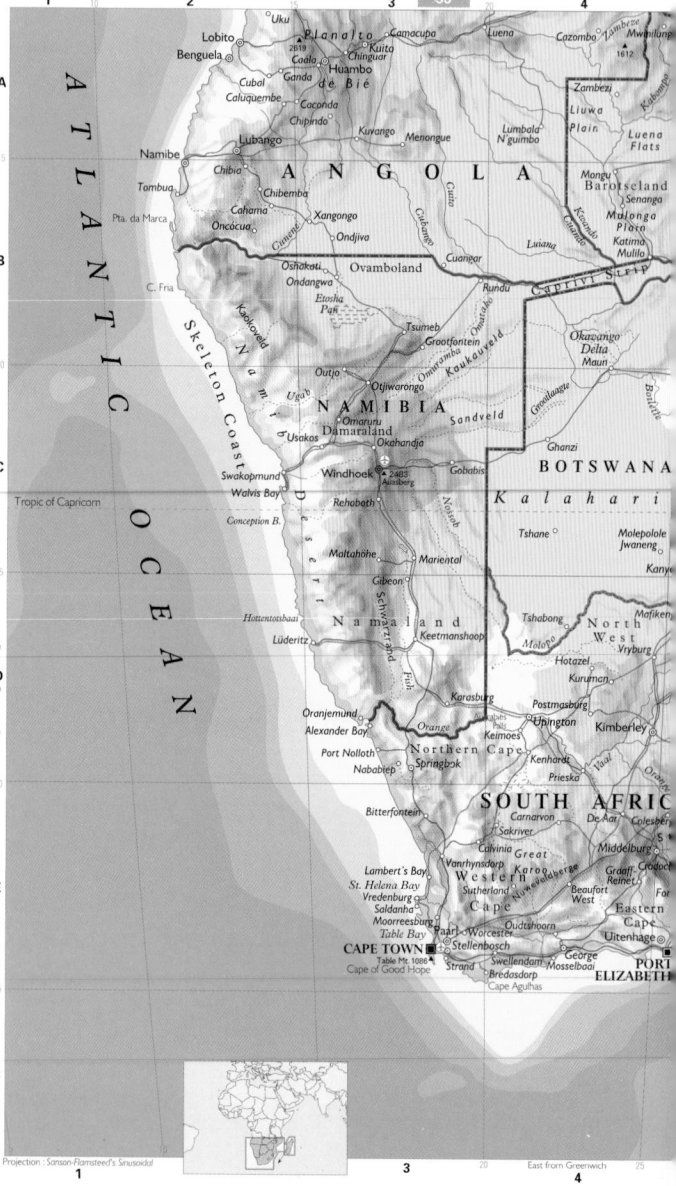
56
1
2
3
4
A
B
C
D
E
F
ATLANTIC OCEAN
Uíuk
Lobito
Benguela
Planalto
2619
Kuito
Chinguar
Camacupa
Luena
Cazombo
Lambezi
Mwinilungi
1612
Cadla
Huambo
Ganda
Cubal
Calúquembe
Caconda
Chipindo
Kuvango
Menongue
Lumbala N'guimbo
Zambezi
Liuwa Plain
Kabompo
Luena Flats
Lubango
Namibe
Chibia
ANGOLA
Tombua
Chibemba
Cahama
Pta. da Marca
Oncócua
Xangongo
Ondjiva
Cunene
Cubango
Cuito
Cuando
Kasando
Luiana
Mangu
Barotseland
Senanga
Mulonga Plain
Katima Mulilo
Caprivi Strip
Cuanavale
C. Fria
Oshakati
Ovamboland
Ondangwa
Etosha Pan
Rundu
Kaokoveld
Skeleton Coast
Namib Desert
Tsumeb
Grootfontein
Omaruru
Koukauveld
Okavango Delta
Maun
Outjo
Otjiwarongo
Ugab
NAMIBIA
Omaruru
Damaraland
Usakos
Okahandja
Sandveld
Gwaikwe
Boteti
Ghanzi
Swakopmund
Windhoek
2483
Auas Berg
Gobabis
BOTSWANA
Walvis Bay
Tropic of Capricorn
Rehoboth
Kalahari
Conception B.
Nossob
Tshane
Molepolole
Jwaneng
Kanye
Maltahöhe
Mariental
Gibeon
Hottentotsbaai
Namaland
Keetmanshoop
Tshabong
North West
Mafikeng
Lüderitz
Sehonghong
Fish
Molopo
Vryburg
Hotazel
Kuruman
Karasburg
Postmasburg
Oranjemund
Alexander Bay
Orange
Upington
Kimberley
Kakamas
Keimoes
Port Nolloth
Northern Cape
Nababerp
Springbok
Kenhardt
Vaal
Prieska
Orange
SOUTH AFRIC
Bitterfontein
Carnarvon
De Aar
Colesberg
Sakriver
Great Karoo
Middelburg
Cavinia
Vanrhynsdorp
Nuweveldberge
Graaff-Reinet
Lambert's Bay
St. Helena Bay
Western Cape
Sutherland
Beaufort West
Vredenburg
Saldanha
Moorreesburg
Eastern Cape
Table Bay
Worcester
Oudtshoorn
Paarl
Stellenbosch
Uitenhage
CAPE TOWN
Table Mt. 1086
Cape of Good Hope
Strand
Swellendam
George
Mossel Baai
PORT ELIZABETH
Bredasdorp
Cape Agulhas
ft
m
12 000
4000
9000
3000
6000
2000
4500
1500
3000
1000
1200
400
600
200
0
0
-200
-600
1000
3000
2000
6000
4000
12 000
Projection : Sanson-Flamsteed's Sinusoidal
East from Greenwich

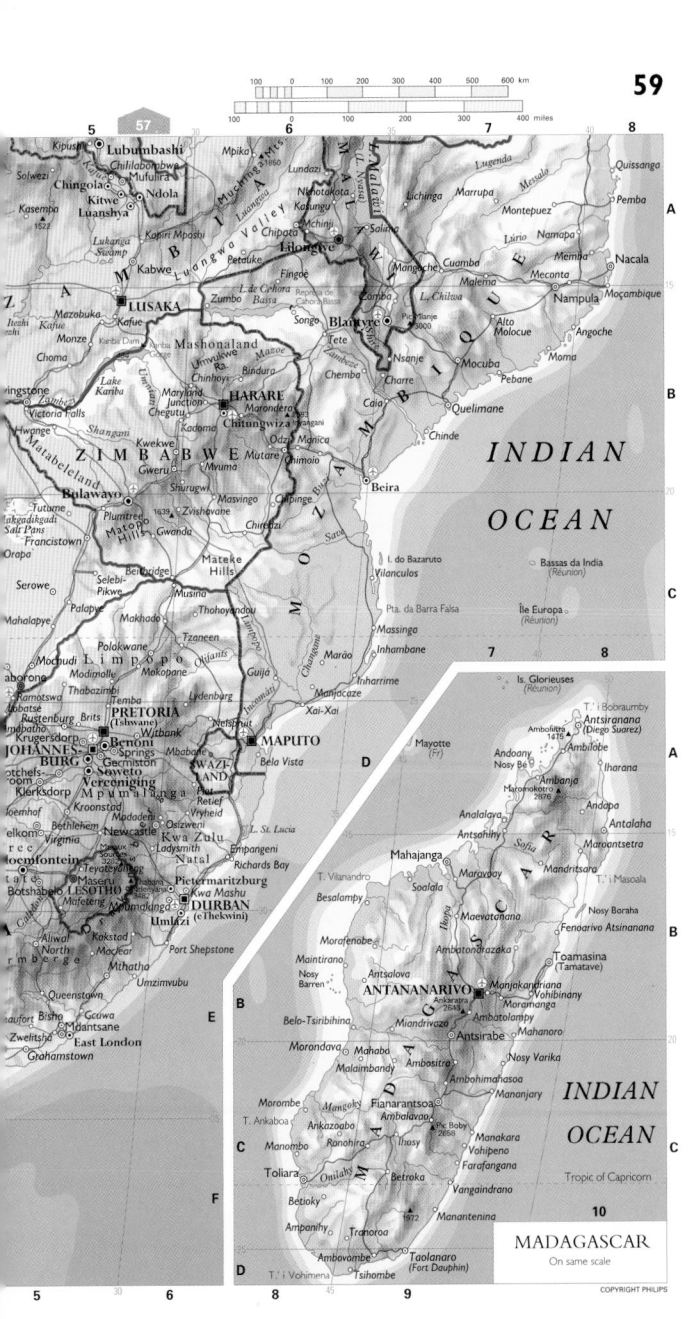
100 0 100 200 300 400 500 600 km
100 0 100 200 300 400 miles
57
Lubumbashi
Kipushi
Mufulira
Chingola
Ndola
Kitwe
Luanshya
Kasempa
Solwezi
Mpika
Lundazi
Nchelenge
Kasama
Mbala
Nyika Plateau
Mzuzu
Nkhotakota
Kasungu
Lilongwe
Chipata
Mchinji
Salima
Lichinga
Marrupa
Montepuez
Pemba
Quissanga
Lugenda
Messalo
Lúrio
Namapa
Nacala
Memba
Mecanhelas
Cuamba
Mandimba
Malema
Meconta
Nampula
Moçambique
Alto Molocue
Angoche
Moma
Mocuba
Pebane
Quelimane
Chinde
Beira
Mocimboa da Praia
Pemba
Kabwe
Petauke
Fingoe
Lake Cahora Bassa
Reservoir de Cahora-Bassa
Zumbo
Tete
Blantyre
Mt. Mlanje 3000
L. Chilwa
Nsanje
Chemba
Charre
Caia
Lake Malawi
Lake Nyasa
Mazabuka
Kafue
Lusaka
Kafue Dam
Kariba Dam
Kariba
Monze
Choma
Mashonaland
Umvukwe Mts.
Mazoe
Zambezi
Bindura
Chinhoyi
Maryland Junction
Harare
Marondera
Chitungwiza
Chegutu
Kadoma
Kwekwe
Gweru
Mutare
Odzi
Mutoko
Chimoio
Mt. Gorongoza
Masvingo
Chipinge
Zvishavane
Chiredzi
Gwanda
Mt. Mavuradonha
Victoria Falls
Hwange
Shangani
Matabeleland
Bulawayo
Tutume
Plumtree
Francistown
Salt Pans
Mt. Hillers
Mateke Hills
Belmondo
Selebi-Pikwe
Serowe
Palapye
Mahalapye
Makhado
Musina
Thohoyandou
Tzaneen
Polokwane
Mochudi
Limpopo
Mokopane
Modimolle
Thabazimbi
Temba
Lydenburg
Rustenburg
Brits
Pretoria (Tshwane)
Witbank
Krugersdorp
Johannesburg
Benoni
Springs
Germiston
Soweto
Vereeniging
Mpumalanga
Kroonstad
Mafeteng
Maseru
Lesotho
Botshabelo
Bethlehem
Newcastle
Ladysmith
Virginia
Qwaqwa
Sasolburg
Vanderbijlpark
Vaal Dam
Oswezwi
Kwa Zulu
Natal
Empangeni
Richards Bay
Pietermaritzburg
Kwa Mashu
Durban (eThekwini)
Umlazi
Umbumbulu
Port Shepstone
Umzimvubu
Mthatha
Mooi River
Kokstad
Aliwal North
Queenstown
Bisho
East London
Grahamstown
Mdantsane
Zwelitsha
Gcuwa
Mozambique
Nampula
Tete
Beira
Inhambane
Maputo
Xai-Xai
Chibuto
Chókwe
Guijá
Maríos
Massinga
Inharrime
Manjacaze
Bela Vista
Swaziland
Mbabane
Nelspruit
Lake Cahora Bassa
Zambezi
Pungwe
Buzi
Save
Limpopo
Olifants
Changane
Ilo Bazaruto
Vilanculos
Pta. da Barra Falsa
Bassas da India (Réunion)
Île Europa (Réunion)
Is. Glorieuses (Réunion)
Tromelin (Fr)
Mayotte (Fr)
Antsiranana (Diego Suarez)
Ambolitra 1478
Ambilobe
Andoany Nosy Be
Iharana
Ambanja
Maromokotro 2876
Andapa
Antalaha
Analalava
Antsohihy
Mahajanga
Mandritsara
Mascala
Maroantsetra
Soalala
Besalampy
Maevatanana
Nosy Boraha
Fenoarivo Atsinanana
Morafenobe
Ambatondrazaka
Toamasina (Tamatave)
Maintirano
Nosy Barren
Antsalova
Antananarivo
Ankaratra 2643
Manjakandriana
Vohibinany
Moramanga
Belo-Tsiribihina
Miandrivazo
Ambatolampy
Antsirabe
Mahanoro
Morondava
Mahabo
Malaimbandy
Ambositra
Nosy Varika
Ambohimahasoa
Mananjary
Morombe
Mangoky
Fianarantsoa
Ambalavao
Ankazoabo
Pic Boby 2658
Manakara
Vohipeno
Manombo
Ranohira
Ihosy
Farafangana
Toliara
Onilahy
Betroka
Betioky
Vangaindrano
Ampanihy
Tranoroa
Ambovombe
Taolanaro (Fort Dauphin)
Tsihombe
T. i Vohimena
Tropic of Capricorn
Indian Ocean
Madagascar
On same scale
COPYRIGHT PHILIPS

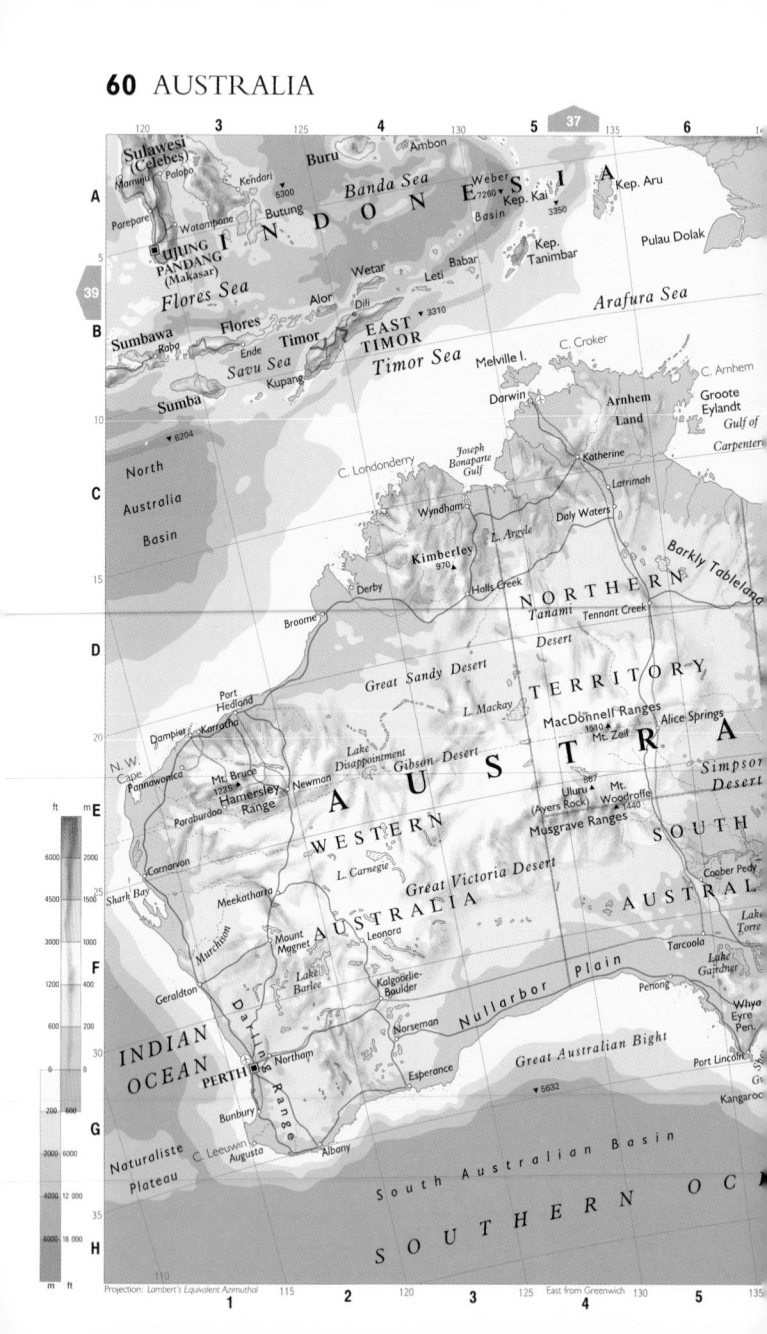
Sulawesi (Celebes)
Mamuju
Palopo
Kendari
5300
Buru
Ambon
Banda Sea
Weber
7260
Kep. Kai
3350
Basin
Kep. Aru
Parepare
Watampone
Butung
I N D O N E S I A
UJUNG PANDANG (Makasar)
Flores Sea
Wetar
Leti
Babar
Kep. Tanimbar
Pulau Dolak
Alor
Dili
3310
Arafura Sea
Sumbawa
Flores
Timor
EAST TIMOR
Timor Sea
Melville I.
C. Croker
Ende
Savu Sea
Kupang
Sumba
Darwin
Arnhem Land
C. Arnhem
Groote Eylandt
Gulf of Carpentaria
6304
North Australia Basin
C. Londonderry
Joseph Bonaparte Gulf
Katherine
Larrimah
Wyndham
Daly Waters
L. Argyle
Kimberley
970
Barkly Tableland
Derby
Halls Creek
NORTHERN TERRITORY
Broome
Tanami Desert
Tennant Creek
Great Sandy Desert
Port Hedland
L. Mackay
MacDonnell Ranges
1510
Mt. Zeil
Alice Springs
Dampier
Karratha
Lake Disappointment
Gibson Desert
N.W. Cape
Pannawonica
Mt. Bruce
1235
Hamersley Range
Newman
Simpson Desert
Paraburdoo
A U S T R A L I A
Uluru (Ayers Rock)
867
Mt. Woodroffe
1440
Musgrave Ranges
WESTERN
SOUTH
Carnarvon
L. Carnegie
Great Victoria Desert
Coober Pedy
Shark Bay
Meekatharra
AUSTRALIA
AUSTRAL
Lake Torrens
Marchison
Mount Magnet
Leonora
Tarcoola
Lake Gairdner
Geraldton
Lake Barlee
Kalgoorlie-Boulder
Penong
Whyalla
Eyre Pen.
Darling Range
Norseman
Nullarbor Plain
INDIAN OCEAN
PERTH
Northam
Esperance
Great Australian Bight
Port Lincoln
Kangaroo
Bunbury
5632
C. Leeuwin
Augusta
Albany
Naturaliste Plateau
South Australian Basin
SOUTHERN OC
S O U T H E R N
Projection: Lambert's Equivalent Azimuthal
East from Greenwich

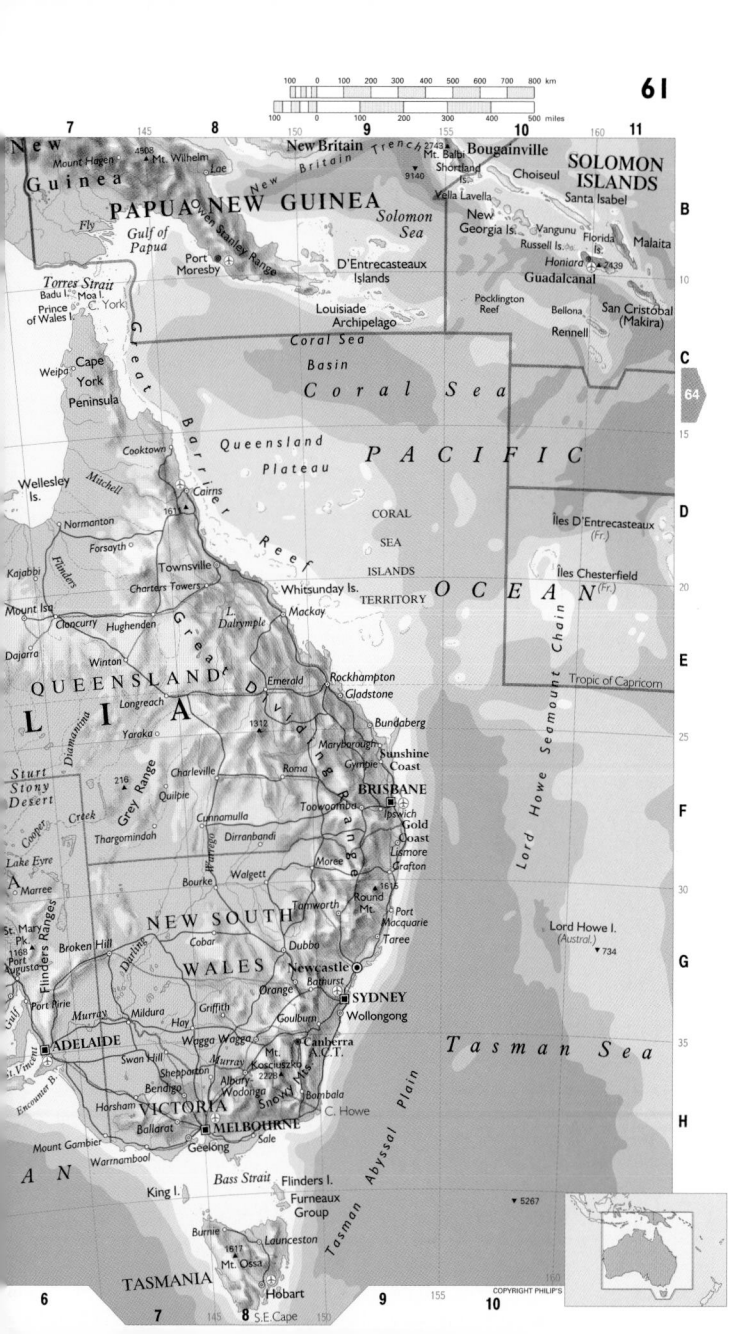
100 0 100 200 300 400 500 600 700 800 km
100 0 100 200 300 400 500 miles
New Guinea
Mount Hagen
4508
Mt. Wilhelm
Lae
New Britain
Trench
2743
Mt. Balbi
Bougainville
Shortland
9140
Choiseul
SOLOMON ISLANDS
Santa Isabel
PAPUA NEW GUINEA
Fly
Gulf of Papua
Owen Stanley Range
Port Moresby
Solomon Sea
Yella Lavella
New Georgia Is.
Vangunu
Russell Is.
Florida Is.
Malaita
Honiara
2439
Guadalcanal
D'Entrecasteaux Islands
Torres Strait
Badu I.
Moa I.
C. York
Prince of Wales I.
Great Barrier Reef
Louisiade Archipelago
Pocklington Reef
Bellona
Rennell
San Cristóbal (Makira)
Coral Sea Basin
Coral Sea
Cape York Peninsula
Weipa
Cooktown
Queensland Plateau
PACIFIC
Wellesley Is.
Mitchell
Cairns
1611
Normanton
Forsayth
Flinders
Kajabbi
Townsville
Charters Towers
CORAL SEA ISLANDS TERRITORY
Whitsunday Is.
Îles D'Entrecasteaux (Fr.)
Îles Chesterfield (Fr.)
OCEAN
Mount Isa
Cloncurry
Hughenden
L. Dalrymple
Mackay
Great Dividing Range
Dajarra
Winton
Emerald
Rockhampton
Gladstone
Tropic of Capricorn
QUEENSLAND
Longreach
Diamantina
Yaraka
1312
Bundaberg
Maryborough
Sunshine Coast
Gympie
Sturt Stony Desert
216
Grey Range
Charleville
Roma
BRISBANE
Quilpie
Toowoomba
Ipswich
Gold Coast
Cooper Creek
Cunnamulla
Thargomindah
Dirranbandi
Lake Eyre
Warrego
Moree
Lismore
Grafton
Marree
Bourke
Walgett
Lord Howe Seamount Chain
1615
Round Mt.
Tamworth
Port Macquarie
NEW SOUTH WALES
St. Mary Pk
1168
Port Augusta
Flinders Ranges
Broken Hill
Darling
Cobar
Dubbo
Taree
Lord Howe I. (Austral.)
734
Newcastle
Bathurst
Orange
SYDNEY
Port Pirie
Murray
Mildura
Griffith
Hay
Goulburn
Wollongong
Wagga Wagga
Canberra A.C.T.
ADELAIDE
Swan Hill
Murray
Mt. Kosciuszko 2228
Snowy
Tasman Sea
Sheppatton
Albury
Wodonga
Bendigo
Bombala
Harsham
VICTORIA
C. Howe
Ballarat
MELBOURNE
Sale
Geelong
Mount Gambier
Warrnambool
Tasman Abyssal Plain
Bass Strait
Flinders I.
King I.
Furneaux Group
5267
Burnie
Launceston
1617
Mt. Ossa
TASMANIA
Hobart
S.E. Cape
COPYRIGHT PHILIP'S
64

62 SOUTH-EAST AUSTRALIA

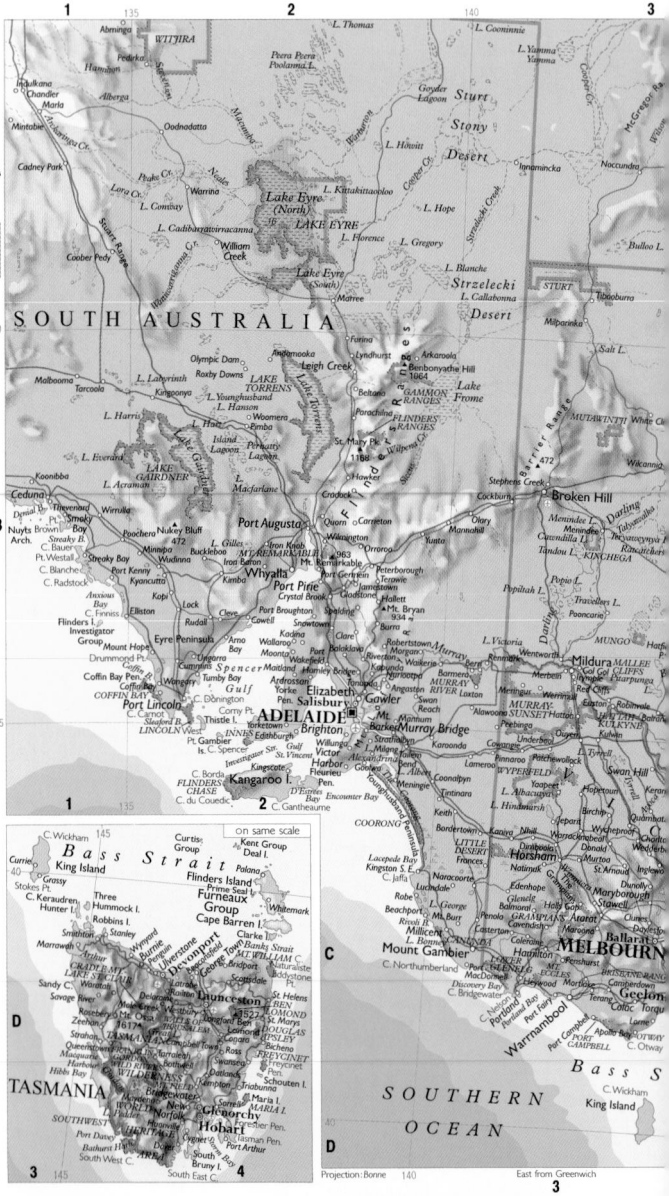

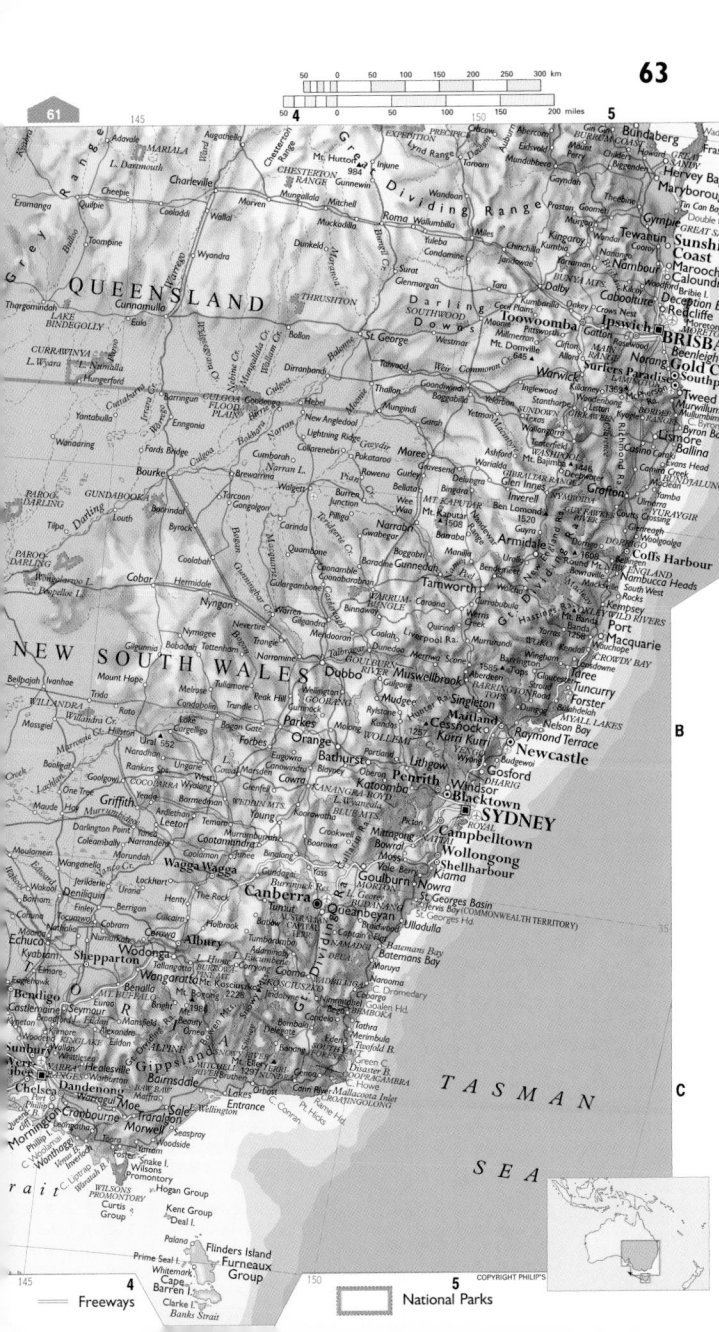
50 0 50 100 150 200 250 300 km
50 0 50 100 150 200 miles
61
4
5
QUEENSLAND
NEW SOUTH WALES
TASMAN SEA
Great Dividing Range
Darling Downs
Grey Range
Bundaberg
Hervey Bay
Maryborough
Gympie
Tewantin
Sunshine Coast
Maroochydore
Caloundra
Nambour
Cooroy
Gympie
Kingaroy
Toowoomba
Ipswich
BRISBANE
Redcliffe
Deception Bay
Beenleigh
Gold Coast
Southport
Surfers Paradise
Tweed Hds
Murwillumbah
Lismore
Ballina
Byron Bay
Grafton
Armidale
Coffs Harbour
Port Macquarie
Tuncurry
Forster
Taree
Kempsey
Nambucca Heads
Tamworth
Gunnedah
Moree
Narrabri
Dubbo
Mudgee
Muswellbrook
Singleton
Maitland
Cessnock
Kurri Kurri
Newcastle
Raymond Terrace
Gosford
Wyong
Windsor
Blacktown
SYDNEY
Campbelltown
Wollongong
Shellharbour
Kiama
Nowra
Goulburn
Bathurst
Orange
Parkes
Forbes
Cowra
Griffith
Leeton
Wagga Wagga
Tumut
Canberra
Queanbeyan
Ulladulla
Batemans Bay
Albury
Wodonga
Shepparton
Wangaratta
Bendigo
Castlemaine
Seymour
Echuca
Kyabram
Sunbury
Melbourne
Geelong
Ballarat
Warrnambool
Portland
Mt Gambier
Bairnsdale
Sale
Morwell
Moe
Warragul
Dandenong
Frankston
Cranbourne
Chelsea
Phillip I.
Wilsons Promontory
Hogan Group
Kent Group
Deal I.
Curtis Group
Flinders Island
Furneaux Group
Prime Seal I.
Whitemark
Cape Barren I.
Clarke I.
Banks Strait
Freeways
National Parks
COPYRIGHT PHILIP'S

64 NEW ZEALAND, CENTRAL AND SOUTH-WEST PACIFIC

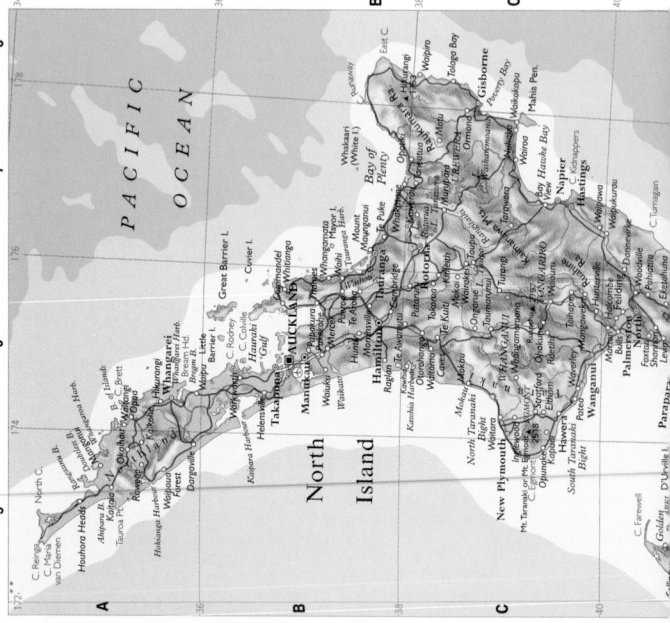
PACIFIC OCEAN
North Island
AUCKLANDS
Hamilton
Rotorua
Tauranga
Gisborne
Napier
Hastings
Wellington
Wanganui
New Plymouth
Whangarei
Whangaroa
Bay of Plenty
Great Barrier I.
Cuvier I.
Mt. Taranaki (Egmont)
Mt. Ruapehu
Mt. Tongariro
Mt. Ngauruhoe
Mt. Tarawera
Mt. Edgecumbe

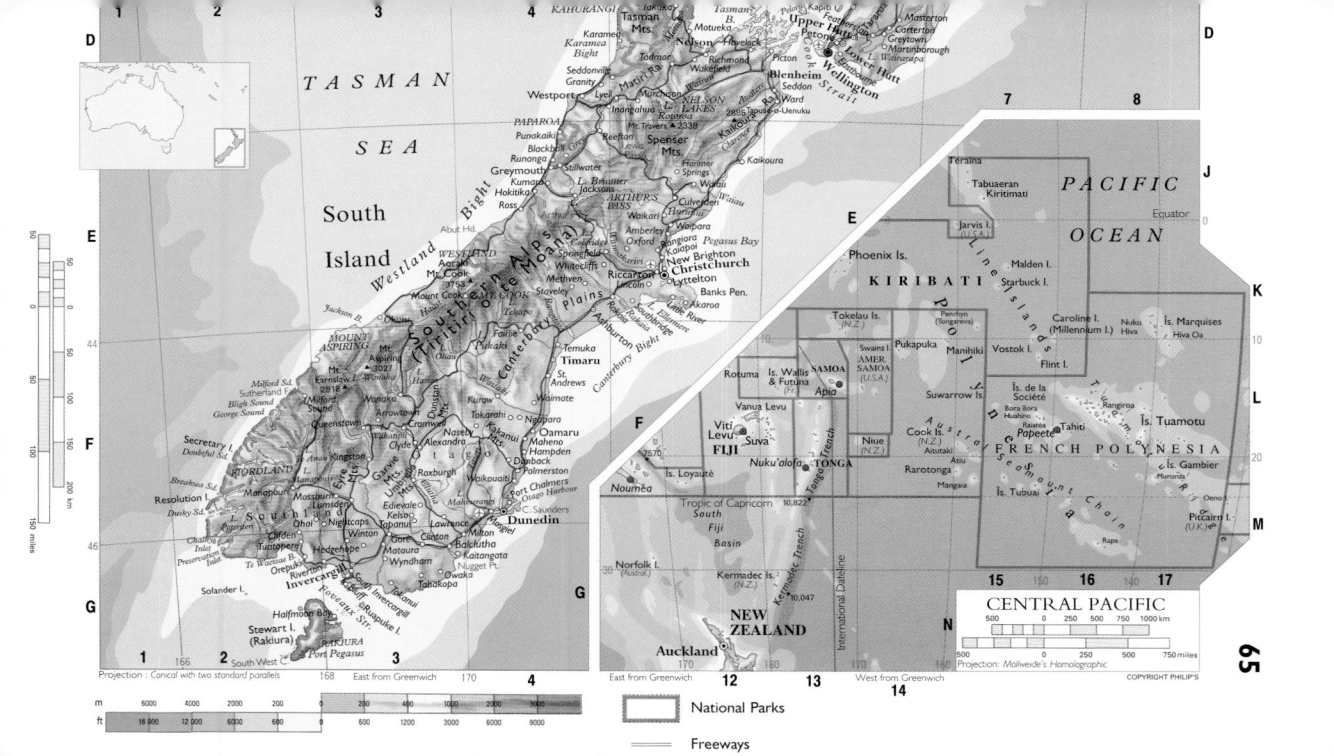
TASMAN SEA
South Island
Tasman Mts.
Nelson
Blenheim
Wellington
Westport
Greymouth
Hokitika
Ross
Kaikoura
Spenser Mts.
Christchurch
Timaru
Oamaru
Dunedin
Invercargill
Stewart I. (Rakiura)
Southern Alps (Tiritiri o te Moana)
Mt. Cook 3764
Mt. Aspiring 3027
Mt. Earnslaw 2819
Mt. Tasman
Mt. Cook
Mt. Aspiring
Mt. Earnslaw
Westland Bight
Canterbury Bight
Canterbury Plains
Pegasus Bay
Cook Strait
Projection : Conical with two standard parallels
East from Greenwich
South West C.
Port Pegasus
Auckland
NEW ZEALAND
Norfolk I.
Kermadec Is.
Kermadec Trench
Tonga Trench
Tropic of Capricorn
South Fiji Basin
Nouméa
Suva
Nuku'alofa
TONGA
FIJI
Apia
SAMOA
Niue
Rarotonga
Papeete
Tahiti
Tuvalu
Tokelau Is.
Wallis & Futuna
Vanua Levu
Viti Levu
Rotuma
Phoenix Is.
KIRIBATI
Tabuaeran
Kiritimati
Jarvis I.
Malden I.
Starbuck I.
Caroline I. (Millennium I.)
Vostok I.
Flint I.
Suwarrow Is.
Is. de la Société
Is. Tuamotu
Is. Gambier
Is. Tubuai
Is. Marquises
Pukapuka
Manihiki
Penrhyn (Tongareva)
Swains I.
AMER. SAMOA (U.S.A.)
Cook Is. (N.Z.)
Aitutaki
Atiu
Mangaia
Rapa
Pitcairn I. (U.K.)
Oeno I.
Raiatea
Bora Bora
Huahine
Rangiroa
Nuku Hiva
Hiva Oa
Terains
Equator
PACIFIC OCEAN
Line Islands
Phoenix Is.
Tuamotu Archipelago
Austral Islands
Marquesas Islands
Tubuai Chain
FRENCH POLYNESIA
CENTRAL PACIFIC
Projection: Mallweide's Homalographic
COPYRIGHT PHILIP'S
International Dateline
East from Greenwich
West from Greenwich
National Parks
Freeways
65

ICELAND
Reykjavik
Denmark Strait
GREENLAND
(Denmark)
Davis Strait
Baffin Island
Baffin Bay
Hudson Strait
Ellesmere I.
Queen Elizabeth Is.
Victoria I.
ARCTIC
OCEAN
Beaufort Sea
International Date Line
Hudson Bay
NUNAVUT
NUNAVIK
LABRADOR
NEWFOUNDLAND
QUEBEC
Fontinent
NOVA SCOTIA
Halifax
MAINE
Quebec
Montreal
ONTARIO
Ottawa
Toronto
Winnipeg
MANITOBA
Churchill
SASKATCHEWAN
Regina
Saskatchewan
Edmonton
ALBERTA
Calgary
Athabasca
Great Slave L.
Yellowknife
Great Bear L.
Mackenzie
NORTHWEST TERRITORIES
Dubawnt L.
Baker L.
Churchill
Nelson
Saskatchewan
Peace
Athabasca
Fraser
Columbia
Kootenay
BRITISH COLUMBIA
Vancouver
Victoria
Olympia
Seattle
Portland
Mult-nomah
Pelly
Liard
Mackenzie
YUKON TERRITORY
Whitehorse
Porcupine
Yukon
Kuskokwim
Nushagak
Kodiak I.
Gulf of Alaska
ALASKA
Fairbanks
Tanana
McKinley
Bering Sea
St. Lawrence
Bering Strait
RUSSIA
Asia
C
B
A
D
E
60
70
80
50
40

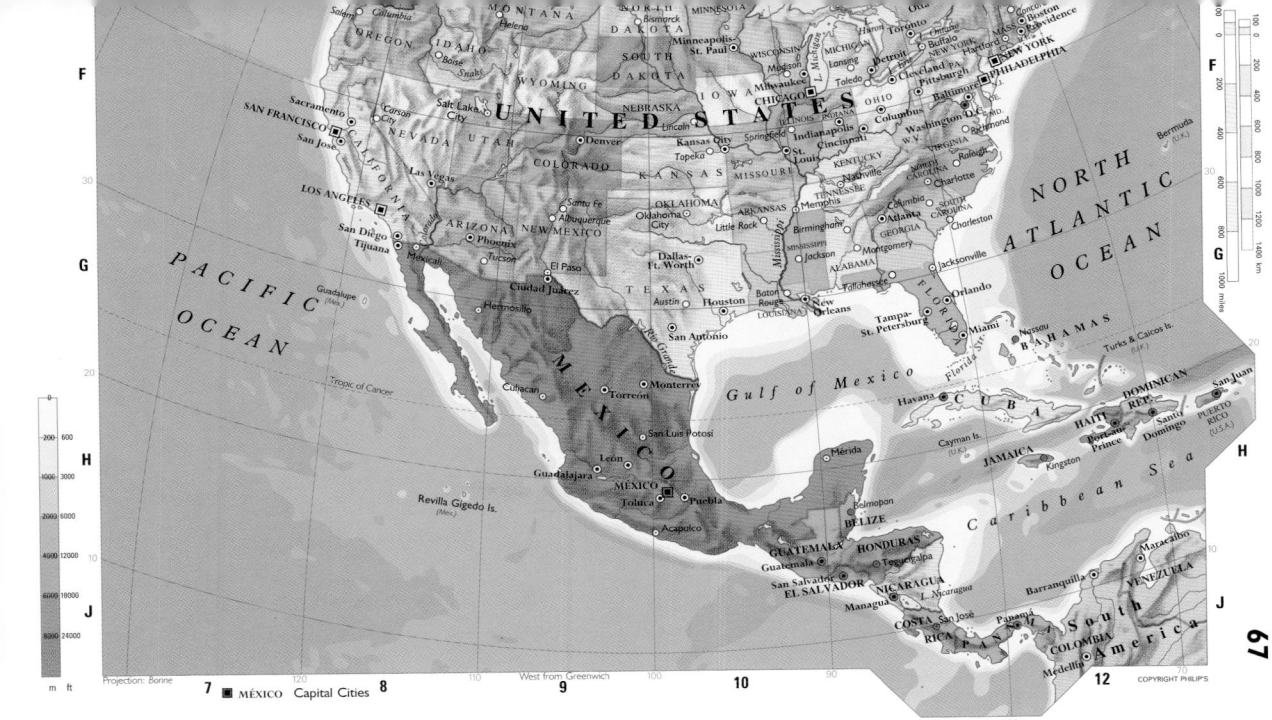
UNITED STATES
MEXICO
CANADA
CUBA
BAHAMAS
HAITI
DOMINICAN REP.
JAMAICA
BELIZE
GUATEMALA
HONDURAS
NICARAGUA
COSTA RICA
PANAMÁ
EL SALVADOR
VENEZUELA
COLOMBIA
South America
PACIFIC OCEAN
ATLANTIC OCEAN
Gulf of Mexico
Caribbean Sea
Tropic of Cancer
Rio Grande
Mississippi
Florida Str.
Revilla Gigedo Is. (Mex.)
Cayman Is. (U.K.)
Turks & Caicos Is. (U.K.)
Bermuda (U.K.)
Guadalupe (Mex.)
Nassau
Havana
Kingston
Port-au-Prince
Santo Domingo
San Juan
PUERTO RICO (U.S.A.)
Belmopan
Guatemala
Tegucigalpa
San Salvador
Managua
L. Nicaragua
San José
Panamá
Barranquilla
Maracaibo
Medellín
Mérida
Monterrey
Torreón
Guadalajara
MÉXICO
Puebla
Tolluca
Acapulco
San Luis Potosí
Ciudad Juárez
Hermosillo
Culiacán
Mexicali
Tijuana
Ensenada
Guaymas
Mazatlán
Tampico
Veracruz
Villahermosa
Oaxaca
Tuxtla Gutierrez
Chihuahua
Durango
Saltillo
Zacatecas
Aguascalientes
Morelia
Toluca
Cancún
Chetumal
Tapachula
Salina Cruz
Coatzacoslcos
Ciudad Del Carmen
Matamoros
Nuevo Laredo
Reynosa
Campeche
Mérida

Hudson Bay
Victoria Island
Banks Island
Prince of Wales I.
Somerset Island
Prince Albert Pen.
Bathurst Pen.
Boothia Pen.
King William I.
Melville Sound
Viscount
M'Clintock Channel
Amundsen Gulf
Coronation Gulf
Dease Arm
Great Bear L.
Great Slave L.
Athabasca
Lake Athabasca
Mackenzie Mts.
Selwyn Mts.
Cassiar Mountains
Rocky Mts.
Wrangell Mts.
St. Elias Mts.
Alexander Archipelago
Queen Charlotte Is.
PACIFIC
Anchorage
Fairbanks
Yukon
Mackenzie
Peace
Slave
Hay
Liard
Nelson
Churchill
Thelon
Coppermine
Kuskokwim
Tanana
Copper
Stikine
Skeena
Fraser
Nass
Kitimat
Prince Rupert
Ketchikan
Juneau
Skagway
Whitehorse
Dawson
Yellowknife
Fort Smith
Fort Nelson
Fort Simpson
Fort Liard
Fort Resolution
Fort Chipewyan
Fort McMurray
Fort McPherson
Fort Good Hope
Norman Wells
Inuvik
Tuktoyaktuk
Cambridge Bay
Coppermine
Kugluktuk
Pond Inlet
Resolute
Eureka
Alert
Ellesmere I.
Baffin I.
Melville Pen.
Victoria I.
Banks I.

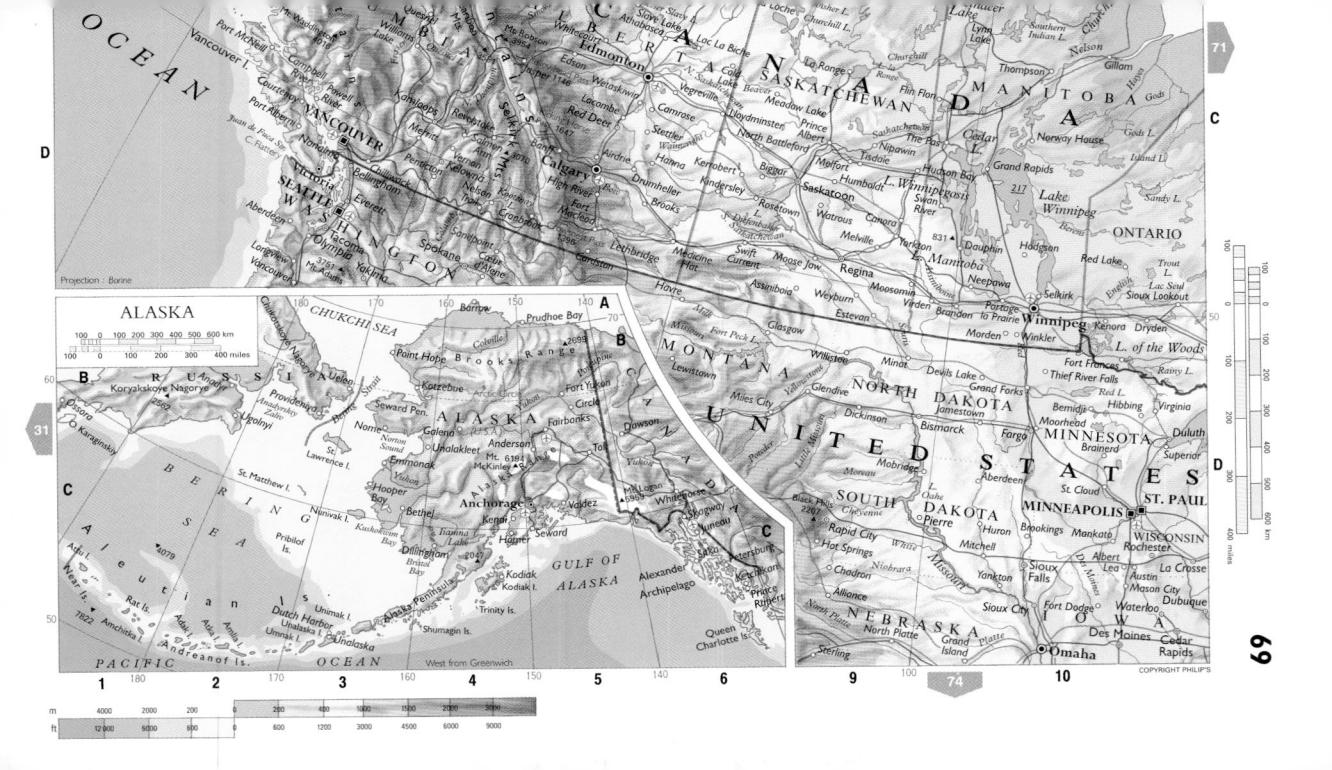
OCEAN
Vancouver I.
Port McNeill
Campbell River
Port Alberni
VANCOUVER
Victoria
SEATTLE
WASHINGTON
Bellingham
Everett
Aberdeen
Olympia
Longview
Vancouver
Spokane
Coeur d'Alene
Yakima
Kamloops
Kelowna
Penticton
Vernon
Nelson
Trail
Cranbrook
Calgary
High River
Fort Macleod
Lethbridge
Medicine Hat
Swift Current
Moose Jaw
Regina
Estevan
Edmonton
Jasper
Banff
Red Deer
Lloydminster
Saskatoon
Prince Albert
Melfort
Humboldt
Watrous
Melville
Yorkton
Moosomin
Weyburn
Assiniboia
Hoyle
Brooks
Drumheller
Kindersley
Rosetown
Swift Current
Grande Prairie
Dawson Creek
Fort St John
Churchill
Thompson
Flin Flon
Lynn Lake
Southern Indian L.
Churchill L.
Nelson
Gillam
Norway House
Cedar L.
Grand Rapids
Nipawin
The Pas
Tadoule
Hudson Bay
L. Winnipegosis
Swan River
Dauphin
Lake Winnipeg
Sandy L.
Gods L.
Island L.
Hodgson
Red Lake
Trout L.
Lac Seul
Sioux Lookout
ONTARIO
Selkirk
Winnipeg
Portage la Prairie
Brandon
Neepawa
Morden
Winkler
Kenora
Dryden
L. of the Woods
Fort Frances
Thief River Falls
Rainy L.
Red L.
Hibbing
Virginia
Duluth
Superior
Brainerd
Moorhead
Bemidji
MINNESOTA
MINNEAPOLIS
ST. PAUL
WISCONSIN
Rochester
La Crosse
Austin
Mason City
Dubuque
Albert Lea
Mankato
St. Cloud
Aberdeen
Fargo
Grand Forks
Jamestown
Devils Lake
Minot
Williston
NORTH DAKOTA
Bismarck
Dickinson
Glendive
Miles City
Glasgow
Havre
Lewistown
Fort Peck L.
Great Falls
Cut Bank
Shelby
Kalispell
Missoula
Helena
Butte
Bozeman
Billings
Sheridan
Gillette
Rapid City
Pierre
Huron
Brookings
Mitchell
Sioux Falls
Yankton
Sioux City
Fort Dodge
Waterloo
Des Moines
Cedar Rapids
Omaha
Lincoln
Grand Island
North Platte
Scottsbluff
Sterling
Alliance
Chadron
Hot Springs
Cheyenne
Laramie
Casper
Rawlins
Rock Springs
Green River
Evanston
Salt Lake City
Provo
Ogden
Logan
Pocatello
Idaho Falls
Twin Falls
Boise
Nampa
Caldwell
Lewiston
Tacoma
Nanaimo
Courtenay
Prince Rupert
Queen Charlotte Is.
Alexander Archipelago
Ketchikan
Prince Rupert
Juneau
Skagway
Whitehorse
Dawson

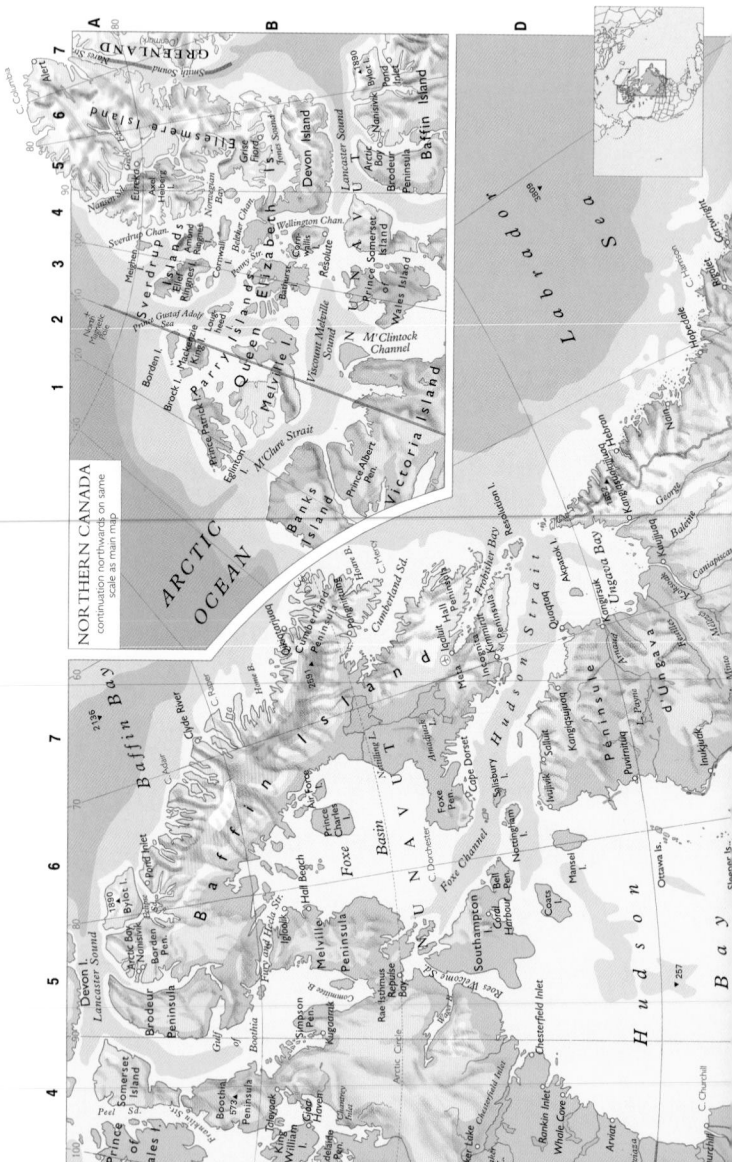
NORTHERN CANADA
continuation northwards on same scale as main map
ARCTIC OCEAN
GREENLAND
Ellesmere Island
Sverdrup Islands
Queen Elizabeth Is.
Parry Islands
Melville I.
Devon Island
Baffin Island
Victoria Island
Banks Island
M'Clintock Channel
Prince of Wales I.
Somerset Island
Prince Patrick I.
Borden I.
Brock I.
Mackenzie King I.
Lancaster Sound
Baffin Bay
Baffin Island
Foxe Basin
Foxe Channel
Hudson Strait
Hudson Bay
Labrador Sea
Ungava Peninsula
Melville Peninsula
Southampton I.
Coats I.
Mansel I.
Ottawa Is.
Akpatok I.
Quaqtaq
Kangiqsujuaq
Kangiqsualujjuaq
Inukjuak
Povungnituk
Salluit
Ivujivik
Cape Dorset
Frobisher Bay
Cumberland Sd.
Pangnirtung
Clyde River
Pond Inlet
Arctic Bay
Nanisivik
Brodeur Peninsula
Bylot I.
Borden Pen.
Arctic Circle
Churchill
Chesterfield Inlet
Rankin Inlet
Whale Cove
Baker Lake
Repulse Bay
Rae Isthmus
Hall Beach
Igloolik
Pond Inlet
Resolute
Grise Fiord
Eureka
Alert
Cape Columbia
Cape Chidley
Cape Churchill
Hudson Strait
Ungava Bay
Hopedale
Nain
Cape Harrison
Cape Dyer
Cape Mercy

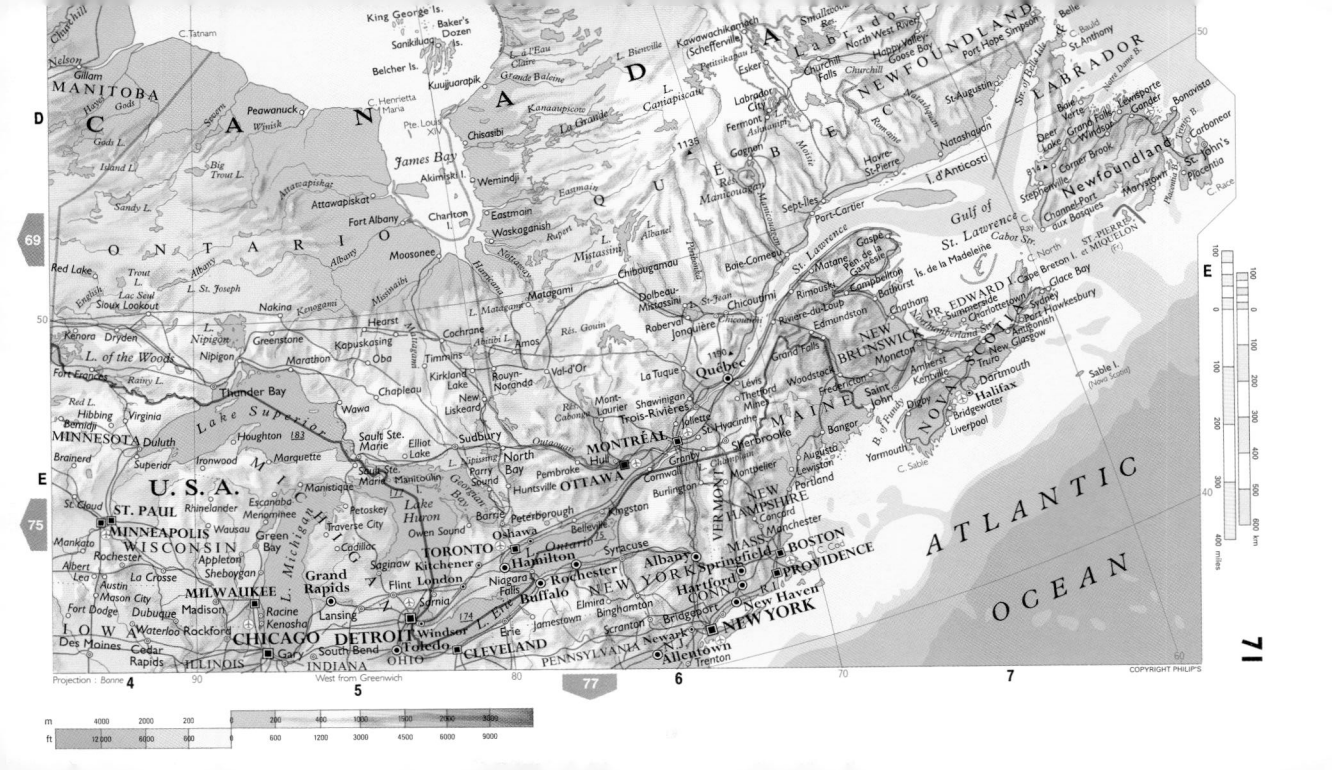
MANITOBA
ONTARIO
QUÉBEC
Labrador
NEWFOUNDLAND
LABRADOR
Newfoundland
NEW BRUNSWICK
NOVA SCOTIA
PR. EDWARD I.
MAINE
VERMONT
NEW HAMPSHIRE
MASS.
CONN.
R.I.
NEW YORK
PENNSYLVANIA
NJ
OHIO
INDIANA
ILLINOIS
IOWA
WISCONSIN
MINNESOTA
U.S.A.
ATLANTIC OCEAN
Gulf of St. Lawrence
James Bay
Hudson Bay
Lake Superior
Lake Michigan
Lake Huron
L. Erie
L. Ontario
MONTREAL
OTTAWA
TORONTO
Québec
Halifax
BOSTON
PROVIDENCE
NEW YORK
CHICAGO
DETROIT
CLEVELAND
MILWAUKEE
MINNEAPOLIS
ST. PAUL
Thunder Bay
Winnipeg
Saint John
Moncton
Fredericton
Sydney
Charlottetown
Sept-Îles
Chibougamau
Matagami
Timmins
Sudbury
North Bay
Kingston
Hamilton
Rochester
Buffalo
Albany
Springfield
Hartford
New Haven
Bridgeport
Newark
Allentown
Scranton
Binghamton
Jamestown
Erie
Toledo
Windsor
Gary
South Bend
Madison
Milwaukee
Chicago
Des Moines
Cedar Rapids
Duluth
Marquette
Green Bay
Grand Rapids
Lansing
Flint
Saginaw
Sarnia
Kitchener
London
Hamilton
Niagara Falls
Elmira
Syracuse
Burlington
Montpelier
Concord
Portland
Augusta
Bangor
Lewiston
Sherbrooke
Trois-Rivières
Rimouski
Gaspé
Baie-Comeau
Roberval
Jonquière
Rouyn-Noranda
Val-d'Or
Amos
Cochrane
Kirkland Lake
Timmins
Sault Ste. Marie
Elliot Lake
Wawa
Chapleau
Hearst
Kapuskasing
Oba
Moosonee
Fort Albany
Attawapiskat
Wemindji
Chisasibi
Kuujjuarapik
Sanikiluaq
Iqaluit
Kangiqsujuaq
Kangiqsualujjuaq
Schefferville
Labrador City
Fermont
Gagnon
Mont-Laurier
Shawinigan
Drummondville
Granby
Cornwall
Pembroke
Huntsville
Barrie
Peterborough
Oshawa
Belleville
Owen Sound
Kenora
Dryden
Red Lake
Sioux Lookout
Nakina
Greenstone
Marathon
Nipigon
Fort Frances
Rainy L.
Hibbing
Virginia
Brainerd
Superior
Ironwood
Houghton
Escanaba
Menominee
Rhinelander
Wausau
Appleton
Sheboygan
Racine
Kenosha
Waterloo
Rockford
Cedar Rapids
Dubuque
Mankato
Rochester
Austin
La Crosse
Mason City
Fort Dodge
Gary
South Bend
Lake Ste. Marie
Manitoulin
Parry Sound
Huntsville
Petoskey
Traverse City
Cadillac
Saint Cloud
Minneapolis
St. Paul
Duluth
Bemidji
Red L.
Manistique

NORTH-WEST USA

VANCOUVER
Nanaimo
Coquitlam
Surrey
New Westminster
Chilliwack
Victoria
Esquimalt
Port Angeles
Port Townsend
Bellingham
Anacortes
Mount Vernon
Everett
Arlington
Snohomish
Monroe
Redmond
SEATTLE
Bremerton
Belleville
Renton
Kent
Puyallup
Tacoma
Olympia
Aberdeen
Hoquiam
Shelton
Kelso
Longview
Cathlamet
Astoria
Seaside
Tillamook
Newport
Lincoln City
Waldport
Florence
Reedsport
Coos Bay
Bandon
Gold Beach
Brookings
Crescent City
Klamath
Yreka
Mt. Shasta
Weed
Dunsmuir
McKinleyville
Eureka
Fortuna
Scotia
Weott
Garberville
Redding
Anderson
Red Bluff
Susanville
Chester
Westwood
Greenville
Quincy
Portola
Truckee
Reno
Sparks
Carson
Virginia City
Fallon
Yerington
Gardnerville
Minden
Stateline
South Lake Tahoe
Mt. Grant 3426 m
Hawthorne
Lovelock
Winnemucca
Gerlach
Rye Patch Res.
Imlay
Battle Mountain
Dunphy
Elko
Spring Creek
Wells
Ely
Currant
Eureka
Austin
Nevada City
Auburn
Roseville
Arden
Rancho Cordova
SACRAMENTO
Vacaville
Elk Grove
Fairfield
Concord
Richmond
Berkeley
San Rafael
Vallejo
Napa
Petaluma
Santa Rosa
Healdsburg
Windsor
Woodland
Davis
Clearlake
Lakeport
Ukiah
Yuba City
Marysville
Oroville
Chico
Paradise
Corning
Orland
Willows
Colusa
Arbuckle
Williams
Gridley
Olivehurst
Grass Valley

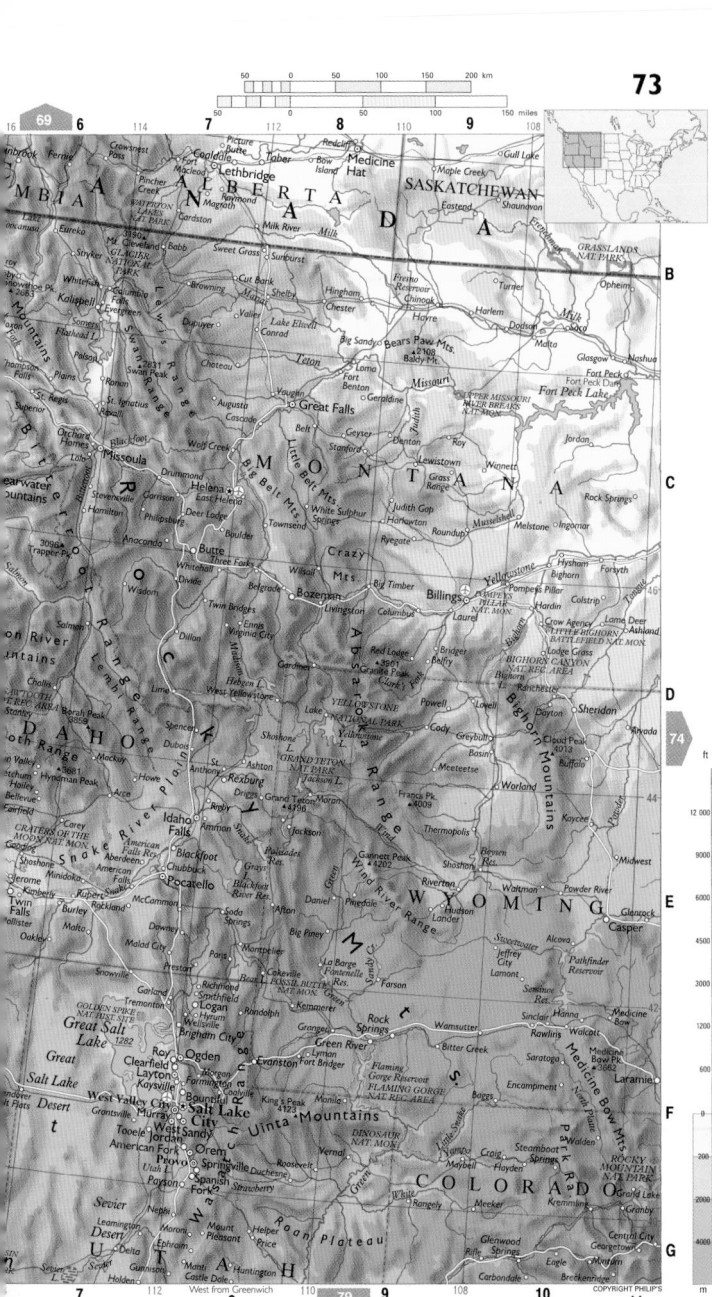
50 0 50 100 150 200 km
50 0 50 100 150 miles
69
74
79
ALBERTA
CANADA
SASKATCHEWAN
MONTANA
IDAHO
WYOMING
COLORADO
UTAH
Medicine Hat
Lethbridge
Cardston
Milk River
Sweet Grass
Sunburst
Cut Bank
Shelby
Havre
Chinook
Harlem
Malta
Glasgow
Opheim
Fort Peck Lake
Great Falls
Helena
Missoula
Butte
Bozeman
Billings
Livingston
Cody
Sheridan
Buffalo
Casper
Laramie
Rock Springs
Green River
Evanston
Ogden
Salt Lake City
Provo
Vernal
Grand Junction
Glenwood Springs
Aspen
Leadville
Salmon
Idaho Falls
Pocatello
Blackfoot
Rexburg
Jackson
Thermopolis
Worland
Lander
Riverton
Powell
Cheyenne
Great Salt Lake
Bear River Range
Wind River Range
Big Horn Mountains
Medicine Bow Mts.
Uinta Mountains
Wasatch Range
Bitterroot Range
Little Belt Mts.
Big Belt Mts.
Crazy Mts.
Absaroka Range
Teton Range
Lemhi Range
Salmon River Range
Snake River Plain
Great Salt Lake Desert
Great Basin
Roan Plateau
Bear Paws Mts.
Sweetgrass Hills
Bighorn Canyon National Recreation Area
Yellowstone National Park
Grand Teton National Park
Glacier National Park
Grasslands National Park
Upper Missouri River Breaks National Monument
Dinosaur National Monument
Rocky Mountain National Park
Flaming Gorge National Recreation Area
Flaming Gorge Reservoir
Fossil Butte National Monument
Craters of the Moon National Monument
Golden Spike National Historic Site
Great Salt Lake 1282
Gannett Peak 4205
Francis Pk. 4009
Cloud Peak 4013
Big Sandy Peak 2709
Bears Paw Mts. 2165
Baldy Pk.
Mt. Cleveland 3561
Glacier National Park
Kalispell
Flathead L.
Swan Range
Mission Range
Bitterroot Range
Lewis Range
Rocky Mountains
Missouri
Yellowstone
Snake
Green
Platte
Bighorn
Powder River
Tongue
Little Missouri
Milk
Marias
Sun
Clark Fork
Bear
Madison
Gallatin
Jefferson
Big Hole
Salmon
Lemhi
Snake
Bear
Weber
Provo
Sevier
Colorado
Dolores
Gunnison
Arkansas
Platte
Cheyenne
Little Snake
Yampa
Green
Bear
Bear River Res.
Flaming Gorge Res.
Pathfinder Reservoir
Seminoe Res.
Alcova
Glendo
Guernsey
Keyhole
Pilot Butte
Fontenelle
Kemmerer
Cokeville
Montpelier
Paris
Preston
Malad City
Downey
Oakley
Burley
Rupert
Twin Falls
Jerome
Shoshone
Gooding
Hailey
Ketchum
Stanley
Challis
Salmon
Lemhi
Dubois
Lander
Riverton
Shoshoni
Thermopolis
Worland
Meeteetse
Cody
Greybull
Basin
Lovell
Dayton
Ranchester
Sheridan
Buffalo
Kaycee
Midwest
Powder River
Glenrock
Douglas
Wheatland
Chugwater
Torrington
Lusk
Newcastle
Hot Springs
Edgemont
Rapid City
Spearfish
Deadwood
Lead
Sturgis
Belle Fourche
Gillette
Sundance
Moorcroft
Upton
Newcastle
Yellowstone National Park
Grand Teton National Park
Pinedale
Afton
Soda Springs
Logan
Brigham City
Ogden
Roy
Clearfield
Layton
Kaysville
Bountiful
Salt Lake City
West Valley City
Murray
West Jordan
Sandy
Tooele
Orem
Provo
Springville
Spanish Fork
Payson
Nephi
Delta
Gunnison
Glenwood Springs
Rifle
Delta
Meeker
Rangely
Craig
Steamboat Springs
Hayden
Maybell
Dinosaur
Vernal
Roosevelt
Duchesne
Manila
Green River
Lyman
Fort Bridger

74 NORTH-CENTRAL USA

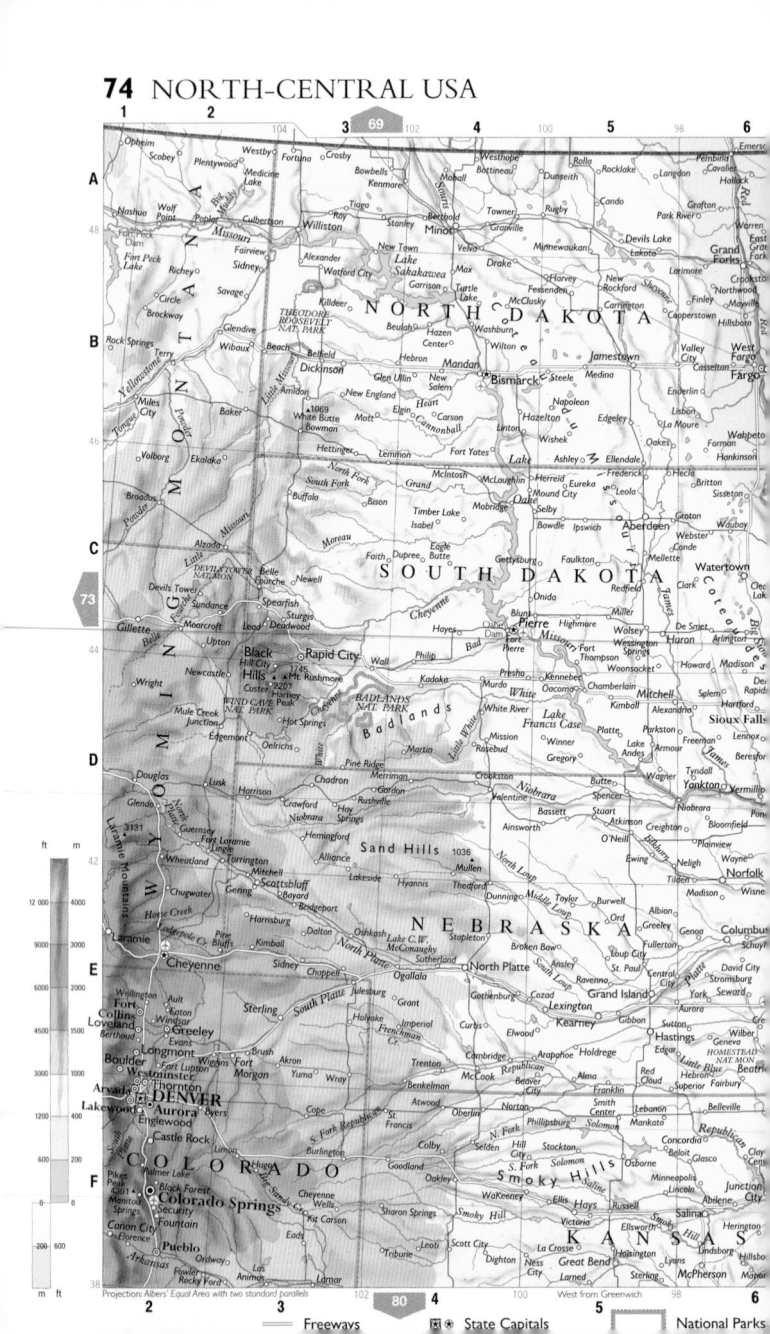
NORTH DAKOTA
SOUTH DAKOTA
MONTANA
WYOMING
NEBRASKA
COLORADO
KANSAS
Williston
Minot
Bismarck
Mandan
Dickinson
Jamestown
Fargo
Grand Forks
Devils Lake
Minneapolis
Aberdeen
Watertown
Pierre
Huron
Rapid City
Black Hills
Sioux Falls
Yankton
Norfolk
Sand Hills
Scottsbluff
Cheyenne
North Platte
Grand Island
Lincoln
Omaha
Sterling
Fort Collins
Loveland
Greeley
Longmont
Boulder
Westminster
Thornton
Arvada
DENVER
Lakewood
Aurora
Englewood
Castle Rock
Colorado Springs
Security
Fountain
Pueblo
Hays
Salina
Great Bend
McPherson
Hastings
Kearney
Lexington
Badlands
Lake Sakakawea
Lake Oahe
Lake Francis Case
Lake C. W. McConaughy
Smoky Hills
Flint Hills
Platte
Yellowstone
Missouri
Cheyenne
Little Missouri
Little Missouri
Powder
Tongue
Bighorn
Little Bighorn
Musselshell
Milk
Madison
Yellowstone
Belle Fourche
Niobrara
Platte
Loup
Elkhorn
Little Blue
Republican
Smoky Hill
Saline
Solomon
Kansas
Arkansas
Brazos

50 0 50 100 150 200 km
50 0 50 100 150 miles
CANADA
LAKE SUPERIOR
MINNESOTA
WISCONSIN
MICHIGAN
IOWA
ILLINOIS
MISSOURI
LAKE MICHIGAN
Thunder Bay
Duluth
Superior
Apostle Is.
Eau Claire
Rochester
La Crosse
Green Bay
Sheboygan
Milwaukee
Racine
Kenosha
Waukegan
North Chicago
Highland Park
Wilmette
Evanston
CHICAGO
Oshkosh
Appleton
Two Rivers
Manitowoc
Fond du Lac
Madison
Janesville
Beloit
Rockford
Dubuque
Waterloo
Cedar Falls
Cedar Rapids
Davenport
Moline
Rock Island
Peoria
Bloomington
Springfield
Decatur
Champaign
Urbana
Joliet
Aurora
Elgin
Kankakee
Streator
Pontiac
Normal
Rantoul
Quincy
Hannibal
Macomb
Keokuk
Burlington
Fort Madison
Galesburg
Moline
Muscatine
Iowa City
Marshalltown
Ames
Boone
Des Moines
Council Bluffs
Omaha
Lincoln
Sioux City
Sioux Falls
Mankato
St. Cloud
Duluth
Minneapolis
ST. PAUL
Bloomington
Burnsville
Lakeville
Northfield
Faribault
Owatonna
Winona
Austin
Albert Lea
Fairmont
Worthington
Marshall
New Ulm
Le Sueur
St. Peter
Mankato
N. Mankato
Waseca
Blue Earth
Estherville
Spencer
Emmetsburg
Algona
Mason City
Clear Lake
Garner
Humboldt
Pocahontas
Storm Lake
Fort Dodge
Webster City
Eldora
Grundy Center
Iowa City
Cedar Falls
Waterloo
Independence
Manchester
Dubuque
Monticello
Maquoketa
Anamosa
Marion
Cedar Rapids
Vinton
Marshalltown
Nevada
Ames
Boone
Carroll
Denison
Onawa
Harlan
Atlantic
Winterset
Indianola
Pella
Oskaloosa
Ottumwa
Fairfield
Mount Pleasant
Burlington
Keokuk
Fort Madison
Centerville
Bloomfield
Corydon
Chariton
Creston
Shenandoah
Clarinda
Bedford
Leon
Grant City
Princeton
Unionville
Kahoka
Canton
Macomb
Carthage
Havana
Lewistown
Kirksville
Edina
Milan
Trenton
Chillicothe
Macon
Monroe City
Palmyra
Louisiana
Vandalia
Mexico
Moberly
Centralia
Fayette
Brunswick
Carrollton
Lexington
Richmond
Marshall
Independence
Liberty
Kansas City
Overland Park
Leavenworth
Atchison
Holton
Topeka
Lawrence
Olathe
Ottawa
Paola
Harrisonville
Leawood
Warrensburg
Boonville
Columbia
Fulton
Jefferson City
Washington
Hermann
Sedalia
California
Clinton
Butler
Harry S. Truman Res.
Lake of the Ozarks
Osage
Vienna
Eldon
Sullivan
Union
Festus
Mehlville
Belleville
Waterloo
Pinckneyville
Du Quoin
De Soto
Ste. Genevieve
Fairfield
Mount Vernon
McLeansboro
Benton
West Frankfort
Salem
Flora
Centralia
Vandalia
Effingham
Litchfield
Carlinville
Taylorville
Pana
Shelbyville
Mattoon
Tuscola
Sullivan
Charleston
Paris
Danville
Hoopeston
Watseka
Kankakee
Bradley
Bourbonnais
Pontiac
Streator
Ottawa
Morris
La Salle
Peru
Princeton
Geneseo
Kewanee
Galesburg
Aledo
Galva
Henry
Chillicothe
Peoria
Pekin
Washington
Lexington
Newton
Jackson
Springfield
Nevada
Ottawa
Lawrence
Topeka
Emporia
Burlington
Sterling
Sterling
Hastings
Superior
Ashland
Wahoo
Fremont
Blair
Tekamah
Logan
Harlan
Missouri
Valley
Council Bluffs
Omaha
Bellevue
Plattsmouth
Nebraska City
Syracuse
Auburn
Falls City
Marysville
Hiawatha
Blue Rapids
Frankfort
Onaga
Tuttle Creek
Manhattan
Wamego
Alma
Council Grove
Osage City
Burlington
Emporia

NORTH-EAST USA

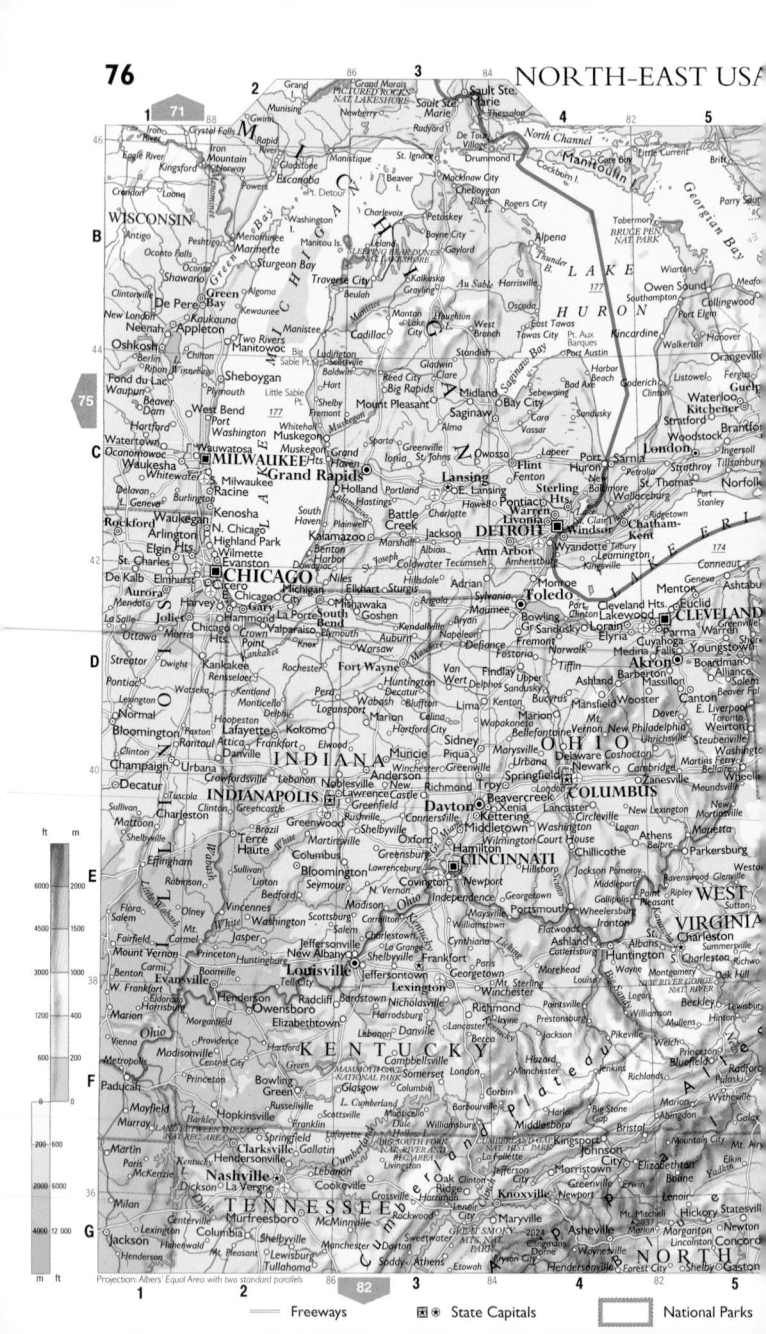
WISCONSIN
MICHIGAN
LAKE MICHIGAN
LAKE HURON
LAKE ERIE
LAKE ONTARIO
Georgian Bay
Green Bay
Saginaw Bay
Lake St. Clair
Sault Ste. Marie
Mackinaw City
Traverse City
Alpena
Cadillac
Saginaw
Bay City
Midland
Mount Pleasant
Flint
Lansing
Owosso
Port Huron
Sarnia
London
Kitchener
Brantford
Toronto
Hamilton
Niagara Falls
Buffalo
Rochester
Syracuse
Utica
Albany
Binghamton
Scranton
Wilkes-Barre
Allentown
Reading
Harrisburg
Lancaster
Philadelphia
Trenton
Atlantic City
Dover
Baltimore
Annapolis
Washington
Alexandria
Fairfax
Arlington
Richmond
Petersburg
Norfolk
Virginia Beach
Chesapeake
Newport News
Hampton
Williamsburg
Fredericksburg
Charlottesville
Lynchburg
Roanoke
Blacksburg
Bristol
Kingsport
Johnson City
Knoxville
Chattanooga
Nashville
Murfreesboro
Clarksville
Jackson
Memphis
Tupelo
Oxford
Hattiesburg
Appalachian Mountains
Great Smoky Mts. Nat. Park
Mammoth Cave National Park
Cumberland Gap National Park
Big South Fork National River and Recreation Area
Land Between the Lakes National Recreation Area
Great Smoky Mts. Nat. Park
Mt. Mitchell
Mt. Pleasant
Mt. Vernon
Mt. Sterling
Mt. Carmel
Mt. Airy

50 0 50 100 150 200 km
50 0 50 100 150 miles
CANADA
ONTARIO
QUEBEC
NEW YORK
VERMONT
NEW HAMPSHIRE
MASS.
CONN.
R.I.
PENNSYLVANIA
NEW JERSEY
MARYLAND
DELAWARE
WASHINGTON D.C.
VIRGINIA
NORTH CAROLINA
MAINE
LAKE ONTARIO
LAKE ERIE
LAKE HURON
LAKE MICHIGAN
LAKE SUPERIOR
ATLANTIC OCEAN
Gulf of Maine
Chesapeake Bay
Delaware Bay
Pamlico Sound
TORONTO
MONTREAL
OTTAWA
QUEBEC
BOSTON
PHILADELPHIA
BALTIMORE
NORFOLK
Virginia Beach
Richmond
Raleigh
Durham
Greensboro
Charlotte
Buffalo
Rochester
Albany
Hartford
Providence
Springfield
Worcester
Lowell
Lawrence
Cambridge
Quincy
Brockton
Fall River
Taunton
New Bedford
Cape Cod
Nantucket I.
Martha's Vineyard
Block I.
Montauk Pt.
Long Island
Manhattan
Bronx
Queens
Brooklyn
Staten Island
Newark
Jersey City
Trenton
Atlantic City
Ocean City
Dover
Wilmington
Baltimore
Annapolis
Washington
Alexandria
Arlington
Richmond
Norfolk
Portsmouth
Chesapeake
Hampton
Newport News
Williamsburg
Petersburg
Lynchburg
Roanoke
Danville
Greensboro
Durham
Raleigh
Wilmington
Charlotte
Bangor
Portland
Augusta
Lewiston
Bath
Brunswick
Rockland
Belfast
Bar Harbor
Mt. Desert I.
Acadia Nat. Park
Kittery
Portsmouth
Newburyport
Dover
Rochester
Concord
Manchester
Nashua
Keene
Lebanon
Hanover
Burlington
Montpelier
Rutland
Bennington
Brattleboro
Newport
Saint John
Fredericton
Moncton
Halifax
Charlottetown
Sydney
Edmundston
Grand Falls
Perth-Andover
Mars Hill
Houlton
Woodstock
Millinocket
Lincoln
Calais
Eastport
Machias
Ellsworth
Belfast
Rockland
Camden
Bath
Brunswick
Lewiston
Auburn
Augusta
Waterville
Bangor
Old Town
Orono
Brewer
Dexter
Dover-Foxcroft
Greenville
Rangeley
Farmington
Rumford
Berlin
Lakes
Moosehead L.
Sebago L.
Kennebec R.
Penobscot R.
Aroostook R.
St. John R.
St. Croix R.
St. Lawrence R.
Hudson R.
Delaware R.
Susquehanna R.
Potomac R.
Rappahannock R.
James R.
Roanoke R.
Niagara Falls
Hamilton
Kingston

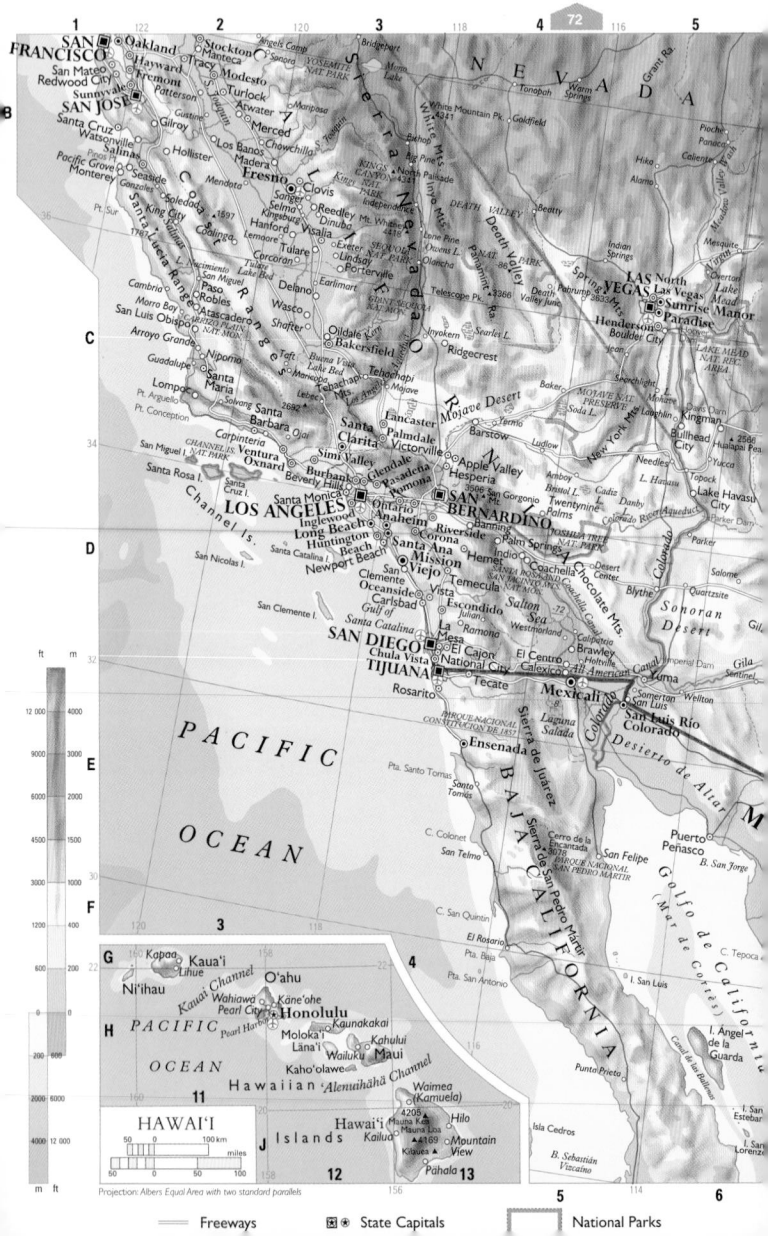
SAN FRANCISCO
Oakland
San Mateo
Redwood City
Hayward
Fremont
Sunnyvale
SAN JOSE
Santa Cruz
Watsonville
Salinas
Pacific Grove
Monterey
Stockton
Manteca
Tracy
Modesto
Turlock
Atwater
Gilroy
Hollister
Los Banos
Chowchilla
Madera
Fresno
Clovis
Selma
Kingsburg
Reedley
Dinuba
Visalia
Tulare
Hanford
Lemoore
Corcoran
Delano
Wasco
Shafter
Bakersfield
Taft
Maricopa
Mojave
Tehachapi
Lancaster
Palmdale
Victorville
Barstow
Apple Valley
Hesperia
Ridgecrest
Mojave Desert
Death Valley
Furnace Creek
Beatty
Tonopah
Goldfield
Warm Springs
NEVADA
LAS VEGAS
North Las Vegas
Sunrise Manor
Paradise
Henderson
Boulder City
Bullhead City
Kingman
Needles
Lake Havasu City
Yucca
Topock
Parker
Blythe
Quartzsite
Yuma
Mexicali
San Luis Río Colorado
Ensenada
Tijuana
Tecate
Rosarito
SAN DIEGO
Chula Vista
National City
El Cajon
El Centro
Calexico
Brawley
Imperial
Calipatria
Westmorland
Salton Sea
Indio
Palm Springs
Coachella
Desert Center
Banning
Riverside
Corona
Hemet
Temecula
Escondido
Vista
Oceanside
Carlsbad
Encinitas
Clemente
San Juan Capistrano
Mission Viejo
Santa Ana
Anaheim
Orange
Newport Beach
Huntington Beach
Long Beach
Inglewood
Ontario
Pomona
Glendale
Pasadena
Burbank
Beverly Hills
Santa Monica
LOS ANGELES
SAN BERNARDINO
Redlands
Yucaipa
Barstow
Needles
Ventura
Oxnard
Simi Valley
Santa Barbara
Santa Maria
Lompoc
Guadalupe
Arroyo Grande
San Luis Obispo
Morro Bay
Paso Robles
Atascadero
Cambria
Cayucos
Pt. Arguello
Pt. Conception
Santa Rosa I.
San Miguel I.
Santa Cruz I.
Channel Is.
San Nicolas I.
Santa Catalina I.
San Clemente I.
Santa Catalina
Gulf of California
Sierra Nevada
Sierra de Juárez
Sierra San Pedro Mártir
BAJA CALIFORNIA
Desierto de Altar
Sonoran Desert
Colorado
Chocolate Mts.
Gila
Golfo de California (Mar de Cortés)
Puerto Peñasco
San Felipe
Cerro de la Encantada
Isla Cedros
B. Sebastián Vizcaíno
PACIFIC OCEAN
Pta. Santo Tomás
Santo Tomás
C. Colonet
San Telmo
C. San Quintín
El Rosario
Pta. Baja
Pta. San Antonio
Puntal Prieto
I. Angel de la Guarda
I. San Esteban
I. San Lorenzo
Kapaa
Kaua'i
Lihue
Ni'ihau
Kaua'i Channel
O'ahu
Wahiawa
Pearl City
Honolulu
Pearl Harbor
Kaunakakai
Molokai
Kahului
Lāna'i
Wailuku
Maui
Kaho'olawe
Alenuihāhā Channel
Hawaiian Islands
Waimea (Kamuela)
Hilo
Hawai'i
Kailua
Mauna Loa
Mauna Kea
Mountain View
Kīlauea
Pāhala
HAWAI'I
Projection: Albers Equal Area with two standard parallels
Freeways
State Capitals
National Parks

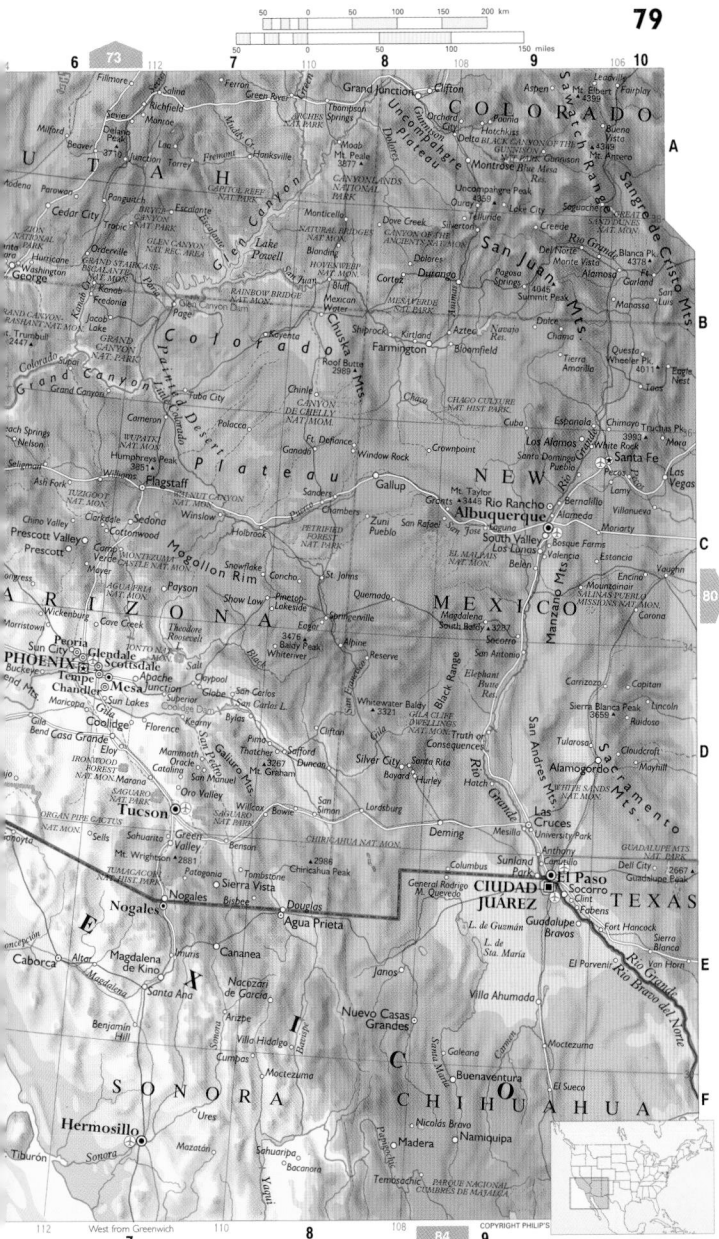
50 0 50 100 150 200 km
50 0 50 100 150 miles
73
80
84
6
7
8
9
10
A
B
C
D
E
F
112
110
108
106
COLORADO
UTAH
ARIZONA
NEW MEXICO
TEXAS
SONORA
CHIHUAHUA
Grand Junction
Clifton
Aspen
Leadville
Mt. Elbert 4399
Fairplay
Salina
Ferron
Green River
Thompson Springs
Orchard City
Delta
Hotchkiss
Buena Vista
Mt. Antero
Nucla
Montrose
Ouray
Lake City
Saguache
Creede
Del Norte
Monte Vista
Alamosa
Blanca Pk. 4378
Garland
San Luis
Mosca
Mabasso
Taos
Questa
Wheeler Pk. 4011
Eagle Nest
Chama
Dolce
Tierra Amarilla
Chimayo
Truchas Pk. 3992
Mora
Espanola
Los Alamos
White Rock
Santa Fe
Pecos
Las Vegas
Pueblo
Cortez
Durango
Dolores
Aztec
Farmington
Bloomfield
Kirtland
Shiprock
Gallup
Grants
Mt. Taylor 3446
Rio Rancho
Bernalillo
Alameda
Albuquerque
Los Lunas
Belen
Bosque Farms
Valencia
Estancia
Mountainair
Encino
Vaughn
Corona
Moriarty
Villanueva
Larry
Tucumcari
Cedar City
Parowan
Panguitch
Escalante
Tropic
Hurricane
Washington
St. George
Kanab
Fredonia
Jacob Lake
Page
Tuba City
Chinle
Kayenta
Roof Rock 2969
Cameron
Polacca
Ganado
Ft. Defiance
Window Rock
Crownpoint
Chaco
Cuba
Nacimiento
Jemez
Bernalillo
Sandia
Sandia Park
Tijeras
Carrizozo
Capitan
Ruidoso
Lincoln
Sierra Blanca Peak 3658
Tularosa
Cloudcroft
Mayhill
Alamogordo
Las Cruces
University Park
Anthony
Sunland Park
Dell City
Socorro
Clint
Fabens
El Paso
Ciudad Juárez
Guadalupe Peak 2667
Fort Hancock
Sierra Blanca
Van Horn
El Porvenir
Deming
Mesilla
Columbus
Lordsburg
Silver City
Santa Rita
Bayard
Hurley
Hatch
Truth or Consequences
Elephant Butte Res.
Socorro
San Antonio
Magdalena
South Baldy 3287
Springerville
Eagar
Alpine
Reserve
Whitewater Baldy 3321
Clifton
Duncan
Safford
Thatcher
Pima
Mt. Graham
Willcox
Bowie
San Simon
Bisbee
Douglas
Tombstone
Chiricahua Peak 2386
Sierra Vista
Nogales
Agua Prieta
Cananea
Nacozari de García
Janos
Villa Ahumada
Nuevo Casas Grandes
Galeana
Moctezuma
Buenaventura
El Sueco
Nicolás Bravo
Madera
Namiquipa
Temosachic
Ojinaga
Presidio
Marfa
Alpine
Fort Davis
Hueco Tanks
Tornillo
Guadalupe Bravos
L. de Guzmán
L. de Sta. María
Rio Grande
Rio Bravo del Norte
Sierra Madre Occidental
Rio Grande
Rio Yaqui
Rio Sonora
Rio Magdalena
Rio Grande
Rio Pecos
Rio Grande
Rio Chama
Rio Puerco
Rio Grande

COLORADO
KANSAS
OKLAHOMA
NEW MEXICO
TEXAS
MEXICO
COAHUILA
CHIHUAHUA
Sierra de Cristo Mts.
Raton
Trinidad
Springfield
Garden City
Dodge City
Wichita
Hutchinson
Newton
Liberal
Elkhart
Guymon
Boise City
Dalhart
Amarillo
Borger
Pampa
Dumas
Canadian
Tucumcari
Conchas Dam
Santa Rosa
Hereford
Canyon
Tulia
Clovis
Portales
Plainview
Lubbock
Levelland
Roswell
Artesia
Carlsbad
Hobbs
Lamesa
Big Spring
Midland
Odessa
Sweetwater
Abilene
Brownwood
San Angelo
Ozona
Fort Stockton
Marfa
Presidio
Ojinaga
Ciudad Acuña
Del Rio
Piedras Negras
Eagle Pass
Zaragoza
Nueva Rosita
Sabinas
Nuevo Laredo
Laredo
Oklahoma City
Norman
Lawton
Altus
Enid
Woodward
Stillwater
Edmond
Ardmore
Denton
Arlington
Fort Worth
Waco
Killeen
Temple
Austin
San Antonio
Corpus Christi
Brownsville
Kerrville
Lockhart
Seguin
Gonzales
Victoria
Alice
Kingsville
Pecos
Las Cruces
El Paso
Chihuahua
Ciudad Juárez
Monterrey
Saltillo
Torreón
Durango
Mapimí
Bolsón de
Stockton Plateau
Edwards Plateau
Balcones Escarpment
Rio Grande
Pecos
Canadian
Red
Brazos
Colorado
Nueces
Frio
Guadalupe
Llano
Sabinas
Salado
Cimarron
Arkansas
Rio Salado
Rio Sabinas
Rio Grande
Presa de la Amistad

50 0 50 100 150 200 km
50 0 50 100 150 miles
MISSOURI
ARKANSAS
TENNESSEE
MISSISSIPPI
LOUISIANA
GULF OF MEXICO
Springfield
Joplin
Rolla
Cape Girardeau
Paducah
Jonesboro
Paragould
Memphis
Little Rock
North Little Rock
Pine Bluff
Fayetteville
Fort Smith
Tulsa
Shreveport
Monroe
Alexandria
Lafayette
Lake Charles
Baton Rouge
New Orleans
Houston
Galveston
Brownsville
McAllen
Laredo
Mississippi River Delta
Mississippi Sd.
Chandeleur Sd.
Matagorda I.
Aransas
Padre I.
TEXAS
continuation southwards on same scale
COPYRIGHT PHILIP'S
State Capitals
National Parks

82 SOUTH-EAST USA

50 0 50 100 150 200 km
50 0 50 100 150 miles
77
86
6
7
8
9
10
A
B
C
D
E
F
G
NORTH CAROLINA
SOUTH CAROLINA
GEORGIA
FLORIDA
ATLANTIC OCEAN
BAHAMAS
Charlotte
Raleigh
Durham
Greensboro
Winston-Salem
Fayetteville
Wilmington
Columbia
Charleston
Savannah
Jacksonville
ORLANDO
TAMPA
MIAMI
Atlanta
Macon
Augusta
Tallahassee
St. Petersburg
Sarasota
Cape Coral
Naples
Key West
Freeport
Grand Bahama
Abaco I.
Pamlico Sound
Albemarle Sd.
Onslow Bay
Long Bay
Gulf of Mexico
COPYRIGHT PHILIP'S

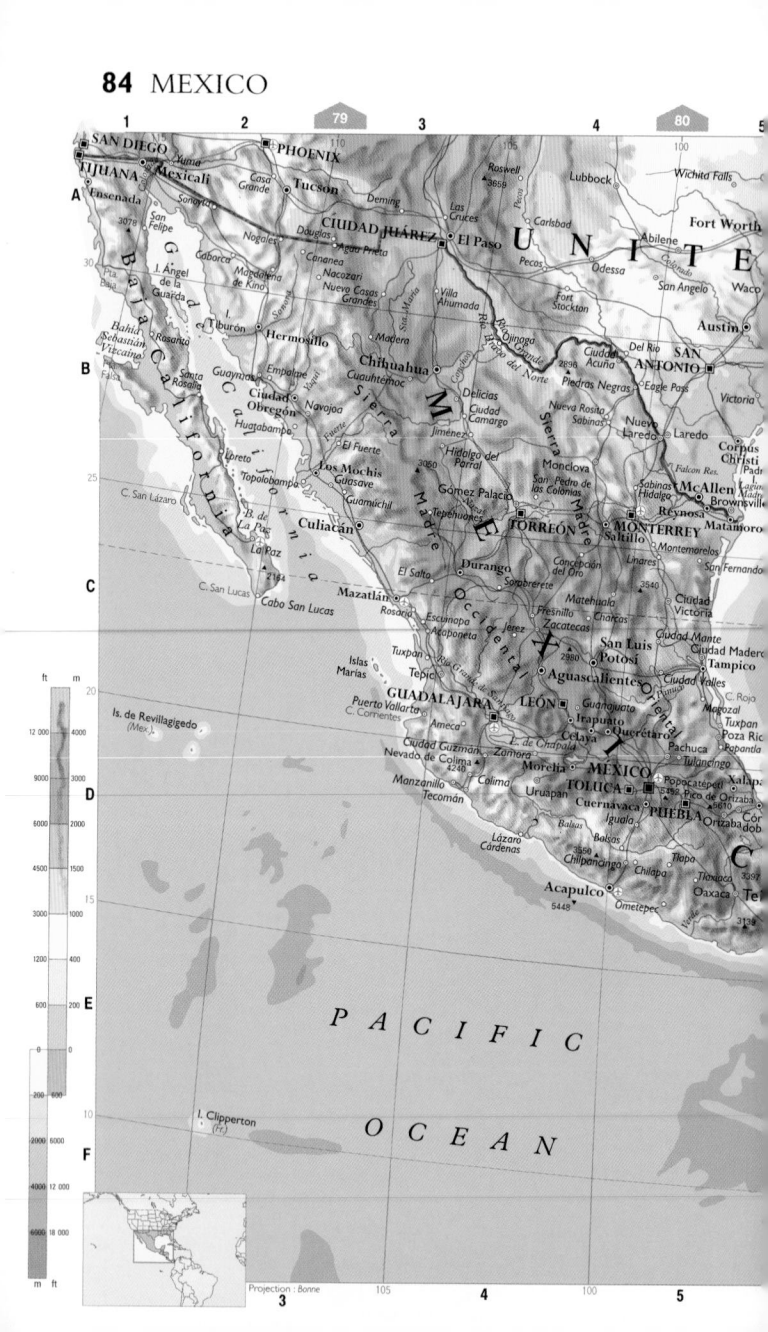
SAN DIEGO
TIJUANA
Mexicali
Ensenada
San Felipe
PHOENIX
Tucson
Yuma
Casa Grande
Sonoyta
Nogales
Douglas
Agua Prieta
Cananea
Nacozari
Nuevo Casas Grandes
CIUDAD JUÁREZ
El Paso
Las Cruces
Deming
Roswell
Lubbock
Carlsbad
Pecos
Odessa
Abilene
Fort Worth
Wichita Falls
San Angelo
Waco
Austin
SAN ANTONIO
Del Rio
Ciudad Acuña
Piedras Negras
Eagle Pass
Victoria
Laredo
Nuevo Laredo
Corpus Christi
Fort Stockton
Villa Ahumada
Ojinaga
Boquillas del Norte
Madera
Hermosillo
Chihuahua
Cuauhtémoc
Delicias
Ciudad Camargo
Jiménez
Hidalgo del Parral
Nueva Rosita
Sabinas
Monclova
San Pedro de las Colonias
Sabinas Hidalgo
McAllen
Brownsville
Reynosa
Matamoros
MONTERREY
Saltillo
Montemorelos
Linares
San Fernando
TORREÓN
Gómez Palacio
Tepehuanes
Durango
Sombrerete
El Salto
Mazatlán
Rosario
Concepción del Oro
Matehuala
Fresnillo
Zacatecas
Charcas
Ciudad Victoria
Ciudad Mante
Ciudad Maderos
Tampico
Ciudad Valles
San Luis Potosí
Aguascalientes
Escuinapa
Mocorito
Jerez
Tepic
Islas Marías
Puerto Vallarta
C. Corrientes
GUADALAJARA
Ameca
LEÓN
Guanajuato
Irapuato
Celaya
Querétaro
Morelia
Zamora
Lago de Chapala
Nevado de Colima
Colima
Manzanillo
Tecomán
Uruapan
TOLUCA
MÉXICO
Cuernavaca
PUEBLA
Pico de Orizaba
Orizaba
Popocatépetl
Iguala
Balsas
Lázaro Cárdenas
Chilpancingo
Chilapa
Tlapa
Tlaxiaco
Oaxaca
Acapulco
Ometepec
Tuxtla
Tuxpan
Poza Rica
Papantla
Pachuca
Tulancingo
Xalapa
Córdoba
Tehuacán
Huatabampo
Navojoa
Guaymas
Empalme
Ciudad Obregón
Sahuaripa
Sierra Madre Occidental
Sierra Madre Oriental
Sierra Madre Occ.
Sierra Madre Or.
Baja California
Golfo de California
Bahía Sebastián Vizcaíno
Bahía de Ancla
I. Angel de la Guarda
I. Tiburón
Santa Rosalía
Loreto
Topolobampo
Los Mochis
Guasave
Guamúchil
El Fuerte
Culiacán
B. de La Paz
La Paz
C. San Lázaro
C. San Lucas
Cabo San Lucas
Is. de Revillagigedo (Mex.)
I. Clipperton (Fr.)
PACIFIC OCEAN
Projection: Bonne
ft
m
12 000
4000
9000
3000
6000
2000
4500
1500
3000
1000
1200
400
600
200
0
0
-200
-600
-2000
-6000
-4000
-12 000
-6000
-18 000
m
ft

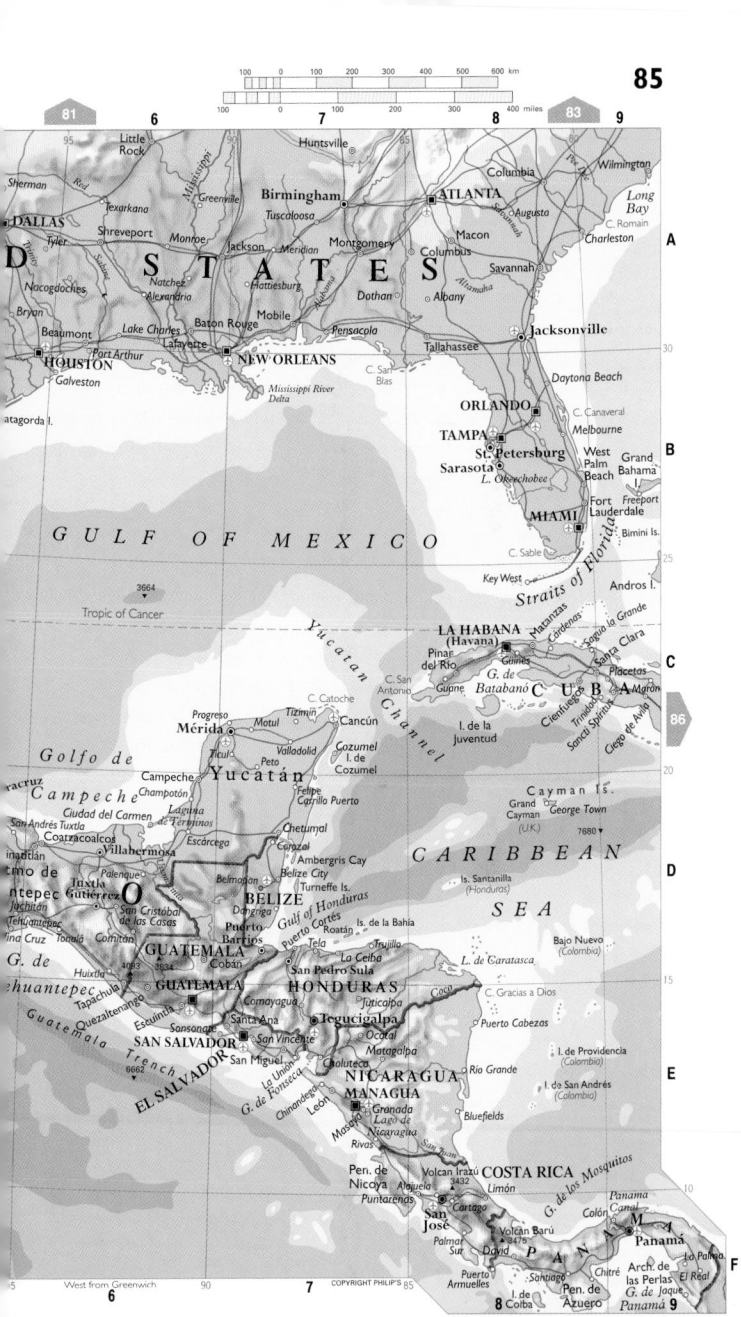
85
100 0 100 200 300 400 500 600 km
100 0 100 200 300 400 miles
81
83
86
6
7
8
9
A
B
C
D
E
F
Little Rock
Huntsville
Sherman
Red
Mississippi
Greenville
Birmingham
ATLANTA
Columbia
Pee Dee
Wilmington
Long Bay
DALLAS
Texarkana
Tuscaloosa
Augusta
Savannah
C. Romain
Shreveport
Monroe
Macon
Charleston
Tyler
Jackson
Meridian
Montgomery
Columbus
Pearl
Sabine
Nacogdoches
Natchez
Alexandria
Hattiesburg
Alabama
Dothan
Albany
Alatamaha
Bryan
Mobile
Beaumont
Lake Charles
Baton Rouge
Pensacola
Jacksonville
Lafayette
Tallahassee
Port Arthur
HOUSTON
NEW ORLEANS
Galveston
C. San Blas
Mississippi River Delta
Daytona Beach
ORLANDO
C. Canaveral
Melbourne
TAMPA
St. Petersburg
West Palm Beach
Grand Bahama I.
Sarasota
L. Okeechobee
Fort Lauderdale
Freeport
MIAMI
Bimini Is.
GULF OF MEXICO
C. Sable
Straits of Florida
Key West
Andros I.
3664
Tropic of Cancer
Yucatan Channel
LA HABANA (Havana)
Matanzas
Cárdenas
Laguna la Grande
Pinar del Rio
Guines
Santa Clara
Placetas
C. San Antonio
Guane
G. de Batabanó
CUBA
Cienfuegos
Trinidad
Sancti Spíritus
Marón
Ciego de Avila
Progreso
Mérida
Motul
Tizimín
C. Catoche
Cancún
I. de la Juventud
Tikul
Valladolid
Cozumel
I. de Cozumel
Peto
Golfo de Campeche
Campeche
Champotón
Yucatán
Felipe Carrillo Puerto
Laguna de Términos
Ciudad del Carmen
Cayman Is.
Grand Cayman (U.K.)
George Town
7680
San Andrés Tuxtla
Escárcega
Chetumal
Coatzacoalcos
Villahermosa
Corozal
Ambergris Cay
CARIBBEAN SEA
Palenque
Belmopan
Belize City
Turneffe Is.
Tuxtla Gutiérrez
Is. Santanilla (Honduras)
San Cristóbal de las Casas
BELIZE
Dangriga
Gulf of Honduras
Puerto Cortés
Is. de la Bahía
Roatán
Comitán
Puerto Barrios
Tela
Trujillo
Bajo Nuevo (Colombia)
GUATEMALA
Cobán
La Ceiba
L. de Caratasca
3837
San Pedro Sula
Huixtla
Tapachula
GUATEMALA
HONDURAS
Comayagua
Tegucigalpa
Coco
C. Gracias a Dios
Quetzaltenango
Escuintla
Santa Ana
Sonsonate
San Vicente
Ocotal
Puerto Cabezas
SAN SALVADOR
San Miguel
Matagalpa
Guatemala Trench
6662
EL SALVADOR
Cholutecа
I. de Providencia (Colombia)
La Unión
G. de Fonseca
NICARAGUA
Rio Grande
I. de San Andrés (Colombia)
Chinandega
León
MANAGUA
Granada
Masaya
Lago de Nicaragua
Bluefields
Rivas
San Juan
Pen. de Nicoya
Volcan Irazú
3432
COSTA RICA
Alajuela
Limón
G. de los Mosquitos
Puntarenas
Cartago
Panama Canal
Colón
San José
Volcan Barú
3475
Palmar Sur
David
PANAMA
Panamá
La Palma
Puerto Armuelles
Santiago
Chitré
Arch. de las Perlas
El Real
I. de Coiba
Pen. de Azuero
G. de Jaque
Panamá
West from Greenwich
COPYRIGHT PHILIP'S

86 CARIBBEAN AND CENTRAL AMERICA

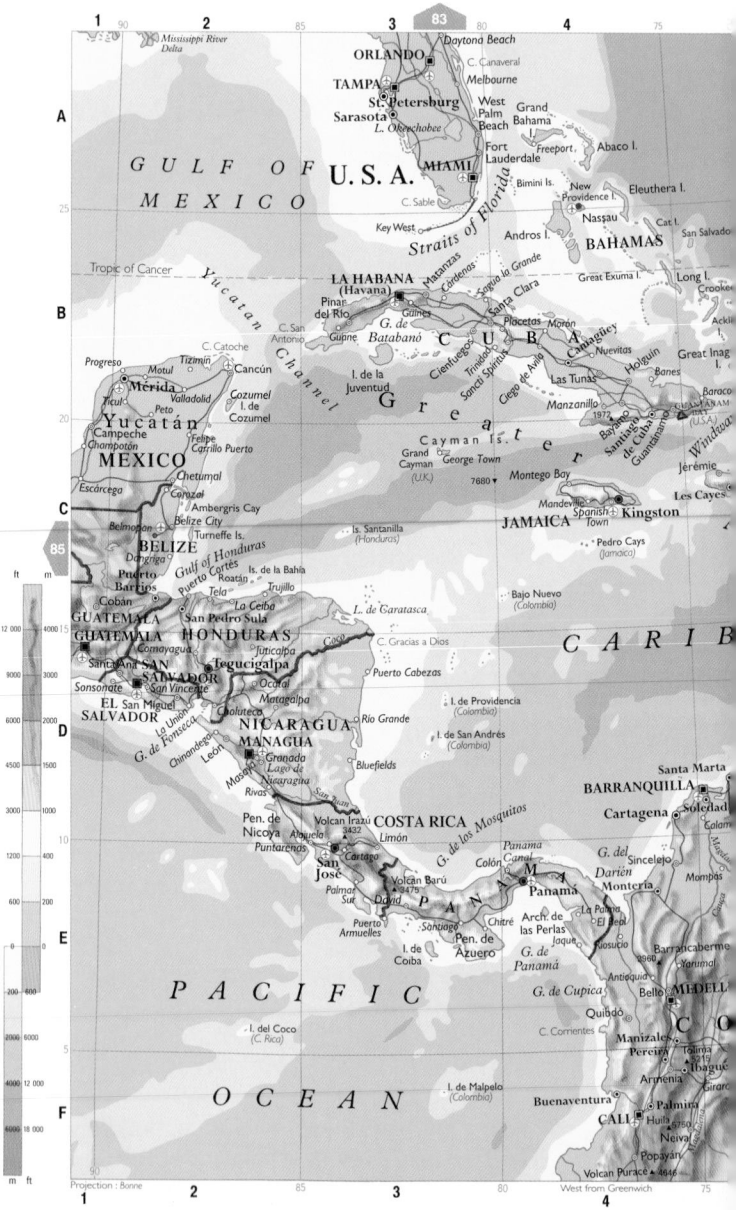

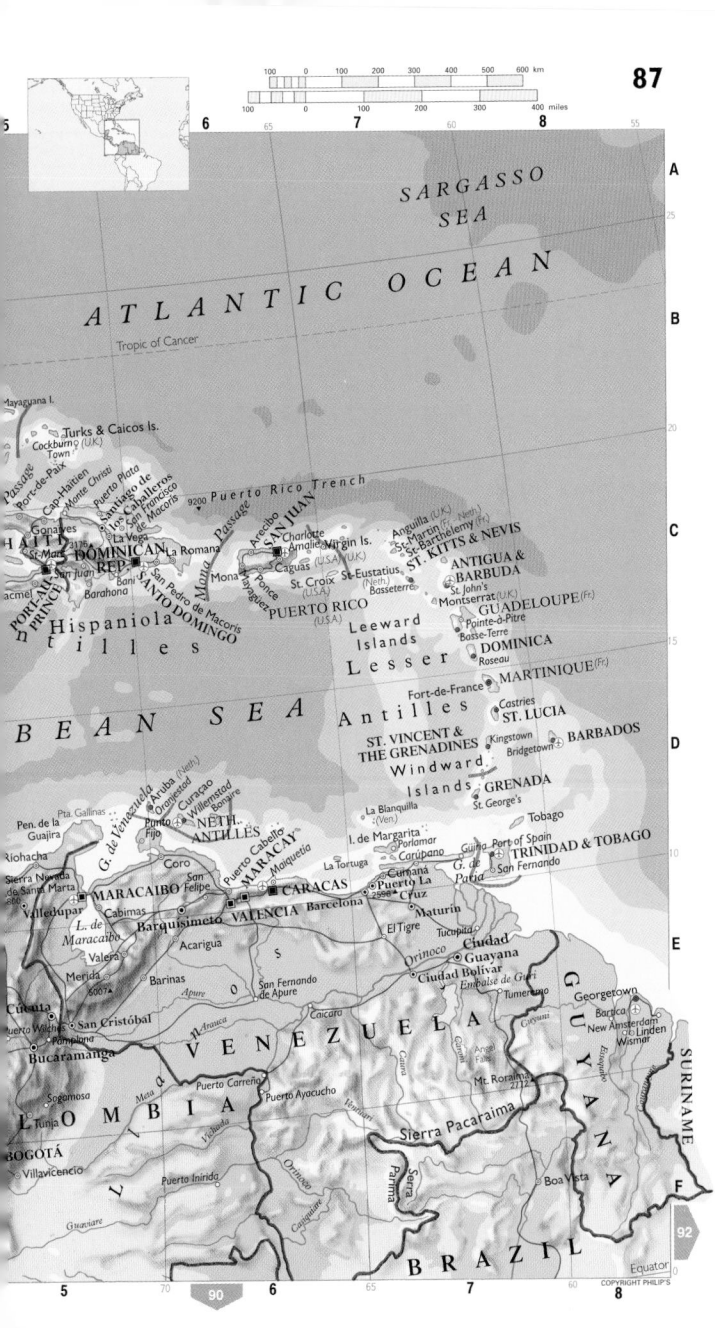
100 0 100 200 300 400 500 600 km
100 0 100 200 300 400 miles
SARGASSO SEA
ATLANTIC OCEAN
Tropic of Cancer
Mayaguana I.
Turks & Caicos Is.
Cockburn Town (U.K.)
Passage Port-de-Paix
Cap-Haïtien
Monte Christi
Puerto Plata
Santiago de los Caballeros
San Francisco de Macorís
Puerto Rico Trench
9200
SAN JUAN
Anegada Passage
Arecibo
Charlotte Amalie
Virgin Is.
Anguilla (U.K.)
St. Martin (Neth.)
St. Barthélemy (Fr.)
ST. KITS & NEVIS
Gonaïves
St. Marc
HAITI
DOMINICAN REP.
La Romana
La Vega
San Juan
PORT-AU-PRINCE
Bani
Barahona
San Pedro de Macorís
SANTO DOMINGO
Mona Passage
Mona
Aguadilla
Ponce
St. Croix (U.S.A.)
Caguas (U.S.A.)
St. Eustatius (Neth.)
Basseterre
ANTIGUA & BARBUDA
St. John's
Montserrat (U.K.)
GUADELOUPE (Fr.)
Pointe-à-Pitre
Basse-Terre
PUERTO RICO (U.S.A.)
Hispaniola
Antilles
Leeward Islands
Lesser Antilles
DOMINICA
Roseau
MARTINIQUE (Fr.)
Fort-de-France
Castries
ST. LUCIA
CARIBBEAN SEA
ST. VINCENT & THE GRENADINES
Kingstown
Bridgetown
BARBADOS
Windward Islands
GRENADA
St. George's
Tobago
Pta. Gallinas
Pen. de la Guajira
Aruba (Neth.)
Oranjestad
Curaçao
Willemstad
Bonaire
Punto Fijo
NETH. ANTILLES
G. de Venezuela
La Blanquilla (Ven.)
I. de Margarita
Porlamar
Carúpano
Guiria
Port of Spain
TRINIDAD & TOBAGO
San Fernando
G. de Paria
Riohacha
Coro
Puerto Cabello
MARACAY
Moiquetia
La Tortuga
Curaçao
Puerto La Cruz
Sierra Nevada de Santa Marta
MARACAIBO
San Felipe
CARACAS
Valledupar
Cabimas
Barquisimeto
VALENCIA
Barcelona
Maturín
L. de Maracaibo
El Tigre
Tucupita
Acarigua
Ciudad Guayana
Orinoco
Ciudad Bolívar
Embalse de Guri
Mérida
Valera
Barinas
San Fernando de Apure
Apure
Tumeremo
Georgetown
Barima
New Amsterdam
Linden
Wismar
Cúcuta
San Cristóbal
Puerto Wilches
Pamplona
Bucaramanga
Arauca
Caicara
VENEZUELA
GUYANA
Cuyuni
Angel Falls
Caura
Caroni
Essequibo
Courantyne
SURINAME
Mt. Roraima 2,772
Sogamoso
Puerto Carreño
Puerto Ayacucho
Meta
Vichada
Negro
COLOMBIA
Tunja
Sierra Pacaraima
BOGOTÁ
Villavicencio
Puerto Inírida
Orinoco
Serra Parima
Boa Vista
Guaviare
Caquetá
BRAZIL
Equator
COPYRIGHT PHILIP'S
5 6 7 8
90 92
A B C D E F

NORTH ATLANTIC OCEAN
Caribbean Sea
Tropic of Cancer
Equator
MEXICO
BELIZE
GUATEMALA
HONDURAS
EL SALVADOR
NICARAGUA
COSTA RICA
PANAMA
CUBA
BAHAMAS
Havana
Turks & Caicos Is. (UK)
Cayman Is. (UK)
JAMAICA
Kingston
HAITI
Port-au-Prince
DOMINICAN REP.
Santo Domingo
San Juan
PUERTO RICO (USA)
Virgin Is. (UK) (US)
Anguilla (UK)
St. Martin (Neth.)
St. Maarten (Fr.)
Saba (Neth.)
St. Eustatius (Neth.)
St. Barthélemy (Fr.)
ST. KITTS & NEVIS
ANTIGUA & BARBUDA
DOMINICA
GUADELOUPE (Fr.)
Basse-Terre
Pointe-à-Pitre
Fort-de-France
MARTINIQUE
Castries
ST. LUCIA
ST. VINCENT
Kingstown
BARBADOS
Bridgetown
GRENADA
St. George's
PANAMA
Panama
TRINIDAD & TOBAGO
Port-of-Spain
Aruba
Oranjestad
NETH. ANTILLES
Willemstad
Curaçao
Caracas
Maracaibo
Barquisimeto
Valencia
Barranquilla
Cartagena
Gulf of Darien
Medellín
Cali
Quito
Guayaquil
G. of Guayaquil
Galápagos Is. (Ecuador)
Gulf of Panama
Cucuta
San Cristóbal
Bucaramanga
BOGOTÁ
Magdalena
Orinoco
Guaviare
Putumayo
Napo
Tajuno
Tigre
Marañón
Ucayali
Mamoré
Madeira
Tapajós
Xingu
Tocantins
Araguaia
Paraguay
Paraná
Uruguay
Paraíba
Parnaíba
Jaguaribe
Rio Negro
Rio Purus
Rio Juruá
Rio Jurua
Rio Madeira
Rio Tapajós
Rio Xingu
Rio Tocantins
Rio Araguaia
Rio Paraguay
Rio Paraná
Rio Uruguay
Rio Paraíba
Rio Parnaíba
Rio Jaguaribe
VENEZUELA
COLOMBIA
ECUADOR
PERU
BRAZIL
BOLIVIA
PARAGUAY
URUGUAY
GUYANA
SURINAME
FRENCH GUIANA
Cayenne
C. Orange
Paramaribo
Georgetown
Ciudad Guayana
RORAIMA
AMAPÁ
AMAZONAS
PARÁ
MARANHÃO
PIAUÍ
CEARÁ
RIO GRANDE DO NORTE
PARAÍBA
PERNAMBUCO
ALAGOAS
SERGIPE
BAHIA
TOCANTINS
MATO GROSSO
RONDÔNIA
ACRE
Belém
Santarém
Manaus
Porto Velho
Tocantins
Fortaleza
São Luís
Teresina
Natal
João Pessoa
Recife
Maceió
Aracaju
Campina Grande
Cuiabá
Iquitos
Pucallpa
Cusco
Lima
Callao
Chiclayo
Trujillo
Arequipa
Tacna
Puerto Maldonado
Cobija
Santa Cruz
Sucre
La Paz
Oruro
Cochabamba
Tarija
Potosí
Asunción
Ciudad del Este
Montevideo
Colonia del Sacramento
Rio de Janeiro
Belo Horizonte
Vitória
Salvador
Feira de Santana
Ilhéus
Vitória da Conquista
Porto Alegre
Pelotas
Rio Grande
Santa Maria
Uruguaiana
Chuí
Rio Grande do Sul
Santa Catarina
Paraná
São Paulo
Campinas
Santos
Sorocaba
Ribeirão Preto
Uberaba
Uberlândia
Goiânia
Brasília
Cuiabá
Campo Grande
Dourados
Corumbá
Tres Lagoas
Ponta Porã

PACIFIC
OCEAN
SOUTH
ATLANTIC
OCEAN
BOLIVIA
PARAGUAY
CHILE
ARGENTINA
URUGUAY
MATO GROSSO
DO SUL
MINAS GERAIS
ESPIRITO
SANTO
SÃO PAULO
PARANÁ
SANTA CATARINA
RIO GRANDE
DO SUL
Arequipa
La Paz
Cochabamba
Santa Cruz
Sucre
Iquique
Antofagasta
Tropic of Capricorn
San Félix
(Chile)
San Ambrosio
(Chile)
Arch. de Juan Fernández
(Chile)
Salta
San Miguel
de Tucumán
Asunción
Resistencia
Corrientes
Córdoba
San Juan
Santa Fe
Paraná
Mendoza
Rosario
Viña del Mar
Valparaíso
SANTIAGO
Talca
Concepción
Valdivia
Puerto Montt
Bahía
Blanca
Mar del Plata
Viedma
Comodoro Rivadavia
Gulf of San Jorge
Gulf of Penas
West Falkland
FALKLAND IS.
(U.K.)
Stanley
East Falkland
Magellan's Str.
Punta Arenas
Tierra del Fuego
C. Horn
South Georgia
(U.K.)
Goiânia
Brasília
Belo
Horizonte
Ribeirão
Prêto
Juiz
de Fora
Campinas
SÃO
PAULO
Santos
RIO DE
JANEIRO
Niterói
Vitória
Campos
Curitiba
Porto Alegre
Pelotas
Montevideo
BUENOS AIRES
La Plata
Rio de la Plata
Paraná
Paraguay
Pilcomayo
Salado
Uruguay
Colorado
Negro
Chubut
Iguazú
Projection: Lambert's Azimuthal Equal Area
LIMA Capital Cities
West from Greenwich
m ft
COPYRIGHT PHILIP'S

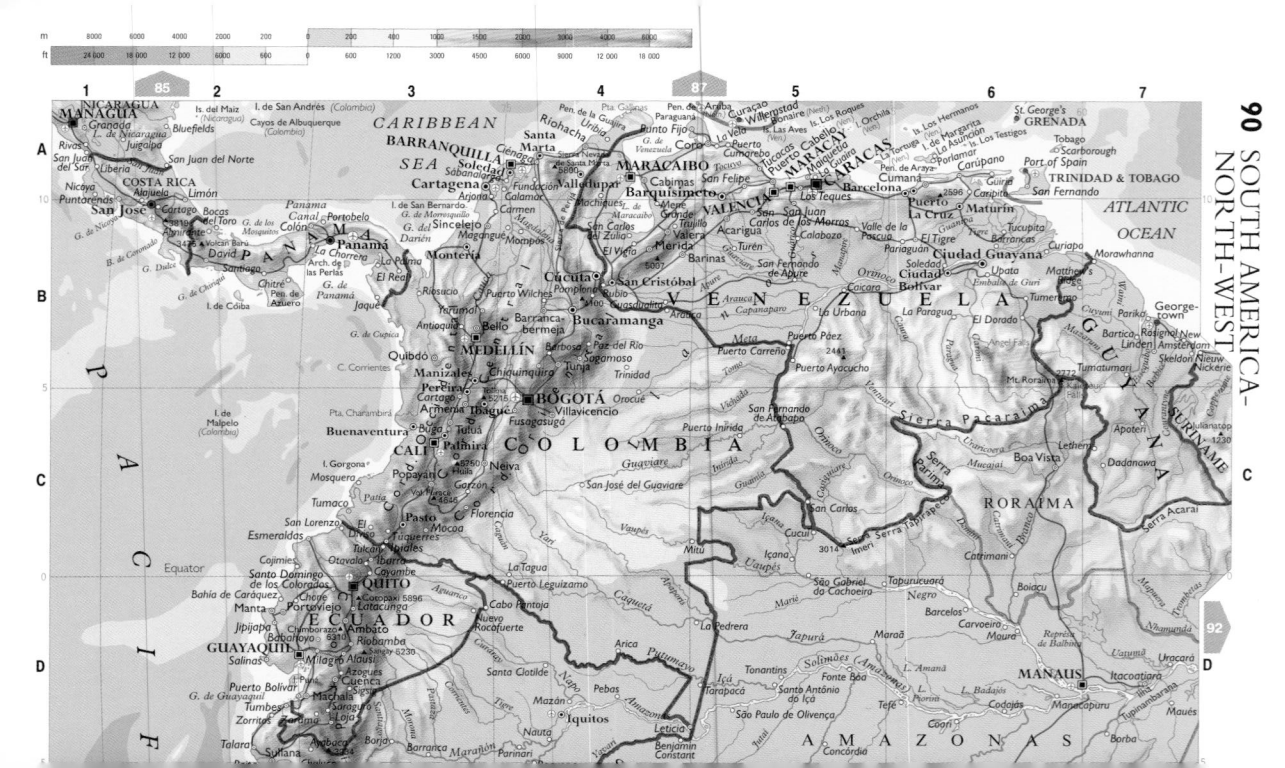
m 8000 6000 4000 2000 200 0 200 400 1000 1500 2000 3000 4000 6000
ft 24 000 18 000 12 000 6000 600 0 600 1200 3000 4500 6000 9000 12 000 18 000
85
87
92
1 2 3 4 5 6 7
A B C D
CARIBBEAN SEA
ATLANTIC OCEAN
PACIFIC
NICARAGUA
MANAGUA
Granada
Bluefields
Rivas
San Juan del Sur
Liberia
San Juan del Norte
COSTA RICA
Alajuela
Limón
Nicoya
Puntarenas
San José
Cartago
Bocas del Toro
Colón
Panama Canal
Portobelo
PANAMA
Panamá
David
Santiago
Chitre
Pen. de Azuero
I. de Coiba
I. de Malpelo (Colombia)
I. de Maiz (Nicaragua)
I. de San Andrés (Colombia)
Cayos de Albuquerque (Colombia)
BARRANQUILLA
Soledad
Sabanalarga
Cartagena
Arjona
Sincelejo
Montería
Riohacha
Santa Marta
Ciénaga
Valledupar
MARACAIBO
Cabimas
Barquisimeto
VALENCIA
Maracay
CARACAS
Los Teques
Barcelona
Puerto La Cruz
Maturín
Cumaná
Carúpano
Pen. de Araya
Coro
Punto Fijo
Curaçao
Willemstad
Aruba
Bonaire
Los Roques
Los Hermanos
Los Testigos
Margarita
La Asunción
Porlamar
St. George's
GRENADA
Tobago
Scarborough
Port of Spain
TRINIDAD & TOBAGO
San Fernando
Ciudad Guayana
Ciudad Bolívar
Tucupita
Curiapo
Morawhanna
Matthews Ridge
Tumeremo
VENEZUELA
Cúcuta
San Cristóbal
Mérida
Barinas
Acarigua
Turén
Valera
Trujillo
Maracaibo
Bucaramanga
Barrancabermeja
Bello
MEDELLÍN
Pereira
Manizales
Armenia
Ibagué
BOGOTÁ
Villavicencio
Tunja
Sogamoso
Paez del Río
Barbosa
Puerto Carreño
Puerto Ayacucho
Puerto Páez
Buenaventura
CALI
Palmira
Buga
Tuluá
Popayán
Neiva
Pasto
Mocoa
Florencia
COLOMBIA
Tumaco
Esmeraldas
Ipiales
Tulcán
Otavalo
Ibarra
Cayambe
Santo Domingo de los Colorados
QUITO
Bahía de Caráquez
Manta
Portoviejo
Latacunga
Ambato
Riobamba
Chimborazo
Cotopaxi 5896
ECUADOR
GUAYAQUIL
Milagro
Alausí
Azogues
Cuenca
Machala
Zaruma
Loja
Tumbes
Zorritos
Talara
Sullana
Puerto Bolívar
Arica
Pisagua
Iquitos
Leticia
Benjamin Constant
Tarapacá
Tonantins
Fonte Boa
Santo Antônio do Içá
São Paulo de Olivença
Tefé
Coari
Codajás
Manacapuru
MANAUS
Itacoatiara
Parintins
Barcelos
Carvoeiro
Maura
Boa Vista
RORAIMA
Lethem
Apoteri
Dadanawa
Sierra Pacaraima
Sierra Parima
Sierra Tapirapeco
Sierra Acaraí
Cucui
Mitú
Caruru
Tapurucuara
São Gabriel da Cachoeira
Cabo Pantoja
Nuevo Rocafuerte
La Pedrera
Puerto Leguizamo
San José del Guaviare
San Carlos
Puerto Inírida
San Fernando de Atabapo
Caicara
Upata
Caripito
Valle de la Pascua
Paramaribo
Nieuw Nickerie
Skeldon
Amsterdam
Linden
Rosignol
Bartica
Parikai
Georgetown
GUYANA
SURINAME
Mt. Roraima
Tumatumari
Kaieteur Falls
Julianatop 1230
Equator
Caquetá
Putumayo
Japurá
Negro
Solimões (Amazonas)
Madeira
Tapajós
Xingu
Tocantins
Orinoco
Meta
Apure
Caroni
Essequibo
Courantyne
Corantijn
Ucayali
Marañón
Pastaza
Napo
Putumayo
Caquetá
Guaviare
Vichada
Meta
Arauca
Zulia
Magdalena
Cauca
Darién
Mosquitos
Gulf of Darien
Gulf of Panama
Gulf of Guayaquil
Gulf of Venezuela
Gulf of Morrosquillo
Gulf of Cupica
Gulf of Chiriquí
Gulf of Nicoya

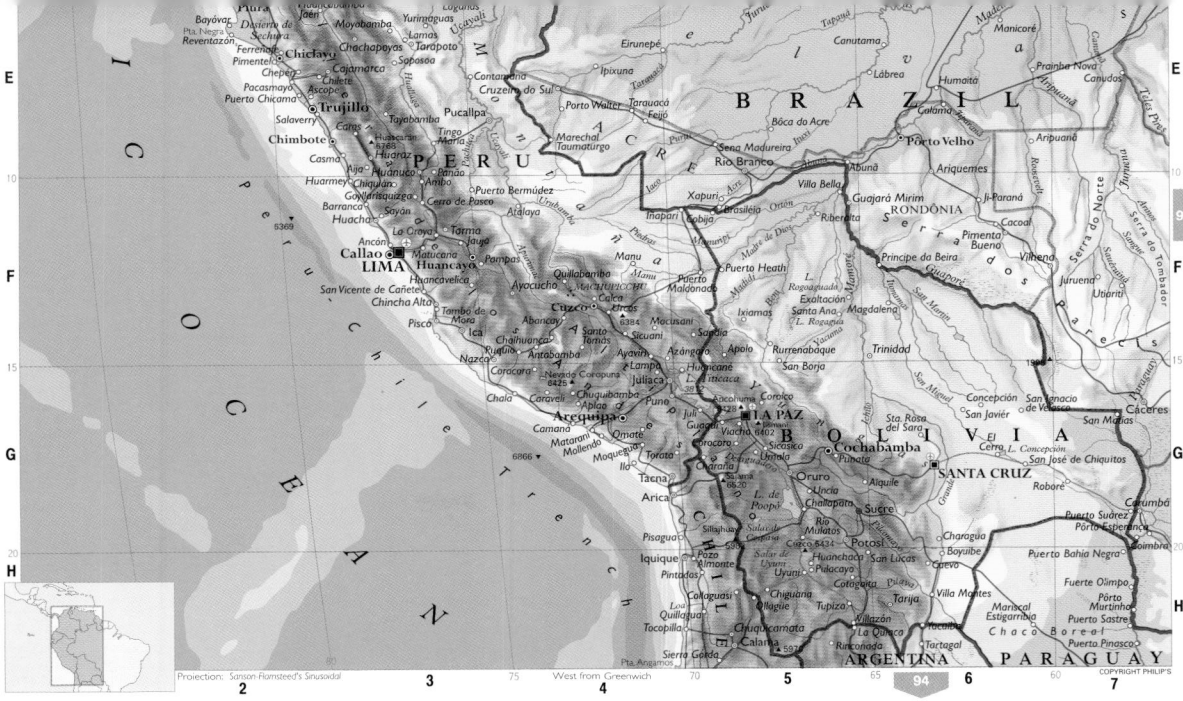
PERU
BRAZIL
BOLIVIA
CHILE
ARGENTINA
PARAGUAY
PACIFIC OCEAN
LIMA
Callao
Trujillo
Chiclayo
Chimbote
Cajamarca
Iquitos
Pucallpa
Cuzco
Arequipa
LA PAZ
Cochabamba
SANTA CRUZ
Oruro
Sucre
Potosí
Tacna
Arica
Iquique
Calama
Tarija
Puerto Maldonado
Puerto Heath
Rio Branco
Porto Velho
Manaus
Belém
Cáceres
Puerto Suárez
Corumbá
Puerto Bahia Negra
Fuerte Olimpo
Pôrto Murtinho
Puerto Pinasco
Puerto Suárez
Pôrto Esperança
Trinidad
Santa Cruz
Chaco Boreal
Serra do Norte
Serra dos Parecis
Serra do Tombador
RONDÔNIA
Proiection: Sanson-Flamsteed's Sinusoidal
West from Greenwich
COPYRIGHT PHILIP'S
91
93
94

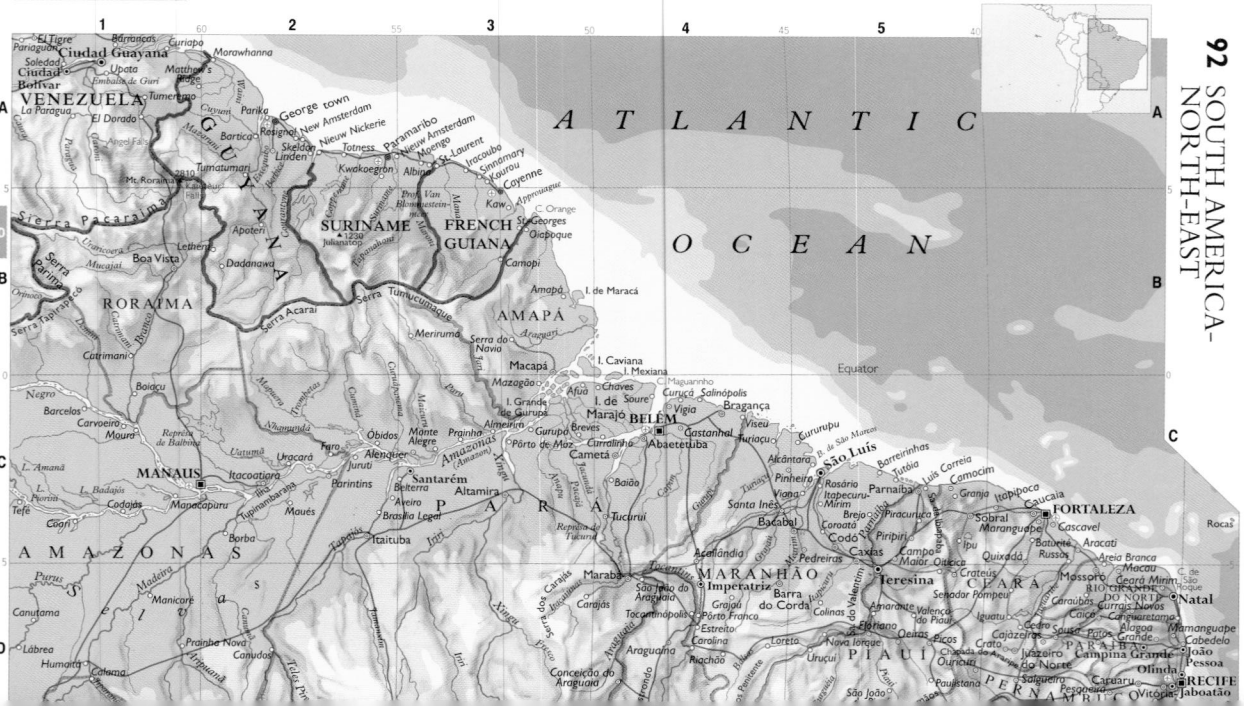
m 4000 2000 200 0 200 400 1000 1500 2000 3000 4000
ft 12 000 6000 600 0 600 1200 3000 4500 6000 9000 12 000
ATLANTIC OCEAN
VENEZUELA
GUYANA
SURINAME
FRENCH GUIANA
RORAIMA
AMAPÁ
AMAZONAS
PARÁ
MARANHÃO
PIAUÍ
CEARÁ
RIO GRANDE DO NORTE
PARAÍBA
PERNAMBUCO
Ciudad Guayana
Paramaribo
Georgetown
Cayenne
Boa Vista
MANAUS
BELÉM
São Luís
Teresina
FORTALEZA
Natal
RECIFE
Equator
Sierra Pacaraima
Serra Parima
Serra Tumucumaque
Serra Acaraí
Serra do Navio
Serra Tapirapeco
Serra Grande
Serra Dos Carajás
Serra Do Araripe
Serra Do Ibiapaba

BRAZIL
BOLIVIA
PARAGUAY
ARGENTINA
RONDÔNIA
MATO GROSSO
MATO GROSSO DO SUL
GOIÁS
TOCANTINS
MINAS GERAIS
BAHIA
SERGIPE
ALAGOAS
PARANÁ
SÃO PAULO
RIO DE JANEIRO
ESPÍRITO SANTO
Serra dos Parecis
Planalto do Mato Grosso
Pantanal
Chaco Boreal
Chaco Central
Serra do Roncador
Serra Geral de Goiás
Serra do Espinhaço
Serra do Mar
Serra do Norte
Serra do Tombador
Serra Formosa
Serra dos Apiacás
Serra do Cachimbo
Serra do Sincorá
Serra do Espinaço

PARAGUAY
ASUNCIÓN
BUENOS AIRES
MONTEVIDEO
URUGUAY
SANTIAGO
CÓRDOBA
ROSARIO
Santa Fe
Mendoza
San Miguel de Tucumán
Santiago del Estero
Salta
Jujuy
Antofagasta
Iquique
Arica
Tacna
Puno
Cuzco
Arequipa
La Paz
Oruro
Cochabamba
Santa Cruz
Sucre
Potosí
Tarija
Corrientes
Resistencia
Formosa
Posadas
Paraná
Concepción
Chillán
Temuco
Valdivia
Puerto Montt
Coquimbo
La Serena
Copiapó
Mar del Plata
Bahía Blanca
Neuquén
Bariloche
Comodoro Rivadavia
Río Gallegos
Ushuaia
Punta Arenas
Talcahuano
Valparaíso
Viña del Mar
Rio Grande
Pelotas
Porto Alegre
Florianópolis
Curitiba
São Paulo
Rio de Janeiro
Campinas
Santos
Belo Horizonte
Brasília
Goiânia
Cuiabá
Campo Grande
Rio Branco
Porto Velho
Pacific Ocean
Atlantic Ocean
Tropic of Capricorn
Equator
Andes
Chaco Boreal
Chaco Central
Chaco Austral
Pampas
Patagonia
Puna de Atacama
Altiplano
Pantanal
Amazonas
Paraná
Paraguay
Uruguay
Parana
Negro
Colorado
Chubut
Santa Cruz
Perú-Chile Trench
Antarctica
SOUTH

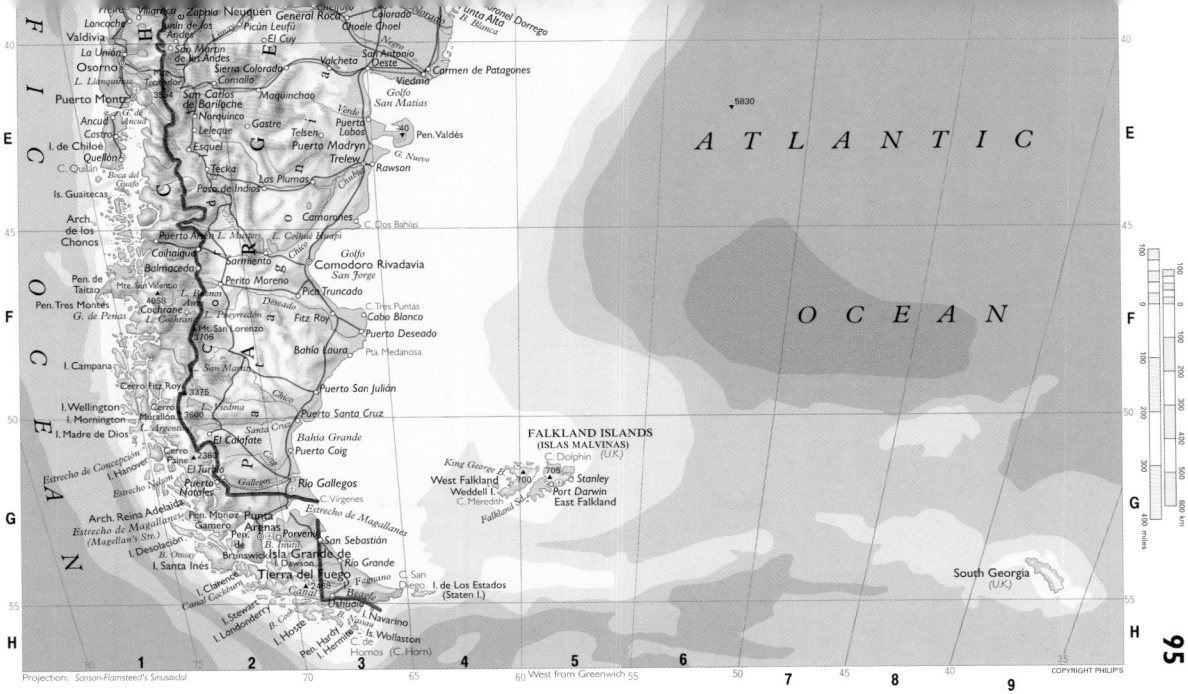
ATLANTIC
OCEAN
PACIFIC OCEAN
CHILE
ARGENTINA
FALKLAND ISLANDS
(ISLAS MALVINAS)
(U.K.)
South Georgia
(U.K.)
Zapala
Neuquen
General Roca
Viedma
Carmen de Patagones
Puerto Madryn
Rawson
Puerto Deseado
Puerto San Julián
Puerto Santa Cruz
Rio Gallegos
Punta Arenas
Isla Grande de Tierra del Fuego
Ushuaia
Puerto Montt
Valdivia
Osorno
Puerto Natales
Comodoro Rivadavia
Pen. Valdés
Golfo San Jorge
Golfo San Matías
Estrecho de Magallanes
(Magellan's Str.)
Estrecho de Magallanes
Estrecho de Concepción
Arch. Reina Adelaida
Pen. Tres Montes
Arch. de los Chonos
Is. Guaitecas
I. de Chiloé
I. Wellington
I. Mornington
I. Madre de Dios
I. Campana
I. Santa Inés
I. Navarino
Is. Wollaston
Pen. Hardy
C. de Hornos (C. Horn)
I. de Los Estados
(Staten I.)
West Falkland
Weddell I.
C. Meredith
Falkland Sd.
King George B.
C. Dolphin
Stanley
Port Darwin
East Falkland
C. Virgenes
C. Dos Bahías
C. Tres Puntas
Cabo Blanco
Pta. Medanosa
Bahía Laura
Bahía Grande
Puerto Coig
Fitz Roy
Cerro Fitz Roy
Mt. San Lorenzo
Cerro Paine
Cerro Mirador
Cerro Pico
Cerro Tronador
Mt. San Valentín
Pico Truncado
Perito Moreno
Sarmiento
Comodoro Rivadavia
Camarones
Las Plumas
Paso de Indios
Esquel
Trelew
Puerto Lobos
Telsen
Gastre
Maquinchao
Sierra Colorado
Viedma
Valcheta
San Antonio Oeste
Choele Choel
Cipolletti
Neuquen
Zapala
Temuco
Valdivia
Osorno
Puerto Montt
Ancud
Castro
Quellón
C. Quilán
Boca del Guafo
Lancoche
Freire
Villarrica
Pucón
Picún Leufú
El Cuy
Ingeniero Jacobacci
Dorrego
Bahía Blanca
Tornquist
Sierra Ventana
Tandil
Mar del Plata
Necochea
Bariloche
Nahuel Huapi
Puerto Aysén
Coihaique
Balmaceda
Cochrane
Isla Grande de Tierra del Fuego
Pen. Tres Montes
Pen. de Taitao
G. de Penas
I. Madre de Dios

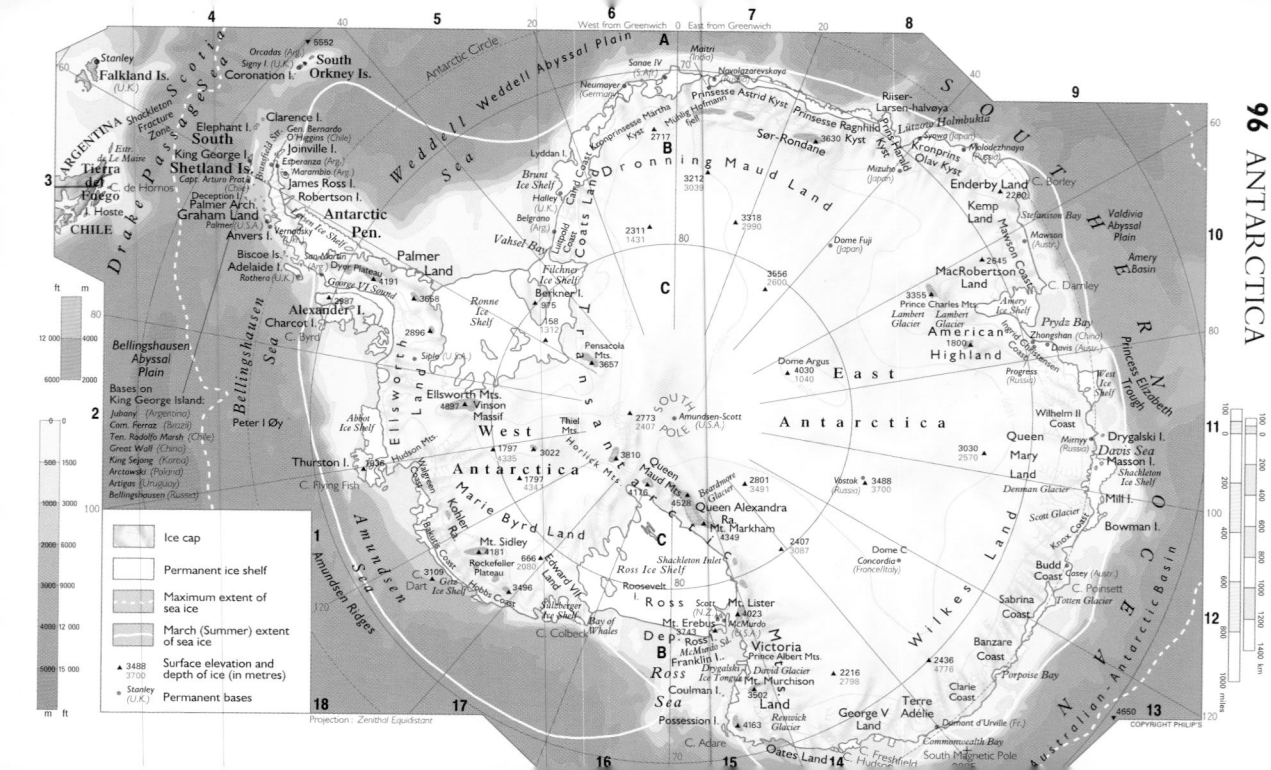
Ice cap
Permanent ice shelf
Maximum extent of sea ice
March (Summer) extent of sea ice
Surface elevation and depth of ice (in metres)
Permanent bases
Bases on King George Island:
Jubany (Argentina)
Com. Ferraz (Brazil)
Ten. Rodolfo Marsh (Chile)
Great Wall (China)
King Sejong (Korea)
Arctowski (Poland)
Artigas (Uruguay)
Bellingshausen (Russia)
Antarctic Circle
West from Greenwich 0 East from Greenwich
Weddell Abyssal Plain
Weddell Sea
Scotia Sea
Falkland Is. (U.K.)
South Orkney Is.
South Shetland Is.
Antarctic Pen.
Palmer Land
Alexander I.
Bellingshausen Sea
Bellingshausen Abyssal Plain
Peter I Øy
Ellsworth Land
Ellsworth Mts.
Vinson Massif
West Antarctica
Marie Byrd Land
Amundsen Sea
Amundsen Ridges
Ross Dependency
Ross Sea
Victoria Land
Queen Alexandra Ra.
Mt. Markham
Mt. Erebus
Mt. Lister
Mt. Sidley
Rockefeller Plateau
Dronning Maud Land
East Antarctica
Enderby Land
Kemp Land
MacRobertson Land
Prince Charles Mts.
American Highland
Dome Argus
Dome Fuji
Dome C
Vostok
Amundsen-Scott
Pensacola Mts.
Queen Mary Land
Wilhelm II Coast
Drygalski I.
Davis Sea
Masson I.
Mill I.
Bowman I.
Budd Coast
Sabrina Coast
Banzare Coast
Wilkes Land
Terre Adélie
George V Land
Oates Land
Australian Antarctic Basin
Princess Elizabeth Trough
Prince Olav Kyst
Prinsesse Ragnhild Kyst
Prinsesse Astrid Kyst
Sør-Rondane
Riiser-Larsen-halvøya
Lützow-Holmbukta
Valdivia Abyssal Plain
Amery Basin
Scott Coast
Knox Coast
Mawson Coast
Queen Maud Land
Queen Maud Mts.
Beardmore Glacier
Shackleton Inlet
Ross Ice Shelf
Roosevelt I.
Bay of Whales
Ellsworth Mts.
Hudson Mts.
Thurston I.
Charcot I.
Palmer Arch.
Graham Land
Antarctic Peninsula
Scotia Sea
Drake Passage
Tierra del Fuego
Cape Horn
Falkland Is.
Stanley
Orcadas (Arg.)
Signy I. (U.K.)
Coronation I.
Elephant I.
King George I.
Clarence I.
Joinville I.
James Ross I.
Robertson I.
Anvers I.
Biscoe Is.
Adelaide I.
Rothera (U.K.)
Palmer (U.S.A.)
Esperanza (Arg.)
Marambio (Arg.)
Deception I.
Vernadsky
Sanae IV (S.Af.)
Maitri (India)
Novolazarevskaya
Neumayer (Germany)
Kohnprinsesse Martha Kyst
Mühlig Hofmann fjell
Lyddan I.
Brunt Ice Shelf
Halley (U.K.)
Belgrano (Arg.)
Vahsel Bay
Filchner Ice Shelf
Berkner I.
Ronne Ice Shelf
Siple (U.S.A.)
Abbot Ice Shelf
Thiel Mts.
Horlick Mts.
Shackleton Range
Hobbs Coast
Walgreen Coast
Kohler Rs.
Edward VII Land
Dart I.
Colbeck
Coats Land
Coulman I.
Possession I.
C. Adare
Commonwealth Bay
Dumont d'Urville (Fr.)
South Magnetic Pole
Fresnel (Fr.)
Hudson
Projection: Zenithal Equidistant
COPYRIGHT PHILIP'S

Index to Map Pages

The index contains the names of all the principal places and features shown on the world maps. Physical features composed of a proper name (Erie) and a description (Lake) are positioned alphabetically by the proper name. The description is positioned after the proper name and is usually abbreviated:

Erie, L. **76 C5**

Where a description forms part of a settlement or administrative name, however, it is always written in full and put in its true alphabetical position:

Lake Charles **81 D7**

Names beginning St. are alphabetized under Saint, but Sankt, Sant, Santa and San are all spelt in full and are alphabetized accordingly.

The number in bold type which follows each name in the index refers to the number of the map page where that feature or place will be found. This is usually the largest scale at which the place or feature appears.

The letter and figure which are in bold type immediately after the page number give the grid square on the map page, within which the feature is situated.

Rivers are indexed to their mouths or confluences, and carry the symbol ➔ after their names. The following symbols are also used in the index: ■ country, ⧄ overseas territory or dependency, □ first order administrative area, △ national park.

A

A Coruña **18 A1**
A Estrada **18 A1**
A Fonsagrada **18 A2**
Aachen **14 C4**
Aalborg **9 D7**
Aalen **14 D6**
Aarhus = Århus **9 D8**
Aba **53 G7**
Abaco I. **86 A4**
Ābādān **47 E7**
Ābādeh **44 D3**
Abadla **52 B5**
Abaetetuba **92 C4**
Abakan **30 D7**
Abancay **91 F4**
Abarqū **44 D3**
Abashiri **32 A9**
Abashiri-Wan **32 B9**
Ābay = Nīl el Azraq ➔ **55 E5**
Abay **29 E8**
Abaya, L. **57 C7**
Abbay = Nīl el Azraq ➔ **55 E5**
Abbeville **12 A4**
Abbieglassie **63 A4**
Abbot Ice Shelf **96 B2**
ABC Islands = Netherlands Antilles ⧄ **87 D6**
Abd al Kūrī **49 E5**
Abéché **55 F3**
Abel Tasman △ **64 D5**
Abeokuta **53 G6**
Abercorn **63 A5**
Aberdeen *Australia* **63 B5**
Aberdeen *U.K.* **10 C5**
Aberdeen *S. Dak., U.S.A.* **74 C5**
Aberdeen *Wash., U.S.A.* **72 C2**
Aberystwyth **11 E4**
Abidjan **53 G5**
Abilene **80 C4**
Abitibi, L. **71 E6**
Abkhaz Republic = Abkhazia □ **25 E5**
Abkhazia □ **25 E5**
Abminga **62 A1**
Åbo = Turku **9 C10**
Abohar **42 D9**
Abomey **53 G6**
Abong-Mbang **56 D2**
Abou-Deïa **55 F2**
Absaroka Range **73 D9**
Abū 'Alī **47 F7**
Abu Dhabi = Abū Ẓāby **44 E3**
Abu Hamed **55 E5**
Abū Kamāl **46 D5**
Abū Madd, Ra's **47 F4**
Abu Rudeis **47 E3**
Abū Ẓabad **55 F4**
Abū Ẓāby **44 E3**
Abuja **53 G7**
Abunā **91 E5**
Abunā ➔ **91 E5**
Abut Hd. **65 E4**
Acaponeta **84 C3**
Acapulco **84 D5**
Acarigua **90 B5**
Accra **53 G5**
Aceh □ **38 D1**
Achalpur **43 J10**
Acharnes **23 E4**
Acheloos ➔ **23 E3**
Achill I. **11 E1**
Achinsk **30 D7**
Acireale **21 F5**
Acklins I. **86 B5**
Aconcagua, Cerro **94 C3**
Aconquija, Mt. **94 B3**
Açores, Is. dos **50 C1**
Acraman, L. **62 B2**
Acre = 'Akko **46 D3**
Acre □ **91 E4**
Acre ➔ **91 E5**
Ad Dahnā **47 F7**
Ad Dammām **47 F7**
Ad Dawādimī **47 F6**
Ad Dawḩah **44 E2**
Ad Dilam **47 G6**
Ad Dīwānīyah **47 E6**
Ada **81 B5**
Adair, C. **70 B6**
Adaja ➔ **18 B3**
Adam **44 F4**
Adamaoua, Massif de l' **55 G1**
Adamawa Highlands = Adamaoua, Massif de l' **55 G1**
Adamello, Mte. **13 C9**
Adaminaby **63 C4**
Adams, Mt. **72 C3**
Adam's Bridge **43 Q11**
Adana **46 C3**
Adapazarı = Sakarya **25 E3**
Adarama **55 E5**
Adare, C. **96 B15**
Adaut **37 F4**
Adavale **63 A3**
Adda ➔ **13 D8**
Addis Ababa = Addis Abeba **49 F2**
Addis Abeba **49 F2**
Adelaide **62 B2**
Adelaide I. **96 A3**
Adelaide Pen. **68 B10**
Adélie, Terre **96 A14**
Adelie Land = Adélie, Terre **96 A14**
Aden = Al 'Adan **49 E4**
Aden, G. of **49 E4**
Adi **37 E4**
Adige ➔ **20 B4**
Adilabad **43 K11**
Adirondack Mts. **77 C8**
Adis Abeba = Addis Abeba **49 F2**
Admiralty I. **68 C6**
Admiralty Is. **64 K9**
Adonara **37 F2**
Adoni **43 M10**
Adour ➔ **12 E3**
Adra **18 D4**
Adrano **21 F5**
Adrar **52 D6**
Adrar des Iforas **52 E6**
Adriatic Sea **20 C5**
Adua **37 E3**
Adzhar Republic = Ajaria □ **25 E5**
Ægean Sea **23 E5**
Aerhtai Shan **34 B4**

Afghanistan ■ 45 C6
'Afif 47 G5
Afuá 92 C3
Afyon 46 C2
Afyonkarahisar = Afyon 46 C2
Agadès = Agadez 53 E7
Agadez 53 E7
Agadir 52 B4
Agapa 30 B6
Agartala 41 F8
Agats 37 F5
Agboville 53 G5
Agde 13 E5
Agen 12 D4
Aghios Efstratios 23 E5
Aghiou Orous, Kolpos 23 D5
Agra 42 F10
Ağri 25 F5
Agri ➔ 21 D6
Ağrı Dağı 25 F5
Ağri Karakose = Ağri 25 F5
Agrigento 21 F4
Agrinio 23 E3
Água Clara 93 G3
Agua Prieta 84 A3
Aguarico ➔ 90 D3
Aguas Blancas 94 A3
Aguascalientes 84 C4
Aguilas 19 D5
Agulhas, C. 58 E4
Agung, Gunung 39 F5
Agusan ➔ 36 C3
Ahaggar 52 D7
Ahar 46 C6
Ahipara B. 64 A5
Ahiri 43 K12
Ahmadabad 43 H8
Ahmadnagar 43 K9
Ahmadpur 42 E7
Ahmedabad = Ahmadabad 43 H8
Ahmednagar = Ahmadnagar 43 K9
Ahväz 47 E7
Ahvenanmaa = Åland 9 C10
Aḩwar 49 E4
Aigues-Mortes 13 E6
Aihui = Heihe 35 A7
Aija 91 E3
Aikawa 33 D6
Aiken 83 C7
Aimere 37 F2
Ain Banaiyan 44 F2
Aïn Ben Tili 52 C4
Aïn Sefra 52 B5
Aïr 53 E7
Air Force I. 70 C6
Aisne ➔ 13 B5
Aitutaki 65 L14
Aix-en-Provence 13 E6
Aix-la-Chapelle = Aachen 14 C4
Aix-les-Bains 13 D6
Aizawl 41 F9
Aizuwakamatsu 33 E6
Ajaccio 13 F8
Ajanta Ra. 43 J9
Ajari Rep. = Ajaria □ 25 E5
Ajaria □ 25 E5
Ajdābiyā 54 B3
Ajka 16 E3
'Ajmān 44 E3
Ajmer 42 F9
Ajo, C. de 18 A4
Akaroa 65 E5
Akelamo 37 D3
Aketi 56 D4
Akhisar 23 E6
Akimiski I. 71 D5
Akita 32 D7
Akjoujt 53 E3
Akkeshi 32 B9
'Akko 46 D3
Akkol = Aqköl 29 E8
Aklavik 68 B6
Akola 43 J10
Akordat 57 A7
Akpatok I. 70 C7
Akranes 8 C1
Akron 76 D5
Aksai Chin 42 B11
Aksaray 46 C3
Aksarka 28 C7
Akşehir 46 C2
Aksu 34 B3
Aktsyabrski 17 B9
Aktyubinsk = Aqtöbe 29 D6
Akure 53 G7
Akureyri 8 B2
Akyab = Sittwe 41 G9
Al 'Adan 49 E4
Al Aḥsā = Hasa 47 F7
Al Amādīyah 46 C5
Al 'Amārah 47 E6
Al 'Aqabah 47 E3
Al 'Aramah 47 F6
Al Ashkhara 45 F4
Al Badī' 47 G6
Al Baḥral Mayyit = Dead Sea 47 E3
Al Baṣrah 47 E6
Al Batinah 44 F4
Al Bayḍā 54 B3
Al Faḍilī 47 F7
Al Fallūjah 46 D5
Al Fāw 47 E7
Al Fujayrah 44 E4
Al Hābah 47 F6
Al Ḥaddār 47 G6
Al Hāmad 47 E4
Al Ḥamar 47 G6
Al Ḥamrā' 47 F4
Al Ḥarīq 47 G6
Al Ḥasakah 46 C5
Al Ḥayy 47 D6
Al Ḥillah *Iraq* 47 D6
Al Ḥillah *Si. Arabia* 47 G6
Al Hoceïma 52 A5
Al Ḥudaydah 49 E3
Al Hufūf 47 F7
Al Ḥulwah 47 G6
Al Jāfūrah 47 F7
Al Jaghbūb 54 C3
Al Jahrah 47 E6
Al Jalāmīd 47 E4
Al Jawf *Libya* 54 D3
Al Jawf *Si. Arabia* 47 E4
Al Jazair = Algeria ■ 52 C6
Al Jazirah 46 D5
Al Jubayl 47 F7
Al Jubaylah 47 F6
Al Junaynah 55 F3
Al Khābūra 44 F4
Al Khalīl 47 E3
Al Kharfah 47 G6
Al Kharsānīyah 47 F7
Al Khaṣab 44 E4
Al Kufrah 54 D3
Al Kūt 47 D6
Al Kuwayt 47 E7
Al Lādhiqīyah 46 D3
Al Luḥayyah 49 D3
Al Madīnah 47 F4
Al Maghreb = Morocco ■ 52 B4
Al Majma'ah 47 F6
Al Manāmah 44 E2
Al Marj 54 B3
Al Mawṣil 46 C5
Al Midhnab 47 F6
Al Mish'āb 47 E7
Al Mubarraz 47 F7
Al Muḥarraq 44 E2
Al Mukallā 49 E4
Al Mukhā 49 E3
Al Musayyib 47 D6
Al Muwayliḥ 47 F3
Al Qaḍīmah 47 G4
Al Qā'iyah 47 F5
Al Qāmishlī 46 C5
Al Qaṣīm □ 47 F5
Al Qaṭīf 47 F7
Al Qaṭrūn 54 D2
Al Quaisūmah 47 E6
Al Quds = Jerusalem 47 E3
Al Qurayyāt 45 F4
Al Qurnah 47 E6
Al 'Ulā 47 F4
Al 'Uqayr 47 F7
Al 'Uthmānīyah 47 F7
Al 'Uwaynid 47 F6
Al 'Uwayqīlah 47 E5
Al 'Uyūn 47 F5
Al Wakrah 44 E2
Al Yamāmah 47 F6
Al Yaman = Yemen ■ 49 D4
Alabama □ 82 C4
Alabama ➔ 82 D4
Alaçam Dağları 23 E7
Alacant = Alicante 19 C5
Alagoa Grande 92 D6
Alagoas □ 93 D6
Alagoinhas 93 E6
Alajuela 86 D3
Alamosa 79 B10
Åland 9 C10
Alania = North Ossetia □ 25 E5
Alanya 46 C2
Alapayevsk 29 D7
Alappuzha = Alleppey 43 Q10
Alaşehir 23 E7
Alaska □ 69 B4
Alaska, G. of 69 C5
Alaska Peninsula 69 C4
Alaska Range 69 B4
Alataw Shankou 34 B3
Alatyr 24 C6
Alausi 90 D3
Alawoona 62 B3
Alba 13 D8
Albacete 19 C5
Albacutya, L. 62 C3
Albanel, L. 71 D6
Albania ■ 23 D3
Albany *Australia* 60 H2
Albany *Ga., U.S.A.* 83 D5
Albany *N.Y., U.S.A.* 77 C9
Albany *Oreg., U.S.A.* 72 D2
Albany ➔ 71 D5
Albardón 94 C3
Albemarle 83 B7
Alberche ➔ 18 C3
Alberga ➔ 62 A2
Albert, L. *Africa* 57 D6
Albert, L. *Australia* 62 C2
Albert Nile ➔ 57 D6
Albertville 13 D7
Albi 12 E5
Albina 92 A3
Alborán 18 E4
Ålborg = Aalborg 9 D7
Alborz, Reshteh-ye Kūhhā-ye 44 B3
Albuquerque 79 C9
Albury 63 C4
Alcalá de Henares 18 B4
Alcalá la Real 18 D4
Álcamo 21 F4
Alcaníz 19 B5
Alcântara 92 C5
Alcántara, Embalse de 18 C2
Alcantarilla 19 D5
Alcaraz, Sierra de 19 C4
Alcaudete 18 D3
Alcázar de San Juan 18 C4
Alchevsk 25 D4
Alcira = Alzira 19 C5
Alcoy 19 C5
Aldabra Is. 51 G8
Aldan ➔ 31 C10
Alderney 11 G5
Aleg 53 E3
Alegrete 94 B5
Aleksandriya = Oleksandriya 17 C8
Aleksandrovskoye 29 C8
Alençon 12 B4
Aleppo = Ḥalab 46 C4
Alert 70 A7
Alès 13 D6
Alessándria 13 D8
Ålesund 8 C7
Aleutian Is. 69 C2
Alexander Arch. 69 C6
Alexander I. 96 A3
Alexandra *Australia* 63 C4
Alexandra *N.Z.* 65 F3

Alexandria = El Iskandarîya **54 B4**
Alexandria *Romania* **22 C5**
Alexandria *La., U.S.A.* **81 D7**
Alexandria *Va., U.S.A.* **77 E7**
Alexandrina, L. **62 C2**
Alexandroupoli **22 D5**
Aleysk **29 D9**
Alga **29 E6**
Algarve **18 D1**
Algeciras **18 D3**
Algemesí **19 C5**
Alger **52 A6**
Algeria ■ **52 C6**
Alghero **21 D2**
Algiers = Alger **52 A6**
Alhucemas = Al Hoceïma **52 A5**
'Alī al Gharbī **47 D6**
'Alī Khēl **42 C6**
Aliağa **23 E6**
Alicante **19 C5**
Alice Springs **60 E5**
Aligarh **42 F11**
Alīgūdarz **46 D7**
Alipur **42 E7**
Alipur Duar **41 D7**
Aliwal North **59 E5**
Aljustrel **18 D1**
Alkmaar **14 B3**
All American Canal **78 D5**
Allahabad **40 E3**
Allegheny ➔ **77 D5**
Allegheny Mts. **77 F5**
Allentown **77 D8**
Alleppey **43 Q10**
Aller ➔ **14 B5**
Allier ➔ **13 C5**
Allora **63 A5**
Alma Ata = Almaty **29 E8**
Almada **18 C1**
Almadén **18 C3**
Almansa **19 C5**
Almanzor, Pico **18 B3**
Almanzora ➔ **19 D5**
Almaty **29 E8**
Almazán **19 B4**
Almeirim **92 C3**
Almelo **14 B4**
Almendralejo **18 C2**
Almería **19 D4**
Almora **42 E11**
Alnwick **10 D6**
Alon **41 F10**
Alor **37 F2**
Alor Setar **38 C2**
Alps **14 E5**
Alsace □ **13 B7**
Alsask **69 C9**
Alsasua **19 A4**
Alta Gracia **94 C4**
Altai = Aerhtai Shan **34 B4**
Altai = Gorno-Altay □ **29 D9**
Altamira **92 C3**
Altamura **21 D6**
Altanbulag **35 A5**
Altay **34 B3**
Altea **19 C5**
Alto Araguaia **93 F3**
Alto Molocue **59 B7**
Alton **75 F9**
Alton Downs **62 A2**
Altoona **77 D6**
Altun Shan **34 C3**
Alusi **37 F4**
Alvear **94 B5**
Alvie **62 C3**
Alwar **42 F10**
Alxa Zuoqi **35 C5**
Alzira **19 C5**
Am Timan **55 F3**
Amâdi **55 G5**
Amadjuak **70 C6**
Amadjuak L. **70 C6**
Amagasaki **33 F4**
Amahai **37 E3**
Amakusa-Shotō **33 G2**
Amaliada **23 F3**
Amalner **43 J9**
Amambay, Cordillera de **94 A5**
Amankeldi **29 D7**
Amapá **92 B3**
Amapá □ **92 B3**
Amarante **92 D5**
Amarillo **80 B3**
Amaro, Mte. **20 C5**
Amasra **46 B3**
Amazon = Amazonas ➔ **92 C3**
Amazonas □ **90 D6**
Amazonas ➔ **92 C3**
Ambala **42 D10**
Ambalavao **59 C9**
Ambanja **59 A9**
Ambartsevo **29 D9**
Ambato **90 D3**
Ambatolampy **59 B9**
Ambatondrazaka **59 B9**
Amberg **15 D6**
Ambergris Cay **85 D7**
Amberley **65 E5**
Ambikapur **40 F4**
Ambilobé **59 A9**
Ambo **91 F3**
Amboise **12 C4**
Ambon **37 E3**
Ambositra **59 C9**
Ambovombe **59 D9**
Amboyna Cay **38 C4**
Ambriz **56 F2**
Amby **63 A4**
Amchitka I. **69 C1**
Amderma **28 C7**
Ameca **84 C4**
Ameland **14 B3**
American Highland **96 B10**
American Samoa ⊠ **65 L13**
Americus **83 C5**
Amery **69 C10**
Amery Ice Shelf **96 A10**
Ames **75 D8**
Amherst *Burma* **41 J11**
Amherst *Canada* **71 E7**
Amiata, Mte. **20 C3**
Amiens **12 B5**
Amirante Is. **26 K9**
'Ammān **47 E3**
Ammochostos = Famagusta **46 D3**
Amorgos **23 F5**
Amos **71 E6**
Amoy = Xiamen **35 D6**
Ampanihy **59 C8**
Ampenan **39 F5**
Amper ➔ **15 D6**
Amravati **43 J10**
Amreli **43 J7**
Amritsar **42 D9**
Amroha **42 E11**
Amsterdam **14 B3**
Amstetten **15 D8**
Amudarya ➔ **29 E6**
Amund Ringnes I. **70 B4**
Amundsen Gulf **68 A7**
Amundsen Sea **96 B1**
Amuntai **39 E5**
Amur ➔ **31 D12**
Amurang **37 D2**
Amyderya = Amudarya ➔ **29 E6**
An Nafūd **47 E5**
An Najaf **47 D6**
An Nhon **38 B3**
An Nu'ayrīyah **47 F7**
Anabar ➔ **30 B9**
Anaconda **73 C7**
Anadolu **25 F3**
'Ānah **46 D5**
Anaheim **78 D4**
Anakapalle **40 J4**
Anambas, Kepulauan **39 D3**
Anambas Is. = Anambas, Kepulauan **39 D3**
Anamur **46 C3**
Anan **33 G4**
Anantnag **42 C9**
Ananyiv **17 E9**
Anápolis **93 F4**
Anār **44 D3**
Anārak **44 C3**
Anatolia = Anadolu **25 F3**
Añatuya **94 B4**
Anchorage **69 B5**
Ancohuma, Nevado **91 G5**
Ancón **91 F3**
Ancona **20 C4**
Ancud **95 E2**
Ancud, G. de **95 E2**
Andalgalá **94 B3**
Andalucía □ **18 D3**
Andalusia = Andalucía □ **18 D3**
Andalusia **82 D4**
Andaman Is. **27 G11**
Andaman Sea **38 B1**
Andapa **59 A9**
Anderson **76 D3**
Anderson ➔ **68 B7**
Andes, Cord. de los **91 G4**
Andhra Pradesh □ **43 L11**
Andijon **29 E8**
Andikithira = Antikythira **23 G4**
Andizhan = Andijon **29 E8**
Andkhvoy **45 B6**
Andoany **59 A9**
Andorra ■ **19 A6**
Andorra La Vella **12 E4**
Andreanof Is. **69 C2**
Andrewilla **62 A2**
Ándria **20 D6**
Andros **23 F5**
Andros I. **86 B4**
Andújar **18 C3**
Andulo **56 G3**
Aneto, Pico de **19 A6**
Ang'angxi **35 B7**
Angara ➔ **30 D7**
Angarsk **30 D8**
Angaston **62 B2**
Ånge **8 C9**
Angeles **36 A2**
Angellala **63 A4**
Ångermanälven ➔ **8 C9**
Angers **12 C3**
Anglesey **11 E4**
Ango **57 D5**
Angoche **59 B7**
Angola ■ **58 A3**
Angoulême **12 D4**
Angoumois **12 D4**
Angren **29 E8**
Anguilla ⊠ **87 C7**
Anhui □ **35 C6**
Anhwei = Anhui □ **35 C6**
Anjou **12 C3**
Ankaboa, Tanjona **59 C8**
Ankang **35 C5**
Ankara **25 F3**
Ankaratra **59 B9**
Ann Arbor **76 C4**
Annaba **52 A7**
Annan **11 D5**
Annapolis **77 E7**
Annecy **13 D7**
Anning **34 D5**
Anniston **82 C5**
Annobón **51 G4**
Annuello **62 B3**
Anqing **35 C6**
Ansbach **14 D6**
Anshan **35 B7**
Anshun **35 D5**
Ansongo **53 E6**
Ansudu **37 E5**
Antabamba **91 F4**
Antakya = Hatay **46 C4**
Antalaha **59 A10**
Antalya **46 C2**
Antalya Körfezi **46 C2**
Antananarivo **59 B9**
Antarctic Pen. **96 A4**
Antarctica **96 C**
Antequera **18 D3**
Anti Atlas **52 C4**
Antibes **13 E7**
Anticosti, Î. d' **71 E7**
Antigonish **71 E7**
Antigua & Barbuda ■ **87 C7**
Antikythira **23 G4**
Antioquia **90 B3**
Antofagasta **94 A2**

Antonina 94 B7
Antrim 11 D3
Antsirabe 59 B9
Antsiranana 59 A9
Antsohihy 59 A9
Antwerp = Antwerpen 14 C3
Antwerpen 14 C3
Anupgarh 42 E8
Anvers = Antwerpen 14 C3
Anvers I. 96 A3
Anxi 34 B4
Anxious B. 62 B1
Anyang 35 C6
Anzhero-Sudzhensk 29 D9
Ânzio 20 D4
Aoga-Shima 33 G6
Aomen = Macau 35 D6
Aomori 32 C7
Aoraki Mount Cook 65 E4
Aosta 13 D7
Aotearoa = New Zealand ■ 64 D7
Aouk, Bahr ➔ 56 C3
Apalachicola ➔ 82 E5
Apaporis ➔ 90 D5
Aparri 36 A2
Apeldoorn 14 B3
Apennines = Appennini 20 B3
Apia 65 L13
Apiacás, Serra dos 91 E7
Aplao 91 G4
Apo, Mt. 36 C3
Apolo 91 F5
Apoteri 90 C7
Appalachian Mts. 77 F5
Appennini 20 B3
Appleton 76 B1
Aprília 20 D4
Apucarana 94 A6
Apure ➔ 90 B5
Apurimac ➔ 91 F4
Aqaba = Al 'Aqabah 47 E3
Aqaba, G. of 47 E3
'Aqabah, Khalīj al = Aqaba, G. of 47 E3
Äqchah 45 B6
Aqköl 29 E8
'Aqrah 46 C5
Aqtöbe 29 D6
Aqtoghay 29 E8
Aquidauana 93 G2
Aquitain, Bassin 12 D3
Ar Rachidiya = Er Rachidia 52 B5
Ar Ramādī 46 D5
Ar Raqqah 46 D4
Ar Rass 47 F5
Ar Rifā'ī 47 E6
Ar Riyāḑ 47 F6
Ar Ruṭbah 46 D5
Ar Ruwayḑah 47 G6
Ara 40 E5
'Arab, Bahr el ➔ 55 G4
Arab, Shatt al ➔ 47 E7
Arabian Desert = Es Sahrâ' Esh Sharqīya 54 C5
Arabian Gulf = Persian Gulf 44 E2
Arabian Sea 26 G8
Araç 46 B3
Aracaju 93 E6
Aracati 92 C6
Araçatuba 93 G3
Aracena 18 D2
Araçuaí 93 F5
Arad 16 E5
Arafura Sea 37 F4
Aragón □ 19 B5
Aragón ➔ 19 A5
Araguacema 92 D4
Araguaia ➔ 92 D4
Araguari 93 F4
Araguari ➔ 92 B4
Arak 52 C6
Arakan Coast 41 H9
Arakan Yoma 41 H10
Araks = Aras, Rüd-e ➔ 46 B7
Aral 29 E7
Aral Sea 29 E6
Aral Tengizi = Aral Sea 29 E6
Aralsk = Aral 29 E7
Aralskoye More = Aral Sea 29 E6
Aran I. 10 D2
Aran Is. 11 E2
Aranda de Duero 18 B4
Aranjuez 18 B4
Arapgir 46 C4
Arapiraca 93 D6
Arapongas 94 A6
Araraquara 93 G4
Ararat 62 C3
Ararat, Mt. = Ağrı Dağı 25 F5
Araripe, Chapada do 92 D6
Aras, Rüd-e ➔ 46 B7
Arauca 90 B4
Arauca ➔ 90 B5
Araxá 93 F4
Araya, Pen. de 90 A6
Árbatax 21 E2
Arbīl 46 C6
Arbroath 10 C5
Arcachon 12 D3
Archangel = Arkhangelsk 28 C5
Arckaringa 62 A1
Arckaringa Cr. ➔ 62 A2
Arcos de la Frontera 18 D3
Arcot 43 N11
Arctic Bay 70 B5
Arctic Red River = Tsiigehtchic 68 B6
Arda ➔ 22 D6
Ardabīl 46 C7
Ardahan 46 B5
Ardenne 14 D3
Ardennes = Ardenne 14 D3
Ardestān 44 C3
Ardlethan 63 B4
Ardmore 80 B5
Ardrossan 62 B2
Arecibo 87 C6
Areia Branca 92 C6
Arendal 9 D7
Arequipa 91 G4
Arévalo 18 B3
Arezzo 20 C3
Arganda 18 B4
Argentan 12 B3
Argentário, Mte. 20 C3
Argentina ■ 94 D3
Argentina Is. 96 A3
Argentino, L. 95 G2
Argeş ➔ 22 B6
Arghandab ➔ 42 D4
Argolikos Kolpos 23 F4
Argos 23 F4
Argostoli 23 E3
Ārhus 9 D8
Ariadnoye 32 A4
Arica *Chile* 91 G4
Arica *Colombia* 90 D4
Aridh 47 F6
Arinos ➔ 91 F7
Aripuanã 91 E6
Aripuanã ➔ 90 E6
Ariquemes 91 E6
Arizona 94 D3
Arizona □ 79 C7
Arjona 90 A3
Arkalyk = Arqalyk 29 D7
Arkansas □ 81 B7
Arkansas ➔ 81 C8
Arkansas City 80 A5
Arkhangelsk 28 C5
Arklow 11 E3
Arkticheskiy, Mys 30 A7
Arlanzón ➔ 18 A3
Arlbergpass 14 E6
Arles 13 E6
Arlington *Va., U.S.A.* 77 E7
Arlington *Wash., U.S.A.* 72 B2
Arlon 14 D3
Armagh 11 D3
Armavir 25 D5
Armenia 90 C3
Armenia ■ 25 E5
Armidale 63 B5
Arnaud ➔ 70 C6
Arnauti, C. 46 D3
Arnhem 14 C3
Arnhem, C. 60 C6
Arnhem Land 60 C5
Arno ➔ 20 C3
Arno Bay 62 B2
Arnsberg 14 C5
Arqalyk 29 D7
Arrabury 62 A3
Arrah = Ara 40 E5
Arran 10 D4
Arras 13 A5
Arrecife 52 C3
Arrée, Mts. d' 12 B2
Arrowtown 65 F3
Arsenev 32 A3
Arta 23 E3
Artem 32 B3
Arthur ➔ 62 D3
Arthur's Pass 65 E4
Arthur's Pass △ 65 E4
Artigas 94 D5
Artois 12 A5
Artsyz 17 E9
Artvin 25 E5
Aru, Kepulauan 37 F4
Aru Is. = Aru, Kepulauan 37 F4
Arua 57 D6
Aruanã 93 E3
Aruba ⌀ 87 D6
Arunachal Pradesh □ 41 C10
Arusha 57 E7
Aruwimi ➔ 56 D4
Arviat 68 B10
Arxan 35 B6
Arys 29 E7
Arzamas 24 B5
As Saffānīyah 47 E7
As Samāwah 47 E6
As Sohar = Ṣuḥār 44 E4
As Sulaymānīyah *Iraq* 46 D6
As Sulaymānīyah *Si. Arabia* 47 F6
As Summān 47 F6
As Sūq 47 G5
As Suwaydā' 46 D4
As Suwayḥ 45 F4
Aş Şuwayrah 47 D6
Asahigawa 32 B8
Asansol 40 F6
Ascension I. 51 G2
Aschaffenburg 14 D5
Aschersleben 15 C6
Áscoli Piceno 20 C4
Ascope 91 E3
Aseb 49 E3
Asenovgrad 22 C5
Aşgabat = Ashgabat 29 F6
Ash Shāmīyah 47 E6
Ash Shāriqah 44 E3
Ash Shaṭrah 47 E6
Ash Shu'aybah 47 F6
Ash Shu'bah 47 E6
Ashburton 65 E4
Asheville 83 B6
Ashford *Australia* 63 A5
Ashford *U.K.* 11 F7
Ashgabat 29 F6
Ashizuri-Zaki 33 G3
Ashkhabad = Ashgabat 29 F6
Ashmyany 17 A7
Ashqelon 47 E3
Ashtabula 76 D5
Ashuanipi, L. 71 D7
Asia, Kepulauan 37 D4
Asifabad 43 K11
Asinara 20 D2
Asinara, G. dell' 20 D2
Asino 29 D9
Asipovichy 17 B9
'Asīr 48 D3
Asir, Ras 49 E5
Asmara = Asmera 57 A7
Asmera 57 A7
Aspiring, Mt. 65 F3
Assab = Aseb 49 E3

Assam □ 41 D9
Assen 14 B4
Assiniboia 69 D9
Assiniboine → 69 D10
Assis 94 A6
Assisi 20 C4
Astana 29 D8
Asti 13 D8
Astipalea 23 F6
Astorga 18 A2
Astoria 72 C2
Astrakhan 25 D6
Astrakhan-Bazàr 25 F6
Asturias □ 18 A3
Asunción 94 B5
Aswân 54 D5
Aswan Dam = Sadd el Aali 54 D5
Asyût 54 C5
At Ṭafilah 47 E3
Aṭ Tā'if 48 C3
Atacama, Desierto de 94 A3
Atacama, Salar de 94 A3
Atalaya 91 F4
Atamyrat 29 F7
Atapupu 37 F2
Atâr 52 D3
Atasū 29 E8
Atauro 37 F3
Atbara 55 E5
'Atbara, Nahr → 55 E5
Atbasar 29 D7
Athabasca 69 C8
Athabasca → 68 C8
Athabasca, L. 68 C8
Athens = Athina 23 F4
Athens *Ala., U.S.A.* 82 B4
Athens *Ga., U.S.A.* 83 C6
Athina 23 F4
Athínai = Athina 23 F4
Athlone 11 E3
Athos 23 D5
Athy 11 E3
Ati 55 F2
Atlanta 83 C5
Atlantic City 77 E8
Atlas Mts. = Haut Atlas 52 B4
Atrak = Atrek → 44 B3
Atrek → 44 B3
Atsuta 32 B7
Attapu 38 B3
Attawapiskat 71 D5
Attawapiskat → 71 D5
Attock 42 C8
Attopeu = Attapu 38 B3
Attur 43 P11
Atuel → 94 D3
Atyraū 29 E6
Aubagne 13 E6
Aube → 13 B5
Auburn 82 C5
Auburn Ra. 63 A5
Aubusson 12 D5
Auch 12 E4
Auckland 64 B6
Aude → 13 E5
Augathella 63 A4
Augsburg 14 D6
Augusta *Italy* 21 F5
Augusta *Ga., U.S.A.* 83 C7
Augusta *Maine, U.S.A.* 77 B11
Aujuittuq = Grise Fiord 70 B5
Aunis 12 C3
Auponhia 37 E3
Aurangabad *Bihar, India* 40 E5
Aurangabad *Maharashtra, India* 43 K9
Aurich 14 B4
Aurillac 12 D5
Aurora *Colo., U.S.A.* 74 F2
Aurora *Ill., U.S.A.* 76 D1
Austin *Minn., U.S.A.* 75 D8
Austin *Tex., U.S.A.* 80 D5
Austral Is. = Tubuaï, Îs. 65 M16
Austral Seamount Chain 65 M16
Australia ■ 60 E6
Australian Alps 63 C4
Australian Capital Territory □ 63 C4
Austria ■ 15 E8
Autun 13 C6
Auvergne □ 13 D5
Auvergne, Mts. d' 13 D5
Auxerre 13 C5
Avallon 13 C5
Aveiro *Brazil* 92 C2
Aveiro *Portugal* 18 B1
Āvej 46 D7
Avellaneda 94 C5
Avellino 21 D5
Aversa 21 D5
Avesta 9 C9
Avezzano 20 C4
Aviemore 10 C5
Avignon 13 E6
Ávila 18 B3
Avilés 18 A3
Avoca → 62 C3
Avola 21 F5
Avranches 12 B3
Awaji-Shima 33 F4
Awash 49 F3
Awatere → 65 D6
Awbārī 54 C1
Awbārī, Idehan 54 C1
Awjilah 54 C3
Axel Heiberg I. 70 B5
Axim 53 H5
Axios → 23 D4
Ayabaca 90 D3
Ayabe 33 F4
Ayacucho *Argentina* 94 D5
Ayacucho *Peru* 91 F4
Ayaguz → Ayaköz 29 E9
Ayaköz 29 E9
Ayamonte 18 D2
Ayaviri 91 F4
Áybak 45 B7
Aydın 23 F6
Ayers Rock = Uluru 60 F5
Ayeyarwady = Irrawaddy → 41 K10
Aylmer, L. 68 B8
Ayn Dār 47 F7
Ayr 10 D4
Aytos 22 C6
Ayu, Kepulauan 37 D4
Ayvacık 23 E6
Ayvalık 23 E6
Aẓ Ẓahrān 47 F7
Az Zarqā 46 D4
Az Zilfī 47 F6
Az Zubayr 47 E6
Azamgarh 40 D4
Azārbayjan = Azerbaijan ■ 25 E6
Āzarbāyjān-e Gharbī □ 46 C6
Āzarbāyjān-e Sharqī □ 46 C6
Azare 53 F8
Azbine = Aïr 53 E7
Azerbaijan ■ 25 E6
Azogues 90 D3
Azores = Açores, Is. dos 50 C1
Azov 25 D4
Azov, Sea of 25 D4
Azovskoye More = Azov, Sea of 25 D4
Azovy 28 C7
Azuaga 18 C3
Azuero, Pen. de 86 E3
Azul 94 D5

B

Ba Don 38 A3
Ba Ria 38 B3
Baardeere = Bardera 49 G3
Bab el Mandeb 49 E3
Bābā, Koh-i- 42 B5
Baba Burnu 23 E6
Babadag 22 B7
Babadayhan 29 F7
Babaeski 22 D6
Babahoyo 90 D3
Babar 37 F3
Babo 37 E4
Bābol 44 B3
Bābol Sar 44 B3
Babruysk 17 B9
Babuyan Chan. 36 A2
Babylon 47 D6
Bacabal 92 C5
Bacan, Kepulauan 37 E3
Bacarra 36 A2
Bacău 17 E8
Bachelina 29 D7
Back → 68 B9
Bacolod 36 B2
Bad Ischl 15 E7
Bad Kissingen 14 C6
Badagara 43 P9
Badajoz 18 C2
Badalona 19 B7
Badampahar 40 F6
Badanah 47 E5
Badarinath 42 D11
Badas 38 D4
Badas, Kepulauan 39 D3
Baddo → 42 E4
Bade 37 F5
Baden 15 D9
Baden-Baden 14 D5
Baden-Württemberg □ 14 D5
Badgastein 15 E7
Bādghīs □ 42 B3
Badin 43 G6
Badlands 74 D3
Baena 18 D3
Baeza 18 D4
Baffin B. 70 B7
Baffin I. 70 C6
Bafia 53 H8
Bafing → 53 F3
Bafoulabé 53 F3
Bāfq 44 D3
Bāft 44 D4
Bafwasende 57 D5
Bagamoyo 57 F7
Baganga 36 C3
Bagansiapiapi 39 D2
Bagdarin 30 D9
Bagé 94 C6
Baghdād 46 D6
Bagheria 21 E4
Baghlān 42 A6
Baghlān □ 45 C7
Bago = Pegu 41 J11
Baguio 36 A2
Bahamas ■ 86 A4
Baharampur 40 E7
Bahawalpur 42 E7
Bahía = Salvador 93 E6
Bahía □ 93 E5
Bahía Blanca 94 D4
Bahía de Caráquez 90 D2
Bahía Laura 95 F3
Bahía Negra 91 H7
Bahraich 40 D3
Bahrain ■ 44 E2
Baia Mare 17 E6
Baïbokoum 55 G2
Baidoa 49 G3
Baie-Comeau 71 E7
Baie Verte 71 E8
Ba'ijī 46 D5
Baikal, L. = Baykal, Oz. 30 D8
Baikonur = Bayqongyr 29 E7
Baile Atha Cliath = Dublin 11 E3
Băileşti 22 B4
Bā'ir 47 E4
Bairiki = Tarawa 64 J12
Bairnsdale 63 C4
Baitadi 40 C3
Baiyin 35 C5
Baja 16 E4
Baja, Pta. 84 B1
Baja California 84 A1
Bajimba, Mt. 63 A5
Bakala 55 G3
Bakchar 29 D9
Bakel 53 F3
Baker, L. 68 B10
Baker, Mt. 72 B3
Baker I. 64 J13
Baker Lake 68 B10

Bakers Dozen Is. **71 D6**
Bakersfield **78 C3**
Bākhtarān = Kermānshāh **46 D6**
Bakı **25 E6**
Bakony **16 E3**
Bakony Forest = Bakony **16 E3**
Bakouma **55 G3**
Baku = Bakı **25 E6**
Bakutis Coast **96 B1**
Baky = Bakı **25 E6**
Balabac I. **38 C5**
Balabac Str. **38 C5**
Balabalangan, Kepulauan **39 E5**
Balaghat Ra. **43 K10**
Balaguer **19 B6**
Balaklava **25 E3**
Balakovo **24 C6**
Balashov **24 C5**
Balasore = Baleshwar **40 G6**
Balaton **16 E3**
Balbina, Reprêsa de **90 D7**
Balchik **22 C7**
Balclutha **65 G3**
Baleares, Is. **19 C7**
Balearic Is. = Baleares, Is. **19 C7**
Baleine = Whale ➔ **70 D7**
Baler **36 A2**
Baleshwar **40 G6**
Bali **39 F5**
Bali □ **39 F5**
Baliem ➔ **37 F5**
Balikeşir **23 E6**
Balikpapan **39 E5**
Balimbing **36 C1**
Balipara **41 D9**
Balkan Mts. = Stara Planina **22 C4**
Balkanabat **29 F6**
Balkh **45 B6**
Balkhash = Balqash **29 E8**
Balkhash, Ozero = Balqash Köli **29 E8**
Balla **41 E8**
Ballarat **62 C3**
Ballater **10 C5**
Ballina *Australia* **63 A5**
Ballina *Ireland* **11 D2**
Ballinasloe **11 E2**
Ballymena **11 D3**
Balmaceda **95 F2**
Balmoral **62 C3**
Balochistan = Baluchistan □ **42 F4**
Balonne ➔ **63 A4**
Balqash **29 E8**
Balqash Köli **29 E8**
Balrampur **40 D4**
Balranald **62 B3**
Balsas ➔ **84 D4**
Balta **17 D9**
Bālţi **17 E8**
Baltic Sea **9 D9**
Baltimore **77 E7**
Baluchistan □ **42 F4**
Balya **23 E6**
Bam **44 D4**
Bama **55 F1**
Bamako **53 F4**
Bambari **55 G3**
Bamberg **14 D6**
Bamenda **53 G8**
Bāmīān □ **42 B5**
Bampūr **45 E5**
Ban Don = Surat Thani **38 C1**
Ban Kantang **38 C1**
Ban Mê Thuôt = Buon Ma Thuot **38 B3**
Banaba **64 K11**
Banalia **57 D5**
Bananal, I. do **93 E3**
Banaras = Varanasi **40 E4**
Bānâs, Ras **54 D6**
Band-e Torkestan **45 C6**
Banda, Kepulauan **37 E3**
Banda Aceh **38 C1**
Banda Banda, Mt. **63 B5**
Banda Elat **37 F4**
Banda Is. = Banda, Kepulauan **37 E3**
Banda Sea **37 F3**
Bandanaira **37 E3**
Bandar = Machilipatnam **40 J3**
Bandar-e Abbās **44 E4**
Bandar-e Anzalī **46 C7**
Bandar-e Bushehr = Būshehr **44 D2**
Bandar-e Chārak **44 E3**
Bandar-e Deylam **47 E7**
Bandar-e Emām Khomeynı **47 E7**
Bandar-e Lengeh **44 E3**
Bandar-e Nakhīlū **44 E3**
Bandar-e Rīg **44 D2**
Bandar-e Torkeman **44 B3**
Bandar Lampung **39 F3**
Bandar Maharani = Muar **39 D2**
Bandar Penggaram = Batu Pahat **39 D2**
Bandar Seri Begawan **38 D5**
Bandar Sri Aman = Sri Aman **39 D4**
Bandera **94 B4**
Bandırma **23 D7**
Bandjarmasin = Banjarmasin **39 E4**
Bandon **11 F2**
Bandundu **56 E3**
Bandung **39 F3**
Banff *Canada* **69 C8**
Banff *U.K.* **10 C5**
Bang Saphan **38 B1**
Bangalore **43 N10**
Bangassou **56 D4**
Banggai, Kepulauan **37 E2**
Banggai Arch. = Banggai, Kepulauan **37 E2**
Banggi, Pulau **38 C5**
Banghāzī **54 B3**
Bangka *Sulawesi, Indonesia* **37 D3**
Bangka *Sumatera, Indonesia* **39 E3**
Bangka, Selat **39 E3**
Bangkinang **39 D2**
Bangko **39 E2**
Bangkok **38 B2**
Bangladesh ■ **41 E7**
Bangong Co **42 B11**
Bangor *Down, U.K.* **11 D4**
Bangor *Gwynedd, U.K.* **11 E4**
Bangor *U.S.A.* **77 B11**
Bangued **36 A2**
Bangui **56 D3**
Bangweulu, L. **57 G6**
Baní **87 C5**
Banī Walīd **54 B1**
Bāniyās **46 D3**
Banja Luka **20 B6**
Banjarmasin **39 E4**
Banjul **53 F2**
Bankipore **40 E5**
Banks I. **68 A7**
Banks Pen. **65 E5**
Banks Str. **62 D4**
Bankura **40 F6**
Bannu **42 C7**
Banswara **43 H9**
Bantry **11 F2**
Banu **42 B6**
Banyak, Kepulauan **39 D1**
Banzare Coast **96 A13**
Baoding **35 C6**
Baoji **35 C5**
Baoshan **34 D4**
Baotou **35 B6**
Bapatla **40 K3**
Ba'qūbah **46 D6**
Bar *Montenegro* **22 C2**
Bar *Ukraine* **17 D8**
Bar-le-Duc **13 B6**
Barabai **39 E5**
Barabinsk **29 D8**
Baracoa **86 B5**
Barahona **87 C5**
Barail Range **41 E9**
Barakaldo **19 A4**
Barakhola **41 E9**
Barakpur **41 F7**
Barakula **63 A5**
Baramula **42 B9**
Baran **43 G10**
Baranavichy **17 B8**
Baranof I. **69 C6**
Barapasi **37 E5**
Barat Daya, Kepulauan **37 F3**
Barbacena **93 G5**
Barbados ■ **87 D8**
Barbastro **19 A6**
Barcellona Pozzo di Gotto **21 E5**
Barcelona *Spain* **19 B7**
Barcelona *Venezuela* **90 A6**
Barcelos **90 D6**
Bardaï **54 D2**
Barddhaman **40 F6**
Bardera **49 G3**
Bardīyah **54 B4**
Bareilly **42 E11**
Barfleur, Pte. de **12 B3**
Barga **34 C3**
Barhi **40 E5**
Bari **20 D6**
Bari Doab **42 D8**
Barīdī, Ra's **47 F4**
Barinas **90 B4**
Baring, C. **68 B8**
Barisal **41 F8**
Barisan, Pegunungan **39 E2**
Barito ➔ **39 E4**
Barkly Tableland **60 D6**
Bārlad ➔ **17 F8**
Barlee, L. **60 F2**
Barletta **20 D6**
Barmedman **63 B4**
Barmer **42 G7**
Barmera **62 B3**
Barnaul **29 D9**
Barnsley **11 E6**
Barnstaple **11 F4**
Baro **53 G7**
Baroda = Vadodara **43 H8**
Barotseland **58 B4**
Barpeta **41 D8**
Barquísimeto **90 A5**
Barra *Brazil* **93 E5**
Barra *U.K.* **10 C3**
Barra do Corda **92 D4**
Barra Falsa, Pta. da **59 C7**
Barraba **63 B5**
Barrackpur = Barakpur **41 F7**
Barraigh = Barra **10 C3**
Barranca *Lima, Peru* **91 F3**
Barranca *Loreto, Peru* **90 D3**
Barrancabermeja **90 B4**
Barrancas **90 B6**
Barrancos **18 C2**
Barranqueras **94 B5**
Barranquilla **90 A4**
Barreiras **93 E5**
Barreirinhas **92 C5**
Barreiro **18 C1**
Barretos **93 G4**
Barrie **71 E6**
Barrier Ra. **62 B3**
Barrington Tops **63 B5**
Barringun **63 A4**
Barrow **69 A4**
Barrow-in-Furness **11 D5**
Barry **11 F5**
Barsi **43 K9**
Barsoi **40 E6**
Barstow **78 C4**
Bartica **90 B7**
Bartin **46 B3**
Bartlesville **81 A6**
Barysaw **17 A9**
Bāsa'idū **44 E3**
Basankusa **56 D3**
Basarabeasca **17 E9**
Basarabia = Bessarabiya **17 E9**
Basel **14 E4**
Bashkir Republic = Bashkortostan □ **29 D6**

Bashkortostan □ 29 D6
Basilan 36 C2
Basilan Str. 36 C2
Basildon 11 F7
Basim = Washim 43 J10
Basingstoke 11 F6
Basle = Basel 14 E4
Basoko 56 D4
Basque Provinces = País Vasco □ 19 A4
Basra = Al Baṣrah 47 E6
Bass Str. 61 H8
Bassano del Grappa 20 B3
Bassas da India 59 C7
Basse-Terre 87 C7
Bassein 41 J10
Basseterre 87 C7
Bastak 44 E3
Bastar 40 H3
Basti 40 D4
Bastia 13 E8
Bastogne 14 C3
Bata 56 D1
Bataan □ 36 B2
Batabanó, G. de 86 B3
Batac 36 A2
Batagai 31 C11
Batamay 31 C10
Batangafo 55 G2
Batangas 36 B2
Batanta 37 E4
Batdambang 38 B2
Batemans B. 63 C5
Batemans Bay 63 C5
Bath 11 F5
Bathurst *Australia* 63 B4
Bathurst *Canada* 71 E7
Bathurst, C. 68 A7
Bathurst Harb. 62 D4
Bathurst I. 70 B3
Bathurst Inlet 68 B9
Batlow 63 C4
Batman 46 C5
Batna 52 A7
Baton Rouge 81 D8
Batouri 56 D2
Battambang = Batdambang 38 B2
Battipáglia 21 D5
Battle Creek 76 C3
Batu 49 F2
Batu, Kepulauan 39 E1
Batu Is. = Batu, Kepulauan 39 E1
Batu Pahat 39 D2
Batuata 37 F2
Baturaja 39 E2
Baturité 92 C6
Bau 39 D4
Baubau 37 F2
Baucau 37 F3
Bauchi 53 F7
Bauer, C. 62 B1
Baukau = Baucau 37 F3
Bauld, C. 71 D8
Bauru 93 G4
Bautzen 15 C8
Bavaria = Bayern □ 15 D6
Bawdwin 41 F11
Bawean 39 F4
Bawku 53 F5
Bawlake 41 H11
Bay City 76 C4
Bay View 64 C7
Bayamo 86 B4
Bayan Har Shan 34 C4
Bayan Hot = Alxa Zuoqi 35 C5
Bayanaüyl 29 D8
Bayanhongor 35 B5
Bayázeh 44 C3
Baybay 36 B2
Baydhabo = Baidoa 49 G3
Bayern □ 15 D6
Bayeux 12 B3
Bayındır 23 E6
Baykal, Oz. 30 D8
Baykit 30 C7
Bayombong 36 A2
Bayonne 12 E3
Bayovar 91 E2
Bayqongyr 29 E7
Bayram-Ali = Baýramaly 29 F7
Baýramaly 29 F7
Bayramiç 23 E6
Bayreuth 15 D6
Bayrūt 46 D3
Baytown 81 E6
Baza 19 D4
Bazaruto, I. do 59 C7
Beachport 62 C2
Beagle, Canal 95 G3
Beardmore Glacier 96 C14
Béarn 12 E3
Beauce, Plaine de la 12 B4
Beaudesert 63 A5
Beaufort 38 C5
Beaufort Sea 66 B6
Beaufort West 58 E4
Beaumont 81 D6
Beaune 13 C6
Beauvais 12 B5
Beaver ➔ 69 C9
Beawar 42 F9
Bečej 22 B3
Béchar 52 B5
Bedford 11 E6
Beenleigh 63 A5
Be'er Sheva 47 E3
Beersheba = Be'er Sheva 47 E3
Befale 56 D4
Bega 63 C4
Behbehān 47 E7
Behshahr 44 B3
Bei Jiang ➔ 35 D6
Bei'an 35 B7
Beihai 35 D5
Beijing 35 C6
Beilpajah 63 B3
Beinn na Faoghla = Benbecula 10 C3
Beira 59 B6
Beirut = Bayrūt 46 D3
Beitbridge 59 C6
Beja *Portugal* 18 C2
Béja *Tunisia* 54 A1
Bejaïa 52 A7
Béjar 18 B3
Bejestān 44 C4
Békéscsaba 16 E5
Bela *India* 40 E4
Bela *Pakistan* 42 F5
Bela Crkva 22 B3
Bela Vista *Brazil* 94 A5
Bela Vista *Mozam.* 59 D6
Belarus ■ 24 C2
Belau = Palau ■ 36 C4
Belawan 39 D1
Belaya Tserkov = Bila Tserkva 17 D10
Belcher Chan. 70 B4
Belcher Is. 71 D6
Beled Weyne = Belet Uen 49 G4
Belém 92 C4
Belet Uen 49 G4
Belev 24 C4
Belfast 11 D4
Belfort 13 C7
Belgaum 43 M9
Belgium ■ 14 C3
Belgorod 24 C4
Belgorod-Dnestrovskiy = Bilhorod-Dnistrovskyy 25 D3
Belgrade = Beograd 22 B3
Beli Drim ➔ 22 C3
Belinyu 39 E3
Beliton Is. = Belitung 39 E3
Belitung 39 E3
Belize ■ 85 D7
Belize City 85 D7
Belkovskiy, Ostrov 30 B11
Bell Bay 62 D4
Bell Peninsula 70 C5
Bell Ville 94 C4
Bella Unión 94 C5
Bella Vista 94 B5
Bellary 43 M10
Bellata 63 A4
Belle-Île 12 C2
Belle Isle 71 D8
Belle Isle, Str. of 71 D8
Belleville *Canada* 71 E6
Belleville *U.S.A.* 75 F10
Bellin = Kangirsuk 70 D7
Bellingen 63 B5
Bellingham 72 B2
Bellingshausen Sea 96 A2
Bellinzona 13 C8
Belluno 20 A4
Belmonte 93 F6
Belmopan 85 D7
Belo Horizonte 93 F5
Belo-Tsiribihina 59 B8
Beloit 75 D10
Belokorovichi 17 C9
Belomorsk 28 C4
Belonia 41 F8
Belorussia = Belarus ■ 24 C2
Belovo 29 D9
Beloye, Ozero 24 A4
Beloye More 8 B13
Belozersk 24 A4
Beltana 62 B2
Belterra 92 C3
Beltsy = Bălţi 17 E8
Belukha 29 E9
Beluran 38 C5
Belyy, Ostrov 28 B8
Belyy Yar 29 D9
Bembéréke 53 F6
Bemidji 75 B7
Ben Lomond *N.S.W., Australia* 63 B5
Ben Lomond *Tas., Australia* 62 D4
Ben Nevis 10 C4
Bena 53 F7
Bena-Dibele 56 E4
Benalla 63 C4
Benares = Varanasi 40 E4
Benavente 18 A3
Benbecula 10 C3
Benbonyathe Hill 62 B2
Bend 72 D3
Bender Beila 49 F5
Bendery = Tighina 17 E9
Bendigo 63 C3
Benevento 20 D5
Bengal, Bay of 41 J7
Bengalūru = Bangalore 43 N10
Bengbu 35 C6
Benghazi = Banghāzī 54 B3
Bengkalis 39 D2
Bengkulu 39 E2
Bengkulu □ 39 E2
Benguela 58 A2
Beni 57 D5
Beni ➔ 91 F5
Beni Mellal 52 B4
Beni Suef 54 C5
Benidorm 19 C5
Benin ■ 53 G6
Benin, Bight of 53 H6
Benin City 53 G7
Benjamin Constant 90 D4
Benoni 59 D5
Bent 44 E4
Benteng 37 F2
Benton Harbor 76 C2
Benue ➔ 53 G7
Benxi 35 B7
Beo 36 D3
Beograd 22 B3
Beppu 33 G2
Berat 23 D2
Berau, Teluk 37 E4
Berber 55 E5
Berbera 49 E4
Berbérati 56 D3
Berbice ➔ 90 B7
Berdichev = Berdychiv 17 D9
Berdsk 29 D9
Berdyansk 25 D4
Berdychiv 17 D9
Berebere 37 D3
Bereda 49 E5
Berehove 17 D6
Berekum 53 G5

Berestechko 17 C7
Bereza = Byaroza 17 B7
Berezhany 17 D7
Berezina = Byarezina ➔ 17 B10
Berezniki 28 D6
Berezovo 28 C7
Berga 19 A6
Bergama 23 E6
Bérgamo 13 D8
Bergen 8 C7
Bergerac 12 D4
Berhala, Selat 39 E2
Berhampore = Baharampur 40 E7
Berhampur = Brahmapur 40 H5
Bering Sea 69 C1
Bering Strait 69 B3
Berja 19 D4
Berkeley 72 H2
Berkner I. 96 B4
Berlin 15 B7
Bermejo ➔ *Formosa, Argentina* 94 B5
Bermejo ➔ *San Juan, Argentina* 94 C3
Bermejo, Paso = Uspallata, P. de 94 C3
Bermuda ⌀ 67 F13
Bern 14 E4
Bernburg 15 C6
Berne = Bern 14 E4
Bernina, Piz 13 C8
Beroun 16 D2
Berri 62 B3
Berry *Australia* 63 B5
Berry *France* 12 C5
Bershad 17 D9
Bertoua 56 D2
Berwick-upon-Tweed 10 D6
Besalampy 59 B8
Besançon 13 C7
Besar 39 E5
Bessarabiya 17 E9
Bessarabka = Basarabeasca 17 E9
Bessemer 82 C4
Betanzos 18 A1
Bétaré Oya 56 C2
Bethel 69 B3
Bethlehem *S. Africa* 59 D5
Bethlehem *U.S.A.* 77 D8
Béthune 13 A5
Betong 39 D4
Betroka 59 C9
Bettiah 40 D5
Betul 43 J10
Beverley 11 E6
Beverly Hills 78 C3
Beyneu 29 E6
Beypazarı 25 E3
Beyşehir Gölü 46 C2
Bezhitsa 24 C3
Béziers 13 E5
Bezwada = Vijayawada 40 J3
Bhachau 43 H7
Bhadrakh 40 G6
Bhadravati 43 N9
Bhagalpur 40 E6
Bhakra Dam 42 D10
Bhamo 41 E11
Bhandara 43 J11
Bhanrer Ra. 43 H11
Bharat = India ■ 43 J10
Bharatpur 42 F10
Bhatpara 41 F7
Bhaunagar = Bhavnagar 43 J8
Bhavnagar 43 J8
Bhawanipatna 40 H4
Bhilai = Bhilainagar-Durg 40 G3
Bhilainagar-Durg 40 G3
Bhilsa = Vidisha 43 H10
Bhilwara 43 G9
Bhima ➔ 43 L10
Bhind 42 F11
Bhiwandi 43 K8
Bhiwani 42 E10
Bhola 41 F8
Bhopal 43 H10
Bhubaneshwar 40 G5
Bhuj 43 H6
Bhumiphol Dam = Phumiphon, Khuan 38 A1
Bhusawal 43 J9
Bhutan ■ 41 D8
Biafra, B. of = Bonny, Bight of 56 D1
Biak 37 E5
Biała Podlaska 17 B6
Białogard 16 A2
Białystok 17 B6
Biaro 37 D3
Biarritz 12 E3
Bibai 32 B7
Biberach 14 D5
Bida 53 G7
Bidar 43 L10
Biddeford 77 C10
Bié, Planalto de 58 A3
Bielefeld 14 B5
Biella 13 D8
Bielsk Podlaski 17 B6
Bielsko-Biała 16 D4
Bien Hoa 38 B3
Bienville, L. 71 D6
Big Horn Mts. = Bighorn Mts. 73 D10
Big Spring 80 C3
Big Trout L. 71 D5
Biğa 23 D6
Bigadiç 23 E7
Biggar 69 C9
Biggenden 63 A5
Bighorn ➔ 73 C10
Bighorn Mts. 73 D10
Bihać 20 B5
Bihar 40 E5
Bihar □ 40 E5
Bihor, Munţii 17 E6
Bijagós, Arquipélago dos 53 F2
Bijapur *Chhattisgarh, India* 40 H3
Bijapur *Karnataka, India* 43 L9
Bijār 46 D6
Bijeljina 20 B7
Bijnor 42 E11
Bikaner 42 E8
Bikini Atoll 64 H11
Bila Tserkva 17 D10
Bilara 42 F8
Bilaspur 40 F4
Bilauk Taungdan 38 B1
Bilbao 19 A4
Bilbo = Bilbao 19 A4
Bilecik 25 E3
Bilhorod-Dnistrovskyy 25 D3
Bilir 31 C11
Billings 73 D9
Billiton Is. = Belitung 39 E3
Bilma 55 E1
Biloxi 81 D9
Biltine 55 F3
Bima 37 F1
Bina-Etawah 43 G11
Binalbagan 36 B2
Binalong 63 B4
Bīnālūd, Kūh-e 44 B4
Binatang = Bintangau 39 D4
Binda 63 A4
Bindle 63 A4
Bindura 59 B6
Bingara *N.S.W., Australia* 63 A5
Bingara *Queens., Australia* 63 A3
Binghamton 77 C8
Bingöl 46 C5
Binh Dinh = An Nhon 38 B3
Binh Son 38 A3
Binjai 39 D1
Binnaway 63 B4
Binongko 37 F2
Bintan 39 D2
Bintangau 39 D4
Bintulu 39 D4
Bintuni 37 E4
Binzert = Bizerte 54 A1
Bioko 53 H7
Bir 43 K9
Bir Atrun 55 E4
Bîr Mogreïn 52 C3
Birāk 54 C1
Birchip 62 C3
Birecik 46 C4
Bireuen 38 C1
Birlik 29 E8
Birmingham *U.K.* 11 E6
Birmingham *U.S.A.* 82 C4
Birmitrapur 40 F5
Birni Nkonni 53 F7
Birnin Kebbi 53 F6
Birr 11 E3
Birrie ➔ 63 A4
Birsk 29 D6
Birur 43 N9
Bisa 37 E3
Biscay, B. of 12 D2
Biscoe Bay 96 B17
Biscoe Is. 96 A3
Bishkek 29 E8
Biskra 52 B7
Bislig 36 C3
Bismarck 74 B4
Bismarck Arch. 64 K9
Bissagos = Bijagós, Arquipélago dos 53 F2
Bissau 53 F2
Bistriţa 17 E7
Bistriţa ➔ 17 E8
Bitlis 46 C5
Bitola 22 D3
Bitolj = Bitola 22 D3
Bitterfontein 58 E3
Bitterroot Range 73 D6
Biu 55 F1
Biwa-Ko 33 F5
Biysk 29 D9
Bizerte 54 A1
Bjelovar 20 B6
Björneborg = Pori 8 C10
Black Forest = Schwarzwald 14 D5
Black Hills 74 D3
Black Sea 25 E3
Black Volta ➔ 53 G5
Blackball 65 E4
Blackburn 11 E5
Blackpool 11 E5
Blackwater ➔ 11 E2
Blagodarnoye = Blagodarnyy 25 D5
Blagodarnyy 25 D5
Blagoevgrad 22 C4
Blagoveshchensk 31 D10
Blanc, Mont 13 D7
Blanca, B. 95 D4
Blanca Peak 79 B10
Blanche, C. 62 B1
Blanche, L. 62 A2
Blanes 19 B7
Blantyre 59 B6
Blayney 63 B4
Blednaya, Gora 28 B7
Blenheim 65 D5
Blida 52 A6
Bligh Sound 65 F2
Blodgett Iceberg Tongue 96 A13
Bloemfontein 59 D5
Bloemhof 59 D5
Blois 12 C4
Bloomington *Ill., U.S.A.* 75 E10
Bloomington *Ind., U.S.A.* 76 E2
Blue Mts. 72 D4
Blue Nile = Nīl el Azraq ➔ 55 E5
Blue Ridge 83 A7
Bluefields 86 D3
Bluff 65 G3
Blumenau 94 B7
Bo 53 G3
Bo Hai 35 C6
Boa Vista 90 C6
Boatman 63 A4
Bobadah 63 B4
Bobbili 40 H4
Bobo-Dioulasso 53 F5

Bóbr ➔ 16 B2
Bobraomby, Tanjon' i 59 A9
Bobruysk = Babruysk 17 B9
Boby, Pic 59 C9
Bôca do Acre 91 E5
Boca Raton 83 F7
Bocaranga 55 G2
Bochum 14 C4
Bodaybo 30 D9
Boden 8 B10
Bodensee 13 C8
Bodhan 43 K10
Bodø 8 B8
Bodrog ➔ 16 D5
Bodrum 23 F6
Boende 56 E4
Bogalusa 81 D9
Bogan Gate 63 B4
Boggabilla 63 A5
Boggabri 63 B5
Bogo 36 B2
Bogong, Mt. 63 C4
Bogor 39 F3
Bogotá 90 C4
Bogotol 29 D9
Bogra 41 E7
Bohemian Forest = Böhmerwald 15 D7
Böhmerwald 15 D7
Bohol □ 36 C2
Bohol Sea 36 C2
Boise 72 E5
Boise City 80 A2
Bojador, C. 52 C3
Bojana ➔ 22 D2
Bojnūrd 44 B4
Bokhara ➔ 63 A4
Bokoro 55 F2
Bolan Pass 42 E5
Bolbec 12 B4
Bole 34 B3
Bolekhiv 17 D6
Bolesławiec 16 C2
Bolgrad = Bolhrad 17 F9
Bolhrad 17 F9
Bolivia ■ 91 G6
Bollon 63 A4
Bolobo 56 E3
Bologna 20 B3
Bologoye 24 B3
Bolsena, L. di 20 C3
Bolshereche 29 D8
Bolshevik, Ostrov 30 B8
Bolshoy Atlym 28 C7
Bolshoy Begichev, Ostrov 30 B9
Bolshoy Kavkas = Caucasus Mountains 25 E5
Bolshoy Lyakhovskiy, Ostrov 31 B12
Bolton 11 E5
Bolu 25 E3
Bolvadin 46 C2
Bolzano 20 A3
Bom Jesus da Lapa 93 E5
Boma 56 F2
Bombala 63 C4
Bombay = Mumbai 43 K8
Bomboma 56 D3
Bomu ➔ 56 D4
Bon, C. 21 F3
Bonaire 87 D6
Bonang 63 C4
Bonavista 71 E8
Bondo 56 D4
Bondoukou 53 G5
Bone, Teluk 37 E2
Bonerate 37 F2
Bonerate, Kepulauan 37 F2
Bong Son = Hoai Nhon 38 B3
Bongor 55 F2
Bonifacio 13 F8
Bonin Is. = Ogasawara Gunto 27 F16
Bonn 14 C4
Bonney, L. 62 C3
Bonny, Bight of 56 D1
Bonoi 37 E5
Bontang 39 D5
Bonthain 37 F1
Bonthe 53 G3
Bontoc 36 A2
Booloboolka L. 62 B3
Booligal 63 B3
Boonah 63 A5
Boorindal 63 B4
Boorowa 63 B4
Boosaaso = Bosaso 49 E4
Boothia, Gulf of 70 B5
Boothia Pen. 68 A10
Booué 56 E2
Bor *Serbia* 22 B4
Bôr *Sudan* 55 G5
Borås 9 D8
Boräzjän 44 D2
Borba 90 D7
Borda, C. 62 C2
Bordeaux 12 D3
Borden I. 70 B2
Borden Pen. 70 B5
Bordertown 62 C3
Bordj Fly Ste. Marie 52 C5
Bordj-in-Eker 52 D7
Bordj Omar Driss 52 C7
Borger 80 B3
Borhoyn Tal 35 B6
Borisoglebsk 24 C5
Borisov = Barysaw 17 A9
Borja 90 D3
Borkou 55 E2
Borkum 14 B4
Borley, C. 96 A9
Borneo 39 D4
Bornholm 9 D9
Borongan 36 B3
Borovichi 24 B3
Borşa 17 E7
Borüjerd 46 D7
Boryslav 17 D6
Bosa 21 D2
Bosanska Gradiška 20 B6
Bosaso 49 E4
Boshrüyeh 44 C4
Bosna ➔ 20 B7
Bosna i Hercegovina = Bosnia-Herzegovina ■ 20 B6
Bosnia-Herzegovina ■ 20 B6
Bosnik 37 E5
Bosobolo 56 D3
Bosporus = İstanbul Boğazı 22 D7
Bossangoa 55 G2
Bosso 55 F1
Bosten Hu 34 B3
Boston *U.K.* 11 E6
Boston *U.S.A.* 77 C10
Bothnia, G. of 8 C10
Bothwell 62 D4
Botletle ➔ 58 C4
Botoşani 17 E8
Botswana ■ 58 C4
Botucatu 93 G4
Bouaké 53 G4
Bouar 56 C3
Bouârfa 52 B5
Bouca 55 G2
Bougainville I. 64 K10
Bougie = Bejaïa 52 A7
Bougouni 53 F4
Boulder 74 E2
Boulder Dam = Hoover Dam 78 B5
Boulogne-sur-Mer 12 A4
Bouna 53 G5
Boundiali 53 G4
Bourbonnais 13 C5
Bourem 53 E5
Bourg-en-Bresse 13 C6
Bourg-St-Maurice 13 D7
Bourgas = Burgas 22 C6
Bourges 12 C5
Bourgogne □ 13 C6
Bourke 63 B4
Bournemouth 11 F6
Bowen Mts. 63 C4
Bowman I. 96 A12
Bowmans 62 B2
Bowral 63 B5
Bowraville 63 B5
Boyne ➔ 11 E3
Boyoma, Chutes 57 D5
Boz Dağları 23 E7
Bozburun 23 F7
Bozcaada 23 E6
Bozdoğan 23 F7
Bozeman 73 D8
Bozen = Bolzano 20 A3
Bozoum 55 G2
Bra 13 D7
Brač 20 C6
Bracciano, L. di 20 C4
Bräcke 8 C9
Bradenton 83 F6
Bradford 11 E6
Braga 18 B1
Bragança *Brazil* 92 C4
Bragança *Portugal* 18 B2
Brahestad = Raahe 8 C10
Brahmanbaria 41 F8
Brahmani ➔ 40 G6
Brahmapur 40 H5
Brahmaputra ➔ 41 F7
Braidwood 63 C4
Brăila 17 F8
Branco ➔ 90 D6
Brandenburg = Neubrandenburg 15 B7
Brandenburg 15 B7
Brandenburg □ 15 B7
Brandon 69 D10
Braniewo 16 A4
Bransfield Str. 96 A4
Brantford 76 C5
Brasil = Brazil ■ 93 E4
Brasiléia 91 F5
Brasília 93 F4
Braşov 17 F7
Brassey, Banjaran 38 D5
Bratislava 16 D3
Bratsk 30 D8
Braunau 15 D7
Braunschweig 14 B6
Bravo del Norte, Rio = Grande, Rio ➔ 84 B5
Brawley 78 D5
Bray 11 E3
Bray, Pays de 12 B4
Brazil ■ 93 E4
Brazos ➔ 81 E6
Brazzaville 56 E3
Brčko 20 B7
Breaksea Sd. 65 F2
Bream B. 64 A6
Bream Hd. 64 A6
Brecon 11 F5
Breda 14 C3
Bredasdorp 58 E4
Bregenz 14 E5
Breiðafjörður 8 B1
Brejo 92 C5
Bremen 14 B5
Bremerhaven 14 B5
Bremerton 72 C2
Brennerpass 15 E6
Brescia 13 D9
Breslau = Wrocław 16 C3
Bressanone 20 A3
Brest *Belarus* 17 B6
Brest *France* 12 B1
Brest-Litovsk = Brest 17 B6
Bretagne □ 12 B2
Brett, C. 64 A6
Brewarrina 63 A4
Bria 55 G3
Briançon 13 D7
Bribie I. 63 A5
Bridgeport 77 D9
Bridgetown 87 D8
Bridgewater 71 E7
Bridgewater, C. 62 C3
Bridlington 11 D6
Bridport 62 D4
Brigham City 73 F7
Bright 63 C4
Brighton *Australia* 62 C2
Brighton *U.K.* 11 F6
Brindisi 21 D6
Brisbane 63 A5
Brisbane ➔ 63 A5
Bristol *U.K.* 11 F5
Bristol *U.S.A.* 83 A6
Bristol B. 69 C3
Bristol Channel 11 F4
British Indian Ocean Terr. = Chagos Arch. ☑ 26 J9

British Isles **11 D4**
British Virgin Is. ⊠ **87 C7**
Brittany = Bretagne □ **12 B2**
Brive-la-Gaillarde **12 D4**
Brixen = Bressanone **20 A3**
Brlik = Birlik **29 E8**
Brno **16 D3**
Brock I. **70 B2**
Brocken **14 C6**
Brodeur Pen. **70 B5**
Brodnica **16 B4**
Brody **17 C7**
Broken Hill **62 B3**
Bronte Park **62 D4**
Brooks Range **69 B5**
Brooloo **63 A5**
Broome **60 D3**
Broughton Island = Qikiqtarjuaq **70 C7**
Brown, Pt. **62 B1**
Brownsville **81 G5**
Brownwood **80 D4**
Bruay-la-Buissière **13 A5**
Bruce, Mt. **60 E2**
Bruck an der Mur **15 E8**
Bruges = Brugge **14 C2**
Brugge **14 C2**
Brumado **93 E5**
Brunei = Bandar Seri Begawan **38 D5**
Brunei ■ **38 D4**
Brunner, L. **65 E4**
Brunswick = Braunschweig **14 B6**
Brunswick **83 D7**
Brunswick, Pen. de **95 G2**
Brussel **14 C3**
Brussels = Brussel **14 C3**
Bruthen **63 C4**
Bruxelles = Brussel **14 C3**
Bryan **81 D5**
Bryan, Mt. **62 B2**
Bryansk **24 C3**
Bu Craa **52 C3**
Buapinang **37 E2**
Buayan **36 C3**
Bucak **46 C2**
Bucaramanga **90 B4**
Buchach **17 D7**
Buchanan **53 G3**
Bucharest = București **22 B6**
Buckie **10 C5**
Buckleboo **62 B2**
București **22 B6**
Budalin **41 F10**
Budapest **16 E4**
Budd Coast **96 A12**
Bude **11 F4**
Budennovsk **25 E5**
Budgewoi **63 B5**
Budjala **56 D3**
Buenaventura **90 C3**
Buenos Aires **94 C5**
Buenos Aires, L. **95 F2**
Buffalo **77 C6**
Bug = Buh ➔ **25 D3**
Bug ➔ **16 B5**
Buga **90 C3**
Bugel, Tanjung **39 F4**
Bugsuk I. **38 C5**
Bugun Shara **35 B5**
Buguruslan **29 D6**
Buh ➔ **25 D3**
Buir Nur **35 B6**
Bujumbura **57 E5**
Bukavu **57 E5**
Bukhara = Bukhoro **29 F7**
Bukhoro **29 F7**
Bukittinggi **39 E2**
Bukoba **57 E6**
Bula **37 E4**
Bulahdelah **63 B5**
Bulan **36 B2**
Bulandshahr **42 E10**
Bulawayo **59 C5**
Buldan **23 E7**
Bulgan **35 B5**
Bulgaria ■ **22 C5**
Bulgroo **63 A3**
Bulgunnia **62 B1**
Buli, Teluk **37 D3**
Buliluyan, C. **38 C5**
Bulloo ➔ **63 A3**
Bulloo Downs **62 A3**
Bulloo L. **62 A3**
Bulls **64 D6**
Bulsar = Valsad **43 J8**
Bulukumba **37 F2**
Bulun **30 B10**
Bumba **56 D4**
Bumhpa Bum **41 D11**
Bunbury **60 G2**
Buncrana **11 D3**
Bundaberg **63 A5**
Bundi **43 G9**
Bundoran **11 D2**
Bungo-Suidō **33 G3**
Bunia **57 D6**
Bunji **42 B9**
Buntok **39 E4**
Bunyu **39 D5**
Buol **37 D2**
Buon Ma Thuot **38 B3**
Buorkhaya, Mys **31 B11**
Buqayq **47 F7**
Bur Acaba **49 G3**
Bûr Safâga **54 C5**
Bûr Sa'īd **54 B5**
Bûr Sûdân **55 E6**
Burao **49 F4**
Buraydah **47 F5**
Buraymī, Al Wāhāt al **44 E3**
Burdur **46 C2**
Burdwan = Barddhaman **40 F6**
Burgas **22 C6**
Burgos **18 A4**
Burgundy = Bourgogne □ **13 C6**
Burhaniye **23 E6**
Burhanpur **43 J10**
Burias I. **36 B2**
Buriram **38 A2**
Burkina Faso ■ **53 F5**
Burlington *Iowa, U.S.A.* **75 E9**
Burlington *N.C., U.S.A.* **83 A8**
Burlington *Vt., U.S.A.* **77 B9**
Burlyu-Tyube **29 E8**
Burma ■ **41 G11**
Burnie **62 D4**
Burnley **11 E5**
Burnside ➔ **68 B9**
Burqān **47 E6**
Burqin **34 B3**
Burra **62 B2**
Burren Junction **63 B4**
Burrendong Dam **63 B4**
Burrinjuck Res. **63 C4**
Burruyacú **94 B4**
Bursa **23 D7**
Buru **37 E3**
Burundi ■ **57 E6**
Burutu **53 G7**
Bury St. Edmunds **11 E7**
Busan **35 C7**
Büshehr **44 D2**
Büshehr □ **44 D2**
Bushire = Büshehr **44 D2**
Businga **56 D4**
Buşra ash Shām **46 D4**
Busto Arsízio **13 D8**
Busu Djanoa **56 D4**
Busuanga I. **36 B1**
Buta **57 D4**
Butare **57 E5**
Butaritari **64 J12**
Butembo **57 D5**
Butha Qi **35 B7**
Buton **37 E2**
Butte **73 C7**
Butterworth = Gcuwa **59 E5**
Butterworth **38 C2**
Butuan **36 C3**
Butung = Buton **37 E2**
Buturlinovka **24 C5**
Buur Hakaba = Bur Acaba **49 G3**
Buxoro = Bukhoro **29 F7**
Buxtehude **14 B5**
Buy **24 B5**
Buyant-Uhaa **35 B6**
Büyük Menderes ➔ **23 F6**
Büyükçekmece **22 D7**
Buzău **17 F8**
Buzău ➔ **17 F8**
Buzen **33 G2**
Buzi ➔ **59 B6**
Buzuluk **29 D6**
Byarezina ➔ **17 B10**
Byaroza **17 B7**
Bydgoszcz **16 B3**
Byelorussia = Belarus ■ **24 C2**
Bykhaw **17 B10**
Bykhov = Bykhaw **17 B10**
Bylot I. **70 B6**
Byrd, C. **96 A3**
Byrock **63 B4**
Byron Bay **63 A5**
Byrranga, Gory **30 B8**
Byrranga Mts. = Byrranga, Gory **30 B8**
Bytom **16 C4**
Bytów **16 A3**

C

Ca Mau **38 C3**
Caála **58 A3**
Cabanatuan **36 A2**
Cabedelo **92 D7**
Cabimas **90 A4**
Cabinda **56 F2**
Cabinda □ **56 F2**
Cabinet Mts. **73 C6**
Cabo Blanco **95 F3**
Cabo Frio **93 G5**
Cabo Pantoja **90 D3**
Cabo Verde = Cape Verde Is. ■ **50 E1**
Cabonga, Réservoir **71 E6**
Caboolture **63 A5**
Cabora Bassa Dam = Cahora Bassa, Reprêsa de **59 B6**
Cabot Str. **71 E8**
Cabra **18 D3**
Cabrera **19 C7**
Cabriel ➔ **19 C5**
Čačak **22 C3**
Cáceres *Brazil* **91 G7**
Cáceres *Spain* **18 C2**
Cachimbo, Serra do **93 D2**
Cachoeira **93 E6**
Cachoeira do Sul **94 C6**
Cachoeiro de Itapemirim **93 G5**
Cacólo **56 G3**
Caconda **58 A3**
Cadibarrawirracanna, L. **62 A2**
Cadiz *Phil.* **36 B2**
Cádiz *Spain* **18 D2**
Cádiz, G. de **18 D2**
Cadney Park **62 A1**
Caen **12 B3**
Caetité **93 E5**
Cagayan de Oro **36 C2**
Cágliari **21 E2**
Cágliari, G. di **21 E2**
Caguas **87 C6**
Cahora Bassa, Reprêsa de **59 B6**
Cahors **12 D4**
Cahul **17 F9**
Caicara **90 B5**
Caicó **92 D6**
Caird Coast **96 B5**
Cairns **61 D8**
Cairo = El Qâhira **54 B5**
Cairo **81 A9**
Cajamarca **91 E3**
Cajàzeiras **92 D6**
Calabar **53 H7**
Calábria □ **21 E6**
Calafate **95 G2**
Calahorra **19 A5**
Calais **12 A4**
Calama *Brazil* **91 E6**
Calama *Chile* **94 A3**
Calamar **90 A4**
Calamian Group **36 B1**
Calamocha **19 B5**
Calang **38 D1**
Calapan **36 B2**

Călăraşi 22 B6
Calatayud 19 B5
Calauag 36 B2
Calavite, C. 36 B2
Calbayog 36 B2
Calca 91 F4
Calcutta = Kolkata 41 F7
Caldas da Rainha 18 C1
Caldera 94 B2
Caldwell 72 E5
Caledon ➔ 59 E5
Calgary 69 C8
Cali 90 C3
Calicut 43 P9
California □ 78 B3
California, G. de 84 B2
Calingasta 94 C3
Callabonna, L. 62 A3
Callao 91 F3
Caloundra 63 A5
Caltagirone 21 F5
Caltanissetta 21 F5
Calulo 56 G2
Calvi 13 E8
Calviá 19 C7
Calvinia 58 E3
Camabatela 56 F3
Camacupa 58 A3
Camagüey 86 B4
Camaná 91 G4
Camargue 13 E6
Camarones 95 E3
Cambay = Khambhat 43 H8
Cambay, G. of = Khambhat, G. of 43 J8
Cambodia ■ 38 B3
Cambrai 13 A5
Cambrian Mts. 11 E5
Cambridge *N.Z.* 64 B6
Cambridge *U.K.* 11 E7
Cambridge *U.S.A.* 77 C10
Cambridge Bay = Ikaluktutiak 68 B9
Cambundi-Catembo 56 G3
Camden *Ark., U.S.A.* 81 C7
Camden *N.J., U.S.A.* 77 E8
Cameroon ■ 56 C2
Cameroun, Mt. 53 H7
Cametá 92 C4
Caminha 18 B1
Camira Creek 63 A5
Camocim 92 C5
Campana, I. 95 F1
Campánia □ 21 D5
Campbell Town 62 D4
Campbellton 71 E7
Campbelltown 63 B5
Campbeltown 10 D4
Campeche 85 D6
Campeche, Golfo de 85 D6
Camperdown 62 C3
Câmpina 17 F7
Campina Grande 92 D6
Campinas 94 A7
Campo Grande 93 G3
Campo Maior 92 C5
Campobasso 20 D5
Campos 93 G5
Campos Belos 93 E4
Câmpulung 17 F7
Camrose 69 C8
Çan 23 D6
Can Tho 38 B3
Canada ■ 68 C8
Cañada de Gómez 94 C4
Çanakkale 23 D6
Çanakkale Boğazı 23 D6
Cananea 84 A2
Canarias, Is. 52 C2
Canary Is. = Canarias, Is. 52 C2
Canavieiras 93 F6
Canberra 63 C4
Candelo 63 C4
Candia = Iraklio 23 G5
Canea = Chania 23 G5
Canelones 94 C5
Cañete *Chile* 94 D2
Cañete *Peru* 91 F3
Cangas de Narcea 18 A2
Canguaretama 92 D6
Canguçu 94 C6
Caniapiscau ➔ 70 D7
Caniapiscau, L. 71 D7
Canicattì 21 F4
Canigou, Mt. 12 E5
Canipaan 38 C5
Çankırı 25 E3
Cann River 63 C4
Cannanore 43 P9
Cannes 13 E7
Canoas 94 B6
Canora 69 C9
Canowindra 63 B4
Cantabria □ 18 A4
Cantabrian Mts. = Cantábrica, Cordillera 18 A3
Cantábrica, Cordillera 18 A3
Cantal, Plomb du 13 D5
Canterbury 11 F7
Canterbury Bight 65 F4
Canterbury Plains 65 E4
Canton = Guangzhou 35 D6
Canton 76 D5
Canudos 91 E7
Canutama 91 E6
Cap-Haïtien 87 C5
Capanaparo ➔ 90 B5
Cape Barren I. 62 D4
Cape Breton I. 71 E7
Cape Coast 53 G5
Cape Dorset 70 C6
Cape Dyer 70 D7
Cape Girardeau 81 A9
Cape Lisburne = Wevok 69 B3
Cape Town 58 E3
Cape Verde Is. ■ 50 E1
Cape York Peninsula 61 C7
Capela 93 E6
Capim ➔ 92 C4
Capraia 13 E8
Capri 21 D5
Caprivi Strip 58 B4
Captain's Flat 63 C4
Caquetá ➔ 90 D5
Caracal 22 B5
Caracas 90 A5
Caracol 93 D5
Caradoc 62 B3
Carajás, Serra dos 92 D3
Caransebeş 17 F6
Caratasca, L. 86 C3
Caratinga 93 F5
Caraúbas 92 D6
Caravaca de la Cruz 19 C5
Caravelas 93 F6
Caraveli 91 G4
Carballo 18 A1
Carbonara, C. 21 E2
Carbondale 81 A9
Carbonear 71 E8
Carbónia 21 E2
Carcassonne 12 E5
Carcross 68 B6
Cardamon Hills 43 Q10
Cárdenas 86 B3
Cardiff 11 F5
Cardigan B. 11 E4
Cardston 69 D8
Carei 17 E6
Carhué 94 D4
Caria 23 F7
Cariacica 93 G5
Caribbean Sea 86 D5
Cariboo Mts. 69 C7
Carinda 63 B4
Carinhanha 93 E5
Carinthia = Kärnten □ 15 E7
Caripito 90 A6
Carlisle 11 D5
Carlow 11 E3
Carlsbad 80 C1
Carmacks 68 B6
Carmarthen 11 F4
Carmaux 12 D5
Carmen 90 B3
Carmen de Patagones 95 E4
Carmona 18 D3
Carnac 12 C2
Carnarvon *Australia* 60 E1
Carnarvon *S. Africa* 58 E4
Carnegie, L. 60 F3
Carnot 56 D3
Carnot, C. 62 B2
Carolina 92 D4
Caroline I. 65 K15
Caroline Is. 64 J10
Caroni ➔ 90 B6
Caroníe = Nébrodi, Monti 21 F5
Caroona 63 B5
Carpathians 16 D5
Carpaţii Meridionali 17 F7
Carpentaria, G. of 60 C6
Carpentras 13 D6
Carpi 20 B3
Carpolac = Morea 62 C3
Carrara 13 D9
Carrauntoohill 11 E2
Carrick-on-Suir 11 E3
Carrieton 62 B2
Carrizal Bajo 94 B2
Carson City 72 G4
Cartagena *Colombia* 90 A3
Cartagena *Spain* 19 D5
Cartago *Colombia* 90 C3
Cartago *Costa Rica* 86 E3
Carterton 65 D6
Carthage 81 A6
Cartwright 70 D8
Caruaru 92 D6
Carúpano 90 A6
Carvoeiro 90 D6
Carvoeiro, C. 18 C1
Casablanca 52 B4
Cascade Ra. 72 C3
Cascais 18 C1
Cascavel 94 A6
Cáscina 20 C3
Caserta 20 D5
Caseyr, Raas = Asir, Ras 49 E5
Casiguran 36 A2
Casilda 94 C4
Casino 63 A5
Casiquiare ➔ 90 C5
Casma 91 E3
Caspe 19 B5
Casper 73 E10
Caspian Sea 29 E6
Castellammare di Stábia 21 D5
Castelló de la Plana 19 C5
Castelo Branco 18 C2
Castelsarrasin 12 D4
Castelvetrano 21 F4
Casterton 62 C3
Castilla-La Mancha □ 18 C4
Castilla y Leon □ 18 A3
Castlebar 11 E2
Castleblaney 11 D3
Castlemaine 63 C3
Castlereagh ➔ 63 B4
Castres 12 E5
Castries 87 D7
Castro 95 E2
Castro Alves 93 E6
Castuera 18 C3
Cat I. 86 B4
Catalão 93 F4
Çatalca 22 D7
Catalonia = Cataluña □ 19 B6
Cataluña □ 19 B6
Catamarca 94 B3
Catanduanes □ 36 B2
Catanduva 93 G4
Catánia 21 F5
Catanzaro 21 E6
Cataman 36 B2
Cateel 36 C3
Catoche, C. 85 C7
Catrimani 90 C6
Catskill Mts. 77 C8
Cauca ➔ 90 B4

Caucaia 92 C6
Caucasus Mountains 25 E5
Caungula 56 F3
Cauquenes 94 D2
Caura ➔ 90 B6
Cauvery ➔ 43 P11
Caux, Pays de 12 B4
Cavan 11 D3
Cavendish 62 C3
Caviana, I. 92 B3
Cavite 36 B2
Cawndilla L. 62 B3
Cawnpore = Kanpur 40 D3
Caxias 92 C5
Caxias do Sul 94 B6
Cayambe 90 C3
Cayenne 92 A3
Cayman Is. ☑ 86 C3
Cazombo 58 A4
Ceanannus Mor 11 E3
Ceará = Fortaleza 92 C6
Ceará □ 92 D6
Ceará Mirim 92 D6
Cebollar 94 B3
Cebu 36 B2
Cecil Plains 63 A5
Cedar L. 69 C10
Cedar Rapids 75 E9
Cedro 92 D6
Ceduna 62 B1
Ceerigaabo = Erigavo 49 E4
Cefalù 21 E5
Cegléd 16 E4
Celaya 84 C4
Celebes = Sulawesi 37 E2
Celebes Sea 37 D2
Celje 20 A5
Celle 14 B6
Celtic Sea 11 F2
Central, Cordillera 90 C3
Central African Rep. ■ 56 C4
Central Makran Range 42 F4
Cephalonia = Kefalonia 23 E3
Ceram = Seram 37 E3
Ceram Sea = Seram Sea 37 E3
Ceres 94 B4
Cerignola 20 D5
Cerigo = Kythira 23 F4
Çerkeş 46 B3
Çerkezköy 22 D6
Cervera 19 B6
Cesena 20 B4
Ceská Rep. = Czech Rep. ■ 16 D2
České Budějovice 16 D2
Českomoravská Vrchovina 16 D2
Çeşme 23 E6
Cessnock 63 B5
Cetinje 22 C2
Cetraro 21 E5
Ceuta 18 E3
Cévennes 13 D5
Ceylon = Sri Lanka ■ 43 R12
Chachapoyas 91 E3
Chachran 42 E7
Chad ■ 55 E2
Chad, L. = Tchad, L. 55 F1
Chadileuvú ➔ 94 D3
Chadyr-Lunga = Ciadâr-Lunga 17 E9
Chagai Hills = Chāh Gay Hills 42 E3
Chagos Arch. ☑ 26 J9
Chāh Bahar 45 E5
Chāh Gay Hills 42 E3
Chahār Borjak 42 D3
Chaibasa 40 F5
Chakhānsūr 42 D3
Chakradharpur 40 F5
Chakwal 42 C8
Chala 91 G4
Chalcis = Halkida 23 E4
Chalhuanca 91 F4
Chalisgaon 43 J9
Chalky Inlet 65 G2
Challapata 91 G5
Chalon-sur-Saône 13 C6
Châlons-en-Champagne 13 B6
Chaman 42 D5
Chamba 42 C10
Chambal ➔ 42 F11
Chambéry 13 D6
Chamical 94 C3
Chamonix-Mont Blanc 13 D7
Champagne 13 B6
Champaign 76 D1
Champlain, L. 77 B9
Chañaral 94 B2
Chandigarh 42 D10
Chandler 62 A1
Chandmani 34 B4
Chandpur 41 F8
Chandrapur 43 K11
Ch'ang Chiang = Chang Jiang ➔ 35 C7
Chang Jiang ➔ 35 C7
Changanacheri 43 Q10
Changane ➔ 59 C6
Changchiak'ou = Zhangjiakou 35 B6
Ch'angchou = Changzhou 35 C6
Changchun 35 B7
Changde 35 D6
Changhai = Shanghai 35 C7
Changhua 35 D7
Changsha 35 D6
Changzhi 35 C6
Changzhou 35 C6
Chania 23 G5
Chanion, Kolpos 23 G4
Channapatna 43 N10
Channel Is. 11 G5
Channel-Port aux Basques 71 E8
Chantada 18 A2
Chanthaburi 38 B2
Chantrey Inlet 68 B10
Chanute 81 A6
Chao Phraya ➔ 38 B2
Chaozhou 35 D6
Chapala, L. de 84 C4
Chapayevsk 24 C6
Chapleau 71 E5
Chapra = Chhapra 40 E5
Chara 31 D9
Charagua 91 G6
Charaña 91 G5
Chardara 29 E7
Chardzhou = Türkmenabat 29 F7
Charente ➔ 12 D3
Chari ➔ 55 F1
Chārīkār 42 B6
Chārjew = Türkmenabat 29 F7
Charleroi 14 C3
Charles, C. 77 F8
Charleston *S.C., U.S.A.* 83 C8
Charleston *W. Va., U.S.A.* 76 E5
Charlesville 56 F4
Charleville 63 A4
Charleville-Mézières 13 B6
Charlotte 83 B7
Charlotte Amalie 87 C6
Charlottesville 77 E6
Charlottetown 71 E7
Charlton 62 C3
Charlton I. 71 D6
Charolles 13 C6
Charters Towers 61 E8
Chartres 12 B4
Chascomús 94 D5
Châteaubriant 12 C3
Châteaulin 12 B1
Châteauroux 12 C4
Châtellerault 12 C4
Chatham = Chatham-Kent 71 E5
Chatham = Miramichi 71 E7
Chatham 11 F7
Chatham-Kent 71 E5
Chatrapur 40 H5
Châttagâm = Chittagong 41 F8
Chattahoochee ➔ 82 D5
Chattanooga 82 B5
Chaukan Pass 41 D11
Chaumont 13 B6
Chaves *Brazil* 92 C4
Chaves *Portugal* 18 B2
Cheb 16 C1
Cheboksary 24 B6
Chech, Erg 52 D5
Chechenia □ 25 E6
Checheno-Ingush Republic = Chechenia □ 25 E6
Chechnya = Chechenia □ 25 E6
Cheduba I. 41 H9
Cheepie 63 A4
Chegga 52 C4
Chegutu 59 B6
Chehalis 72 C2
Cheju-do = Jeju-do 35 C7
Chekiang = Zhejiang □ 35 D7
Cheleken = Hazar 29 F6
Chelforó 95 D3
Chelkar = Shalqar 29 E6
Chelkar Tengiz, Solonchak 29 E7
Chełm 17 C6
Chełmno 16 B4
Chelmsford 11 F7
Cheltenham 11 F5
Chelyabinsk 29 D7
Chelyuskin, C. = Chelyuskin, Mys 30 B8
Chelyuskin, Mys 30 B8
Chemba 59 B6
Chemnitz 15 C7
Chenab ➔ 42 D7
Chengchou = Zhengzhou 35 C6
Chengde 35 B6
Chengdu 35 C5
Chengjiang 34 D5
Ch'engtu = Chengdu 35 C5
Chennai 43 N12
Chenzhou 35 D6
Cheo Reo 38 B3
Cheom Ksan 38 B2
Cheongju 35 C7
Chepén 91 E3
Chepes 94 C3
Cher ➔ 12 C4
Cherbourg 12 B3
Cherdyn 28 C6
Cherepanovo 29 D9
Cherepovets 24 B4
Chergui, Chott ech 52 B6
Cherikov = Cherykaw 17 B10
Cherkasy 24 D3
Cherlak 29 D8
Chernaya 30 B6
Chernigov = Chernihiv 24 C3
Chernihiv 24 C3
Chernivtsi 17 D7
Chernobyl = Chornobyl 17 C10
Chernovtsy = Chernivtsi 17 D7
Cherrapunji 41 E8
Cherven 17 B9
Chervonohrad 17 C7
Cherykaw 17 B10
Chesapeake 77 F7
Chesapeake B. 77 E7
Cheshskaya Guba 28 C5
Chester *U.K.* 11 E5
Chester *U.S.A.* 77 E8
Chesterfield 11 E6
Chesterfield, Is. 64 L10
Chesterfield Inlet 68 B10
Chesterton Ra. 63 A4
Chetumal 85 D7
Cheviot Hills 10 D5
Chew Bahir 55 H6
Cheyenne 74 E2

Cheyenne ➔ 74 C4
Chhapra 40 E5
Chhatarpur 43 G11
Chhindwara 43 H11
Chi ➔ 38 A2
Chiai 35 D7
Chiávari 13 D8
Chiavenna 13 C8
Chiba 33 F7
Chibemba 58 B2
Chibia 58 B2
Chibougamau 71 E6
Chicacole = Srikakulam 40 H4
Chicago 76 D2
Chichagof I. 69 C6
Chichester 11 F6
Ch'ich'ihaerh = Qiqihar 35 B7
Chickasha 80 B5
Chiclana de la Frontera 18 D2
Chiclayo 91 E3
Chico 72 G3
Chico ➔ *Chubut, Argentina* 95 E3
Chico ➔ *Santa Cruz, Argentina* 95 F3
Chicoutimi 71 E6
Chidambaram 43 P11
Chidley, C. 70 C7
Chiemsee 15 E7
Chiese ➔ 13 D9
Chieti 20 C5
Chiguana 91 H5
Chihli, G. of = Bo Hai 35 C6
Chihuahua 84 B3
Chiili = Shīeli 29 E7
Chik Bollapur 43 N10
Chikmagalur 43 N9
Chilapa 84 D5
Chilas 42 B9
Chilaw 43 R11
Childers 63 A5
Chile ■ 94 D2
Chilete 91 E3
Chililabombwe 59 A5
Chilin = Jilin 35 B7
Chilka L. 40 H5
Chillán 94 D2
Chiloé, I. de 95 E2
Chilpancingo 84 D5
Chilung 35 D7
Chilwa, L. 59 B7
Chimbay 29 E6
Chimborazo 90 D3
Chimbote 91 E3
Chimkent = Shymkent 29 E7
Chimoio 59 B6
Chin □ 41 F9
China ■ 35 C5
Chinan = Jinan 35 C6
Chinandega 85 E7
Chincha Alta 91 F3
Chinchilla 63 A5
Chinchou = Jinzhou 35 B7
Chinde 59 B7
Chindwin ➔ 41 G10
Chingola 59 A5
Ch'ingtao = Qingdao 35 C7
Chinguetti 52 D3
Chinhoyi 59 B6
Chiniot 42 D8
Chinnampo = Namp'o 35 C7
Chinon 12 C4
Chióggia 20 B4
Chíos = Hios 23 E6
Chipata 59 A6
Chiquián 91 F3
Chiquinquira 90 B4
Chirchiq 29 E7
Chiredzi 59 C6
Chirmiri 40 F4
Chisapani Garhi 40 D5
Chisasibi 71 D6
Chisimaio 49 H3
Chişinău 17 E9
Chistopol 24 B7
Chita 30 D9
Chitral 42 B7
Chitré 86 E3
Chittagong 41 F8
Chittagong □ 41 E8
Chittaurgarh 43 G9
Chittoor 43 N11
Chitungwiza 59 B6
Chiusi 20 C3
Chivasso 13 D7
Chivilcoy 94 B4
Chkalov = Orenburg 29 D6
Choele Choel 95 D3
Chojnice 16 B3
Cholet 12 C3
Choluteca 85 E7
Choma 59 B5
Chomolungma = Everest, Mt. 40 C6
Chomutov 16 C1
Chon Buri 38 B2
Chone 90 D3
Ch'öngjin 35 B7
Chongqing 35 D5
Chongui 30 F
Chonos, Arch. de los 95 F2
Chop 17 D6
Chora Sfakion 23 G5
Chornobyl 17 C10
Chortkiv 17 D7
Chorzów 16 C4
Chos-Malal 94 D2
Choszczno 16 B2
Chotila 43 H7
Choybalsan 35 B6
Christchurch 65 E5
Christmas I. = Kiritimati 65 J15
Chū = Shū 29 E8
Ch'uanchou = Quanzhou 35 D6
Chubut ➔ 95 E3
Chudskoye, Ozero 24 B2
Chūgoku-Sanchi 33 F3
Chula Vista 78 D4
Chulucanas 90 E2
Chulym ➔ 29 D9
Chumbicha 94 B3
Chumphon 38 B1
Chuna ➔ 30 D7
Chuncheon 35 C7
Chungking = Chongqing 35 D5
Chunya 57 F6
Chuquibamba 91 G4
Chuquicamata 94 A3
Chur 13 C8
Churachandpur 41 E9
Churchill 68 C10
Churchill ➔ *Man., Canada* 68 C10
Churchill ➔ *Nfld. & L., Canada* 71 D7
Churchill, C. 68 C10
Churchill Falls 71 D7
Churchill L. 69 C9
Churu 42 E9
Chushal 42 C11
Chusovoy 28 D6
Chuuk = Truk 64 J10
Chuvash Republic = Chuvashia □ 24 B6
Chuvashia □ 24 B6
Ciadâr-Lunga 17 E9
Cicero 76 D2
Ciechanów 16 B5
Ciego de Ávila 86 B4
Ciénaga 90 A4
Cienfuegos 86 B3
Cieza 19 C5
Cijara, Embalse de 18 C3
Cilician Gates P. 46 C3
Cill Chainnigh = Kilkenny 11 E3
Cimişlia 17 E9
Cimone, Mte. 20 B3
Cinca ➔ 19 B6
Cincar 20 C6
Cincinnati 76 E3
Çine 23 F7
Cinto, Mte. 13 E8
Circle 69 B5
Cirebon 39 F3
Citlaltépetl = Orizaba, Pico de 84 D5
Città del Vaticano = Vatican City ■ 20 D4
Città di Castello 20 C4
Ciudad Bolívar 90 B6
Ciudad de México 84 D5
Ciudad del Carmen 85 D6
Ciudad Delicias = Delicias 84 B3
Ciudad Guayana 90 B6
Ciudad Juárez 84 A3
Ciudad Madero 84 C5
Ciudad Mante 84 C5
Ciudad Obregón 84 B3
Ciudad Real 18 C4
Ciudad Rodrigo 18 B2
Ciudad Victoria 84 C5
Civitanova Marche 20 C4
Civitavécchia 20 C3
Cizre 46 C5
Clare 62 B2
Clarence ➔ *Australia* 63 A5
Clarence ➔ *N.Z.* 65 E5
Clarence, I. 95 G2
Clarence I. 96 A4
Clarie Coast 96 A13
Clarke I. 62 D4
Clarksdale 81 B8
Clarksville 82 A4
Claveria 36 A2
Clear, C. 11 F2
Clearwater 83 F6
Clearwater Mts. 73 C6
Clermont-Ferrand 13 D5
Cleveland *Australia* 63 A5
Cleveland *U.S.A.* 76 D5
Clifden 65 G2
Clifton 63 A5
Clifton Hills 62 A2
Clinton *N.Z.* 65 G3
Clinton *U.S.A.* 75 E9
Clinton Colden L. 68 B9
Clones 11 D3
Clonmel 11 E3
Clovis 80 B2
Cluj-Napoca 17 E6
Clunes 62 C3
Clutha ➔ 65 G3
Clyde 65 F3
Clyde ➔ 10 D4
Clyde, Firth of 10 D4
Clyde River 70 B7
Coari 90 D6
Coast Mts. 68 C7
Coast Ranges 72 F2
Coats I. 70 C5
Coats Land 96 B5
Coatzacoalcos 85 D6
Cobar 63 B4
Cóbh 11 F2
Cobham 62 B3
Cobija 91 F5
Cobram 63 C4
Coburg 15 C6
Cocanada = Kakinada 40 J4
Cochabamba 91 G5
Cochin 43 Q10
Cochin China = Nam-Phan 38 B3
Cochrane 71 E5
Cochrane, L. 95 F2
Cockburn 62 B3
Cockburn, Canal 95 G2
Coco ➔ 86 D3
Cocobeach 56 D1
Cod, C. 77 C10
Codajás 90 D6
Codó 92 C5
Coeur d'Alene 72 C5
Coffeyville 81 A6
Coffin B. 62 B2
Coffin Bay Peninsula 62 B2
Coffs Harbour 63 B5
Cognac 12 D3
Cohuna 63 C3
Coiba, I. de 86 E3
Coig ➔ 95 G3
Coihaique 95 F2
Coimbatore 43 P10
Coimbra *Brazil* 91 G7

Coimbra *Portugal* **18 B1**
Coin **18 D3**
Cojimies **90 C3**
Colac **62 C3**
Colatina **93 F5**
Colbeck, C. **96 B17**
Colbinabbin **63 C3**
Colchester **11 F7**
Colebrook **62 D4**
Coleman **69 D8**
Coleraine *Australia* **62 C3**
Coleraine *U.K.* **11 D3**
Coleridge, L. **65 E4**
Colesberg **59 E5**
Colhué Huapi, L. **95 F3**
Colima **84 D4**
Colinas **92 D5**
Coll **10 C3**
Collaguasi **91 H5**
Collarenebri **63 A4**
Collina, Passo di **20 B3**
Collingwood **64 D5**
Colmar **13 B7**
Colo ➔ **63 B5**
Cologne = Köln **14 C4**
Colomb-Béchar = Béchar **52 B5**
Colombia ■ **90 C4**
Colombo **43 R11**
Colón *Cuba* **86 B3**
Colón *Panama* **85 F9**
Colonia del Sacramento **94 C5**
Colonia Dora **94 B4**
Colonsay **10 C3**
Colorado □ **79 A10**
Colorado ➔ *Argentina* **95 D4**
Colorado ➔ *N. Amer.* **78 E5**
Colorado Plateau **79 B7**
Colorado Springs **74 F2**
Columbia *Mo., U.S.A.* **75 F8**
Columbia *S.C., U.S.A.* **83 B7**
Columbia *Tenn., U.S.A.* **82 B4**
Columbia ➔ **72 C1**
Columbia, C. **70 A7**
Columbia, District of □ **77 E7**
Columbia Basin **72 C4**
Columbretes, Is. **19 C6**
Columbus *Ga., U.S.A.* **82 C5**
Columbus *Miss., U.S.A.* **82 C3**
Columbus *Ohio, U.S.A.* **76 E4**
Colville ➔ **69 A4**
Colville, C. **64 B6**
Colwyn Bay **11 E5**
Comácchio **20 B4**
Comallo **95 E2**
Comilla **41 F8**
Comino, C. **21 D2**
Committee B. **70 C5**
Commonwealth B. **96 A14**
Commoron Cr. ➔ **63 A5**
Communism Pk. = imeni Ismail Samani, Pik **29 F8**
Como **13 D8**
Como, Lago di **13 D8**
Comodoro Rivadavia **95 F3**
Comorin, C. = Kanyakumari **43 Q10**
Comoros ■ **51 H8**
Compiègne **13 B5**
Compton Downs **63 B4**
Comrat **17 E9**
Conakry **53 G3**
Conara **62 D4**
Concarneau **12 C2**
Conceição da Barra **93 F6**
Concepción *Bolivia* **91 G6**
Concepción *Chile* **94 D2**
Concepción *Paraguay* **94 A5**
Concepción, L. **91 G6**
Concepción del Oro **84 C4**
Concepción del Uruguay **94 C5**
Conchos ➔ **84 B3**
Concord *N.C., U.S.A.* **83 B7**
Concord *N.H., U.S.A.* **77 C10**
Concordia *Argentina* **94 C5**
Concórdia *Brazil* **90 D5**
Condamine **63 A5**
Condeúba **93 E5**
Condobolin **63 B4**
Conegliano **20 B4**
Confuso ➔ **94 B5**
Congo (Brazzaville) = Congo ■ **56 E3**
Congo (Kinshasa) = Congo, Dem. Rep. of the ■ **56 E4**
Congo ■ **56 E3**
Congo ➔ **56 F2**
Congo, Dem. Rep. of the ■ **56 E4**
Conjeeveram = Kanchipuram **43 N11**
Conlea **63 B3**
Conn, L. **11 D2**
Connacht □ **11 E2**
Connecticut □ **77 D9**
Connecticut ➔ **77 D9**
Connemara **11 E2**
Conran, C. **63 C4**
Conselheiro Lafaiete **93 G5**
Constance = Konstanz **14 E5**
Constance, L. = Bodensee **13 C8**
Constanța **22 B7**
Constantine **52 A7**
Constitución **94 D2**
Contai **40 G6**
Contamana **91 E4**
Contas ➔ **93 E6**
Conway, L. **62 A2**
Coober Pedy **62 A1**
Cooch Behar = Koch Bihar **41 D7**
Cook, B. **95 H2**
Cook, Mt. = Aoraki Mount Cook **65 E4**
Cook Inlet **69 C4**
Cook Is. **65 L14**
Cook Strait **65 D6**
Cooktown **61 D8**
Coolabah **63 B4**
Cooladdi **63 A4**
Coolah **63 B4**
Coolamon **63 B4**
Coolangatta **63 A5**
Cooma **63 C4**
Coonabarabran **63 B4**
Coonamble **63 B4**
Coondapoor **43 N9**
Coongie **62 A3**
Coongoola **63 A4**
Cooninnie, L. **62 A2**
Cooper Cr. ➔ *N. Terr., Australia* **60 C5**
Cooper Cr. ➔ *S. Austral., Australia* **62 A2**
Coorong, The **62 C2**
Cooroy **63 A5**
Cootamundra **63 B4**
Cooyar **63 A5**
Copenhagen = København **9 D8**
Copiapó **94 B2**
Copiapó ➔ **94 B2**
Coppermine = Kugluktuk **68 B8**
Coppermine ➔ **68 B8**
Coquimbo **94 C2**
Corabia **22 C5**
Coracora **91 G4**
Coral Harbour **70 C5**
Coral Sea **64 L10**
Corato **21 D6**
Corby **11 E6**
Corcaigh = Cork **11 F2**
Corcubión **18 A1**
Córdoba *Argentina* **94 C4**
Córdoba *Spain* **18 D3**
Córdoba, Sierra de **94 C4**
Cordova **69 B5**
Corfu = Kerkyra **23 E2**
Coria **18 C2**
Corigliano Cálabro **21 E6**
Corinna **62 D4**
Corinth = Korinthos **23 F4**
Corinth, G. of = Korinthiakos Kolpos **23 E4**
Corinto **93 F5**
Cork **11 F2**
Çorlu **22 D6**
Corner Brook **71 E8**
Cornești **17 E9**
Cornwall **71 E6**
Cornwall I. **70 B4**
Cornwallis I. **70 B4**
Corny Pt. **62 B2**
Coro **90 A5**
Coroatá **92 C5**
Corocoro **91 G5**
Coroico **91 G5**
Coromandel **64 B6**
Corona **62 B3**
Coronation Gulf **68 B8**
Coronation I. **96 A4**
Coronel **94 D2**
Coronel Dorrego **94 D4**
Coronel Suárez **94 D4**
Corowa **63 C4**
Corpus Christi **80 F5**
Corrib, L. **11 E2**
Corrientes **94 B5**
Corrientes ➔ **90 D4**
Corrientes, C. *Colombia* **90 B3**
Corrientes, C. *Mexico* **84 C3**
Corriverton **90 B7**
Corse □ **13 E8**
Corse, C. **13 E8**
Corsica = Corse □ **13 E8**
Corsicana **81 C5**
Corte **13 E8**
Cortés, Mar de = California, G. de **84 B2**
Çorum **25 E3**
Corumbá **91 G7**
Corunna = A Coruña **18 A1**
Corvallis **72 D2**
Cosenza **21 E6**
Costa Blanca **19 C5**
Costa Brava **19 B7**
Costa del Sol **18 D3**
Costa Dorada **19 B6**
Costa Rica ■ **86 E3**
Cotabato **36 C2**
Cotagaita **91 H5**
Côte d'Azur **13 E7**
Côte-d'Ivoire = Ivory Coast ■ **53 G4**
Cotentin **12 B3**
Cotonou **53 G6**
Cotopaxi **90 D3**
Cotswold Hills **11 F5**
Cottbus **15 C8**
Couedic, C. du **62 C2**
Coulman I. **96 B15**
Council Bluffs **75 E7**
Courantyne ➔ **90 B7**
Courtrai = Kortrijk **14 C2**
Coventry **11 E6**
Covilhã **18 B2**
Covington **76 E3**
Cowal, L. **63 B4**
Cowangie **62 C3**
Cowarie **62 A2**
Cowell **62 B2**
Cowra **63 B4**
Coxim **93 F3**
Cox's Bazar **41 G8**
Cozumel, Isla **85 C7**
Craboon **63 B4**
Cracow = Kraków **16 C4**
Cracow **63 A5**
Cradock **59 E5**
Craigavon **11 D3**
Crailsheim **14 D6**
Craiova **22 B4**
Cranbrook *Australia* **62 D4**
Cranbrook *Canada* **69 D8**

Crateús 92 D5
Crato 92 D6
Crawley 11 F6
Crazy Mts. 73 C8
Crema 13 D8
Cremona 13 D9
Cres 20 B5
Crete = Kriti 23 G5
Créteil 12 B5
Creus, C. de 19 A7
Creuse ➔ 12 C4
Crewe 11 E5
Criciúma 94 B7
Crimean Pen. = Krymskyy Pivostriv 25 D3
Crişul Negru ➔ 16 E5
Crna ➔ 22 D3
Crna Gora = Montenegro ■ 22 C2
Crna Gora 22 C3
Crna Reka = Crna ➔ 22 D3
Croatia ■ 20 B6
Crocker, Banjaran 38 C5
Croker, C. 60 C5
Cromer 11 E7
Cromwell 65 F3
Cronulla 63 B5
Crookwell 63 B4
Cross Sound 69 C6
Crotone 21 E6
Crows Nest 63 A5
Crowsnest Pass 69 D8
Cruz Alta 94 B6
Cruz del Eje 94 C4
Cruzeiro do Sul 91 E4
Crystal Brook 62 B2
Csongrád 16 E5
Cuamba 59 A7
Cuando ➔ 58 B4
Cuango = Kwango ➔ 56 E3
Cuanza ➔ 56 F2
Cuba ■ 86 B4
Cubango ➔ 58 B4
Cúcuta 90 B4
Cuddalore 43 P11
Cuddapah 43 M11
Cuenca *Ecuador* 90 D3
Cuenca *Spain* 19 B4
Cuenca, Serranía de 19 C5
Cuernavaca 84 D5
Cuevas del Almanzora 19 D5
Cuevo 91 H6
Cuiabá 93 F2
Cuiabá ➔ 93 F2
Cuito ➔ 58 B4
Culcairn 63 C4
Culgoa ➔ 63 A4
Culiacán 84 C3
Culion 36 B2
Cullarin Ra. 63 B4
Cullera 19 C5
Culuene ➔ 93 E3
Culverden 65 E5
Cumaná 90 A6
Cumberland 77 E6
Cumberland Pen. 70 C7
Cumberland Plateau 76 F3
Cumberland Sd. 70 C7
Cumborah 63 A4
Cumbum 43 M11
Cummins 62 B2
Cumnock 63 B4
Cunene ➔ 58 B2
Cúneo 13 D7
Cunnamulla 63 A4
Cupica, G. de 90 B3
Curaçao 87 D6
Curaray ➔ 90 D4
Curiapo 90 B6
Curicó 94 C2
Curitiba 94 B7
Currabubula 63 B5
Currais Novos 92 D6
Curralinho 92 C4
Currie 62 C3
Curtea de Argeş 17 F7
Curtis Group 62 C4
Curuápanema ➔ 92 C2
Curuçá 92 C4
Curup 39 E2
Cururupu 92 C5
Curuzú Cuatiá 94 B5
Cusco = Cuzco 91 F4
Cuttaburra ➔ 63 A3
Cuttack 40 G5
Cuvier I. 64 B6
Cuxhaven 14 B5
Cuyo 36 B2
Cuzco *Bolivia* 91 H5
Cuzco *Peru* 91 F4
Cwmbran 11 F5
Cyclades 23 F5
Cygnet 62 D4
Cyprus ■ 46 D3
Cyrenaica 54 C3
Czech Rep. ■ 16 D2
Częstochowa 16 C4

D

Da Hinggan Ling 35 B7
Da Lat 38 B3
Da Nang 38 A3
Da Qaidam 34 C4
Daba Shan 35 C5
Dabo = Pasirkuning 39 E2
Dabola 53 F3
Dacca = Dhaka 41 F8
Dacca = Dhaka □ 41 E8
Dachau 15 D6
Dadanawa 90 C7
Dadra & Nagar Haveli □ 43 J8
Dadu 42 F5
Daegu 35 C7
Daejeon 35 C7
Daet 36 B2
Dagana 53 E2
Dagestan □ 25 E6
Daghestan Republic = Dagestan □ 25 E6
Dagö = Hiiumaa 24 B1
Dagupan 36 A2
Dahlak Kebir 49 D3
Dahod 43 H9
Daiō-Misaki 33 F5
Daisetsu-Zan 32 B8
Dakar 53 F2
Dakhla 52 D2
Dakhla, El Wâhât el- 54 C4
Dakhovskaya 25 E5
Đakovica 22 C3
Dalälven ➔ 9 C9
Dalaman ➔ 23 F7
Dalandzadgad 35 B5
Dalap-Uliga-Darrit = Majuro 64 J12
Dālbandīn 42 E4
Dalby 63 A5
Dali 34 D5
Dalian 35 C7
Daliang Shan 34 D5
Dallarnil 63 A5
Dallas 81 C5
Dalmacija 20 C6
Dalmatia = Dalmacija 20 C6
Dalnegorsk 32 A4
Daloa 53 G4
Dalton 82 B5
Dalton Iceberg Tongue 96 A13
Daly Waters 60 D5
Daman 43 J8
Damanhûr 54 B5
Damar 37 F3
Damaraland 58 C3
Damascus = Dimashq 46 D4
Damāvand 44 C3
Damāvand, Qolleh-ye 44 C3
Damba 56 F3
Dâmboviţa ➔ 22 B6
Dāmghān 44 B3
Damiel 18 C4
Damietta = Dumyât 54 B5
Dammam = Ad Dammām 47 F7
Damoh 43 H11
Dampier 60 E2
Dampier, Selat 37 E4
Danbury 77 D9
Dandeldhura 40 C3
Dandeli 43 M9
Dandenong 63 C4
Dandong 35 B7
Danger Is. = Pukapuka 65 L14
Dangla Shan = Tanggula Shan 34 C4
Danilov 24 B5
Dankhar Gompa 42 C11
Danmark = Denmark ■ 9 D7
Dannemora 9 F11
Dannevirke 64 D7
Danube = Dunărea ➔ 17 F9
Danville 83 A8
Danzig = Gdańsk 16 A4
Dao = Tobias Fornier 36 B2
Dar el Beida = Casablanca 52 B4
Dar es Salaam 57 F7
Dārāb 44 D3
Daraj 54 B1
Darband 42 B8
Darbhanga 40 D5
Dardanelles = Çanakkale Boğazı 23 D6
Dârfûr 55 F3
Dargai 42 B7
Darganata 29 E7
Dargaville 64 A5
Darica 22 D7
Darién, G. del 90 B3
Darjeeling = Darjiling 40 D7
Darjiling 40 D7
Darling ➔ 62 B3
Darling Downs 63 A5
Darling Ra. 60 G2
Darlington 11 D6
Darłowo 16 A3
Darmstadt 14 D5
Darnah 54 B3
Darnley, C. 96 A10
Darnley B. 68 B7
Dart, C. 96 B18
Dartmoor 11 F5
Dartmouth 71 E7
Dartmouth Res. 63 A4
Darvaza 29 E6
Darvel, Teluk = Lahad Datu, Telok 36 D1
Darwha 43 J10
Darwin 60 C5
Daryoi Amu = Amudarya ➔ 29 E6
Dās 44 E3
Dashen, Ras 57 B7
Dashoguz 29 E6
Dasht ➔ 42 G2
Datça 23 F6
Datia 43 G11
Datong 35 B6
Datu, Tanjung 39 D3
Datu Piang 36 C2
Datuk, Tanjong = Datu, Tanjung 39 D3
Daugava ➔ 24 B1
Daugavpils 24 B2
Daulpur 42 F10
Dauphin 69 C9
Dauphiné 13 D6
Davangere 43 M9
Davao 36 C3
Davao G. 36 C3
Dāvar Panāh = Sarāvān 45 E5
Davenport 75 E9
David 86 E3
David Gorodok = Davyd Haradok 17 B8
Davis Sea 96 A11
Davis Str. 6 C14
Davos 13 C8
Davyd Haradok 17 B8
Dawei = Tavoy 38 B1
Dawna Ra. 41 J12
Dawson 68 B6
Dawson, I. 95 G2
Dax 12 E3

Daxian **35 C5**
Daxue Shan **34 C5**
Daylesford **62 C3**
Dayr az Zawr **46 D5**
Dayton **76 E3**
Daytona Beach **83 E7**
De Aar **58 E4**
Dead Sea **47 E3**
Deakin **60 G4**
Deal I. **62 C4**
Deán Funes **94 C4**
Death Valley **78 B4**
Debar **22 D3**
Debre Markos **55 F6**
Debrecen **16 E5**
Decatur *Ala., U.S.A.* **82 B4**
Decatur *Ill., U.S.A.* **75 F10**
Deccan **43 L11**
Děčín **16 C2**
Dedéagach = Alexandroupoli **22 D5**
Dee ➔ **10 C5**
Deepwater **63 A5**
Deer Lake **71 E8**
Deggendorf **15 D7**
Deh Bīd **44 D3**
Dehi Titan **42 C3**
Dehibat **54 B1**
Dehkareqan **46 C6**
Dehra Dun **42 D11**
Dej **17 E6**
Dekese **56 E4**
Delano **78 C3**
Delaware □ **77 E8**
Delegate **63 C4**
Delgado, C. **57 G8**
Delgo **55 D5**
Delhi **42 E10**
Delice ➔ **25 F3**
Delicias **84 B3**
Déline **68 B7**
Delmenhorst **14 B5**
Deloraine **62 D4**
Delungra **63 A5**
Delvinë **23 E3**
Demanda, Sierra de la **18 A4**
Demavend = Damāvand, Qolleh-ye **44 C3**
Dembidolo **55 G5**
Demini ➔ **90 D6**
Demirci **23 E7**
Demirköy **22 D6**
Dempo **39 E2**
Den Bosch = 's-Hertogenbosch **14 C3**
Den Haag = 's-Gravenhage **14 B3**
Den Helder **14 B3**
Denali = McKinley, Mt. **69 B4**
Denau **29 F7**
Dendang **39 E3**
Denia **19 C6**
Denial B. **62 B1**
Deniliquin **63 C3**
Denizli **46 C2**
Denman Glacier **96 A11**
Denmark ■ **9 D7**
Denmark Str. **66 C17**
Denpasar **39 F5**
Denton **80 C5**
D'Entrecasteaux Is. **61 B9**
Denver **74 F2**
Deoghar **40 E6**
Deolali **43 K8**
Deoria **40 D4**
Deosai Mts. **42 B9**
Dera Ghazi Khan **42 D7**
Dera Ismail Khan **42 D7**
Derbent **25 E6**
Derby *Australia* **60 D3**
Derby *U.K.* **11 E6**
Derg, L. **11 E2**
Dergaon **41 D9**
Derry = Londonderry **11 D3**
Des Moines **75 E8**
Des Moines ➔ **75 E9**
Desaguadero ➔ **91 G5**
Dese **49 E2**
Desna ➔ **17 C10**
Desolación, I. **95 G2**
Despeñaperros, Paso **18 C4**
Dessau **15 C7**
Dessye = Dese **49 E2**
D'Estrees B. **62 C2**
Detmold **14 C5**
Detroit **76 C4**
Deutsche Bucht **14 A5**
Deutschland = Germany ■ **14 C6**
Deva **17 F6**
Devakottai **43 Q11**
Deventer **14 B4**
Devon I. **70 B5**
Devonport *Australia* **62 D4**
Devonport *N.Z.* **64 B6**
Dewas **43 H10**
Deyhūk **44 C4**
Deyyer **44 E2**
Dezfūl **47 D7**
Dezhneva, Mys **31 C16**
Dhafra **44 F3**
Dhahira **44 F4**
Dhahran = Aẓ Ẓahrān **47 F7**
Dhaka **41 F8**
Dhaka □ **41 E8**
Dhamtari **40 G3**
Dhanbad **40 F6**
Dhangarhi **40 C3**
Dhankuta **40 D6**
Dhar **43 H9**
Dharmapuri **43 N11**
Dhaulagiri **40 C4**
Dhenkanal **40 G5**
Dhodhekánisos = Dodecanese **23 F6**
Dhrol **43 H7**
Dhubaibah **44 F3**
Dhuburi **41 D7**
Dhule **43 J9**
Dhut ➔ **49 E5**
Diafarabé **53 F5**
Diamantina **93 F5**
Diamantina ➔ **62 A2**
Diamantino **93 E2**
Diamond Harbour **40 F7**
Dibaya-Lubue **56 E3**
Dibbi **49 G3**
Dibrugarh **41 D10**
Didiéni **53 F4**
Diefenbaker, L. **69 C9**
Diego Suarez = Antsiranana **59 A9**
Dieppe **12 B4**
Digby **71 E7**
Dighinala **41 F9**
Digne-les-Bains **13 D7**
Digos **36 C3**
Digul ➔ **37 F5**
Dihang = Brahmaputra ➔ **41 F7**
Dijlah, Nahr ➔ **47 E6**
Dijon **13 C6**
Dikimdya **31 D10**
Dikson **28 B9**
Dikti Oros **23 G5**
Dili **37 F3**
Dilli = Delhi **42 E10**
Dillingham **69 C4**
Dilolo **56 G4**
Dilston **62 D4**
Dimashq **46 D4**
Dimboola **62 C3**
Dîmboviţa = Dâmboviţa ➔ **22 B6**
Dimitrovgrad *Bulgaria* **22 C5**
Dimitrovgrad *Russia* **24 C6**
Dimitrovo = Pernik **22 C4**
Dinagat **36 B3**
Dinajpur **41 E7**
Dinan **12 B2**
Dinant **14 C3**
Dinar **46 C2**
Dīnār, Kūh-e **44 D2**
Dinara Planina **20 B6**
Dinard **12 B2**
Dinaric Alps = Dinara Planina **20 B6**
Dindigul **43 P11**
Dingle **11 E1**
Dingwall **10 C4**
Dinosaur ⌓ **73 F9**
Dipolog **36 C2**
Dir **42 B7**
Dire Dawa **49 F3**
Dirfis Oros **23 E4**
Dirranbandi **63 A4**
Disa **43 G8**
Disappointment, L. **60 E3**
Disaster B. **63 C4**
Discovery B. **62 C3**
Disteghil Sar **42 A9**
District of Columbia □ **77 E7**
Distrito Federal □ **93 F4**
Diu **43 J7**
Divinópolis **93 G5**
Divnoye **25 D5**
Diyarbakır **46 C5**
Diz Chah **44 C3**
Djakarta = Jakarta **39 F3**
Djambala **56 E2**
Djanet **52 D7**
Djawa = Jawa **39 F3**
Djelfa **52 B6**
Djerba, Ī. de **54 B1**
Djerid, Chott **52 B7**
Djibouti **49 E3**
Djibouti ■ **49 E3**
Djolu **56 D4**
Djoum **56 D2**
Djourab, Erg du **55 E2**
Dmitriya Lapteva, Proliv **31 B12**
Dnepr = Dnipro ➔ **25 D3**
Dneprodzerzhinsk = Dniprodzerzhynsk **25 D3**
Dnepropetrovsk = Dnipropetrovsk **25 D4**
Dnestr = Dnister ➔ **17 E10**
Dnieper = Dnipro ➔ **25 D3**
Dniester = Dnister ➔ **17 E10**
Dnipro ➔ **25 D3**
Dniprodzerzhynsk **25 D3**
Dnipropetrovsk **25 D4**
Dnister ➔ **17 E10**
Dnistrovskyy Lyman **17 E10**
Dnyapro = Dnipro ➔ **25 D3**
Doba **55 G2**
Doberai, Jazirah **37 E4**
Dobo **37 F4**
Doboj **20 B7**
Dobrich **22 C6**
Dobruja **22 B7**
Dobrush **17 B10**
Dodecanese **23 F6**
Dodekanisa = Dodecanese **23 F6**
Dodge City **80 A3**
Dodoma **57 F7**
Doha = Ad Dawḥah **44 E2**
Dohazari **41 F9**
Doi **37 D3**
Dois Irmãos, Sa. **93 D5**
Dolak, Pulau **37 F5**
Dolbeau-Mistassini **71 E6**
Dole **13 C6**
Dolomites = Dolomiti **20 A3**
Dolomiti **20 A3**
Dolores **94 D5**
Dolphin, C. **95 G5**
Dolphin and Union Str. **68 B8**
Dombarovskiy **29 D6**
Dominica ■ **87 C7**
Dominican Rep. ■ **87 C5**
Domodóssola **13 C8**
Domville, Mt. **63 A5**
Don ➔ *Russia* **25 D4**
Don ➔ *U.K.* **10 C5**
Don Benito **18 C3**
Donald **62 C3**
Donau = Dunărea ➔ **17 F9**
Donauwörth **14 D6**
Doncaster **11 E6**
Dondo, Teluk **37 D2**

Donegal **11 D2**
Donets ➔ **25 D5**
Donetsk **25 D4**
Donggala **37 E1**
Dongola **55 E5**
Dongting Hu **35 D6**
Donington, C. **62 B2**
Donnelly's Crossing **64 A5**
Donostia = Donostia-San Sebastián **19 A5**
Donostia-San Sebastián **19 A5**
Dora Báltea ➔ **13 D8**
Dorchester, C. **70 C6**
Dordogne ➔ **12 D3**
Dordrecht **14 C3**
Dori **53 F5**
Dornbirn **14 E5**
Doro, Kavo **23 E5**
Dorohoi **17 E8**
Döröö Nuur **34 B4**
Dorrigo **63 B5**
Dortmund **14 C4**
Dos Bahías, C. **95 E3**
Dos Hermanas **18 D3**
Dosso **53 F6**
Dothan **82 D5**
Douai **13 A5**
Douala **53 H7**
Douarnenez **12 B1**
Double Island Pt. **63 A5**
Doubs ➔ **13 C6**
Doubtful Sd. **65 F2**
Doubtless B. **64 A5**
Douglas *I. of Man* **11 D4**
Douglas *U.S.A.* **79 E8**
Dourados **94 A6**
Douro ➔ **18 B1**
Dover *Australia* **62 D4**
Dover *U.K.* **11 F7**
Dover, Str. of **11 F7**
Dovrefjell **8 C7**
Dowlat Yār **45 C6**
Dowlatābād **44 D4**
Drăgăşani **22 B5**
Dragichyn **17 B7**
Dragoman, Prokhod **22 C4**
Draguignan **13 E7**
Drake **63 A5**
Drakensberg **59 E5**
Drama **22 D5**
Drammen **9 D8**
Drau = Drava ➔ **20 B7**
Drava ➔ **20 B7**
Dresden **15 C7**
Dreux **12 B4**
Drin ➔ **22 C2**
Drina ➔ **20 B7**
Drobeta-Turnu Severin **22 B4**
Drochia **17 D8**
Drogheda **11 E3**
Drogichin = Dragichyn **17 B7**
Drogobych = Drohobych **17 D6**
Drohobych **17 D6**
Droichead Atha = Drogheda **11 E3**
Dromedary, C. **63 C5**
Dronning Maud Land **96 B7**
Druk Yul = Bhutan ■ **41 D8**
Drumheller **69 C8**
Drummond Pt. **62 B2**
Drut ➔ **17 B10**
Drygalski I. **96 A11**
Ḍubā **47 F3**
Dubai = Dubayy **44 E3**
Dubăsari **17 E9**
Dubăsari Vdkhr. **17 E9**
Dubawnt ➔ **68 B9**
Dubawnt L. **68 B9**
Dubayy **44 E3**
Dubbo **63 B4**
Dublin *Ireland* **11 E3**
Dublin *U.S.A.* **83 C6**
Dubno **17 C7**
Dubossary = Dubăsari **17 E9**
Dubossary Vdkhr. = Dubăsari Vdkhr. **17 E9**
Dubovka **24 D5**
Dubréka **53 G3**
Dubrovitsa = Dubrovytsya **17 C8**
Dubrovnik **20 C7**
Dubrovytsya **17 C8**
Dudhi **40 E4**
Dudinka **30 C6**
Duero = Douro ➔ **18 B1**
Dūghī Kalā **42 C3**
Dugi Otok **20 B5**
Duisburg **14 C4**
Dujiangyan **34 C5**
Dukhān **44 E2**
Duki **42 D6**
Dulce ➔ **94 C4**
Dulit, Banjaran **39 D4**
Duluth **75 B8**
Dum Duma **41 D10**
Dumaguete **36 C2**
Dumai **39 D2**
Dumaran **36 B1**
Dumfries **11 D5**
Dumyāt **54 B5**
Dún Dealgan = Dundalk **11 D3**
Dún Laoghaire **11 E3**
Duna = Dunărea ➔ **17 F9**
Dunaj = Dunărea ➔ **17 F9**
Dunakeszi **16 E4**
Dunărea ➔ **17 F9**
Dunaújváros **16 E4**
Dunav = Dunărea ➔ **17 F9**
Dunback **65 F4**
Dunbar **10 D5**
Duncan **80 B5**
Dundalk **11 D3**
Dundee **10 C5**
Dundoo **63 A3**
Dunedin **65 F4**
Dunfermline **10 C5**
Dungarvan **11 E3**
Dungog **63 B5**
Dungu **57 D5**
Dunhuang **34 B4**
Dunkerque **12 A5**
Dunkirk = Dunkerque **12 A5**
Dúnleary = Dún Laoghaire **11 E3**
Dunolly **62 C3**
Dunstan Mts. **65 F3**
Durance ➔ **13 E6**
Durango *Mexico* **84 C4**
Durango *Spain* **19 A4**
Durazno **94 C5**
Durazzo = Durrës **22 D2**
Durban **59 D6**
Düren **14 C4**
Durg = Bhilainagar-Durg **40 G3**
Durgapur **40 F6**
Durham *U.K.* **11 D6**
Durham *U.S.A.* **83 B8**
Durham Downs **63 A4**
Durmitor **22 C2**
Durrës **22 D2**
Dursunbey **23 E7**
D'Urville, Tanjung **37 E5**
D'Urville I. **65 D5**
Dushak **29 F7**
Dushanbe **29 F7**
Dusky Sd. **65 F2**
Düsseldorf **14 C4**
Dutch Harbor **69 C3**
Duyun **35 D5**
Dvina, Severnaya ➔ **28 C5**
Dvinsk = Daugavpils **24 B2**
Dwarka **43 H6**
Dyatlovo = Dzyatlava **17 B7**
Dyer, C. **70 C7**
Dyer Plateau **96 B3**
Dyersburg **81 A9**
Dymer **17 C10**
Dynevor Downs **63 A3**
Dzerzhinsk **24 B5**
Dzhambul = Taraz **29 E8**
Dzhankoy **25 D3**
Dzhardzhan **30 C10**
Dzhezkazgan = Zhezqazghan **29 E7**
Dzhizak = Jizzakh **29 E7**
Działdowo **16 B5**
Dzierżoniów **16 C3**
Dzungaria = Junggar Pendi **34 B3**
Dzungarian Basin = Junggar Pendi **34 B3**
Dzungarian Gate = Alataw Shankou **34 B3**
Dzüünmod **35 B5**
Dzyarzhynsk **17 B8**
Dzyatlava **17 B7**

E

Earnslaw, Mt. **65 F3**
East Bengal **41 E7**
East Beskids = Vychodné Beskydy **17 D5**
East C. = Dezhneva, Mys **31 C16**
East C. **64 B8**
East China Sea **35 C7**
East Falkland **95 G5**
East Kilbride **10 D4**
East London **59 E5**
East Main = Eastmain **71 D6**
East Orange **77 D8**
East St. Louis **75 F9**
East Sea = Japan, Sea of **32 D4**
East Timor ■ **37 F3**
East Toorale **63 B4**
Eastbourne *N.Z.* **65 D6**
Eastbourne *U.K.* **11 F7**
Eastern Ghats **43 N11**
Eastmain **71 D6**
Eastmain ➔ **71 D6**
Eau Claire **75 C9**
Eau Claire, L. à l' **71 D6**
Eberswalde-Finow **15 B7**
Ebetsu **32 B7**
Ebolowa **56 D2**
Ebro ➔ **19 B6**
Eceabat **23 D6**
Ech Chéliff **52 A6**
Echo Bay **68 B8**
Echuca **63 C3**
Ecija **18 D3**
Eclipse Sd. **70 B6**
Ecuador ■ **90 D3**
Ed Dar el Beida = Casablanca **52 B4**
Ed Debba **55 E5**
Ed Dueim **55 F5**
Eddystone Pt. **62 D4**
Édéa **53 H8**
Eden **63 C4**
Eder ➔ **14 C5**
Edessa **23 D4**
Édhessa = Edessa **23 D4**
Edievale **65 F3**
Edinburg **80 F4**
Edinburgh **10 D5**
Edineţ **17 D8**
Edirne **22 D6**
Edithburgh **62 C2**
Edmonton **69 C8**
Edmundston **71 E7**
Edremit **23 E6**
Edremit Körfezi **23 E6**
Edson **69 C8**
Edward ➔ **62 C3**
Edward, L. **57 E5**
Edward VII Land **96 C17**
Edwards Plateau **80 D3**
Eesti = Estonia ■ **24 B2**
Égadi, Isole **21 F4**
Eger = Cheb **16 C1**
Eger **16 E5**
Egio **23 E4**
Eglinton I. **70 B2**
Egmont, C. **64 C5**
Egmont, Mt. = Taranaki, Mt. **64 C6**
Egmont △ **64 C6**
Eğridir **46 C2**
Eğridir Gölü **46 C2**
Egypt ■ **54 C5**
Eibar **19 A4**

Eidsvold 63 A5
Eifel 14 C4
Eigg 10 C3
Eil 49 F4
Eildon, L. 63 C4
Eindhoven 14 C3
Eire = Ireland ■ 11 E3
Eirunepé 91 E5
Eisenach 14 C6
Eisenerz 15 E8
Eivissa 19 C6
Ekaterinburg = Yekaterinburg 29 D7
Eketahuna 64 D6
Ekibastuz 29 D8
El Aaiún 52 C3
El 'Alamein 54 B4
El Asnam = Ech Chéliff 52 A6
El Bayadh 52 B6
El Centro 78 D5
El Cerro 91 G6
El Cuy 95 D3
El Dere 49 G4
El Diviso 90 C3
El Djouf 53 D4
El Dorado *Ark., U.S.A.* 81 C7
El Dorado *Kans., U.S.A.* 80 A5
El Dorado *Venezuela* 90 B6
El Escorial 18 B3
El Faiyûm 54 C5
El Fâsher 55 F4
El Ferrol = Ferrol 18 A1
El Fuerte 84 B3
El Gal 49 E5
El Geneina = Al Junaynah 55 F3
El Gîza 54 C5
El Homeur 52 C6
El Iskandarîya 54 B4
El Jadida 52 B4
El Khârga 54 C5
El Khartûm 55 E5
El Lucero 84 A3
El Maestrazgo 19 B5
El Mahalla el Kubra 54 B5
El Mansûra 54 B5
El Minyâ 54 C5
El Obeid 55 F5
El Odaiya 55 F4
El Oued 52 B7
El Paso 79 E9
El Prat de Llobregat 19 B7
El Puerto de Santa María 18 D2
El Qâhira 54 B5
El Reno 80 B5
El Salvador ■ 85 E7
El Suweis 54 C5
El Tigre 90 B6
El Turbio 95 G2
El Uqsur 54 C5
El Vigía 90 B4
El Wak 57 D8
El Wuz 55 E5
Elat 47 E3
Elâzığ 46 C4
Elba 20 C3
Elbasan 22 D3
Elbe ➔ 14 B5
Elbert, Mt. 79 A9
Elbeuf 12 B4
Elbing = Elbląg 16 A4
Elbląg 16 A4
Elbrus 25 E5
Elburz Mts. = Alborz, Reshteh-ye Kühhā-ye 44 B3
Elche 19 C5
Elda 19 C5
Elde ➔ 15 B6
Eldoret 57 D7
Elefantes ➔ 59 C6
Elektrostal 24 B4
Elephant I. 96 A4
Eleuthera 86 A4
Elgin *U.K.* 10 C5
Elgin *U.S.A.* 76 C1
Elgon, Mt. 57 D6
Eliase 37 F4
Elista 25 D5
Elizabeth *Australia* 62 B2
Elizabeth *U.S.A.* 77 D8
Elizabeth City 83 A9
Elizabethton 83 A6
Elk 16 B6
Elkhart 76 D3
Elkhovo 22 C6
Elko 72 F6
Ellas = Greece ■ 23 E4
Ellef Ringnes I. 70 B3
Ellery, Mt. 63 C4
Ellesmere, L. 65 G5
Ellesmere I. 70 B6
Ellice Is. = Tuvalu ■ 64 K12
Elliot Lake 71 E5
Elliston 62 B1
Ellore = Eluru 40 J3
Ellsworth Land 96 B2
Ellsworth Mts. 96 B2
Elmore 63 C3
Elmshorn 14 B5
Eltham 64 C6
Eluru 40 J3
Elvas 18 C2
Elx = Elche 19 C5
Ely 11 E7
eMalahleni 59 D5
Emämrüd 44 B3
Embarcación 94 A4
Embetsu 32 A7
Embi 29 E6
Embi ➔ 29 E6
Embrun 13 D7
Emden 14 B4
Emet 23 E7
Emi Koussi 55 E2
Emine, Nos 22 C6
Emissi, Tarso 54 D2
Emmen 14 B4
Empalme 84 B2
Empangeni 59 D6
Empedrado 94 B5
Empty Quarter = Rub' al Khālī 48 D4
Ems ➔ 14 B4
En Nahud 55 F4
Enare = Inarijärvi 8 B11
Enarotali 37 E5
Encanto, C. 36 A2
Encarnación 94 B5
Encounter B. 62 C2
Ende 37 F2
Enderby Land 96 A9
Enewetak Atoll 64 H11
Enez 23 D6
Engaño, C. 36 A2
Engaru 32 A8
Engels 24 C6
Enggano 39 F2
England □ 11 E6
Englewood 74 F2
English Bazar = Ingraj Bazar 40 E7
English Channel 11 F5
Enid 80 A5
Enna 21 F5
Ennedi 55 E3
Enngonia 63 A4
Ennis 11 E2
Enniskillen 11 D3
Enns ➔ 15 D8
Enschede 14 B4
Ensenada 84 A1
Entebbe 57 D6
Entre Ríos □ 94 C5
Entroncamento 18 C1
Enugu 53 G7
Eólie, Îs. 21 E5
Épernay 13 B5
Ephesus 23 F6
Épinal 13 B7
Equatorial Guinea ■ 56 D1
Er Rachidia 52 B5
Er Rahad 55 F5
Er Rif 52 A5
Erāwadī Myit = Irrawaddy ➔ 41 K10
Erāwadī Myitwanya = Irrawaddy, Mouths of the 41 K10
Erbil = Arbīl 46 C6
Ercıyaş Dağı 46 C3
Érd 16 E4
Erdek 23 D6
Erebus, Mt. 96 B15
Erechim 94 B6
Ereğli *Konya, Turkey* 46 C3
Ereğli *Zonguldak, Turkey* 25 E3
Eresma ➔ 18 B3
Erfurt 15 C6
Ergani 46 C4
Érice 21 E4
Erie 77 C5
Erie, L. 76 C5
Erigavo 49 E4
Erimanthos 23 F3
Erimo-misaki 32 C8
Eritrea ■ 49 E2
Erlangen 15 D6
Ermenek 46 C3
Erne, Lower L. 11 D3
Erode 43 P10
Eromanga 63 A3
Erramala Hills 43 M11
Ertis = Irtysh ➔ 28 C7
Erzgebirge 15 C7
Erzincan 25 F4
Erzurum 25 F5
Es Sahrā' Esh Sharqīya 54 C5
Es Sînâ' 54 C5
Esan-Misaki 32 C7
Esashi *Hokkaidō, Japan* 32 A8
Esashi *Hokkaidō, Japan* 32 C7
Esbjerg 9 D7
Esbo = Espoo 9 C10
Esch-sur-Alzette 13 B6
Escuinapa de Hidalgo 84 C3
Esenguly 29 F6
Eṣfahān 44 C2
Esh Sham = Dimashq 46 D4
Esil = Ishim ➔ 29 D8
Esker 71 D7
Eskilstuna 9 D9
Eskimo Point = Arviat 68 B10
Eskişehir 25 F3
Esla ➔ 18 B2
Eslāmābād-e Gharb 46 D6
Eşme 23 E7
Esmeraldas 90 C3
España = Spain ■ 18 C4
Esperance 60 G3
Espichel, C. 18 C1
Espinazo, Sierra del = Espinhaço, Serra do 93 F5
Espinhaço, Serra do 93 F5
Espírito Santo □ 93 G5
Espíritu Santo 64 L11
Espoo 9 C10
Esquel 95 E2
Esquina 94 C5
Essaouira 52 B4
Essen 14 C4
Essequibo ➔ 90 B7
Esslingen 14 D5
Estados, I. de Los 95 G4
Estância 93 E6
Estevan 69 D9
Estonia ■ 24 B2
Estrela, Serra da 18 B2
Estremoz 18 C2
Estrondo, Serra do 92 D4
Esztergom 16 E4
Etadunna 62 A2
Étampes 12 B5
Etawah 42 F11
eThekwini = Durban 59 D6
Ethiopia ■ 49 F2
Ethiopian Highlands 49 F2
Etna 21 F5
Etosha Pan 58 B3
Euboea = Evia 23 E5
Eucumbene, L. 63 C4
Eufaula 82 D5
Eugene 72 E2
Eugowra 63 B4

Eulo **63 A4**
Euphrates = Furāt, Nahr al ➔ **47 E6**
Eureka *Canada* **70 B5**
Eureka *U.S.A.* **72 F1**
Euroa **63 C4**
Europa, Île **59 C8**
Europa, Picos de **18 A3**
Europa, Pt. **18 D3**
Evans Head **63 A5**
Evanston **76 C2**
Evansville **76 F2**
Everard, L. **62 B1**
Everest, Mt. **40 C6**
Everett **72 C2**
Everglades △ **83 G7**
Evia **23 E5**
Évora **18 C2**
Évreux **12 B4**
Evros ➔ **22 D6**
Évry **12 B5**
Évvoia = Evia **23 E5**
Ewo **56 E2**
Exaltación **91 F5**
Exeter **11 F5**
Exmoor **11 F5**
Exmouth **11 F5**
Extremadura □ **18 C2**
Eyasi, L. **57 E6**
Eyre (North), L. **62 A2**
Eyre (South), L. **62 A2**
Eyre, L. **60 F6**
Eyre Mts. **65 F3**
Eyre Pen. **62 B2**
Ezine **23 E6**

F

F.Y.R.O.M. = Macedonia ■ **22 D3**
Fabriano **20 C4**
Fada **55 E3**
Fada-n-Gourma **53 F6**
Faddeyevskiy, Ostrov **31 B12**
Faenza **20 B3**
Færoe Is. = Føroyar ⧄ **6 C4**
Făgăras **17 F7**
Fagnano, L. **95 G3**
Fahraj **45 D4**
Fahüd **44 F4**
Fair Isle **10 B6**
Fairbanks **69 B5**
Fairfield *Ala., U.S.A.* **82 C4**
Fairfield *Calif., U.S.A.* **72 G2**
Fairlie **65 F4**
Fairweather, Mt. **69 C6**
Faisalabad **42 D8**
Faizabad **40 D4**
Fakfak **37 E4**
Falaise **12 B3**
Falam **41 F9**
Falconara Maríttima **20 C4**
Falcone, C. del **20 D2**
Faleshty = Fălești **17 E8**
Fălești **17 E8**
Falkland Is. ⧄ **95 G5**
Falkland Sd. **95 G5**
Fall River **77 D10**
Falmouth **11 F4**
Fālticeni **17 E8**
Falun **9 C9**
Famagusta **46 D3**
Fano **20 C4**
Fao = Al Fāw **47 E7**
Faradje **57 D5**
Farafangana **59 C9**
Farāh **42 C3**
Farāh □ **42 C3**
Faranah **53 F3**
Farasān, Jazā'ir **49 D3**
Farasan Is. = Farasān, Jazā'ir **49 D3**
Fareham **11 F6**
Farewell, C. **64 D5**
Farghona **29 E8**
Fargo **74 B6**
Farīmān **45 C4**
Farina **62 B2**
Faro *Brazil* **92 C2**
Faro *Portugal* **18 D2**
Farrāshband **44 D3**
Farrukhabad-cum-Fatehgarh **42 F11**
Fārs □ **44 D3**
Farsala **23 E4**
Fartak, Rās **47 E3**
Fāryāb □ **45 B6**
Fasā **44 D3**
Fasano **21 D6**
Fastiv **17 C9**
Fastov = Fastiv **17 C9**
Fatagar, Tanjung **37 E4**
Fatehgarh **42 F11**
Fatehpur *Raj., India* **42 F9**
Fatehpur *Ut. P., India* **40 E3**
Favara **21 F4**
Favignana **21 F4**
Faxaflói **8 C1**
Faya-Largeau **55 E2**
Fayd **47 F5**
Fayetteville *Ark., U.S.A.* **81 A6**
Fayetteville *N.C., U.S.A.* **83 B8**
Fazilka **42 D9**
Fdérik **52 D3**
Feather ➔ **72 G3**
Featherston **65 D6**
Fécamp **12 B4**
Fehmarn **15 A6**
Feilding **64 D6**
Feira de Santana **93 E6**
Feldkirch **14 E5**
Felipe Carrillo Puerto **85 D7**
Felixstowe **11 F7**
Fenoarivo Atsinanana **59 B9**
Fenyang **35 C6**
Feodosiya **25 D4**
Ferdows **44 C4**
Ferfer **49 F4**
Fergana = Farghona **29 E8**
Fermo **20 C4**
Fermont **71 D7**
Fernando de Noronha **92 C7**
Fernando Póo = Bioko **53 H7**
Ferozepore = Firozpur **42 D9**
Ferrara **20 B3**
Ferreñafe **91 E3**
Ferret, C. **12 D3**
Ferrol **18 A1**
Fès **52 B5**
Feteşti **22 B6**
Fetlar **10 A6**
Feuilles ➔ **70 D6**
Fez = Fès **52 B5**
Fezzan **54 C2**
Fianarantsoa **59 C9**
Fier **23 D2**
Figeac **12 D5**
Figueira da Foz **18 B1**
Figueres **19 A7**
Figuig **52 B5**
Fiji ■ **64 L12**
Filiatra **23 F3**
Filyos Cayi ➔ **46 B3**
Fíngoè **59 A6**
Finike **46 C2**
Finisterre, C. = Fisterra, C. **18 A1**
Finland ■ **8 C11**
Finland, G. of **9 D11**
Finlay ➔ **68 C7**
Finley **63 C4**
Finniss, C. **62 B1**
Fiora ➔ **20 C3**
Fiordland △ **65 F2**
Firat = Furāt, Nahr al ➔ **47 E6**
Firenze **20 C3**
Firozabad **42 F11**
Firozpur **42 D9**
Fīrūzābād **44 D3**
Fīrūzkūh **44 C3**
Fish ➔ **58 D3**
Fishguard **11 E4**
Fisterra, C. **18 A1**
Fitz Roy **95 F3**
Fiume = Rijeka **20 B5**
Fizi **57 E5**
Flagstaff **79 C7**
Flåm **8 C7**
Flaming Gorge Res. **73 F9**
Flamingo, Teluk **37 F5**
Flanders = Flandre **14 C2**
Flandre **14 C2**
Flathead L. **73 C7**
Flattery, C. **72 B1**
Flensburg **14 A5**
Flers **12 B3**
Flesko, Tanjung **37 D2**
Flin Flon **69 C9**
Flinders ➔ **61 D7**
Flinders I. **62 C4**
Flinders Ranges **62 B2**
Flint **76 C4**
Flint I. **65 L15**
Flinton **63 A4**
Florence = Firenze **20 C3**
Florence *Ala., U.S.A.* **82 B4**
Florence *S.C., U.S.A.* **83 B8**
Florence, L. **62 A2**
Flores **37 F2**
Flores Sea **37 F2**
Floreşti **17 E9**
Floriano **92 D5**
Florianópolis **94 B7**
Florida **94 C5**
Florida □ **83 F6**
Florida, Straits of **86 B3**
Florina **23 D3**
Florø **8 C7**
Fluk **37 E3**
Flushing = Vlissingen **14 C2**
Fly ➔ **61 B7**
Flying Fish, C. **96 B1**
Foça **23 E6**
Focşani **17 F8**
Fóggia **20 D5**
Föhr **14 A5**
Foix **12 E4**
Folda **8 B8**
Foligno **20 C4**
Folkestone **11 F7**
Fond du Lac **75 D10**
Fondi **20 D4**
Fongafale **64 K12**
Fonsagrada = A Fonsagrada **18 A2**
Fonseca, G. de **85 E7**
Fontainebleau **13 B5**
Fonte Boa **90 D5**
Fontenay-le-Comte **12 C3**
Foochow = Fuzhou **35 D6**
Forbes **63 B4**
Fords Bridge **63 A4**
Forestier Pen. **62 D4**
Forfar **10 C5**
Forlì **20 B4**
Formentera **19 C6**
Formentor, C. de **19 C7**
Former Yugoslav Republic of Macedonia = Macedonia ■ **22 D3**
Fórmia **20 D4**
Formosa = Taiwan ■ **35 D7**
Formosa **94 B5**
Formosa, Serra **93 E3**
Formosa B. = Ungwana B. **57 E8**
Føroyar ⧄ **6 C4**
Forsayth **61 D7**
Forst **15 C8**
Fort Albany **71 D5**
Fort Collins **74 E2**
Fort Dauphin = Taolanaro **59 D9**
Fort-de-France **87 D7**
Fort Dodge **75 D7**
Fort Franklin = Déline **68 B7**
Fort George = Chisasibi **71 D6**
Fort Good Hope **68 B7**
Fort Lauderdale **83 F7**
Fort Liard **68 B7**
Fort Macleod **69 D8**
Fort McPherson **68 B6**

Fort Myers **83 F7**
Fort Norman = Tulita **68 B7**
Fort Peck L. **73 C10**
Fort Pierce **83 F7**
Fort Providence **68 B8**
Fort Resolution **68 B8**
Fort Rupert = Waskaganish **71 D6**
Fort Scott **81 A6**
Fort Shevchenko **29 E6**
Fort Simpson **68 B7**
Fort Smith *Canada* **68 B8**
Fort Smith *U.S.A.* **81 B6**
Fort Walton Beach **82 D4**
Fort Wayne **76 D3**
Fort William **10 C4**
Fort Worth **80 C5**
Fort Yukon **69 B5**
Fortaleza **92 C6**
Forür **44 E3**
Foshan **35 D6**
Fossano **13 D7**
Fougères **12 B3**
Foula **10 A5**
Fourni **23 F6**
Fouta Djallon **53 F3**
Foveaux Str. **65 G3**
Foxe Basin **70 C6**
Foxe Chan. **70 C5**
Foxe Pen. **70 C6**
Foxton **64 D6**
Foz do Iguaçu **94 B6**
Franca **93 G4**
Francavilla Fontana **21 D6**
France ■ **13 C5**
Frances **62 C3**
Franceville **56 E2**
Franche-Comté □ **13 C6**
Francistown **59 C5**
Frankfurt *Brandenburg, Germany* **15 B8**
Frankfurt *Hessen, Germany* **14 C5**
Fränkische Alb **15 D6**
Franklin B. **68 B7**
Franklin I. **96 B15**
Franklin Mts. **68 B7**
Franklin Str. **68 A10**
Frankston **63 C4**
Frantsa Iosifa, Zemlya **28 A6**
Franz Josef Land = Frantsa Iosifa, Zemlya **28 A6**
Fraser ➔ **69 D7**
Fraser I. **63 A5**
Fraserburgh **10 C5**
Fray Bentos **94 C5**
Fredericksburg **77 E7**
Fredericton **71 E7**
Frederikshavn **9 D8**
Fredrikstad **9 D8**
Free State □ **59 D5**
Freeport *Bahamas* **86 A4**
Freeport *U.S.A.* **75 D10**
Freetown **53 G3**
Fregenal de la Sierra **18 C2**
Freiburg **14 E4**
Freire **95 D2**
Freising **15 D6**
Freistadt **15 D8**
Fréjus **13 E7**
Fremont **78 B2**
French Guiana ⧄ **92 B3**
French Polynesia ⧄ **65 M16**
Fresco ➔ **92 D3**
Freshfield, C. **96 A14**
Fresnillo **84 C4**
Fresno **78 B3**
Freycinet Pen. **62 D4**
Fria, C. **58 B2**
Frías **94 B3**
Friedrichshafen **14 E5**
Frobisher B. **70 C7**
Frobisher Bay = Iqaluit **70 C7**
Frome ➔ **62 A2**
Frome, L. **62 B2**
Frosinone **20 D4**
Frunze = Bishkek **29 E8**
Frutal **93 F4**
Frýdek-Místek **16 D4**
Fuchou = Fuzhou **35 D6**
Fuchü **33 F3**
Fuengirola **18 D3**
Fuentes de Oñoro **18 B2**
Fuerte ➔ **84 B3**
Fuerte Olimpo **91 H7**
Fuerteventura **52 C3**
Fuhai **34 B3**
Fuji **33 F6**
Fuji-San **33 F6**
Fujian □ **35 D6**
Fujiyama, Mt. = Fuji-San **33 F6**
Fukien = Fujian □ **35 D6**
Fukuchiyama **33 F4**
Fukue-Shima **33 G1**
Fukui **33 E5**
Fukuoka **33 G2**
Fukushima **33 E7**
Fukuyama **33 F3**
Fulda **14 C5**
Fulda ➔ **14 C5**
Funabashi **33 F7**
Funafuti = Fongafale **64 K12**
Funchal **52 B2**
Fundación **90 A4**
Fundão **18 B2**
Fundy, B. of **71 E7**
Funtua **53 F7**
Furāt, Nahr al ➔ **47 E6**
Furneaux Group **62 D4**
Fürstenwalde **15 B8**
Fürth **14 D6**
Furukawa **32 D7**
Fury and Hecla Str. **70 C5**
Fusagasuga **90 C4**
Fushun **35 B7**
Futuna **64 L12**
Fuxin **35 B7**
Fuyuan **35 B8**
Fuzhou **35 D6**
Fyn **9 D8**

G

Gabela **56 G2**
Gabès **54 B1**
Gabès, G. de **54 B1**
Gabon ■ **56 E2**
Gaborone **59 C5**
Gabrovo **22 C5**
Gachsārān **44 D2**
Gadag **43 M9**
Gadarwara **43 H11**
Gadhada **43 J7**
Gadsden **82 B4**
Gadwal **43 L10**
Gafsa **52 B7**
Gagnoa **53 G4**
Gagnon **71 D7**
Gaillimh = Galway **11 E2**
Gainesville *Fla., U.S.A.* **83 E6**
Gainesville *Ga., U.S.A.* **83 B6**
Gainesville *Tex., U.S.A.* **80 C5**
Gairdner, L. **62 B2**
Galashiels **10 D5**
Galaţi **17 F9**
Galatina **21 D7**
Galcaio **49 F4**
Galdhøpiggen **8 C7**
Galela **37 D3**
Galesburg **75 E9**
Galich **24 B5**
Galicia □ **18 A2**
Galilee, Sea of = Yam Kinneret **46 D3**
Gállego ➔ **19 B5**
Gallegos ➔ **95 G3**
Gallinas, Pta. **90 A4**
Gallipoli = Gelibolu **23 D6**
Gallipoli **21 D6**
Gällivare **8 B10**
Galloway, Mull of **11 D4**
Galveston **81 E6**
Gálvez **94 C4**
Galway **11 E2**
Galway B. **11 E2**
Gambia ■ **53 F2**
Gambia ➔ **53 F2**
Gambier, Îs. **65 M17**
Gambier Is. **62 C2**
Gamboma **56 E3**
Gan Jiang ➔ **35 D6**
Ganāveh **44 D2**
Gäncä **25 E6**
Gand = Gent **14 C2**
Ganda **58 A2**
Gandak ➔ **40 E5**
Gandava **42 E5**
Gander **71 E8**
Gandhi Sagar **43 G9**
Gandía **19 C5**
Ganedidalem = Gani **37 E3**
Ganga ➔ **41 F8**
Ganganagar **42 E8**
Gangaw **41 F10**
Gangdisê Shan **40 B3**
Ganges = Ganga ➔ **41 F8**
Gangneung **35 C7**
Gangtok **41 D7**
Gani **37 E3**
Gansu □ **34 C5**
Ganta **53 G4**
Gantheaume, C. **62 C2**
Gantsevichi = Hantsavichy **17 B8**
Ganyem = Genyem **37 E6**
Ganzhou **35 D6**
Gaoua **53 F5**
Gaoual **53 F3**
Gaoxiong = Kaohsiung **35 D7**
Gap **13 D7**
Gar **34 C2**
Garabogazköl Aylagy **29 E6**
Garagum **29 F6**
Garanhuns **92 D6**
Garda, L. di **20 B3**
Garden City **80 A3**
Gardēz **42 C6**
Gardo **49 F4**
Gargano, Mte. **20 D5**
Garigliano ➔ **20 D4**
Garland **73 F7**
Garm **29 F8**
Garmisch-Partenkirchen **14 E6**
Garmsār **44 C3**
Garoe **49 F4**
Garonne ➔ **12 D3**
Garoowe = Garoe **49 F4**
Garoua **55 G1**
Garrison Res. = Sakakawea, L. **74 B4**
Garry, L. **68 B9**
Garvie Mts. **65 F3**
Garwa = Garoua **55 G1**
Gary **76 D2**
Garzê **34 C5**
Garzón **90 C3**
Gasan Kuli = Esenguly **29 F6**
Gascogne **12 E4**
Gascogne, G. de **12 D2**
Gascony = Gascogne **12 E4**
Gaspé **71 E7**
Gaspé, C. **71 E7**
Gaspé Pen. = Gaspésie, Pén. de la **71 E7**
Gaspésie, Pén. de la **71 E7**
Gasteiz = Vitoria-Gasteiz **19 A4**
Gastonia **83 B7**
Gastre **95 E3**
Gata, C. de **19 D4**
Gata, Sierra de **18 B2**
Gateshead **11 D6**
Gauhati = Guwahati **41 D8**
Gavāter **45 E5**
Gavdos **23 G5**
Gâvle **9 C9**
Gawilgarh Hills **43 J10**
Gawler **62 B2**
Gaxun Nur **34 B5**
Gaya *India* **40 E5**
Gaya *Niger* **53 F6**

Gayndah 63 A5
Gaysin = Haysyn 17 D9
Gayvoron = Hayvoron 17 D9
Gaza 47 E3
Gaza Strip ■ 47 E3
Gaziantep 46 C4
Gazimağosa = Famagusta 46 D3
Gazli 29 E7
Gcuwa 59 E5
Gdańsk 16 A4
Gdańska, Zatoka 16 A4
Gdov 24 B2
Gdynia 16 A4
Gebe 37 D3
Gebze 22 D7
Gedaref 55 F6
Gediz ➔ 23 E6
Gedser 9 E8
Geelong 63 C3
Geesthacht 14 B6
Geidam 55 F1
Gejiu 34 D5
Gela 21 F5
Gelibolu 23 D6
Gelsenkirchen 14 C4
Gemena 56 D3
Gemerek 46 C4
Gemlik 23 D7
General Acha 94 D4
General Alvear *B. Aires, Argentina* 94 D5
General Alvear *Mendoza, Argentina* 94 D3
General Belgrano 94 D5
General Juan Madariaga 94 D5
General La Madrid 94 D4
General MacArthur 36 B3
General Pico 94 D4
General Pinedo 94 B4
General Santos 36 C3
General Villegas 94 D4
Geneva = Genève 14 E4
Geneva, L. = Léman, L. 13 C7
Genève 14 E4
Genil ➔ 18 D3
Gennargentu, Mti. del 21 D2
Genoa = Génova 13 D8
Genoa 63 C4
Génova 13 D8
Génova, G. di 20 C2
Gent 14 C2
Genyem 37 E6
Georga, Zemlya 28 A5
George 58 E4
George ➔ 70 D7
George, L. *N.S.W., Australia* 63 C4
George, L. *S. Austral., Australia* 62 C3
George River = Kangiqsualujjuaq 70 D7
George Sound 65 F2
George Town *Cayman Is.* 86 C3
George Town *Malaysia* 38 C2
George V Land 96 A14
George VI Sound 96 B3
Georgetown = Janjanbureh 53 F3
Georgetown 90 B7
Georgia □ 83 C6
Georgia ■ 25 E5
Georgian B. 71 E5
Georgiyevsk 25 E5
Gera 15 C7
Geral de Goiás, Serra 93 E4
Geraldton 60 F1
Gerede 46 B3
Gereshk 42 D4
Germany ■ 14 C6
Germiston 59 D5
Gernika-Lumo 19 A4
Gerona = Girona 19 B7
Geser 37 E4
Getafe 18 B4
Gettysburg 77 E7
Getxo 19 A4
Getz Ice Shelf 96 B18
Ghaghara ➔ 40 E5
Ghana ■ 53 G5
Ghanzi 58 C4
Ghardaïa 52 B6
Gharyān 54 B1
Ghat 54 D1
Ghats, Eastern 43 N11
Ghats, Western 43 N9
Ghawdex = Gozo 21 F5
Ghayl 47 G6
Ghazal, Bahr el ➔ *Chad* 55 F2
Ghazāl, Bahr el ➔ *Sudan* 55 G5
Ghaziabad 42 E10
Ghazipur 40 E4
Ghazni 42 C6
Ghazni □ 42 C6
Ghent = Gent 14 C2
Gheorghe Gheorghiu-Dej = Onești 17 E8
Ghowr □ 42 C4
Ghugus 43 K11
Ghūrīān 42 B2
Gia Lai = Plei Ku 38 B3
Gian 36 C3
Gianitsa 23 D4
Giarabub = Al Jaghbūb 54 C3
Giarre 21 F5
Gibeon 58 D3
Gibraltar ⊠ 18 D3
Gibraltar, Str. of 18 E3
Gibson Desert 60 E4
Giebnegáisi = Kebnekaise 8 B9
Giessen 14 C5
Gifu 33 F5
Gíglio 20 C3
Gijón 18 A3
Gila ➔ 78 D5
Gilān □ 46 C7
Gilbert Is. 64 J12
Gilgandra 63 B4
Gilgit 42 B9
Gilles, L. 62 B2
Gilmore 63 C4
Gin Gin 63 A5
Ginir 49 F3
Giona, Oros 23 E4
Giresun 25 E4
Girga 54 C5
Giridih 40 E6
Girne = Kyrenia 46 D3
Giron = Kiruna 8 B10
Girona 19 B7
Gironde ➔ 12 D3
Girvan 10 D4
Gisborne 64 C8
Gisenyi 57 E5
Gitega 57 E5
Githio 23 F4
Giuba ➔ 49 G3
Giurgiu 22 C5
Giza = El Gīza 54 C5
Gizab 42 C4
Giżycko 16 A5
Gjirokastër 23 D3
Gjoa Haven 68 B10
Glace Bay 71 E8
Gladstone *Queens., Australia* 61 E9
Gladstone *S. Austral., Australia* 62 B2
Glåma = Glomma ➔ 9 C8
Glasgow 10 D4
Glazov 28 D6
Gleiwitz = Gliwice 16 C4
Glen Canyon ⌓ 79 B7
Glen Innes 63 A5
Glendale 78 C3
Glenelg ➔ 62 C3
Glenmorgan 63 A4
Glenorchy 62 D4
Glenreagh 63 B5
Glenrothes 10 C5
Glens Falls 77 C9
Gliwice 16 C4
Głogów 16 C3
Glomma ➔ 9 C8
Glorieuses, Îs. 59 A9
Gloucester *Australia* 63 B5
Gloucester *U.K.* 11 F5
Glusk 17 B9
Gmünd 15 D8
Gmunden 15 E7
Gniezno 16 B3
Goa 43 M8
Goa □ 43 M8
Goalen Hd. 63 C5
Goalpara 41 D8
Goba 49 F2
Gobabis 58 C3
Gobi 35 B6
Godavari ➔ 40 J4
Godavari Pt. 40 J4
Godhra 43 H8
Gods ➔ 69 C10
Gods L. 69 C10
Godthåb = Nuuk 66 C14
Goeie Hoop, Kaap die = Good Hope, C. of 58 E3
Gogra = Ghaghara ➔ 40 E5
Goiânia 93 F4
Goiás 93 F3
Goiás □ 93 E4
Goio-Erê 94 A6
Gojra 42 D8
Gökçeada 23 D5
Gökova Körfezi 23 F6
Gokteik 41 F11
Gold Coast 63 A5
Golden B. 64 D5
Golden Gate 72 H2
Goldsboro 83 B9
Goleniów 16 B2
Golfo Aranci 20 D2
Golspie 10 C5
Goma 57 E5
Gomel = Homyel 17 B10
Gomera 52 C2
Gómez Palacio 84 B4
Gomogomo 37 F4
Gomoh 40 F6
Gompa = Ganta 53 G4
Gonābād 44 C4
Gonaïves 87 C5
Gonbad-e Kāvūs 44 B3
Gonda 40 D3
Gonder 55 F6
Gönen 23 D6
Gonghe 34 C5
Gongolgon 63 B4
Good Hope, C. of 58 E3
Goodooga 63 A4
Goolgowi 63 B4
Goombalie 63 A4
Goondiwindi 63 A5
Gooray 63 A5
Gop 43 H6
Göppingen 14 D5
Gorakhpur 40 D4
Goražde 20 C7
Gordon ➔ 62 D4
Gore *Australia* 63 A5
Gore *Ethiopia* 55 G6
Gore *N.Z.* 65 G3
Gorgān 44 B3
Gorgona, I. 90 C3
Gorizia 20 B4
Gorkiy = Nizhniy Novgorod 24 B5
Gorkovskoye Vdkhr. 24 B5
Görlitz 15 C8
Gorlovka = Horlivka 25 D4
Gorna Dzhumayo = Blagoevgrad 22 C4
Gorna Oryakhovitsa 22 C5
Gorno-Altay □ 29 D9
Gorno-Altaysk 29 D9
Gorno Slinkino = Gornopravdinsk 29 C8
Gornopravdinsk 29 C8
Gornyy 32 A3
Gorodenka = Horodenka 17 D7
Gorodok = Horodok 17 D6
Gorokhov = Horokhiv 17 C7
Gorontalo 37 D2
Gorzów Wielkopolski 16 B2
Gosford 63 B5
Goshogawara 32 C7

Goslar **14 C6**
Gospič **20 B5**
Göta kanal **9 D9**
Göteborg **9 D8**
Gotha **14 C6**
Gothenburg = Göteborg **9 D8**
Gotland **9 D9**
Gotō-Rettō **33 G1**
Göttingen **14 C5**
Gottwaldov = Zlín **16 D3**
Gouda **14 B3**
Gouin, Rés. **71 E6**
Goulburn **63 B4**
Gouro **55 E2**
Governador Valadares **93 F5**
Goya **94 B5**
Goyder Lagoon **62 A2**
Goyllarisquisga **91 F3**
Goz Beïda **55 F3**
Gozo **21 F5**
Graaff-Reinet **58 E4**
Gračac **20 B5**
Gracias a Dios, C. **86 D3**
Grado **18 A2**
Gradule **63 A4**
Grafton **63 A5**
Graham Bell, Ostrov = Greem-Bell, Ostrov **28 A7**
Graham Land **96 A3**
Grahamstown **59 E5**
Grajaú **92 D4**
Grajaú ➔ **92 C5**
Grampian Highlands = Grampian Mts. **10 C4**
Grampian Mts. **10 C4**
Grampians, The **62 C3**
Gran Canaria **52 C2**
Gran Chaco **94 B4**
Gran Paradiso **13 D7**
Gran Sasso d'Itália **20 C4**
Granada *Nic.* **85 E7**
Granada *Spain* **18 D4**
Granby **71 E6**
Grand Bahama I. **86 A4**
Grand Bassam **53 G5**
Grand Canyon **79 B6**
Grand Cayman **86 C3**
Grand Coulee Dam **72 C4**
Grand Falls **71 E7**
Grand Falls-Windsor **71 E8**
Grand Forks **74 B6**
Grand Island **74 E5**
Grand Rapids *Canada* **69 C10**
Grand Rapids *U.S.A.* **76 C3**
Grand St-Bernard, Col du **13 D7**
Grand Teton **73 E8**
Grande ➔ *Bolivia* **91 G6**
Grande ➔ *Bahia, Brazil* **93 E5**
Grande ➔ *Minas Gerais, Brazil* **93 G3**
Grande, B. **95 G3**
Grande, Rio ➔ **84 B5**
Grande Baleine, R. de la ➔ **71 D6**
Granite City **75 F9**
Granity **65 D4**
Granja **92 C5**
Granollers **19 B7**
Grantham **11 E6**
Granville **12 B3**
Grasse **13 E7**
Grassmere **62 B3**
Graulhet **12 E4**
's-Gravenhage **14 B3**
Gravesend **63 A5**
Graz **15 E8**
Great Abaco I. = Abaco I. **86 A4**
Great Australian Bight **60 G4**
Great Barrier I. **64 B6**
Great Barrier Reef **61 D8**
Great Basin **72 G5**
Great Bear ➔ **68 B7**
Great Bear L. **68 B7**
Great Belt = Store Bælt **9 D8**
Great Divide, The = Great Dividing Ra. **61 E8**
Great Dividing Ra. **61 E8**
Great Falls **73 C8**
Great Inagua I. **86 B5**
Great Indian Desert = Thar Desert **42 F7**
Great Karoo **58 E4**
Great Khingan Mts. = Da Hinggan Ling **35 B7**
Great Lake **62 D4**
Great Ouse ➔ **11 E7**
Great Ruaha ➔ **57 F7**
Great Saint Bernard Pass = Grand St-Bernard, Col du **13 D7**
Great Salt Desert = Kavīr, Dasht-e **44 C3**
Great Salt L. **73 F7**
Great Salt Lake Desert **73 F7**
Great Sandy Desert **60 E3**
Great Sangi = Sangihe, Pulau **37 D3**
Great Slave L. **68 B8**
Great Smoky Mts. △ **83 B6**
Great Victoria Desert **60 F4**
Great Wall **35 C5**
Great Yarmouth **11 E7**
Great Zab = Zāb al Kabīr ➔ **46 C5**
Greater Antilles **86 C5**
Greater Sudbury = Sudbury **71 E5**
Greater Sunda Is. **39 F4**
Gredos, Sierra de **18 B3**
Greece ■ **23 E4**
Greeley **74 E2**
Greely Fd. **70 A5**
Greem-Bell, Ostrov **28 A7**
Green ➔ **79 A8**
Green Bay **76 B2**
Green C. **63 C5**
Greenland ⊠ **66 C9**
Greenock **10 D4**
Greensboro **83 A8**
Greenville *Ala., U.S.A.* **82 D4**
Greenville *Miss., U.S.A.* **81 C8**
Greenville *N.C., U.S.A.* **83 B9**
Greenville *S.C., U.S.A.* **83 B6**
Greenwood *Miss., U.S.A.* **81 C8**
Greenwood *S.C., U.S.A.* **83 B6**
Gregory, L. **62 A2**
Greifswald **15 A7**
Greiz **15 C7**
Gremikha **28 C4**
Grenada ■ **87 D7**
Grenfell **63 B4**
Grenoble **13 D6**
Grey ➔ **65 E4**
Grey Ra. **63 A3**
Greymouth **65 E4**
Greytown **65 D6**
Griffin **83 C5**
Griffith **63 B4**
Grimari **55 G3**
Grimaylov = Hrymayliv **17 D8**
Grimsby **11 E6**
Gris-Nez, C. **12 A4**
Grise Fiord **70 B5**
Grodno = Hrodna **17 B6**
Grodzyanka = Hrodzyanka **17 B9**
Grójec **16 C5**
Groningen **14 B4**
Grootfontein **58 B3**
Grosser Arber **15 D7**
Grosseto **20 C3**
Grossglockner **15 E7**
Groznyy **25 E6**
Grudziądz **16 B4**
Gryazi **24 C4**
Gryazovets **28 D5**
Gua **40 F5**
Guadalajara *Mexico* **84 C4**
Guadalajara *Spain* **18 B4**
Guadalcanal **64 K11**
Guadalete ➔ **18 D2**
Guadalquivir ➔ **18 D2**
Guadalupe = Guadeloupe ⊠ **87 C7**
Guadalupe, Sierra de **18 C3**
Guadarrama, Sierra de **18 B4**
Guadeloupe ⊠ **87 C7**
Guadiana ➔ **18 D2**
Guadix **18 D4**
Guafo, Boca del **95 E2**
Guaira **94 A6**
Guaitecas, Is. **95 E2**
Guajará-Mirim **91 F5**
Guajira, Pen. de la **90 A4**
Gualeguaychú **94 C5**
Guam ⊠ **64 H9**
Guamúchil **84 B3**
Guanahani = San Salvador I. **86 B5**
Guanajuato **84 C4**
Guandacol **94 B3**
Guane **86 B3**
Guangdong □ **35 D6**
Guangxi Zhuangzu Zizhiqu □ **35 D5**
Guangzhou **35 D6**
Guanipa ➔ **90 B6**
Guantánamo **86 B4**
Guantánamo B. **86 B5**
Guaporé ➔ **91 F5**
Guaqui **91 G5**
Guarapuava **94 B6**
Guarda **18 B2**
Guardafui, C. = Asir, Ras **49 E5**
Guasdualito **90 B4**
Guatemala **85 E6**
Guatemala ■ **85 D6**
Guaviare ➔ **90 C5**
Guaxupé **93 G4**
Guayaquil **90 D3**
Guayaquil, G. de **90 D2**
Guaymas **84 B2**
Guddu Barrage **42 E6**
Gudur **43 M11**
Guecho = Getxo **19 A4**
Guelph **76 C5**
Guéret **12 C4**
Guernica = Gernika-Lumo **19 A4**
Guernsey **11 G5**
Guidónia-Montecélio **20 C4**
Guijá **59 C6**
Guildford **11 F6**
Guilin **35 D6**
Guimarães **18 B1**
Guimaras □ **36 B2**
Guinea ■ **53 F3**
Guinea, Gulf of **51 F3**
Guinea-Bissau ■ **53 F3**
Guingamp **12 B2**
Güiria **90 A6**
Guiuan **36 B3**
Guiyang **35 D5**
Guizhou □ **35 D5**
Gujarat □ **43 H7**
Gujranwala **42 C9**
Gujrat **42 C9**
Gulbarga **43 L10**
Gulf, The = Persian Gulf **44 E2**
Gulgong **63 B4**
Güllük **23 F6**
Gülshat **29 E8**
Gulu **57 D6**
Gümüşhane **46 B4**
Gumzai **37 F4**
Guna **43 G10**
Gunnedah **63 B5**
Gunningbar Cr. ➔ **63 B4**
Gunsan **35 C7**
Guntakal **43 M10**
Guntur **40 J3**
Gunungapi **37 F3**
Gunungsitoli **39 D1**
Gunza **56 G2**

Gupis 42 A8
Gürchän 46 D7
Gurdaspur 42 C9
Gurkha 40 C5
Gurley 63 A4
Gurupá 92 C3
Gurupá, I. Grande de 92 C3
Gurupi ➔ 92 C4
Guryev = Atyraü 29 E6
Gusau 53 F7
Güstrow 15 B7
Gütersloh 14 C5
Guthrie 80 B5
Guwahati 41 D8
Guyana ■ 90 B7
Guyane française = French Guiana ⊠ 92 B3
Guyenne 12 D4
Guyra 63 B5
Güzelyurt = Morphou 46 D3
Gwa 41 J10
Gwabegar 63 B4
Gwädar 42 G3
Gwalior 42 F11
Gwanda 59 C5
Gwangju 35 C7
Gwanju = Gwangju 35 C7
Gweru 59 B5
Gwydir ➔ 63 A4
Gyandzha = Gäncä 25 E6
Gyaring Hu 34 C4
Gydanskiy Poluostrov 28 B8
Gympie 63 A5
Gyöngyös 16 E4
Győr 16 E3
Gyula 16 E5
Gyumri 25 E5
Gyzylarbat = Serdar 29 F6

H

Haarlem 14 B3
Haast ➔ 65 E3
Haboro 32 A7
Hachijō-Jima 33 G6
Hachinohe 32 C7
Hadarba, Ras 54 D6
Ḥadd, Ra's al 45 F4
Hadejia 53 F7
Haden 63 A5
Ḥadera 46 D3
Hadhramaut = Ḥaḍramawt 49 D4
Ḥaḍramawt 49 D4
Haeju 35 C7
Haerhpin = Harbin 35 B7
Hafar al Bāṭin 47 E6
Hafizabad 42 C8
Haflong 41 E9
Haft Gel 47 E7
Hagen 14 C4
Hagerstown 77 E7
Hagi 33 F2
Hagondange 13 B7
Hague, C. de la 12 B3
Hague, The = 's-Gravenhage 14 B3
Haguenau 13 B7
Haidarâbâd = Hyderabad 43 L11
Haifa = Ḥefa 46 D3
Haikou 35 D6
Ḥā'il 47 F5
Hailar 35 B6
Hailun 35 B7
Hailuoto 8 B10
Hainan □ 35 E5
Haiphong 35 D5
Haiti ■ 87 C5
Haiya 55 E6
Hajdúböszörmény 16 E5
Haji Ibrahim 46 C6
Hajnówka 17 B6
Hakodate 32 C7
Hala 42 G6
Ḥalab 46 C4
Ḥalabjah 46 D6
Halaib 54 D6
Halberstadt 15 C6
Halcombe 64 D6
Halcon 36 B2
Halden 9 D8
Haldia 40 F7
Haldwani 42 E11
Halfmoon Bay 65 G3
Halifax *Canada* 71 E7
Halifax *U.K.* 11 E6
Hālī ➔ 44 E4
Halkida 23 E4
Hall Beach = Sanirajak 70 C5
Hall Pen. 70 C7
Hallāniyat, Jazā'ir al 49 D6
Halle 15 C6
Hallett 62 B2
Halmahera 37 D3
Halmstad 9 D8
Hälsingborg = Helsingborg 9 D8
Ḥālūl 44 E3
Hamada 33 F3
Hamadān 46 D7
Hamadān □ 46 D7
Ḥamāh 46 D4
Hamamatsu 33 F5
Hamar 8 C8
Hamburg 14 B5
Hämeenlinna 8 C10
Hameln 14 B5
Hamersley Ra. 60 E2
Hamhüng 35 C7
Hami 34 B4
Hamilton *Australia* 62 C3
Hamilton *Canada* 71 E6
Hamilton *N.Z.* 64 B6
Hamilton *U.K.* 10 D4
Hamilton ➔ 62 A2
Hamley Bridge 62 B2
Hamlin = Hameln 14 B5
Hamm 14 C4
Hammerfest 8 A10
Hammond 76 D2
Hampden 65 F4
Hampton 77 F7
Han Pijesak 20 B7
Hanamaki 32 D7
Hanau 14 C5
Hancock 75 C7
Handan 35 C6
Hangayn Nuruu 34 B4
Hangchou = Hangzhou 35 C7
Hangzhou 35 C7
Hangzhou Wan 35 C7
Hania = Chania 23 G5
Ḥanīsh 49 E3
Hankö 9 D10
Hanle 42 C11
Hanmer Springs 65 E5
Hanna 69 C8
Hannibal 75 F9
Hannover 14 B5
Hanoi 35 D5
Hanover = Hannover 14 B5
Hanover, I. 95 G2
Hansi 42 E9
Hanson, L. 62 B2
Hantsavichy 17 B8
Hanzhong 35 C5
Haora 40 F7
Haparanda 8 B10
Happy Valley-Goose Bay 71 D7
Hapur 42 E10
Ḥaql 47 E3
Har 37 F4
Har Hu 34 C4
Har Us Nuur 34 B4
Ḥaraḍ 47 F7
Haraisan Plateau = Hurayṣān 47 G6
Haranomachi 33 E7
Harare 59 B6
Haraz 55 F2
Harbin 35 B7
Hardangerfjorden 8 C7
Hardwar = Haridwar 42 E11
Hardy, Pen. 95 H3
Harer 49 F3
Hargeisa 49 F3
Hari ➔ 39 E2
Haridwar 42 E11
Haringhata ➔ 41 G7
Harīrūd 45 C5
Harīrūd ➔ 42 A2
Harlingen 80 F5
Harlow 11 F7
Harney Basin 72 E4
Härnösand 8 C9
Harricana ➔ 71 D6
Harris 10 C3
Harris, L. 62 B2
Harrisburg 77 D7
Harrison, C. 70 D8
Harrogate 11 D6
Hart, L. 62 B2
Hartford 77 D9
Hartlepool 11 D6
Harvey 76 D2
Harwich 11 F7
Haryana □ 42 E10
Haryn ➔ 17 B8
Harz 14 C6
Hasa 47 F7
Haskovo = Khaskovo 22 D5
Hassi Messaoud 52 B7
Hastings *N.Z.* 64 C7
Hastings *U.K.* 11 F7
Hastings *U.S.A.* 74 E5
Hastings Ra. 63 B5
Hatay 46 C4
Hatfield P.O. 62 B3
Hatgal 34 A5
Hathras 42 F11
Hatia 41 F8
Hattah 62 B3
Hatteras, C. 83 B10
Hattiesburg 81 D9
Hatvan 16 E4
Hau Bon = Cheo Reo 38 B3
Haugesund 9 D7
Hauraki G. 64 B6
Haut Atlas 52 B4
Hautah, Wahāt al 47 G6
Havana = La Habana 86 B3
Havant 11 F6
Havel ➔ 15 B7
Havelock 65 D5
Haverfordwest 11 F4
Havlíčkův Brod 16 D2
Havre 73 B9
Havre-St.-Pierre 71 D7
Havza 46 B3
Hawai'i □ 78 H12
Hawaiian Is. 78 H12
Hawea, L. 65 F3
Hawera 64 C6
Hawick 10 D5
Hawke B. 64 C7
Hawker 62 B2
Hawkwood 63 A5
Hay 63 B3
Hay River 68 B8
Haya = Tehoru 37 E3
Hayastan = Armenia ■ 25 E5
Hayes ➔ 69 C10
Hayrabolu 22 D6
Haysyn 17 D9
Hayvoron 17 D9
Hazar 29 F6
Hazārān, Küh-e 44 D4
Hazaribag 40 F5
Healesville 63 C4
Hearst 71 E5
Hebei □ 35 C6
Hebel 63 A4
Hebron = Al Khalīl 47 E3
Hebron 70 D7
Hechi 35 D5
Hechuan 35 C5
Heerlen 13 A6
Ḥefa 46 D3
Hefei 35 C6
Hegang 35 B8
Heidelberg 14 D5
Heihe 35 A7
Heilbronn 14 D5
Heilongjiang □ 35 B7
Heilunkiang = Heilongjiang □ 35 B7
Heimaey 8 C1
Heinze Kyun 41 K11

Hejaz = Ḥijāz **47 F4**
Hekımhan **46 C4**
Hekou **34 D5**
Helena *Ark., U.S.A.* **81 B8**
Helena *Mont., U.S.A.* **73 C7**
Helensville **64 B6**
Helgoland **14 A4**
Heligoland = Helgoland **14 A4**
Heligoland B. = Deutsche Bucht **14 A5**
Hellas = Greece ■ **23 E4**
Hellespont = Çanakkale Boğazı **23 D6**
Hellín **19 C5**
Helmand □ **42 D3**
Helmand ➔ **42 D2**
Helmand, Hamun **45 D5**
Helmsdale **10 B5**
Helsingborg **9 D8**
Helsingfors = Helsinki **9 C11**
Helsinki **9 C11**
Helwân **54 C5**
Hemel Hempstead **11 F6**
Henan □ **35 C6**
Henares ➔ **18 B4**
Henashi-Misaki **32 C6**
Henderson **83 A8**
Hendon **63 A5**
Hengyang **35 D6**
Henrietta Maria, C. **71 D5**
Hentiyn Nuruu **35 B5**
Henty **63 C4**
Henzada **41 J10**
Heraklion = Iraklio **23 G5**
Herät **42 B3**
Herät □ **42 B3**
Herceg-Novi **22 C2**
Hereford **11 E5**
Herford **14 B5**
Hermidale **63 B4**
Hermite, I. **95 H3**
Hermon, Mt. = Shaykh, J. ash **46 D3**
Hermosillo **84 B2**
Hernád ➔ **16 E5**
Heroica Nogales = Nogales **84 A2**
Herrick **62 D4**
's-Hertogenbosch **14 C3**
Hesse = Hessen □ **14 C5**
Hessen □ **14 C5**
Hexham **11 D5**
Heywood **62 C3**
Hialeah **83 G7**
Hibbing **75 B8**
Hibbs B. **62 D4**
Hickory **83 B7**
Hicks, Pt. **63 C4**
Hidalgo del Parral **84 B3**
Higashiajima-San **33 E7**
Higashiōsaka **33 F4**
High Point **83 B8**
High River **69 C8**
High Tatra = Tatry **16 D4**
High Wycombe **11 F6**
Hiiumaa **24 B1**
Ḥijārah, Ṣaḥrā' al **47 E6**
Ḥijāz **47 F4**
Hijo = Tagum **36 C3**
Hikurangi *Gisborne, N.Z.* **64 C7**
Hikurangi *Northland, N.Z.* **64 A6**
Hildesheim **14 B5**
Hillston **63 B4**
Hilo **78 J13**
Hilversum **14 B3**
Himachal Pradesh □ **42 D10**
Himalaya **40 C5**
Himatnagar **43 H8**
Himeji **33 F4**
Himi **33 E5**
Ḥimṣ **46 D4**
Hindmarsh, L. **62 C3**
Hindu Bagh **42 D5**
Hindu Kush **42 B7**
Hindupur **43 N10**
Hinganghat **43 J11**
Hingoli **43 K10**
Hinna = Imi **49 F3**
Hinojosa del Duque **18 C3**
Hinthada = Henzada **41 J10**
Hios **23 E6**
Hirakud Dam **40 G4**
Hiroo **32 B8**
Hirosaki **32 C7**
Hiroshima **33 F3**
Hisar **42 E9**
Hispaniola **87 C5**
Hitachi **33 E7**
Hjälmaren **9 D9**
Hkakabo Razi **41 C11**
Hlyboka **17 D7**
Ho Chi Minh City = Thanh Pho Ho Chi Minh **38 B3**
Hoai Nhon **38 B3**
Hoare B. **70 C7**
Hobart **62 D4**
Hobbs Coast **96 B18**
Hodaka-Dake **33 E5**
Hodeida = Al Ḥudaydah **49 E3**
Hodgson **69 C10**
Hódmezővásárhely **16 E5**
Hodna, Chott el **52 A6**
Hodonín **16 D3**
Hoek van Holland **14 B3**
Hof **15 C6**
Hofsjökull **8 C2**
Höfu **33 F2**
Hogan Group **62 C4**
Hoggar = Ahaggar **52 D7**
Hoh Xil Shan **34 C3**
Hoher Rhön = Rhön **14 C5**
Hohhot **35 B6**
Hoi An **38 A3**
Hokianga Harbour **64 A5**
Hokitika **65 E4**
Hokkaidō □ **32 B8**
Holbrook **63 C4**
Holguín **86 B4**
Hollywood **83 G7**
Holman **68 A8**
Holstebro **9 D7**
Holyhead **11 E4**
Homalin **41 E10**
Hombori **53 E5**
Home B. **70 C7**
Homer **69 C4**
Homs = Ḥimṣ **46 D4**
Homyel **17 B10**
Hon Chong **38 B2**
Honan = Henan □ **35 C6**
Honbetsu **32 B8**
Honduras ■ **85 E7**
Honduras, G. de **85 D7**
Hønefoss **9 C8**
Honfleur **12 B4**
Hong Kong □ **35 D6**
Hongjiang **35 D5**
Hongshui He ➔ **35 D5**
Hongze Hu **35 C6**
Honiara **64 K10**
Honjō **32 D7**
Honolulu **78 H12**
Honshū **33 F4**
Hood, Mt. **72 D3**
Hooghly = Hugli ➔ **40 G7**
Hook of Holland = Hoek van Holland **14 B3**
Hoorn **14 B3**
Hoover Dam **78 B5**
Hope, L. **62 A2**
Hopedale **70 D7**
Hopei = Hebei □ **35 C6**
Hopetoun **62 C3**
Hopetown **58 D4**
Hoquiam **72 C2**
Horlick Mts. **96 C1**
Horlivka **25 D4**
Hormoz **44 E3**
Hormoz, Jaz.-ye **44 E4**
Hormozgān □ **44 E3**
Hormuz, Str. of **44 E4**
Horn **15 D8**
Horn, Cape = Hornos, C. de **95 H3**
Hornavan **8 B9**
Hornos, C. de **95 H3**
Horodenka **17 D7**
Horodok *Khmelnytskyy, Ukraine* **17 D8**
Horodok *Lviv, Ukraine* **17 D6**
Horokhiv **17 C7**
Horqin Youyi Qianqi **35 B7**
Horqueta **94 A5**
Horsham **62 C3**
Horton ➔ **68 B7**
Hose, Gunung-Gunung **39 D4**
Hoshangabad **43 H10**
Hoshiarpur **42 D9**
Hospet **43 M10**
Hoste, I. **95 H3**
Hot Springs **81 B7**
Hotan **34 C2**
Hotazel **58 D4**
Houhora Heads **64 A5**
Houlton **77 A12**
Houma **81 E8**
Houston **81 E6**
Hovd □ **34 B4**
Hövsgöl Nuur **34 A5**
Howard **63 A5**
Howe, C. **63 C5**
Howitt, L. **62 A2**
Howrah = Haora **40 F7**
Höxter **14 C5**
Hoy **10 B5**
Høyanger **8 C7**
Hoyerswerda **15 C8**
Hpa-an = Pa-an **41 J11**
Hpunan Pass **41 D11**
Hradec Králové **16 C2**
Hrodna **17 B6**
Hrodzyanka **17 B9**
Hrvatska = Croatia ■ **20 B6**
Hrymayliv **17 D8**
Hsenwi **41 F11**
Hsiamen = Xiamen **35 D6**
Hsian = Xi'an **35 C5**
Hsinhailien = Lianyungang **35 C6**
Hsüchou = Xuzhou **35 C6**
Hua Hin **38 B1**
Huacho **91 F3**
Huai He ➔ **35 C6**
Huainan **35 C6**
Huallaga ➔ **90 E3**
Huambo **58 A3**
Huancabamba **91 E3**
Huancane **91 G5**
Huancavelica **91 F3**
Huancayo **91 F3**
Huang Hai = Yellow Sea **35 C7**
Huang He ➔ **35 C6**
Huangliu **35 E5**
Huangshan **35 D6**
Huangshi **35 C6**
Huánuco **91 E3**
Huaraz **91 E3**
Huarmey **91 F3**
Huascarán, Nevado **91 E3**
Huasco **94 B2**
Huatabampo **84 B3**
Hubei □ **35 C6**
Hubli **43 M9**
Huddersfield **11 E6**
Hudiksvall **8 C9**
Hudson ➔ **77 D8**
Hudson Bay **70 C5**
Hudson Mts. **96 B2**
Hudson Str. **70 C7**
Hue **38 A3**
Huelva **18 D2**
Huesca **19 A5**
Hughenden **61 E7**
Hugli ➔ **40 G7**
Huila, Nevado del **90 C3**
Huinca Renancó **94 C4**
Huize **34 D5**
Hukawng Valley **41 D11**
Hulan **35 B7**
Ḥulayfā' **47 F5**
Hull = Kingston upon Hull **11 E6**
Hull **71 E6**
Hulun Nur **35 B6**
Humahuaca **94 A3**
Humaitá **91 E6**
Humber ➔ **11 E6**
Humboldt **69 C9**

Humboldt ➔ 72 F4
Hume, L. 63 C4
Hün 54 C2
Húnaflói 8 B1
Hunan □ 35 D6
Hunedoara 17 F6
Hungary ■ 16 E4
Hungerford 63 A3
Hüngnam 35 C7
Hunsrück 14 D4
Hunter I. 62 D3
Hunter Ra. 63 B5
Hunterville 64 C6
Huntington 76 E4
Huntington Beach 78 D3
Huntly *N.Z.* 64 B6
Huntly *U.K.* 10 C5
Huntsville *Canada* 71 E6
Huntsville *U.S.A.* 82 B4
Huonville 62 D4
Hupeh = Hubei □ 35 C6
Huraysān 47 G6
Huron, L. 76 B4
Hurunui ➔ 65 E5
Húsavík 8 B2
Huşi 17 E9
Hutchinson 80 A5
Hutton, Mt. 63 A4
Hvar 20 C6
Hwang Ho = Huang He ➔ 35 C6
Hwange 59 B5
Hyargas Nuur 34 B4
Hyderabad *India* 43 L11
Hyderabad *Pakistan* 42 G6
Hydra 23 F4
Hyères 13 E7
Hyères, Îs. d' 13 E7
Hyūga 33 G2

I

I-n-Gall 53 E7
Iaco ➔ 91 E5
Ialomiţa ➔ 22 B6
Iaşi 17 E8
Iba 36 A2
Ibadan 53 G6
Ibagué 90 C3
Ibar ➔ 22 C3
Ibarra 90 C3
Ibiá 93 F4
Ibiapaba, Sa. da 92 C5
Ibiza = Eivissa 19 C6
Ibonma 37 E4
Ibotirama 93 E5
Ibu 37 D3
Ibusuki 33 H2
Ica 91 F3
Iça ➔ 90 D5
Içana 90 C5
İçel 46 C3
Iceland ■ 8 B2
Ich'ang = Yichang 35 C6
Ichchapuram 40 H5
Ichihara 33 F7
Ichilo ➔ 91 G6
Ichinomiya 33 F5
Ichinoseki 32 D7
Idaho □ 73 D7
Idaho Falls 73 E7
Idar-Oberstein 14 D4
Idensalmi = Iisalmi 8 C11
Idfû 54 D5
Īdhra = Hydra 23 F4
Idi 38 C1
Idi, Oros = Psiloritis, Oros 23 G5
Idiofa 56 E3
Idlib 46 D4
Idlip 46 D4
Ierapétra 23 G5
Iesi 20 C4
Ife 53 G6
Iforas, Adrar des 52 E6
Igarapava 93 G4
Igarka 28 C9
Iglésias 21 E2
Igloolik 70 C5
Igluligaarjuk = Chesterfield Inlet 68 B10
Iglulik = Igloolik 70 C5
Iğneada Burnu 22 D7
Igoumenitsa 23 E3
Iguaçu ➔ 94 B6
Iguaçu, Cat. del 94 B6
Iguaçu Falls = Iguaçu, Cat. del 94 B6
Iguala 84 D5
Igualada 19 B6
Iguassu = Iguaçu ➔ 94 B6
Iguatu 92 D6
Iharana 59 A10
Ihosy 59 C9
Iida 33 F5
Iisalmi 8 C11
Ijebu-Ode 53 G6
IJsselmeer 14 B3
Ikaluktutiak 68 B9
Ikaria 23 F6
Ikeda 33 F3
Ikela 56 E4
Iki 33 G1
Ikopa ➔ 59 B9
Ikparjuk = Arctic Bay 70 B5
Ilagan 36 A2
Īlām 46 D6
Iława 16 B4
Ile ➔ 29 E8
Île-de-France □ 12 B5
Ilebo 56 E4
Ilesha 53 G6
Ilhéus 93 E6
Ili = Ile ➔ 29 E8
Iligan 36 C2
Illampu = Ancohuma, Nevado 91 G5
Illana B. 36 C2
Illapel 94 C2
Iller ➔ 14 D5
Illimani, Nevado 91 G5
Ilmen, Ozero 24 B3
Ilo 91 G4
Iloilo 36 B2
Ilorin 53 G6
Ilwaki 37 F3
Imabari 33 F3
Imandra, Ozero 28 C4
Imari 33 G1
Imatra 8 C11
imeni 26 Bakinskikh Komissarov = Neftçala 46 C7
imeni Ismail Samani, Pik 29 F8
Imeri, Serra 90 C5
Imi 49 F3
Ímola 20 B3
Imperatriz 92 D4
Império 13 E8
Imperial Dam 78 D5
Impfondo 56 D3
Imphal 41 E9
Ímroz = Gökçeada 23 D5
Imuruan B. 36 B1
In Salah 52 C6
Ina 33 F5
Inangahua 65 D4
Inanwatan 37 E4
Iñapari 91 F5
Inari 8 B11
Inarijärvi 8 B11
Inca 19 C7
Ince Burun 25 E3
Incheon 35 C7
İncirliova 23 F6
Incomáti ➔ 59 D6
Indalsälven ➔ 8 C9
Indaw 41 E11
Independence *Kans., U.S.A.* 81 A6
Independence *Mo., U.S.A.* 75 F7
India ■ 43 J10
Indian ➔ 83 F7
Indiana □ 76 D3
Indianapolis 76 E2
Indigirka ➔ 31 B12
Indira Gandhi Canal 42 F8
Indonesia ■ 39 E4
Indore 43 H9
Indravati ➔ 40 H3
Indre ➔ 12 C4
Indus ➔ 43 G5
İnebolu 25 E3
Inglewood *Queens., Australia* 63 A5
Inglewood *Vic., Australia* 62 C3
Inglewood *N.Z.* 64 C6
Ingolstadt 15 D6
Ingraj Bazar 40 E7
Ingrid Christensen Coast 96 A10
Ingulec = Inhulec 25 D3
Inhambane 59 C7
Inharrime 59 C7
Inhulec 25 D3
Ining = Yining 29 E9
Inírida ➔ 90 C5
Injune 63 A4
Inland Kaikoura Ra. 65 D5
Inland Sea = Setonaikai 33 F3
Inle L. 41 G11
Inn ➔ 15 D7
Innamincka 62 A3
Inner Hebrides 10 C3
Inner Mongolia = Nei Monggol Zizhiqu □ 35 B6
Innsbruck 15 E6
Inongo 56 E3
Inoucdjouac = Inukjuak 70 D6
Inowrocław 16 B4
Insein 41 J11
International Falls 75 A8
Inukjuak 70 D6
Inútil, B. 95 G2
Inuvik 68 B6
Invercargill 65 G3
Inverell 63 A5
Invergordon 10 C4
Inverness 10 C4
Inverurie 10 C5
Investigator Group 62 B1
Investigator Str. 62 C2
Inya 29 D9
Inza 24 C6
Ioannina 23 E3
Ionian Is. = Ionioi Nisoi 23 E3
Ionian Sea 21 F6
Ionioi Nisoi 23 E3
Ios 23 F5
Iowa □ 75 D8
Iowa City 75 E9
Ipameri 93 F4
Ipatinga 93 F5
Ipiales 90 C3
Ipin = Yibin 35 D5
Ipixuna 91 E4
Ipoh 38 D2
Ippy 55 G3
Ipsala 22 D6
Ipswich *Australia* 63 A5
Ipswich *U.K.* 11 E7
Ipu 92 C5
Iqaluit 70 C7
Iquique 91 H4
Iquitos 90 D4
Iracoubo 92 A3
Iraklio 23 G5
Iráklion = Iraklio 23 G5
Iran ■ 44 C3
Iran, Pegunungan 39 D4
Iran Ra. = Iran, Pegunungan 39 D4
Īrānshahr 45 E5
Irapuato 84 C4
Iraq ■ 46 D5
Ireland ■ 11 E3
Irian Jaya = Papua □ 37 E5
Iringa 57 F7
Iriri ➔ 92 C3
Irish Republic ■ 11 E3
Irish Sea 11 E4
Irkineyeva 30 D7
Irkutsk 30 D8
Irō-Zaki 33 F6
Iron Baron 62 B2
Iron Gate = Portile de Fier 22 B4
Iron Knob 62 B2
Ironwood 75 B9
Irpin 17 C10

Irrara Cr. ➔ 63 A4
Irrawaddy □ 41 J10
Irrawaddy ➔ 41 K10
Irrawaddy, Mouths of the 41 K10
Irtysh ➔ 28 C7
Irún 19 A5
Irunea = Pamplona 19 A5
Irvine 10 D4
Irymple 62 B3
Isabela 36 C2
Ísafjörður 8 B1
Isahaya 33 G2
Isar ➔ 15 D7
Ischia 21 D4
Ise-Wan 33 F5
Isère ➔ 13 D6
Isérnia 20 D5
Isfahan = Eşfahān 44 C2
Ishikari-Gawa ➔ 32 B7
Ishikari-Wan 32 B7
Ishim ➔ 29 D8
Ishinomaki 32 D7
Ishkuman 42 A8
Isil Kul 29 D8
Isiro 57 D5
İskenderun 46 C4
Iskŭr ➔ 22 C5
Islamabad 42 C8
Island = Iceland ■ 8 B2
Island L. 69 C10
Island Lagoon 62 B2
Islands, B. of 64 A6
Islay 10 D3
Isle ➔ 12 D3
Isle of Wight □ 11 F6
Ismail = Izmayil 17 F9
Ismâ'ilīya 47 E3
Isparta 46 C2
Ispica 21 F5
Israel ■ 46 E3
Issoire 13 D5
Issyk-Kul, Ozero = Ysyk-Köl 29 E8
İstanbul 22 D7
İstanbul Boğazı 22 D7
Istiea 23 E4
Istra 20 B4
Istres 13 E6
Istria = Istra 20 B4
Itaberaba 93 E5
Itabira 93 F5
Itabuna 93 E6
Itaipú, Reprêsa de 94 B6
Itaituba 92 C2
Itajaí 94 B7
Italy ■ 20 C4
Itapecuru-Mirim 92 C5
Itaperuna 93 G5
Itapicuru ➔ *Bahia, Brazil* 93 E6
Itapicuru ➔ *Maranhão, Brazil* 92 C5
Itapipoca 92 C6
Itaquí 94 B5
Ithaca = Ithaki 23 E3
Ithaki 23 E3
Itō 33 F6
Itonamas ➔ 91 F6
Ituiutaba 93 F4
Itumbiara 93 F4
Iturbe 94 A3
Itzehoe 14 B5
Ivanava 17 B7
Ivanhoe 63 B3
Ivano-Frankivsk 17 D7
Ivanovo = Ivanava 17 B7
Ivanovo 24 B5
Ivatsevichy 17 B7
Ivory Coast ■ 53 G4
Ivrea 13 D7
Ivujivik 70 C6
Iwahig 38 C5
Iwaizumi 32 D7
Iwaki 33 E7
Iwakuni 33 F3
Iwamizawa 32 B7
Iwanai 32 B7
Iwata 33 F5
Iwate-San 32 D7
Iwo 53 G6
Ixiamas 91 F5
Izhevsk 28 D6
Izmayil 17 F9
İzmir 23 E6
İzmit = Kocaeli 25 E2
İznik Gölü 23 D7
Izu-Shotō 33 F7
Izumi-Sano 33 F4
Izumo 33 F3
Izyaslav 17 C8

J

Jabalpur 43 H11
Jablah 46 D4
Jablanica 22 D3
Jablonec nad Nisou 16 C2
Jaboatão 92 D6
Jaca 19 A5
Jacareí 94 A7
Jackson *Australia* 63 A4
Jackson *Mich., U.S.A.* 76 C3
Jackson *Miss., U.S.A.* 81 C8
Jackson *Tenn., U.S.A.* 82 B3
Jackson B. 65 E3
Jacksons 65 E4
Jacksonville *Fla., U.S.A.* 83 D7
Jacksonville *Ill., U.S.A.* 75 F9
Jacksonville *N.C., U.S.A.* 83 B9
Jacmel 87 C5
Jacobabad 42 E6
Jacobina 93 E5
Jacundá ➔ 92 C3
Jade Mt. = Yü Shan 35 D7
Jaén *Peru* 91 E3
Jaén *Spain* 18 D4
Jaffa = Tel Aviv-Yafo 46 D3
Jaffa, C. 62 C2
Jaffna 43 Q12
Jagadhri 42 D10
Jagdalpur 40 H3
Jagodina 22 B3
Jagraon 42 D9
Jagtial 43 K11
Jaguariaíva 94 A7
Jaguaribe ➔ 92 C6
Jahrom 44 D3
Jailolo 37 D3
Jailolo, Selat 37 D3
Jaipur 42 F9
Jakarta 39 F3
Jalālābād 42 B7
Jalapa Enríquez = Xalapa 84 D5
Jalas, Jabal al 47 F4
Jalgaon *Maharashtra, India* 43 J10
Jalgaon *Maharashtra, India* 43 J9
Jalna 43 K9
Jalón ➔ 19 B5
Jalpaiguri 41 D7
Jaluit I. 64 J11
Jamaica ■ 86 C4
Jamalpur *Bangla.* 41 E7
Jamalpur *India* 40 E6
Jamanxim ➔ 92 C2
Jambe 37 E4
Jambi 39 E2
Jambi □ 39 E2
Jambongan, Pulau 38 C5
James ➔ 74 D6
James B. 71 D5
James Ross I. 96 A4
Jamestown *Australia* 62 B2
Jamestown *N. Dak., U.S.A.* 74 B5
Jamestown *N.Y., U.S.A.* 77 C6
Jaṃkhandi 43 L9
Jammu 42 C9
Jammu & Kashmir □ 42 B10
Jamnagar 43 H7
Jamshedpur 40 F6
Jand 42 C8
Jandaq 44 C3
Jandowae 63 A5
Janesville 75 D10
Janjanbureh 53 F3
Januária 93 F5
Jaora 43 H9
Japan ■ 33 F5
Japan, Sea of 32 D4
Japen = Yapen 37 E5
Japurá ➔ 90 D5
Jaqué 90 B3
Jarama ➔ 18 B4
Jarvis I. 65 K15
Jarwa 40 D4
Jāsk 44 E4
Jasper 82 C4
Jászberény 16 E4
Jataí 93 F3
Játiva = Xátiva 19 C5
Jaú 93 G4
Jauja 91 F3
Jaunpur 40 E4
Java = Jawa 39 F3
Java Sea 39 E3
Jawa 39 F3
Jaya, Puncak 37 E5
Jayanti 41 D7
Jayapura 37 E6
Jayawijaya, Pegunungan 37 E5
Jaynagar 40 D6
Jebel, Bahr el ➔ 55 G5
Jedburgh 10 D5
Jedda = Jiddah 47 G4
Jędrzejów 16 C5
Jefferson City 75 F8
Jega 53 F6
Jeju-do 35 C7
Jelenia Góra 16 C2
Jelgava 24 B1
Jena 15 C6
Jeonju 35 C7
Jeparit 62 C3
Jequié 93 E5
Jequitinhonha 93 F5
Jequitinhonha ➔ 93 F6
Jérémie 86 C5
Jerez de la Frontera 18 D2
Jerez de los Caballeros 18 C2
Jerid, Chott el = Djerid, Chott 52 B7
Jerilderie 63 C4
Jersey 11 G5
Jersey City 77 D8
Jerusalem 47 E3
Jervis B. 63 C5
Jesi = Iesi 20 C4
Jessore 41 F7
Jeypore 40 H4
Jhal Jhao 42 F4
Jhalawar 43 G10
Jhang Maghiana 42 D8
Jhansi 43 G11
Jharsuguda 40 G5
Jhelum 42 C8
Jhelum ➔ 42 D8
Jhunjhunu 42 E9
Jiamusi 35 B8
Ji'an 35 D6
Jiangmen 35 D6
Jiangsu □ 35 C6
Jiangxi □ 35 D6
Jiao Xian = Jiaozhou 35 C7
Jiaozhou 35 C7
Jiaxing 35 C7
Jiayi = Chiai 35 D7
Jibuti = Djibouti ■ 49 E3
Jiddah 47 G4
Jido 41 C10
Jihlava 16 D2
Jihlava ➔ 16 D3
Jijiga 49 F3
Jilin 35 B7
Jilong = Chilung 35 D7
Jima 55 G6
Jiménez 84 B4
Jinan 35 C6
Jindabyne 63 C4
Jindřichův Hradec 16 D2
Jingdezhen 35 D6
Jinggu 34 D5
Jinhua 35 D6
Jining *Nei Monggol Zizhiqu, China* 35 B6

Jining *Shandong, China* **35 C6**
Jinja **57 D6**
Jinnah Barrage **42 C7**
Jinzhou **35 B7**
Jiparaná ➔ **91 E6**
Jipijapa **90 D2**
Jiu ➔ **22 C4**
Jiujiang **35 D6**
Jiuquan **34 C4**
Jixi **35 B8**
Jizzakh **29 E7**
Joaçaba **94 B6**
João Pessoa **92 D7**
Joaquín V. González **94 B4**
Jodhpur **42 F8**
Joensuu **8 C11**
Jogjakarta = Yogyakarta **39 F4**
Johannesburg **59 D5**
Johnson City **83 A6**
Johnston Falls = Mambilima Falls **57 G5**
Johnstown **77 D6**
Johor Bahru **39 D2**
Joinville **94 B7**
Joinville I. **96 A4**
Joliet **76 D1**
Joliette **71 E6**
Jolo **36 C2**
Jome **37 E3**
Jones Sound **70 B5**
Jonesboro **81 B8**
Jönköping **9 D8**
Jonquière **71 E6**
Joplin **81 A6**
Jordan ■ **47 E4**
Jorhat **41 D10**
Jorong **39 E4**
Jos **53 G7**
Jotunheimen **8 C7**
Jowzjān □ **45 B6**
Juan de Fuca, Str of. **72 B1**
Juan Fernández, Arch. de **89 G3**
Juárez **94 D5**
Juàzeiro **93 D5**
Juàzeiro do Norte **92 D6**
Juba = Giuba ➔ **49 G3**
Jubbulpore = Jabalpur **43 H11**
Juby, C. **52 C3**
Júcar = Xúquer ➔ **19 C5**
Juchitán de Zaragoza **85 D5**
Jugoslavia = Serbia ■ **22 B3**
Juiz de Fora **93 G5**
Juli **91 G5**
Juliaca **91 G4**
Jullundur **42 D9**
Jumilla **19 C5**
Jumla **40 C4**
Jumna = Yamuna ➔ **40 E3**
Junagadh **43 J7**
Jundiaí **94 A7**
Juneau **69 C6**
Junee **63 B4**
Junggar Pendi **34 B3**
Junín **94 C4**
Junín de los Andes **95 D2**
Jüniyah **46 D3**
Jur, Nahr el ➔ **55 G4**
Jura = Jura, Mts. du **13 C7**
Jura = Schwäbische Alb **14 D5**
Jura **10 D4**
Jura, Mts. du **13 C7**
Juruá ➔ **90 D5**
Juruena ➔ **91 E7**
Juruti **92 C2**
Justo Daract **94 C3**
Jutland = Jylland **9 D7**
Juventud, I. de la **86 B3**
Jwaneng **58 C4**
Jylland **9 D7**
Jyväskylä **8 C11**

K

K2 **42 B10**
Kaapstad = Cape Town **58 E3**
Kabaena **37 F2**
Kabala **53 G3**
Kabale **57 E6**
Kabalo **57 F5**
Kabanjahe **39 D1**
Kabarai **37 E4**
Kabardino-Balkar Republic = Kabardino-Balkaria □ **25 E5**
Kabardino-Balkaria □ **25 E5**
Kabarega Falls = Murchison Falls **57 D6**
Kabasalan **36 C2**
Kabīr Küh **47 D6**
Kabompo ➔ **58 A4**
Kabongo **57 F5**
Kabūd Gonbad **44 B4**
Kābul **42 B6**
Kābul □ **42 B6**
Kābul ➔ **42 C8**
Kaburuang **37 D3**
Kabwe **59 A5**
Kachchh, Gulf of **43 H6**
Kachchh, Rann of **43 G6**
Kachin □ **41 D11**
Kachiry **29 D8**
Kaçkar **25 E5**
Kadan Kyun **38 B1**
Kadina **62 B2**
Kadiyevka = Stakhanov **25 D4**
Kadoma **59 B5**
Kâdugli **55 F4**
Kaduna **53 F7**
Kaédi **53 E3**
Kaesŏng **35 C7**
Käf **47 E4**
Kafan = Kapan **25 F6**
Kafanchan **53 G7**
Kafue ➔ **59 B5**
Kaga Bandoro **55 G2**
Kagan **29 F7**
Kağızman **46 B5**
Kagoshima **33 H2**
Kagul = Cahul **17 F9**
Kahayan ➔ **39 E4**
Kahnūj **44 E4**
Kaho'olawe **78 H12**
Kahramanmaraş **46 C4**
Kahurangi △ **65 D5**
Kai, Kepulauan **37 F4**
Kai Besar **37 F4**
Kai Is. = Kai, Kepulauan **37 F4**
Kai Kecil **37 F4**
Kaiapoi **65 E5**
Kaieteur Falls **90 B7**
Kaifeng **35 C6**
Kaikohe **64 A5**
Kaikoura **65 E5**
Kaimana **37 E4**
Kaimanawa Mts. **64 C6**
Kainji Res. **53 F6**
Kaipara Harbour **64 B6**
Kaironi **37 E4**
Kairouan **54 A1**
Kaiserslautern **14 D4**
Kaitaia **64 A5**
Kaitangata **65 G3**
Kajaani **8 C11**
Kajabbi **61 D6**
Kajana = Kajaani **8 C11**
Kajo Kaji **55 H5**
Kakamega **57 D6**
Kakanui Mts. **65 F4**
Kakhovka **25 D3**
Kakhovske Vdskh. **25 D3**
Kakinada **40 J4**
Kalaallit Nunaat = Greenland ⧄ **66 C9**
Kalabagh **42 C7**
Kalabahi **37 F2**
Kalach **24 C5**
Kaladan ➔ **41 G9**
Kalahari **58 C4**
Kalakan **31 D9**
K'alak'unlun Shank'ou = Karakoram Pass **42 B10**
Kalamata **23 F4**
Kalamazoo **76 C3**
Kalan **46 C4**
Kalao **37 F2**
Kalaotoa **37 F2**
Kalat **42 E5**
Kalce **20 B5**
Kale **23 F7**
Kalegauk Kyun **41 K11**
Kalemie **57 F5**
Kalewa **41 F10**
Kalgoorlie-Boulder **60 G3**
Kaliakra, Nos **22 C7**
Kalianda **39 F3**
Kalibo **36 B2**
Kalima **57 E5**
Kalimantan **39 E4**
Kalimantan Barat □ **39 D4**
Kalimantan Selatan □ **39 E5**
Kalimantan Tengah □ **39 E4**
Kalimantan Timur □ **39 D5**
Kálimnos **23 F6**
Kaliningrad **24 C1**
Kalinkavichy **17 B9**
Kalinkovichi = Kalinkavichy **17 B9**
Kalispell **73 B6**
Kalisz **16 C4**
Kallsjön **8 C8**
Kalmar **9 D9**
Kalmyk Republic = Kalmykia □ **25 D6**
Kalmykia □ **25 D6**
Kalocsa **16 E4**
Kaluga **24 C4**
Kalush **17 D7**
Kalutara **43 R11**
Kama ➔ **29 D6**
Kamaishi **32 D7**
Kamarān **49 D3**
Kamchatka, Poluostrov **31 D13**
Kamchatka Pen. = Kamchatka, Poluostrov **31 D13**
Kamchiya ➔ **22 C6**
Kamen **29 D9**
Kamen-Rybolov **32 A3**
Kamenjak, Rt **20 B4**
Kamenka Bugskaya = Kamyanka-Buzka **17 C7**
Kamensk Uralskiy **29 D7**
Kamin-Kashyrskyy **17 C7**
Kamina **57 F5**
Kamloops **69 C7**
Kampala **57 D6**
Kampar ➔ **39 D2**
Kampen **14 B3**
Kampong Chhnang **38 B2**
Kampong Saom **38 B2**
Kampot **38 B2**
Kampuchea = Cambodia ■ **38 B3**
Kampungbaru = Tolitoli **37 D2**
Kamrau, Teluk **37 E4**
Kamui-Misaki **32 B7**
Kamyanets-Podilskyy **17 D8**
Kamyanka-Buzka **17 C7**
Kamyshin **24 C6**
Kanaaupscow **71 D6**
Kanagi **32 C7**
Kananga **56 F4**
Kanash **24 B6**
Kanastraíon, Ákra = Paliouri, Akra **23 E4**
Kanazawa **33 E5**
Kanchanaburi **38 B1**
Kanchenjunga **40 D7**
Kanchipuram **43 N11**
Kandahār **42 D4**
Kandahār □ **42 D4**
Kandalaksha **8 B12**
Kandalu **42 E3**
Kandangan **39 E5**
Kandi **53 F6**
Kandla **43 H7**
Kandos **63 B4**
Kandy **43 R12**
Kangaroo I. **62 C2**
Kangāvar **46 D7**
Kangean, Kepulauan **39 F5**

Kangean Is. = Kangean, Kepulauan **39 F5**
Kangiqliniq = Rankin Inlet **68 B10**
Kangiqsualujjuaq **70 D7**
Kangiqsujuaq **70 C6**
Kangiqtugaapik = Clyde River **70 B7**
Kangirsuk **70 D7**
Kangto **41 D9**
Kaniapiskau = Caniapiscau ➔ **70 D7**
Kaniapiskau, L. = Caniapiscau, L. **71 D7**
Kanin, Poluostrov **28 C5**
Kanin Nos, Mys **28 C5**
Kanin Pen. = Kanin, Poluostrov **28 C5**
Kaniva **62 C3**
Kankakee **76 D2**
Kankan **53 F4**
Kankendy = Xankändi **25 F6**
Kanker **40 G3**
Kannapolis **83 B7**
Kannauj **42 F11**
Kannod **43 H10**
Kano **53 F7**
Kanowit **39 D4**
Kanoya **33 H2**
Kanpetlet **41 G9**
Kanpur **40 D3**
Kansas □ **74 F5**
Kansas City *Kans., U.S.A.* **75 F7**
Kansas City *Mo., U.S.A.* **75 F7**
Kansk **30 D7**
Kansu = Gansu □ **34 C5**
Kanyakumari **43 Q10**
Kanye **59 C5**
Kaohsiung **35 D7**
Kaolack **53 F2**
Kapan **25 F6**
Kapanga **56 F4**
Kapchagai = Qapshaghay **29 E8**
Kapela = Velika Kapela **20 B5**
Kapfenberg **15 E8**
Kapiri Mposhi **59 A5**
Käpīsā □ **45 C7**
Kapit **39 D4**
Kapiti I. **65 D6**
Kapoeta **55 H5**
Kaposvár **16 E3**
Kaptai L. **41 F9**
Kapuas ➔ **39 E3**
Kapuas Hulu, Pegunungan **39 D4**
Kapuas Hulu Ra. = Kapuas Hulu, Pegunungan **39 D4**
Kapunda **62 B2**
Kapuni **64 C6**
Kaputar, Mt. **63 B5**
Kara **28 C7**
Kara Bogaz Gol, Zaliv = Garabogazköl Aylagy **29 E6**
Kara Kalpak Republic = Qoraqalpoghistan □ **29 E6**
Kara Kum = Garagum **29 F6**
Kara Sea **28 B8**
Karabiğa **23 D6**
Karabük **46 B3**
Karaburun **23 E6**
Karabutak = Qarabutaq **29 E7**
Karacabey **23 D7**
Karacasu **23 F7**
Karachi **43 G5**
Karad **43 L9**
Karaganda = Qaraghandy **29 E8**
Karagayly = Qaraghayly **29 E8**
Karaikal **43 P11**
Karaikkudi **43 P11**
Karakalpakstan = Qoraqalpoghistan □ **29 E6**
Karakas **29 E9**
Karakelong **36 D3**
Karakitang **37 D3**
Karakol **29 E8**
Karakoram Pass **42 B10**
Karakoram Ra. **42 B10**
Karalon **30 D9**
Karaman **46 C3**
Karamay **34 B3**
Karambu **39 E5**
Karamea Bight **65 D4**
Karasburg **58 D3**
Karasino **28 C9**
Karasuk **29 D8**
Karatau, Khrebet = Qarataŭ **29 E7**
Karatsu **33 G2**
Karawanken **20 A5**
Karazhal = Qarazhal **29 E8**
Karbalā' **47 D6**
Karcag **16 E5**
Karditsa **23 E3**
Karelia □ **8 C12**
Karelian Republic = Karelia □ **8 C12**
Kargānrūd **46 C7**
Kargasok **29 D9**
Kargat **29 D9**
Kargil **42 B10**
Kariba, L. **59 B5**
Kariba Dam **59 B5**
Kariba Gorge **59 B5**
Karimata, Kepulauan **39 E3**
Karimata, Selat **39 E3**
Karimata Is. = Karimata, Kepulauan **39 E3**
Karimnagar **43 K11**
Karimunjawa, Kepulauan **39 F4**
Karin **49 E4**
Karkaralinsk = Qarqaraly **29 E8**
Karkinitska Zatoka **25 D3**
Karkinitskiy Zaliv = Karkinitska Zatoka **25 D3**
Karkuk = Kirkūk **46 D6**
Karlovac **20 B5**
Karlovo **22 C5**
Karlovy Vary **16 C1**
Karlsbad = Karlovy Vary **16 C1**
Karlskrona **9 D9**
Karlsruhe **14 D5**
Karlstad **9 D8**
Karnal **42 E10**
Karnali ➔ **40 C3**
Karnaphuli Res. = Kaptai L. **41 F9**
Karnataka □ **43 N10**
Kärnten □ **15 E7**
Karonga **57 F6**
Karoonda **62 C2**
Karora **55 E6**
Karpathos **23 G6**
Kars **25 E5**
Karsakpay **29 E7**
Karshi = Qarshi **29 F7**
Karsun **24 C6**
Karufa **37 E4**
Karungu **57 E6**
Karviná **16 D4**
Karwar **43 M9**
Kasai ➔ **56 E3**
Kasama **57 G6**
Kasandra Kolpos **23 D4**
Kasaragod **43 N9**
Kasba L. **68 B9**
Kasempa **59 A5**
Kasenga **57 G5**
Kāshān **44 C2**
Kashgar = Kashi **34 C2**
Kashi **34 C2**
Kashk-e Kohneh **42 B3**
Kāshmar **44 C4**
Kashun Noerh = Gaxun Nur **34 B5**
Kasimov **24 C5**
Kasiruta **37 E3**
Kasongo **57 E5**
Kasongo Lunda **56 F3**
Kasos **23 G6**
Kassalâ **55 E6**
Kassel **14 C5**
Kastamonu **25 E3**
Kasur **42 D9**
Katanga □ **57 F4**
Katangi **43 J11**
Katerini **23 D4**
Katha **41 E11**
Kathiawar **43 H7**
Kathmandu = Katmandu **40 D5**
Katihar **40 E6**
Katima Mulilo **58 B4**
Katingan = Mendawai ➔ **39 E4**
Katiola **53 G4**
Katmandu **40 D5**
Katoomba **63 B5**
Katowice **16 C4**
Katsina **53 F7**
Kattegat **9 D8**
Kaua'i **78 G11**
Kaunas **24 C1**
Kavala **22 D5**
Kavalerovo **32 A4**
Kavīr, Dasht-e **44 C3**
Kaw **92 B3**
Kawagoe **33 F6**
Kawaguchi **33 F6**
Kawardha **40 G3**
Kawasaki **33 F6**
Kawasi **37 E3**
Kawawachikamach **71 D7**
Kawerau **64 C7**
Kawhia **64 C6**
Kawhia Harbour **64 C6**
Kawio, Kepulauan **36 D3**
Kawnro **41 F12**
Kawthoolei = Kayin □ **41 H11**
Kawthule = Kayin □ **41 H11**
Kaya **53 F5**
Kayah □ **41 H11**
Kayan ➔ **39 D5**
Kayeli **37 E3**
Kayes **53 F3**
Kayin □ **41 H11**
Kayoa **37 D3**
Kayrunnera **62 B3**
Kayseri **46 C3**
Kazachye **31 B11**
Kazakhstan ■ **29 E7**
Kazan **24 B6**
Kazanlŭk **22 C5**
Kazatin = Kozyatyn **17 D9**
Käzerūn **44 D2**
Kazym ➔ **28 C7**
Kea **23 F5**
Kebnekaise **8 B9**
Kebri Dehar **49 F3**
Kecskemét **16 E4**
Kediri **39 F4**
Keelung = Chilung **35 D7**
Keetmanshoop **58 D3**
Kefalonia **23 E3**
Kefamenanu **37 F2**
Keffi **53 G7**
Keflavík **8 C1**
Keighley **11 E6**
Keimoes **58 D4**
Keith **62 C3**
Kekri **42 G9**
Kël **30 C10**
Kelang = Klang **39 D2**
Kells = Ceanannus Mor **11 E3**
Kelowna **69 D8**
Kelso **65 F3**
Keluang = Kluang **39 D2**
Kem **28 C4**
Kema **37 D3**
Kemah **46 C4**
Kemerovo **29 D9**
Kemi **8 B10**
Kemi älv = Kemijoki ➔ **8 B10**
Kemi träsk = Kemijärvi **8 B11**
Kemijärvi **8 B11**
Kemijoki ➔ **8 B10**
Kemp Land **96 A9**
Kempsey **63 B5**
Kempten **14 E6**

Kendal 39 F4
Kendall 63 B5
Kendari 37 E2
Kendawangan 39 E4
Kendrapara 40 G6
Kenema 53 G3
Keng Tawng 41 G12
Keng Tung 41 G12
Kenitra 52 B4
Kennedy, Mt. 41 F9
Kennewick 72 C4
Kenogami ➔ 71 D5
Kenosha 76 C2
Kent Group 62 C4
Kent Pen. 68 B9
Kentaū 29 E7
Kentucky □ 76 F3
Kentville 71 E7
Kenya ■ 57 D7
Kenya, Mt. 57 E7
Kepi 37 F5
Kerala □ 43 P10
Kerang 62 C3
Kerch 25 D4
Kericho 57 E7
Kerinci 39 E2
Kerki = Atamyrat 29 F7
Kerkyra 23 E2
Kermadec Is. 64 M13
Kermadec Trench 65 N13
Kermān 44 D4
Kermān □ 44 D4
Kermānshāh 46 D6
Kerrobert 69 C9
Kerulen ➔ 35 B6
Kerzaz 52 C5
Keşan 22 D6
Kesennuma 32 D7
Kestenga 28 C4
Ket ➔ 29 D9
Ketapang 39 E4
Ketchikan 69 C6
Kętrzyn 16 A5
Key West 86 B3
Khabarovo 28 C7
Khabarovsk 31 E11
Khābūr ➔ 46 D5
Khairpur 42 F6
Khakassia □ 30 D6
Khalkhāl 46 C7
Khalkís = Halkida 23 E4
Khalmer Yu 28 C7
Khalturin 24 B6
Khalūf 48 C6
Khambhat 43 H8
Khambhat, G. of 43 J8
Khamir 49 D3
Khānābād 45 B7
Khānaqīn 46 D6
Khandwa 43 J10
Khanewal 42 D7
Khaniá = Chania 23 G5
Khanka, L. 32 A3
Khankendy = Xankändi 25 F6
Khanty-Mansiysk 29 C7
Khapcheranga 30 E9
Kharagpur 40 F6
Kharan Kalat 42 E4
Kharānaq 44 C3
Kharda 43 K9
Kharg = Khārk, Jazīreh-ye 47 E7
Khârga, El Wâhât-el 54 C5
Khargon 43 J9
Khārk, Jazīreh-ye 47 E7
Kharkiv 24 D4
Kharkov = Kharkiv 24 D4
Kharovsk 24 B5
Kharta 22 D7
Khartoum = El Khartûm 55 E5
Khasan 32 B2
Khāsh 42 E2
Khashm el Girba 55 F6
Khaskovo 22 D5
Khatanga 30 B8
Khatanga ➔ 30 B8
Khaybar, Ḥarrat 47 F5
Khed Brahma 43 G8
Khemmarat 38 A3
Khenchela 52 A7
Kherson 25 D3
Kheta ➔ 30 B8
Khilok 30 D9
Khíos = Hios 23 E6
Khiuma = Hiiumaa 24 B1
Khiva 29 E7
Khīyāv 46 C6
Khmelnik 17 D8
Khmelnitskiy = Khmelnytskyy 17 D8
Khmelnytskyy 17 D8
Khmer Rep. = Cambodia ■ 38 B3
Khodoriv 17 D7
Khodzent = Khūjand 29 E7
Khojak Pass 42 D5
Kholm *Afghan.* 45 B6
Kholm *Russia* 24 B3
Khomeyn 44 C2
Khon Kaen 38 A2
Khorat = Nakhon Ratchasima 38 B2
Khorramābād 46 D7
Khorrāmshahr 47 E7
Khotyn 17 D8
Khouribga 52 B4
Khowst 42 C6
Khoyniki 17 C9
Khu Khan 38 B2
Khudzhand = Khūjand 29 E7
Khūgīānī 42 D4
Khūjand 29 E7
Khulna 41 F7
Khulna □ 41 F7
Khūr 44 C4
Khurayṣ 47 F7
Khush 42 C3
Khushab 42 C8
Khust 17 D6
Khuzdar 42 F5
Khvor 44 C3
Khvormūj 44 D2
Khvoy 46 C6
Khyber Pass 42 B7
Kiama 63 B5
Kiamba 36 C2
Kiangsi = Jiangxi □ 35 D6
Kiangsu = Jiangsu □ 35 C6
Kibombo 57 E5
Kibris = Cyprus ■ 46 D3
Kibwezi 57 E7
Kicking Horse Pass 69 C8
Kidal 53 E6
Kidnappers, C. 64 C7
Kiel 14 A6
Kiel Canal = Nord-Ostsee-Kanal 14 A5
Kielce 16 C5
Kieler Bucht 14 A6
Kiev = Kyyiv 17 C10
Kiffa 53 E3
Kifrī 46 D6
Kigali 57 E6
Kigoma-Ujiji 57 E5
Kihee 62 A3
Kii-Sanchi 33 F5
Kikinda 22 B3
Kikládhes = Cyclades 23 F5
Kikwit 56 E3
Kilcoy 63 A5
Kilimanjaro 57 E7
Kilis 46 C4
Kiliya 17 F9
Kilkenny 11 E3
Kilkis 23 D4
Killarney *Australia* 63 A5
Killarney *Ireland* 11 E2
Killeen 80 D5
Killini 23 F4
Kilmarnock 10 D4
Kilmore 63 C3
Kilosa 57 F7
Kilrush 11 E2
Kilwa Kivinje 57 F7
Kimaam 37 F5
Kimba 62 B2
Kimberley *Australia* 60 D4
Kimberley *S. Africa* 58 D4
Kimmirut 70 C7
Kimry 24 B4
Kinabalu, Gunung 38 C5
Kindia 53 F3
Kindu 57 E5
Kineshma 24 B5
King George B. 95 G4
King George I. 96 A4
King George Is. 71 D5
King I. = Kadan Kyun 38 B1
King I. 62 C3
King William I. 68 B10
Kingait = Cape Dorset 70 C6
Kingaok = Bathurst Inlet 68 B9
Kingaroy 63 A5
Kingoonya 62 B2
Kings Canyon △ 78 B3
King's Lynn 11 E7
Kingscote 62 C2
Kingsport 83 A6
Kingston *Canada* 71 E6
Kingston *Jamaica* 86 C4
Kingston *N.Z.* 65 F3
Kingston South East 62 C2
Kingston upon Hull 11 E6
Kingstown 87 D7
Kingsville 80 F5
Kınık 23 E6
Kinkala 56 E2
Kinleith 64 C6
Kinsale 11 F2
Kinsha = Chang Jiang ➔ 35 C7
Kinshasa 56 E3
Kinston 83 B9
Kiparissia 23 F3
Kiparissiakos Kolpos 23 F3
Kipushi 59 A5
Kirghizia = Kyrgyzstan ■ 29 E8
Kiribati ■ 64 K12
Kırıkkale 25 F3
Kirillov 24 B4
Kirin = Jilin 35 B7
Kirinyaga = Kenya, Mt. 57 E7
Kiritimati 65 J15
Kirkcaldy 10 C5
Kirkcudbright 11 D4
Kirkee 43 K8
Kirkland Lake 71 E5
Kırklareli 22 D6
Kirkük 46 D6
Kirkwall 10 B5
Kirov 28 D5
Kirovabad = Gäncä 25 E6
Kirovograd = Kirovohrad 25 D3
Kirovohrad 25 D3
Kirovsk = Babadayhan 29 F7
Kirovskiy 32 A3
Kirsanov 24 C5
Kırşehir 25 F3
Kirthar Range 42 F5
Kiruna 8 B10
Kiryū 33 E6
Kisangani 57 D5
Kisar 37 F3
Kiselevsk 29 D9
Kishanganj 40 D7
Kishangarh 42 F7
Kishb, Ḥarrat al 47 G5
Kishinev = Chişinău 17 E9
Kishtwar 42 C9
Kisii 57 E6
Kiskőrös 16 E4
Kiskunfélegyháza 16 E4
Kiskunhalas 16 E4
Kislovodsk 25 E5
Kismayu = Chisimaio 49 H3
Kiso-Gawa ➔ 33 F5
Kissidougou 53 G3
Kisumu 57 E6
Kita 53 F4
Kitaibaraki 33 E7
Kitakyūshū 33 G2
Kitale 57 D7
Kitami 32 B8
Kitchener 71 E5

Kitega = Gitega **57 E5**
Kithira = Kythira **23 F4**
Kithnos **23 F5**
Kitikmeot □ **68 B9**
Kittakittaoolooo, L. **62 A2**
Kitui **57 E7**
Kitwe **59 A5**
Kivertsi **17 C7**
Kivu, L. **57 E5**
Kiyev = Kyyiv **17 C10**
Kiyevskoye Vdkhr. = Kyyivske Vdskh. **17 C10**
Kızıl Irmak ➔ **25 E4**
Kizlyar **25 E6**
Kizyl-Arvat = Serdar **29 F6**
Kladno **16 C2**
Klagenfurt **15 E8**
Klaipėda **24 B1**
Klamath Falls **72 E3**
Klamath Mts. **72 F2**
Klang **39 D2**
Klarälven ➔ **9 C8**
Klatovy **16 D1**
Klerksdorp **59 D5**
Kletsk = Klyetsk **17 B8**
Kłodzko **16 C3**
Klondike **68 B6**
Klouto **53 G6**
Kluane L. **68 B6**
Kluang **39 D2**
Kluczbork **16 C4**
Klyetsk **17 B8**
Knossos **23 G5**
Knox Coast **96 A12**
Knoxville **83 B6**
Koartac = Quaqtaq **70 C7**
Koba **37 F4**
Kobarid **20 A4**
Köbe **33 F4**
København **9 D8**
Koblenz **14 C4**
Kobroor **37 F4**
Kobryn **17 B7**
Kocaeli **25 E2**
Kočani **22 D4**
Koch Bihar **41 D7**
Kochi = Cochin **43 Q10**
Köchi **33 G3**
Kochiu = Gejiu **34 D5**
Kodiak **69 C4**
Kodiak I. **69 C4**
Kofiau **37 E3**
Koforidua **53 G5**
Köfu **33 F6**
Kogan **63 A5**
Kohat **42 C7**
Kohima **41 E10**
Kohkīlūyeh va Būyer Aḥmadi □ **44 D2**
Kohler Ra. **96 B1**
Kokand = Qūqon **29 E8**
Kokas **37 E4**
Kokchetav = Kökshetaū **29 D7**
Koko Kyunzu **41 K9**
Kokomo **76 D2**
Kökshetaū **29 D7**
Koksoak ➔ **70 D7**
Kokstad **59 E5**
Kola **37 F4**
Kola Pen. = Kolskiy Poluostrov **8 B13**
Kolaka **37 E2**
Kolar **43 N11**
Kolar Gold Fields **43 N11**
Kolayat **42 F8**
Kolepom = Dolak, Pulau **37 F5**
Kolguyev, Ostrov **28 C5**
Kolhapur **43 L9**
Kolín **16 C2**
Kolkata **41 F7**
Kollam = Quilon **43 Q10**
Köln **14 C4**
Koło **16 B4**
Kołobrzeg **16 A2**
Kolomna **24 B4**
Kolomyya **17 D7**
Kolonodale **37 E2**
Kolosib **41 E9**
Kolpashevo **29 D9**
Kolpino **24 B3**
Kolskiy Poluostrov **8 B13**
Kolwezi **57 G5**
Kolyma ➔ **31 C13**
Komatsu **33 E5**
Komi □ **28 C6**
Kommunarsk = Alchevsk **25 D4**
Kommunizma, Pik = imeni Ismail Samani, Pik **29 F8**
Komodo **37 F1**
Komoran, Pulau **37 F5**
Komotini **22 D5**
Kompong Cham **38 B3**
Kompong Chhnang = Kampong Chhnang **38 B2**
Kompong Som = Kampong Saom **38 B2**
Komrat = Comrat **17 E9**
Komsomolets, Ostrov **30 A7**
Kon Tum **38 B3**
Konar □ **42 B7**
Konch **42 G11**
Kondoa **57 E7**
Kondoz **45 B7**
Kondoz □ **45 B7**
Köneürgench **29 E6**
Kong **53 G5**
Kong, Koh **38 B2**
Konglu **41 D11**
Kongolo **57 F5**
Konin **16 B4**
Konjic **20 C6**
Konosha **28 C5**
Konotop **24 C3**
Konqi He ➔ **34 B4**
Końskie **16 C5**
Konstanz **14 E5**
Kontagora **53 F7**
Konya **46 C3**
Konya Ovası **46 C3**
Kooloonong **62 B3**
Koonibba **62 B1**
Koorawatha **63 B4**
Kootenay L. **69 D8**
Kopaonik **22 C3**
Koper **20 B4**
Kopi **62 B2**
Koprivnica **20 A6**
Kopychyntsi **17 D7**
Korab **22 D3**
Korçë **23 D3**
Korčula **20 C6**
Kordestan = Kurdistan **46 D5**
Kordestān □ **46 D6**
Kordofān **55 F4**
Korea, North ■ **35 C7**
Korea, South ■ **35 C7**
Korea Bay **35 C7**
Korea Strait **35 C7**
Korets **17 C8**
Korhogo **53 G4**
Korinthiakos Kolpos **23 E4**
Korinthos **23 F4**
Köriyama **33 E7**
Korneshty = Cornești **17 E9**
Koro **53 G4**
Korogwe **57 F7**
Koror = Melekeok **36 C4**
Körös ➔ **16 E5**
Korosten **17 C9**
Korostyshev **17 C9**
Kortrijk **14 C2**
Kos **23 F6**
Kościan **16 B3**
Kosciuszko, Mt. **63 C4**
Kosha **54 D5**
K'oshih = Kashi **34 C2**
Koshiki-Rettō **33 H1**
Košice **16 D5**
Kosovo ■ **22 C3**
Kosovska Mitrovica **22 C3**
Kõstĩ **55 F5**
Kostopil **17 C8**
Kostroma **24 B5**
Kostrzyn **16 B2**
Koszalin **16 A3**
Kota **43 G9**
Kota Belud **38 C5**
Kota Bharu **38 C2**
Kota Kinabalu **38 C5**
Kota Kubu Bharu **39 D2**
Kota Tinggi **39 D2**
Kotaagung **39 F2**
Kotaboru **39 E5**
Kotabumi **39 E2**
Kotamobagu **37 D2**
Kotelnich **24 B6**
Kotelnyy, Ostrov **31 B11**
Kotka **9 C11**
Kotlas **28 C5**
Kotor **22 C2**
Kotovsk **17 E9**
Kotri **42 G6**
Kotturu **43 M10**
Kotuy ➔ **30 B8**
Kotzebue **69 B3**
Koudougou **53 F5**
Kouilou ➔ **56 E2**
Koula Moutou **56 E2**
Koulen = Kulen **38 B2**
Koumra **55 G2**
Kounradskiy **29 E8**
Kousseri **55 F1**
Kouvola **8 C11**
Kovel **17 C7**
Kovrov **24 B5**
Koyampattur = Coimbatore **43 P10**
Köyceğiz **23 F7**
Kozan **46 C3**
Kozani **23 D3**
Kozhikode = Calicut **43 P9**
Kozyatyn **17 D9**
Kra, Isthmus of = Kra, Kho Khot **38 B1**
Kra, Kho Khot **38 B1**
Kracheh **38 B3**
Kragujevac **22 B3**
Krajina **20 B6**
Krakatau = Rakata, Pulau **39 F3**
Krakatoa = Rakata, Pulau **39 F3**
Kraków **16 C4**
Kraljevo **22 C3**
Kramatorsk **25 D4**
Kranj **20 A5**
Kraśnik **16 C6**
Krasnoarmeysk **29 D5**
Krasnodar **25 D4**
Krasnoperekopsk **25 D3**
Krasnoselkup **28 C9**
Krasnoturinsk **28 D7**
Krasnoyarsk **30 D7**
Krasnyy Luch **25 D4**
Krasnyy Yar **25 D6**
Kratie = Kracheh **38 B3**
Krau **37 E6**
Krefeld **14 C4**
Kremen **20 B5**
Kremenchuk **24 D3**
Kremenchuksk Vdskh. **24 D3**
Kremenets **17 C7**
Krems **15 D8**
Kribi **56 D1**
Krichev = Krychaw **17 B10**
Krishna ➔ **40 K3**
Krishnanagar **41 F7**
Kristiansand **9 D7**
Kristiansund **8 C7**
Kriti **23 G5**
Krivoy Rog = Kryvyy Rih **25 D3**
Krk **20 B5**
Kronprins Olav Kyst **96 A9**
Kronshtadt **24 B2**
Kroonstad **59 D5**
Kropotkin *Irkutsk, Russia* **30 D9**
Kropotkin *Krasnodar, Russia* **25 D5**
Krotoszyn **16 C3**
Krung Thep = Bangkok **38 B2**
Krupki **17 A9**
Kruševac **22 C3**
Krychaw **17 B10**
Krymskiy Poluostrov = Krymskyy Pivostriv **25 D3**
Krymskyy Pivostriv **25 D3**
Kryvyy Rih **25 D3**

Ksar el Kebir 52 B4
Ksar es Souk = Er Rachidia 52 B5
Kuala Lipis 39 D2
Kuala Lumpur 39 D2
Kuala Sepetang 38 D2
Kuala Terengganu 38 C2
Kualajelai 39 E4
Kualakapuas 39 E4
Kualakurun 39 E4
Kualapembuang 39 E4
Kualasimpang 39 D1
Kuandang 37 D2
Kuangchou = Guangzhou 35 D6
Kuantan 39 D2
Kuba = Quba 25 E6
Kuban ➔ 25 D4
Kuching 39 D4
Kucing = Kuching 39 D4
Kuda 43 H7
Kudat 38 C5
Kudymkar 28 D6
Kueiyang = Guiyang 35 D5
Kufra Oasis = Al Kufrah 54 D3
Kufstein 15 E7
Kugaaruk = Pelly Bay 70 C5
Kugluktuk 68 B8
Küh-e 'Alijūq 44 D2
Küh-e Sorkh 44 C4
Kühak 42 F3
Kühhā-ye-Bashākerd 45 E4
Kühpāyeh 44 C3
Kuito 58 A3
Kuji 32 C7
Kukës 22 C3
Kula 23 E7
Kulasekarappattinam 43 Q11
Kulen 38 B2
Külob 29 F7
Kulsary 29 E6
Kulunda 29 D8
Kulwin 62 C3
Kulyab = Külob 29 F7
Kum Tekei 29 E8
Kuma ➔ 25 E6
Kumagaya 33 E6
Kumai 39 E4
Kumamba, Kepulauan 37 E5
Kumamoto 33 G2
Kumanovo 22 C3
Kumara 65 E4
Kumasi 53 G5
Kumba 53 H7
Kumbakonam 43 P11
Kumbarilla 63 A5
Kumon Bum 41 D11
Kunama 63 C4
Kungala 63 A5
Kungrad = Qūnghirot 29 E6
Kungur 29 D6
Kunlong 41 F12
Kunlun Shan 34 C3
Kunming 34 D5
Kunya-Urgench = Köneürgench 29 E6
Kuopio 8 C11
Kupa ➔ 20 B6
Kuqa 34 B3
Kür ➔ 25 E6
Kura = Kür ➔ 25 E6
Kurdistan 46 D5
Kürdzhali 22 D5
Kure 33 F3
Kurgaldzhinskiy 29 D8
Kurgan 29 D7
Kuria Maria Is. = Hallāniyat, Jazā'ir al 49 D6
Kurigram 41 E7
Kuril Is. = Kurilskiye Ostrova 31 E12
Kurilskiye Ostrova 31 E12
Kurnool 43 L11
Kurow 65 F4
Kurri Kurri 63 B5
Kursk 24 C4
Kuruktag 34 B3
Kuruman 58 D4
Kurume 33 G2
Kus Gölü 23 D6
Kuşadası 23 F6
Kushimoto 33 G4
Kushiro 32 B9
Kushtia 41 F7
Kuskokwim B. 69 C3
Kustanay = Qostanay 29 D7
Kütahya 25 F3
Kutaisi 25 E5
Kutaraja = Banda Aceh 38 C1
Kutch, Gulf of = Kachchh, Gulf of 43 H6
Kutch, Rann of = Kachchh, Rann of 43 G6
Kutno 16 B4
Kutu 56 E3
Kutum 55 F3
Kuujjuaq 70 D7
Kuujjuarapik 71 D6
Kuusamo 8 B11
Kuwait = Al Kuwayt 47 E7
Kuwait ■ 47 E6
Kuybyshev = Samara 24 C7
Kuybyshev 29 D8
Kuybyshevskoye Vdkhr. 24 B6
Kuyumba 30 C7
Kuzey Anadolu Dağları 25 E4
Kuznetsk 24 C6
Kvarner 20 B5
Kvarnerić 20 B5
Kwajalein 64 J11
Kwakoegron 92 A2
KwaMashu 59 D6
Kwando ➔ 58 B4
Kwangchow = Guangzhou 35 D6
Kwango ➔ 56 E3
Kwangsi-Chuang = Guangxi Zhuangzu Zizhiqu □ 35 D5
Kwangtung = Guangdong □ 35 D6
Kwatisore 37 E4
KwaZulu Natal □ 59 D6
Kweichow = Guizhou □ 35 D5
Kwekwe 59 B5
Kwidzyn 16 B4
Kwoka 37 E4
Kyabra Cr. ➔ 63 A3
Kyabram 63 C4
Kyancutta 62 B2
Kyaukpadaung 41 G10
Kyaukpyu 41 H9
Kyaukse 41 G11
Kyneton 63 C3
Kyō-ga-Saki 33 F4
Kyoga, L. 57 D6
Kyogle 63 A5
Kyonpyaw 41 J10
Kyōto 33 F4
Kypros = Cyprus ■ 46 D3
Kyrenia 46 D3
Kyrgyzstan ■ 29 E8
Kyrtylakh 31 C10
Kystatyam 30 C10
Kythira 23 F4
Kyunhla 41 F10
Kyūshū 33 G2
Kyustendil 22 C4
Kyusyur 30 B10
Kyyiv 17 C10
Kyyivske Vdskh. 17 C10
Kyzyl Kum 29 E7
Kyzyl-Kyya 29 E8
Kyzyl-Orda = Qyzylorda 29 E7

L

La Alcarria 19 B4
La Asunción 90 A6
La Banda 94 B4
La Carlota 94 C4
La Ceiba 85 D7
La Cocha 94 B3
La Coruña = A Coruña 18 A1
La Crosse 75 D9
La Estrada = A Estrada 18 A1
La Grande ➔ 71 D6
La Grange 82 C5
La Guaira 90 A5
La Habana 86 B3
La Línea de la Concepción 18 D3
La Mancha 19 C4
La Palma 52 C2
La Palma del Condado 18 D2
La Paragua 90 B6
La Paz *Entre Ríos, Argentina* 94 C5
La Paz *San Luis, Argentina* 94 C3
La Paz *Bolivia* 91 G5
La Paz *Mexico* 84 C2
La Pedrera 90 D5
La Plata 94 D5
La Quiaca 94 A3
La Rioja 94 B3
La Rioja □ 19 A4
La Robla 18 A3
La Roche-sur-Yon 12 C3
La Rochelle 12 C3
La Roda 19 C4
La Romana 87 C6
La Serena 94 B2
La Seu d'Urgell 19 A6
La Seyne-sur-Mer 13 E6
La Spézia 13 D8
La Tortuga 87 D6
La Tuque 71 E6
La Unión 95 E2
La Urbana 90 B5
La Vall d'Uixó 19 C5
La Vega 87 C5
Laas Caanood = Las Anod 49 F4
Labe = Elbe ➔ 14 B5
Labé 53 F3
Laboulaye 94 C4
Labrador 71 D7
Labrador City 71 D7
Labrador Sea 70 D8
Lábrea 91 E6
Labuan 38 C5
Labuan, Pulau 38 C5
Labuha 37 E3
Labuhanbajo 37 F2
Labuk, Telok 38 C5
Labyrinth, L. 62 B2
Labytnangi 28 C7
Lac La Biche 69 C8
Lac la Martre = Wha Ti 68 B8
Lacanau 12 D3
Laccadive Is. = Lakshadweep Is. 26 G9
Lacepede B. 62 C2
Lachlan ➔ 63 B3
Lacombe 69 C8
Ladakh Ra. 42 B10
Lādīz 45 D5
Ladoga, L. = Ladozhskoye Ozero 8 C12
Ladozhskoye Ozero 8 C12
Ladysmith 59 D5
Lae 61 B8
Lafayette 81 D7
Lafia 53 G7
Laghmān □ 45 C7
Laghouat 52 B6
Lagonoy G. 36 B2
Lagos *Nigeria* 53 G6
Lagos *Portugal* 18 D1
Laguna 94 B7
Lagunas 90 E3
Lahad Datu 36 C1
Lahad Datu, Telok 36 D1
Lahat 39 E2
Lahewa 39 D1
Lāhījān 46 C7
Lahn ➔ 14 C4
Lahore 42 D9
Lahti 8 C11
Lahtis = Lahti 8 C11
Laï 55 G2
Laidley 63 A5

Laila = Layla **47 G6**
Lairg **10 B4**
Laizhou **35 C6**
Lajes **94 B6**
Lake Cargelligo **63 B4**
Lake Charles **81 D7**
Lake City **83 D6**
Lake Harbour = Kimmirut **70 C7**
Lake Worth **83 F7**
Lakeland **83 E7**
Lakes Entrance **63 C4**
Lakewood **76 D5**
Lakhnau = Lucknow **40 D3**
Lakonikos Kolpos **23 F4**
Lakor **37 F3**
Lakota **53 G4**
Lakshadweep Is. **26 G9**
Lalaghat **41 E9**
L'Albufera **19 C5**
Lalín **18 A1**
Lalitapur **40 D5**
Lamaing **41 K11**
Lamas **91 E3**
Lambaréné **56 E2**
Lambert Glacier **96 B10**
Lamego **18 B2**
Lameroo **62 C3**
Lamia **23 E4**
Lamon B. **36 B2**
Lampa **91 G4**
Lampedusa **21 G4**
Lampione **21 G4**
Lampung □ **39 F2**
Lamu **57 E8**
Lāna'i **78 H12**
Lanak La **42 B11**
Lanak'o Shank'ou = Lanak La **42 B11**
Lancaster *U.K.* **11 D5**
Lancaster *U.S.A.* **77 D7**
Lancaster Sd. **70 B5**
Lanchow = Lanzhou **35 C5**
Lanciano **20 C5**
Landeck **14 E6**
Landes **12 D3**
Landi Kotal **42 B7**
Land's End **11 F4**
Landshut **15 D7**
La'nga Co **40 B3**
Langjökull **8 C2**
Langkawi, Pulau **38 C1**
Langkon **38 C5**
Langreo **18 A3**
Langres **13 C6**
Langres, Plateau de **13 C6**
Langsa **38 D1**
Languedoc **13 E5**
Lannion **12 B2**
Lansdowne **63 B5**
Lansing **76 C3**
Lanusei **21 E2**
Lanzarote **52 C3**
Lanzhou **35 C5**
Laoag **36 A2**
Laoang **36 B3**
Laohekou **35 C6**
Laon **13 B5**
Laos ■ **38 A3**
Laparan **36 C1**
Lapland = Lappland **8 B10**
Lappland **8 B10**
Lapseki **23 D6**
Laptev Sea **30 B10**
L'Àquila **20 C4**
Lär **44 E3**
Laramie **74 E2**
Larantuka **37 F2**
Larap **36 B2**
Larat **37 F4**
Laredo **80 F4**
Lariang **37 E1**
Larisa **23 E4**
Larnaca **46 D3**
Larne **11 D4**
Larrimah **60 D5**
Larsen Ice Shelf **96 A3**
Larvik **9 D8**
Laryak **29 C8**
Las Anod **49 F4**
Las Cruces **79 D9**
Las Flores **94 D5**
Las Lajas **94 D2**
Las Lomitas **94 A4**
Las Palmas **52 C2**
Las Plumas **95 E3**
Las Varillas **94 C4**
Las Vegas **78 B5**
Lash-e Joveyn **42 D2**
Lashio **41 F11**
Lassen Pk. **72 F3**
Lastoursville **56 E2**
Lastovo **20 C6**
Latacunga **90 D3**
Latakia = Al Lādhiqīyah **46 D3**
Latina **20 D4**
Latium = Lazio □ **20 C4**
Latrobe **62 D4**
Latvia ■ **24 B1**
Lauchhammer **15 C7**
Launceston **62 D4**
Laurel **81 D9**
Lauria **21 D5**
Lausanne **14 E4**
Laut **38 D3**
Laut Kecil, Kepulauan **39 E5**
Laval **12 B3**
Lavrio **23 F5**
Lawas **38 D5**
Lawele **37 F2**
Lawng Pit **41 E11**
Lawrence *N.Z.* **65 F3**
Lawrence *U.S.A.* **75 F7**
Lawton **80 B4**
Layla **47 G6**
Lazio □ **20 C4**
Lazo **32 B3**
Le Creusot **13 C6**
Le Havre **12 B4**
Le Mans **12 C4**
Le Mont-St-Michel **12 B3**
Le Puy-en-Velay **13 D5**
Le Touquet-Paris-Plage **12 A4**
Le Tréport **12 A4**
Le Verdon-sur-Mer **12 D3**
Leamington Spa = Royal Leamington Spa **11 E6**
Leavenworth **75 F7**
Lebak **36 C2**
Lebanon ■ **46 D3**
Lębork **16 A3**
Lebrija **18 D2**
Lebu **94 D2**
Lecce **21 D7**
Lecco **13 D8**
Lech ➜ **14 D6**
Łęczyca **16 B4**
Leeds **11 E6**
Leer **14 B4**
Leeton **63 B4**
Leeuwarden **14 B3**
Leeuwin, C. **60 G2**
Leeward Is. **87 C7**
Lefkada **23 E3**
Leganés **18 B4**
Legazpi **36 B2**
Leghorn = Livorno **20 C3**
Legionowo **16 B5**
Legnago **20 B3**
Legnica **16 C3**
Legume **63 A5**
Leh **42 B10**
Leicester **11 E6**
Leiden **14 B3**
Leie ➜ **14 C2**
Leine ➜ **14 B5**
Leinster □ **11 E3**
Leipzig **15 C7**
Leiria **18 C1**
Leitrim **11 D2**
Leizhou Bandao **35 D6**
Leleque **95 E2**
Léman, L. **13 C7**
Lemhi Ra. **73 D7**
Lena ➜ **30 B10**
Leninogorsk **29 D9**
Leninsk **25 D6**
Leninsk-Kuznetskiy **29 D9**
Lenmalu **37 E4**
Lens **13 A5**
Lentini **21 F5**
Leoben **15 E8**
Leodhas = Lewis **10 B3**
León *Mexico* **84 C4**
León *Nic.* **85 E7**
León *Spain* **18 A3**
León, Montes de **18 A2**
Leongatha **63 C4**
Leova **17 E9**
Lepel = Lyepyel **24 C2**
Lepikha **31 C10**
Lérida = Lleida **19 B6**
Lerwick **10 A6**
Les Cayes **86 C5**
Les Sables-d'Olonne **12 C3**
Lesbos **23 E6**
Leskovac **22 C3**
Lesotho ■ **59 D5**
Lesozavodsk **32 A3**
Lesser Antilles **87 D7**
Lesser Sunda Is. **37 F2**
Lésvos = Lesbos **23 E6**
Leszno **16 C3**
Lethbridge **69 D8**
Leti, Kepulauan **37 F3**
Leti Is. = Leti, Kepulauan **37 F3**
Leticia **90 D4**
Letpadan **41 J10**
Letpan **41 H10**
Letterkenny **11 D3**
Leuser, G. **39 D1**
Leuven **14 C3**
Levanger **8 C8**
Levin **64 D6**
Lévis **71 E6**
Levka Oros **23 G5**
Levkás = Lefkada **23 E3**
Levkôsia = Nicosia **46 D3**
Levskigrad = Karlovo **22 C5**
Lewis **10 B3**
Lewisporte **71 E8**
Lewiston *Idaho, U.S.A.* **72 C5**
Lewiston *Maine, U.S.A.* **77 B10**
Lexington *Ky., U.S.A.* **76 E3**
Lexington *N.C., U.S.A.* **83 B7**
Leyte □ **36 B2**
Lezhë **22 D2**
Lhasa **34 D4**
Lhazê **34 D3**
Lhokkruet **38 D1**
Lhokseumawe **38 C1**
L'Hospitalet de Llobregat **19 B7**
Liancourt Rocks **33 E2**
Lianga **36 C3**
Lianyungang **35 C6**
Liaoning □ **35 B7**
Liaoyuan **35 B7**
Liard ➜ **68 B7**
Libau = Liepāja **24 B1**
Libenge **56 D3**
Liberal **80 A3**
Liberec **16 C2**
Liberia ■ **53 G4**
Lībīya, Sahrā' **54 C4**
Libobo, Tanjung **37 E3**
Libourne **12 D3**
Libreville **56 D1**
Libya ■ **54 C2**
Libyan Desert = Lībīya, Sahrā' **54 C4**
Licantén **94 D2**
Licata **21 F4**
Lichinga **59 A7**
Lida **17 B7**
Liechtenstein ■ **14 E5**
Liège **14 C3**
Liegnitz = Legnica **16 C3**
Lienyünchiangshih = Lianyungang **35 C6**
Lienz **15 E7**
Liepāja **24 B1**
Lietuva = Lithuania ■ **24 B1**
Liffey ➜ **11 E3**
Lifford **11 D3**
Lightning Ridge **63 A4**
Liguria □ **13 D8**

Ligurian Sea 20 C2
Lijiang 34 D5
Likasi 57 G5
Lille 13 A5
Lillehammer 8 C8
Lilongwe 59 A6
Liloy 36 C2
Lim ➔ 20 C7
Lima *Indonesia* 37 E3
Lima *Peru* 91 F3
Lima *U.S.A.* 76 D3
Lima ➔ 18 B1
Limassol 46 D3
Limay Mahuida 94 D3
Limbang 38 D5
Limbe 53 H7
Limbri 63 B5
Limburg 14 C5
Limeira 93 G4
Limerick 11 E2
Limfjorden 9 D7
Limia = Lima ➔ 18 B1
Limnos 23 E5
Limoges 12 D4
Limón 86 E3
Limousin □ 12 D4
Limoux 12 E5
Limpopo ➔ 59 D6
Limuru 57 E7
Linares *Chile* 94 D2
Linares *Mexico* 84 C5
Linares *Spain* 18 C4
Lincoln *Argentina* 94 C4
Lincoln *N.Z.* 65 E5
Lincoln *U.K.* 11 E6
Lincoln *U.S.A.* 75 E6
Linden 90 B7
Lindesnes 9 D7
Lindi 57 F7
Lindos 23 F7
Lingayen 36 A2
Lingayen G. 36 A2
Lingen 14 B4
Lingga 39 E2
Lingga, Kepulauan 39 E2
Lingga Arch. = Lingga, Kepulauan 39 E2
Linguère 53 E2
Linhai 35 D7
Linhares 93 F5
Linköping 9 D9
Linosa 21 G4
Lins 93 G4
Linville 63 A5
Linxia 34 C5
Linz 15 D8
Lion, G. du 13 E6
Lions, G. of = Lion, G. du 13 E6
Lipa 36 B2
Lípari 21 E5
Lípari, Is. = Eólie, Îs. 21 E5
Lipcani 17 D8
Lipetsk 24 C4
Lipkany = Lipcani 17 D8
Lipovets 17 D9
Lippe ➔ 14 C4
Liptrap, C. 63 C4
Lira 57 D6
Liria = Lliria 19 C5
Lisala 56 D4
Lisboa 18 C1
Lisbon = Lisboa 18 C1
Lisburn 11 D3
Lisichansk = Lysychansk 25 D4
Lisieux 12 B4
Liski 24 C4
Lismore 63 A5
Lister, Mt. 96 B15
Liston 63 A5
Listowel 11 E2
Litani ➔ *Lebanon* 46 D3
Litani ➔ *S. Amer.* 30 E
Lithgow 63 B5
Lithino, Akra 23 G5
Lithuania ■ 24 B1
Litoměřice 16 C2
Little Barrier I. 64 B6
Little Khingan Mts. = Xiao Hinggan Ling 35 B7
Little Laut Is. = Laut Kecil, Kepulauan 39 E5
Little Missouri ➔ 74 B3
Little River 65 E5
Little Rock 81 B7
Little Zab = Zāb aş Şaghīr ➔ 46 D5
Liukang Tenggaja = Sabalana, Kepulauan 37 F1
Liuwa Plain 58 A4
Liuzhou 35 D5
Livadia 23 E4
Liverpool *Canada* 71 E7
Liverpool *U.K.* 11 E5
Liverpool Plains 63 B5
Liverpool Ra. 63 B5
Livingstone 59 B5
Livny 24 C4
Livorno 20 C3
Ljubljana 20 A5
Llancanelo, Salina 94 D3
Llanelli 11 F4
Llanes 18 A3
Llano Estacado 80 C2
Llanos 90 C4
Lleida 19 B6
Lliria 19 C5
Llobregat ➔ 19 B7
Lloret de Mar 19 B7
Llucmajor 19 C7
Llullaillaco, Volcán 94 A3
Loa ➔ 94 A2
Lobatse 59 D5
Lobería 94 D5
Lobito 58 A2
Locarno 13 C8
Loch Garman = Wexford 11 E3
Loches 12 C4
Lock 62 B2
Lodhran 42 E7
Lodi *Italy* 13 D8
Lodi *U.S.A.* 72 G3
Lodja 56 E4
Lodwar 57 D7
Łódź 16 C4
Lofoten 8 B9
Logan 73 F8
Logan, Mt. 68 B5
Logone ➔ 55 F2
Logroño 19 A4
Lohardaga 40 F5
Loi-kaw 41 H11
Loir ➔ 12 C3
Loire ➔ 12 C2
Loja *Ecuador* 90 D3
Loja *Spain* 18 D3
Loji = Kawasi 37 E3
Lokitaung 57 D7
Lokkan tekojärvi 8 B11
Lokoja 53 G7
Lom 22 C4
Lomami ➔ 56 D4
Lombárdia □ 13 D8
Lombardy = Lombárdia □ 13 D8
Lomblen 37 F2
Lombok 39 F5
Lomé 53 G6
Lomela 56 E4
Lomela ➔ 56 E4
Lomond, L. 10 C4
Lompobatang 37 F1
Łomża 16 B6
Loncoche 95 D2
Londa 43 M9
London *Canada* 71 E5
London *U.K.* 11 F6
Londonderry 11 D3
Londonderry, C. 60 C4
Londonderry, I. 95 H2
Londrina 94 A6
Long Beach 78 D3
Long I. *Bahamas* 86 B4
Long I. *U.S.A.* 77 D9
Long Xuyen 38 B3
Longford *Australia* 62 D4
Longford *Ireland* 11 E3
Longiram 39 E5
Longnawan 39 D4
Longreach 61 E7
Longview *Tex., U.S.A.* 81 C6
Longview *Wash., U.S.A.* 72 C2
Lons-le-Saunier 13 C6
Lop Nor = Lop Nur 34 B4
Lop Nur 34 B4
Lopez, C. 56 E1
Lora ➔ 42 D4
Lora, Hāmūn-i- 42 E4
Lora Cr. ➔ 62 A2
Lora del Río 18 D3
Lorain 76 D4
Loralai 42 D6
Lorca 19 D5
Lord Howe I. 64 N10
Lord Howe Rise 64 N11
Lorestān □ 46 D6
Loreto 92 D4
Lorient 12 C2
Lorne 62 C3
Lorraine □ 13 B7
Los Alamos 79 C9
Los Andes 94 C2
Los Angeles *Chile* 94 D2
Los Angeles *U.S.A.* 78 C3
Los Blancos 94 A4
Los Hermanos Is. 90 A6
Los Mochis 84 B3
Los Roques Is. 90 A5
Los Testigos, Is. 90 A6
Los Vilos 94 C2
Lošinj 20 B5
Lot ➔ 12 D4
Lota 94 D2
Loubomo 56 E2
Louga 53 E2
Lougheed I. 70 B3
Louis Trichardt 59 C5
Louis XIV, Pte. 71 D6
Louisiade Arch. 61 C9
Louisiana □ 81 D8
Louisville 76 E3
Loulé 18 D1
Lourdes 12 E3
Louth *Australia* 63 B4
Louth *U.K.* 11 E6
Louvain = Leuven 14 C3
Lovech 22 C5
Lowell 77 C10
Lower California = Baja California 84 A1
Lower Hutt 65 D6
Lower Saxony = Niedersachsen □ 14 B5
Lower Tunguska = Tunguska, Nizhnyaya ➔ 30 C6
Lowestoft 11 E7
Lowgar □ 45 C7
Łowicz 16 B4
Loxton 62 B3
Loyalty Is. = Loyauté, Îs. 64 M11
Loyang = Luoyang 35 C6
Loyauté, Îs. 64 M11
Loyev = Loyew 17 C10
Loyew 17 C10
Luachimo 56 F4
Lualaba ➔ 57 D5
Luanda 56 F2
Luangwa ➔ 59 A6
Luanshya 59 A5
Luapula ➔ 57 F5
Luarca 18 A2
Luau 56 G4
Lubang Is. 36 B2
Lubango 58 A2
Lubbock 80 C3
Lübeck 15 B6
Lubero = Luofu 57 E5
Lubin 16 C3
Lublin 17 C6
Lubnān = Lebanon ■ 46 D3
Lubuk Antu 39 D4
Lubuklinggau 39 E2
Lubuksikaping 39 D2
Lubumbashi 59 A5
Lubutu 57 E5
Lucca 20 C3
Lucena *Phil.* 36 B2
Lucena *Spain* 18 D3
Lucerne = Luzern 13 C8
Luckenwalde 15 B7
Lucknow 40 D3
Lüda = Dalian 35 C7

Lüderitz 58 D3
Ludhiana 42 D9
Ludwigsburg 14 D5
Ludwigshafen 14 D5
Lufira ➔ 57 F5
Lufkin 81 D6
Luga 24 B2
Lugano 13 C8
Lugansk = Luhansk 25 D4
Lugh Ganana 49 G3
Lugo *Italy* 20 B3
Lugo *Spain* 18 A2
Lugoj 17 F5
Lugovoy = Qulan 29 E8
Luhansk 25 D4
Luichow Pen. = Leizhou Bandao 35 D6
Luimneach = Limerick 11 E2
Luís Correia 92 C5
Luitpold Coast 96 B5
Luiza 56 F4
Lukanga Swamp 59 A5
Lukenie ➔ 56 E3
Łuków 17 C6
Luleå 8 B10
Luleälven ➔ 8 B10
Lüleburgaz 22 D6
Lulonga ➔ 56 D3
Lulua ➔ 56 E4
Lumbala N'guimbo 58 A4
Lumsden 65 F3
Lumut, Tanjung 39 E3
Lund 9 D8
Lundazi 59 A6
Lundu 39 D3
Lüneburg 14 B6
Lüneburg Heath = Lüneburger Heide 14 B6
Lüneburger Heide 14 B6
Lunéville 13 B7
Lunglei 41 F9
Luni 42 G8
Luni ➔ 43 G7
Luninets = Luninyets 17 B8
Luninyets 17 B8
Luofu 57 E5
Luoyang 35 C6
Lurgan 11 D3
Lusaka 59 B5
Lusambo 56 E4
Lushnjë 23 D2
Luta = Dalian 35 C7
Lutherstadt Wittenberg 15 C7
Luton 11 F6
Łutselk'e 68 B8
Lutsk 17 C7
Lützow Holmbukta 96 A8
Luuq = Lugh Ganana 49 G3
Luwuk 37 E2
Luxembourg 13 B7
Luxembourg ■ 14 D4
Luxor = El Uqsur 54 C5
Luza 24 A6
Luzern 13 C8
Luzhou 35 D5
Luziânia 93 F4
Luzon 36 A2
Lviv 17 D7
Lvov = Lviv 17 D7
Lyakhavichy 17 B8
Lyakhovskiye, Ostrova 31 B12
Lydenburg 59 D6
Lydia 23 E7
Lyell 65 D5
Lyepyel 24 C2
Łyna ➔ 16 A5
Lynchburg 77 F6
Lynd Ra. 63 A4
Lyndhurst 62 B2
Lynn Lake 69 C9
Lyon 13 D6
Lyonnais 13 D6
Lyons = Lyon 13 D6
Lys = Leie ➔ 14 C2
Lysychansk 25 D4
Lyttelton 65 E5
Lyubertsy 24 B4
Lyuboml 17 C7

M

Ma'alah 47 F6
Ma'ān 47 E3
Ma'anshan 35 C6
Ma'arrat an Nu'mān 46 D4
Maas ➔ 14 C3
Maastricht 13 A6
McAllen 80 F4
Macao = Macau 35 D6
Macapá 92 B3
Macau *Brazil* 92 D6
Macau *China* 35 D6
M'Clintock Chan. 68 A9
M'Clure Str. 70 B2
McComb 81 D8
MacDonnell Ranges 60 E5
McDouall Peak 62 A1
Macdougall L. 68 B10
Macedonia □ 23 D4
Macedonia ■ 22 D3
Maceió 93 D6
Macerata 20 C4
Macfarlane, L. 62 B2
Macgillycuddy's Reeks 11 F2
McGregor Ra. 62 A3
Mach 42 E5
Machado = Jiparaná ➔ 91 E6
Machakos 57 E7
Machala 90 D3
Machilipatnam 40 J3
Machiques 90 A4
Machupicchu 91 F4
Macintyre ➔ 63 A5
Mackay 61 E8
Mackay, L. 60 E4
Mackenzie ➔ 68 B6
Mackenzie City = Linden 90 B7
Mackenzie King I. 70 B2
Mackenzie Mts. 68 B6
McKinley, Mt. 69 B4
McKinney 81 C5
Macksville 63 B5
Maclean 63 A5
Maclear 59 E5
Macleay ➔ 63 B5
McMurdo Sd. 96 B15
Mâcon *France* 13 C6
Macon *U.S.A.* 83 C6
McPherson Ra. 63 A5
Macquarie Harbour 62 D4
MacRobertson Land 96 B10
Macumba ➔ 62 A2
Madadeni 59 D6
Madagascar ■ 59 C9
Madā'in Sālih 47 F4
Madama 54 D1
Madang 61 B8
Madaripur 41 F8
Madauk 41 J11
Madaya 41 F11
Maddalena 20 D2
Madeira 52 B2
Madeira ➔ 90 D7
Madeleine, Îs. de la 71 E7
Madha 43 L9
Madhya Pradesh □ 43 H10
Madikeri 43 N9
Madimba 56 E3
Madingou 56 E2
Madison 75 D10
Madiun 39 F4
Madras = Chennai 43 N12
Madras = Tamil Nadu □ 43 P10
Madre, L. 80 F5
Madre, Sierra 36 A2
Madre de Dios ➔ 91 F5
Madre de Dios, I. 95 G1
Madre Occidental, Sierra 84 B3
Madrid 18 B4
Madurai 43 Q11
Madurantakam 43 N11
Mae Sot 38 A1
Maebashi 33 E6
Maevatanana 59 B9
Mafeteng 59 D5
Maffra 63 C4
Mafia I. 57 F7
Mafra *Brazil* 94 B7
Mafra *Portugal* 18 C1
Magadan 31 D13
Magallanes, Estrecho de 95 G2
Magangué 90 B4
Magdalen Is. = Madeleine, Îs. de la 71 E7
Magdalena *Argentina* 94 D5
Magdalena *Bolivia* 91 F6
Magdalena ➔ 90 A4
Magdeburg 15 B6
Magelang 39 F4
Magellan's Str. = Magallanes, Estrecho de 95 G2
Maggiore, Lago 13 D8
Magnetic Pole (North) 70 A2
Magnetic Pole (South) 96 A13
Magnitogorsk 29 D6
Magoša = Famagusta 46 D3
Maguarinho, C. 92 C4
Mağusa = Famagusta 46 D3
Magwe 41 G10
Magyarorszag = Hungary ■ 16 E4
Mahābād 46 C6
Mahabo 59 C8
Mahajanga 59 B9
Mahakam ➔ 39 E5
Mahalapye 59 C5
Maḥallāt 44 C2
Mahanadi ➔ 40 G6
Maharashtra □ 43 J9
Mahbubnagar 43 L10
Mahdia 54 A1
Mahenge 57 F7
Maheno 65 F4
Mahesana 43 H8
Mahia Pen. 64 C7
Mahilyow 17 B10
Mahinerangi, L. 65 F3
Mahón = Maó 19 C8
Mai-Ndombe, L. 56 E3
Maicurú ➔ 92 C3
Maidstone 11 F7
Maiduguri 55 F1
Maijdi 41 F8
Maikala Ra. 40 G3
Main ➔ 14 D5
Maine 12 C3
Maingkwan 41 D11
Mainit, L. 36 C3
Mainland *Orkney, U.K.* 10 B5
Mainland *Shet., U.K.* 10 A6
Mainz 14 C5
Maipú 94 D5
Maiquetía 90 A5
Mairabari 41 D9
Maitland *N.S.W., Australia* 63 B5
Maitland *S. Austral., Australia* 62 B2
Maizuru 33 F4
Majene 37 E1
Majorca = Mallorca 19 C7
Majuro 64 J12
Makale 37 E1
Makarikari = Makgadikgadi Salt Pans 59 C5
Makasar = Ujung Pandang 37 F1
Makasar, Selat 37 E1
Makasar, Str. of = Makasar, Selat 37 E1
Makat = Maqat 29 E6
Makedonija = Macedonia ■ 22 D3
Makeyevka = Makiyivka 25 D4
Makgadikgadi Salt Pans 59 C5
Makhachkala 25 E6
Makhado = Louis Trichardt 59 C5

Makhfar al Buşayyah **47 E6**
Makian **37 D3**
Makĭnsk **29 D8**
Makiyivka **25 D4**
Makkah **47 G4**
Makó **16 E5**
Makokou **56 D2**
Makrai **43 H10**
Makran **45 E5**
Makran Coast Range **42 G4**
Maksimkin Yar **29 D9**
Mäkü **46 C6**
Makurazaki **33 H2**
Makurdi **53 G7**
Malabar Coast **43 P9**
Malacca, Straits of **38 D1**
Maladzyechna **17 A8**
Málaga **18 D3**
Malagasy Rep. = Madagascar ■ **59 C9**
Malakâl **55 G5**
Malakand **42 B7**
Malang **39 F4**
Malanje **56 F3**
Mälaren **9 D9**
Malargüe **94 D3**
Malaryta **17 C7**
Malatya **46 C4**
Malawi ■ **59 A6**
Malawi, L. **59 A6**
Malay Pen. **38 C2**
Malaybalay **36 C3**
Malāyer **46 D7**
Malaysia ■ **38 D4**
Malazgirt **25 F5**
Malbooma **62 B1**
Malbork **16 A4**
Malden I. **65 K15**
Maldives ■ **26 H9**
Maldonado **94 C6**
Maleas, Akra **23 F4**
Malegaon **43 J9**
Malema **59 A7**
Malha **55 E4**
Mali ■ **53 E5**
Mali ➔ **41 E11**
Maliku **37 E2**
Malili **37 E2**
Malin Hd. **10 D3**
Malindi **57 E8**
Malines = Mechelen **14 C3**
Malino **37 D2**
Malita **36 C3**
Malkara **22 D6**
Mallacoota Inlet **63 C4**
Mallaig **10 C4**
Mallawi **54 C5**
Mallorca **19 C7**
Mallow **11 E2**
Malmö **9 D8**
Malolos **36 B2**
Malpelo, I. de **90 C2**
Malta ■ **21 G5**
Maltahöhe **58 C3**
Maluku **37 E3**
Maluku □ **37 E3**
Maluku Sea = Molucca Sea **37 E2**
Malvan **43 L8**
Malvinas, Is. = Falkland Is. ⊠ **95 G5**
Malyn **17 C9**
Malyy Lyakhovskiy, Ostrov **31 B12**
Mamahatun **46 C5**
Mamanguape **92 D6**
Mamasa **37 E1**
Mamberamo ➔ **37 E5**
Mambilima Falls **57 G5**
Mamburao **36 B2**
Mamoré ➔ **91 F5**
Mamou **53 F3**
Mamuju **37 E1**
Man **53 G4**
Man, I. of **11 D4**
Man Na **41 F11**
Manaar, G. of = Mannar, G. of **43 Q11**
Manacapuru **90 D6**
Manacor **19 C7**
Manado **37 D2**
Managua **85 E7**
Manakara **59 C9**
Manama = Al Manāmah **44 E2**
Mananjary **59 C9**
Manaos = Manaus **90 D7**
Manapouri **65 F2**
Manapouri, L. **65 F2**
Manas **34 B3**
Manas ➔ **41 D8**
Manasir **44 E2**
Manaung **41 H9**
Manaus **90 D7**
Manchester *U.K.* **11 E5**
Manchester *U.S.A.* **77 C10**
Mand ➔ **44 D3**
Mandal **9 D7**
Mandala, Puncak **37 E6**
Mandalay **41 F11**
Mandale = Mandalay **41 F11**
Mandalī **46 D6**
Mandar, Teluk **37 E1**
Mandaue **36 B2**
Mandi **42 D10**
Mandimba **59 A7**
Mandioli **37 E3**
Mandla **40 F3**
Mandritsara **59 B9**
Mandsaur **43 G9**
Mandvi **43 H6**
Mandya **43 N10**
Manfalût **54 C5**
Manfredónia **20 D5**
Mangalia **22 C7**
Mangalore **43 N9**
Mangaweka **64 C6**
Manggar **39 E3**
Manggawitu **37 E4**
Mangghystaŭ Tübegi **29 E6**
Mangkalihat, Tanjung **37 D1**
Mangla Dam **42 C8**
Mangnai **34 C4**
Mango **53 F6**
Mangoche **59 A7**
Mangoky ➔ **59 C8**
Mangole **37 E3**
Mangonui **64 A5**
Mangueira, L. da **94 C6**
Mangyshlak, Poluostrov = Mangghystaŭ Tübegi **29 E6**
Manica **59 B6**
Manicoré **91 E6**
Manicouagan ➔ **71 E7**
Manicouagan, Rés. **71 D7**
Manĭfah **47 F7**
Manihiki **65 L14**
Manila **36 B2**
Manila B. **36 B2**
Manilla **63 B5**
Manipur □ **41 E9**
Manipur ➔ **41 F10**
Manisa **23 E6**
Manitoba □ **69 C10**
Manitoba, L. **69 C10**
Manitoulin I. **71 E5**
Manitowoc **76 B2**
Manizales **90 B3**
Manjhand **42 G6**
Manjra ➔ **43 K10**
Manmad **43 J9**
Manna **39 E2**
Mannahill **62 B3**
Mannar **43 Q11**
Mannar, G. of **43 Q11**
Mannar I. **43 Q11**
Mannheim **14 D5**
Mannum **62 B2**
Manokwari **37 E4**
Manono **57 F5**
Manosque **13 E6**
Manresa **19 B6**
Mansa **57 G5**
Mansel I. **70 C5**
Mansfield *Australia* **63 C4**
Mansfield *U.K.* **11 E6**
Mansfield *U.S.A.* **76 D4**
Manta **90 D2**
Mantalingajan, Mt. **38 C5**
Mantes-la-Jolie **12 B4**
Manthani **43 K11**
Mántova **20 B3**
Mantua = Mántova **20 B3**
Manu **91 F4**
Manuel Alves ➔ **93 E4**
Manui **37 E2**
Manukau **64 B6**
Manych-Gudilo, Ozero **25 D5**
Manzai **42 C7**
Manzanares **18 C4**
Manzanillo *Cuba* **86 B4**
Manzanillo *Mexico* **84 D4**
Manzhouli **35 B6**
Mao *Chad* **55 F2**
Maó *Spain* **19 C8**
Maoke, Pegunungan **37 E5**
Maoming **35 D6**
Mapam Yumco **40 B3**
Mapia, Kepulauan **37 D4**
Mapuera ➔ **90 D7**
Maputo **59 D6**
Maqat **29 E6**
Maqnā **47 E3**
Maquan He = Brahmaputra ➔ **41 F7**
Maquela do Zombo **56 F3**
Maquinchao **95 E3**
Mar Chiquita, L. **94 C4**
Mar del Plata **94 D5**
Mar Menor **19 D5**
Maraã **90 D5**
Marabá **92 D4**
Maracá, I. de **92 B3**
Maracaibo **90 A4**
Maracaibo, L. de **90 B4**
Maracay **90 A5**
Maradi **53 F7**
Marāgheh **46 C6**
Marāh **47 F6**
Marajó, I. de **92 C4**
Marand **46 C6**
Maranguape **92 C6**
Maranhão = São Luís **92 C5**
Maranhão □ **92 D4**
Maranoa ➔ **63 A4**
Marañón ➔ **90 D4**
Marão **59 C6**
Maraş = Kahramanmaraş **46 C4**
Maratua **37 D1**
Marbella **18 D3**
Marburg **14 C5**
Marche **12 C4**
Marchena **18 D3**
Mardan **42 B8**
Mardin **46 C5**
Marek = Stanke Dimitrov **22 C4**
Margarita, I. de **90 A6**
Margaritovo **32 B4**
Margate **11 F7**
Marghilon **29 E8**
Mārgow, Dasht-e **42 D3**
Mari El □ **24 B6**
Mari Republic = Mari El □ **24 B6**
Maria I. **62 D4**
Maria van Diemen, C. **64 A5**
Mariana Trench **64 H9**
Maribor **20 A5**
Marie Byrd Land **96 B18**
Mariecourt = Kangiqsujuaq **70 C6**
Mariental **58 C3**
Mariinsk **29 D9**
Marília **93 G3**
Marín **18 A1**
Marinduque **36 B2**
Maringá **94 A6**
Marion **81 A9**
Mariscal Estigarribia **91 H6**
Maritime Alps = Maritimes, Alpes **13 D7**
Maritimes, Alpes **13 D7**
Maritsa = Evros ➔ **22 D6**
Mariupol **25 D4**
Marīvān **46 D6**
Marka = Merca **49 G3**
Markham, Mt. **96 C15**

Marks 24 C6
Marla 62 A1
Marmagao 43 M8
Marmara 23 D6
Marmara, Sea of = Marmara Denizi 22 D7
Marmara Denizi 22 D7
Marmaris 23 F7
Marmolada, Mte. 20 A3
Marne ➔ 12 B5
Maroantsetra 59 B9
Marondera 59 B6
Maroni ➔ 92 A3
Maroochydore 63 A5
Maroona 62 C3
Maroua 55 F1
Marovoay 59 B9
Marquesas Is. = Marquises, Ìs. 65 K17
Marquises, Ìs. 65 K17
Marrakech 52 B4
Marrawah 62 D3
Marree 62 A2
Marrowie Cr. ➔ 63 B4
Marrupa 59 A7
Marsá Matrûh 54 B4
Marsabit 57 D7
Marsala 21 F4
Marsden 63 B4
Marseille 13 E6
Marseilles = Marseille 13 E6
Marshall 81 C6
Marshall Is. ■ 64 J12
Marshalltown 75 D8
Martaban 41 J11
Martaban, G. of 41 J11
Martapura *Kalimantan, Indonesia* 39 E4
Martapura *Sumatera, Indonesia* 39 E2
Martigues 13 E6
Martinborough 65 D6
Martinique ⊠ 87 D7
Martinsville 83 A8
Marton 64 D6
Martos 18 D4
Marudi 39 D4
Maruf 42 D5
Marugame 33 F3
Marwar 42 G8
Mary 29 F7
Maryborough = Port Laoise 11 E3
Maryborough *Queens., Australia* 63 A5
Maryborough *Vic., Australia* 62 C3
Maryland □ 77 E7
Marystown 71 E8
Maryvale 63 A5
Marzüq 54 C1
Marzüq, Idehān 54 D1
Masaka 57 E6
Masalembo, Kepulauan 39 F4
Masalima, Kepulauan 39 F5
Masamba 37 E2
Masan 35 C7
Masandam, Ra's 44 E4
Masasi 57 G7
Masaya 85 E7
Masbate 36 B2
Mascara 52 A6
Masela 37 F3
Maseru 59 D5
Mashābih 47 F4
Mashhad 44 B4
Māshkel, Hāmūn-i- 42 E3
Mashki Chāh 42 E3
Mashonaland 59 B6
Masindi 57 D6
Masjed Soleyman 47 E7
Mask, L. 11 E2
Maskin 44 F4
Masoala, Tanjon' i 59 B10
Masohi = Amahai 37 E3
Mason City 75 D8
Masqat 45 F4
Massa 13 D9
Massachusetts □ 77 C9
Massakory 55 F2
Massangena 59 C6
Massena 77 B8
Massénya 55 F2
Massif Central 13 D5
Massinga 59 C7
Masson I. 96 A11
Mastanli = Momchilgrad 22 D5
Masterton 65 D6
Mastuj 42 A8
Mastung 42 E5
Masty 17 B7
Masuda 33 F2
Masvingo 59 C6
Mata-au = Clutha ➔ 65 G3
Matabeleland 59 B5
Matad 35 B6
Matadi 56 F2
Matagalpa 85 E7
Matagami 71 E6
Matagami, L. 71 E6
Matak 39 D3
Matam 53 E3
Matamoros *Coahuila, Mexico* 84 B4
Matamoros *Tamaulipas, Mexico* 84 B5
Ma'ṭan as Sarra 54 D3
Matane 71 E7
Matanzas 86 B3
Matapan, C. = Tenaro, Akra 23 F4
Mataram 39 F5
Matarani 91 G4
Mataró 19 B7
Mataura 65 G3
Matehuala 84 C4
Matera 21 D6
Mathraki 21 E7
Mathura 42 F10
Mati 36 C3
Matiri Ra. 65 D5
Mato Grosso □ 93 E3
Mato Grosso, Planalto do 93 F3
Mato Grosso do Sul □ 93 F3
Matochkin Shar 28 B6
Matosinhos 18 B1
Maṭruḥ 45 F4
Matsue 33 F3
Matsumae 32 C7
Matsumoto 33 E6
Matsusaka 33 F5
Matsuyama 33 G3
Mattagami ➔ 71 D5
Mattancheri 43 Q10
Matthews Ridge 90 B6
Matucana 91 F3
Matūn = Khowst 42 C6
Maturín 90 B6
Mau Ranipur 43 G11
Maubeuge 13 A5
Maude 63 B3
Maudin Sun 41 K10
Maués 90 D7
Mauganj 40 E3
Maui 78 H12
Maulamyaing = Moulmein 41 J11
Maumere 37 F2
Maun 58 B4
Maungmagan Kyunzu 41 K11
Mauritania ■ 53 E3
Mauritius ■ 51 H9
Mawk Mai 41 G11
Mawlaik 41 F10
Mawlamyine = Moulmein 41 J11
Mawson Coast 96 A10
Mayaguana 87 B5
Mayagüez 87 C6
Maydena 62 D4
Mayenne ➔ 12 C3
Maykop 25 E5
Mayo 68 B6
Mayo L. 68 B6
Mayon Volcano 36 B2
Mayor I. 64 B7
Mayotte ⊠ 59 A9
Mayu 37 D3
Mazabuka 59 B5
Mazagán = El Jadida 52 B4
Mazagão 92 C3
Mazán 90 D4
Māzandarān □ 44 B3
Mazār-e Sharīf 45 B6
Mazara del Vallo 21 F4
Mazarrón 19 D5
Mazaruni ➔ 90 B7
Mazatlán 84 C3
Māzhān 44 C4
Mazīnān 44 B4
Mazoe ➔ 59 B6
Mazurian Lakes = Mazurski, Pojezierze 16 B5
Mazurski, Pojezierze 16 B5
Mazyr 17 C9
Mbabane 59 D6
Mbaïki 56 D3
Mbala 57 F6
Mbale 57 D6
Mbalmayo 56 D2
Mbandaka 56 D3
Mbanza Congo 56 F2
Mbanza Ngungu 56 F2
Mbarara 57 E6
Mbeya 57 F6
Mbini = Río Muni □ 56 D2
Mbour 53 F2
Mbuji-Mayi 56 F4
Mdantsane 59 E5
Mead, L. 78 B5
Mearim ➔ 92 C5
Meaux 13 B5
Mecca = Makkah 47 G4
Mechelen 14 C3
Mecheria 52 B5
Mecklenburg 15 B6
Mecklenburger Bucht 15 A6
Medan 39 D1
Medanosa, Pta. 95 F3
Médéa 52 A6
Medellín 90 B3
Medford 72 E2
Medgidia 22 B7
Medicine Bow Mts. 73 F10
Medicine Hat 69 C8
Medina = Al Madīnah 47 F4
Medina del Campo 18 B3
Medina Sidonia 18 D3
Medinipur 40 F6
Mediterranean Sea 50 C5
Médoc 12 D3
Medveditsa ➔ 24 D5
Medvezhyegorsk 28 C4
Meekatharra 60 F2
Meerut 42 E10
Megara 23 F4
Meghalaya □ 41 E8
Meighen I. 70 B4
Meiktila 41 G10
Meissen 15 C7
Meizhou 35 D6
Mejillones 94 A2
Mekhtar 42 D6
Meknès 52 B4
Mekong ➔ 38 C3
Mekongga 37 E2
Mekvari = Kür ➔ 25 E6
Melagiri Hills 43 N10
Melaka 39 D2
Melalap 38 C5
Melanesia 64 K10
Melbourne *Australia* 63 C3
Melbourne *U.S.A.* 83 E7
Melekeok 36 C4
Mélèzes ➔ 70 D6
Melfort 69 C9
Melilla 19 E4
Melitopol 25 D4
Melk 15 D8
Melo 94 C6
Melolo 37 F2
Melrose 63 B4
Melun 13 B5
Melville 69 C9
Melville I. *Australia* 60 C5
Melville I. *Canada* 70 B2
Melville Pen. 70 C5
Memboro 37 F1

Memel = Klaipėda **24 B1**
Memmingen **14 E6**
Mempawah **39 D3**
Memphis *Tenn., U.S.A.* **82 B3**
Memphis *Tex., U.S.A.* **80 B3**
Ménaka **53 E6**
Menan = Chao Phraya ➔ **38 B2**
Mendawai ➔ **39 E4**
Mende **13 D5**
Mendocino, C. **72 F1**
Mendoza **94 C3**
Mene Grande **90 B4**
Menemen **23 E6**
Menggala **39 E3**
Mengzi **34 D5**
Menindee **62 B3**
Menindee L. **62 B3**
Meningie **62 C2**
Menominee **76 B2**
Menongue **58 A3**
Menorca **19 C7**
Mentawai, Kepulauan **39 E1**
Menton **13 E7**
Meppel **14 B4**
Meran = Merano **20 A3**
Merano **20 A3**
Merauke **37 F6**
Merbein **62 B3**
Merca **49 G3**
Merced **78 B2**
Mercedes *B. Aires, Argentina* **94 C5**
Mercedes *Corrientes, Argentina* **94 B5**
Mercedes *San Luis, Argentina* **94 C3**
Mercedes *Uruguay* **94 C5**
Mercer **64 B6**
Mercy, C. **70 C7**
Meredith, C. **95 G4**
Mergui Arch. = Myeik Kyunzu **38 B1**
Mérida *Mexico* **85 C7**
Mérida *Spain* **18 C2**
Mérida *Venezuela* **90 B4**
Meridian **82 C3**
Merirumā **92 B3**
Merriwa **63 B5**
Merseburg **15 C6**
Mersin = Içel **46 C3**
Mersing **39 D2**
Merthyr Tydfil **11 F5**
Mértola **18 D2**
Meru **57 D7**
Mesa **79 D7**
Meshed = Mashhad **44 B4**
Mesologi **23 E3**
Mesopotamia = Al Jazirah **46 D5**
Messina = Musina **59 C6**
Messina **21 E5**
Messina, Str. di **21 E5**
Messini **23 F4**
Messiniakos Kolpos **23 F4**
Mesta ➔ **22 D5**
Meta ➔ **90 B5**
Meta Incognita Pen. **70 C7**
Metairie **81 E8**
Metán **94 B4**
Methven **65 E4**
Metlakatla **69 C6**
Mettur Dam **43 P10**
Metz **13 B7**
Meulaboh **39 D1**
Meureudu **38 C1**
Meuse ➔ **13 A6**
Mexiana, I. **92 C4**
Mexicali **84 A1**
México **84 D5**
Mexico ■ **84 C4**
México, Ciudad de **84 D5**
Mexico, G. of **85 B7**
Meymaneh **42 B4**
Mezen **28 C5**
Mezen ➔ **28 C5**
Mézenc, Mt. **13 D6**
Mezőkövesd **16 E5**
Mezőtúr **16 E5**
Mhow **43 H9**
Miami **83 G7**
Miami Beach **83 G7**
Miāndowāb **46 C6**
Miandrivazo **59 B9**
Miāneh **46 C6**
Mianwali **42 C7**
Miass **29 D7**
Michigan □ **76 C3**
Michigan, L. **76 C2**
Michurin **22 C6**
Michurinsk **24 C5**
Micronesia **64 H11**
Micronesia, Federated States of ■ **64 J10**
Middelburg **58 E5**
Middlesbrough **11 D6**
Midi, Canal du ➔ **12 E4**
Midland **80 D3**
Midyat **46 C5**
Midzŏr **22 C4**
Międzychód **16 B2**
Międzyrzec Podlaski **17 C6**
Mielec **16 C5**
Mieres **18 A3**
Mikhaylovgrad = Montana **22 C4**
Mikines **23 F4**
Mikonos = Mykonos **23 F5**
Milagro **90 D3**
Milan = Milano **13 D8**
Milang **62 B2**
Milano **13 D8**
Milâs **23 F6**
Milazzo **21 E5**
Mildura **62 B3**
Miles **63 A5**
Miletus **23 F6**
Milford Haven **11 F4**
Milford Sd. **65 F2**
Milford Sound **65 F2**
Milḥ, Baḥr al = Razāzah, Buḥayrat ar **47 D5**
Mill I. **96 A12**
Millau **13 D5**
Millennium I. = Caroline I. **65 K15**
Millicent **62 C3**
Millinocket **77 B11**
Millmerran **63 A5**
Milne Inlet **70 B5**
Milos **23 F5**
Milparinka **62 A3**
Milton **65 G3**
Milton Keynes **11 E6**
Milwaukee **76 C2**
Min Jiang ➔ *Fujian, China* **35 D6**
Min Jiang ➔ *Sichuan, China* **35 D5**
Mīnā Su'ud **47 E7**
Mīnā'al Aḥmadī **47 E7**
Mīnāb **44 E4**
Minamata **33 G2**
Minas **94 C5**
Minas Gerais □ **93 F4**
Minbu **41 G10**
Mindanao **36 C2**
Mindanao Sea = Bohol Sea **36 C2**
Mindanao Trench **36 B3**
Minden **14 B5**
Mindiptana **37 F6**
Mindoro **36 B2**
Mindoro Str. **36 B2**
Mingāçevir Su Anbarı **25 E6**
Mingechaurskoye Vdkhr. = Mingāçevir Su Anbarı **25 E6**
Mingin **41 F10**
Mingteke Daban = Mintaka Pass **42 A9**
Minho = Miño ➔ **18 B1**
Minho **18 B1**
Minna **53 G7**
Minneapolis **75 C8**
Minnesota □ **75 B7**
Minnipa **62 B2**
Miño ➔ **18 B1**
Minorca = Menorca **19 C7**
Minot **74 A4**
Minsk **24 C2**
Mińsk Mazowiecki **16 B5**
Mintaka Pass **42 A9**
Minto, L. **70 D6**
Minutang **41 C11**
Mira **20 B4**
Mirabello, Kolpos **23 G5**
Miraj **43 L9**
Miram Shah **42 C7**
Miramichi **71 E7**
Miranda **93 G2**
Miranda de Ebro **19 A4**
Miranda do Douro **18 B2**
Miri **38 D4**
Mirim, L. **94 C6**
Mirpur Khas **42 G6**
Mirzapur **40 E4**
Mirzapur-cum-Vindhyachal = Mirzapur **40 E4**
Mish'āb, Ra's al **47 E7**
Mishan **35 B8**
Miskolc **16 D5**
Misool **37 E4**
Miṣr = Egypt ■ **54 C5**
Miṣrātah **54 B2**
Misriç **46 C5**
Missinaibi ➔ **71 D5**
Mississippi □ **81 C9**
Mississippi ➔ **81 E9**
Mississippi River Delta **81 E9**
Missoula **73 C7**
Missouri □ **75 F8**
Missouri ➔ **75 F9**
Mistassini, L. **71 D6**
Misurata = Miṣrātah **54 B2**
Mitchell *Australia* **63 A4**
Mitchell *U.S.A.* **74 D5**
Mitchell ➔ **61 D7**
Mitilini **23 E6**
Mito **33 E7**
Mitrovica = Kosovska Mitrovica **22 C3**
Mittagong **63 B5**
Mittimatalik = Pond Inlet **70 B6**
Mitú **90 C4**
Mitumba, Mts. **57 F5**
Mitwaba **57 F5**
Miyake-Jima **33 F6**
Miyako **32 D7**
Miyakonojō **33 H2**
Miyazaki **33 H2**
Miyet, Bahr el = Dead Sea **47 E3**
Mizal **47 G6**
Mizdah **54 B1**
Mizoram □ **41 F9**
Mjøsa **8 C8**
Mladá Boleslav **16 C2**
Mlange = Mulanje **59 B7**
Mława **16 B5**
Mljet **20 C6**
Mmabatho **59 D5**
Mo i Rana **8 B8**
Moa **37 F3**
Moalie Park **62 A3**
Mobaye **56 D4**
Mobayi **56 D4**
Mobile **82 D3**
Moçambique = Mozambique ■ **59 B7**
Moçambique **59 B8**
Mochudi **59 C5**
Mocimboa da Praia **57 G8**
Mocoa **90 C3**
Mocuba **59 B7**
Modane **13 D7**
Módena **20 B3**
Modesto **78 B2**
Módica **21 F5**
Modimolle **59 C5**
Moe **63 C4**
Moengo **92 A3**
Mogadishu = Muqdisho **49 G4**
Mogador = Essaouira **52 B4**
Mogami-Gawa ➔ **32 D7**
Mogaung **41 E11**
Mogi das Cruzes **94 A7**
Mogilev = Mahilyow **17 B10**
Mogilev-Podolskiy = Mohyliv-Podilskyy **17 D8**

Mogok 41 F11
Mohács 16 F4
Moḥammadābād 44 B4
Mohyliv-Podilskyy 17 D8
Moisie ➔ 71 D7
Mojave Desert 78 C4
Mokai 64 C6
Mokau 64 C6
Mokokchung 41 D10
Mokopane 59 C5
Mokra Gora 22 C3
Molchanovo 29 D9
Moldavia = Moldova ■ 17 E9
Molde 8 C7
Moldova ■ 17 E9
Moldoveanu, Vf. 17 F7
Molepolole 59 C5
Molfetta 20 D6
Moline 75 E9
Mollendo 91 G4
Molodechno = Maladzyechna 17 A8
Moloka'i 78 H12
Molong 63 B4
Molopo ➔ 58 D4
Molu 37 F4
Molucca Sea 37 E2
Moluccas = Maluku 37 E3
Moma 59 B7
Mombasa 57 E7
Mombetsu 32 A8
Momchilgrad 22 D5
Mompós 90 B4
Mon ➔ 41 G10
Mona, Canal de la = Mona Passage 87 C6
Mona Passage 87 C6
Monaco ■ 13 E7
Monahans 80 D2
Monastir = Bitola 22 D3
Moncayo, Sierra del 19 B5
Mönchengladbach 14 C4
Monchique 18 D1
Monclova 84 B4
Moncton 71 E7
Mondego ➔ 18 B1
Mondeodo 37 E2
Mondovì 13 D7
Monforte de Lemos 18 A2
Mong Hsu 41 G12
Mong Kung 41 G11
Mong Nai 41 G11
Mong Pawk 41 F12
Mong Ton 41 G12
Mong Wa 41 G13
Mong Yai 41 F12
Mongalla 55 G5
Monghyr = Munger 40 E6
Mongibello = Etna 21 F5
Mongo 55 F2
Mongolia ■ 35 B5
Mongu 58 B4
Monkoto 56 E4
Monópoli 21 D6
Monroe *La., U.S.A.* 81 C7
Monroe *N.C., U.S.A.* 83 B7
Monrovia 53 G3
Mons 14 C2
Monse 37 E2
Mont-de-Marsan 12 E3
Mont-Laurier 71 E6
Mont-St-Michel, Le 12 B3
Montalbán 19 B5
Montana 22 C4
Montana □ 73 C9
Montargis 13 C5
Montauban 12 D4
Montbéliard 13 C7
Montceau-les-Mines 13 C6
Monte Alegre 92 C3
Monte Azul 93 F5
Monte-Carlo 13 E7
Monte Caseros 94 C5
Monte Comán 94 C3
Monte Santu, C. di 21 D2
Montecristo 20 C3
Montego Bay 86 C4
Montélimar 13 D6
Montemorelos 84 B5
Montenegro ■ 22 C2
Montepuez 59 A7
Monterey 78 B2
Montería 90 B3
Monterrey 84 B4
Montes Claros 93 F5
Montesilvano 20 C5
Montevideo 94 C5
Montgomery 82 C4
Montilla 18 D3
Montluçon 13 C5
Montmorillon 12 C4
Montoro 18 C3
Montpellier 13 E5
Montréal 71 E6
Montrose *U.K.* 10 C5
Montrose *U.S.A.* 79 A9
Montserrat ⊠ 87 C7
Montsinéry 30 E
Monywa 41 F10
Monza 13 D8
Monze 59 B5
Monze, C. 43 G5
Monzón 19 B6
Moolawatana 62 A2
Moomin Cr. ➔ 63 A4
Moonie 63 A5
Moonie ➔ 63 A4
Moonta 62 B2
Moose Jaw 69 C9
Moosomin 69 C9
Moosonee 71 D5
Mopti 53 F5
Moqor 42 C5
Moquegua 91 G4
Mora 8 C8
Moradabad 42 E11
Morafenobe 59 B8
Moramanga 59 B9
Moratuwa 43 R11
Morava ➔ *Serbia* 22 B3
Morava ➔ *Slovak Rep.* 16 D3
Moravian Hts. = Českomoravská Vrchovina 16 D2
Morawhanna 90 B7
Moray Firth 10 C5
Morden 69 D10
Mordovian Republic = Mordvinia □ 24 C5
Mordvinia □ 24 C5
Morea 62 C3
Moree 63 A4
Morelia 84 D4
Morella 19 B5
Morena, Sierra 18 C3
Moreton I. 63 A5
Morgan City 81 E8
Morioka 32 D7
Morlaix 12 B2
Morne Constant 30 C
Mornington 63 C4
Mornington, I. 95 F1
Moro G. 36 C2
Morocco ■ 52 B4
Morogoro 57 F7
Morombe 59 C8
Morón 86 B4
Mörön ➔ 35 B6
Morón de la Frontera 18 D3
Morondava 59 C8
Morotai 37 D3
Moroto 57 D6
Morphou 46 D3
Morrinhos 93 F4
Morrinsville 64 B6
Morristown 83 A6
Morshansk 24 C5
Morteros 94 C4
Mortlake 62 C3
Morundah 63 B4
Moruya 63 C5
Morvan 13 C6
Morven 63 A4
Morwell 63 C4
Moscos Is. 41 L11
Moscow = Moskva 24 B4
Moscow 72 C5
Mosel ➔ 13 A7
Moselle = Mosel ➔ 13 A7
Mosgiel 65 F4
Moshi 57 E7
Mosjøen 8 B8
Moskva 24 B4
Mosonmagyaróvár 16 E3
Mosquera 90 C3
Moss Vale 63 B5
Mossburn 65 F3
Mosselbaai 58 E4
Mossendjo 56 E2
Mossgiel 63 B3
Mossoró 92 D6
Most 16 C1
Mostaganem 52 A6
Mostar 20 C6
Mostardas 94 C6
Mostiska = Mostyska 17 D6
Mosty = Masty 17 B7
Mostyska 17 D6
Mosul = Al Mawṣil 46 C5
Motihari 40 D5
Motril 18 D4
Motueka 65 D5
Motueka ➔ 65 D5
Moudros 23 E5
Mouila 56 E2
Moulamein 63 C3
Moulins 13 C5
Moulmein 41 J11
Moundou 55 G2
Mount Aspiring △ 65 F3
Mount Barker 62 C2
Mount Cook 65 E4
Mount Eba 62 B2
Mount Gambier 62 C3
Mount Hope *N.S.W., Australia* 63 B4
Mount Hope *S. Austral., Australia* 62 B2
Mount Howitt 62 A3
Mount Isa 61 E6
Mount Lofty Ranges 62 B2
Mount Margaret 63 A3
Mount Maunganui 64 B7
Mount Perry 63 A5
Moura *Brazil* 90 D6
Moura *Portugal* 18 C2
Mourdi, Dépression du 55 E3
Moussoro 55 F2
Moutong 37 D2
Moyale 49 G2
Moyen Atlas 52 B4
Moyo 39 F5
Moyyero ➔ 30 C8
Moyynty 29 E8
Mozambique = Moçambique 59 B8
Mozambique ■ 59 B7
Mozambique Chan. 51 H8
Mozdok 25 E5
Mozyr = Mazyr 17 C9
Mpanda 57 F6
Mpika 59 A6
Mpwapwa 57 F7
Mthatha 59 E5
Mu Us Shamo 35 C5
Muar 39 D2
Muarabungo 39 E2
Muaraenim 39 E2
Muarajuloi 39 E4
Muarakaman 39 E5
Muaratebo 39 E2
Muaratembesi 39 E2
Muaratewe 39 E4
Mubarraz = Al Mubarraz 47 F7
Mubi 55 F1
Muckadilla 63 A4
Mucuri 93 F6
Mudanjiang 35 B7
Mudanya 23 D7
Mudgee 63 B4
Mufulira 59 A5
Mugi 33 G4
Muğla 23 F7
Mugu 40 C4
Muhammad Qol 54 D6
Mühlhausen 14 C6
Mühlig Hofmann fjell 96 B7
Mujnak = Muynak 29 E6
Mukacheve 17 D6
Mukachevo = Mukacheve 17 D6

Mukah 39 D4
Mukden = Shenyang 35 B7
Mukomuko 39 E2
Muktsar 42 D9
Mukur = Moqor 42 C5
Mula 19 C5
Mulanje 59 B7
Mulchén 94 D2
Mulde ➔ 15 C7
Mulgathing 62 B1
Mulhacén 18 D4
Mulhouse 13 C7
Mull 10 C4
Mullengudgery 63 B4
Muller, Pegunungan 39 D4
Mullingar 11 E3
Mullumbimby 63 A5
Multan 42 D7
Mumbai 43 K8
Muna 37 F2
München 15 D6
Munchen-Gladbach = Mönchengladbach 14 C4
Muncie 76 D3
Münden 14 C5
Mundo Novo 93 E5
Mungallala 63 A4
Mungallala Cr. ➔ 63 A4
Mungbere 57 D5
Munger 40 E6
Munich = München 15 D6
Muñoz Gamero, Pen. 95 G2
Münster 14 C4
Munster □ 11 E2
Muntok 39 E3
Muqdisho 49 G4
Murallón, Cerro 95 F2
Murang'a 57 E7
Murashi 24 B6
Muratlı 22 D6
Murchison ➔ 60 F1
Murchison, Mt. 96 B15
Murchison Falls 57 D6
Murcia 19 C5
Murcia □ 19 D5
Mureş ➔ 22 A3
Mureşul = Mureş ➔ 22 A3
Murfreesboro 82 B4
Murgap 29 F8
Murghob = Murgap 29 F8
Murgon 63 A5
Müritz 15 B7
Murmansk 8 B12
Murom 24 B5
Muroran 32 B7
Muroto 33 G4
Muroto-Misaki 33 G4
Murray ➔ 62 C2
Murray Bridge 62 C2
Murrumbidgee ➔ 62 B3
Murrumburrah 63 B4
Murrurundi 63 B5
Murtoa 62 C3
Murwara 40 F3
Murwillumbah 63 A5
Mürzzuschlag 15 E8
Muş 46 C5
Mūsa, Gebel 47 E3
Musa Khel 42 D6
Mūsa Qal'eh 42 C4
Musala *Bulgaria* 22 C4
Musala *Indonesia* 39 D1
Muscat = Masqat 45 F4
Muscatine 75 E9
Musgrave Ranges 60 F5
Mushie 56 E3
Musi ➔ 39 E2
Musina 59 C6
Muskogee 81 B6
Musoma 57 E6
Mussoorie 42 D11
Mustafakemalpaşa 23 D7
Mustang 40 C4
Musters, L. 95 F3
Muswellbrook 63 B5
Mût *Egypt* 54 C4
Mut *Turkey* 46 C3
Mutare 59 B6
Muting 37 F6
Mutoray 30 C8
Mutsu 32 C7
Mutsu-Wan 32 C7
Muynak 29 E6
Muzaffarabad 42 B8
Muzaffargarh 42 D7
Muzaffarnagar 42 E10
Muzaffarpur 40 D5
Muzhi 28 C7
Muztag 34 C3
Mvuma 59 B6
Mwanza *Dem. Rep. of the Congo* 57 F5
Mwanza *Tanzania* 57 E6
Mweka 56 E4
Mweru, L. 57 F5
Mwinilunga 58 A4
My Tho 38 B3
Myanaung 41 H10
Myanmar = Burma ■ 41 G11
Myaungmya 41 J10
Mycenæ = Mikines 23 F4
Myeik Kyunzu 38 B1
Myingyan 41 G10
Myitkyina 41 E11
Mykolayiv 25 D3
Mykonos 23 F5
Mymensingh 41 E8
Mýrdalsjökull 8 C2
Mysia 23 E6
Mysore = Karnataka □ 43 N10
Mysore 43 N10
Myszków 16 C4
Mytishchi 24 B4

N

Na Hearadh = Harris 10 C3
Naab ➔ 15 D7
Nababeep 58 D3
Naberezhnyye Chelny 29 D6
Nabeul 54 A1
Nabire 37 E5
Nāblus = Nābulus 46 D3
Nābulus 46 D3
Nacala 59 A8
Nachingwea 57 G7
Nacogdoches 81 D6
Nacozari de García 84 A3
Nadiad 43 H8
Nadūshan 44 C3
Nadvirna 17 D7
Nadvornaya = Nadvirna 17 D7
Nadym 28 C8
Nadym ➔ 28 C8
Nafpaktos 23 E3
Nafplio 23 F4
Nafūd ad Dahy 47 G6
Nafud Desert = An Nafūd 47 E5
Naga 36 B2
Nagaland □ 41 E10
Nagano 33 E6
Nagaoka 33 E6
Nagappattinam 43 P11
Nagar Parkar 43 G7
Nagasaki 33 G1
Nagaur 42 F8
Nagercoil 43 Q10
Nagīneh 44 C4
Nagoya 33 F5
Nagpur 43 J11
Nagykanizsa 16 E3
Nagykőrös 16 E4
Naha 35 D7
Nahāvand 46 D7
Nä'īfah 48 D5
Nain *Canada* 70 D7
Nä'īn *Iran* 44 C3
Nairn 10 C5
Nairobi 57 E7
Najaf = An Najaf 47 D6
Najafābād 44 C2
Najd 47 F5
Najibabad 42 E11
Nakamura 33 G3
Nakashibetsu 32 B9
Nakhichevan = Naxçıvan 25 F6
Nakhichevan Rep. = Naxçıvan □ 25 F6
Nakhodka 32 B3
Nakhon Phanom 38 A2
Nakhon Ratchasima 38 B2
Nakhon Sawan 38 A2
Nakhon Si Thammarat 38 C2
Nakina 71 D5
Nakuru 57 E7
Nal ➔ 42 G4
Nalchik 25 E5
Nalgonda 43 L11
Nallamalai Hills 43 M11
Nam Co 34 C4
Nam-Phan 38 B3
Namak, Daryācheh-ye 44 C3
Namak, Kavir-e 44 C4
Namaland 58 D3
Namangan 29 E8
Namapa 59 A7
Namber 37 E4
Nambour 63 A5
Nambucca Heads 63 B5
Namib Desert 58 C2
Namibe 58 B2
Namibia ■ 58 C3
Namibwoestyn = Namib Desert 58 C2
Namlea 37 E3
Namoi ➔ 63 B4
Nampa 72 E5
Namp'o 35 C7
Nampō-Shotō 33 H7
Nampula 59 B7
Namrole 37 E3
Namse Shankou 40 C4
Namtu 41 F11
Namur 14 C3
Nan-ch'ang = Nanchang 35 D6
Nanaimo 69 D7
Nanango 63 A5
Nanao 33 E5
Nanchang 35 D6
Nanching = Nanjing 35 C6
Nanchong 35 C5
Nancy 13 B7
Nanda Devi 42 D11
Nanded 43 K10
Nandewar Ra. 63 B5
Nandurbar 43 J9
Nandyal 43 M11
Nanga-Eboko 56 D2
Nanga Parbat 42 B9
Nangapinoh 39 E4
Nangarhār □ 42 B7
Nangatayap 39 E4
Nanjing 35 C6
Nanking = Nanjing 35 C6
Nanning 35 D5
Nanping 35 D6
Nansei-Shotō = Ryūkyū-rettō 35 D7
Nansen Sd. 70 A4
Nantes 12 C3
Nantucket I. 77 D10
Nanuque 93 F5
Nanusa, Kepulauan 36 D3
Nanyang 35 C6
Nanyuki 57 D7
Nao, C. de la 19 C6
Napa 72 G2
Napier 64 C7
Naples = Nápoli 21 D5
Naples 83 F7
Napo ➔ 90 D4
Nápoli 21 D5
Nappa Merrie 62 A3
Nara 53 E4
Naracoorte 62 C3
Naradhan 63 B4
Narasapur 40 J3
Narathiwat 38 C2
Narayanganj 41 F8
Narayanpet 43 L10
Narbonne 13 E5
Nardò 21 D7
Narew ➔ 16 B5
Narin 42 A6
Narmada ➔ 43 J8
Narodnaya 28 C6
Narooma 63 C5
Narrabri 63 B4

Narran ➔ 63 A4
Narrandera 63 B4
Narromine 63 B4
Narsimhapur 43 H11
Naruto 33 F4
Narva 24 B2
Narvik 8 B9
Naryan-Mar 28 C6
Naryilco 62 A3
Narym 29 D9
Narymskoye 29 E9
Naryn 29 E8
Naseby 65 F4
Naser, Buheirat en 54 D5
Nashville 82 A4
Nasik 43 K8
Nasirabad 42 F9
Nassarawa 53 G7
Nassau 86 A4
Nassau, B. 95 H3
Nasser, L. = Naser, Buheirat en 54 D5
Natal *Brazil* 92 D6
Natal *Indonesia* 39 D1
Naṭanz 44 C2
Natashquan 71 D7
Natashquan ➔ 71 D7
Natchez 81 D8
Nathalia 63 C4
Nathdwara 43 G8
Natitingou 53 F6
Natkyizin 41 K11
Natron, L. 57 E7
Natuna Besar, Kepulauan 39 D3
Natuna Is. = Natuna Besar, Kepulauan 39 D3
Natuna Selatan, Kepulauan 39 D3
Naturaliste, C. 62 D4
Naujaat = Repulse Bay 70 C5
Naumburg 15 C6
Nauru ■ 64 K11
Naushahra = Nowshera 42 B8
Nauta 90 D4
Nautanwa 40 D4
Navahrudak 17 B7
Navalmoral de la Mata 18 C3
Navarino, I. 95 H3
Navarra □ 19 A5
Nāvodari 22 B7
Navoi = Nawoiy 29 E7
Navojoa 84 B3
Navsari 43 J8
Nawabshah 42 F6
Nawakot 40 D5
Nawalgarh 42 F9
Nawāsīf, Ḥarrat 47 G5
Nawoiy 29 E7
Naxçıvan 25 F6
Naxçıvan □ 25 F6
Naxos 23 F5
Nāy Band 44 E3
Naypyidaw 41 H11
Nayoro 32 A8
Nazas ➔ 84 B4
Nazilli 23 F7
Ndalatando 56 F2
Ndélé 55 G3
Ndjamena 55 F1
Ndola 59 A5
Neagh, Lough 11 D3
Neales ➔ 62 A2
Near Is. 69 C1
Neath 11 F5
Nebine Cr. ➔ 63 A4
Nebitdag = Balkanabat 29 F6
Nebraska □ 74 E5
Nébrodi, Monti 21 F5
Neckar ➔ 14 D5
Necochea 94 D5
Nederland = Netherlands ■ 14 B3
Neemuch = Nimach 43 G9
Neepawa 69 C10
Neftçala 46 C7
Negapatam = Nagappattinam 43 P11
Negele 49 F2
Negombo 43 R11
Negotin 22 B4
Negrais, C. = Maudin Sun 41 K10
Negro ➔ *Argentina* 95 E4
Negro ➔ *Brazil* 90 D6
Negro ➔ *Uruguay* 94 C5
Negros 36 C2
Nei Monggol Zizhiqu □ 35 B6
Neijiang 35 D5
Neiva 90 C3
Nejd = Najd 47 F5
Nellore 43 M11
Nelson *Canada* 69 D8
Nelson *N.Z.* 65 D5
Nelson ➔ 69 C10
Nelson, C. 62 C3
Nelson, Estrecho 95 G2
Nelson Lakes △ 65 D5
Nelspruit 59 D6
Néma 53 E4
Neman = Nemunas ➔ 24 B1
Nemunas ➔ 24 B1
Nemuro 32 B9
Nemuro-Kaikyō 32 B9
Nenagh 11 E2
Nenjiang 35 B7
Nepal ■ 40 D5
Nepalganj 40 C3
Nereta ➔ 20 C6
Ness, L. 10 C4
Nesterov 17 C6
Nesvizh = Nyasvizh 17 B8
Netherlands ■ 14 B3
Netherlands Antilles ⊘ 87 D6
Nettilling L. 70 C6
Neubrandenburg 15 B7
Neumünster 14 A5
Neunkirchen 14 D4
Neuquén 94 D3
Neuruppin 15 B7
Neustrelitz 15 B7
Neva ➔ 24 B3
Nevada □ 72 G5
Nevers 13 C5
Nevertire 63 B4
Nevinnomyssk 25 E5
Nevşehir 46 C3
New Amsterdam 90 B7
New Angledool 63 A4
New Bedford 77 D10
New Bern 83 B9
New Brighton 65 E5
New Britain *Papua N. G.* 64 K10
New Britain *U.S.A.* 77 D9
New Brunswick □ 71 E7
New Caledonia ⊘ 64 M11
New Castile = Castilla-La Mancha □ 18 C4
New Delhi 42 E10
New England Ra. 63 B5
New Forest △ 11 F6
New Glasgow 71 E7
New Hampshire □ 77 C10
New Haven 77 D9
New Hebrides = Vanuatu ■ 64 L11
New Ireland 64 K10
New Jersey □ 77 E9
New Liskeard 71 E6
New London 77 D9
New Mexico □ 79 C9
New Norfolk 62 D4
New Orleans 81 E8
New Plymouth 64 C6
New Providence 86 A4
New Siberian Is. = Novosibirskiye Ostrova 31 B12
New South Wales □ 63 B4
New York 77 D9
New York □ 77 C8
New Zealand ■ 64 D7
Newark 77 D8
Newburgh 77 D8
Newbury 11 F6
Newcastle 63 B5
Newcastle-upon-Tyne 11 D6
Newfoundland & Labrador □ 71 D8
Newman 60 E2
Newport *I. of W., U.K.* 11 F6
Newport *Newport, U.K.* 11 F5
Newport *U.S.A.* 77 D10
Newport News 77 F7
Newquay 11 F4
Newry 11 D3
Newton Boyd 63 A5
Neya 24 B5
Neyrīz 44 D3
Neyshābūr 44 B4
Nezhin = Nizhyn 24 C3
Ngabang 39 D3
Ngabordamlu, Tanjung 37 F4
Nganglong Kangri 40 A3
Ngaoundéré 56 C2
Ngapara 65 F4
Ngoring Hu 34 C4
Nguigmi 55 F1
Nha Trang 38 B3
Nhill 62 C3
Niagara Falls *Canada* 71 E6
Niagara Falls *U.S.A.* 77 C6
Niah 39 D4
Niamey 53 F6
Nias 39 D1
Nicaragua ■ 85 E7
Nicaragua, L. de 85 E7
Nicastro 21 E6
Nice 13 E7
Nichinan 33 H2
Nicobar Is. 27 H11
Nicosia 46 D3
Nicoya, Pen. de 85 F7
Niedersachsen □ 14 B5
Niemen = Nemunas ➔ 24 B1
Nienburg 14 B5
Nieuw Amsterdam 92 A2
Nieuw Nickerie 92 A2
Niğde 46 C3
Niger ■ 53 E7
Niger ➔ 53 G7
Nigeria ■ 53 G7
Nightcaps 65 F3
Nihon = Japan ■ 33 F5
Nii-Jima 33 F6
Niigata 33 E6
Ni'ihau 78 H10
Niitsu 33 E6
Nijmegen 14 C3
Nikiniki 37 F2
Nikolayev = Mykolayiv 25 D3
Nikolayevsk 24 C6
Nikopol 25 D3
Nīkshahr 45 E5
Nikšić 22 C2
Nīl, Nahr en ➔ 54 B5
Nīl el Abyad ➔ 55 E5
Nīl el Azraq ➔ 55 E5
Nile = Nīl, Nahr en ➔ 54 B5
Nimach 43 G9
Nîmes 13 E6
Nimfaíon, Ákra = Pines, Akra 23 D5
Nimmitabel 63 C4
Nīmrūz □ 45 D5
Nīnawá 46 C5
Nindigully 63 A4
Nineveh = Nīnawá 46 C5
Ningbo 35 D7
Ningpo = Ningbo 35 D7
Ningsia Hui A.R. = Ningxia Huizu Zizhiqu □ 35 C5
Ningxia Huizu Zizhiqu □ 35 C5
Niobrara ➔ 74 D5
Nioro du Sahel 53 E4
Niort 12 C3
Nipawin 69 C9
Nipigon, L. 71 E5
Nipissing, L. 71 E6
Nippon = Japan ■ 33 F5
Niquelândia 93 E4
Nirmal 43 K11
Nirmali 40 D6
Niš 22 C3

Niṣāb *Sí. Arabia* **47 E6**
Niṣāb *Yemen* **49 E4**
Nistru = Dnister ➔ **17 E10**
Niṭā' **47 F7**
Niterói **93 G5**
Niue **65 L14**
Niut **39 D4**
Nivernais **13 C5**
Nizamabad **43 K11**
Nizamghat **41 C10**
Nizhnevartovsk **29 C8**
Nizhneyansk **31 B11**
Nizhniy Novgorod **24 B5**
Nizhniy Tagil **29 D6**
Nizhyn **24 C3**
Nkhata Bay **57 G6**
Nkhotakota **59 A6**
Nkongsamba **53 H7**
Nmai ➔ **41 E11**
Noakhali = Maijdi **41 F8**
Nobeoka **33 G2**
Nocera Inferiore **21 D5**
Nockatunga **62 A3**
Nogales *Mexico* **84 A2**
Nogales *U.S.A.* **79 E7**
Nōgata **33 G2**
Noginsk **30 C7**
Noires, Mts. **12 B2**
Noirmoutier, Î. de **12 C2**
Nojima-Zaki **33 F6**
Nok Kundi **42 E3**
Nokhtuysk **30 C9**
Nola **56 D3**
Nome **69 B3**
Nong Khai **38 A2**
Noondoo **63 A4**
Noranda = Rouyn-Noranda **71 E6**
Nord-Ostsee-Kanal **14 A5**
Norderney **14 B4**
Norderstedt **14 B5**
Nordfriesische Inseln **14 A5**
Nordhausen **14 C6**
Nordkapp **8 A11**
Nordrhein-Westfalen ☐ **14 C4**
Nordvik **30 B9**
Norfolk **77 F7**
Norfolk I. **64 M11**
Norge = Norway ■ **8 C8**
Norilsk **30 C6**
Norley **63 A3**
Norman **80 B5**
Norman Wells **68 B7**
Normandie **12 B4**
Normandy = Normandie **12 B4**
Normanton **61 D7**
Norquinco **95 E2**
Norrköping **9 D9**
Norrland **8 C9**
Norseman **60 G3**
North, C. **71 E7**
North Battleford **69 C9**
North Bay **71 E6**
North Bend **72 E1**
North C. **64 A5**
North Cape = Nordkapp **8 A11**
North Carolina ☐ **83 B7**
North Channel **11 D4**
North Dakota ☐ **74 B4**
North East Frontier Agency = Arunachal Pradesh ☐ **41 C10**
North Frisian Is. = Nordfriesische Inseln **14 A5**
North I. **64 B5**
North Korea ■ **35 C7**
North Lakhimpur **41 D10**
North Magnetic Pole **70 A2**
North Minch **10 B4**
North Ossetia ☐ **25 E5**
North Pagai, I. = Pagai Utara, Pulau **39 E2**
North Platte **74 E4**
North Platte ➔ **74 E4**
North Rhine Westphalia = Nordrhein-Westfalen ☐ **14 C4**
North Saskatchewan ➔ **69 C8**
North Sea **10 D8**
North Taranaki Bight **64 C6**
North Thompson ➔ **69 C7**
North Uist **10 C3**
North West C. **60 E1**
North West Frontier ☐ **42 B8**
North West Highlands **10 C4**
North West River **71 D7**
Northampton **11 E6**
Northern Circars **40 J4**
Northern Ireland ☐ **11 D3**
Northern Marianas ☑ **64 H9**
Northern Sporades **23 E4**
Northern Territory ☐ **60 D5**
Northland ☐ **64 A5**
Northumberland, C. **62 C3**
Northumberland Str. **71 E7**
Northwest Territories ☐ **68 B9**
Norton Sd. **69 B3**
Norway ■ **8 C8**
Norway House **69 C10**
Norwegian B. **70 B5**
Norwegian Sea **6 B5**
Norwich **11 E7**
Noshiro **32 C7**
Nosok **28 B9**
Noşratābād **45 D4**
Nossob ➔ **58 D4**
Nosy Barren **59 B8**
Nosy Bé **59 A9**
Nosy Boraha **59 B9**
Nosy Varika **59 C9**
Noteć ➔ **16 B2**
Notre Dame B. **71 E8**
Notre-Dame-de-Koartac = Quaqtaq **70 C7**
Notre-Dame-d'Ivugivic = Ivujivik **70 C6**
Nottaway ➔ **71 D6**
Nottingham **11 E6**
Nottingham I. **70 C6**
Nouâdhibou **52 D2**
Nouâdhibou, Râs **52 D2**
Nouakchott **53 E2**
Nouméa **64 M11**
Nouveau Comptoir = Wemindji **71 D6**
Nouvelle-Calédonie = New Caledonia ☑ **64 M11**
Nova Casa Nova **93 D5**
Nova Friburgo **93 G5**
Nova Iguaçu **93 G5**
Nova Iorque **92 D5**
Nova Lima **93 F5**
Nova Scotia ☐ **71 E7**
Nova Venécia **93 F5**
Nova Zagora **22 C5**
Novara **13 D8**
Novaya Ladoga **24 A3**
Novaya Lyalya **29 D7**
Novaya Zemlya **28 B6**
Novgorod **24 B3**
Novgorod-Severskiy = Novhorod-Siverskyy **24 C3**
Novhorod-Siverskyy **24 C3**
Novi Ligure **13 D8**
Novi Pazar **22 C3**
Novi Sad **22 B2**
Novo Mesto **20 B5**
Novo Remanso **93 D5**
Novoaltaysk **29 D9**
Novocherkassk **25 D5**
Novogrudok = Navahrudak **17 B7**
Novohrad-Volynskyy **17 C8**
Novokachalinsk **32 A3**
Novokuybyshevsk **24 C6**
Novokuznetsk **29 D9**
Novomoskovsk **24 C4**
Novorossiysk **25 E4**
Novorybnoye **30 B8**
Novoselytsya **17 D8**
Novoshakhtinsk **25 D4**
Novosibirsk **29 D9**
Novosibirskiye Ostrova **31 B12**
Novotroitsk **29 D6**
Novouzensk **24 C6**
Novovolynsk **17 C7**
Novska **20 B6**
Novyy Port **28 C8**
Nowa Sól **16 C2**
Nowgong **41 D9**
Nowra **63 B5**
Nowshera **42 B8**
Nowy Targ **16 D5**
Nowy Tomyśl **16 B3**
Noyon **13 B5**
Nsanje **59 B7**
Nubian Desert = Nûbîya, Es Sahrâ en **54 D5**
Nûbîya, Es Sahrâ en **54 D5**
Nuboai **37 E5**
Nueltin L. **68 B10**
Nueva Rosita **84 B4**
Nuéve de Julio **94 D4**
Nuevitas **86 B4**
Nuevo, G. **95 E4**
Nuevo Laredo **84 B5**
Nugget Pt. **65 G3**
Nuhaka **64 C7**
Nukey Bluff **62 B2**
Nuku'alofa **65 M13**
Nukus **29 E6**
Nullarbor Plain **60 G4**
Numalla, L. **63 A3**
Numan **55 G1**
Numazu **33 F6**
Numfoor **37 E4**
Numurkah **63 C4**
Nunavut ☐ **70 C5**
Nuneaton **11 E6**
Nunivak I. **69 B3**
Nunkun **42 C10**
Núoro **21 D2**
Nuremberg = Nürnberg **15 D6**
Nuriootpa **62 B2**
Nürnberg **15 D6**
Nurran, L. = Terewah, L. **63 A4**
Nusa Tenggara Barat ☐ **39 F5**
Nusa Tenggara Timur ☐ **37 F2**
Nushki **42 E5**
Nuuk **66 C14**
Nuwakot **40 C4**
Nuweveldberge **58 E4**
Nuyts Arch. **62 B1**
Nyahururu **57 D7**
Nyainqêntanglha Shan **34 C4**
Nyâlâ **55 F3**
Nyasa, L. = Malawi, L. **59 A6**
Nyasvizh **17 B8**
Nyda **28 C8**
Nyíregyháza **17 E5**
Nylstroom = Modimolle **59 C5**
Nymagee **63 B4**
Nyngan **63 B4**
Nyoman = Nemunas ➔ **24 B1**
Nysa **16 C3**
Nysa ➔ **16 B2**
Nyslott = Savonlinna **8 C11**
Nystad = Uusikaupunki **9 C10**
Nyurba **30 C9**
Nzega **57 E6**
Nzérékoré **53 G4**
Nzeto **56 F2**

O

Ō-Shima **33 F6**
Oahe, L. **74 C4**
O'ahu **78 H12**
Oak Ridge **83 A5**
Oakey **63 A5**
Oakland **78 B1**

Oamaru 65 F4
Oates Land 96 A15
Oaxaca 84 D5
Ob ➔ 28 C7
Oba 71 E5
Oban 10 C4
Obbia 49 F4
Oberhausen 14 C4
Oberon 63 B4
Obi, Kepulauan 37 E3
Ōbidos 92 C2
Obihiro 32 B8
Obilatu 37 E3
Obo 57 C5
Obozerskaya = Obozerskiy 28 C5
Obozerskiy 28 C5
Obskaya Guba 28 C8
Obuasi 53 G5
Ocala 83 E6
Ocaña 18 C4
Occidental, Cordillera 90 C3
Ocean I. = Banaba 64 K11
Oceanside 78 D4
Ocniţa 17 D8
Ōda 33 F3
Odate 32 C7
Odawara 33 F6
Ödemiş 23 E7
Odense 9 D8
Oder ➔ 15 B8
Odesa 25 D3
Odessa = Odesa 25 D3
Odessa 80 D2
Odienné 53 G4
Odintsovo 24 B4
Odra = Oder ➔ 15 B8
Odzi 59 B6
Oeiras 92 D5
Ofanto ➔ 20 D6
Offa 53 G6
Offenbach 14 C5
Offenburg 14 D4
Oga 32 D6
Oga-Hantō 32 D6
Ōgaki 33 F5
Ogasawara Gunto 27 F16
Ogbomosho 53 G6
Ogden 73 F7
Ogdensburg 77 B8
Oglio ➔ 20 B3
Ogooué ➔ 56 E1
Ogowe = Ogooué ➔ 56 E1
Ohai 65 F2
Ohakune 64 C6
Ohanet 52 C7
Ohata 32 C7
Ohau, L. 65 F3
Ohio □ 76 D4
Ohio ➔ 76 F1
Ohře ➔ 16 C2
Ohrid 22 D3
Ohridsko Jezero 23 D3
Oise ➔ 12 B5
Ōita 33 G2
Oiticica 92 D5
Ojos del Salado, Cerro 94 B3
Oka ➔ 28 D5
Okaba 37 F5
Okahandja 58 C3
Okanogan ➔ 72 B4
Okara 42 D8
Okavango Delta 58 B4
Okavango Swamp = Okavango Delta 58 B4
Okayama 33 F3
Okazaki 33 F5
Okeechobee, L. 83 F7
Okefenokee Swamp 83 D6
Okhotsk, Sea of 31 D12
Oki-Shotō 33 E3
Okinawa-Jima 35 D7
Oklahoma □ 80 B5
Oklahoma City 80 B5
Okmulgee 81 B6
Oknitsa = Ocniţa 17 D8
Oksibil 37 E6
Oktabrsk = Oktyabrsk 29 E6
Oktyabrsk 29 E6
Oktyabrskiy = Aktsyabrski 17 B9
Oktyabrskoy Revolyutsii, Ostrov 30 B7
Oktyabrskoye 28 C7
Okuru 65 E3
Okushiri-Tō 32 B6
Öland 9 D9
Olary 62 B3
Olavarría 94 D4
Oława 16 C3
Ólbia 20 D2
Old Castile = Castilla y Leon □ 18 A3
Old Crow 68 B6
Oldenburg 14 B5
Oldham 11 E5
Olekma ➔ 31 C10
Olekminsk 31 C10
Oleksandriya 17 C8
Olenek 30 C9
Olenek ➔ 30 B10
Oléron, Î. d' 12 D3
Oleśnica 16 C3
Olevsk 17 C8
Olhão 18 D2
Olifants = Elefantes ➔ 59 C6
Ólimbos, Óros = Olympos Oros 23 D4
Olinda 92 D7
Olivenza 18 C2
Ollagüe 91 H5
Olomouc 16 D3
Olongapo 36 B2
Olot 19 A7
Olsztyn 16 B5
Olt ➔ 22 C5
Oltenița 22 B6
Olympos Oros 23 D4
Olympia *Greece* 23 F3
Olympia *U.S.A.* 72 C2
Olympic Mts. 72 C2
Olympus, Mt. = Olympos Oros 23 D4
Olympus, Mt. = Uludağ 23 D7
Om ➔ 29 D8
Ōmagari 32 D7
Omagh 11 D3
Omaha 75 E7
Oman ■ 48 C6
Oman, G. of 45 E4
Omaruru 58 C3
Omate 91 G4
Ombai, Selat 37 F2
Omboué 56 E1
Ombrone ➔ 20 C3
Omdurmān 55 E5
Ometepec 84 D5
Omo ➔ 55 G6
Omsk 29 D8
Ōmu 32 A8
Omul, Vf. 17 F7
Omuramba Omatako ➔ 58 B4
Ōmuta 33 G2
Onang 37 E1
Onda 19 C5
Ondangwa 58 B3
Öndörhaan 35 B6
Onega 28 C4
Onega, L. = Onezhskoye Ozero 8 C13
Oneşti 17 E8
Onezhskoye Ozero 8 C13
Ongarue 64 C6
Onilahy ➔ 59 C8
Onitsha 53 G7
Ontario □ 71 E5
Ontario, L. 77 C7
Oodnadatta 62 A2
Oostende 14 C2
Ootacamund = Udagamandalam 43 P10
Opala 56 E4
Opava 16 D3
Opole 16 C3
Oporto = Porto 18 B1
Opotiki 64 C7
Opua 64 A6
Opunake 64 C5
Opunohu, B. d' 30 H
Oradea 17 E5
Öræfajökull 8 C2
Orai 42 G11
Oral = Zhayyq ➔ 29 E6
Oral 24 C7
Oran 52 A5
Orange *Australia* 63 B4
Orange *France* 13 D6
Orange *U.S.A.* 81 D7
Orange ➔ 58 D3
Orange, C. 92 B3
Orange Free State = Free State □ 59 D5
Orangeburg 83 C7
Oranienburg 15 B7
Oranje = Orange ➔ 58 D3
Orapa 59 C5
Oras 36 B3
Orbetello 20 C3
Orbost 63 C4
Orchila, I. 90 A5
Ordos = Mu Us Shamo 35 C5
Ordu 46 B4
Ore Mts. = Erzgebirge 15 C7
Örebro 9 D9
Oregon □ 72 E3
Orekhovo-Zuyevo 24 B4
Orel 24 C4
Ören 23 F6
Orenburg 29 D6
Orense = Ourense 18 A2
Orepuki 65 G2
Orfanos Kolpos 23 D5
Orgaz 18 C4
Orgeyev = Orhei 17 E9
Orhaneli 23 E7
Orhangazi 23 D7
Orhei 17 E9
Orhon Gol ➔ 35 A5
Orient 62 A3
Oriental, Cordillera 90 B4
Orihuela 19 C5
Orinoco ➔ 90 B6
Orissa □ 40 G5
Oristano 21 E2
Oristano, G. di 21 E2
Orizaba 84 D5
Orizaba, Pico de 84 D5
Orkney Is. 10 B5
Orlando 83 E7
Orléanais 12 C5
Orléans 12 C4
Ormara 42 G4
Ormoc 36 B2
Ormond 64 C7
Örnsköldsvik 8 C9
Orocué 90 C4
Orol Dengizi = Aral Sea 29 E6
Oroquieta 36 C2
Orosháza 16 E5
Orroroo 62 B2
Orsha 24 C3
Orsk 29 D6
Orşova 22 B4
Ortaca 23 F7
Ortegal, C. 18 A2
Orthez 12 E3
Ortigueira 18 A2
Ortles 13 C9
Ortón ➔ 91 F5
Orūmīyeh 46 C6
Orūmīyeh, Daryācheh-ye 46 C6
Oruro 91 G5
Oruzgān □ 42 C5
Orvieto 20 C4
Oryakhovo 22 C4
Ōsaka 33 F4
Ösel = Saaremaa 24 B1
Osh 29 E8
Oshakati 58 B3
Oshawa 71 E6
Oshkosh 74 E3
Oshmyany = Ashmyany 17 A7
Oshogbo 53 G6
Oshwe 56 E3
Osijek 20 B7
Osipovichi = Asipovichy 17 B9

Osizweni 59 D6
Oskarshamn 9 D9
Öskemen 29 E9
Oslo 9 D8
Oslofjorden 9 D8
Osmanabad 43 K10
Osmaniye 46 C4
Osnabrück 14 B5
Osorno 95 E2
Ossa, Mt. 62 D4
Ossa, Oros 23 E4
Ostend = Oostende 14 C2
Oster 17 C10
Österdalälven 8 C8
Österreich = Austria ■ 15 E8
Östersund 8 C8
Ostfriesische Inseln 14 B4
Ostrava 16 D4
Ostróda 16 B4
Ostroh 17 C8
Ostrołęka 16 B5
Ostrów Mazowiecka 16 B5
Ostrów Wielkopolski 16 C3
Ostrowiec-Świętokrzyski 16 C5
Ostuni 21 D6
Osuna 18 D3
Oswego 77 C7
Otago □ 65 F3
Otago Harbour 65 F4
Otaki 64 D6
Otaru 32 B7
Otaru-Wan = Ishikari-Wan 32 B7
Otavalo 90 C3
Otjiwarongo 58 C3
Otoineppu 32 A8
Otorohanga 64 C6
Otranto 21 D7
Otranto, C. d' 21 D7
Otranto, Str. of 21 D7
Ōtsu 33 F4
Ottawa = Outaouais ➔ 71 E6
Ottawa 71 E6
Ottawa Is. 70 D5
Ottumwa 75 E8
Oturkpo 53 G7
Otway, B. 95 G2
Otway, C. 62 C3
Otwock 16 B5
Ouachita Mts. 81 B6
Ouadda 55 G3
Ouagadougou 53 F5
Ouahran = Oran 52 A5
Ouallene 52 D6
Ouanda Djallé 55 G3
Ouaqui 30 E
Ouargla 52 B7
Ouarzazate 52 B4
Oubangi ➔ 56 E3
Oudtshoorn 58 E4
Ouessant, Î. d' 12 B1
Ouesso 56 D3
Ouest, Pte. de l' 30 A
Ouezzane 52 B4
Oujda 52 B5
Oulu 8 B11
Oulujärvi 8 C11
Oulujoki ➔ 8 B11
Oum Chalouba 55 E3
Oum Hadjer 55 F2
Ouniang Sérir 55 E3
Ourense 18 A2
Ouricuri 92 D5
Ouro Prêto 93 G5
Ouse 62 D4
Outaouais ➔ 71 E6
Outer Hebrides 10 C3
Outjo 58 C3
Ouyen 62 C3
Ovalle 94 C2
Ovamboland 58 B3
Oviedo 18 A3
Ovruch 17 C9
Owaka 65 G3
Owambo = Ovamboland 58 B3
Owase 33 F5
Owbeh 42 B3
Owen Sound 71 E5
Owen Stanley Ra. 61 B8
Owo 53 G7
Owyhee ➔ 72 E5
Oxford *N.Z.* 65 E5
Oxford *U.K.* 11 F6
Oxnard 78 C3
Oxus = Amudarya ➔ 29 E6
Oya 39 D4
Oyama 33 E6
Oyem 56 D2
Oyo 53 G6
Ozamiz 36 C2
Ozark Plateau 81 A8
Özd 16 D5

P

Pa-an 41 J11
Paarl 58 E3
Pab Hills 42 F5
Pabianice 16 C4
Pabna 41 E7
Pacaja ➔ 92 C3
Pacaraima, Sa. 90 C6
Pacasmayo 91 E3
Pachpadra 42 G8
Pachuca 84 C5
Padaido, Kepulauan 37 E5
Padang 39 E2
Padangpanjang 39 E2
Padangsidempuan 39 D1
Paderborn 14 C5
Padloping Island 70 C7
Pádova 20 B3
Padua = Pádova 20 B3
Paducah 76 F1
Paeroa 64 B6
Pag 20 B5
Pagadian 36 C2
Pagai Selatan, Pulau 39 E2
Pagai Utara, Pulau 39 E2
Pagalu = Annobón 51 G4
Pagastikos Kolpos 23 E4
Pagatan 39 E5
Pahiatua 64 D6
Päijänne 8 C11
Painan 39 E2
Paint Hills = Wemindji 71 D6
Painted Desert 79 C7
País Vasco □ 19 A4
Paisley 10 D4
Paita 90 E2
Pajares, Puerto de 18 A3
Pakistan ■ 42 E7
Pakokku 41 G10
Paktīā □ 42 C6
Pakxe 38 A3
Pala 55 G2
Palagruža 20 C6
Palam 43 K10
Palampur 42 C10
Palana 62 C4
Palanan 36 A2
Palanan Pt. 36 A2
Palangkaraya 39 E4
Palani Hills 43 P10
Palanpur 43 G8
Palapye 59 C5
Palau ■ 36 C4
Palawan 38 C5
Palayankottai 43 Q10
Paleleh 37 D2
Palembang 39 E2
Palencia 18 A3
Palermo 21 E4
Palestine 81 D6
Paletwa 41 G9
Palghat 43 P10
Pali 42 G8
Palikir 64 J10
Paliouri, Akra 23 E4
Palitana 43 J7
Palk Bay 43 Q11
Palk Strait 43 Q11
Pallanza = Verbánia 13 D8
Palm Springs 78 D4
Palma, B. de 19 C7
Palma de Mallorca 19 C7
Palmares 92 D6
Palmas, C. 53 H4
Pálmas, G. di 21 E2
Palmeira dos Índios 93 D6
Palmer 69 B5
Palmer Arch. 96 A3
Palmer Land 96 B3
Palmerston 65 F4
Palmerston North 64 D6
Palmi 21 E5
Palmira 90 C3
Palmyra = Tudmur 46 D4
Palopo 37 E2
Palos, C. de 19 D5
Palu *Indonesia* 37 E1
Palu *Turkey* 46 C5
Pamiers 12 E4
Pamir 29 F8
Pamlico Sd. 83 B10
Pampa 80 B3
Pampanua 37 E2
Pampas *Argentina* 94 D4
Pampas *Peru* 91 F4
Pamplona *Colombia* 90 B4
Pamplona *Spain* 19 A5
Panaji 43 M8
Panamá 85 F9
Panama ■ 86 E4
Panamá, G. de 86 E4
Panama Canal 86 E4
Panama City 82 D5
Panão 91 E3
Panay 36 B2
Panay G. 36 B2
Pančevo 22 B3
Pandan 36 B2
Pandharpur 43 L9
Pando, L. = Hope, L. 62 A2
Panevėžys 24 B1
Pang-Long 41 F12
Pang-Yang 41 F12
Pangani 57 F7
Pangfou = Bengbu 35 C6
Pangkajene 37 E1
Pangkalanbrandan 39 D1
Pangkalanbuun 39 E4
Pangkalpinang 39 E3
Pangnirtung 70 C7
Pangutaran Group 36 C2
Panjgur 42 F4
Panjim = Panaji 43 M8
Panjnad Barrage 42 E7
Pannirtuuq = Pangnirtung 70 C7
Panorama 94 A6
Pantar 37 F2
Pante Macassar 37 F2
Pante Makasar = Pante Macassar 37 F2
Pantelleria 21 F3
Paoting = Baoding 35 C6
Paot'ou = Baotou 35 B6
Paoua 55 G2
Pápa 16 E3
Papakura 64 B6
Papantla 84 C5
Papar 38 C5
Paparoa △ 65 E4
Papeete 65 L16
Papua □ 37 E5
Papua New Guinea ■ 64 K9
Papudo 94 C2
Papun 41 H11
Pará = Belém 92 C4
Pará □ 92 C3
Paracatu 93 F4
Paracel Is. 38 A4
Parachilna 62 B2
Paradip 40 G6
Parado 37 F1
Paragua ➔ 90 B6
Paraguaçu ➔ 93 E6
Paraguaná, Pen. de 90 A4
Paraguari 94 B5
Paraguay ■ 94 A5
Paraguay ➔ 94 B5
Paraíba = João Pessoa 92 D7
Paraíba □ 92 D6
Parakou 53 G6
Paramaribo 92 A2
Paraná *Argentina* 94 C4

Paraná *Brazil* **93 E4**
Paraná □ **94 A6**
Paraná ➔ **94 C5**
Paranaguá **94 B7**
Paranaíba **93 F3**
Paranaíba ➔ **93 G3**
Paranapanema ➔ **94 A6**
Paranas **36 B3**
Parang *Maguindanao, Phil.* **36 C2**
Parang *Sulu, Phil.* **36 C2**
Parângul Mare, Vf. **17 F6**
Paraparaumu **64 D6**
Paratinga **93 E5**
Parattah **62 D4**
Parbhani **43 K10**
Parchim **15 B6**
Pardo ➔ *Bahia, Brazil* **93 F6**
Pardo ➔ *Mato Grosso, Brazil* **93 G3**
Pardubice **16 C2**
Parecis, Serra dos **91 F7**
Parepare **37 E1**
Parga **23 E3**
Pariaguán **90 B6**
Parigi **37 E2**
Parika **90 B7**
Parima, Serra **90 C6**
Parinari **90 D4**
Parintins **92 C2**
Pariparit Kyun **41 K9**
Paris *France* **12 B5**
Paris *U.S.A.* **81 C6**
Park Range **73 G10**
Parkersburg **76 E5**
Parkes **63 B4**
Parla **18 B4**
Parma **13 D9**
Parnaguá **93 E5**
Parnaíba **92 C5**
Parnaíba ➔ **92 C5**
Parnassos **23 E4**
Pärnu **24 B1**
Paroo ➔ **63 B3**
Paros **23 F5**
Parral **94 D2**
Parry Is. **70 B3**
Parry Sound **71 E6**
Partinico **21 E4**
Paru ➔ **92 C3**
Parvân □ **42 B6**
Parvatipuram **40 H4**
Pas, The **69 C9**
Pasadena *Calif., U.S.A.* **78 C3**
Pasadena *Tex., U.S.A.* **81 E6**
Pascagoula **81 D9**
Paşcani **17 E8**
Pasco **72 C4**
Pasco, Cerro de **91 F3**
Pasirkuning **39 E2**
Pašman **20 C5**
Pasni **42 G3**
Paso de Indios **95 E3**
Passau **15 D7**
Passero, C. **21 F5**
Passo Fundo **94 B6**
Passos **93 G4**
Pastaza ➔ **90 D3**
Pasto **90 C3**
Patagonia **95 F3**
Patan = Lalitapur **40 D5**
Patan **43 H8**
Patani **37 D3**
Patchewollock **62 C3**
Patea **64 C6**
Paternò **21 F5**
Paterson **77 D8**
Pathankot **42 C9**
Pathein = Bassein **41 J10**
Patiala **42 D10**
Patkai Bum **41 D10**
Patmos **23 F6**
Patna **40 E5**
Patos, L. dos **94 C6**
Patos de Minas **93 F4**
Patquía **94 C3**
Patra **23 E3**
Patraikos Kolpos **23 E3**
Patras = Patra **23 E3**
Patrocínio **93 F4**
Pattani **38 C2**
Patuakhali **41 F8**
Pau **12 E3**
Pauk **41 G10**
Paulistana **92 D5**
Paulo Afonso **93 D6**
Pavia **13 D8**
Pavlodar **29 D8**
Pavlograd = Pavlohrad **25 D4**
Pavlohrad **25 D4**
Pavlovo **24 B5**
Pavlovsk **24 C5**
Pawtucket **77 D10**
Paxi **23 E3**
Payakumbuh **39 E2**
Payne Bay = Kangirsuk **70 D7**
Payne L. **70 D6**
Paysandú **94 C5**
Paz, B. de la **84 C2**
Pazar **46 B5**
Pazardzhik **22 C5**
Peace ➔ **68 C8**
Peak Hill **63 B4**
Peake Cr. ➔ **62 A2**
Peawanuck **71 D5**
Pebane **59 B7**
Pebas **90 D4**
Peć **22 C3**
Pechenga **28 C4**
Pechenizhyn **17 D7**
Pechora ➔ **28 C6**
Pechorskaya Guba **28 C6**
Pecos ➔ **80 E3**
Pécs **16 E4**
Pedder, L. **62 D4**
Pedirka **62 A2**
Pedra Azul **93 F5**
Pedreiras **92 C5**
Pedro Afonso **93 D4**
Pedro Juan Caballero **94 A5**
Peebinga **62 B3**
Peel ➔ *Australia* **63 B5**
Peel ➔ *Canada* **68 B6**
Peera Peera Poolanna L. **62 A2**
Pegasus Bay **65 E5**
Pegu **41 J11**
Pegu Yoma **41 H10**
Pehuajó **94 D4**
Peine **14 B6**
Peip'ing = Beijing **35 C6**
Peipus, L. = Chudskoye, Ozero **24 B2**
Peixe **93 E4**
Pekalongan **39 F3**
Pekanbaru **39 D2**
Pekin **75 E10**
Peking = Beijing **35 C6**
Pelagie, Is. **21 G4**
Pelaihari **39 E4**
Peleaga, Vf. **17 F6**
Peleng **37 E2**
Pelješac **20 C6**
Pelly ➔ **68 B6**
Pelly Bay **70 C5**
Peloponnese □ **23 F4**
Peloro, C. **21 E5**
Pelorus Sd. **65 D5**
Pelotas **94 C6**
Pelvoux, Massif du **13 D7**
Pematangsiantar **39 D1**
Pemba **59 A8**
Pemba I. **57 F7**
Pembroke *Canada* **71 E6**
Pembroke *U.K.* **11 F4**
Penang = Pinang **38 C2**
Penápolis **94 A6**
Peñarroya-Pueblonuevo **18 C3**
Peñas, C. de **18 A3**
Peñas, G. de **95 F2**
Pench'i = Benxi **35 B7**
Pend Oreille, L. **72 C5**
Pendembu **53 G3**
Pendleton **72 D4**
Penedo **93 E6**
Penguin **62 D4**
Peniche **18 C1**
Penida, Nusa **39 F5**
Peninsular Malaysia □ **39 D2**
Penmarch, Pte. de **12 C1**
Pennines **11 D5**
Pennsylvania □ **77 D7**
Penny Str. **70 B4**
Penola **62 C3**
Penong **60 G5**
Penrhyn **65 K15**
Penrith **63 B5**
Pensacola **82 D4**
Pensacola Mts. **96 C4**
Penshurst **62 C3**
Penticton **69 D8**
Pentland Firth **10 B5**
Penza **24 C6**
Penzance **11 F4**
Peoria **75 E10**
Perabumulih **39 E2**
Perche, Collines du **12 B4**
Perdido, Mte. **19 A6**
Perdu, Mt. = Perdido, Mte. **19 A6**
Pereira **90 C3**
Perekerten **62 B3**
Pereyaslav-Khmelnytskyy **24 C3**
Pergamino **94 C4**
Péribonka ➔ **71 E6**
Perico **94 A3**
Périgueux **12 D4**
Perijá, Sierra de **90 B4**
Perlas, Arch. de las **86 E4**
Perm **29 D6**
Pernambuco = Recife **92 D7**
Pernatty Lagoon **62 B2**
Pernik **22 C4**
Perpendicular Pt. **63 B5**
Perpignan **13 E5**
Persepolis **44 D3**
Pershotravensk **17 C8**
Persia = Iran ■ **44 C3**
Persian Gulf **44 E2**
Perth *Australia* **60 G2**
Perth *U.K.* **10 C5**
Perth Amboy **77 D8**
Peru ■ **90 C3**
Perúgia **20 C4**
Pervomaysk **25 D3**
Pervouralsk **29 D6**
Pésaro **20 C4**
Pescara **20 C5**
Peshawar **42 B7**
Peshkopi **22 D3**
Pesqueira **92 D6**
Petah Tiqwa **46 D3**
Petauke **59 A6**
Peter I. Øy **96 A2**
Peterborough *Australia* **62 B2**
Peterborough *Canada* **71 E6**
Peterborough *U.K.* **11 E6**
Peterhead **10 C6**
Petersburg *Alaska, U.S.A.* **69 C6**
Petersburg *Va., U.S.A.* **77 F7**
Petit Barachois **30 A**
Petitsikapau L. **71 D7**
Petlad **43 H8**
Peto **85 C7**
Petone **65 D6**
Petra Velikogo, Zaliv **32 B3**
Petrich **22 D4**
Petrikov = Pyetrikaw **17 B9**
Petrolândia **93 D6**
Petrolina **93 D5**
Petropavl **29 D7**
Petropavlovsk = Petropavl **29 D7**
Petropavlovsk-Kamchatskiy **31 D13**
Petrópolis **93 G5**
Petroşani **17 F6**
Petrovaradin **22 B2**
Petrovsk **24 C6**
Petrozavodsk **8 C12**
Peureulak **38 D1**
Pforzheim **14 D5**
Phagwara **42 D9**
Phalodi **42 F8**
Phan Rang **38 B3**
Phangan, Ko **38 C2**
Phangnga **38 C1**

Phatthalung 38 C2
Phetchabun 38 A2
Philadelphia 77 E8
Philippine Trench = Mindanao Trench 36 B3
Philippines ■ 36 B2
Philippopolis = Plovdiv 22 C5
Phillip I. 63 C4
Phillott 63 A4
Phitsanulok 38 A2
Phnom Dangrek 38 B2
Phnom Penh 38 B2
Phnum Penh = Phnom Penh 38 B2
Phoenix 79 D6
Phra Nakhon Si Ayutthaya 38 B2
Phuket 38 C1
Phumiphon, Khuan 38 A1
Piacenza 13 D8
Pialba 63 A5
Pian Cr. ➔ 63 B4
Pianosa 20 C3
Piatra Neamţ 17 E8
Piauí □ 92 D5
Piave ➔ 20 B4
Pibor Post 55 G5
Picardie □ 13 B5
Picardy = Picardie □ 13 B5
Pichilemu 94 C2
Pico Truncado 95 F3
Picton *Australia* 63 B5
Picton *N.Z.* 65 D6
Picún Leufú 95 D3
Piedmont = Piemonte □ 13 D7
Piedras, R. de las ➔ 91 F5
Piedras Negras 84 B4
Pielinen 8 C11
Piemonte □ 13 D7
Piet Retief 59 D6
Pietermaritzburg 59 D6
Pietersburg = Polokwane 59 C5
Pietrosul, Vf. *Maramureş, Romania* 17 E7
Pietrosul, Vf. *Suceava, Romania* 17 E7
Pigüe 94 D4
Piła 16 B3
Pilar 94 B5
Pilcomayo ➔ 94 B5
Pilibhit 42 E11
Pilica ➔ 16 C5
Pilipinas = Philippines ■ 36 B2
Pilos 23 F3
Pimba 62 B2
Pimenta Bueno 91 F6
Pimentel 91 E3
Pinang 38 C2
Pinar del Río 86 B3
Pınarhisar 22 D6
Pińczów 16 C5
Pindos Oros 23 E3
Pindus Mts. = Pindos Oros 23 E3
Pine Bluff 81 B7
Pine Point 68 B8
Pinega ➔ 28 C5
Pinerolo 13 D7
Pines, Akra 23 D5
Ping ➔ 38 A2
Pingdong 35 D7
Pingliang 35 C5
Pingxiang 35 D5
Pinhel 18 B2
Pini 39 D1
Pinios ➔ 23 E4
Pinnaroo 62 C3
Pinrang 37 E1
Pinsk 17 B8
Pintados 91 H5
Pinyug 24 A6
Piombino 20 C3
Pioner, Ostrov 30 B7
Piopiotaki = Milford Sd. 65 F2
Piorini, L. 90 D6
Piotrków Trybunalski 16 C4
Pīp 45 E5
Piquiri ➔ 94 A6
Piracicaba 94 A7
Piracuruca 92 C5
Piræus = Pireas 23 F4
Piraiévs = Pireas 23 F4
Piraṇé 94 B5
Pirapora 93 F5
Pireas 23 F4
Pirgos 23 F3
Pirin Planina 22 D4
Pirineos = Pyrénées 12 E4
Piripiri 92 C5
Pirmasens 14 D4
Pirot 22 C4
Piru 37 E3
Pisa 20 C3
Pisagua 91 G4
Pisciotta 21 D5
Pisco 91 F3
Písek 16 D2
Pishan 34 C2
Pising 37 F2
Pistóia 20 C3
Pisuerga ➔ 18 B3
Pitarpunga L. 62 B3
Pitcairn I. 65 M17
Piteå 8 B10
Piteşti 22 B5
Pithapuram 40 J4
Pittsburg 81 A6
Pittsburgh 77 D5
Pittsworth 63 A5
Piura 90 E2
Placentia 71 E8
Placentia B. 71 E8
Plainview 80 B3
Plaka, Akra 23 G6
Plakhino 28 C9
Plasencia 18 B2
Plastun 32 A5
Plata, Río de la ➔ 94 C5
Plátani ➔ 21 F4
Platte ➔ 75 F7
Plauen 15 C7
Plei Ku 38 B3
Plenty, B. of 64 B7
Pleven 22 C5
Plevlja 22 C2
Płock 16 B4
Plöckenstein 15 D7
Ploieşti 22 B6
Plovdiv 22 C5
Plumtree 59 C5
Plymouth 11 F4
Plzeň 16 D1
Po ➔ 20 B4
Po Hai = Bo Hai 35 C6
Pobedy, Pik 29 E8
Pocatello 73 E7
Poços de Caldas 93 G4
Podgorica 22 C2
Podilska Vysochyna 17 D8
Podolsk 24 B4
Poh 37 E2
Pohnpei 64 J10
Poinsett, C. 96 A12
Pointe-à-Pitre 87 C7
Pointe-Noire 56 E2
Poitiers 12 C4
Poitou 12 C3
Pokaran 42 F7
Pokataroo 63 A4
Pola = Pula 20 B4
Polan 45 E5
Poland ■ 16 B5
Polatsk 24 B2
Polesye = Pripet Marshes 17 B9
Police 16 B2
Poligiros 23 D4
Polillo Is. 36 B2
Pollachi 43 P10
Polnovat 28 C7
Polokwane 59 C5
Polonne 17 C8
Polonnoye = Polonne 17 C8
Poltava 24 D3
Polunochnoye 28 C7
Polynesia 65 L15
Polynésie française = French Polynesia ⊠ 65 M16
Pombal 18 C1
Pomézia 20 D4
Pomorskie, Pojezierze 16 B3
Ponape = Pohnpei 64 J10
Ponca City 80 A5
Ponce 87 C6
Pond Inlet 70 B6
Pondicherry = Puducherry 43 P11
Ponferrada 18 A2
Ponnani 43 P9
Ponnyadaung 41 F10
Ponta Grossa 94 B6
Ponta Pora 94 A5
Pontarlier 13 C7
Pontchartrain, L. 81 D8
Ponte Nova 93 G5
Pontevedra 18 A1
Pontiac 76 C4
Pontianak 39 E3
Pontine Is. = Ponziane, Ísole 21 D4
Pontine Mts. = Kuzey Anadolu Dağları 25 E4
Pontivy 12 B2
Pontoise 12 B5
Ponziane, Ísole 21 D4
Poochera 62 B1
Poole 11 F6
Poona = Pune 43 K8
Pooncarie 62 B3
Poopelloe L. 63 B3
Poopó, L. de 91 G5
Popayán 90 C3
Popigay 30 B9
Popiltah L. 62 B3
Popio L. 62 B3
Poplar Bluff 81 A8
Popocatépetl, Volcán 84 D5
Popokabaka 56 F3
Porbandar 43 J6
Porcupine ➔ 69 B5
Pordenone 20 B4
Pori 8 C10
Porkala = Porkkala 9 G12
Porkkala 9 G12
Porlamar 90 A6
Poroshiri-Dake 32 B8
Porpoise B. 96 A13
Port Alberni 69 D7
Port Angeles 72 B2
Port Arthur *Australia* 62 D4
Port Arthur *U.S.A.* 81 E7
Port-au-Prince 87 C5
Port Augusta 62 B2
Port Augusta West 62 B2
Port Broughton 62 B2
Port-Cartier 71 D7
Port Chalmers 65 F4
Port Darwin 95 G5
Port Davey 62 D4
Port Dickson 39 D2
Port Elizabeth 59 E5
Port Fairy 62 C3
Port-Gentil 56 E1
Port Harcourt 53 H7
Port Harrison = Inukjuak 70 D6
Port Hawkesbury 71 E7
Port Hedland 60 E2
Port Hope Simpson 71 D8
Port Huron 76 C4
Port Kenny 62 B1
Port Lairge = Waterford 11 E3
Port Laoise 11 E3
Port Lincoln 62 B2
Port Loko 53 G3
Port Louis 51 J9
Port MacDonnell 62 C3
Port Macquarie 63 B5
Port Moresby 61 B8
Port Nelson 69 C10
Port Nolloth 58 D3
Port Nouveau-Québec = Kangiqsualujjuaq 70 D7
Port of Spain 87 D7
Port Pegasus 65 G2
Port Phillip B. 63 C3
Port Pirie 62 B2
Port Safaga = Bûr Safâga 54 C5
Port Said = Bûr Sa'īd 54 B5

Port St. Johns = Umzimvubu **59 E5**
Port Shepstone **59 E6**
Port Stanley = Stanley **95 G5**
Port Sudan = Bûr Sûdân **55 E6**
Port Talbot **11 F5**
Port-Vendres **13 E5**
Port Vila **64 L11**
Port Wakefield **62 B2**
Porta Orientalis **22 B4**
Portadown **11 D3**
Portage la Prairie **69 D10**
Portalegre **18 C2**
Portbou **19 A7**
Portile de Fier **22 B4**
Portimão **18 D1**
Portland *N.S.W., Australia* **63 B4**
Portland *Vic., Australia* **62 C3**
Portland *Maine, U.S.A.* **77 C10**
Portland *Oreg., U.S.A.* **72 D2**
Portland B. **62 C3**
Porto **18 B1**
Pôrto Alegre **94 C6**
Pôrto de Móz **92 C3**
Porto Empédocle **21 F4**
Pôrto Esperança **91 G7**
Pôrto Franco **92 D4**
Pôrto Mendes **94 A6**
Pôrto Murtinho **91 H7**
Pôrto Nacional **93 E4**
Porto-Novo **53 G6**
Porto Santo, I. de **52 B2**
Pôrto Seguro **93 F6**
Porto Tórres **20 D2**
Pôrto União **94 B6**
Pôrto Válter **91 E4**
Porto-Vecchio **13 F8**
Pôrto Velho **91 E6**
Portoferráio **20 C3**
Portoscuso **21 E2**
Portoviejo **90 D2**
Portree **10 C3**
Portsmouth *U.K.* **11 F6**
Portsmouth *U.S.A.* **77 F7**
Porttipahdan tekojärvi **8 B11**
Portugal ■ **18 C1**
Porvenir **95 G2**
Posadas **94 B5**
Poso **37 E2**
Posse **93 E4**
Possession I. **96 B15**
Poste-de-la-Baleine = Kuujjuarapik **71 D6**
Postmasburg **58 D4**
Postojna **20 B5**
Potchefstroom **59 D5**
Potenza **21 D5**
Poteriteri, L. **65 G2**
Potgietersrus = Mokopane **59 C5**
Poti **25 E5**
Potomac ➔ **77 E7**
Potosí **91 G5**
Pototan **36 B2**
Potrerillos **94 B3**
Potsdam **15 B7**
Poughkeepsie **77 D9**
Považská Bystrica **16 D4**
Poverty B. **64 C8**
Póvoa de Varzim **18 B1**
Povungnituk = Puvirnituq **70 C6**
Powder ➔ **74 B2**
Powell, L. **79 B7**
Poyang Hu **35 D6**
Požarevac **22 B3**
Poznań **16 B3**
Pozo Almonte **91 H5**
Pozoblanco **18 C3**
Pozzuoli **21 D5**
Prachuap Khiri Khan **38 B1**
Prado **93 F6**
Prague = Praha **16 C2**
Praha **16 C2**
Prainha *Amazonas, Brazil* **91 E6**
Prainha *Pará, Brazil* **92 C3**
Prairies **69 C9**
Prapat **39 D1**
Prata **93 F4**
Prato **20 C3**
Pravia **18 A2**
Praya **39 F5**
Preobrazheniye **32 B3**
Preparis North Channel **41 K9**
Preparis South Channel **41 K9**
Přerov **16 D3**
Preservation Inlet **65 G2**
Presidencia Roque Saenz Peña **94 B4**
Presidente Epitácio **93 G3**
Presidente Prudente **93 G3**
Prespa, L. = Prespansko Jezero **23 D3**
Prespansko Jezero **23 D3**
Presque Isle **77 A11**
Preston **11 E5**
Pretoria **59 D5**
Preveza **23 E3**
Příbram **16 D2**
Prichard **82 D3**
Prieska **58 D4**
Prilep **22 D3**
Priluki = Pryluky **24 C3**
Prime Seal I. **62 D4**
Prince Albert **69 C9**
Prince Albert Mts. **96 B15**
Prince Albert Pen. **68 A8**
Prince Albert Sd. **68 A8**
Prince Alfred, C. **70 B1**
Prince Charles I. **70 C6**
Prince Charles Mts. **96 B10**
Prince Edward I. □ **71 E7**
Prince of Wales I. **68 A10**
Prince Patrick I. **70 B2**
Principe da Beira **91 F6**
Prins Harald Kyst **96 B8**
Prinsesse Astrid Kyst **96 B7**
Prinsesse Ragnhild Kyst **96 B8**
Pripet = Prypyat ➔ **17 C10**
Pripet Marshes **17 B9**
Pripyat Marshes = Pripet Marshes **17 B9**
Pripyats = Prypyat ➔ **17 C10**
Priština **22 C3**
Privas **13 D6**
Privolzhskaya Vozvyshennost **24 C6**
Prizren **22 C3**
Proddatur **43 M11**
Progreso **85 C7**
Prokopyevsk **29 D9**
Prokuplje **22 C3**
Prome **41 H10**
Propriá **93 E6**
Prosna ➔ **16 B3**
Prostějov **16 D3**
Proston **63 A5**
Provence **13 E6**
Providence **77 D10**
Providencia, I. de **86 D3**
Provins **13 B5**
Provo **73 F8**
Pruszków **16 B5**
Prut ➔ **17 F9**
Pruzhany **17 B7**
Prydz B. **96 A10**
Pryluky **24 C3**
Prypyat ➔ **17 C10**
Przhevalsk = Karakol **29 E8**
Psara **23 E5**
Psiloritis, Oros **23 G5**
Pskov **24 B2**
Ptich = Ptsich ➔ **17 B9**
Ptsich ➔ **17 B9**
Puán **94 D4**
Pucallpa **91 E4**
Puducherry **43 P11**
Pudukkottai **43 P11**
Puebla **84 D5**
Pueblo **74 F2**
Puelches **94 D3**
Puente Alto **94 C2**
Puente-Genil **18 D3**
Puerto Aisén **95 F2**
Puerto Ayacucho **90 B5**
Puerto Barrios **85 D7**
Puerto Bermúdez **91 F4**
Puerto Bolívar **90 D3**
Puerto Cabello **90 A5**
Puerto Cabezas **86 D3**
Puerto Carreño **90 B5**
Puerto Chicama **91 E3**
Puerto Coig **95 G3**
Puerto Cortés **85 D7**
Puerto Cumarebo **90 A5**
Puerto Deseado **95 F3**
Puerto Heath **91 F5**
Puerto La Cruz **90 A6**
Puerto Leguízamo **90 D4**
Puerto Lobos **95 E3**
Puerto Madryn **95 E3**
Puerto Maldonado **91 F5**
Puerto Montt **95 E2**
Puerto Natales **95 G2**
Puerto Páez **90 B5**
Puerto Pinasco **94 A5**
Puerto Plata **87 C5**
Puerto Princesa **36 C1**
Puerto Rico ☑ **87 C6**
Puerto Sastre **91 H7**
Puerto Suárez **91 G7**
Puerto Wilches **90 B4**
Puertollano **18 C3**
Pueyrredón, L. **95 F2**
Pugachev **24 C6**
Puget Sound **72 C2**
Puigcerdà **19 A6**
Pukaki, L. **65 F4**
Pukapuka **65 L14**
Pukekohe **64 B6**
Pula **20 B4**
Pulandian **35 C7**
Puławy **16 C5**
Pullman **72 C5**
Pulog, Mt. **36 A2**
Pułtusk **16 B5**
Puná, I. **90 D2**
Punakaiki **65 E4**
Punakha Dzong **41 D7**
Punata **91 G5**
Punch **42 C9**
Pune **43 K8**
Punjab □ *India* **42 D9**
Punjab □ *Pakistan* **42 D8**
Puno **91 G4**
Punta Alta **94 D4**
Punta Arenas **95 G2**
Punta de Díaz **94 B2**
Puntabie **62 B1**
Puntarenas **86 E3**
Punto Fijo **90 A4**
Puquio **91 F4**
Pur ➔ **28 C8**
Puracé, Vol. **90 C3**
Puralia = Puruliya **40 F6**
Puri **40 H5**
Purnia **40 E6**
Purukcahu **39 E4**
Puruliya **40 F6**
Purus ➔ **90 D6**
Pusan = Busan **35 C7**
Pushkino **24 C6**
Putao **41 D11**
Putaruru **64 C6**
Puthein Myit ➔ **41 K10**
Putignano **21 D6**
Puting, Tanjung **39 E4**
Putorana, Gory **30 C7**
Puttalam **43 Q11**
Puttgarden **15 A6**
Putumayo ➔ **90 D5**
Putussibau **39 D4**
Puvirnituq **70 C6**
Puy-de-Dôme **13 D5**
Pwllheli **11 E4**
Pyapon **41 J10**
Pyasina ➔ **30 B6**
Pyatigorsk **25 E5**
Pyè = Prome **41 H10**
Pyetrikaw **17 B9**
Pyinmana **41 H11**
P'yŏngyang **35 C7**
Pyrénées **12 E4**
Pyu **41 H11**

Q

Qā'emshahr **44 B3**
Qahremānshahr = Kermānshāh **46 D6**
Qaidam Pendi **34 C4**
Qal'at al Akhḍar **47 E4**
Qalāt-i-Ghilzai **45 C6**
Qal'eh Shaharak **42 B4**
Qamani'tuaq = Baker Lake **68 B10**
Qamruddin Karez **42 D6**
Qandahār = Kandahār **42 D4**
Qandahār = Kandahār □ **42 D4**
Qapshaghay **29 E8**
Qarabutaq **29 E7**
Qarachuk **46 C5**
Qaraghandy **29 E8**
Qaraghayly **29 E8**
Qarataū *Kazakhstan* **29 E7**
Qarataū *Zhambyl, Kazakhstan* **29 E8**
Qarazhal **29 E8**
Qardho = Gardo **49 F4**
Qarqan **34 C3**
Qarqan He ➔ **34 C3**
Qarqaraly **29 E8**
Qarshi **29 F7**
Qaṣr-e Qand **45 E5**
Qasr Farāfra **54 C4**
Qatar ■ **44 E2**
Qattāra, Munkhafed el **54 C4**
Qattāra Depression = Qattāra, Munkhafed el **54 C4**
Qausiuittuq = Resolute **70 B4**
Qāyen **44 C4**
Qazaqstan = Kazakhstan ■ **29 E7**
Qazvīn **46 C7**
Qena **54 C5**
Qeshm **44 E4**
Qikiqtarjuaq **70 C7**
Qila Saifullāh **42 D6**
Qilian Shan **34 C4**
Qingdao **35 C7**
Qinghai □ **34 C4**
Qinghai Hu **34 C5**
Qinhuangdao **35 C6**
Qinzhou **35 D5**
Qiqihar **35 B7**
Qitai **34 B3**
Qom **44 C2**
Qomolangma Feng = Everest, Mt. **40 C6**
Qomsheh **44 C2**
Qondūz = Kondoz **45 B7**
Qondūz = Kondoz □ **45 B7**
Qoqon = Qūqon **29 E8**
Qoraqalpoghistan □ **29 E6**
Qostanay **29 D7**
Quambatook **62 C3**
Quambone **63 B4**
Quan Long = Ca Mau **38 C3**
Quang Ngai **38 A3**
Quanzhou **35 D6**
Quaqtaq **70 C7**
Quartu Sant'Élena **21 E2**
Quba **25 E6**
Qūchān **44 B4**
Queanbeyan **63 C4**
Québec **71 E6**
Québec □ **71 E6**
Queen Alexandra Ra. **96 C15**
Queen Charlotte Is. **68 C6**
Queen Charlotte Sd. **69 C7**
Queen Elizabeth Is. **66 B9**
Queen Mary Land **96 B11**
Queen Maud G. **68 B9**
Queen Maud Land = Dronning Maud Land **96 B7**
Queen Maud Mts. **96 C16**
Queenscliff **63 C3**
Queensland □ **61 E7**
Queenstown *Australia* **62 D4**
Queenstown *N.Z.* **65 F3**
Queenstown *S. Africa* **59 E5**
Queimadas **93 E6**
Quelimane **59 B7**
Quelpart = Jeju-do **35 C7**
Querétaro **84 C4**
Quetta **42 D5**
Quezon City **36 B2**
Qui Nhon **38 B3**
Quibaxe **56 F2**
Quibdo **90 B3**
Quiberon **12 C2**
Quilán, C. **95 E2**
Quillabamba **91 F4**
Quillagua **91 H5**
Quillota **94 C2**
Quilon **43 Q10**
Quilpie **63 A3**
Quimilí **94 B4**
Quimper **12 B1**
Quimperlé **12 C2**
Quincy **75 F9**
Quines **94 C3**
Quintanar de la Orden **18 C4**
Quinyambie **62 B3**
Quipungo **58 A2**
Quirindi **63 B5**
Quissanga **59 A8**
Quito **90 D3**
Quixadá **92 C6**
Qulan **29 E8**
Qūnghirot **29 E6**
Quondong **62 B3**
Quorn **62 B2**
Qūqon **29 E8**
Quseir **54 C5**
Quzhou **35 D6**
Qyzylorda **29 E7**

R

Raahe **8 C10**
Raba **37 F1**
Rába ➔ **16 E3**
Rabat *Malta* **21 G5**
Rabat *Morocco* **52 B4**
Rabaul **64 K10**
Rābigh **47 G4**
Rābniţa **17 E9**
Race, C. **71 E8**
Rach Gia **38 B3**
Racine **76 C2**
Rādāuţi **17 E7**
Radekhiv **17 C7**
Radekhov = Radekhiv **17 C7**
Radom **16 C5**
Radomsko **16 C4**
Radomyshl **17 C9**
Radstock, C. **62 B1**
Rae **68 B8**
Rae Bareli **40 D3**
Rae Isthmus **70 C5**
Raetihi **64 C6**
Rafaela **94 C4**
Rafḥā **47 E5**
Rafsanjān **44 D4**
Ragachow **17 B10**
Ragama **43 R11**
Raglan **64 B6**
Ragusa **21 F5**
Raha **37 E2**
Rahaeng = Tak **38 A1**
Rahimyar Khan **42 E7**
Raichur **43 L10**
Raigarh **40 G4**
Railton **62 D4**
Rainier, Mt. **72 C3**
Raipur **40 G3**
Ra'is **47 G4**
Raj Nandgaon **40 G3**
Raja, Ujung **39 D1**
Raja Ampat, Kepulauan **37 E3**
Rajahmundry **40 J3**
Rajang ➔ **39 D4**
Rajapalaiyam **43 Q10**
Rajasthan □ **42 F8**
Rajasthan Canal = Indira Gandhi Canal **42 F8**
Rajgarh **43 G10**
Rajkot **43 H7**
Rajpipla **43 J8**
Rajshahi **41 E7**
Rakaia **65 E5**
Rakaia ➔ **65 E5**
Rakan, Ra's **44 E2**
Rakaposhi **42 A9**
Rakata, Pulau **39 F3**
Rakhiv **17 D7**
Rakitnoye **32 A4**
Rakiura △ **65 G2**
Raleigh **83 B8**
Ramanathapuram **43 Q11**
Rame Hd. **63 C4**
Ramechhap **40 D6**
Ramelau **37 F3**
Ramgarh *Jharkhand, India* **40 F5**
Ramgarh *Raj., India* **42 F7**
Ramnad = Ramanathapuram **43 Q11**
Rāmnicu Sărat **17 F8**
Rāmnicu Vâlcea **17 F7**
Rampur **42 E11**
Rampur Hat **40 E6**
Ramree I. **41 H9**
Ramtek **43 J11**
Ranaghat **41 F7**
Ranau **38 C5**
Rancagua **94 C2**
Ranchi **40 F5**
Randers **9 D8**
Rangaunu B. **64 A5**
Rangia **41 D8**
Rangiora **65 E5**
Rangitaiki ➔ **64 B7**
Rangitata ➔ **65 E4**
Rangitoto ke te tonga = D'Urville I. **65 D5**
Rangon ➔ **41 J11**
Rangoon **41 J11**
Rangpur **41 E7**
Ranibennur **43 M9**
Raniganj **40 F6**
Raniwara **43 G8**
Rankin Inlet **68 B10**
Rankins Springs **63 B4**
Ranohira **59 C9**
Ranong **38 C1**
Ransiki **37 E4**
Rantauprapat **39 D1**
Rantemario **37 E1**
Rapa **65 M16**
Rapallo **13 D8**
Rāpch **45 E4**
Raper, C. **70 C7**
Rapid City **74 C3**
Rarotonga **65 M14**
Ra's al Khaymah **44 E4**
Ra's Lānūf **54 B2**
Rasht **46 C7**
Rat Islands **69 C1**
Ratangarh **42 E9**
Rathenow **15 B7**
Ratlam **43 H9**
Ratnagiri **43 L8**
Raukumara Ra. **64 C7**
Rauma **8 C10**
Raumo = Rauma **8 C10**
Raurkela **40 F5**
Rausu-Dake **32 A9**
Rava-Ruska **17 C6**
Rava Russkaya = Rava-Ruska **17 C6**
Rāvar **44 D4**
Ravenna **20 B4**
Ravensburg **14 E5**
Ravi ➔ **42 D7**
Rawalpindi **42 C8**
Rawene **64 A5**
Rawlins **73 F10**
Rawson **95 E3**
Ray, C. **71 E8**
Rayadurg **43 M10**
Rayagada **40 H4**
Raz, Pte. du **12 B1**
Razāzah, Buḥayrat ar **47 D5**
Razazah, L. = Razāzah, Buḥayrat ar **47 D5**
Razdel'naya = Rozdilna **17 E10**

Razgrad 22 C6
Razim, Lacul 22 B7
Ré, Î. de 12 C3
Reading *U.K.* 11 F6
Reading *U.S.A.* 77 D8
Realicó 94 D4
Rebi 37 F4
Rebiana 54 D3
Rebun-Tō 32 A7
Rechytsa 17 B10
Recife 92 D7
Reconquista 94 B5
Recreo 94 B3
Red ➔ 81 D8
Red Cliffs 62 B3
Red Deer 69 C8
Red River of the North ➔ 74 A6
Red Sea 48 C2
Red Tower Pass = Turnu Roşu, P. 17 F7
Redcar 11 D6
Redcliffe 63 A5
Redding 72 F2
Redditch 11 E6
Redon 12 C2
Redondela 18 A1
Redwood City 78 B1
Ree, L. 11 E3
Reefton 65 E4
Regensburg 15 D7
Reggâne = Zaouiet Reggâne 52 C6
Réggio di Calábria 21 E5
Réggio nell'Emilia 20 B3
Reghin 17 E7
Regina 69 C9
Rehoboth 58 C3
Rehovot 46 E3
Reichenbach 15 C7
Reidsville 83 A8
Reigate 11 F6
Reims 13 B6
Reina Adelaida, Arch. 95 G2
Reindeer L. 69 C9
Reinga, C. 64 A5
Reinosa 18 A3
Remarkable, Mt. 62 B2
Remeshk 45 E4
Rendsburg 14 A5
Rengat 39 E2
Reni 17 F9
Renmark 62 B3
Rennes 12 B3
Reno 72 G4
Reno ➔ 20 B4
Rentería 19 A5
Republican ➔ 74 F6
Repulse Bay 70 C5
Requena *Peru* 90 E4
Requena *Spain* 19 C5
Reşadiye = Datça 23 F6
Resht = Rasht 46 C7
Resistencia 94 B5
Reşiţa 17 F5
Resolute 70 B4
Resolution I. *Canada* 70 C7
Resolution I. *N.Z.* 65 F2
Rethimno 23 G5
Réunion ☑ 51 J9
Reus 19 B6
Reutlingen 14 D5
Reval = Tallinn 24 B1
Revelstoke 69 C8
Revillagigedo, Is. de 84 D2
Rewa 40 E3
Rewari 42 E10
Rey Bouba 55 G1
Rey Malabo 53 H7
Reykjavík 8 C1
Reynosa 84 B5
Rhein ➔ 14 C4
Rhein-Main-Donau-Kanal 15 D6
Rheine 14 B4
Rheinland-Pfalz □ 14 C4
Rhin = Rhein ➔ 14 C4
Rhine = Rhein ➔ 14 C4
Rhineland-Palatinate = Rheinland-Pfalz □ 14 C4
Rhode Island □ 77 D10
Rhodes 23 F7
Rhodope Mts. = Rhodopi Planina 22 D5
Rhodopi Planina 22 D5
Rhön 14 C5
Rhondda 11 F5
Rhône ➔ 13 E6
Rhum 10 C3
Riachão 92 D4
Riasi 42 C9
Riau □ 39 E2
Riau, Kepulauan 39 D2
Riau Arch. = Riau, Kepulauan 39 D2
Ribadeo 18 A2
Ribeirão Prêto 93 G4
Riberalta 91 F5
Riccarton 65 E5
Richards Bay 59 D6
Richland 72 C4
Richmond *N.Z.* 65 D5
Richmond *Calif., U.S.A.* 72 H2
Richmond *Va., U.S.A.* 77 F7
Richmond Ra. 63 A5
Ridder = Leninogorsk 29 D9
Ried 15 D7
Riesa 15 C7
Rieti 20 C4
Rif = Er Rif 52 A5
Rīga 24 B1
Riga, G. of 24 B1
Rīgas Jūras Līcis = Riga, G. of 24 B1
Rīgestān 42 D4
Rigolet 70 D8
Riiser-Larsen-halvøya 96 A8
Rijeka 20 B5
Rimah, Wadi ar ➔ 47 F5
Rimini 20 B4
Rimouski 71 E7
Rinca 37 F1
Rinconada 94 A3
Rinjani 39 F5
Rio Branco *Brazil* 91 E5
Río Branco *Uruguay* 94 C6
Río Cuarto 94 C4
Rio de Janeiro 93 G5
Rio de Janeiro □ 93 G5
Rio do Sul 94 B7
Río Gallegos 95 G3
Rio Grande *Argentina* 95 G3
Rio Grande *Brazil* 94 C6
Rio Grande ➔ 84 B5
Río Grande de Santiago ➔ 84 C3
Rio Grande do Norte □ 92 D6
Rio Grande do Sul □ 94 B6
Rio Largo 93 D6
Rio Mulatos 91 G5
Río Muni □ 56 D2
Rio Negro 94 B7
Rio Verde 93 F3
Riobamba 90 D3
Riohacha 90 A4
Riosucio *Caldas, Colombia* 90 B3
Riosucio *Choco, Colombia* 90 B3
Rishiri-Tō 32 A7
Riva del Garda 20 B3
Rivadavia 94 B2
Rivera 94 C5
Riverside 78 D4
Riverton *Australia* 62 B2
Riverton *N.Z.* 65 G2
Riviera di Levante 13 D8
Riviera di Ponente 13 D8
Rivière-du-Loup 71 E7
Rivne 17 C8
Rívoli 13 D7
Rivoli B. 62 C3
Riyadh = Ar Riyāḍ 47 F6
Rize 25 E5
Rizzuto, C. 21 E6
Roanne 13 C6
Roanoke 77 F6
Robbins I. 62 D4
Robertson I. 96 A4
Robertstown 62 B2
Roberval 71 E6
Robinvale 62 B3
Roboré 91 G7
Robson, Mt. 69 C8
Roca, C. da 18 C1
Rocas, I. 92 C7
Rocha 94 C6
Rochefort 12 D3
Rochester *Minn., U.S.A.* 75 C8
Rochester *N.Y., U.S.A.* 77 C7
Rock, The 63 C4
Rock Hill 83 B7
Rock Island 75 E9
Rock Springs 73 F9
Rockefeller Plateau 96 C18
Rockford 75 D10
Rockhampton 61 E9
Rocky Mount 83 B9
Rocky Mts. 68 C7
Rod 42 E3
Rodez 13 D5
Ródhos = Rhodes 23 F7
Rodney, C. 64 B6
Roes Welcome Sd. 70 C5
Rogachev = Ragachow 17 B10
Rogagua, L. 91 F5
Rogatyn 17 D7
Rogoaguado, L. 91 F5
Rohri 42 F6
Rohtak 42 E10
Roi Et 38 A2
Rojo, C. 84 C5
Rokan ➔ 39 D2
Rolândia 94 A6
Roma *Australia* 63 A4
Roma *Italy* 20 D4
Romaine ➔ 71 D7
Roman 17 E8
Romang 37 F3
Romania ■ 22 B5
Romans-sur-Isère 13 D6
Romblon 36 B2
Rome = Roma 20 D4
Rome 82 B5
Romorantin-Lanthenay 12 C4
Roncador, Serra do 93 E3
Ronda 18 D3
Rondônia □ 91 F6
Rondonópolis 93 F3
Ronge, L. la 69 C9
Roniu, Mt. 30 H
Ronne Ice Shelf 96 B3
Roorkee 42 E10
Roosevelt ➔ 91 E6
Roosevelt I. 96 B16
Roquetas de Mar 19 D4
Roraima □ 90 C6
Roraima, Mt. 90 B6
Rosa, Monte 13 D7
Rosario *Argentina* 94 C4
Rosário *Brazil* 92 C5
Rosario *Mexico* 84 C3
Rosario *Paraguay* 94 A5
Rosario de la Frontera 94 B3
Rosário do Sul 94 C6
Roscommon 11 E2
Roseau *Dominica* 87 C7
Roseau *U.S.A.* 75 A7
Rosebery 62 D4
Roseburg 72 E2
Rosenheim 15 E7
Roses, G. de 19 A7
Rosetown 69 C9
Roseville 72 G3
Rosewood 63 A5
Rosignano Marittimo 20 C3
Rosignol 90 B7
Roşiori de Vede 22 B5
Roslavl 24 C3
Roslyn 63 B4
Ross *Australia* 62 D4
Ross *N.Z.* 65 E4

Ross I. 96 B15
Ross Ice Shelf 96 C16
Ross Sea 96 B15
Rossano 21 E6
Rossiya = Russia ■ 26 C10
Rosslare 11 E3
Rosso 53 E2
Rossosh 24 C4
Rostock 15 A7
Rostov *Don, Russia* 25 D4
Rostov *Yaroslavl, Russia* 24 B4
Roswell 80 C1
Rotherham 11 E6
Roto 63 B4
Rotondo, Mte. 13 E8
Rotoroa, L. 65 D5
Rotorua 64 C7
Rotorua, L. 64 C7
Rotterdam 14 C3
Rottweil 14 D5
Rotuma 64 L12
Roubaix 13 A5
Rouen 12 B4
Round Mt. 63 B5
Rousse = Ruse 22 C5
Roussillon 13 E5
Rouyn-Noranda 71 E6
Rovaniemi 8 B11
Rovereto 20 B3
Rovigo 20 B3
Rovinj 20 B4
Rovno = Rivne 17 C8
Rovuma = Ruvuma ➔ 57 G8
Rowena 63 A4
Roxas 36 B2
Roxburgh 65 F3
Royal Leamington Spa 11 E6
Royan 12 D3
Rozdilna 17 E10
Rozhyshche 17 C7
Rtishchevo 24 C5
Ruahine Ra. 64 C7
Ruapehu 64 C6
Ruapuke I. 65 G3
Rub' al Khālī 48 D4
Rubio 90 B4
Rubtsovsk 29 D9
Rudall 62 B2
Rudolfa, Ostrov 28 A6
Rufiji ➔ 57 F7
Rufino 94 C4
Rugby 11 E6
Rügen 15 A7
Ruhr ➔ 14 C4
Rukwa, L. 57 F6
Rum = Rhum 10 C3
Rumāḩ 47 F6
Rumania = Romania ■ 22 B5
Rumbêk 55 G4
Rumia 16 A4
Rumoi 32 B7
Runanga 65 E4
Runaway, C. 64 B7
Rundu 58 B3
Ruoqiang 34 C3
Rupa 41 D9
Rupat 39 D2
Rupert ➔ 71 D6
Rupert House = Waskaganish 71 D6
Rurrenabaque 91 F5
Ruschuk = Ruse 22 C5
Ruse 22 C5
Russas 92 C6
Russellkonda 40 H5
Russia ■ 26 C10
Russkaya Polyana 29 D8
Rustavi 25 E6
Rustenburg 59 D5
Ruteng 37 F2
Ruvuma ➔ 57 G8
Ruwenzori 57 D5
Rwanda ■ 57 E6
Ryazan 24 C4
Ryazhsk 24 C5
Rybache = Rybachye 29 E9
Rybachye 29 E9
Rybinsk 24 B4
Rybinskoye Vdkhr. 24 B4
Rybnitsa = Râbniţa 17 E9
Rylstone 63 B4
Ryötsu 32 D6
Rypin 16 B4
Ryukyu Is. = Ryükyü-rettö 35 D7
Ryükyü-rettö 35 D7
Rzeszów 16 C5
Rzhev 24 B3

S

Sa Dec 38 B3
Sa'ādatābād 44 D3
Saale ➔ 15 C6
Saalfeld 15 C6
Saar ➔ 13 B7
Saarbrücken 14 D4
Saaremaa 24 B1
Šabac 22 B2
Sabadell 19 B7
Sabah □ 38 C5
Ṣabāḩ, Wadi ➔ 47 G7
Sabalān, Kühhā-ye 46 C6
Sabalana, Kepulauan 37 F1
Sábanalarga 90 A4
Sabang 38 C1
Sabará 93 F5
Saberania 37 E5
Sabhā 54 C1
Sabinas 84 B4
Sabinas Hidalgo 84 B4
Sablayan 36 B2
Sable, C. *Canada* 71 E7
Sable, C. *U.S.A.* 86 A3
Sable I. 71 E8
Sabrina Coast 96 A12
Sabulubbek 39 E1
Sabzevār 44 B4
Sabzvārān 44 D4
Săcele 17 F7
Sachsen □ 15 C7
Sachsen-Anhalt □ 15 C7
Sacramento 72 G3
Sacramento ➔ 72 G3
Sacramento Mts. 79 D10
Sadd el Aali 54 D5
Sado 32 E6
Sadon 41 E11
Safi 52 B4
Safid Kūh 42 B3
Saga 33 G2
Sagar 43 M9
Sagarmatha = Everest, Mt. 40 C6
Sagil 34 A4
Saginaw 76 C4
Saglouc = Salluit 70 C6
Sagua la Grande 86 B3
Sagunt 19 C5
Sagunto = Sagunt 19 C5
Sahagún 18 A3
Sahand, Kūh-e 46 C6
Sahara 52 D6
Saharan Atlas = Saharien, Atlas 52 B6
Saharanpur 42 E10
Saharien, Atlas 52 B6
Sahiwal 42 D8
Sahrawi = Western Sahara ■ 52 D3
Sa'id Bundās 55 G3
Sa'īdābād = Sirjān 44 D3
Sa'īdīyeh 46 C7
Saidpur 41 E7
Saidu Sharif 42 B8
Saigon = Thanh Pho Ho Chi Minh 38 B3
Saikhoa Ghat 41 D10
Saiki 33 G2
Sailolof 37 E4
Saimaa 8 C11
Saimen = Saimaa 8 C11
St. Andrews 10 C5
St. Anthony 71 D8
St. Arnaud 62 C3
St-Augustin 71 D8
St. Augustine 83 E7
St. Austell 11 F4
St. Boniface 69 D10
St-Brieuc 12 B2
St. Catharines 77 C6
St-Chamond 13 D6
St. Christopher-Nevis = St. Kitts & Nevis ■ 87 C7
St. Cloud 75 C7
St. Croix 87 C7
St-Denis 12 B5
St-Dizier 13 B6
St. Elias, Mt. 68 B5
St-Étienne 13 D6
St-Flour 13 D5
St. Gallen = Sankt Gallen 13 C8
St-Gaudens 12 E4
St. George 63 A4
St-Georges 92 B3
St. George's 87 D7
St. George's Channel 11 F3
St. Georges Hd. 63 C5
St. Gotthard P. = San Gottardo, P. del 13 C8
St. Helena 51 H3
St. Helena B. 58 E3
St. Helens 62 D4
St. Helier 11 G5
St-Hyacinthe 71 E6
St-Jean, L. 71 E6
St. John 71 E7
St. John's *Antigua & B.* 87 C7
St. John's *Canada* 71 E8
St. Johns ➔ 83 D7
St. Joseph 75 F7
St. Joseph, L. 71 D4
St. Kilda 10 C2
St. Kitts & Nevis ■ 87 C7
St-Laurent 92 A3
St. Lawrence ➔ 71 E7
St. Lawrence, Gulf of 71 E7
St. Lawrence I. 69 B2
St-Lô 12 B3
St. Louis *Senegal* 53 E2
St. Louis *U.S.A.* 75 F9
St. Lucia ■ 87 D7
St-Malo 12 B2
St-Marc 87 C5
St. Mary Pk. 62 B2
St. Marys 62 D4
St-Mathieu, Pte. 12 B1
St-Nazaire 12 C2
St-Omer 12 A5
St. Paul 75 C8
St. Peter Port 11 G5
St. Petersburg = Sankt-Peterburg 24 B3
St. Petersburg 83 F6
St-Pierre-et-Miquelon ⊠ 71 E8
St-Quentin 13 B5
St-Tropez 13 E7
St. Vincent, G. 62 C2
St. Vincent & the Grenadines ■ 87 D7
Ste-Marie, Ile = Nosy Boraha 59 B9
Saintes 12 D3
Saintonge 12 D3
Saipan 64 H9
Sairang 41 F9
Sajama 91 G5
Sajószentpéter 16 D5
Sakākah 47 E5
Sakakawea, L. 74 B4
Sakartvelo = Georgia ■ 25 E5
Sakarya 25 E3
Sakata 32 D6
Sakhalin 31 D12
Sakon Nakhon 38 A2
Sala 9 D9
Sala Consilina 21 D5
Saladillo 94 D5
Salado ➔ *B. Aires, Argentina* 94 D5
Salado ➔ *La Pampa, Argentina* 94 D3
Salado ➔ *Santa Fe, Argentina* 94 C4
Salaga 53 G5
Salālah 49 D5
Salamanca *Chile* 94 C2

Salamanca *Spain* **18 B3**
Salamina **23 F4**
Salar de Atacama **94 A3**
Salar de Uyuni **91 H5**
Salaverry **91 E3**
Salawati **37 E4**
Salayar **37 F2**
Saldanha **58 E3**
Sale *Australia* **63 C4**
Salé *Morocco* **52 B4**
Salekhard **28 C7**
Salem *India* **43 P11**
Salem *U.S.A.* **72 D2**
Salerno **21 D5**
Salgótarján **16 D4**
Salihli **23 E7**
Salihorsk **17 B8**
Salima **59 A6**
Salina *Italy* **21 E5**
Salina *U.S.A.* **74 F6**
Salina Cruz **85 D5**
Salinas *Brazil* **93 F5**
Salinas *Ecuador* **90 D2**
Salinas *U.S.A.* **78 B2**
Salinas Grandes **94 C3**
Salinópolis **92 C4**
Salisbury *Australia* **62 B2**
Salisbury *U.K.* **11 F6**
Salisbury *U.S.A.* **83 B7**
Salisbury I. **70 C6**
Salliq = Coral Harbour **70 C5**
Salluit **70 C6**
Salmās **46 C6**
Salmon ➔ **72 D5**
Salmon River Mts. **73 D6**
Salon-de-Provence **13 E6**
Salonica = Thessaloniki **23 D4**
Salonta **16 E5**
Salsk **25 D5**
Salso ➔ **21 F4**
Salt Creek **62 C2**
Salt L. **62 B3**
Salt Lake City **73 F8**
Salta **94 A3**
Saltillo **84 B4**
Salto **94 C5**
Salto ➔ **20 C4**
Salton Sea **78 D5**
Salūm **54 B4**
Salur **40 H4**
Salvador **93 E6**
Salvador, El ■ **85 E7**
Salwa **44 E2**
Salween ➔ **41 J11**
Salyan **25 F6**
Salzach ➔ **15 D7**
Salzburg **15 E7**
Salzgitter **14 B6**
Salzwedel **15 B6**
Sama **28 C7**
Sama de Langreo = Langreo **18 A3**
Samales Group **36 C2**
Samangān □ **45 B7**
Samani **32 B8**
Samar **36 B3**
Samara **24 C7**
Samarinda **39 E5**
Samarkand = Samarqand **29 F7**
Samarqand **29 F7**
Sāmarrā' **46 D5**
Sambalpur **40 G5**
Sambar, Tanjung **39 E4**
Sambas **39 D3**
Sambhal **42 E11**
Sambhar **42 F9**
Sambiase **21 E6**
Sambir **17 D6**
Samoa ■ **65 L13**
Samokov **22 C4**
Samos **23 F6**
Samothráki = Mathraki **21 E7**
Samothraki **23 D5**
Sampit **39 E4**
Sampit, Teluk **39 E4**
Samra **47 F5**
Samsun **25 E4**
Samui, Ko **38 C2**
Samut Prakan **38 B2**
Samut Songkhram **38 B2**
San **53 F5**
San Agustin, C. **36 C3**
San Andrés, I. de **86 D3**
San Andrés Tuxtla **85 D5**
San Angelo **80 D3**
San Antonio *Chile* **94 C2**
San Antonio *U.S.A.* **80 E4**
San Antonio, C. **94 D5**
San Antonio Oeste **95 E4**
San Benedetto del Tronto **20 C4**
San Bernardino **78 C4**
San Bernardino Str. **36 B2**
San Bernardo **94 C2**
San Bernardo, I. de **90 B3**
San Borja **91 F5**
San Buenaventura = Ventura **78 C3**
San Carlos *Argentina* **94 C3**
San Carlos *Chile* **94 D2**
San Carlos *Phil.* **36 B2**
San Carlos *Amazonas, Venezuela* **90 C5**
San Carlos *Cojedes, Venezuela* **90 B5**
San Carlos de Bariloche **95 E2**
San Carlos del Zulia **90 B4**
San Cristóbal *Argentina* **94 C4**
San Cristóbal *Venezuela* **90 B4**
San Cristóbal de las Casas **85 D6**
San Diego **78 D4**
San Diego, C. **95 G3**
San Felipe *Chile* **94 C2**
San Felipe *Venezuela* **90 A5**
San Fernando *Chile* **94 C2**
San Fernando *La Union, Phil.* **36 A2**
San Fernando *Pampanga, Phil.* **36 A2**
San Fernando *Spain* **18 D2**
San Fernando *Trin. & Tob.* **87 D7**
San Fernando *U.S.A.* **78 C3**
San Fernando de Apure **90 B5**
San Fernando de Atabapo **90 C5**
San Francisco *Argentina* **94 C4**
San Francisco *U.S.A.* **78 B1**
San Francisco de Macorís **87 C5**
San Gottardo, P. del **13 C8**
San Ignacio *Bolivia* **91 G6**
San Ignacio *Paraguay* **94 B5**
San Ildefonso, C. **36 A2**
San Javier **91 G6**
San Joaquin ➔ **78 A2**
San Jorge, G. **95 F3**
San José *Costa Rica* **86 E3**
San Jose *Mind. Occ., Phil.* **36 B2**
San Jose *Nueva Ecija, Phil.* **36 A2**
San Jose *U.S.A.* **78 B2**
San José de Chiquitos **91 G6**
San José de Jáchal **94 C3**
San José de Mayo **94 C5**
San José del Guaviare **90 C4**
San Juan *Argentina* **94 C3**
San Juan *Phil.* **36 C3**
San Juan *Puerto Rico* **87 C6**
San Juan ➔ **86 D3**
San Juan de los Morros **90 B5**
San Juan Mts. **79 B9**
San Justo **94 C4**
San Leandro **78 B1**
San Lorenzo **90 C3**
San Lorenzo, Mte. **95 F2**
San Lucas **91 H5**
San Lucas, C. **84 C2**
San Luis **94 C3**
San Luis Obispo **78 C2**
San Luis Potosí **84 C4**
San Marino **20 C4**
San Marino ■ **20 C4**
San Martín, L. **95 F2**
San Matías **91 G7**
San Matías, G. **95 E4**
San Miguel **85 E7**
San Miguel ➔ **91 F6**
San Miguel de Tucumán **94 B3**
San Narciso **36 A2**
San Nicolás de los Arroyas **94 C4**
San Pedro **53 H4**
San Pedro de las Colonias **84 B4**
San Pedro de Macorís **87 C6**
San Pedro del Paraná **94 B5**
San Pedro Sula **85 D7**
San Pietro **21 E2**
San Rafael *Argentina* **94 C3**
San Rafael *U.S.A.* **72 H2**
San Remo **13 E7**
San Roque *Argentina* **94 B5**
San Roque *Spain* **18 D3**
San Rosendo **94 D2**
San Salvador **85 E7**
San Salvador de Jujuy **94 A4**
San Salvador I. **86 B5**
San Sebastián = Donostia-San Sebastián **19 A5**
San Sebastián **95 G3**
San Severo **20 D5**
San Valentin, Mte. **95 F2**
San Vicente de la Barquera **18 A3**
Sana' **49 D3**
Sana ➔ **20 B6**
Sanaga ➔ **56 D1**
Sanana **37 E3**
Sanandaj **46 D6**
Sancti Spiritus **86 B4**
Sancy, Puy de **13 D5**
Sandakan **38 C5**
Sandanski **22 D4**
Sanday **10 B5**
Sandgate **63 A5**
Sandía **91 F5**
Sandıklı **46 C2**
Sandoa **56 F4**
Sandomierz **16 C5**
Sandoway = Thandwe **41 H10**
Sandusky **76 D4**
Sandwip Chan. **41 F8**
Sandy C. **62 D3**
Sandy L. **69 C10**
Sanford *Fla., U.S.A.* **83 E7**
Sanford *N.C., U.S.A.* **83 B8**
Sanford, Mt. **69 B5**
Sanga ➔ **56 E3**
Sangamner **43 K9**
Sangar **31 C10**
Sangeang **37 F1**
Sangerhausen **15 C6**
Sanggau **39 D4**
Sangihe, Pulau **37 D3**
Sangkapura **39 F4**
Sangli **43 L9**
Sangmélima **56 D2**
Sangre de Cristo Mts. **80 A1**
Sanikiluaq **71 D6**
Sanirajak **70 C5**
Sanjo **33 E6**
Sankt Gallen **13 C8**
Sankt Moritz **13 C8**
Sankt-Peterburg **24 B3**
Sankt Pölten **15 D8**
Sankuru ➔ **56 E4**
Sanliurfa **46 C4**
Sanlúcar de Barrameda **18 D2**

Sanmenxia 35 C6
Sannicandro Gargánico 20 D5
Sant Antoni de Portmany 19 C6
Sant Feliu de Guíxols 19 B7
Sant Jordi, G. de 19 B6
Santa Ana *Bolivia* 91 F5
Santa Ana *El Salv.* 85 E7
Santa Ana *U.S.A.* 78 D4
Sant' Antioco 21 E2
Santa Barbara 78 C3
Santa Catalina I. 78 D3
Santa Catarina □ 94 B7
Santa Clara 86 B4
Santa Clotilde 90 D4
Santa Coloma de Gramenet 19 B7
Santa Cruz *Argentina* 95 G3
Santa Cruz *Bolivia* 91 G6
Santa Cruz *Phil.* 36 B2
Santa Cruz *U.S.A.* 78 B1
Santa Cruz ➔ 95 G3
Santa Cruz de Tenerife 52 C2
Santa Cruz do Sul 94 B6
Santa Cruz Is. 64 L11
Santa Eugenia, Pta. 84 B1
Santa Fé *Argentina* 94 C4
Santa Fe *U.S.A.* 79 C10
Santa Filomena 93 D4
Santa Inés, I. 95 G2
Santa Isabel 94 D3
Santa Isabel do Morro 93 E3
Santa Lucia Range 78 C2
Santa Maria *Brazil* 94 B6
Santa Maria *U.S.A.* 78 C2
Santa María ➔ 84 A3
Santa Maria da Vitória 93 E5
Santa Maria di Léuca, C. 21 E7
Santa Marta 90 A4
Santa Marta, Sierra Nevada de 90 A4
Santa Maura = Lefkada 23 E3
Santa Rosa *La Pampa, Argentina* 94 D4
Santa Rosa *San Luis, Argentina* 94 C3
Santa Rosa *Brazil* 94 B6
Santa Rosa *U.S.A.* 72 G2
Santa Vitória do Palmar 94 C6
Santai 35 C5
Santana, Coxilha de 94 C5
Santana do Livramento 94 C5
Santander 18 A4
Santarém *Brazil* 92 C3
Santarém *Portugal* 18 C1
Santiago = Río Grande de Santiago ➔ 84 C3
Santiago *Brazil* 94 B6
Santiago *Chile* 94 C2
Santiago ➔ 90 D3
Santiago de Compostela 18 A1
Santiago de Cuba 86 C4
Santiago de los Caballeros 87 C5
Santiago del Estero 94 B4
Santo Amaro 93 E6
Santo Ângelo 94 B6
Santo Antônio do Leverger 93 F2
Santo Domingo 87 C6
Santo Tomás 91 F4
Santo Tomé 94 B5
Santo Tomé de Guayana = Ciudad Guayana 90 B6
Santoña 18 A4
Santorini 23 F5
Santos 94 A7
São Bernardo do Campo 93 G4
São Borja 94 B5
São Carlos 94 A7
São Cristóvão 93 E6
São Domingos 93 E4
São Francisco 93 F5
São Francisco ➔ 93 E6
São Francisco do Sul 94 B7
São Gabriel 94 C6
São João da Madeira 18 B1
São João del Rei 93 G5
São João do Araguaia 92 D4
São João do Piauí 92 D5
São José do Rio Prêto 93 G4
São Leopoldo 94 B6
São Lourenço 93 G4
São Lourenço ➔ 93 F2
São Luís 92 C5
São Marcos ➔ 93 F4
São Marcos, B. de 92 C5
São Mateus 93 F6
São Paulo 94 A7
São Paulo □ 94 A7
São Roque, C. de 92 D6
São Sebastião, I. de 94 A7
São Tomé & Príncipe ■ 51 F4
São Vicente, C. de 18 D1
Saône ➔ 13 D6
Saonek 37 E4
Saparua 37 E3
Sapele 53 G7
Saposoa 91 E3
Sapporo 32 B7
Sapulpa 81 B5
Saqqez 46 C6
Sar-e Pol 45 B6
Sar-e Pol □ 45 B6
Sar Planina 22 C3
Sarāb 46 C6
Saragossa = Zaragoza 19 B5
Saraguro 90 D3
Sarajevo 20 C7
Saran, Gunung 39 E4
Sarangani B. 36 C3
Sarangani Is. 36 C3
Sarangarh 40 G4
Saransk 24 C6
Sarapul 29 D6
Sarasota 83 F6
Saratov 24 C6
Sarāvān 45 E5
Saravane 38 A3
Sarawak □ 39 D4
Saray 22 D6
Sarayköy 23 F7
Sarbāz 45 E5
Sarbīsheh 45 C4
Sarda ➔ 40 D3
Sardarshahr 42 E9
Sardegna □ 21 D2
Sardinia = Sardegna □ 21 D2
Sardis 23 E7
Sargodha 42 C8
Sarh 55 G2
Sārī 44 B3
Sarıgöl 23 E7
Sarikamiş 46 B5
Sarikei 39 D4
Sark 11 G5
Şarköy 23 D6
Sarlat-la-Canéda 12 D4
Sarmi 37 E5
Sarmiento 95 F3
Sarnia 71 E5
Sarny 24 C2
Sarolangun 39 E2
Saronikos Kolpos 23 F4
Sarre = Saar ➔ 13 B7
Sarreguemines 13 B7
Sarthe ➔ 12 C3
Sartynya 28 C7
Sarvestān 44 D3
Sary-Tash 29 F8
Saryshaghan 29 E8
Sasaram 40 E5
Sasebo 33 G1
Saser 42 B10
Saskatchewan □ 69 C9
Saskatchewan ➔ 69 C9
Saskatoon 69 C9
Saskylakh 30 B9
Sasovo 24 C5
Sassandra 53 H4
Sassandra ➔ 53 H4
Sássari 21 D2
Sassnitz 15 A7
Sassuolo 20 B3
Sasyk, Ozero 17 F9
Sata-Misaki 33 H2
Satadougou 53 F3
Satara 43 L8
Satmala Hills 43 J9
Satna 40 E3
Sátoraljaújhely 16 D5
Satpura Ra. 43 J10
Satu Mare 17 E6
Satui 39 E5
Saturnina ➔ 91 F7
Sauðarkrókur 8 B2
Saudi Arabia ■ 47 F6
Sauerland 14 C4
Sault Ste. Marie *Canada* 71 E5
Sault Ste. Marie *U.S.A.* 76 A3
Saumlaki 37 F4
Saumur 12 C3
Saunders, C. 65 F4
Saurimo 56 F4
Sava ➔ 22 B3
Savage I. = Niue 65 L14
Savalou 53 G6
Savannah 83 C7
Savannah ➔ 83 C7
Savannakhet 38 A2
Save ➔ 59 C6
Säveh 46 D7
Savelugu 53 G5
Savoie □ 13 D7
Savona 13 D8
Savonlinna 8 C11
Savoy = Savoie □ 13 D7
Sawahlunto 39 E2
Sawai 37 E3
Sawai Madhopur 42 F10
Sawatch Range 79 A9
Sawu 37 F2
Sawu Sea 37 F2
Saxony = Sachsen □ 15 C7
Saxony, Lower = Niedersachsen □ 14 B5
Sayán 91 F3
Sayan, Zapadnyy 30 D7
Saydā 46 D3
Sayghān 45 C6
Sayḩūt 49 D5
Saylac = Zeila 49 E3
Saynshand = Buyant-Uhaa 35 B6
Sazanit 23 D2
Sázava ➔ 16 D2
Sazin 42 B8
Scandicci 20 C3
Scandinavia 8 C8
Scarborough 11 D6
Scebeli, Wabi ➔ 49 G3
Schaffhausen 13 C8
Schefferville = Kawawachikamach 71 D7
Schelde ➔ 14 C3
Schenectady 77 C9
Schiermonnikoog 14 B4
Schio 20 B3
Schleswig 14 A5
Schleswig-Holstein □ 14 A5
Schouten I. 62 D4
Schouten Is. = Supiori 37 E5
Schwäbische Alb 14 D5
Schwaner, Pegunungan 39 E4
Schwarzwald 14 D5
Schwedt 15 B8
Schweinfurt 14 C6
Schweiz = Switzerland ■ 13 C8
Schwenningen = Villingen-Schwenningen 14 D5
Schwerin 15 B6
Schwyz 13 C8

Sciacca 21 F4
Scilla 21 E5
Scilly, Isles of 11 G3
Scone 63 B5
Scotland □ 10 C4
Scott Glacier 96 A12
Scott Inlet 70 B6
Scottsbluff 74 E3
Scottsdale 62 D4
Scranton 77 D8
Scunthorpe 11 E6
Scutari = Shkodër 22 C2
Seaspray 63 C4
Seattle 72 C2
Sebastopol = Sevastopol 25 E3
Sebha = Sabhā 54 C1
Şebinkarahisar 46 B4
Sebta = Ceuta 18 E3
Sebuku 39 E5
Sebuku, Teluk 39 D5
Secretary I. 65 F2
Secunderabad 43 L11
Sedalia 75 F8
Sedan 13 B6
Seddon 65 D6
Seddonville 65 D5
Sédhiou 53 F2
Sedova, Pik 28 B6
Seferihisar 23 E6
Segamat 39 D2
Segesta 21 F4
Seget 37 E4
Ségou 53 F4
Segovia = Coco → 86 D3
Segovia 18 B3
Segre → 19 B6
Séguéla 53 G4
Segura → 19 C5
Sehore 43 H10
Seinäjoki → 8 C10
Seine → 12 B4
Seistan = Sīstān 45 D5
Seistan, Daryācheh-ye = Sīstān, Daryācheh-ye 45 D5
Sekayu 39 E2
Sekondi-Takoradi 53 H5
Selaru 37 F4
Selçuk 23 F6
Sele → 21 D5
Selebi-Pikwe 59 C5
Selenga = Selenge Mörön → 35 A5
Selenge Mörön → 35 A5
Seletan, Tanjung 39 E4
Sélibabi 53 E3
Selīma, El Wāhāt el 54 D4
Selkirk 69 C10
Selkirk Mts. 69 C8
Selma 83 B8
Selpele 37 E4
Selu 37 F4
Selva 94 B4
Selvas 91 E5
Seman → 23 D2
Semarang 39 F4
Semey 29 D9
Semiozernoye 29 D7
Semipalatinsk = Semey 29 D9
Semirara Is. 36 B2
Semitau 39 D4
Semiyarka 29 D8
Semiyarskoye = Semiyarka 29 D8
Semmering P. 15 E8
Semnān 44 C3
Semnān □ 44 C3
Semporna 36 D1
Semuda 39 E4
Sena Madureira 91 E5
Senador Pompeu 92 D6
Senanga 58 B4
Sendai *Kagoshima, Japan* 33 H2
Sendai *Miyagi, Japan* 32 D7
Sendai-Wan 32 D7
Senegal ■ 53 F3
Sénégal → 53 E2
Senge Khambab = Indus → 43 G5
Senhor-do-Bonfim 93 E5
Senigállia 20 C4
Senj 20 B5
Senja 8 B9
Senlis 13 B5
Senmonorom 38 B3
Sens 13 B5
Senta 22 B3
Sentani 37 E6
Seo de Urgel = La Seu d'Urgell 19 A6
Seoul 35 C7
Sept-Îles 71 D7
Sequoia △ 78 B3
Seram 37 E3
Seram Laut 37 E4
Seram Sea 37 E3
Serasan 39 D3
Serbia ■ 22 B3
Serdar 29 F6
Serdobsk 24 C5
Seremban 39 D2
Sereth = Siret → 17 F9
Sergipe □ 93 E6
Sergiyev Posad 24 B4
Seria 38 D4
Serian 39 D4
Seribu, Kepulauan 39 F3
Serifos 23 F5
Sermata 37 F3
Serov 28 D7
Serowe 59 C5
Serpukhov 24 C4
Serres 22 D4
Serrinha 93 E6
Serua 37 F4
Serui 37 E5
Sesepe 37 E3
Setana 32 B6
Sète 13 E5
Sete Lagôas 93 F5
Sétif 52 A7
Setonaikai 33 F3
Settat 52 B4
Setúbal 18 C1
Setúbal, B. de 18 C1
Sevan, Ozero = Sevana Lich 25 E6
Sevana Lich 25 E6
Sevastopol 25 E3
Severn → *Canada* 71 D5
Severn → *U.K.* 11 F5
Severnaya Zemlya 30 B7
Severnyye Uvaly 24 B6
Severo-Yeniseyskiy 30 C7
Severodvinsk 28 C4
Sevilla 18 D2
Seville = Sevilla 18 D2
Sevlievo 22 C5
Seward 69 B5
Seward Peninsula 69 B3
Sewer 37 F4
Seychelles ■ 26 J7
Seyðisfjörður 8 B3
Seymour 63 C4
Sfântu Gheorghe 17 F7
Sfax 54 B1
Shaanxi □ 35 C5
Shaba = Katanga □ 57 F4
Shaballe = Scebeli, Wabi → 49 G3
Shache 34 C2
Shackleton Ice Shelf 96 A11
Shackleton Inlet 96 C15
Shadrinsk 29 D7
Shāhābād 44 B4
Shahdād 44 D4
Shahdād, Namakzār-e 44 D4
Shahdadkot 42 F5
Shahgarh 42 F6
Shahjahanpur 42 F11
Shahr-e Kord 44 C2
Shahrig 42 D5
Shajapur 43 H10
Shakhty 25 D5
Shakhunya 24 B6
Shaki 53 G6
Shalqar 29 E6
Shām, Bādiyat ash 47 D4
Shām, J. ash 44 F4
Shamīl 44 E4
Shammar, Jabal 47 F5
Shamo = Gobi 35 B6
Shamo, L. 55 G6
Shan □ 41 G12
Shandong □ 35 C6
Shangani → 59 B5
Shanghai 35 C7
Shangqiu 35 C6
Shangrao 35 D6
Shangshui 35 C6
Shannon 64 D6
Shannon → 11 E2
Shansi = Shanxi □ 35 C6
Shantou 35 D6
Shantung = Shandong □ 35 C6
Shanxi □ 35 C6
Shaoguan 35 D6
Shaoxing 35 C7
Shaoyang 35 D6
Shaqra' *Sí. Arabia* 47 F6
Shaqrā' *Yemen* 49 E4
Shari 32 B9
Sharjah = Ash Shāriqah 44 E3
Sharon 76 D5
Sharya 24 B6
Shashi 35 C6
Shasta, Mt. 72 F2
Shatt al Arab 47 E7
Shawan 34 B3
Shawinigan 71 E6
Shaykh, J. ash 46 D3
Shchūchīnsk 29 D8
Shebele = Scebeli, Wabi → 49 G3
Sheboygan 76 C2
Sheffield 11 E6
Shekhupura 42 D8
Shelby 83 B7
Shelbyville 82 B4
Shellharbour 63 B5
Shenandoah → 77 E7
Shendam 53 G7
Shendī 55 E5
Shensi = Shaanxi □ 35 C5
Shenyang 35 B7
Sheopur Kalan 42 G10
Shepetivka 17 C8
Shepetovka = Shepetivka 17 C8
Shepparton 63 C4
Sherbro I. 53 G3
Sherbrooke 71 E6
Sheridan 73 D10
Sherman 81 C5
Shetland Is. 10 A6
Shibām 49 D4
Shibata 33 E6
Shibecha 32 B9
Shibetsu 32 A8
Shīeli 29 E7
Shihchiachuangi = Shijiazhuang 35 C6
Shijiazhuang 35 C6
Shikarpur 42 F6
Shikoku □ 33 G3
Shikotsu-Ko 32 B7
Shilabo 49 F3
Shiliguri 40 D7
Shillong 41 E8
Shimla 42 D10
Shimoga 43 N9
Shimonoseki 33 G2
Shīndand 42 C3
Shingū 33 G4
Shinyanga 57 E6
Shio-no-Misaki 33 G4
Shipchenski Prokhod 22 C5
Shipki La 42 D11
Shiquan He = Indus → 43 G5
Shīr Kūh 44 D3
Shiragami-Misaki 32 C7
Shīrāz 44 D3
Shire → 59 B7
Shiriya-Zaki 32 C7
Shīrvān 44 B4
Shirwa, L. = Chilwa, L. 59 B7
Shivpuri 43 G10
Shizuoka 33 F6
Shklov = Shklow 17 A10
Shklow 17 A10

Shkodër 22 C2
Shkumbini ➔ 23 D2
Shmidta, Ostrov 30 A7
Sholapur = Solapur 43 L9
Shoshone Mts. 72 G5
Shqipëria = Albania ■ 23 D3
Shreveport 81 C7
Shrewsbury 11 E5
Shrirampur 40 F7
Shū 29 E8
Shuangyashan 35 B8
Shule 34 C2
Shumagin Is. 69 C4
Shumen 22 C6
Shür ➔ 44 D3
Shurugwi 59 B6
Shūsf 45 D5
Shūshtar 47 D7
Shwebo 41 F10
Shwegu 41 E11
Shweli ➔ 41 F11
Shymkent 29 E7
Shyok 42 B11
Shyok ➔ 42 B9
Si Kiang = Xi Jiang ➔ 35 D6
Si-ngan = Xi'an 35 C5
Siah 47 G6
Siahan Range 42 F4
Siaksriindrapura 39 D2
Sialkot 42 C9
Siam = Thailand ■ 38 A2
Sian = Xi'an 35 C5
Siantan 39 D3
Siargao I. 36 C3
Siasi 36 C2
Siau 37 D3
Šiauliai 24 B1
Šibenik 20 C5
Siberia 30 C8
Siberut 39 E1
Sibi 42 E5
Sibil = Oksibil 37 E6
Sibirtsevo 32 A3
Sibiti 56 E2
Sibiu 17 F7
Sibolga 39 D1
Sibsagar 41 D10
Sibu 39 D4
Sibuco 36 C2
Sibuguey B. 36 C2
Sibut 55 G2
Sibutu 36 D1
Sibutu Passage 36 D1
Sibuyan I. 36 B2
Sibuyan Sea 36 B2
Sichuan □ 34 C5
Sicilia 21 F5
Sicily = Sicilia 21 F5
Sicuani 91 F4
Siddipet 43 K11
Sidi-bel-Abbès 52 A5
Sidi Ifni 52 C3
Sidley, Mt. 96 B18
Sidon = Saydā 46 D3
Sidra, G. of = Surt, Khalīj 54 B2
Siedlce 17 B6
Sieg ➔ 14 C4
Siegen 14 C5
Siem Reap = Siemreab 38 B2
Siemreab 38 B2
Siena 20 C3
Sieradz 16 C4
Sierra Colorada 95 E3
Sierra Gorda 94 A3
Sierra Leone ■ 53 G3
Sierra Madre Occidental 84 B3
Sierra Nevada *Spain* 18 D4
Sierra Nevada *U.S.A.* 72 G3
Sifnos 23 F5
Sighetu-Marmaţiei 17 E6
Sigli 38 C1
Siglufjörður 8 B2
Sigsig 90 D3
Sigüenza 19 B4
Sigiuri 53 F4
Sikar 42 F9
Sikasso 53 F4
Sikhote Alin, Khrebet 32 A5
Sikhote Alin Ra. = Sikhote Alin, Khrebet 32 A5
Sikinos 23 F5
Sikkim □ 40 D7
Sil ➔ 18 A2
Silchar 41 E9
Silesia = Śląsk 16 C3
Silgarhi Doti 40 C3
Silghat 41 D9
Silifke 46 C3
Siliguri = Shiliguri 40 D7
Siling Co 34 C3
Silistra 22 B6
Silivri 22 D7
Sillajhuay, Cordillera 91 G5
Simanggang = Sri Aman 39 D4
Simav 23 E7
Simbirsk 24 C6
Simeria 17 F6
Simeulue 39 D1
Simferopol 25 E3
Simi 23 F6
Simikot 40 C3
Simla = Shimla 42 D10
Simpson Desert 60 F6
Simpson Pen. 70 C5
Sinabang 39 D1
Sinadogo 49 F4
Sinai = Es Sīnā' 54 C5
Sinai, Mt. = Mūsa, Gebel 47 E3
Sinaloa de Leyva 84 B3
Sincelejo 90 B3
Sincorá, Serra do 93 E5
Sind = Sindh □ 42 F6
Sind Sagar Doab 42 D7
Sindangan 36 C2
Sindh □ 42 F6
Sines 18 D1
Sines, C. de 18 D1
Singa 55 F5
Singapore ■ 39 D2
Singaraja 39 F5
Singida 57 E6
Singkaling Hkamti 41 E10
Singkang 37 E2
Singkawang 39 D3
Singleton 63 B5
Singora = Songkhla 38 C2
Sinjai 37 F2
Sinjär 46 C5
Sinkat 55 E6
Sinkiang = Xinjiang Uygur Zizhiqu □ 34 B3
Sinni ➔ 21 D6
Sinop 25 E4
Sintang 39 D4
Sintra 18 C1
Siocon 36 C2
Siófok 16 E4
Sioux City 75 D6
Sioux Falls 74 D6
Sioux Lookout 69 C10
Siping 35 B7
Sipura 39 E1
Siquijor 36 C2
Siracusa 21 F5
Sirajganj 41 E7
Siret ➔ 17 F9
Sīrjān 44 D3
Sirohi 43 G8
Sironj 43 G10
Síros = Syros 23 F5
Sirsa 42 E9
Sisak 20 B6
Sisaket 38 A2
Sisophon 38 B2
Sīstān 45 D5
Sīstān, Daryācheh-ye 45 D5
Sīstān va Balūchestān □ 45 E5
Sitapur 40 D3
Sitges 19 B6
Sitia 23 G6
Sitka 69 C6
Sittang Myit ➔ 41 J11
Sittoung = Sittang Myit ➔ 41 J11
Sittwe 41 G9
Siuri 40 F6
Sivas 25 F4
Siverek 46 C4
Sivrihisar 25 F3
Siwa 54 C4
Siwalik Range 40 D4
Siwan 40 D5
Sjælland 9 D8
Sjumen = Shumen 22 C6
Skadarsko Jezero 22 C2
Skagen 9 D8
Skagerrak 9 D7
Skagway 69 C6
Skala-Podilska 17 D8
Skala Podolskaya = Skala-Podilska 17 D8
Skalat 17 D7
Skardu 42 B9
Skarżysko-Kamienna 16 C5
Skeena ➔ 68 C6
Skegness 11 E7
Skeldon = Corriverton 90 B7
Skeleton Coast 58 C2
Skellefteå 8 C10
Skellefteälven ➔ 8 C10
Skiathos 23 E4
Skien 9 D7
Skierniewice 16 C5
Skikda 52 A7
Skiros 23 E5
Skole 17 D6
Skopelos 23 E4
Skopje 22 C3
Skvyra 17 D9
Skye 10 C3
Skyros = Skiros 23 E5
Śląsk 16 C3
Slatina 22 B5
Slave ➔ 68 B8
Slavgorod 29 D8
Slavonski Brod 20 B7
Slavuta 17 C8
Slavyanka 32 B2
Slavyansk = Slovyansk 25 D4
Slawharad 17 B10
Sleaford B. 62 B2
Sleeper Is. 70 D5
Sligeach = Sligo 11 D2
Sligo 11 D2
Sliven 22 C6
Slobodskoy 24 B7
Slobozia 22 B6
Slonim 17 B7
Slough 11 F6
Slovak Rep. ■ 16 D4
Slovakia = Slovak Rep. ■ 16 D4
Slovakian Ore Mts. = Slovenské Rudohorie 16 D4
Slovenia ■ 20 B5
Slovenija = Slovenia ■ 20 B5
Slovenska = Slovak Rep. ■ 16 D4
Slovenské Rudohorie 16 D4
Slovyansk 25 D4
Sluch ➔ 17 C8
Słupsk 16 A3
Slutsk 17 B8
Smallwood Res. 71 D7
Smara 52 B4
Smarhon 17 A8
Smederevo 22 B3
Smithton 62 D4
Smithtown 63 B5
Smoky Bay 62 B1
Smolensk 24 C3
Smolikas, Oros 23 D3
Smolyan 22 D5
Smorgon = Smarhon 17 A8
Smyrna = İzmir 23 E6
Snake ➔ 72 C4
Snake I. 63 C4
Snake River Plain 73 E7
Sneek 14 B3
Sněžka 16 C2

Snøhetta 8 C7
Snowdon 11 E4
Snowdrift = Łutselk'e 68 B8
Snowtown 62 B2
Snowy ➔ 63 C4
Snowy Mts. 63 C4
Snyatyn 17 D7
Snyder 80 C3
Sobat, Nahr ➔ 55 G5
Sobral 92 C5
Soc Trang 38 C3
Soch'e = Shache 34 C2
Sochi 25 E4
Société, Îs. de la 65 L15
Society Is. = Société, Îs. de la 65 L15
Socompa, Portezuelo de 94 A3
Socotra 49 E5
Söderhamn 8 C9
Sodiri 55 F4
Sofia = Sofiya 22 C4
Sofia ➔ 59 B9
Sofiya 22 C4
Sogamoso 90 B4
Sognefjorden 8 C7
Sohâg 54 C5
Soissons 13 B5
Sokal 17 C7
Söke 23 F6
Sokhumi 25 E5
Sokodé 53 G6
Sokol 24 B5
Sokółka 17 B6
Sokołów Podlaski 17 B6
Sokoto 53 F7
Solander I. 65 G2
Solano 36 A2
Solapur 43 L9
Soledad 90 B6
Soligalich 24 B5
Soligorsk = Salihorsk 17 B8
Solikamsk 28 D6
Solimões = Amazonas ➔ 92 C3
Solingen 14 C4
Sóller 19 C7
Sologne 12 C4
Solok 39 E2
Solomon Is. ■ 64 K10
Solomon Sea 61 B9
Solon 35 B7
Solor 37 F2
Šolta 20 C6
Solţānābād 44 B4
Solunska Glava 22 D3
Solwezi 59 A5
Sōma *Japan* 32 E7
Soma *Turkey* 23 E6
Somali Rep. ■ 49 F4
Somalia = Somali Rep. ■ 49 F4
Somaliland □ 49 E4
Sombor 22 B2
Sombrerete 84 C4
Somerset I. 68 A10
Someş ➔ 17 E6
Sommariva 63 A4
Somme ➔ 12 A4
Somosierra, Puerto de 18 B4
Somport, Puerto de 12 E3
Sóndrio 13 C8
Sonepur 40 G4
Song Cau 38 B3
Songea 57 G7
Songhua Jiang ➔ 35 B8
Songkhla 38 C2
Songo 59 B6
Songpan 34 C5
Sonipat 42 E10
Sonmiani 42 G5
Sono ➔ 93 D4
Sonora ➔ 84 B2
Sonsonate 85 E7
Soochow = Suzhou 35 C7
Soomaaliya = Somali Rep. ■ 49 F4
Sopi 37 D3
Sopot 16 A4
Sopron 16 E3
Sør-Rondane 96 B8
Sorel-Tracy 71 E6
Sórgono 21 D2
Soria 19 B4
Sorkh, Kuh-e 44 C4
Soroca 17 D9
Sorocaba 94 A7
Soroki = Soroca 17 D9
Sorong 37 E4
Soroti 57 D6
Sørøya 8 A10
Sorrento 63 C3
Sorsogon 36 B2
Sosnowiec 16 C4
Souanké 56 D2
Soudas, Ormos 23 G5
Sŏul = Seoul 35 C7
Sources, Mt. aux 59 D5
Soure 92 C4
Souris ➔ 69 D10
Sousa 92 D6
Sousse 54 A1
South Africa ■ 58 E4
South Australia □ 62 B2
South Bend 76 D2
South Carolina □ 83 C7
South China Sea 38 C4
South Dakota □ 74 C4
South East C. 62 D4
South Horr 57 D7
South I. 65 E3
South Invercargill 65 G3
South Korea ■ 35 C7
South Magnetic Pole 96 A13
South Nahanni ➔ 68 B7
South Natuna Is. = Natuna Selatan, Kepulauan 39 D3
South Orkney Is. 96 A4
South Pagai, I. = Pagai Selatan, Pulau 39 E2
South Platte ➔ 74 E4
South Pole 96 C
South Ronaldsay 10 B5
South Saskatchewan ➔ 69 C9
South Shetland Is. 96 A4
South Shields 11 D6
South Taranaki Bight 64 C6
South Uist 10 C3
South West C. *Australia* 62 D4
South West C. *N.Z.* 65 G2
Southampton 11 F6
Southampton I. 70 C5
Southbridge 65 E5
Southend-on-Sea 11 F7
Southern Alps 65 E4
Southern Indian L. 69 C10
Southern Ocean 96 A9
Southern Uplands 10 D5
Southland □ 65 F3
Southport 63 A5
Sovetsk *Kaliningrad, Russia* 24 B1
Sovetsk *Kirov, Russia* 24 B6
Soweto 59 D5
Sozh ➔ 17 C10
Spain ■ 18 C4
Spalding 62 B2
Spanish Town 86 C4
Sparta = Sparti 23 F4
Spartanburg 83 B7
Sparti 23 F4
Spartivento, C. *Calabria, Italy* 21 F6
Spartivento, C. *Sard., Italy* 21 E2
Spassk Dalniy 32 A3
Spatha, Akra 23 G4
Spence Bay = Taloyoak 68 B10
Spencer, C. 62 C2
Spencer G. 62 B2
Spenser Mts. 65 E5
Spey ➔ 10 C5
Speyer 14 D5
Split 20 C6
Spokane 72 C5
Spoleto 20 C4
Sporyy Navolok, Mys 28 B7
Spratly Is. 38 C4
Spree ➔ 15 B7
Springfield *N.Z.* 65 E4
Springfield *Ill., U.S.A.* 75 F10
Springfield *Mass., U.S.A.* 77 C9
Springfield *Mo., U.S.A.* 81 A7
Springfield *Ohio, U.S.A.* 76 E4
Springfield *Oreg., U.S.A.* 72 D2
Springhurst 63 C4
Springs 59 D5
Srbija = Serbia ■ 22 B3
Sre Ambel 38 B2
Sre Umbell = Sre Ambel 38 B2
Srebrenica 20 B7
Sredinny Ra. = Sredinnyy Khrebet 31 D14
Sredinnyy Khrebet 31 D14
Srednevilyuysk 31 C10
Śrem 16 B3
Sremska Mitrovica 22 B2
Sri Aman 39 D4
Sri Lanka ■ 43 R12
Srikakulam 40 H4
Srinagar 42 B9
Stade 14 B5
Stafford 11 E5
Stakhanov 25 D4
Stalowa Wola 17 C6
Stamford 77 D9
Stanke Dimitrov 22 C4
Stanley *Australia* 62 D4
Stanley *Falk. Is.* 95 G5
Stanovoy Khrebet 31 D10
Stanovoy Ra. = Stanovoy Khrebet 31 D10
Stanthorpe 63 A5
Stara Planina 22 C4
Stara Zagora 22 C5
Starachowice 16 C5
Staraya Russa 24 B3
Starbuck I. 65 K15
Stargard Szczeciński 16 B2
Staritsa 24 B3
Starogard Gdański 16 B4
Starokonstantinov = Starokonstyantyniv 17 D8
Starokonstyantyniv 17 D8
Staryy Chartoriysk 17 C7
Staryy Oskol 24 C4
State College 77 D7
Staten, I. = Estados, I. de Los 95 G4
Statesville 83 B7
Stavanger 9 D7
Staveley 65 E4
Stavropol 25 D5
Stawell 62 C3
Stefanie L. = Chew Bahir 55 H6
Stefansson Bay 96 A9
Steiermark □ 15 E8
Steinkjer 8 C8
Stendal 15 B6
Steornabhaigh = Stornoway 10 B3
Stepanakert = Xankändi 25 F6
Stephens Creek 62 B3
Stephenville 71 E8
Stepnyak 29 D8
Sterlitamak 29 D6
Stettin = Szczecin 16 B2
Stettiner Haff 15 B8
Stettler 69 C8
Steubenville 76 D5
Stevenage 11 F6
Stevenson ➔ 62 A2
Stewart ➔ 68 B6
Stewart, I. 95 G2
Stewart I. 65 G2
Steyr 15 D8
Stillwater *N.Z.* 65 E4
Stillwater *U.S.A.* 80 A5
Štip 22 D4

Stirling **10 C5**
Stockerau **15 D9**
Stockholm **9 D9**
Stockport **11 E5**
Stockton **78 B2**
Stockton-on-Tees **11 D6**
Stoeng Treng **38 B3**
Stoke-on-Trent **11 E5**
Stokes Pt. **62 D3**
Stolac **20 C6**
Stolbovoy, Ostrov **30 B11**
Stolbtsy = Stowbtsy **17 B8**
Stolin **17 C8**
Stonehaven **10 C5**
Stony Tunguska = Tunguska, Podkamennaya ➔ **30 C7**
Stora Lulevatten **8 B9**
Storavan **8 B9**
Store Bælt **9 D8**
Store Creek **63 B4**
Storm B. **62 D4**
Stormberge **59 E5**
Stornoway **10 B3**
Storozhinets = Storozhynets **17 D7**
Storozhynets **17 D7**
Storsjön **8 C8**
Storuman **8 B9**
Stowbtsy **17 B8**
Strahan **62 D4**
Stralsund **15 A7**
Stranraer **11 D4**
Strasbourg **13 B7**
Stratford *Canada* **76 C5**
Stratford *N.Z.* **64 C6**
Strathalbyn **62 C2**
Straubing **15 D7**
Streaky B. **62 B1**
Streaky Bay **62 B1**
Strelka **30 D7**
Strezhevoy **29 C8**
Strimonas ➔ **23 D4**
Strómboli **21 E5**
Stronsay **10 B5**
Stroud Road **63 B5**
Strumica **22 D4**
Stryy **17 D6**
Strzelecki Cr. ➔ **62 A2**
Stuart Ra. **62 A1**
Stung Treng = Stoeng Treng **38 B3**
Stuttgart **14 D5**
Styria = Steiermark □ **15 E8**
Suakin **55 E6**
Subansiri ➔ **41 D9**
Subi **39 D3**
Subotica **16 E4**
Suceava **17 E8**
Suchou = Suzhou **35 C7**
Süchow = Xuzhou **35 C6**
Sucre **91 G5**
Sudair **47 F6**
Sudan ■ **55 E4**
Sudbury **71 E5**
Sûdd **55 G4**
Sudeten Mts. = Sudety **16 C3**
Sudety **16 C3**
Sudirman, Pegunungan **37 E5**
Sueca **19 C5**
Suez = El Suweis **54 C5**
Suez, G. of = Suweis, Khalīg el **54 C5**
Sugluk = Salluit **70 C6**
Şuḩār **44 E4**
Sühbaatar **35 A5**
Suhl **14 C6**
Suihua **35 B7**
Suisse = Switzerland ■ **13 C8**
Sukadana **39 E3**
Sukagawa **33 E7**
Sukaraja **39 E4**
Sukhona ➔ **28 C5**
Sukhumi = Sokhumi **25 E5**
Sukkur **42 F6**
Sukkur Barrage **42 F6**
Sukumo **33 G3**
Sula, Kepulauan **37 E3**
Sulaiman Range **42 D6**
Sulawesi **37 E2**
Sulawesi Sea = Celebes Sea **37 D2**
Sulawesi Tengah □ **37 E2**
Sulawesi Tenggara □ **37 E2**
Sulima **53 G3**
Sulina **17 F9**
Sullana **90 D2**
Sultanpur **40 D4**
Sulu Arch. **36 C2**
Sulu Sea **36 C2**
Suluq **54 B3**
Sulzberger Ice Shelf **96 B17**
Sumalata **37 D2**
Sumatera **39 D2**
Sumatra = Sumatera **39 D2**
Sumba **37 F1**
Sumba, Selat **37 F1**
Sumbawa **39 F5**
Sumbawa Besar **39 F5**
Sumbe **56 G2**
Šumen = Shumen **22 C6**
Sumgait = Sumqayıt **25 E6**
Summerside **71 E7**
Šumperk **16 D3**
Sumqayıt **25 E6**
Sumter **83 C7**
Sumy **24 C3**
Sunbury **63 C3**
Sunda, Selat **39 F3**
Sunda Str. = Sunda, Selat **39 F3**
Sundarbans **41 G7**
Sundargarh **40 F5**
Sunderland **11 D6**
Sundsvall **8 C9**
Sungaigerong **39 E2**
Sungailiat **39 E3**
Sungaipakning **39 D2**
Sungaipenuh **39 E2**
Sungari = Songhua Jiang ➔ **35 B8**
Sunghua Chiang = Songhua Jiang ➔ **35 B8**
Sungurlu **46 B3**
Sunnyvale **78 B1**
Suntar **30 C9**
Suomi = Finland ■ **8 C11**
Supaul **40 D6**
Superior **75 B8**
Superior, L. **71 E5**
Suphan Dağı **46 C5**
Supiori **37 E5**
Suquṭra = Socotra **49 E5**
Sūr *Lebanon* **46 D3**
Ṣūr *Oman* **45 F4**
Sura ➔ **24 B6**
Surabaja = Surabaya **39 F4**
Surabaya **39 F4**
Surakarta **39 F4**
Surat *Australia* **63 A4**
Surat *India* **43 J8**
Surat Thani **38 C1**
Suratgarh **42 E8**
Surgut **29 C8**
Suriapet **43 L11**
Surigao **36 C3**
Surinam = Suriname ■ **92 B2**
Suriname ■ **92 B2**
Suriname ➔ **92 A2**
Surt **54 B2**
Surt, Khalīj **54 B2**
Surtsey **8 C1**
Suruga-Wan **33 F6**
Süsangerd **47 E7**
Susanville **72 F3**
Susquehanna ➔ **77 E7**
Susques **94 A3**
Susunu **37 E4**
Susurluk **23 E7**
Sutherland **58 E4**
Sutherland Falls **65 F2**
Sutlej ➔ **42 E7**
Suttsu **32 B7**
Suva **64 L12**
Suva Planina **22 C4**
Suvorov Is. = Suwarrow Is. **65 L14**
Suwałki **17 A6**
Suwarrow Is. **65 L14**
Suweis, Khalīg el **54 C5**
Suzdal **24 B5**
Suzhou **35 C7**
Suzu **33 E5**
Suzu-Misaki **33 E5**
Svealand □ **9 D9**
Sverdrup Chan. **70 B4**
Sverdrup Is. **70 B4**
Sverige = Sweden ■ **9 D9**
Svetlogorsk = Svyetlahorsk **17 B9**
Svishtov **22 C5**
Svislach **17 B7**
Svizzera = Switzerland ■ **13 C8**
Svyetlahorsk **17 B9**
Swabian Alps = Schwäbische Alb **14 D5**
Swakopmund **58 C2**
Swan Hill **62 C3**
Swansea **11 F5**
Swatow = Shantou **35 D6**
Swaziland ■ **59 D6**
Sweden ■ **9 D9**
Sweetwater **80 C3**
Swellendam **58 E4**
Świdnica **16 C3**
Świdnik **17 C6**
Świebodzin **16 B2**
Świecie **16 B4**
Swift Current **69 C9**
Swindon **11 F6**
Swinemünde = Świnoujście **16 B2**
Świnoujście **16 B2**
Switzerland ■ **13 C8**
Sydney *Australia* **63 B5**
Sydney *Canada* **71 E7**
Sydra, G. of = Surt, Khalīj **54 B2**
Syktyvkar **28 C6**
Sylhet **41 E8**
Sylt **14 A5**
Sym **29 C9**
Syracuse **77 C7**
Syrdarya ➔ **29 E7**
Syria ■ **46 D4**
Syrian Desert = Shām, Bādiyat ash **47 D4**
Syros **23 F5**
Syzran **24 C6**
Szczecin **16 B2**
Szczecinek **16 B3**
Szczeciński, Zalew = Stettiner Haff **15 B8**
Szczytno **16 B5**
Szechwan = Sichuan □ **34 C5**
Szeged **16 E5**
Székesfehérvár **16 E4**
Szekszárd **16 E4**
Szentes **16 E5**
Szolnok **16 E5**
Szombathely **16 E3**

T

Tabacal **94 A4**
Tabaco **36 B2**
Ṭābah **47 F5**
Ṭabas *Khorāsān, Iran* **45 C5**
Ṭabas *Yazd, Iran* **44 C4**
Tabatinga, Serra da **93 E5**
Tablas **36 B2**
Table B. **58 E3**
Table Mt. **58 E3**
Tábor **16 D2**
Tabora **57 F6**
Tabou **53 H4**
Tabrīz **46 C6**
Tabük **47 E4**
Tacheng **34 B3**
Tacloban **36 B2**
Tacna **91 G4**
Tacoma **72 C2**
Tacuarembó **94 C5**
Tademaït, Plateau du **52 C6**

Tadjoura 49 E3
Tadmor 65 D5
Tadzhikistan = Tajikistan ■ 29 F8
Taegu = Daegu 35 C7
Taejŏn = Daejeon 35 C7
Tafalla 19 A5
Tafelbaai = Table B. 58 E3
Tafermaar 37 F4
Taft 36 B3
Taftan 42 E2
Taftān, Küh-e 45 D5
Taga Dzong 41 D7
Taganrog 25 D4
Tagbilaran 36 C2
Tagliamento ➔ 20 B4
Taguatinga 93 E5
Tagum 36 C3
Tagus = Tejo ➔ 18 C1
Tahakopa 65 G3
Tahan, Gunung 38 D2
Tahat 52 D7
Tāherī 44 E3
Tahiti 65 L16
Tahoe, L. 72 G3
Tahoua 53 F7
Tahta 54 C5
Tahulandang 37 D3
Tahuna 37 D3
Taibei = T'aipei 35 D7
T'aichung 35 D7
Taidong 35 D7
Taieri ➔ 65 G4
Taihape 64 C6
Tailem Bend 62 C2
Taimyr Peninsula = Taymyr, Poluostrov 30 B7
Tain 10 C4
T'ainan 35 D7
T'aipei 35 D7
Taiping 38 D2
Taitao, Pen. de 95 F1
Taiwan ■ 35 D7
Taiyuan 35 C6
Taizhong = T'aichung 35 D7
Ta'izz 49 E3
Tajikistan ■ 29 F8
Tajima 33 E6
Tajo = Tejo ➔ 18 C1
Tak 38 A1
Takada 33 E6
Takaka 65 D5
Takamatsu 33 F4
Takaoka 33 E5
Takapuna 64 B6
Takasaki 33 E6
Takayama 33 E5
Takefu 33 F5
Takengon 38 D1
Takeshima = Liancourt Rocks 33 E2
Täkestän 46 D7
Takev 38 B2
Takhār □ 45 B7
Takikawa 32 B7
Takla Makan 34 C3
Taklamakan Shamo = Takla Makan 34 C3
Talara 90 D2
Talas 29 E8
Talaud, Kepulauan 36 D3
Talaud Is. = Talaud, Kepulauan 36 D3
Talavera de la Reina 18 C3
Talayan 36 C2
Talbragar ➔ 63 B4
Talca 94 D2
Talcahuano 94 D2
Talcher 40 G5
Taldy Kurgan = Taldyqorghan 29 E8
Taldyqorghan 29 E8
Tālesh, Kühhā-ye 46 C7
Tali Post 55 G5
Talibon 36 B2
Taliwang 39 F5
Tall 'Afar 46 C5
Talladega 82 C4
Tallahassee 83 D5
Tallangatta 63 C4
Tallinn 24 B1
Taloyoak 68 B10
Taltal 94 B2
Talwood 63 A4
Talyawalka Cr. ➔ 62 B3
Tamale 53 G5
Tamanrasset 52 D7
Tamarang 63 B5
Tamatave = Toamasina 59 B9
Tambacounda 53 F3
Tambelan, Kepulauan 39 D3
Tambo de Mora 91 F3
Tambora 39 F5
Tambov 24 C5
Tâmega ➔ 18 B1
Tamenglong 41 E9
Tamgak, Mts. 53 E7
Tamil Nadu □ 43 P10
Tammerfors = Tampere 8 C10
Tamo Abu, Banjaran 39 D5
Tampa 83 F6
Tampere 8 C10
Tampico 84 C5
Tamsagbulag 35 B6
Tamu 41 E10
Tamworth 63 B5
Tana ➔ *Kenya* 57 E8
Tana ➔ *Norway* 8 A11
Tana, L. 55 F6
Tanabe 33 G4
Tanahbala 39 E1
Tanahgrogot 39 E5
Tanahjampea 37 F2
Tanahmasa 39 E1
Tanahmerah 37 F6
Tanakura 33 E7
Tanami Desert 60 D5
Tanana ➔ 69 B4
Tananarive = Antananarivo 59 B9
Tánaro ➔ 13 D8
Tandag 36 C3
Tandil 94 D5
Tando Adam 42 G6
Tandou L. 62 B3
Taneatua 64 C7
Tanen Tong Dan = Dawna Ra. 41 J12
Tanezrouft 52 D6
Tanga 57 F7
Tanganyika, L. 57 F5
Tanger 52 A4
Tanggula Shan 34 C4
Tanghla Range = Tanggula Shan 34 C4
Tangier = Tanger 52 A4
Tangshan 35 C6
Tanimbar, Kepulauan 37 F4
Tanimbar Is. = Tanimbar, Kepulauan 37 F4
Taninthari = Tenasserim 38 B1
Tanjay 36 C2
Tanjore = Thanjavur 43 P11
Tanjung 39 E5
Tanjungbalai 39 D1
Tanjungbatu 39 D5
Tanjungkarang Telukbetung = Bandar Lampung 39 F3
Tanjungpandan 39 E3
Tanjungpinang 39 D2
Tanjungredeb 39 D5
Tanjungselor 39 D5
Tanout 53 F7
Tanta 54 B5
Tantung = Dandong 35 B7
Tanunda 62 B2
Tanzania ■ 57 F6
Taolanaro 59 D9
Taoudenni 52 D5
Tapa Shan = Daba Shan 35 C5
Tapajós ➔ 92 C3
Tapaktuan 39 D1
Tapanui 65 F3
Tapauá ➔ 91 E6
Tapeta 53 G4
Tapirapecó, Serra 90 C6
Tapti ➔ 43 J8
Tapuae-o-Uenuku 65 D5
Tapul Group 36 C2
Taquari ➔ 91 G7
Tara *Australia* 63 A5
Tara *Russia* 29 D8
Tara ➔ *Montenegro* 22 C2
Tara ➔ *Russia* 29 D8
Tarābulus *Lebanon* 46 D3
Tarābulus *Libya* 54 B1
Tarakan 39 D5
Taranaki □ 64 C6
Taranaki, Mt. 64 C6
Tarancón 19 B4
Taranga Hill 43 H8
Táranto 21 D6
Táranto, G. di 21 D6
Tarapacá 90 D5
Tararua Ra. 64 D6
Tarashcha 17 D10
Tarauacá 91 E4
Tarauacá ➔ 91 E5
Tarawa 64 J12
Tarawera 64 C7
Tarawera, L. 64 C7
Taraz 29 E8
Tarazona 19 B5
Tarbagatay, Khrebet 29 E9
Tarbela Dam 42 B8
Tarbes 12 E4
Tarcoola 62 B1
Tarcoon 63 B4
Taree 63 B5
Tarfaya 52 C3
Târgovişte 22 B5
Târgu Jiu 17 F6
Târgu Mureş 17 E7
Tarifa 18 D3
Tarija 94 A4
Tariku ➔ 37 E5
Tarim Basin = Tarim Pendi 34 C3
Tarim He ➔ 34 C3
Tarim Pendi 34 C3
Taritatu ➔ 37 E5
Tarkhankut, Mys 25 D3
Tarko Sale 28 C8
Tarkwa 53 G5
Tarlac 36 A2
Tarma 91 F3
Tarn ➔ 12 D4
Tarnobrzeg 16 C5
Tarnów 16 C5
Tarnowskie Góry 16 C4
Taroom 63 A4
Taroudannt 52 B4
Tarragona 19 B6
Tarrasa = Terrassa 19 B7
Tarsus 46 C3
Tartagal 94 A4
Tartu 24 B2
Tartūs 46 D3
Tarutung 39 D1
Tash-Kömür 29 E8
Tash-Kumyr = Tash-Kömür 29 E8
Tashauz = Dashoguz 29 E6
Tashi Chho Dzong = Thimphu 41 D7
Tashkent = Toshkent 29 E7
Tashtagol 29 D9
Tasman B. 65 D5
Tasman Mts. 65 D5
Tasman Pen. 62 D4
Tasmania □ 62 D4
Tatabánya 16 E4
Tatar Republic = Tatarstan □ 29 D6
Tatarbunary 17 F9
Tatarsk 29 D8
Tatarstan □ 29 D6
Tateyama 33 F6
Tathra 63 C4
Tatnam, C. 71 D4
Tatra = Tatry 16 D4
Tatry 16 D4
Tatta 43 G5
Tat'ung = Datong 35 B6

Tatvan **46 C5**
Taubaté **94 A7**
Tauern **15 E7**
Taumarunui **64 C6**
Taumaturgo **91 E4**
Taungdwingyi **41 G10**
Taunggyi **41 G11**
Taungup **41 H10**
Taungup Taunggya **41 H9**
Taunton **11 F5**
Taunus **14 C5**
Taupo **64 C7**
Taupo, L. **64 C6**
Tauranga **64 B7**
Tauranga Harb. **64 B7**
Taurianova **21 E6**
Taurus Mts. = Toros Dağları **46 C3**
Tavastehus = Hämeenlinna **8 C10**
Tavda **29 D7**
Tavda ➔ **29 D7**
Tavira **18 D2**
Tavoy **38 B1**
Tawau **38 D5**
Tawi-Tawi **36 C2**
Tay ➔ **10 C5**
Tayabamba **91 E3**
Taygetos Oros **23 F4**
Taylakova **29 D8**
Taylakovy = Taylakova **29 D8**
Taymä **47 F4**
Taymyr, Oz. **30 B8**
Taymyr, Puluostrov **30 B7**
Taytay **36 B1**
Taz ➔ **28 C8**
Taza **52 B5**
Tazovskiy **28 C8**
Tbilisi **25 E5**
Tchad = Chad ■ **55 E2**
Tchad, L. **55 F1**
Tch'eng-tou = Chengdu **35 C5**
Tchibanga **56 E2**
Tch'ong-k'ing = Chongqing **35 D5**
Tczew **16 A4**
Te Anau, L. **65 F2**
Te Aroha **64 B6**
Te Awamutu **64 C6**
Te Ika a Maui = North I. **64 B5**
Te Kuiti **64 C6**
Te Puke **64 B7**
Te Waewae B. **65 G2**
Te Wai Pounamu = South I. **65 E3**
Tebakang **39 D4**
Tébessa **52 A7**
Tebicuary ➔ **94 B5**
Tebingtinggi **39 D1**
Tecuci **22 B6**
Tedzhen = Tejen **29 F7**
Tefé **90 D6**
Tegal **39 F3**
Tegucigalpa **85 E7**
Tehachapi **78 C3**
Teheran = Tehrān **44 C2**
Tehoru **37 E3**
Tehrān **44 C2**
Tehuantepec **85 D5**
Tehuantepec, G. de **85 D5**
Tehuantepec, Istmo de **85 D6**
Tejen **29 F7**
Tejo ➔ **18 C1**
Tekapo, L. **65 E4**
Tekeli **29 E8**
Tekirdağ **22 D6**
Tekkali **40 H5**
Tel Aviv-Yafo **46 D3**
Tela **85 D7**
Telanaipura = Jambi **39 E2**
Telavi **25 E6**
Telekhany = Tsyelyakhany **17 B7**
Teles Pires ➔ **91 E7**
Telford **11 E5**
Tellicherry **43 P9**
Telsen **95 E3**
Teluk Anson = Teluk Intan **39 D2**
Teluk Betung = Bandar Lampung **39 F3**
Teluk Intan **39 D2**
Telukbutun **39 D3**
Telukdalem **39 D1**
Tema **53 G5**
Temerloh **39 D2**
Temir **29 E6**
Temirtau *Kazakhstan* **29 D8**
Temirtau *Russia* **29 D9**
Temma **62 D3**
Tempe **79 D7**
Temple **80 D5**
Temuco **94 D2**
Temuka **65 F4**
Tenali **40 J3**
Tenaro, Akra **23 F4**
Tenasserim **38 B1**
Tenda, Colle di **13 D7**
Tendaho **49 E3**
Tenerife **52 C2**
Tengah, Kepulauan **39 F5**
Tengchong **34 D4**
Tenggarong **39 E5**
Tengiz Köli **29 D7**
Tenkasi **43 Q10**
Tennessee □ **82 B4**
Tennessee ➔ **76 F1**
Tenom **38 C5**
Tenterfield **63 A5**
Teófilo Otoni **93 F5**
Tepa **37 F3**
Tepic **84 C4**
Teplice **16 C1**
Ter ➔ **19 A7**
Téramo **20 C4**
Terang **62 C3**
Terebovlya **17 D7**
Terek ➔ **25 E6**
Teresina **92 D5**
Terewah, L. **63 A4**
Teridgerie Cr. ➔ **63 B4**
Termez = Termiz **29 F7**
Término Imerese **21 F4**
Termiz **29 F7**
Térmoli **20 C5**
Ternate **37 D3**
Terney **32 A5**
Terni **20 C4**
Ternopil **17 D7**
Ternopol = Ternopil **17 D7**
Terowie *N.S.W., Australia* **63 B4**
Terowie *S. Austral., Australia* **62 B2**
Terracina **20 D4**
Terralba **21 E2**
Terrassa **19 B7**
Terre Haute **76 E2**
Terschelling **14 B3**
Teruel **19 B5**
Teryaweynya L. **62 B3**
Teshio **32 A7**
Teshio-Gawa ➔ **32 A7**
Tesiyn Gol ➔ **34 A4**
Teslin **68 B6**
Tessalit **52 D6**
Tetas, Pta. **94 A2**
Tete **59 B6**
Teterev ➔ **17 C10**
Teteven **22 C5**
Tetiyev **17 D9**
Tétouan **52 A4**
Tetovo **22 C3**
Teuco ➔ **94 B4**
Teun **37 F3**
Teutoburger Wald **14 B5**
Tevere ➔ **20 D4**
Tewantin **63 A5**
Texarkana **81 C6**
Texas **63 A5**
Texas □ **80 D4**
Texas City **81 E6**
Texel **14 B3**
Teyvareh **45 C6**
Tezpur **41 D9**
Thabana Ntlenyana **59 D5**
Thabazimbi **59 C5**
Thailand ■ **38 A2**
Thailand, G. of **38 B2**
Thakhek **38 A2**
Thal **42 C7**
Thala La = Hkakabo Razi **41 C11**
Thallon **63 A4**
Thames **64 B6**
Thames ➔ **11 F7**
Thandwe **41 H10**
Thane **43 K8**
Thanh Pho Ho Chi Minh **38 B3**
Thanjavur **43 P11**
Thar Desert **42 F7**
Tharad **43 G7**
Thargomindah **63 A3**
Tharrawaddy **41 J10**
Thasos **23 D5**
Thaton **41 J11**
Thaungdut **41 E10**
Thayetmyo **41 H10**
Thazi **41 G11**
The Gulf = Persian Gulf **44 E2**
The Hague = 's-Gravenhage **14 B3**
The Pas **69 C9**
The Wash **11 E7**
Thebes = Thiva **23 E4**
Theebine **63 A5**
Thermopylae **23 E4**
Thessaloniki **23 D4**
Thessaloniki, Gulf of = Thessaloniki Kolpos **23 D4**
Thessaloniki Kolpos **23 D4**
Thetford **11 E7**
Thetford Mines **71 E6**
Thevenard **62 B1**
Thiel Mts. **96 C2**
Thiers **13 D5**
Thiès **53 F2**
Thika **57 E7**
Thimphu **41 D7**
Thionville **13 B7**
Thira = Santorini **23 F5**
Thiruvananthapuram = Trivandrum **43 Q10**
Thistle I. **62 C2**
Thiva **23 E4**
Þjórsá ➔ **8 C1**
Thohoyandou **59 C6**
Thomas, L. **62 A2**
Thomasville *Ga., U.S.A.* **83 D6**
Thomasville *N.C., U.S.A.* **83 B7**
Thompson **69 C10**
Thrace **22 D6**
Three Hummock I. **62 D3**
Three Points, C. **53 H5**
Thunder Bay **71 E5**
Thung Song **38 C1**
Thunkar **41 D8**
Thüringer Wald **14 C6**
Thurles **11 E3**
Thurloo Downs **63 A3**
Thurso **10 B5**
Thurston I. **96 B2**
Thylungra **63 A3**
Tia **63 B5**
Tian Shan **34 B3**
Tianjin **35 C6**
Tianshui **35 C5**
Tiaret **52 A6**
Tiber = Tevere ➔ **20 D4**
Tiberias, L. = Yam Kinneret **46 D3**
Tibesti **54 D2**
Tibet = Xizang Zizhiqu □ **34 C3**
Tibooburra **62 A3**
Tiburón, I. **84 B2**
Ticino ➔ **13 D8**
Tiddim **41 F9**
Tidjikja **53 E3**
Tidore **37 D3**
Tien Shan = Tian Shan **34 B3**
Tien-tsin = Tianjin **35 C6**
T'ienching = Tianjin **35 C6**
Tientsin = Tianjin **35 C6**
Tierra de Campos **18 A3**
Tierra del Fuego, I. Gr. de **95 G3**
Tiétar ➔ **18 C2**

Tieyon 62 A1
Tifu 37 E3
Tighina 17 E9
Tigre ➔ 90 D4
Tigris = Dijlah, Nahr ➔ 47 E6
Tigyaing 41 F11
Tijuana 84 A1
Tikamgarh 43 G11
Tikhoretsk 25 D5
Tikiraqjuaq = Whale Cove 68 B10
Tikrīt 46 D5
Tiksi 30 B10
Tilamuta 37 D2
Tilburg 14 C3
Tilos 23 F6
Tilpa 63 B3
Timaru 65 F4
Timbuktu = Tombouctou 53 E5
Timimoun 52 C6
Timiris, Rås 53 E2
Timişoara 16 F5
Timmins 71 E5
Timok ➔ 22 B4
Timor 37 F2
Timor Leste = East Timor ■ 37 F3
Tinaca Pt. 36 C3
Tindouf 52 C4
Tingo Maria 91 E3
Tinian 64 H9
Tinjoub 52 C4
Tinnevelly = Tirunelveli 43 Q10
Tinogasta 94 B3
Tinos 23 F5
Tintinara 62 C3
Tioman, Pulau 39 D2
Tipongpani 41 D10
Tipperary 11 E2
Tirān 44 C2
Tiranë 22 D2
Tiraspol 17 E9
Tire 23 E6
Tirebolu 25 E4
Tiree 10 C3
Tîrgovişte = Târgovişte 22 B5
Tîrgu Jiu = Târgu Jiu 17 F6
Tîrgu Mureş = Târgu Mureş 17 E7
Tirich Mir 42 A7
Tiritiri o te Moana = Southern Alps 65 E4
Tirnavos 23 E4
Tirodi 43 J11
Tirol □ 14 E6
Tirso ➔ 21 E2
Tiruchchirappalli 43 P11
Tirunelveli 43 Q10
Tirupati 43 N11
Tiruppur 43 P10
Tiruvannamalai 43 N11
Tisa ➔ 22 B3
Tisdale 69 C9
Tisza = Tisa ➔ 22 B3
Tit-Ary 30 B10
Titicaca, L. 91 G5
Titule 57 D5
Tivaouane 53 F2
Tivoli 20 D4
Tiwī 45 F4
Tizi-Ouzou 52 A6
Tjirebon = Cirebon 39 F3
Tlaxiaco 84 D5
Tlemcen 52 B5
Toamasina 59 B9
Toay 94 D4
Toba Kakar 42 D6
Tobago 87 D7
Tobelo 37 D3
Tobermory 10 C3
Tobias Fornier 36 B2
Toboali 39 E3
Tobol ➔ 29 D7
Toboli 37 E2
Tobolsk 29 D7
Tobruk = Tubruq 54 B3
Tobyl = Tobol ➔ 29 D7
Tocantinópolis 92 D4
Tocantins □ 93 E4
Tocantins ➔ 92 C4
Tocumwal 63 C4
Tocuyo ➔ 90 A5
Todeli 37 E2
Todos os Santos, B. de 93 E6
Togian, Kepulauan 37 E2
Togliatti 24 C6
Togo ■ 53 G6
Toili 37 E2
Toinya 55 G4
Tojikiston = Tajikistan ■ 29 F8
Tojo 37 E2
Tokala 37 E2
Tōkamachi 33 E6
Tokanui 65 G3
Tokarahi 65 F4
Tokat 46 B4
Tokdo = Liancourt Rocks 33 E2
Tokelau Is. 65 K13
Tokmak 29 E8
Tokushima 33 F4
Tokuyama 33 F2
Tōkyō 33 F6
Tolaga Bay 64 C8
Tolbukhin = Dobrich 22 C6
Toledo *Spain* 18 C3
Toledo *U.S.A.* 76 D4
Toledo, Montes de 18 C3
Toliara 59 C8
Tolima 90 C3
Tolitoli 37 D2
Tolo, Teluk 37 E2
Toluca 84 D5
Tomakomai 32 B7
Tomar 18 C1
Tomaszów Mazowiecki 16 C4
Tombouctou 53 E5
Tombua 58 B2
Tomelloso 18 C4
Tomini 37 D2
Tomini, Teluk 37 E2
Tomorit 23 D3
Tomsk 29 D9
Tonantins 90 D5
Tondano 37 D2
Tonekābon 44 B2
Tonga ■ 65 L13
Tonga Trench 65 L13
Tongareva = Penrhyn 65 K15
Tongariro △ 64 C6
Tongchuan 35 C5
Tonghua 35 B7
Tongjiang 35 B8
Tongking, G. of = Tonkin, G. of 35 D5
Tongoy 94 C2
Tongsa Dzong 41 D8
Tongue ➔ 74 B2
Tonk 42 F9
Tonkin, G. of 35 D5
Tonle Sap 38 B2
Tonnégrande 30 E
Toompine 63 A3
Toora 63 C4
Toowoomba 63 A5
Topeka 75 F7
Topki 29 D9
Topolobampo 84 B3
Torata 91 G4
Torbalı 23 E6
Torbat-e Heydārīyeh 44 C4
Torbat-e Jām 45 C5
Torbay □ 11 F5
Tordesillas 18 B3
Torgau 15 C7
Torino 13 D7
Torit 55 H5
Tormes ➔ 18 B2
Torneå = Tornio 8 E12
Torneälven ➔ 8 B10
Torneträsk 8 B9
Tornio 8 E12
Tornionjoki = Torneälven ➔ 8 B10
Tornquist 94 D4
Toro, Cerro del 94 B3
Toronto 71 E6
Toropets 24 B3
Tororo 57 D6
Toros Dağları 46 C3
Torre de Moncorvo 18 B2
Torre del Greco 21 D5
Torrejón de Ardoz 18 B4
Torrelavega 18 A3
Torremolinos 18 D3
Torrens, L. 62 B2
Torrent 19 C5
Torreón 84 B4
Torres Vedras 18 C1
Torrevieja 19 D5
Tortosa 19 B6
Tortosa, C. 19 B6
Ţorŭd 44 C3
Toruń 16 B4
Tosa-Wan 33 G3
Toscana □ 20 C3
Toshkent 29 E7
Tostado 94 B4
Tosya 46 B3
Totma 24 A5
Totten Glacier 96 A12
Tottenham 63 B4
Tottori 33 F4
Toubkal, Djebel 52 B4
Tougan 53 F5
Tougguort 52 B7
Toul 13 B6
Toulon 13 E6
Toulouse 12 E4
Toummo 54 D1
Toungoo 41 H11
Touraine 12 C4
Tourcoing 13 A5
Tourińán, C. 18 A1
Tournai 14 C2
Tournon-sur-Rhône 13 D6
Tours 12 C4
Towada 32 C7
Towada-Ko 32 C7
Towamba 63 C4
Towang 41 D8
Townsville 61 D8
Toya-Ko 32 B7
Toyama 33 E5
Toyama-Wan 33 E5
Toyohashi 33 F5
Toyooka 33 F4
Toyota 33 F5
Tozeur 52 B7
Tozkhurmato 46 D6
Trá Lí = Tralee 11 E2
Trabzon 25 E4
Trafalgar, C. 18 D2
Trail 69 D8
Tralee 11 E2
Trancas 94 B3
Trang 38 C1
Trangan 37 F4
Trangie 63 B4
Trani 20 D6
Transantarctic Mts. 96 C3
Transilvania 17 F7
Transilvanian Alps = Carpaţii Meridionali 17 F7
Transylvania = Transilvania 17 F7
Trápani 21 E4
Traralgon 63 C4
Trasimeno, L. 20 C4
Traun 15 D8
Travemünde 15 B6
Travers, Mt. 65 E5
Travnik 20 B6
Tŕebbia ➔ 13 D8
Třebíč 16 D2
Trebinje 20 C7
Treinta y Tres 94 C6
Trelew 95 E3
Tremp 19 A6
Trenque Lauquen 94 D4
Trent ➔ 11 E6
Trento 20 A3
Trenton 77 D8
Tres Arroyos 94 D4
Três Lagoas 93 G3
Tres Montes, C. 95 F1
Tres Puntas, C. 95 F3
Três Rios 93 G5

Treviso 20 B4
Triabunna 62 D4
Trichinopoly = Tiruchchirappalli 43 P11
Trichur 43 P10
Trida 63 B4
Trier 14 D4
Trieste 20 B4
Triglav 20 A4
Trikala 23 E3
Trikora, Puncak 37 E5
Trinidad *Bolivia* 91 F6
Trinidad *Cuba* 86 B3
Trinidad *Uruguay* 94 C5
Trinidad *U.S.A.* 80 A1
Trinidad & Tobago ■ 87 D7
Trinity ➔ 81 E6
Trinity B. 71 E8
Trinity Range 72 F4
Trinkitat 55 E6
Tripoli = Tarābulus *Lebanon* 46 D3
Tripoli = Tarābulus *Libya* 54 B1
Tripoli 23 F4
Tripura □ 41 F8
Trivandrum 43 Q10
Troglav 20 C6
Trois-Rivières 71 E6
Troitsko Pechorsk 28 C6
Trollhättan 9 D8
Tromsø 8 B9
Tronador, Mte. 95 E2
Trondheim 8 C8
Trondheimsfjorden 8 C8
Trout L. 68 B7
Trouville-sur-Mer 12 B4
Troy *Turkey* 23 E6
Troy *Ala., U.S.A.* 82 D5
Troy *N.Y., U.S.A.* 77 C9
Troyes 13 B6
Trucial States = United Arab Emirates ■ 44 F3
Trudovoye 32 B3
Trujillo *Honduras* 85 D7
Trujillo *Peru* 91 E3
Trujillo *Spain* 18 C3
Trujillo *Venezuela* 90 B4
Truk 64 J10
Trundle 63 B4
Truro *Canada* 71 E7
Truro *U.K.* 11 F4
Truskavets 17 D6
Trutnov 16 C2
Tsaratanana 59 B9
Tsetserleg 34 B5
Tshabong 58 D4
Tshane 58 C4
Tshela 56 E2
Tshikapa 56 F4
Tshwane = Pretoria 59 D5
Tsiigehtchic 68 B6
Tsimlyansk Res. = Tsimlyanskoye Vdkhr. 25 D5
Tsimlyanskoye Vdkhr. 25 D5
Tsinan = Jinan 35 C6
Tsinghai = Qinghai □ 34 C4
Tsingtao = Qingdao 35 C7
Tsirigo = Kythira 23 F4
Tskhinvali 25 E5
Tsna ➔ 24 C5
Tsuchiura 33 E7
Tsugaru-Kaikyō 32 C7
Tsumeb 58 B3
Tsuruga 33 F5
Tsuruoka 32 D6
Tsushima 33 F1
Tsuyama 33 F4
Tsyelyakhany 17 B7
Tual 37 F4
Tuamotu, Îs. 65 L16
Tuamotu Arch. = Tuamotu, Îs. 65 L16
Tuamotu Ridge 65 M17
Tuao 36 A2
Tuapse 25 E4
Tuatapere 65 G2
Tubarão 94 B7
Tübingen 14 D5
Tubruq 54 B3
Tubuaï, Îs. 65 M16
Tucacas 90 A5
Tucson 79 D7
Tucumcari 80 B2
Tucupita 90 B6
Tucuruí 92 C4
Tucuruí, Reprêsa de 92 C4
Tudela 19 A5
Tudmur 46 D4
Tuen 63 A4
Tuguegarao 36 A2
Tui 18 A1
Tukangbesi, Kepulauan 37 F2
Tuktoyaktuk 68 B6
Tukuyu 57 F6
Tula 24 C4
Tülak 45 C5
Tulare 78 B3
Tulcán 90 C3
Tulcea 17 F9
Tulchyn 17 D9
Tulita 68 B7
Tullamore *Australia* 63 B4
Tullamore *Ireland* 11 E3
Tulle 12 D4
Tullibigeal 63 B4
Tulsa 81 A6
Tulua 90 C3
Tum 37 E4
Tumaco 90 C3
Tumatumari 90 B7
Tumba, L. 56 E3
Tumbarumba 63 C4
Tumbes 90 D2
Tumby Bay 62 B2
Tumeremo 90 B6
Tumkur 43 N10
Tump 42 F3
Tumpat 38 C2
Tumu 53 F5
Tumucumaque, Serra 92 B3
Tumut 63 C4
Tuncurry 63 B5
Tundzha ➔ 22 D6
Tungabhadra ➔ 43 M11
Tunguska, Nizhnyaya ➔ 30 C6
Tunguska, Podkamennaya ➔ 30 C7
Tunis 50 A1
Tunisia ■ 50 B1
Tunja 90 B4
Tunuyán ➔ 94 C3
Tupelo 82 B3
Tupinambaranas 90 D7
Tupiza 94 A3
Tupungato, Cerro 94 C3
Túquerres 90 C3
Tura 30 C8
Turabah 47 E5
Türän 44 C4
Ţurayf 47 E4
Turek 16 B4
Turfan = Turpan 34 B3
Turfan Basin = Turpan Pendi 34 B3
Turfan Depression = Turpan Pendi 34 B3
Türgovishte 22 C6
Turgutlu 23 E6
Turhal 46 B4
Turia ➔ 19 C5
Turiaçu 92 C4
Turiaçu ➔ 92 C4
Turin = Torino 13 D7
Turkana, L. 57 D7
Turkestan = Türkistan 29 E7
Turkey ■ 25 F4
Türkistan 29 E7
Türkmenabat 29 F7
Türkmenbashi 29 E6
Turkmenistan ■ 29 F6
Turks & Caicos Is. ☑ 87 B5
Turku 9 C10
Turnagain, C. 64 D7
Turneffe Is. 85 D7
Turnhout 14 C3
Tŭrnovo = Veliko Tŭrnovo 22 C5
Turnu Măgurele 22 C5
Turnu Roşu, P. 17 F7
Turpan 34 B3
Turpan Pendi 34 B3
Turukhansk 30 C6
Tuscaloosa 82 C4
Tuscany = Toscana □ 20 C3
Tuticorin 43 Q11
Tutóia 92 C5
Tutong 38 D4
Tutrakan 22 B6
Tuttlingen 14 E5
Tutuala 37 F3
Tutuila 65 L13
Tutume 59 C5
Tuvalu ■ 64 K12
Tuxpan 84 C5
Tuxtla Gutiérrez 85 D6
Tuy = Tui 18 A1
Tuz Gölü 46 C3
Ţūz Khurmātū = Tozkhurmato 46 D6
Tuzla 20 B7
Tver 24 B4
Tweed Heads 63 A5
Twin Falls 73 E6
Twofold B. 63 C4
Tyachiv 17 D6
Tychy 16 C4
Tyler 81 C6
Tyre = Sūr 46 D3
Tyrol = Tirol □ 14 E6
Tyrrell ➔ 62 C3
Tyrrell, L. 62 C3
Tyrrhenian Sea 21 E4
Tyumen 29 D7
Tzaneen 59 C6
Tzukong = Zigong 35 D5

U

U.S.A. = United States of America ■ 67 F10
Uato-Udo 37 F3
Uatumã ➔ 90 D7
Uaupés 90 D5
Uaupés ➔ 90 C5
Ubá 93 G5
Ubaitaba 93 E6
Ubangi = Oubangi ➔ 56 E3
Ubauro 42 E6
Ube 33 G2
Ubeda 18 C4
Uberaba 93 F4
Uberlândia 93 F4
Ubon Ratchathani 38 A2
Ubort ➔ 17 B9
Ubundu 57 E5
Ucayali ➔ 90 D4
Uchiura-Wan 32 B7
Udagamandalam 43 P10
Udaipur 43 G8
Udaipur Garhi 40 D6
Udgir 43 K10
Udhampur 42 C9
Ūdine 20 A4
Udmurtia □ 28 D6
Udon Thani 38 A2
Udupi 43 N9
Uele ➔ 57 D4
Uelzen 14 B6
Ufa 29 D6
Ugab ➔ 58 C2
Ugalla ➔ 57 F6
Uganda ■ 57 D6
Ugljan 20 B5
Ugolyak 30 C10
Uibhist a Deas = South Uist 10 C3
Uibhist a Tuath = North Uist 10 C3
Uige 56 F2
Uinta Mts. 73 F8
Uitenhage 59 E5
Ujjain 43 H9
Ujung Pandang 37 F1
Ukhrul 41 E10
Ukhta 28 C6
Ukraine ■ 25 D3
Ulaanbaatar 35 B5
Ulaangom 34 A4

Ulaanjirem **35 B5**
Ulan Bator = Ulaanbaatar **35 B5**
Ulan Ude **30 D8**
Ulcinj **22 D2**
Ule älv = Oulujoki ➔ **8 B11**
Ule träsk = Oulujärvi **8 C11**
Uleåborg = Oulu **8 B11**
Ulhasnagar **43 K8**
Uliastay **34 B4**
Ulladulla **63 C5**
Ullapool **10 C4**
Ulleungdo **33 E2**
Ulm **14 D5**
Ulmarra **63 A5**
Ulster □ **11 D3**
Ulubat Gölü **23 D7**
Uludağ **23 D7**
Ulungur He ➔ **34 B3**
Uluru **60 F5**
Ulutau **29 E7**
Ulverstone **62 D4**
Ulyanovsk = Simbirsk **24 C6**
Ulyasutay = Uliastay **34 B4**
Umala **91 G5**
'Umān = Oman ■ **48 C6**
Uman **17 D10**
Umaria **40 F3**
Umarkot **43 G6**
Umbrella Mts. **65 F3**
Umeå **8 C10**
Umeälven ➔ **8 C10**
Umera **37 E3**
Umlazi **59 E6**
Umm al Qaywayn **44 E3**
Umm Durman = Omdurmân **55 E5**
Umm Lajj **47 F4**
Umm Ruwaba **55 F5**
Umnak I. **69 C3**
Umniati ➔ **59 B5**
Umtata = Mthatha **59 E5**
Umuarama **93 G3**
Umzimvubu **59 E5**
Una ➔ **20 B6**
Unalaska **69 C3**
Uncía **91 G5**
Underbool **62 C3**
Ungarie **63 B4**
Ungarra **62 B2**
Ungava, Pén. d' **70 C6**
Ungava B. **70 D7**
Ungeny = Ungheni **17 E8**
Ungheni **17 E8**
Ungwana B. **57 E8**
União da Vitória **94 B6**
Unimak I. **69 C3**
United Arab Emirates ■ **44 F3**
United Kingdom ■ **11 D5**
United States of America ■ **67 F10**
Unnao **40 D3**
Unst **10 A6**
Ünye **46 B4**
Upata **90 B6**
Upemba, L. **57 F5**
Upington **58 D4**
Upper Hutt **65 D6**
Upper Volta = Burkina Faso ■ **53 F5**
Uppsala **9 D9**
Uqsuqtuuq = Gjoa Haven **68 B10**
Ur **47 E6**
Ural = Zhayyq ➔ **29 E6**
Ural **63 B4**
Ural Mts. = Uralskie Gory **28 D6**
Uralla **63 B5**
Uralsk = Oral **24 C7**
Uralskie Gory **28 D6**
Uranquinty **63 C4**
Uray **29 C7**
Urbana **76 D1**
Urbino **20 C4**
Urbión, Picos de **19 A4**
Urcos **91 F4**
Urda **25 D6**
Urewera △ **64 C7**
Urfa = Sanliurfa **46 C4**
Urganch **29 E7**
Urgench = Urganch **29 E7**
Uribia **90 A4**
Urla **23 E6**
Urmia = Orümīyeh **46 C6**
Uroševac **22 C3**
Urubamba ➔ **91 F4**
Uruçara **90 D7**
Uruçuí **92 D5**
Uruguai ➔ **94 B6**
Uruguaiana **94 B5**
Uruguay ■ **94 C5**
Uruguay ➔ **94 C5**
Urumchi = Ürümqi **29 E9**
Ürümqi **29 E9**
Ürzhar **29 E9**
Usakos **58 C3**
Usedom **15 B8**
Ushant = Ouessant, Î. d' **12 B1**
Ushibuka **33 G2**
Üshtöbe **29 E8**
Ushuaia **95 G3**
Usman **24 C4**
Uspallata, P. de **94 C3**
Uspenskiy **29 E8**
Ussuriysk **32 B2**
Ust-Ishim **29 D8**
Ust-Kamenogorsk = Öskemen **29 E9**
Ust-Karenga **31 D9**
Ust-Kuyga **31 B11**
Ust Muya **30 D9**
Ust-Olenek **30 B10**
Ust-Port **28 C9**
Ust-Tsilma **28 C6**
Ust-Urt = Ustyurt Plateau **29 E6**
Ústí nad Labem **16 C2**
Ústica **21 E4**
Ustinov = Izhevsk **28 D6**
Ustye **30 D7**
Ustyurt Plateau **29 E6**
Usu **34 B3**
Usumacinta ➔ **85 D6**
Usumbura = Bujumbura **57 E5**
Uta **37 E5**
Utah □ **73 G8**
Utiariti **91 F7**
Utica **77 C8**
Utrecht **14 B3**
Utrera **18 D3**
Utsunomiya **33 E6**
Uttar Pradesh □ **42 F11**
Uttaradit **38 A2**
Uusikaupunki **9 C10**
Uvat **29 D7**
Uvinza **57 F6**
Uvira **57 E5**
Uvs Nuur **34 A4**
'Uwairidh, Ḥarrat al **47 F4**
Uwajima **33 G3**
Uyuni **91 H5**
Uzbekistan ■ **29 E7**
Uzerche **12 D4**
Uzh ➔ **17 C10**
Uzhgorod = Uzhhorod **17 D6**
Uzhhorod **17 D6**
Užice **22 C2**
Uzunköprü **22 D6**

V

Vaal ➔ **58 D4**
Vaasa **8 C10**
Vác **16 E4**
Vach = Vakh ➔ **29 C8**
Vadodara **43 H8**
Vadsø **8 D13**
Vaduz **13 C8**
Vahsel B. **96 B5**
Váhtjer = Gällivare **8 B10**
Vaigach **28 B6**
Vakh ➔ **29 C8**
Val-d'Or **71 E6**
Valahia **22 B5**
Valandovo **22 D4**
Valcheta **95 E3**
Valdai Hills = Valdayskaya Vozvyshennost **24 B3**
Valdayskaya Vozvyshennost **24 B3**
Valdepeñas **18 C4**
Valdés, Pen. **95 E4**
Valdez **69 B5**
Valdivia **95 D2**
Valdosta **83 D6**
Valença **93 E6**
Valença do Piauí **92 D5**
Valence **13 D6**
Valencia *Spain* **19 C5**
Valencia *Venezuela* **90 A5**
Valencia □ **19 C5**
Valencia, G. de **19 C6**
Valencia de Alcántara **18 C2**
Valencia I. **11 F1**
Valenciennes **13 A5**
Valentim, Sa. do **92 D5**
Valera **90 B4**
Valjevo **22 B2**
Vall de Uxó = La Vall d'Uixó **19 C5**
Valladolid *Mexico* **85 C7**
Valladolid *Spain* **18 B3**
Valle de la Pascua **90 B5**
Valledupar **90 A4**
Vallejo **72 G2**
Vallenar **94 B2**
Valletta **21 G5**
Valls **19 B6**
Valognes **12 B3**
Valona = Vlorë **23 D2**
Valozhyn **17 A8**
Valparaíso **94 C2**
Vals, Tanjung **37 F5**
Valsad **43 J8**
Valverde del Camino **18 D2**
Van **46 C5**
Van, L. = Van Gölü **46 C5**
Van Gölü **46 C5**
Van Rees, Pegunungan **37 E5**
Vanadzor **25 E5**
Vancouver *Canada* **69 D7**
Vancouver *U.S.A.* **72 D2**
Vancouver I. **69 D7**
Vänern **9 D8**
Vangaindrano **59 C9**
Vännäs **8 C9**
Vannes **12 C2**
Vanrhynsdorp **58 E3**
Vantaa ➔ **9 C11**
Vanua Levu **64 L12**
Vanuatu ■ **64 L11**
Vapnyarka **17 D9**
Varanasi **40 E4**
Varangerfjorden **8 A11**
Varaždin **20 A6**
Varberg **9 D8**
Vardak □ **45 C7**
Vardar = Axios ➔ **23 D4**
Varese **13 D8**
Varna **22 C6**
Varzaneh **44 C3**
Vasa = Vaasa **8 C10**
Vasa Barris ➔ **93 E6**
Vascongadas = País Vasco □ **19 A4**
Vasht = Khāsh **42 E2**
Vasilevichi **17 B9**
Vasilkov = Vasylkiv **17 C10**
Västerås **9 D9**
Västerdalälven ➔ **8 C8**
Västervik **9 D9**
Vasto **20 C5**
Vasylkiv **17 C10**
Vatican City ■ **20 D4**
Vatnajökull **8 C2**
Vatra-Dornei **17 E7**
Vättern **9 D8**
Vaupés = Uaupés ➔ **90 C5**
Vawkavysk **17 B7**
Vaygach, Ostrov **28 C6**
Vedea ➔ **22 C5**
Vega **8 B8**
Vegreville **69 C8**
Vejer de la Frontera **18 D3**
Velebit Planina **20 B5**
Veles **22 D3**
Vélez-Málaga **18 D3**
Vélez Rubio **19 D4**
Velhas ➔ **93 F5**
Velika Kapela **20 B5**

Velikaya ➔ 24 B2
Veliki Ustyug 24 A6
Velikiye Luki 24 B3
Veliko Türnovo 22 C5
Velikonda Range 43 M11
Velletri 20 D4
Vellore 43 N11
Venado Tuerto 94 C4
Vendée □ 12 C3
Vendôme 12 C4
Venézia 20 B4
Venézia, G. di 20 B4
Venezuela ■ 90 B5
Venezuela, G. de 90 A4
Vengurla 43 M8
Venice = Venézia 20 B4
Venkatapuram 40 H3
Ventotène 21 D4
Ventoux, Mt. 13 D6
Ventspils 24 B1
Ventuarí ➔ 90 C5
Ventura 78 C3
Venus B. 63 C4
Vera *Argentina* 94 B4
Vera *Spain* 19 D5
Veracruz 84 D5
Veraval 43 J7
Verbánia 13 D8
Vercelli 13 D8
Verde ➔ 95 E3
Verden 14 B5
Verdun 13 B6
Vereeniging 59 D5
Verga, C. 53 F3
Veria 23 D4
Verín 18 B2
Verkhnevilyuysk 30 C10
Verkhniy Baskunchak 25 D6
Verkhoyansk 31 C11
Verkhoyansk Ra. = Verkhoyanskiy Khrebet 31 C10
Verkhoyanskiy Khrebet 31 C10
Vermont □ 77 C9
Vernon *Canada* 69 C8
Vernon *U.S.A.* 80 B4
Véroia = Veria 23 D4
Verona 20 B3
Versailles 12 B5
Vert, C. 53 F2
Verviers 14 C3
Veselovskoye Vdkhr. 25 D5
Vesoul 13 C7
Vesterålen 8 B9
Vestfjorden 8 B8
Vesuvio 21 D5
Vesuvius, Mt. = Vesuvio 21 D5
Veszprém 16 E3
Vettore, Mte. 20 C4
Vezhen 22 C5
Viacha 91 G5
Viamão 94 C6
Viana 92 C5
Viana do Alentejo 18 C2
Viana do Castelo 18 B1
Viangchan = Vientiane 38 A2
Vianópolis 93 F4
Viaréggio 20 C3
Vibo Valéntia 21 E6
Vic 19 B7
Vicenza 20 B3
Vich = Vic 19 B7
Vichy 13 C5
Vicksburg 81 C8
Victor 43 J7
Victor Harbor 62 C2
Victoria *Canada* 69 D7
Victoria *Chile* 94 D2
Victoria □ 62 C3
Victoria, L. *Africa* 57 E6
Victoria, L. *Australia* 62 B3
Victoria, Mt. 41 G9
Victoria de Durango = Durango 84 C4
Victoria Falls 59 B5
Victoria I. 68 A8
Victoria Ld. 96 B14
Victorica 94 D3
Vicuña 94 C2
Vidin 22 C4
Vidisha 43 H10
Viedma 95 E4
Viedma, L. 95 F2
Vienna = Wien 15 D9
Vienne 13 D6
Vienne ➔ 12 C4
Vientiane 38 A2
Vierzon 12 C5
Vietnam ■ 38 A3
Vieux-Fort, Pte. du 30 C
Vigan 36 A2
Vigévano 13 D8
Vigia 92 C4
Vigo 18 A1
Vijayawada 40 J3
Vijosë ➔ 23 D2
Vikeke = Viqueque 37 F3
Vikna 8 C8
Vila do Bispo 18 D1
Vila Franca de Xira 18 C1
Vila Nova de Gaia 18 B1
Vila Real 18 B2
Vila-real de los Infantes 19 C5
Vila Real de Santo António 18 D2
Vila Velha 93 G5
Vilagarcía de Arousa 18 A1
Vilaine ➔ 12 C2
Vilanculos 59 C7
Vilanova i la Geltrú 19 B6
Vileyka 17 A8
Vilhelmina 8 C9
Vilhena 91 F6
Vilkitskogo, Proliv 30 B8
Vilkovo = Vylkove 17 F9
Villa Ángela 94 B4
Villa Bella 91 F5
Villa de María 94 B4
Villa Dolores 94 C3
Villa Hayes 94 B5
Villa María 94 C4
Villa Mazán 94 B3
Villa Montes 94 A4
Villa Ocampo 94 B5
Villacarrillo 18 C4
Villach 15 E7
Villaguay 94 C5
Villahermosa 85 D6
Villajoyosa 19 C5
Villalba 18 A2
Villanueva de la Serena 18 C3
Villanueva y Geltrú = Vilanova i la Geltrú 19 B6
Villarreal = Vila-real de los Infantes 19 C5
Villarrica *Chile* 95 D2
Villarrica *Paraguay* 94 B5
Villarrobledo 19 C4
Villavicencio 90 C4
Villaviciosa 18 A3
Villazón 94 A3
Villena 19 C5
Villeneuve-d'Ascq 13 A5
Villeneuve-sur-Lot 12 D4
Villingen-Schwenningen 14 D5
Vilnius 24 C2
Vilyuy ➔ 31 C10
Vilyuysk 31 C10
Viña del Mar 94 C2
Vinarós 19 B6
Vindhya Ra. 43 H10
Vineland 77 E8
Vinkovci 20 B7
Vinnitsa = Vinnytsya 17 D9
Vinnytsya 17 D9
Viqueque 37 F3
Virac 36 B2
Viramgam 43 H8
Virden 69 D9
Vire 12 B3
Vírgenes, C. 95 G3
Virgin Is. (British) ☑ 87 C7
Virginia 59 D5
Virginia □ 77 F6
Virginia Beach 77 F8
Virovitica 20 B6
Virudunagar 43 Q10
Vis 20 C6
Visalia 78 B3
Visayan Sea 36 B2
Visby 9 D9
Viscount Melville Sd. 70 B3
Višegrad 20 C7
Viseu *Brazil* 92 C4
Viseu *Portugal* 18 B2
Vishakhapatnam 40 J4
Viso, Mte. 13 D7
Vistula = Wisła ➔ 16 A4
Vitebsk = Vitsyebsk 24 B3
Viterbo 20 C4
Viti Levu 64 L12
Vitigudino 18 B2
Vitória 93 G5
Vitória da Conquista 93 E5
Vitoria-Gasteiz 19 A4
Vitsyebsk 24 B3
Vittória 21 F5
Vittório Véneto 20 B4
Viveiro 18 A2
Vize 22 D6
Vizianagaram 40 H4
Vladikavkaz 25 E5
Vladimir 24 B5
Vladimir Volynskiy = Volodymyr-Volynskyy 17 C7
Vladivostok 32 B2
Vlissingen 14 C2
Vlorë 23 D2
Vltava ➔ 16 C2
Vogelkop = Doberai, Jazirah 37 E4
Vogelsberg 14 C5
Voghera 13 D8
Vohimarina = Iharana 59 A10
Vohimena, Tanjon' i 59 D9
Voi 57 E7
Voiron 13 D6
Vojvodina □ 22 B2
Volga ➔ 25 D6
Volga Hts. = Privolzhskaya Vozvyshennost 24 C6
Volgodonsk 25 D5
Volgograd 25 D5
Volgogradskoye Vdkhr. 24 C6
Volkhov ➔ 24 A3
Volkovysk = Vawkavysk 17 B7
Volochanka 30 B7
Volodymyr-Volynskyy 17 C7
Vologda 24 B4
Volos 23 E4
Volovets 17 D6
Volozhin = Valozhyn 17 A8
Volsk 24 C6
Volta, L. 53 G6
Volta Redonda 93 G5
Volterra 20 C3
Volturno ➔ 20 D4
Volzhskiy 25 D5
Vorkuta 28 C7
Voronezh 24 C4
Vosges 13 B7
Vostok I. 65 L15
Vouga ➔ 18 B1
Voznesensk 25 D3
Vrangelya, Ostrov 31 B15
Vranje 22 C3
Vratsa 22 C4
Vrbas ➔ 20 B6
Vršac 22 B3
Vryburg 58 D4
Vryheid 59 D6
Vukovar 20 B7
Vulcan 17 F6
Vulcanești 17 F9
Vulcano 21 E5
Vulkaneshty = Vulcanești 17 F9
Vung Tau 38 B3
Vyatka = Kirov 28 D5
Vyatskiye Polyany 24 B7
Vyazma 24 B3
Vyborg 28 C3
Vychegda ➔ 28 C5
Vychodné Beskydy 17 D5
Vylkove 17 F9
Vynohradiv 17 D6
Vyshniy Volochek 24 B3
Vyškov 16 D3

W

Waal → 14 C3
Wabash → 76 F1
Waco 80 D5
Wad Hamid 55 E5
Wad Medanī 55 F5
Waddington, Mt. 69 C7
Waddy Pt. 63 A5
Wadi Halfa 54 D5
Wafrah 47 E6
Wager B. 70 C5
Wager Bay 70 C4
Wagga Wagga 63 C4
Waghete 37 E5
Wah 42 C8
Wahai 37 E3
Waiau → 65 E5
Waibeem 37 E4
Waigeo 37 E4
Waihi 64 B6
Waihou → 64 B6
Waikabubak 37 F1
Waikaremoana, L. 64 C7
Waikari 65 E5
Waikato → 64 B6
Waikerie 62 B2
Waikokopu 64 C7
Waikouaiti 65 F4
Waimakariri → 65 E5
Waimate 65 F4
Wainganga → 43 K11
Waingapu 37 F2
Waiouru 64 C6
Waipara 65 E5
Waipawa 64 C7
Waipiro 64 C8
Waipoua Forest 64 A5
Waipu 64 A6
Waipukurau 64 D7
Wairakei 64 C7
Wairarapa, L. 65 D6
Wairoa 64 C7
Waitaki → 65 F4
Waitangi 64 A6
Waitara 64 C6
Waitomo Caves 64 C6
Waiuku 64 B6
Wajima 33 E5
Wajir 57 D8
Wakasa-Wan 33 F4
Wakatipu, L. 65 F3
Wakayama 33 F4
Wakefield 65 D5
Wakkanai 32 A7
Wakool 63 C3
Wakool → 62 C3
Wakre 37 E4
Wałbrzych 16 C3
Walcha 63 B5
Wałcz 16 B3
Wales □ 11 E4
Walgett 63 A4
Walgreen Coast 96 B1
Walla Walla 72 C4
Wallachia = Valahia 22 B5
Wallal 63 A4
Wallaroo 62 B2
Wallis & Futuna, Is. 64 L13
Wallowa Mts. 72 D5
Wallumbilla 63 A4
Walvis Bay 58 C2
Walvisbaai = Walvis Bay 58 C2
Wamba 57 D5
Wamena 37 E5
Wamulan 37 E3
Wana 42 C6
Wanaaring 63 A3
Wanaka 65 F3
Wanaka, L. 65 F3
Wandoan 63 A4
Wangal 37 F4
Wanganella 63 C3
Wanganui 64 C6
Wangaratta 63 C4
Wangary 62 B2
Wangerooge 14 B4
Wangiwangi 37 F2
Warangal 43 L11
Waratah 62 D4
Waratah B. 63 C4
Warburton 63 C4
Warburton → 62 A2
Ward 65 D6
Ward → 63 A4
Wardha 43 J11
Wardha → 43 K11
Warialda 63 A5
Wariap 37 E4
Warkopi 37 E4
Warner Mts. 72 F3
Warracknabeal 62 C3
Warragul 63 C4
Warrego → 63 B4
Warren *Australia* 63 B4
Warren *U.S.A.* 76 C4
Warrenville 63 A4
Warri 53 G7
Warrina 62 A2
Warrington *U.K.* 11 E5
Warrington *U.S.A.* 82 D4
Warrnambool 62 C3
Warsa 37 E5
Warsaw = Warszawa 16 B5
Warszawa 16 B5
Warta → 16 B2
Warthe = Warta → 16 B2
Waru 37 E4
Warwick 63 A5
Wasatch Ra. 73 F8
Wash, The 11 E7
Washim 43 J10
Washington 77 E7
Washington □ 72 C3
Washington, Mt. 77 B10
Wasian 37 E4
Wasior 37 E4
Waskaganish 71 D6
Wasserkuppe 14 C5
Watampone 37 E2
Waterbury 77 D9
Waterford 11 E3
Waterloo 75 D8
Watertown 77 C8
Waterville 77 B11
Watford 11 F6
Watling I. = San Salvador I. 86 B5
Watrous 69 C9
Watsa 57 D5
Watson Lake 68 B7
Watsonville 78 B2
Wattiwarriganna Cr. → 62 A2
Watuata = Batuata 37 F2
Watubela, Kepulauan 37 E4
Watubela Is. = Watubela, Kepulauan 37 E4
Wau = Wāw 55 G4
Wauchope 63 B5
Waukegan 76 C2
Waukesha 76 C1
Wausau 75 C10
Wauwatosa 76 C2
Waverley 64 C6
Wāw 55 G4
Wāw al Kabīr 54 C2
Waxahachie 81 C5
Wayabula 37 D3
Wayatinah 62 D4
Waycross 83 D6
Wazirabad 42 C9
We 38 C1
Weda 37 D3
Weda, Teluk 37 D3
Weddell I. 95 G4
Weddell Sea 96 A4
Wedderburn 62 C3
Wee Waa 63 B4
Weemelah 63 A4
Weiden 15 D7
Weifang 35 C6
Weimar 15 C6
Weipa 61 C7
Weir → 63 A4
Wejherowo 16 A4
Welbourn Hill 62 A1
Welkom 59 D5
Wellesley Is. 60 D6
Wellington *Australia* 63 B4
Wellington *N.Z.* 65 D6
Wellington, I. 95 F1
Wellington, L. 63 C4
Wellington Chan. 70 B4
Wels 15 D8
Welshpool 11 E5
Wemindji 71 D6
Wenatchee 72 C3
Wenchi 53 G5
Wenchow = Wenzhou 35 D7
Wendesi 37 E4
Wensu 34 B3
Wentworth 62 B3
Wenut 37 E4
Wenzhou 35 D7
Weri 37 E4
Werra → 14 C5
Werrimull 62 B3
Werris Creek 63 B5
Wersar 37 E4
Weser → 14 B5
Wesiri 37 F3
West Bank ■ 46 D3
West Bengal □ 40 F7
West Beskids = Západné Beskydy 16 D4
West Falkland 95 G4
West Fjord = Vestfjorden 8 B8
West Ice Shelf 96 A11
West Palm Beach 83 F7
West Pt. 62 C2
West Virginia □ 76 E5
West Wyalong 63 B4
Westall, Pt. 62 B1
Westbury 62 D4
Westerland 14 A5
Western Australia □ 60 F3
Western Dvina = Daugava → 24 B1
Western Ghats 43 N9
Western Sahara ■ 52 D3
Western Samoa = Samoa ■ 65 L13
Western Sierra Madre = Madre Occidental, Sierra 84 B3
Westerwald 14 C4
Westland △ 65 E4
Westland Bight 65 E4
Weston-super-Mare 11 F5
Westport *Ireland* 11 E2
Westport *N.Z.* 65 D4
Westray 10 B5
Wetar 37 F3
Wetaskiwin 69 C8
Wetzlar 14 C5
Wevok 69 B3
Wexford 11 E3
Weyburn 69 D9
Weymouth 11 F5
Wha Ti 68 B8
Whakaari = White I. 64 B7
Whakatane 64 B7
Whale → 70 D7
Whale Cove 68 B10
Whales, B. of 96 B16
Whangamata 64 B6
Whangamomona 64 C6
Whanganui △ 64 C6
Whangarei 64 A6
Whangarei Harb. 64 A6
Wheeling 76 D5
White → *Ark., U.S.A.* 81 C8
White → *Ind., U.S.A.* 76 E2
White Cliffs 62 B3
White I. 64 B7
White Nile = Nīl el Abyad → 55 E5
White Russia = Belarus ■ 24 C2
White Sea = Beloye More 8 B13
Whitecliffs 65 E4
Whitehaven 11 D5
Whitehorse 68 B6
Whitemark 62 D4
Whitianga 64 B6
Whitney, Mt. 78 B3
Whittlesea 63 C4
Wholdaia L. 68 B9
Whyalla 62 B2
Whyjonta 62 A3
Wichita 80 A5
Wichita Falls 80 C4
Wick 10 B5
Wickham, C. 62 C3
Wicklow Mts. 11 E3